DUNDAS AND BARTOS ON THE ARBITRATION (SCOTLAND) ACT 2010

DUNDAS AND BARTOS ON THE ARBITRATION (SCOTLAND) ACT 2010

2ND EDITION

By

Hew R. Dundas, FCIArb, CHARTERED ARBITRATOR
International Arbitrator, Mediator & Expert Determiner

and

David Bartos, FCIArb,
Advocate and Arbitrator

W. GREEN  THOMSON REUTERS

First edition published 2010.

Published in 2014 by W. Green, 21 Alva Street,
Edinburgh EH2 4PS
Part of Thomson Reuters (Professional) UK Limited
(Registered in England & Wales, Company No 1679046.
Registered Office and address for service: Aldgate House,
33 Aldgate High Street, London EC3N 1DL)

http://www.wgreen.thomson.com

Typeset by YHT Ltd

Printed and bound in Great Britain by CPI Group (UK) Ltd, Croydon, CR0 4YY

ISBN 978-0-414-019270

A catalogue record for this title is available
from the British Library

All rights reserved. UK statutory material used in this publication is acknowledged as Crown Copyright. No part of this publication may be reproduced or transmitted, in any form or by any means, electronic, mechanical, photocopying, recording or otherwise, or stored in any retrieval system of any nature, without prior written permission of the copyright holder and the publisher, application for which should be made to the publisher, except for permitted fair dealing under the Copyright, Designs and Patents Act 1988, or in accordance with the terms of a licence issued by the Copyright Licensing Agency in respect of photocopying and/or reprographic reproduction. Full acknowledgement of publisher and source must be given. Material is contained in this publication for which publishing permission has been sought, and for which copyright is acknowledged. Permission to reproduce such material cannot be granted by the publishers and application must be made to the copyright holders.

No natural forests were destroyed to make this product; only farmed timber was used and replanted.

© 2014 Thomson Reuters (Professional) UK Limited

Thomson Reuters and the Thomson Reuters Logo
are trademarks of Thomson Reuters.

FOREWORD

Before the Arbitration (Scotland) Act 2010 was enacted, the Scots law of arbitration was relatively inaccessible and far from user-friendly. Most of its rules were based on elderly (nineteenth century) case law which did not address modern commercial realities; legislative provision was piecemeal; and there were many gaps and uncertainties. Lack of clarity about an arbiter's powers gave rise to avoidable and expensive disputes: see, e.g. *McCrindle Group Ltd v Maclay Murray & Spens* [2013] CSOH 72. In short, it was not fit for purpose.

The authors of this book, which like its first edition provides a valuable commentary on the 2010 Act, were intimately involved in the development of proposals contained in the Act. In their introduction they set out the steps which interested professionals have taken in the last 25 years to promote a modern legislative code for arbitration in Scotland.

The introduction of appeals by stated case in s.3 of the Administration of Justice (Scotland) Act 1972 was on balance not a success. The repeal of that provision is not a matter of regret. It was the preparation of the UNCITRAL Model Law on international commercial arbitration which proved the spur to the updating of arbitration law in the United Kingdom. The legislative introduction of the Model Law in international arbitration in Scotland in 1990 was a step forward. But it was not a comprehensive code; nor did it remove the serious deficiencies in the Scots law of arbitration. Rather the value of the Model Law has been its provision of the principles and the language on which the jurisdictions of the United Kingdom have been able to draw in developing modern legislative codes. First, England, Wales and Northern Ireland adopted a modern code in the Arbitration Act 1996 to replace an earlier statutory code. Secondly, learning from the experience of the operation of the 1996 Act, the promoters of the 2010 Act in Scotland have been able to produce a modern, comprehensive and accessible arbitration code for this jurisdiction.

By drawing on the Model Law and the 1996 Act the framers of the 2010 Act have been able to create a code which is accessible to those with experience in arbitration in other jurisdictions and international arbitration. By taking principles and approaches used in, and terminology from, the 1996 Act they have enabled Scots lawyers to draw on English jurisprudence as persuasive authority. This is welcome because our jurisdiction produces only limited case law and the 2010 Act restricts recourse to the courts (see s.13, rr.41, 42 and Part 8 of the Rules). The model of a short Act of 37 sections, which sets out the basic rules and concepts, and a schedule with the Scottish Arbitration Rules, many of which are default rules which the parties can modify or replace, is a welcome innovation. The Rules set out an arbitration code in a logical and user-friendly manner.

The 2010 Act is also the product of the commitment by major Scottish political parties to encourage arbitration in Scotland. That commitment may blend in well with broader initiatives. The UK Government has been keen in recent years to promote UK legal services internationally as it sees that the legal services sector plays an important role in underpinning economic growth. It is inevitable that the Scottish legal profession does not have the critical mass to compete across the board with the international drawing power of the City of London in unlocking legal disputes. But there are areas of strength and expertise within the legal profession and other professions as well as cost advantages which may be harnessed to attract interesting work to Scotland, whatever the substantive law to be used in deciding the dispute, or to allow Scottish practitioners to offer their services further afield. The creation of a modern code of alternative dispute resolution in the 2010 Act is an important building block in this project.

For those who are familiar with arbitration and also those who wish to learn, the detailed and up-to-date commentary, in which Hew Dundas and David Bartos cite relevant case law from many jurisdictions, will be an invaluable guide. They and W. Green, the publishers, are to be congratulated for compiling the second edition of this very useful book.

Patrick S. Hodge

PREFACE

The authors are very pleased to commend this 2nd edition of our book to you. Much can change in the four years between World Cup football tournaments, Olympic Games and in many countries, parliamentary or presidential elections; the world of arbitration is no exception. Quite apart from the reporting of the first judicial decisions in Scotland under the 2010 Act, case law south of the border and internationally has continued apace since 2010 (the authors have considered over 700 new cases from approximately 20 jurisdictions). In addition, as well as new legislation having been enacted in several countries including (inter alia) Australia, France, Hong Kong, and Việt Nam (and imminently, Canada and Russia), each of UNCITRAL, the ICC and the LCIA have published new, revised sets of rules. It follows that a 2nd edition is wholly necessary. The authors offer this work to all those involved in arbitration in Scotland and throughout the world, both in the belief that it will contribute to a proper understanding of arbitration law and practice in Scotland and in the hope that it will contribute to a fuller understanding of arbitration worldwide.

We take this opportunity to thank, most warmly, all those who responded (often with remarkable celerity!) with assistance, especially cases and other materials. They include (in alphabetical order; UK unless otherwise stated): Professor Louise Barrington (Canada), Professor Rafael Bernal (Colombia), Len Bunton, David Cairns (Spain/New Zealand), Peter Scott Caldwell (Hong Kong), Laurie Craig (USA/France), Louis Flannery, Dr Robert Gaitskell QC, Hamish Goodall, Glenn Haley (Australia/Hong Kong), Professor Mark Hoyle (UK/Dubai), Professor Doug Jones AO RFD (Australia), Professor Mark Kantor (USA), Dr Christian Konrad (Vienna), Dr Stefan Kröll (Germany), Andrew McKenzie and Brandon Malone (both of the Scottish Arbitration Centre), Donald O'Meara (UK/Canada), Professor Datuk Sundra Rajoo Ybhg (Malaysia), J Gordon Reid QC FCIArb, Preeti Sukthanker (India) and two members of the 1995/96 DAC—John Sims and Professor John Uff CBE QC.

We are also most grateful to Professor Fraser Davidson for the valuable work he put in to the 1st edition, which we have been able to build on and develop, and to Lindy Patterson QC of Dundas & Wilson CS.

We are both very honoured and most grateful that the Rt Hon Lord Hodge, Justice of the UK Supreme Court, graciously agreed to write the Foreword.

Further, this 2nd edition could never have happened without the invaluable support from the excellent team at W. Green, namely Janet Campbell, Alan Bett and Lauren McIndoe and the invaluable resources of the Advocates' Library in Edinburgh.

We must also record our warmest thanks, both on our behalf and that of the entire arbitral community in Scotland, to Lord Dervaird for his great efforts over many years in promoting Scottish Arbitration.

Finally, we must record our heartfelt thanks to our families—Vân, Clare, Mark and Thomas—who graciously tolerated our strivings (long hours at the computer, absent from family life) through the highly-pressured gestation of this book. They have all heard so much about arbitration in recent months that they could probably pass the ACIArb examinations without further study.

CONTENTS

	Page
Foreword	v
Preface	vii
Table of Cases	xi
Table of UK Statutes	xxxiii
Table of Scottish Statutes	xxxvii
Table of Abbreviations	xlvii
Introduction	1
Arbitration (Scotland) Act 2010	9
Schedule 1: Scottish Arbitration Rules	159
Schedule 2: Repeals	504
Appendix 1: Arbitration involving consumers	505
Appendix 2: Annotated Rules of the Court of Session Ch.62 Pt IX and Ch.100	507
Index	527

TABLE OF CASES

A v B [2006] EWHC 2006 (Comm); [2007] 1 All E.R. (Comm) 591; [2007] 1 Lloyd's
  Rep. 237; [2007] 2 C.L.C. 157 .... S3–10, S10–26, S10–27
A v B [2011] EWHC 2345 (Comm); [2011] 2 Lloyd's Rep. 591; [2011] Arb. L.R. 43;
  (2011) 161 N.L.J. 1291 .... R12–14
A v B; III ZR 33/00 9th April 2000 .... S10–54
A v R (HCCT No. 54 of 2008) April 30, 2009 .... S20–124
AAMCO Transmissions Inc v Kunz [1996] A.D.R.L.J 32 CA (Saskatchewan) S20–80
Aasma v American Steamship Owners Mutual Protection and Indemnity (2003)
  XXVIII YCA 1140 District Ct (US) S20–83
AB Gotaverken v General National Maritime Transport Co (1981) VI YCA 237 Sup
  Ct (Sweden) S20–83, S20–85, S20–89
ABB AG v Hochtief Airport GmbH [2006] EWHC 388 (Comm); [2006] 1 All E.R.
  (Comm) 529; [2006] 2 Lloyd's Rep. 1 .... R68–20
ABB Lummus Global Ltd v Keppel Fels Ltd (formerly Far East Levingston Ship-
  building Ltd) [1999] 2 Lloyd's Rep. 24 QBD (Comm Ct) S9–10, R19–10
Aberdeen Railway Co v Blaikie Bothers (1853) 15 D. (HL) 20 .... R48–05
Abu Dhabi Investment Co v H Clarkson & Co Ltd [2006] EWHC 1252 (Comm);
  [2006] 2 Lloyd's Rep. 381 .... S10–54, S30–15
ACD Tridon Inc v Tridon Australia Pty Ltd (2004) XIX YCA 533 .... S10–50
Aeroflot - Russian Airlines v Berezovsky; sub nom. Joint Stock Co Aeroflot Russian
  Airlines v Berezovsky [2013] EWCA Civ 784; [2013] 2 Lloyd's Rep. 242 .... S10–26,
                                                                                                    S10–46
AES Ust-Kamenogorsk Hydropower Plant LLP v Ust-Kamenogorsk Hydropower
  Plant JSC; sub nom. Ust-Kamenogorsk Hydropower Plant JSC v AES Ust-
  Kamenogorsk Hydropower Plant LLP [2013] UKSC 35; [2013] 1 W.L.R. 1889;
  [2014] 1 All E.R. 335; [2014] 1 All E.R. (Comm) 1; [2013] Bus. L.R. 1357; [2013] 2
  Lloyd's Rep. 281; [2013] 1 C.L.C. 1069 .... S20–82
Age Ltd v Kwik Save Stores Ltd; sub nom. AGE Ltd v Brown, 2001 S.C. 144; 2001
  S.L.T. 841; 2000 G.W.D. 27–1018 OH S2–03
Agnew v Scott Lithgow Ltd (No.2), 2003 S.C. 448; 2003 S.C.L.R. 426; 2003 G.W.D.
  13-443 IH (Ex Div) R76–10
Agrimex Ltd v Tradigrain SA [2003] EWHC 1656 (Comm); [2003] 2 Lloyd's Rep. 537;
  (2003) 153 N.L.J. 1121 .... R32–08, R51–43, R56–20, R60–15
Agro Industries (P) Ltd v Texuna International Ltd [1994] 1 H.K.L.R. 89 .... S20–107
Aguna v Smith Industries (1983) VIII YCA 360 .... S10–50
AI Trade Finance v Bulgarian Trade Bank (case 1881–99) Unreported October 27,
  2000 Sup Ct R26–09
Air India Ltd v Caribjet Inc [2002] 2 All E.R. (Comm) 76; [2002] 1 Lloyd's Rep. 314
  QBD (Comm) S20–143
Al Haddad Bros Enterprises v M/S Agapi (1987) XII YCA 549 .... S20–58, S20–64
Al-Hadha Trading Co v Tradigrain SA [2002] 2 Lloyd's Rep. 512 QBD (Mer) R51–46,
                                                                                                    R51–51, R58–14
Albon (t/a NA Carriage Co) v Naza Motor Trading Sdn Bhd [2007] EWHC 1879
  (Ch); [2007] 2 Lloyd's Rep. 420 .... S10–47
Ali Shipping Corp v Shipyard Trogir [1999] 1 W.L.R. 314; [1998] 2 All E.R. 136;
  [1998] 1 Lloyd's Rep. 643; [1998] C.L.C. 566 CA (Civ Div) S15–16, S15–17,
                                                    S15–18, S15–20, R26–08, R26–14, R26–15
Allianz SpA (formerly Riunione Adriatica di Sicurta SpA) v West Tankers Inc (C-185/
  07); Front Comor, The; sub nom. West Tankers Inc v Allianz SpA (formerly
  Riunione Adriatica di Sicurta SpA) (C-185/07) [2009] 1 A.C. 1138; [2009] 3
  W.L.R. 696; [2009] All E.R. (EC) 491; [2009] 1 All E.R. (Comm) 435; [2009] 1
  Lloyd's Rep. 413; [2009] 1 C.L.C. 96; [2009] C.E.C. 619; [2009] I.L.Pr. 20; 2009
  A.M.C. 2847 .... S3–22, S3–23
Alston v Chappell (1839) 2 D 348 .... R28–12, R28–58
Amec Building Ltd v Cadmus Investment Co Ltd [1997] C.L.Y. 262 .... R50–11
Amec Civil Engineering Ltd v Secretary of State for Transport [2005] EWCA Civ 291;

Table of Cases

[2005] 1 W.L.R. 2339; [2005] B.L.R. 227; 101 Con. L.R. 26; (2005) 21 Const. L.J. 640; [2005] 12 E.G. 219 (C.S.); (2005) 102(20) L.S.G. 30 15 .... S2–16
American Oil Co v Libya (1981) 20 I.L.M. 893 .... S20–23
Anderson v Gibb, 1993 S.L.T. 726 OH R46–34
Anderson v Wood (1821) 1 S. 31 .... S11–04
AOOT Kalmneft v Glencore International AG. *See* Kalmneft JSC v Glencore International AG
Apollo Engineering Ltd v James Scott Ltd [2013] UKSC 37; 2013 S.C. (U.K.S.C.) 286; 2014 S.L.T. 32; 2013 G.W.D. 21-409 .... R42–05
Apollo Engineering Ltd v James Scott Ltd, 2008 S.L.T. 472; [2009] CSIH 39; 2009 S.C. 525 .... R53–10, R62–11
Arab Business Consortium International Finance & Investment Co v Banque Franco-Tunisienne [1997] 1 Lloyd's Rep. 531 CA (Civ Div) S20–143
Arab National Bank v El-Abdali [2004] EWHC 2381 (Comm); [2005] 1 Lloyd's Rep. 541 .... S3–09, S3–19, S14–05
Arbitration Application No.2 of 2011 [2011] CSOH 186; 2011 Hous. L.R. 72; 2011 G.W.D. 38–785 .... R70–06, A2–40
Arbitration Application No.3 of 2011 [2011] CSOH 164; 2012 S.L.T. 150; 2011 G.W.D. 32–678 OH S13–03, R67–14, R68–12, R70–11, A2–21, A2–27, A2–29, A2–31, A2–33, A2–34, A2–35, A2–40
Arbitration Application No.1 of 2013 [2014] CSOH 83 .... R51–42, R51–46, R51–48, R51–51, R58–13, R58–20, R68–19, R69–19, R70–06, R70–16, R70–20, R70–24
Argyllshire Weavers Ltd v A Macaulay (Tweeds) Ltd (No.1), 1962 S.C. 388; 1962 S.L.T. 310 IH (1 Div) S3–20
Ascot Commodities NV v Olam International Ltd [2002] C.L.C. 277 .... R68–80, R68–85, R70–41
ASM Shipping Ltd of India v TTMI Ltd of England (The Amer Energy); Amer Energy, The [2009] 1 Lloyd's Rep. 293 QBD (Comm Ct) S12–19
ASM Shipping Ltd of India v TTMI Ltd of England [2005] EWHC 2238 (Comm); [2006] 2 All E.R. (Comm) 122; [2006] 1 Lloyd's Rep. 375; [2006] 1 C.L.C. 656 .... R8–11, R10–18, R12–11, R12–14, R13–05, R24–19, R76–11
ASM Shipping Ltd v Harris [2007] EWHC 1513 (Comm); [2008] 1 Lloyd's Rep. 61; [2007] 1 C.L.C. 1017; (2007) 23 Const. L.J. 533; [2007] Bus. L.R. D105 .... R10–18, R13–05
Associated Electric & Gas Insurance Services Ltd v European Reinsurance Co of Zurich [2003] UKPC 11; [2003] 1 W.L.R. 1041; [2003] 1 All E.R. (Comm) 253; [2003] 2 C.L.C. 340; (2003) 100(11) L.S.G. 31; (2003) 147 S.J.L.B. 148 .... S15–05, R26–14, R26–15
AT&T Corp v Saudi Cable Co [2000] 2 All E.R. (Comm) 625; [2000] 2 Lloyd's Rep. 127; [2000] C.L.C. 1309; [2000] B.L.R. 293 CA (Civ Div) R12–15, R24–15, R77–05
Athletic Union of Constantinople (AEK) v National Basketball Association [2002] 1 All E.R. (Comm) 70; [2002] 1 Lloyd's Rep. 305 QBD (Comm Ct) R20–11, R20–17, R76–07
Atlanska Plovidba v Consignaciones Asturianas SA (The Lapad); Lapad, The [2004] EWHC 1273 (Admlty); [2004] 2 Lloyd's Rep. 109; [2004] 2 C.L.C. 886 ... R1–21, R1–24
Atlantic Lines & Navigation Co Inc v Italmare SpA (The Apollon); Apollon, The [1985] 1 Lloyd's Rep. 597 QBD (Comm) R51–54
Attorney General of Ghana v Texaco Overseas Tankships Ltd (The Texaco Melbourne); Texaco Melbourne, The [1994] 1 Lloyd's Rep. 473; [1994] C.L.C. 155 HL R48–12
Austrian Bundesgerichtshof (Supreme Court) decision (1977) I YCA 232 .... S21–04
Azov Shipping Co v Baltic Shipping Co (No.1) [1999] 1 All E.R. 476; [1999] 1 Lloyd's Rep. 68; [1998] C.L.C. 1240 QBD (Comm Ct) R19–16, R67–13
Azov Shipping Co v Baltic Shipping Co (No.2) [1999] 1 All E.R. (Comm.) 716; [1999] 2 Lloyd's Rep. 39; [1999] C.L.C. 624 QBD (Comm Ct) R71–46, R71–47

B v A (Arbitration: Chosen Law); A v B [2010] EWHC 1626 (Comm); [2010] 2 Lloyd's Rep. 681; [2010] 2 C.L.C. 1; 132 Con. L.R. 73; [2011] Bus. L.R. D113 .... R47–17, R47–18, R51–15
B v S [2011] 2 Lloyd's Rep. 18 .... R46–01

Table of Cases

Babanaft International Co SA v Avanti Petroleum Inc (The Oltenia); Oltenia, The; sub nom. Babanaft International Co SA v Avant Petroleum Inc [1982] 1 W.L.R. 871; [1982] 3 All E.R. 244; [1982] 2 Lloyd's Rep. 99; [1982] Com. L.R. 104; [1983] E.C.C. 365; (1982) 79 L.S.G. 953; (1982) 126 S.J. 361 CA (Civ Div) R42–20
Babcock Rosyth Defence Ltd v Grootcon (UK) Ltd, 1998 S.L.T. 1143; 1997 G.W.D. 19–864 OH S4–13
Baillie v Pollock (1829) 7 S. 619 .... S12–31, S15–04
Baird's Trustees v Baird & Co (1877) 4 R. 1005 .... R50–22
Baker Marine (Nigeria) Ltd v Chevron (Nigeria) Ltd, 191 F.3d 194 (1999) S20–97
Baleares, The. *See* Geogas SA v Trammo Gas Ltd (The Baleares)
Bandwidth Shipping Corp v Intaari (A Firm) (The Magdalena Oldendorff); Magdalena Oldendorff, The [2007] EWCA Civ 998; [2008] Bus. L.R. 702; [2008] 1 All E.R. (Comm) 1015; [2008] 1 Lloyd's Rep. 7; [2007] 2 C.L.C. 537 .... R68–19, R68–27
Bank Mellat v GAA Development Construction Co Ltd [1988] 2 Lloyd's Rep. 44; [1988] F.T.L.R. 409 QBD (Comm Ct) R51–09
Barclays Bank Plc v Nylon Capital LLP [2011] EWCA Civ 826; [2012] 1 All E.R. (Comm) 912; [2012] Bus. L.R. 542; [2011] 2 Lloyd's Rep. 347; [2011] B.L.R. 614 .... S2–06
Bargues Agro Industrie SA v Young Pecan Ltd (2005) XXX YCA 499 CA (Paris) ... S20–48
Bavarian Supreme Court (2002) XXVII YCA 44 .... S20–39
Bay Hotel and Resort Ltd v Cavalier Construction Co Ltd [2001] UKPC 34 .... R51–39
Belgravia Property Co Ltd v S&R (London) Ltd [2001] C.L.C. 1626; [2001] B.L.R. 424; 93 Con. L.R. 59; (2003) 19 Const. L.J. 36 QBD (T&CC) R22–05
Benaim (UK) Ltd v Davies Middleton & Davies Ltd (No.2) [2005] EWHC 1370 (TCC); 102 Con. L.R. 1 .... R51–42, R68–22
Bernuth Lines Ltd v High Seas Shipping Ltd (The Eastern Navigator); Eastern Navigator, The [2005] EWHC 3020 (Comm); [2006] 1 All E.R. (Comm) 359; [2006] 1 Lloyd's Rep. 537; [2006] 1 C.L.C. 403; [2006] C.I.L.L. 2343; (2006) 156 N.L.J. 64 .... R1–11, R38–06, R83–13
Bevan Ashford v Geoff Yeandle (Contractors) Ltd (In Liquidation) [1999] Ch. 239; [1998] 3 W.L.R. 172; [1998] 3 All E.R. 238; 59 Con. L.R. 1; [1998] 2 Costs L.R. 15; (1998) 95(16) L.S.G. 27; (1998) 148 N.L.J. 587; (1998) 142 S.J.L.B. 151; [1998] N.P.C. 69 Ch D R59–11
BGH decision of June 4, 1992 BGHZ 118 .... R48–08
BGH decision (1999) XXIV YCA 928 .... S20–17
BGH decision (2001) XXVI YCA 771 .... S21–08
BGH decision (2004) XXIX YCA 700 .... S20–120
BHPB Freight Pty Ltd v Cosco Oceania Chartering Pty Ltd [2008] F.C.A. 551 .... S10–43
Bilta (UK) Ltd (In Liquidation) v Nazir [2010] EWHC 1086 (Ch); [2010] Bus. L.R. 1634; [2010] 2 Lloyd's Rep. 29 .... S10–65
Blair v Gibb (1738) Mor. 664 .... R56 10
BLCT (13096) Ltd v J Sainsbury Plc [2003] EWCA Civ 884; [2004] 1 C.L.C. 24; [2004] 2 P. & C.R. 3; (2003) 147 S.J.L.B. 815 .... S1–05, R70–33
BMBF (No.12) Ltd v Harland & Wolff Shipbuilding & Heavy Industries Ltd [2001] EWCA Civ 862; [2001] 2 All E.R. (Comm) 385; [2001] 2 Lloyd's Rep. 227; [2001] C.L.C. 1552 .... R53–16
Bonnor v Balfour Kilpatrick Ltd, 1974 S.C. 223; 1975 S.L.T. (Notes) 3 IH (1 Div) R69–14
Bottiglieri di Navigazione SpA v Cosco Qingdao Ocean Shipping Co (The Bunga Saga Lima); Bunga Saga Lima, The [2005] EWHC 244 (Comm); [2005] 2 Lloyd's Rep. 1 .... R70–24
Boyd & Forrest (A Firm) v Glasgow & South Western Railway Co (No.1), 1912 S.C. (H.L.) 93; 1912 1 S.L.T. 476 HL R68–65
Boyle v Glasgow Royal Infirmary and Associated Hospitals Board of Management, 1969 S.C. 72; 1969 S.L.T. 137 IH (1 Div) R28–28
BP Chemicals Ltd v Kingdom Engineering (Fife) Ltd [1994] 2 Lloyd's Rep. 373; 69 B.L.R. 113; 38 Con. L.R. 14; (1994) 10 Const. L.J. 116 QBD R50–10
Bradford v McLeod, 1986 S.L.T. 244; 1985 S.C.C.R. 379; [1986] Crim. L.R. 690 HCJ R24–09

Table of Cases

Braes of Doune Wind Farm (Scotland) Ltd v Alfred McAlpine Business Services Ltd [2008] EWHC 426 (TCC); [2008] 2 All E.R. (Comm) 493; [2008] 1 Lloyd's Rep. 608; [2008] 1 C.L.C. 487; [2008] B.L.R. 321; [2008] Bus. L.R. D137 .... S3–05, S3–16, S3–20, S3–21, R70–19
Brakinrig v Menzies (1841) 4 D. 474 IH (2 Div) S2–12
Brandeis Brokers Ltd v Black [2001] 2 All E.R. (Comm) 980; [2001] 2 Lloyd's Rep. 359 QBD (Comm) R32–06
Bremer Handelsgesellschaft mbH v Westzucker GmbH (No.2); sub nom. Bunge GmbH v Westzucker GmbH [1981] 2 Lloyd's Rep. 130; [1981] Com. L.R. 179 CA (Civ Div) R51–39, R51–47, R51–49
Bremner v Elder (1875) 2 R. (HL) 136 .... R3–03
Brockton Capital LLP v Atlantic-Pacific Capital Inc [2014] EWHC 1459 (Comm) . R68–79
Brown v EE Caledonia Ltd, 1993 G.W.D. 24–1478 .... S30–11
Brown v Hamilton DC, 1983 S.C. (H.L.) 1; 1983 S.L.T. 397; (1983) 133 N.L.J. 63 HL S13–05
Bulgarian Foreign Trade Bank Ltd (Bulbank) v Al Trade Finance Inc (2001) XXVI YCA 291 Sup Ct (Sweden); Case 1881-99 Unreported October 27, 2000 Supreme Court S6–13, R26–09, R26–18
Bulk & Metal Transport (UK) LLP v Voc Bulk Ultra Handymax Pool LLC (Voc Gallant); Voc Gallant, The [2009] EWHC 288 (Comm); [2009] 2 All E.R. (Comm) 377; [2009] 1 Lloyd's Rep. 418 .... R1–22
Bulk Ship Union SA v Clipper Bulk Shipping Ltd [2012] EWHC 2595 (Comm) R58–20
Bunge SA v ADM do Brasil Ltda [2009] EWHC 845 (Comm); [2009] 2 Lloyd's Rep. 175; [2009] 1 C.L.C. 608 .... R40–08
Bunge SA v Nibulon Trading BV [2013] EWHC 3936 (Comm) R71–07
Burt v Kirkcaldy [1965] 1 W.L.R. 474; [1965] 1 All E.R. 741; (1965) 129 J.P. 190; (1965) 109 S.J. 33 QBD R83–14
Butera v Pagnan (1979) IV YCA 296 .... S20–91

C v D [2007] EWCA Civ 1282; [2008] 1 All E.R. (Comm) 1001; [2008] Bus. L.R. 843; [2008] 1 Lloyd's Rep. 239; [2008] C.P. Rep. 11; [2007] 2 C.L.C. 930; 116 Con. L.R. 230 .... S6–12, S9–09, S20–30
Calderbank v Calderbank [1976] Fam. 93; [1975] 3 W.L.R. 586; [1975] 3 All E.R. 333; (1975) 5 Fam. Law 190; (1975) 119 S.J. 490 CA (Civ Div) R62–20
Caledonian Insurance Co v Gilmour [1893] A.C. 85; (1892) 20 R. (H.L.) 13 HL S10–69, S10–70
Caledonian Railway Co v Lockhart (1860) 3 Macq 808 .... R34–04, R34–05
Campbell v Campbell (1843) 5 D. 530 IH (2 Div) S2–12
Canada Dalimpex Ltd v Janicki [2003] 172 O.A.C. 321 .... S10–25
Caparo Group Ltd v Fagor Arrasate Sociedad Cooperativa [2000] A.D.R.L.J. 254 ... S14–09
Capital & Counties Plc v Hawa [1991] 2 E.G.L.R. 133; [1991] 46 E.G. 163 Ch D ... R28–16
Cargill International SA Antigua (Geneva Branch) v Sociedad Iberica de Molturacion SA; Sociedad Iberica de Molturacion SA v Cargill International SA; SIMSA v Cargill International SA [1998] 1 Lloyd's Rep. 489; [1998] C.L.C. 231; (1998) 95(4) L.S.G. 33; (1998) 142 S.J.L.B. 34 CA (Civ Div) R51–06, R51–34
Carmichael v Caledonian Railway Co; sub nom. Caledonian Railway v Carmichael (1870-75) L.R. 2 Sc. 56; (1870) 8 M. (H.L.) 119 HL R50–08
Carnegie v Nature Conservancy Council, 1992 S.L.T. 342 OH R62–22, R62–25
Carter (t/a Michael Carter Partnership) v Harold Simpson Associates (Architects) Ltd [2004] UKPC 29; [2005] 1 W.L.R. 919; [2004] 2 Lloyd's Rep. 512; [2004] 2 C.L.C. 1053; (2004) 101(27) L.S.G. 29; (2004) 148 S.J.L.B. 759 .... R72–06
Carters (Merchants) Ltd v Ferraro (1979) IV YCA 275 CA (Naples) S20–50
Case reference 200.005.269/01 April 28, 2009 CA (Amsterdam) S20–98
Case reference 365094/KG RK 07-7 50 February 28, 2008 .... S20–98
Cetelem SA v Roust Holdings Ltd [2005] EWCA Civ 618; [2005] 1 W.L.R. 3555; [2005] 4 All E.R. 52; [2005] 2 All E.R. (Comm) 203; [2005] 2 Lloyd's Rep. 494; [2005] 1 C.L.C. 821 .... R46–55
CGU International Insurance Plc v AstraZeneca Insurance Co Ltd (Permission to Appeal); sub nom. AstraZeneca Insurance Co Ltd v CGU International Insurance Plc (Permission to Appeal) [2006] EWCA Civ 1340; [2007] Bus. L.R. 162;

Table of Cases

[2007] 1 All E.R. (Comm) 501; [2007] 1 Lloyd's Rep. 142; [2007] C.P. Rep. 4; [2006] 2 C.L.C. 441; [2006] H.R.L.R. 43 .... R70–43, R70–49
Channel Tunnel Group Ltd v Balfour Beatty Construction Ltd; France Manche SA v Balfour Beatty Construction Ltd [1993] A.C. 334; [1993] 2 W.L.R. 262; [1993] 1 All E.R. 664; [1993] 1 Lloyd's Rep. 291; 61 B.L.R. 1; 32 Con. L.R. 1; [1993] I.L.Pr. 607; (1993) 137 S.J.L.B. 36; [1993] N.P.C. 8 HL S10–06
Charles M Willie & Co (Shipping) Ltd v Ocean Laser Shipping Ltd (The Smaro); George Roussos Sons SA v Charles M Willie & Co (Shipping) Ltd [1999] 1 Lloyd's Rep. 225; [1999] C.L.C. 301 QBD (Comm Ct) R37–10, R54–06
Checkpoint Ltd v Strathclyde Pension Fund [2003] EWCA Civ 84; [2003] L. & T.R. 22; [2003] 1 E.G.L.R. 1; [2003] 14 E.G. 124; [2003] 8 E.G. 128 (C.S.); (2003) 100(12) L.S.G. 29; (2003) 147 S.J.L.B. 233; [2003] N.P.C. 23 .... R24–32, R51–42
Chimimport Plc v G D'Alesio SAS (The Paula D'Alesio); Paula D'Alesio, The [1994] 2 Lloyd's Rep. 366; [1994] C.L.C. 459 QBD (Comm Ct) R19–10
China Agribusiness Development Corp v Balli Trading [1998] 2 Lloyd's Rep. 76; [1997] C.L.C. 1437 QBD (Comm Ct) S20–06, S20–59
China Merchant Heavy Industry Co Ltd v JGC Corp (2003) XXVIII YCA 267 ...... S10–50
China Nanhai Oil v Gee Tai Holdings Co Ltd [1995] A.D.R.L.J. 127 .... S20–05, S20–60
China Resources Metal Ltd v Anada Non-Ferrous Metals Ltd [1994] 3 H.K.C. 526 .... S10–48
China State Construction Engineering Corp Guandong Branch v Madiford Ltd [1992] 1 H.K.C. 320 .... S10–48
Chromalloy Aeroservices Inc v Arab Republic of Egypt, 939 F.Supp. 907 (1996) District Ct (US) S20–97
City of London v Sancheti [2008] EWCA Civ 1283; [2009] Bus. L.R. 996; [2009] 1 Lloyd's Rep. 117; [2008] 2 C.L.C. 730 .... S10–41
City of Moscow v Bankers Trust Co. See Department of Economic Policy and Development of the City of Moscow v Bankers Trust Co
Clark v Stirling (1839) 1 D. 955 .... R46–54
Clyde & Co LLP v Bates van Winkelhof [2011] EWHC 668 (QB); [2011] C.P. Rep. 31; [2012] I.C.R. 928; [2011] I.R.L.R. 467; [2011] Arb. L.R. 7; (2011) 155(12) S.J.L.B. 30 .... S30–08
CMA CGM SA v Beteiligungs KG MS Northern Pioneer Schiffahrtsgesellschaft mbH & Co (the Northern Pioneer) [2002] EWCA Civ 1878; [2003] 1 W.L.R. 1015; [2003] 3 All E.R. 330; [2003] 1 All E.R. (Comm) 204; [2003] 1 Lloyd's Rep. 212; [2003] 1 C.L.C. 141; (2003) 100(9) L.S.G. 28 .... R69–22, R70–14, R70–16, R70–22, R70–26, R70–27
Coal Authority v Trustees of the Nostell Trust [2005] EWHC 154 (TCC) ... R70–15, R70–28
Cole v Silvermills Estates and Land Ltd [2011] CSIH 37; 2012 S.C. 1; 2011 S.L.T. 779; 2011 G.W.D. 20–461 .... R61–17
Collins (Contractors) Ltd v Baltic Quay Management (1994) Ltd [2004] EWCA Civ 1757; [2005] B.L.R. 63; [2005] T.C.L.R. 3; 99 Con. L.R. 1; (2005) 102(5) L.S.G. 26 .... S2–16
Cominco France SA v Soquiber SL (1983) VIII YCA 408 Sup Ct (Spain) S20–40
COMITAS v SOVAG (1983) VIII YCA 366 .... S20–91
Commerce & Industry Insurance Co (Canada) v Lloyd's Underwriters; sub nom. Viking Insurance Co v Rossdale [2002] 1 W.L.R. 1323; [2002] 2 All E.R. (Comm) 204; [2002] 1 Lloyd's Rep. 219; [2002] C.L.C. 26 QBD (Comm) R45–10
Commerzbank AG v Large, 1977 S.C. 375; 1977 S.L.T. 219 IH (1 Div) R48–09
Commonwealth of Australia v Cockatoo Dockyard Pty Ltd (1995) 36 N.S.W.L.R. 662 .... S15–20
Compagnie de Saint Gobain-Pont a Mousson v Fertilizer Corp of India Ltd (1976) I YCA 184 .... S20–86
Compagnie des Bauxites de Guinee v Hammermills Inc (1993) XVIII YCA 566 District Ct (US) S20–61
Compania Sud-Americana De Vapores SA v Nippon Yusen Kaisha; Nippon Yusen Kaisha v Compania Sud-Americana De Vapores SA [2009] EWHC 1606 (Comm) R68–23
Compton Beauchamp Estates Ltd v Spence [2013] EWHC 1101 (Ch); [2013] 2 P. & C.R. 15; [2013] 20 E.G. 107 (C.S.) R51–49

Table of Cases

Conder Structures v Kvaerner Construction Ltd [1999] A.D.R.L.J. 305 .... R12–07
Continental Enterprises Ltd v Shandong Zhucheng Foreign Trade Group Co [2005] EWHC 92 (Comm) S20–19
Continental Tranfert Technique Ltd v Nigeria [2010] EWHC 780 (Comm) S20–101
Corcoran v AIG Multi-line Syndicate Inc (1990) XV YCA 586 .... S20–26
Corcoran v Ardra Insurance Co Ltd (1989) XIV YCA 733 .... S10–50
Corcoran v Ardra Insurance Co Ltd (1991) XVI YCA 663 .... S20–26
Corporacion Transnacional de Inversiones SA de CV v STET International SpA (2000) O.R. 414 .... S20–03
Corvetina Technology Ltd v Clough Engineering Ltd [2004] N.S.W.S.C. 700 .... S20–116
Cottonex Anstalt v Patriot Spinning Mills Ltd [2013] EWHC 236 (Comm) R68–80
Crudens, Applicants; sub nom. Crudens Ltd, Petitioners, 1971 S.C. 64 IH (1 Div) ... R45–13
Cunninghame v Drummond (1491) Mor. 635 .... R9–02, R24–46, R51–62
Curtis v London Rent Assessment Committee; sub nom. Curtis v Chairman of London Rent Assessment Committee [1999] Q.B. 92; [1998] 3 W.L.R. 1427; [1997] 4 All E.R. 842; (1998) 30 H.L.R. 733; [1998] 1 E.G.L.R. 79; [1998] 15 E.G. 120; [1997] E.G. 132 (C.S.); [1997] N.P.C. 140 CA (Civ Div) R51–49
Czech Republic v CME Unreported May 15, 2003 CA (Sweden) R51–11

DALIMPEX v Janicki [2003] 172 O.A.C. 321 .... S10–55, R68–70
Dallah Real Estate & Tourism Holding Co v Pakistan; sub nom. Dallah Real Estate & Tourism Holding Co v Ministry of Religious Affairs; Dallah v Pakistan [2010] UKSC 46; [2011] 1 A.C. 763; [2010] 3 W.L.R. 1472; [2011] 1 All E.R. 485; [2011] 1 All E.R. (Comm) 383; [2011] Bus. L.R. 158; [2010] 2 Lloyd's Rep. 691; [2010] 2 C.L.C. 793; 133 Con. L.R. 1; (2010) 160 N.L.J. 1569 .... S20–07, S20–31, R67–13
Dalmia Dairy Industries Ltd v National Bank of Pakistan [1978] 2 Lloyd's Rep. 223 .... S20–126
Dalmine SpA v M & M Sheet Metal Forming Machinery (1999) XXIV YCA 709 Corte Suprema di Cassazione (Italy) S20–18
Damond Lock Grabowski v Laing Investments (Bracknell) Ltd, 60 B.L.R. 112 .... R12–08
Danae Air Transport SA v Air Canada [2000] 1 W.L.R. 395; [2000] 2 All E.R. 649; [1999] 2 All E.R. (Comm) 943; [1999] 2 Lloyd's Rep. 547; [2000] C.P. Rep. 25; [1999] C.L.C. 1859; (1999) 96(32) L.S.G. 31; [1999] N.P.C. 108 CA (Civ Div) ... R58–28
Dardana Ltd v Yukos Oil Co (No.1); sub nom. Petroalliance Services Co Ltd v Yukos Oil Co; Yukos Oil Co v Dardana Ltd [2002] EWCA Civ 543; [2002] 1 All E.R. (Comm) 819; [2002] 2 Lloyd's Rep. 326; [2002] C.L.C. 1120 .... S20–136, S20–144, S20–147, S21–09
Dardana Ltd v Yukos Oil Co (No.2) [2002] 2 Lloyd's Rep. 261 QBD (Comm) S20–148
David Wilson Homes Ltd v Survey Services Ltd (In Liquidation) [2001] EWCA Civ 34; [2001] 1 All E.R. (Comm) 449; [2001] B.L.R. 267; (2001) 3 T.C.L.R. 13; 80 Con. L.R. 8 .... S2–06
DDT Trucks of North America Ltd v DDT Holdings Ltd [2007] EWHC 1542 (Comm); [2007] 2 Lloyd's Rep. 213 .... R68–70
Decision (1994) XIX YCA 700 .... S21–07
Decision of August 25, 2004 reported in (2006) Cahiers de l'Arbitrage 441 .... S20–128
Deko Scotland Ltd v Edinburgh Royal Joint Venture, 2003 S.L.T. 727; 2003 G.W.D. 13–396 OH R61–08, R61–15
Della Sanara Kustvaart v Fallimento Cap Giovanni Coppola Srl (1992) XVII YCA 542 CA (Genoa) S10–45
Demco Investments & Commercial SA v SE Banken Forsakring Holding AB [2005] EWHC 1398 (Comm); [2005] 2 Lloyd's Rep. 650 .... R28–16, R28–17, R70–17
Department of Economic Policy and Development of the City of Moscow v Bankers Trust Co; sub nom. Department of Economics, Policy and Development of the City of Moscow v Bankers Trust Co; Moscow City Council v Bankers Trust Co [2004] EWCA Civ 314; [2005] Q.B. 207; [2004] 3 W.L.R. 533; [2004] 4 All E.R. 746; [2004] 2 All E.R. (Comm) 193; [2004] 2 Lloyd's Rep. 179; [2004] 1 C.L.C. 1099; [2004] B.L.R. 229; (2004) 148 S.J.L.B. 389 ...... S15–13, S15–18, S15–19, R26–14, R26–26
Dermajaya Properties Sdn Bhd v Premium Properties Sdn Bhd (2002) 2 S.L.R. 164 High Ct (Sing) S32–02

Table of Cases

Derry v Peek; sub nom. Peek v Derry (1889) 14 App. Cas. 337; (1889) 5 T.L.R. 625 HL R68–65
Deutsche Schachtbau- und Tiefbohrgesellschaft mbH v Ras Al-Khaimah National Oil Co; Deutsche Schachtbau- und Tiefbohrgesellschaft mbH v Ras Al-Khaimah National Oil Co (Garnishee Proceedings); Deutsche Schachtbau- und Tiefbohrgesellschaft mbH v Shell International Petroleum Co Ltd (Nos.1 and 2); sub nom. DST v Rakoil [1990] 1 A.C. 295; [1988] 3 W.L.R. 230; [1988] 2 All E.R. 833; [1988] 2 Lloyd's Rep. 293; (1988) 85(28) L.S.G. 45 HL S20–29, S20–73
Diag Human SA v Czech Republic [2013] EWHC 3190 (Comm); [2014] 1 All E.R. (Comm) 605 .... S19–12
Diamond v PJW Enterprises Ltd. *See* Gillies Ramsay Diamond v PJW Enterprises Ltd
Discain Project Services Ltd v Opecprime Developments Ltd [2001] EWHC 450 (TCC) R17–08
Dolling-Baker v Merrett [1990] 1 W.L.R. 1205; [1991] 2 All E.R. 890; (1990) 134 S.J. 806 CA (Civ Div) R26–07, R26–08, R26–14, R26–20
Dombo Beheer BV v Netherlands (A/274-A) (1994) 18 E.H.R.R. 213 ECtHR R24–27
Donaldson's Hospital Trustees v Esslemont, 1925 S.C. 199 .... R19–03
Double K Oil Products 1996 Ltd v Neste Oil Oyj [2009] EWHC 3380 (Comm); [2010] 1 Lloyd's Rep. 141; (2010) 160 N.L.J. 68 .... R68–66, R68–69, R68–71
Douglas v Douglas's Trs (1867) 5 M 827 .... R50–22
Drummond v Bell-Irving; sub nom. Drummond v Peel's Trustees, 1929 S.C. 484; 1929 S.L.T. 450 IH R46–19
DS v HM Advocate; sub nom. HM Advocate v DS [2007] UKPC D1; 2007 S.C. (P.C.) 1; 2007 S.L.T. 1026; 2007 S.C.C.R. 222; [2007] H.R.L.R. 28; 24 B.H.R.C. 412 .... S1–16, S1–17
Dubai Islamic Bank PJSC v Paymentech Merchant Services Inc [2001] 1 All E.R. (Comm) 514; [2001] 1 Lloyd's Rep. 65; [2001] C.L.C. 173; (2000) 97(47) L.S.G. 39 .... S3–17, S3–18
Dubois & Vanderwalle v Boots Frites BV (1999) XXIV YCA 640 Cour d'Appel (Paris) S20–67
Duffy (John) v Normand, 1995 S.L.T. 1264; 1995 S.C.C.R. 538 HCJ (Appeal) R83–14
Dumbarton Water Commissioners v Lord Blantyre (1884) 12 R. 115 .... R19–03
Dumbarton Water-works Commissioners v The Right Honourable Lord Blantyre (1884) 12 R. 115 IH (1 Div) S10–33
Durham CC v Darlington BC [2003] EWHC 2598 (Admin); [2004] B.L.G.R. 311; [2003] N.P.C. 136 .... R50–10
Durie December 15, 1631 .... S4–07
Dutch Hoge Raad (Supreme Court) (1976) I YCA 195 .... S20–65
Dutco (Pvt) Ltd v Dajen (Pvt) Ltd [1997] 2 Zimbabwe L.R. 199 .... S20–88

EAGLE STAR INSURANCE CO LTD v Yuval Insurance Co [1978] 1 Lloyd's Rep. 357 CA (Civ Div) S10–61
Eco Swiss China Time Ltd v Benetton International NV (C-126/97) [1999] 2 All E.R. (Comm) 44; [1999] E.C.R. I-3055; [1999] U.K.C.L.R. 183; [2000] 5 C.M.L.R. 816 .... S20–128
ECONERG Ltd v National Electricity Company AD (2000) XXV YCA 678 Sup Ct (Bulgaria) S21–04
E D and F Man Sugar Ltd v Unicargo Transportgesellschaft GmbH [2013] EWCA Civ 1449 .... R70–39
EDO Corp v Ultra Electronics Ltd [2009] EWHC 682 (Ch); [2009] Bus. L.R. 1306; [2009] 2 Lloyd's Rep. 349 .... S10–18
Edwards (Inspector of Taxes) v Bairstow; Edwards (Inspector of Taxes) v Harrison [1956] A.C. 14; [1955] 3 W.L.R. 410; [1955] 3 All E.R. 48; 48 R. & I.T. 534; 36 T.C. 207; (1955) 34 A.T.C. 198; [1955] T.R. 209; (1955) 99 S.J. 558 HL R28–16, R41–11
Egypt v SPP Ltd (1985) X YCA 113 .... S20–23
Eitzen Bulk A/S v TTMI Sarl; Bonnie Smithwick, The [2012] EWHC 202 (Comm); [2012] 2 All E.R. 100; [2012] 1 Lloyd's Rep. 407 .... R71–29

xvii

Table of Cases

El Nasharty v J Sainsbury Plc [2007] EWHC 2618 (Comm); [2008] 1 Lloyd's Rep. 360 .... S5–08
Elektrim SA v Vivendi Universal SA [2007] EWHC 11 (Comm); [2007] 2 All E.R. (Comm) 365; [2007] 1 Lloyd's Rep. 693; [2007] 1 C.L.C. 16; [2007] Bus. L.R. D69 .... R68–69
Emmott v Michael Wilson & Partners Ltd; Michael Wilson & Partners Ltd v Emmott [2009] EWHC 1 (Comm); [2009] Bus. L.R. 723; [2009] 2 All E.R. (Comm) 856; [2009] 1 Lloyd's Rep. 233 .... S15–20, R46–12, R46–15
Emmott v Michael Wilson & Partners Ltd. *See* Michael Wilson & Partners Ltd v Emmott
English v Donnelly, 1958 S.C. 494; 1959 S.L.T. 2 IH (1 Div) S6–09
English v Emery Reimbold & Strick Ltd; Verrechia (t/a Freightmaster Commercials) v Commissioner of Police of the Metropolis; DJ&C Withers (Farms) Ltd v Ambic Equipment Ltd [2002] EWCA Civ 605; [2002] 1 W.L.R. 2409; [2002] 3 All E.R. 385; [2002] C.P.L.R. 520; [2003] I.R.L.R. 710; [2002] U.K.H.R.R. 957; (2002) 99(22) L.S.G. 34; (2002) 152 N.L.J. 758; (2002) 146 S.J.L.B. 123 .... R51–49
ERDC Construction Ltd v HM Love & Co, 1994 S.C. 620 .... S4–11
ERDC Construction Ltd v HM Love & Co (No.2), 1996 S.C. 523; 1997 S.L.T. 175; 1996 S.C.L.R. 886 IH (1 Div) S29–01, R28–06, R41–04, R41–12, R41–13, R42–09
Essex CC v Premier Recycling Ltd [2006] EWHC 3594 (TCC); [2007] B.L.R. 233 ... R69–09
Esso Australia Resources v Plowman (1995) 128 A.L.R. 391 .... S15–20, R26–08, R26–09, R26–18
Ethiopia v Baruch Foster Corp (1977) II YCA 252 .... S21–13
Europcar Italia SpA v Maiellano Tours International Inc, 156 F.3d 310 (1998) CA (US) S20–137
European Grain & Shipping Ltd v Johnston [1983] Q.B. 520; [1983] 2 W.L.R. 241; [1982] 3 All E.R. 989; [1982] 2 Lloyd's Rep. 550; [1982] Com. L.R. 246; [1984] E.C.C. 219; (1982) 126 S.J. 783 CA (Civ Div) R51–10
Excelsior Film TV Srl v UGC-PH (1999) XXIV YCA 643 CFI (France) S20–121
Exmar BV v National Iranian Tanker Co (The Trade Fortitude); Trade Fortitude, The [1992] 1 Lloyd's Rep. 169 QBD (Comm Ct) R54–07, R54–08

F Ltd v M Ltd [2009] EWHC 275 (TCC); [2009] 2 All E.R. (Comm) 519; [2009] 1 Lloyd's Rep. 537; [2009] C.I.L.L. 2681 .... R51–15, R51–16, R51–17
F&G Sykes (Wessex) Ltd v Fine Fare Ltd [1967] 1 Lloyd's Rep. 53 CA S2–15
Fairlie Yacht Slip v Lumsden, 1977 S.L.T. (Notes) 41 IH (1 Div) S29–01
Far Eastern Shipping Co v AKP Sovcomflot [1995] 1 Lloyd's Rep. 520 QBD (Comm) S20–143
Fashion Ribbon Co Inc v Iberband SL (2005) XXX YCA 627 Sup Ct (Spain) S20–48
FCLG Enterprises v Golden Margarine Ltd [2004] O.J. 3804 .... R54–10
Federal Insurance Co v Transamerica Occidental Life Insurance Co; Transamerica Occidental Life Insurance Co v Federal Insurance Co [1999] 2 All E.R. (Comm) 138; [1999] 2 Lloyd's Rep. 286; [1999] C.L.C. 1406; (1999) 149 N.L.J. 1037 QBD (Comm Ct) S1–05
Fence Gate Ltd v NEL Construction Ltd [2001] 82 Con. L.R. 41 QBD (T&T Ct) ... R28–16, R62–07
Fertilizer Corp of India v IDI Management Inc (1982) VII YCA 382 District Ct (US) S20–83, S20–86
FIAT SpA v Suriname (1998) XXIII YCA 880 District Ct (US) S20–132
Fidelity Management SA v Myriad International Holdings BV [2005] EWHC 1193 (Comm); [2005] 2 All E.R. (Comm) 312; [2005] 2 Lloyd's Rep. 508 .... R51–48, R68–36
Fife Coal Co Ltd v Feeney; sub nom. Feeney v Fife Coal Co, 1918 S.C. 197; 1918 1 S.L.T. 129 IH (2 Div) R62–18
Fincantieri-Cantieri Navali Italiani SpA v Ministry of Defence of Iraq (1996) XXI YCA 594 CA (Genoa) S30–16, S30–20
Finmoon Ltd v Baltic Reefers Management Ltd [2012] EWHC 920 (Comm); [2012] 2 Lloyd's Rep. 388; [2012] 1 C.L.C. 813 .... R1–23
Fiona Trust & Holding Corp v Privalov; sub nom. Premium Nafta Products Ltd v Fili Shipping Co Ltd [2007] UKHL 40; [2007] Bus. L.R. 1719; [2007] 4 All E.R. 951; [2007] 2 All E.R. (Comm) 1053; [2008] 1 Lloyd's Rep. 254; [2007] 2 C.L.C. 553;

Table of Cases

114 Con. L.R. 69; [2007] C.I.L.L. 2528; (2007) 104(42) L.S.G. 34; (2007) 151 S.J.L.B. 1364 .... S4–08, S4–09, S5–07, S5–11, S14–10, S14–11, S20–79, S20–81, R19–08, R19–11, R46–10, R49–06
Fisher v Colquhoun (1844) 6 D. 1286 .... S25–10
Flannery v Halifax Estate Agencies Ltd (t/a Colleys Professional Services) [2000] 1 W.L.R. 377; [2000] 1 All E.R. 373; [2000] C.P. Rep. 18; [1999] B.L.R. 107; (1999) 11 Admin. L.R. 465; (1999) 15 Const. L.J. 313; (1999) 96(13) L.S.G. 32; (1999) 149 N.L.J. 284; [1999] N.P.C. 22 CA (Civ Div) R51–49
Fleming v Gemmill, 1908 S.C. 340; (1907) 15 S.L.T. 691 IH (1 Div) R60–10
Flight Training International Inc v International Fire Training Equipment Ltd [2004] EWHC 721 (Comm); [2004] 2 All E.R. (Comm) 568 .... S2–10
Fondation M v Banque X, ATF 122 III 139, ASA Bulletin 527, Swiss Fed. Trib. Apr. 29 1996 .... S10–25
Food Corp of India v Marastro Cia Naviera SA (The Trade Fortitude) (No.1); Food Corp of India v Marastro Cia Naviera SA (The Trade Fortitude) (No.2); Trade Fortitude, The (No.1); Trade Fortitude, The (No.2) [1987] 1 W.L.R. 134; [1986] 3 All E.R. 500; [1986] 2 Lloyd's Rep. 209; (1986) 83 L.S.G. 2919; (1986) 136 N.L.J. 607; (1986) 130 S.J. 649 CA (Civ Div) R58–14
Food Services of America Inc v Pan Pacific Specialities Ltd (2004) XXIX YCA 581 Sup Ct (BC) S20–68
Forbes v Underwood (1886) 13 R. 465 .... R15–05, R15–15
Fountain Forestry Holdings Ltd v Sparkes, 1989 S.C. 224; 1989 S.L.T. 853; 1989 S.C.L.R. 509 OH R24–32
Fowler v Merrill Lynch Pierce and Smith Inc (1985) X YCA 499 .... S10–50
Fraser v Pattie (1847) 9 D. 303 .... R46–20
Fraser v Wright (1838) 16 S. 1049 .... R56–11
Frota Oceanica Brasiliera SA v Steamship Mutual Underwriting Association (Bermuda) Ltd (The Frotanorte); Frotanorte, The [1996] 2 Lloyd's Rep. 461; [1997] C.L.C. 230 CA (Civ Div) S4–20
Fuga AG v Bunge AG [1975] 2 Lloyd's Rep. 192 QBD (Comm Ct) R58–14
Fulham Football Club (1987) Ltd v Richards [2011] EWCA Civ 855; [2012] Ch. 333; [2012] 2 W.L.R. 1008; [2012] 1 All E.R. 414; [2012] 1 All E.R. (Comm) 1148; [2012] Bus. L.R. 606; [2011] B.C.C. 910; [2012] 1 B.C.L.C. 335; [2012] 1 C.L.C. 850; [2011] Arb. L.R. 22 .... S10–17
Fun Sang Trading Ltd v Kai Sun Sea Products & Food Co Ltd [1992] A.D.R.L.J. 93 .... S10–25, R19–06, R19–12

G SpA v V SpA (1993) XVIII YCA 143 .... S30–16
G1 Venues Ltd, Petitioners [2013] CSOH 202; 2014 G.W.D. 4-75 ... S1–07, R21–16, R24–52
GA Estates Ltd v Caviapen Trustees Ltd (No.2), 1993 S.L.T. 1051 IH (Ex Div) S23–12
Gall v Bird (1855) 17 D. 1027 .... R4–05
Galloway Water Power Co v Carmichael, 1937 S.C. 135; 1937 S.L.T. 188 IH (2 Div) R46–36, R46–74
Gannet Shipping Ltd v Eastrade Commodities Inc; Eastrade Commodities Inc v Gannet Shipping Ltd [2002] 1 All E.R. (Comm) 297; [2002] 1 Lloyd's Rep. 713; [2002] C.L.C. 365 QBD (Comm Ct) R58–34, R68–28, R68–43
Gao v Keeneye Holdings Ltd [2011] HKCA 459 on appeal from [2011] HKCFI 240 .... S2–08, S20–122, R57–23
Gater Assets Ltd v Nak Naftogaz Ukrainiy [2007] EWCA Civ 988; [2008] Bus. L.R. 388; [2008] 1 All E.R. (Comm) 209; [2007] 2 Lloyd's Rep. 588; [2008] C.P. Rep. 4; [2007] 2 C.L.C. 567 .... S20–148
Gater Assets Ltd v Nak Naftogaz Ukrainiy [2008] EWHC 1108 (Comm); [2009] Bus. L.R. 396; [2009] 1 All E.R. (Comm) 667; [2008] 2 Lloyd's Rep. 295 .... S20–119
Gatoil International Plc v National Iranian Oil Company Unreported February 22, 1990 CA (Civ Div) S10–52
Gatoil v National Iranian Oil Co (1993) Revue de l'Arbitrage 281 CA (Paris) S10–45
Gbangbola v Smith & Sherriff Ltd [1998] 3 All E.R. 730; (1999) 1 T.C.L.R. 136 QBD (T&CC) R58–29
General Feeds Inc Panama v Slobodna Plovidba Yugoslavia (The Krapan J); Krapan J, The [1999] 1 Lloyd's Rep. 688 QBD (Comm) R51–49

Table of Cases

Generica Ltd v Pharmaceuticals Basics Inc, 125 F.3d 1123 (1997) CA (US) S20–49
Geogas SA v Trammo Gas Ltd (The Baleares); Baleares, The [1993] 1 Lloyd's Rep. 215 CA (Civ Div) R28–16
George Cohen Sons & Co Ltd v Jamieson & Paterso, 1963 S.C. 289; 1963 S.L.T. 35 OH R46–22
Gillies Ramsay Diamond v PJW Enterprises Ltd; sub nom. Diamond v PJW Enterprises Ltd, 2004 S.C. 430; 2004 S.L.T. 545; [2004] B.L.R. 131; 2004 G.W.D. 12–262 IH (2 Div) S2–11
Gillies v Secretary of State for Work and Pensions; sub nom. Secretary of State for Work and Pensions v Gillies [2006] UKHL 2; [2006] 1 W.L.R. 781; [2006] 1 All E.R. 731; 2006 S.C. (H.L.) 71; 2006 S.L.T. 77; 2006 S.C.L.R. 276; [2006] I.C.R. 267; (2006) 9 C.C.L. Rep. 404; (2006) 103(9) L.S.G. 33; (2006) 150 S.J.L.B. 127; 2006 G.W.D. 3–66 .... R24–13
Glasgow City and District Railway Company v MacGeorge, Cowan and Galloway (1886) 13 R. 609 .... R71–31
Glencot Development & Design Co Ltd v Ben Barrett & Son (Contractors) Ltd [2001] B.L.R. 207; (2001) 3 T.C.L.R. 11; 80 Con. L.R. 14; (2001) 17 Const. L.J. 336 QBD (TCC) S2–07, R57–22
Glidepath BV v Thompson [2005] EWHC 818 (Comm); [2005] 2 All E.R. (Comm) 833; [2005] 2 Lloyd's Rep. 549; [2005] 1 C.L.C. 1090 .... R26–14
Goel v Amega Ltd [2010] EWHC 2454 (TCC) R24–18
Golden Strait Corp v Nippon Yusen Kubishika Kaisha (The Golden Victory); Golden Victory, The [2007] UKHL 12; [2007] 2 A.C. 353; [2007] 2 W.L.R. 691; [2007] 3 All E.R. 1; [2007] 2 All E.R. (Comm) 97; [2007] Bus. L.R. 997; [2007] 2 Lloyd's Rep. 164; [2007] 1 C.L.C. 352; (2007) 157 N.L.J. 518; (2007) 151 S.J.L.B. 468 .... R69–22
Gray Construction Ltd v Harley Haddow LLP [2012] CSOH 92; 2012 S.L.T. 1035; 2012 G.W.D. 19–377 .... R26–20, R26–22, R26–24
Gray v Brown (1833) 11 S. 353 .... R46–48, R49–08
Groundshire v VHE Construction [2001] B.L.R. 395 QBD (T&CC) R12–06, R12–20, R58–19
Grow Biz International v DLT Holdings Inc (2005) XXX YCA 450 .... S20–59
Guandong New Technology Import and Export Corp v Chiu Sing (1993) XVIII YCA 385 High Ct (HK) S20–41
Guangzhou Dockyards Co Ltd v E.N.E. Aegiali I [2010] EWHC 2826 (Comm) R69–01
Guardcliffe Properties Ltd v City & St James [2003] EWHC 215 (Ch); [2003] 2 E.G.L.R. 16; [2003] 25 E.G. 143; (2003) 147 S.J.L.B. 693 .... R28–16
Guidance Investments Ltd v Guidance Investments Hotel Co BSC (Closed) [2013] EWHC 3413 (Comm) S4–09
GWL Kersten & Co BV v Societe Commerciale Raoul-Duval & Cie (1994) XIX YCA 708 CA (Amsterdam) S20–53

Hackston v Hackston, 1956 S.L.T. (Notes) 38 .... S30–12
Hackwood Ltd v Areen Design Services Ltd [2005] EWHC 2322 (TCC); (2006) 22 Const. L.J. 68 .... S14–12
Händler v Paczy. See Paczy v Händler & Natermann GmbH (No.2); Halfdan Grieg & Co A/S v Sterling Coal & Navigation Corp (The Lysland); Lysland, The [1973] Q.B. 843; [1973] 2 W.L.R. 904; [1973] 2 All E.R. 1073; [1973] 1 Lloyd's Rep. 296; (1973) 117 S.J. 415 CA (Civ Div) R41–12
Hague Court of First Instance decision (1979) IV YCA 305 .... S20–77
Halifax Financial Services Ltd v Intuitive Systems Ltd [1999] 1 All E.R. (Comm) 303; (2000) 2 T.C.L.R. 35; [1999] C.I.L.L. 1467 QBD S4–04, S4–06
Halki Shipping Corp v Sopex Oils Ltd (The Halki); Halki, The [1998] 1 W.L.R. 726; [1998] 2 All E.R. 23; [1998] 1 Lloyd's Rep. 465; [1998] C.L.C. 583; (1998) 142 S.J.L.B. 44; [1998] N.P.C. 4 CA (Civ Div) S1–05, S–16
Hall Street Associates LLC vs Mattel Inc (2008) 552 US 576 Sup Ct R69–02
Halvanon Insurance Co Ltd v Companhia de Seguros do Estado de Sao Paolo [1995] L.R.L.R 403 .... S10–50
Hamilton v Wakefield, 1993 S.L.T. (Sh Ct) 30 Sh Ct S6–08

Table of Cases

Hamlyn & Co v Talisker Distillery; sub nom. Talisker Distillery v Hamlyn & Co [1894]
A.C. 202; (1894) 21 R. (H.L.) 21; (1894) 2 S.L.T.12 HL S3–02, S6–09, S10–02,
S10–07, S12–16, S22–02, R68–55, R68–59
Harbour Assurance Co (UK) Ltd v Kansa General International Insurance Co Ltd
[1993] Q.B. 701; [1993] 3 W.L.R. 42; [1993] 3 All E.R. 897; [1993] 1 Lloyd's Rep.
455 CA (Civ Div) S20–19
Hashwani v Jivraj. *See* Jivraj v Hashwani
Hassneh Insurance Co of Israel v Stuart J Mew [1993] 2 Lloyd's Rep. 243 QBD
(Comm Ct) R26–08, R26–14
Hauschildt v Denmark (A/154) (1990) 12 E.H.R.R. 266 ECtHR R24–11
Hayter v Nelson & Home Insurance Co [1990] 2 Lloyd's Rep. 265; 23 Con. L.R. 88
QBD (Comm Ct) S2–16, S2–17
Hebei Import & Export Corp v Politek Engineering Co Ltd (1998) XXIV YCA 652
CA (HK) S20–38, S20–120, S20–127
Hebei Import & Export Corp v Polytek Engineering Co Ltd (1999) 2 HKCFAR
111 .... S20–125
Heifer International Inc v Christiansen [2007] EWHC 3015 (TCC); [2008] 2 All E.R.
(Comm) 831; [2008] Bus. L.R. D49 .... S4–25, A1–09
Henderson v Maclellan (1874) 1 R. 920 .... R46–54
Henry Boot Construction Ltd v Alstom Combined Cycles Ltd [2005] EWCA Civ 814;
[2005] 1 W.L.R. 3850; [2005] 3 All E.R. 832; [2005] 2 C.L.C. 63; [2005] B.L.R.
437; 101 Con. L.R. 52; (2005) 102(30) L.S.G. 28 .... S25–07
Highland Railway Co v Mitchell (1868) 6 M. 896 .... R45–08
Himpurna California Energy Ltd v PT (Persero) Perusahaan Listruik Negara (2000)
XXV YCA 13 .... R11–07
Hip Hing Construction Co Ltd v Hope Lee Iron Work Co [2002] 633 H.K.C.U. 1 ... S10–56
Hiscox v Outhwaite (No.1) [1992] 1 A.C. 562; [1991] 3 W.L.R. 297; [1991] 3 All E.R.
641; [1991] 2 Lloyd's Rep. 435 HL S18–12, R29–05, R52–02, R52–05, R52–06
Hiskett v Wilson (No.1), 2003 S.L.T. 58; 2003 S.C.L.R. 181; 2002 G.W.D. 33-1095
OH R19–17
HMV UK Ltd v Propinvest Friar LP [2011] EWCA Civ 1708; [2012] 1 Lloyd's Rep.
416; [2013] Bus. L.R. D5 .... R70–20
Hobbs Padgett & Co (Reinsurance) Ltd v JC Kirkland Ltd [1969] 2 Lloyd's Rep. 547;
(1969) 113 S.J. 832 CA (Civ Div) S4–20
Hober, Kraus and Melis v Soyak International Construction & Investment Inc (Case
Ö 4227-06), reported in Mealey's International Arbitration Report, Vol.24 No.3
(March 2009) R56–19
HOK Sport Ltd (formerly Lobb Partnership Ltd) v Aintree Racecourse Co Ltd [2002]
EWHC 3094 (TCC); [2003] B.L.R. 155; 86 Con. L.R. 165; [2003] Lloyd's Rep.
P.N. 148 .... R42–13, R67–33, R69–23
Holland House Property Investments Ltd v Crabbe [2008] CSIH 40; 2008 S.C. 619;
2008 S.L.T. 777; 2008 S.C.L.R. 633; 2008 G.W.D. 23-367 .... S2–05
Holmes v Nursing and Midwifery Council [2009] CSIH 82; 2010 G.W.D. 9-147 ...... R71–16
Home of Homes Ltd v Hammersmith and Fulham LBC [2003] EWHC 807 (TCC); 92
Con. L.R. 48 .... R58–31
Home Office v Harman; sub nom. Harman v Home Office [1983] 1 A.C. 280; [1982] 2
W.L.R. 338; [1982] 1 All E.R. 532; (1982) 126 S.J. 136 HL R26–14
Hope v Crookston Brothers (1890) 17 R. 868 IN (2 Div) R28–58
Hopetoun, Earl of v Scots Mines Co (1856) 18 D. 739 IH (1 Div) S12–17
House of Fraser Ltd v Scottish Widows Plc [2011] EWHC 2800 (Ch); [2012] 1
E.G.L.R. 9; [2012] 7 E.G. 92; [2011] Arb. L.R. 44 .... R28–17, R70–16, R70–17
Hrvatska Elektroprivreda dd v the Republic of Slovenia (ICSID case no.ARBl05
124) R33–06
Hume v Nursing and Midwifery Council [2007] CSIH 53; 2007 S.C. 644 .... R71–16
Hussmann (Europe) Ltd v Al Ameen Development & Trade Co; sub nom. Hussman
(Europe) Ltd v Al Ameen Development & Trade Co [2000] 2 Lloyd's Rep. 83;
[2000] C.L.C. 1243 QBD (Comm Ct) R19–13, R34–10, R51–54, R60–12, R67–29,
R68–23, R68–29, R68–41
Huyton SA v Jakil SpA [1999] 2 Lloyd's Rep. 83; 1998] C.L.C. 937 CA (Civ
Div) R72–03, R72–04

Table of Cases

ICC CASE 5946 (1991) XVI YCA 97 .... R48–07
Insurance Co v Lloyd's Syndicate [1995] 1 Lloyd's Rep. 272; [1994] C.L.C. 1303;
    [1995] 4 Re. L.R. 37 QBD (Comm Ct) R26–08, R26–14
Inter-Arab Investment Guarantee Corp v Banque Arabe et Internationale d'Inves-
    tissements (1997) XXII YCA 643 CFI (Brussels) S20–47
Inter-Arab Investment Guarantee Corp v Banque Arabe et Internationale d'Inves-
    tissements (1999) XXIV YCA 603 .... S20–69
Inter-Arab Investment Guarantee Corp v Banque Arabe et Internationale d'Inves-
    tissements (2001) XXVI YCA 207 Cour de Cassation S20–33
International Civil Aviation Organisation v Tripal Systems Ltd (1998) XXIII YCA
    226 Sup Ct (Quebec) R19–16
International Investor KCSC v Sanghi Polyesters Ltd (2005) XXX YCA 577 High Ct
    (India) S20–36
International Standard Electric Corp v Bridas Sociedad Anonima Petrolera (1992)
    XVII YCA 639 District Ct (US) S20–95
Inverclyde (Mearns) Housing Society Ltd v Lawrence Construction Co Ltd, 1989
    S.L.T. 815; 1989 S.C.L.R. 486 OH S10–11, S10–67
Inverurie Town Council v Sorrie, 1956 S.C. 175; 1956 S.L.T. (Notes) 17 IH (2
    Div) R46–46
IPCO (Nigeria) Ltd v Nigerian National Petroleum Corp [2005] EWHC 726
    (Comm); [2005] 2 Lloyd's Rep. 326; [2005] 1 C.L.C. 613 ..... S20–04, S20–138, S20–139,
                                                                                                                S20–147
IPCO (Nigeria) Ltd v Nigerian National Petroleum Corp; sub nom. Nigerian National
    Petroleum Corp v IPCO (Nigeria) Ltd [2008] EWCA Civ 1157; [2009] Bus. L.R.
    545; [2009] 1 All E.R. (Comm) 611; [2009] 1 Lloyd's Rep. 89; [2008] 2 C.L.C. 550;
    [2009] B.L.R. 71 .... S12–19, S18–07, S19–11, S20–138, S20–142
Iran Aircraft Ind v Avco Corp (1993) XVIII YCA 599 CA (US) S20–54
Irvani v Irvani [2000] 1 Lloyd's Rep. 412; [2000] C.L.C. 477 CA (Civ Div) S19–03
Ispat Industries Ltd v Western Bulk Pte. Ltd [2011] EWHC 93 (Comm) R68–40

J.J. RYAN & SONS v Rhone Poulenc Textile, S.A. [1988] USCA4 2036 .... S10–41
James Miller & Partners Ltd v Whitworth Street Estates (Manchester) Ltd. See
    Whitworth Street Estates (Manchester) Ltd v James Miller & Partners Ltd
Japan Line Ltd v Aggeliki Charis Compania Maritima SA (The Angelic Grace);
    Angelic Grace, The (Arbitrators: Misconduct); sub nom. Japan Line Ltd v Davies
    and Potter [1980] 1 Lloyd's Rep. 288; (1979) 123 S.J. 487 CA (Civ   Div) R53–21
Javor v Francoeur (2004) XXIX YCA 596 .... S21–13
Jean Charbonneau v Les Industries AC Davie Inc Unreported March 14, 1989 Sup Ct
    (Quebec) S10–44
Jivraj v Hashwani; sub nom. Hashwani v Jivraj [2011] UKSC 40; [2011] 1 W.L.R.
    1872; [2012] 1 All E.R. 629; [2012] 1 All E.R. (Comm) 1177; [2011] Bus. L.R.
    1182; [2011] 2 Lloyd's Rep. 513; [2011] 2 C.L.C. 427; [2012] 1 C.M.L.R. 12; [2011]
    I.C.R. 1004; [2011] I.R.L.R. 827; [2011] Eq. L.R. 1088; [2011] Arb. L.R. 28; [2011]
    C.I.L.L. 3076; [2011] 32 E.G. 54 (C.S.) R28–03
John G McGregor (Contractors) Ltd v Grampian RC (No.2), 1991 S.L.T. 136 IH (2
    Div) R50–07
John Holland Pty Ltd v Toyo Engineering Corp (Japan) [2001] SGHC 48 .... S32–02
John Nimmo & Son Ltd, Petitioners (1905) 8 F. 173; (1905) 13 S.L.T. 539 IH (1
    Div) R45–13
Jones v Kaney [2011] UKSC 13; [2011] 2 A.C. 398; [2011] 2 W.L.R. 823; [2011] 2 All
    E.R. 671; [2011] B.L.R. 283; 135 Con. L.R. 1; [2011] 2 F.L.R. 312; [2012] 2 F.C.R.
    372; (2011) 119 B.M.L.R. 167; [2011] P.N.L.R. 21; [2011] C.I.L.L. 3037; [2011]
    Fam. Law 1202; [2011] 14 E.G. 95 (C.S.).; (2011) 108(15) L.S.G. 19; (2011) 161
    N.L.J. 508; (2011) 155(13) S.J.L.B. 30 .... R75–05
Joseph Muller AG v Bergesen (1986) IX YCA 437 .... S20–58
JSC Surgutneftegaz v Harvard College, 2005 WL 1863676 District Ct (US) S30–19
JSC Zestafoni G Nikoladze Ferroalloy Plant v Ronly Holdings Ltd [2004] EWHC 245
    (Comm); [2004] 2 Lloyd's Rep. 335; [2004] 1 C.L.C. 1146 .... R67–27

Table of Cases

K Trading v Bayerische Motoren Werke AG (2005) XXX YCA 568 CA (Bavaria) S20–67
Kahler v Midland Bank Ltd [1950] A.C. 24; [1949] 2 All E.R. 621; 65 T.L.R. 663; [1949] L.J.R. 1687 HL S6–09
Kajo-Erzeugnisse Essenzen GmbH v DO Zdravilisce Radenska (1995) XX YCA 1051 Sup Ct (Austra) S20–95
Kalmneft JSC v Glencore International AG; sub nom. AOOT Kalmneft v Glencore International AG [2002] 1 All E.R. 76; [2001] 2 All E.R. (Comm) 577; [2002] 1 Lloyd's Rep. 128; [2001] C.L.C. 1805 QBD (Comm Ct) R12–05, R12–20, R20–26, R67–22, R71–17, R71–19
Kanoria v Guinness [2006] EWCA Civ 222; [2006] 2 All E.R. (Comm) 413; [2006] 1 Lloyd's Rep. 701 .... S20–07, S20–53
Karaha Bodas Co LLC v Perusahaan Pertambangan Minyak Dan Gas Bumi Negara-Pertamina [2003] 380 H.K.C.U. 1 .... S20–94
Karaha Bodas Co LLC v Perusahaan Pertambangan Minyak Dan Gas Bumi Negara-Pertamina (2003) XXVIII YCA 752 .... S20–06, S20–09, S20–52, S20–75
Karling v Purdue, 2004 S.L.T. 1067; 2005 S.C.L.R. 43; [2005] P.N.L.R. 13; 2004 G.W.D. 30–627 OH R75–04, R75–05
Kastner v Jason; Sherman v Kastner [2004] EWHC 592 (Ch); [2004] 2 Lloyd's Rep. 233; [2004] N.P.C. 47; [2004] 2 P. & C.R. DG2 .... R49–03
Kazakhstan v Istil Group Inc; sub nom. Kazakhstan v Istil Group Ltd [2007] EWCA Civ 471; [2008] Bus. L.R. 878; [2008] 1 All E.R. (Comm) 88; [2007] 2 Lloyd's Rep. 548 .... R67–38, R68–92, R70–51
Kersa Holding Co v Infancourtage (1996) XXI YCA 617 CA (Luxembourg) S20–84
Kid v Bunyan (1842) 5 D. 193 .... R45–31
Kincaid (Mor. 5064) S4–07
Kinetics Technology International SpA v Cross Seas Shipping Corp (The Mosconici); Mosconici, The [2001] 2 Lloyd's Rep. 313 QBD (Comm) R48–12
Kintore (Earl of) v Union Bank of Scotland (1863) 4 Macq. 465 .... S30–11
Krcmar v Czech Republic (35376/97) (2001) 31 E.H.R.R. 41 ECtHR R24–31
Kruppa v Benedetti [2014] EWHC 1877 (Comm) S4–05
Kyocera Corp vs Prudential-Bache Trade Services Inc, 341 F 3d 987 (9th Cir 2003) R69–02

La Pantofola D'Oro SpA v Blane Leisure Ltd (No.1), 2000 S.L.T. 105; 1999 G.W.D. 37–1784 OH S18–03
La Societe National des Hydrocarbures v Shaheen National Resources Inc, 585 F.Supp. 57 (1983) S20–35
Laboratorios Grossman v Forest Laboratories, 295 N.Y. Supp. (2d) 756 (1985) S10–48
Lafarge (Aggregates) Ltd v Newham LBC [2005] EWHC 1337 (Comm); [2005] 2 Lloyd's Rep. 577 .... R83–10
Laminoires-Trefileries-Cableries de Lens SA v Southwire Co, 484 F Supp 1065 (1981) CA (US) S20–49, S20–107
Lapad, The. See Atlanska Plovidba v Consignaciones Asturianas SA (The Lapad)
Leach v Haringey London Borough Council, Times, March 23, 1977 .... R54–11
Ledee v Ceramiche Ragno, 684 F.2d 184 (1981) Ct Appeals (US); (1984) IX YCA 471 CA (US) S6–13, S10–45, S30–21
Lemenda Trading Co Ltd v African Middle East Petroleum Co Ltd [1988] Q.B. 448; [1988] 2 W.L.R. 735; [1988] 1 All E.R. 513; [1988] 1 Lloyd's Rep. 361; [1988] 1 F.T.L.R. 123; (1988) 132 S.J. 538 QBD (Comm) R68–61
Lenmorniiproekt OAO v Arne Larsson & Partner Leasing AB (Case Ö 13-09) April 16, 2010 Sup Ct (Sweden) S20–45
Lesotho Highlands Development Authority v Impregilo SpA [2005] UKHL 43; [2006] 1 A.C. 221; [2005] 3 W.L.R. 129; [2005] 3 All E.R. 789; [2005] 2 All E.R. (Comm) 265; [2005] 2 Lloyd's Rep. 310; [2005] 2 C.L.C. 1; [2005] B.L.R. 351; 101 Con. L.R. 1; [2005] 27 E.G. 220 (C.S.); (2005) 155 N.L.J. 1046 ..... S20–74, R48–10, R50–23, R50–25, R68–33, R68–45
LG Caltex Gas Co Ltd v China National Petroleum Corp; Contigroup Companies Inc (formerly Continental Grain Co) v China Petroleum Technology & Development Corp [2001] EWCA Civ 788; [2001] 1 W.L.R. 1892; [2001] 4 All E.R. 875; [2001] 2

Table of Cases

All E.R. (Comm) 97; [2001] C.L.C. 1392; [2001] B.L.R. 325; (2001) 3 T.C.L.R. 22; (2001) 98(25) L.S.G. 46; (2001) 145 S.J.L.B. 142 .... S1–05
Linlithgow, Earl of v Hamilton (1610) Mor. 636 .... R9–02, R24–47, R51–62
Lithgow v United Kingdom (A/102); sub nom. Lithgow v United Kingdom (9006/80); Vosper Plc v United Kingdom (9262/81); English Electric Co Ltd v United Kingdom (9263/81); Banstonian Co v United Kingdom (9265/81); Yarrow Plc v United Kingdom (9266/81); Vickers Plc v United Kingdom (9313/81); Dowsett Securities Ltd v United Kingdom (9405/81) (1986) 8 E.H.R.R. 329 ECtHR S16–03, S16–05
LKT Industrial Berhad (Malaysia) v Chun [2004] N.S.W.S.C. 820 .... S20–40
Lobb Partnership Ltd v Aintree Racecourse Co Ltd [2000] C.L.C. 431; [2000] B.L.R. 65; 69 Con. L.R. 79 QBD (Comm Ct) R19–13, S4–06
Lobb Partnership Ltd v Aintree Racecourse Co Ltd. *See* HOK Sport Ltd (formerly Lobb Partnership Ltd) v Aintree Racecourse Co Ltd
Lobo Machado v Portugal (1997) 23 E.H.R.R. 79 ECtHR R24–30
Locabail Ltd v Bayfield Properties Ltd [2000] Q.B. 451 .... R76–03
London and Leeds Estates Ltd v Paribas Ltd [1995] 1 E.G.L.R. 102; [1995] 02 E.G. 134 QBD S15–20, R26–14
London Steam Ship Owners Mutual Insurance Association Ltd v Spain (The Prestige); Prestige, The [2013] EWHC 2840 (Comm); [2014] 1 All E.R. (Comm) 300 .... S14–13, S14–14
London Underground Ltd v Citylink Telecommunications Ltd [2007] EWHC 1749 (TCC); [2007] 2 All E.R. (Comm) 694; [2007] B.L.R. 391; 114 Con. L.R. 1 ...... R28–17
Love v Montgomerie, 1982 S.L.T. (Sh. Ct.) 60 Sh Pr R19–17
Lovelock (EJR) v Exportles [1968] 1 Lloyd's Rep. 163 CA (Civ Div) S10–49
Lucky-Goldstar International (HK) Ltd v Ng Moo Kee Engineering Ltd [1994] A.D.R.L.J. 49 .... S10–48
Luzon Hydro Corp v Transfield Philippines Inc [2004] S.G.H.C. 204; [2004] 4 S.L.R. 705 .... R32–15
Lyle v Falconer (1842) 5 D. 236 .... R53–09, R66–05

MACBRYDE v Macrae's Executors (1748) Mor. 657 .... R58–04
MacDonald Estates Plc v National Car Parks Ltd, 2010 S.C. 250; 2010 S.L.T. 36; 2009 G.W.D. 38–639 IH (Ex Div) S2–03, S2–04
Macintyre Bros (A Firm) v Smith, 1913 S.C. 129; 1913 1 S.L.T. 148 IH (Ex Div) ... R60–07, R60–09
Mackenzie v Girvan (1840) 3 D. 318 IH (2 Div) S2–12
Magill v Porter [2001] UKHL 67; [2002] 2 A.C. 357; [2002] 2 W.L.R. 37; [2002] 1 All E.R. 465; [2002] H.R.L.R. 16; [2002] H.L.R. 16; [2002] B.L.G.R. 51; (2001) 151 N.L.J. 1886; [2001] N.P.C. 184 .... R24–10
Malden Mills Inc (US) v Hilaturas Lourdes SA (1979) IV YCA 302 CA (Mexcio) ... S20–43
Mangistaumunaigaz Oil Production Association v United World Trading Inc [1995] 1 Lloyd's Rep. 617 QBD (Comm Ct) R19–13
Manufacturer v Exclusive Distributor (2004) XIX YCA 687 at 696 .... S20–109
Marc Rich & Co AG v Beogradska Plovidba (The Avala); Avala, The [1994] 2 Lloyd's Rep. 363 QBD (Comm) R59–08
Margulead Ltd v Exide Technologies [2004] EWHC 1019 (Comm); [2004] 2 All E.R. (Comm) 727; [2005] 1 Lloyd's Rep. 324 .... R24–42, R51–42, R68–21
Marshall v Edinburgh & Glasgow Railway Co (1853) 15 D. 603 .... R15–05
Martin Dawes v Treasure & Son Ltd [2010] EWHC 3218 (TCC) R57–08, R57–09
Martrade Shipping and Transport Gmbh v United Enterprises Corp [2014] EWHC 1884 (Comm) S1–05, R70–25
Masinimport v Scottish Mechanical Light Industries Ltd, 1976 S.C. 102; 1976 S.L.T. 245 OH S20–119
Matermaco SA v PPM Cranes Inc (2000) XXV YCA 653 Commercial Ct (Brussels) S6–13, S30–16
McArdle v J&R Howie Ltd, 1927 S.C. 779; 1927 S.L.T. 521 IH (2 Div) R62–09
McCallum v Robertson (1825) 4 S. 66 .... R51–11
McCallum v Robertson (1826) 2 W. & S. 344 .... R55–05

Table of Cases

McCosh v Moore; sub nom. Moore v McCosh (1903) 5 F. 946; (1903) 11 S.L.T. 112 IH (2 Div) S10–33, R19–03

McDougall v Argyll & Bute DC (Arbitration Clause), 1987 S.L.T. 7 OH S10–11

McFeetridge v Stewarts & Lloyds Ltd, 1913 S.C. 773; 1913 1 S.L.T. 325 IH (2 Div) S6–07, S20–15

McKenzie v Aberdeen and Inverness Junction Railway Co (1866) 4 M. 810 .... R58–05

McKenzie v Inverness and Ross-shire Railway Co (1861) 24 D. 251 .... R4–05

McMillan v Free Church of Scotland (1862) 24 D. 1282 .... R73–03

McQuater v Fergusson, 1911 S.C. 640; 1911 1 S.L.T. 295 IH (1 Div) R59–06, R59–07

Mediterranean Salvage & Towage Ltd v Seamar Trading & Commerce Inc [2008] 2 Lloyd's Rep. 628; [2008] EWHC 1875 (Comm) R70–26

Mediterranean Salvage & Towage Ltd v Seamar Trading & Commerce Inc (The Reborn); Reborn, The [2009] EWCA Civ 531; [2010] 1 All E.R. (Comm) 1; [2009] 2 Lloyd's Rep. 639; [2009] 1 C.L.C. 909; (2009) 159 N.L.J. 898 .... R69–22

Mendok BV v Cumberland Maritime Corp, 1989 S.L.T. 192 OH R46–07

Merck Canada Inc v Accord Healthcare Ltd Case (C-555/13) ECJ February 14, 2014 .... R41–15

Michael Wilson & Partners Ltd v Emmott; sub nom. Emmott v Michael Wilson & Partners Ltd [2008] EWCA Civ 184; [2008] Bus. L.R. 1361; [2008] 2 All E.R. (Comm) 193; [2008] 1 Lloyd's Rep. 616; [2008] C.P. Rep. 26; [2008] B.L.R. 515 .... R26–10, R26–11, R26–13, R26–17, R26–20, R26–23

Midgulf International Ltd v Groupe Chimiche Tunisien [2009] EWHC 963 (Comm); [2009] 2 Lloyd's Rep. 411; [2009] 1 C.L.C. 984 .... S3–23

Midgulf International Ltd v Groupe Chimiche Tunisien; sub nom. Gulf International Ltd v Groupe Chimique Tunisien [2010] EWCA Civ 66; [2010] 2 Lloyd's Rep. 543; [2010] 1 C.L.C. 113 .... R67–17

Mikuta v William Baird & Co Ltd, 1916 S.C. 194; 1915 2 S.L.T. 396 IH (1 Div) ... R62–23

Milan Nigeria Ltd v Angeliki B Maritime Co; Angeliki B Maritime Co v Milan Nigeria Ltd; Angeliki B, The [2011] EWHC 892 (Comm); [2011] Arb. L.R. 24 .... R48–11, R69–20

Millar (David Cameron) v Dickson; Marshall v Ritchie; Tracey v Heywood; Payne v Heywood; Stewart v Heywood [2001] UKPC D 4; [2002] 1 W.L.R. 1615; [2002] 3 All E.R. 1041; 2002 S.C. (P.C.) 30; 2001 S.L.T. 988; 2001 S.C.C.R. 741; [2001] H.R.L.R. 59; [2001] U.K.H.R.R. 999; 2001 G.W.D. 26–1015 .... R24–09

Minermet SpA Milan v Luckyfield Shipping Corp SA [2004] EWHC 729 (Comm); [2004] 2 Lloyd's Rep. 348; [2004] 2 C.L.C. 421 .... R19–18

Ministere Tunisien de l'Equipment v Bec Freres (1997) XXII YCA 682 Cour d'Appel (Paris) S20–21

Ministry of Defence of the Republic of Iran v Cubic Defense Systems, Inc, 29 F.Supp. 2d 1168 (1998) District Ct (US) S20–75

Minmetals Germany GmbH v Ferco Steel Ltd [1999] 1 All E.R. (Comm.) 315; [1999] C.L.C. 647 QBD (Comm) S20–06, S20–47, S20–74, S20–127

Mitchell v News Group Newspapers Ltd [2013] EWCA Civ 1537; [2013] 6 Costs L.R. 1008; [2014] C.I.L.L. 3452; (2013) 163(7587) N.L.J. 20 .... R65–11

Mitchell-Gill v Buchan, 1921 S.C. 390; 1921 1 S.L.T. 197 IH (1 Div) R42–20

Mitsubishi Motors Corp v Soler Chrysler-Plymouth, Inc, 473 U.S. 614 (1985) Sup Ct (US) S30–18

Molino e Pacifico Ponte San Giovanni Spa v Anrde & Cie SA (1983) VIII YCA 378 Sup Ct (Italy) S10–50

Montgomerie v Carrick (1848) 10 D. 1387 IH (Div) S10–38

Mosconici, The. *See* Kinetics Technology International SpA v Cross Seas Shipping Corp (The Mosconici)

Mosstroyekonombank Joint Stock Commercial Bank CJSC v Kalinka-Stockmann CJSC (Federal Arbitrazh Court of the Moscow Circuit) S20–112

Mowbray v Dickson (1848) 10 D. 1102 .... R28–12, R28–45, R32–03

Municipalite de Khoms El Megreb v Societe Dalico, 1994 Revue de l'Arbitrage 116 .... S6–13, S6–15

Murphy v Farme Coal Co Ltd, 1918 S.C. 659; 1918 2 S.L.T. 8 IH (2 Div) R62–24

Table of Cases

Mylcrist Builders Ltd v Buck [2008] EWHC 2172 (TCC); [2009] 2 All E.R. (Comm) 259; [2008] B.L.R. 611; [2008] C.I.L.L. 2624; (2008) 105(39) L.S.G. 22; (2008) 152(38) S.J.L.B. 29 .... R24–37, A1–06, A1–07

NAGUSINA NAVIERA v Allied Maritime Inc [2002] EWCA Civ 1147; [2003] 2 C.L.C. 1 .... R71–18
Nanjing Cereals, Oils and Foodstuffs Import and Export Corp v Luckmate Commodities Trading Ltd (1999) XXI YCA 542 CFA (HK) S20–47
Nasmyth v Magistrates of Glasgow (1777) 5 Br. Supp. 427 .... R58–04
Nasser v United Bank of Kuwait (Security for Costs) [2001] EWCA Civ 556; [2002] 1 W.L.R. 1868; [2002] 1 All E.R. 401; [2001] C.P. Rep. 105 .... R64–08, R71–45
National Development Co v Khashoggi (1993) XVIII YCA 506 District Ct (NY) ... S20–48
National Trust for Places of Historic Interest or Natural Beauty v Fleming [2009] EWHC 1789 (Ch); [2009] N.P.C. 97 .... R70–20
Naviera Amazonica Peruana SA v Compania Internacional de Seguros de Peru [1988] 1 Lloyd's Rep. 116; [1988] 1 F.T.L.R. 100 CA (Civ Div) S9–10
Navigation Somanar Inc v Algoma Steamships Ltd (1994) XIX YCA 256 Sup Ct (Quebec) R51–47
Navios International Inc v Sangamon Transportation Group; Dimitris L, The [2012] EWHC 166 (Comm); [2012] 1 Lloyd's Rep. 493; [2013] Bus. L.R. D9 .... R71–33
Newfield Construction Ltd v Tomlinson [2004] EWHC 3051 (TCC); 97 Con. L.R. 148 .... R68–22, R68–30
Newton v Marylebone BC (1915) 84 L.J.K.B. 1721 .... S3–07
Norbrook Laboratories Ltd v Tank [2006] EWHC 1055 (Comm); [2006] 2 Lloyd's Rep. 485; [2006] B.L.R. 412 .... R12–10, R28–42, R68–28
Nordsee Deutsche Hochseefischerei GmbH v Reederei Mond Hochseefischerei Nordstern AG & Co KG (102/81) [1982] E.C.R. 1095; [1982] Com. L.R. 154 .... R41–15
North Range Shipping Ltd v Seatrans Shipping Corp (The Western Triumph); Western Triumph, The [2002] EWCA Civ 405; [2002] 1 W.L.R. 2397; [2002] 4 All E.R. 390; [2002] 2 All E.R. (Comm) 193; [2002] 2 Lloyd's Rep. 1; [2002] C.L.C. 992; (2002) 99(20) L.S.G. 31 .... R70–48
Norwest Holst Ltd v Carfin Developments Ltd [2008] CSOH 138; [2009] B.L.R. 167; 2008 G.W.D. 33–493 OH S2–17

O'CALLAGHAN v Coral Racing Ltd, Times, November 26, 1998; Independent, November 26, 1998 CA (Civ Div) S4–19, R19–11
O'Donoghue v Enterprise Inns Plc [2008] EWHC 2273 (Ch); [2009] 1 P. & C.R. 14; [2008] N.P.C. 103 .... S20–51, R28–47
O'Neill v Giffnock Collieries Ltd, 1924 S.C. 376; 1924 S.L.T. 325 IH (2 Div) R62–09
OAO Rosneft v Yukos Capital SARL (Case 09/02565) June 25, 2010 Hoge Raad (First Chamber) S20–98
Oberlandesgericht Cologne decision (1979) IV YCA 258 .... S20–44
Oberlandesgericht of Schleswig decision (2004) XXIX YCA 687 .... S20–43
Omnibridge Consulting Ltd v Clearsprings (Management) Ltd [2004] EWHC 2276 (Comm) R58–11, R68–28
Omnium de Traitement et de Valorisation SA v Hilmarton Ltd [1999] 2 All E.R. (Comm) 146; [1999] 2 Lloyd's Rep. 222 .... S20–117
Osuuskunta METEX Anderlag VS v Turkiye Electric Kurumu Genel Mudurlugu General Directorate (1997) XXII YCA 807 CA (Ankara) S20–70
Overseas Cosmos Inc v NR Vessel Corp (1998) XXIII YCA 1096 District Ct (US) S20–51
Owners of the Bamburi v Compton (The Bamburi); Bamburi, The [1982] 1 Lloyd's Rep. 312; [1982] Com. L.R. 31 .... S25–03
Owners of the Eleftherotria v Owners of the Despina R; Folias, The; Despina R, The; sub nom. Services Europe Atlantique Sud (SEAS) v Stockholms Rederi AB Svea (The Folias) [1979] A.C. 685; [1978] 3 W.L.R. 804; [1979] 1 All E.R. 421; [1979] 1 Lloyd's Rep. 1; (1978) 122 S.J. 758 HL R48–12

Table of Cases

Pacific Basin IHX Ltd v Bulkhandling Handymax AS; Triton Lark, The [2011] EWHC 2862 (Comm); [2012] 1 All E.R. (Comm) 639; [2012] 1 Lloyd's Rep. 151; [2012] 1 C.L.C. 1 .... R23–11
Pacol Ltd v Joint Stock Co Rossakhar [1999] 2 All E.R. (Comm) 778; [2000] 1 Lloyd's Rep. 109; [2000] C.L.C. 315 QBD (Comm) R68–22
Paczy v Händler & Natermann GmbH (No.2) [1981] 1 Lloyd's Rep. 302; [1981] Com. L.R. 12; [1981] F.S.R. 250 CA (Civ Div) S10–53, S25–03
Paczy v Händler. *See* Paczy v Händler & Natermann GmbH (No.2)
Paklito Investment Ltd v Klockner (East Asia) Ltd [1995] A.D.R.L.J 127 High Ct (HK) S20–53
Pan Liberty Navigation Co Ltd v World Link (HK) Resources Ltd (2005) B.C.C.A. 206 .... S21–13
Parsons & Whittemore Overseas Co Inc v Societe Generale de l'Industrie du Papier (RAKTA), 508 F.2d 969 (2nd Cir. 1974) S20–09, S20–108, S20–109
Parsons & Whittemore Overseas Co Inc v Societe Generale de l'Industrie du Papier (RAKTA) (1976) I YCA 205 CA (US) S20–50, S20–52
Pasrederiet m/v Jytte Dania v Mas SA (1989) XIV YCA 704 Sup Ct (Spain) S20–47
Paterson & Son Ltd v Glasgow Corp (1900) 2 F. 1201; (1901) 3 F. (H.L.) 34 HL .. R33–01
Paterson v Paterson, 1919 1 S.L.T. 12 OH R28–29
Paterson v Sanderson (1829) 7 S. 616 .... R61–08
Patley Wood Farm LLP v Brake [2013] EWHC 4035 (Ch) R46–12
Patrick v McCall (1867) 4 S.L.R. 12 .... R58–05
Peterson Farms Inc v C&M Farming Ltd (Payment into Court) [2003] EWHC 2298 (Comm); [2004] 1 Lloyd's Rep. 614 .... R71–55
Peterson Farms Inc v C&M Farming Ltd; sub nom. Petersen Farms Inc v C&M Farming Ltd [2004] EWHC 121 (Comm); [2004] 1 Lloyd's Rep. 603; [2004] N.P.C. 13 .... R47–27, R67–13, R71–55
Peterson v Ayre, 139 E.R. 610; (1855) 15 C.B. 724 CCP R51–09
Petroships Pte Ltd of Singapore v Petec Trading & Investment Corp of Vietnam (The Petro Ranger) [2001] 2 Lloyd's Rep. 348 .... R68–39
Pierreux NV v Transportmaschinen Handelshaus GmbH (1997) XXII YCA 631 ..... S10–56
Pirtek (UK) Ltd v Deanswood Ltd [2005] EWHC 2301 (Comm); [2005] 2 Lloyd's Rep. 728 .... R50–23
Pollich v Heatley (No.2), 1910 S.C. 469; (1910) 1 S.L.T. 203 IH (1 Div) R62–04, R62–13
Positive Software Solutions, Inc v New Century Mortgage Corp, 337 F.Supp. 2d 862 (N.D. Tex. 2004), affirmed 436 F.3d 495 (5th Cir. 2006), rehearing en banc granted, 449 F.3d 616 (5th Cir. 2006), revised 476 F.3d 278 (5th Cir. 2007) (en banc), cert. den. 551 U.S. 1114 (2007) R8–18
President of India v La Pintada Compania Navigacion SA (The La Pintada); La Pintada, The [1985] A.C. 104; [1984] 3 W.L.R. 10; [1984] 2 All E.R. 773; [1984] 2 Lloyd's Rep. 9; [1984] C.I.L.L. 110; (1984) 81 L.S.G. 1999, (1984) 128 S.J. 414 HL R49–04
Presslie v Cochrane McGregor Group Ltd (No.1), 1996 S.C. 289; 1996 S.L.T. 988 IH (2 Div) S10 67
Primetrade AG v Ythan Ltd; Ythan, The [2005] EWHC 2399 (Comm); [2006] 1 All E.R. 367; [2006] 1 All E.R. (Comm) 157; [2006] 1 Lloyd's Rep. 457; [2005] 2 C.L.C. 911 .... R20–18, R67–28, R76–05
Protech Projects Construction (Pty) Ltd v Al-Kharafi & Sons; Mohammed Abdulmohsin Al-Kharafi & Sons WLL v Big Dig Construction (Proprietary) Ltd (In Liquidation) [2005] EWHC 2165 (Comm); [2005] 2 Lloyd's Rep. 779 .... R59–12

Quintette Coal Ltd v Nippon Steel Corp (1993) XVIII YCA 159 CA (BC) S30–18

R v V [2008] EWHC 1531 (Comm); [2009] 1 Lloyd's Rep. 97; 119 Con. L.R. 73 .... R68–61
R. (on the application of Anufrijeva) v Secretary of State for the Home Department [2003] UKHL 36; [2004] 1 A.C. 604; [2003] 3 W.L.R. 252; [2003] 3 All E.R. 827; [2003] H.R.L.R. 31; [2003] Imm. A.R. 570; [2003] I.N.L.R. 521; (2003) 100(33) L.S.G. 29 .... R21–09, R71–13
R. v Secretary of State for Transport Ex p. Factortame Ltd (No.2) [1991] 1 A.C. 603; [1990] 3 W.L.R. 818; [1991] 1 All E.R. 70; [1991] 1 Lloyd's Rep. 10; [1990] 3

Table of Cases

C.M.L.R. 375; (1991) 3 Admin. L.R. 333; (1990) 140 N.L.J. 1457; (1990) 134 S.J. 1189 HL R49–12
Ramsay v Hay (1624) Mor. 16245 .... S30–05
Ransohoff & Wissler v Burrell (1897) 25 R. 284 IH (2 Div) S5–04, S5–06
RC Pillar & Sons v Edwards [2002] C.I.L.L. 1799 .... R58–25, R58–33
Rederi Aktiebolaget Sally v Srl Termarea (1979) IV YCA 294 CA (Florence) S20–63
Rena K, The; Rena K, The [1979] Q.B. 377; [1978] 3 W.L.R. 431; [1979] 1 All E.R. 397; [1978] 1 Lloyd's Rep. 545; (1978) 122 S.J. 315 QBD (Admlty Ct) S10–53
Resort Condominiums International Inc v Bolwell (1994) XX YCA 628 Sup Ct (Qld) S18–08, S20–86
Rhone Mediterranee v Achille Lauro, 712 F.2d 50 (1983) S10–47, S10–56
Riley v Kingsley Underwriting Agencies, 969 F.2d 953 (1992) S10–49
Rio Algom Ltd v Sammi Steel Co (1991) 47 C.P.C. 251 .... R19–12
Robert Brown & Son Ltd (In Liquidation) v Associated Fireclay Companies Ltd, 1937 S.C. (H.L.) 42; 1937 S.L.T. 435 HL R28–45
Rosseel NV v Oriental Commercial & Shipping Co (UK) Ltd [1991] 2 Lloyd's Rep. 625 QBD (Comm) S20–87
Rostock Court of Appeal decision (2000) XXV YCA 717 .... S21–09
Roussel-Uclaf v GD Searle & Co Ltd (No.2) [1978] 1 Lloyd's Rep. 225; [1978] F.S.R. 95; [1978] R.P.C. 747 Ch D S10–61
Roxburgh v Dinardo, 1981 S.L.T. 291 OH S10–05, S30–12
Royal Bank of Scotland Plc v Theobald Unreported January 10, 2007 EAT R76–10
RSA v A Ltd (2001) XXVI YCA 863 .... S21–15
Ruiz Torija v Spain (A/303-A) (1995) 19 E.H.R.R. 553 ECtHR R51–33
Ruiz-Mateos v Spain (A/262) (1993) 16 E.H.R.R. 505 ECtHR R24–30
Russell v Russell (1880) (1880) L.R. 14 Ch. D. 471 Ch D R26–11
Rustal Trading Ltd v Gill & Duffus SA [2000] 1 Lloyd's Rep. 14; [2000] C.L.C. 231 QBD (Comm Ct) R12–12

Safeway Stores Plc v Legal and General Assurance Society Ltd [2004] EWHC 415 (Ch); [2005] 1 P. & C.R. 9 .... R70–16
Sanderson (A) & Son v Armour & Co Ltd; sub nom. Sanderson & Son v Armour & Co Ltd, 1922 S.C. (H.L.) 117; 1922 S.L.T. 285 HL S4–10, S5–05, S10–02, S10–05, S10–06
Santa Fe International Corp v Napier Shipping SA (No.1), 1985 S.L.T. 430 OH R26–23
Save Britain's Heritage v Number 1 Poultry Ltd; sub nom. Save Britain's Heritage v Secretary of State for the Environment [1991] 1 W.L.R. 153; [1991] 2 All E.R. 10; 89 L.G.R. 809; (1991) 3 Admin. L.R. 437; (1991) 62 P. & C.R. 105; [1991] 3 P.L.R. 17; (1991) 155 L.G. Rev. 429; [1991] E.G. 24 (C.S.); (1991) 88(15) L.S.G. 31; (1991) 135 S.J. 312 HL R51–49
Scarth v United Kingdom (1999) 27 E.H.R.R. CD37 ECtHR R26–03
Schiffahrtsgesellschaft Detlev von Appen GmbH v Voest Alpine Intertrading GmbH (The Jay Bola); Schiffahrtsgesellschaft Detlev von Appen GmbH v Wiener Allianz Versicherungs AG; Jay Bola, The [1997] 2 Lloyd's Rep. 279; [1997] C.L.C. 993 CA (Civ Div) S10–39
Schreter v Gasmac Inc (1992) 89 D.L.R. (4th) 365 .... S20–87
Schwebel v Schwebel [2010] EWHC 3280 (TCC); [2011] 2 All E.R. (Comm) 1048; (2011) 161 N.L.J. 29; [2012] Bus. L.R. D21 .... R68–34, R69–16
Science Research Council v Nassé; Leyland Cars (BL Cars Ltd) v Vyas; Science Research Council v Nassé; sub nom. Nassé v Science Research Council; Vyas v Leyland Cars [1980] A.C. 1028; [1979] 3 W.L.R. 762; [1979] 3 All E.R. 673; [1979] I.C.R. 921; [1979] I.R.L.R. 465; (1979) 123 S.J. 768 HL R26–14, R26–23
Scott Lithgow Ltd v Secretary of State for Defence, 1989 S.C. (H.L.) 9; 1989 S.L.T. 236; 45 B.L.R. 1 HL S25–06
Scott v Avery, 10 E.R. 1121; (1856) 5 H.L. Cas. 811 HL S10–69, S10–70, S10–71
Sea Traders SA v Participaciones, Proyectos y Estudios SA (1996) XXI YCA 676 .. S21–07
Seabridge Shipping AB v AC Orssleff's Eftf's A/S; sub nom. Seabridge Shipping AB v AC Orsleff's EFTS A/S [2000] 1 All E.R. (Comm) 415; [1999] 2 Lloyd's Rep. 685; [2000] C.L.C. 656 QBD (Comm) R1–14

Table of Cases

Secretary of State for the Environment v Reed International [1994] 1 E.G.L.R. 22; [1994] 06 E.G. 137 .... R28–16
SEEE v Yugoslavia (1986) XI YCA 491 CA (Rouen) S20–65
Sesostris v Transportes Navales, 727 F.Supp. 737 (1989) District Ct (US) S20–39
SGL Carbon Fibres Ltd, Petitioners [2013] CSOH 21; 2013 S.L.T. 307; 2013 G.W.D. 6-142 .... R45–06
Shalson v DF Keane Ltd [2003] EWHC 599 (Ch); [2003] B.P.I.R. 1045; (2003) 19 Const. L.J. 290 .... S10–18
Sharrat v London Bus Co Ltd [2003] EWCA Civ 718 .... R59–12
Shashoua v Sharma [2009] EWHC 957 (Comm); [2009] 2 All E.R. (Comm) 477; [2009] 2 Lloyd's Rep. 376; [2009] 1 C.L.C. 716 .... S3–23
Shell Egypt West Manzala GmbH v Dana Gas Egypt Ltd (formerly Centurion Petroleum Corp) [2009] EWHC 2097 (Comm); [2010] 1 Lloyd's Rep. 109; [2009] 2 C.L.C. 481; 127 Con. L.R. 27 .... R69–10
Shepherd v Elliot (1896) 23 R. 695 .... R62–17
Shin-Etsu Chemical Co v Aksh Opticfibre Ltd (2006) XXXI YCA 747 .... S10–25
Siemens AG and BKMI Industrienlagen GmbH v Dutco Construction Co, French Cass. Civ. 1ere, January 7, 1992 (1992) 1 Bull Civ. R6–18, R6–19
Simpson v Strachan (1736) Mor. 17007 .... R58–04
Sinclair v Woods of Winchester Ltd [2005] EWHC 1631 (QB); 102 Con. L.R. 127 ... R12–16, R28–47, R51–46, R58–29, R71–19
SL Sethia Liners v Naviagro Maritime Corp (The Kostas Melas; Kostas Melas, The [1981] 1 Lloyd's Rep. 18; [1980] Com. L.R. 3 QBD (Comm) R54–08
Small Business Ltd v Big Multinational Plc R33–04
Smits Leslie v Roach [2006] H.C.A. 36 .... R24–17, R77–05
Societe Arabe des Engrais Phosphates v Gemanco Srl (1997) XXII YCA 737 Corte Cassizione (Italy) S20–20
Société Commerciale de Reassurance v Eras International Ltd (formerly Eras (UK)); sub nom. Eras EIL Actions, Re [1992] 2 All E.R. 82 (Note); [1992] 1 Lloyd's Rep. 570 CA (Civ Div) S10–52
Societe Tunisienne d'Electricitee et de Gaz v Societe Entrepose (1978) III YCA 283 .... S20–21
SODIME v Schuurmans & Van Ginneken BV (1996) XXI YCA 607 Sup Ct (Italy) S21–04
Soeximex SAS v Agrocorp International Pte Ltd [2011] EWHC 2743 (Comm) R68–44
Soinco SACI v Novokuznetsk Aluminium Plant (No.1) [1998] 2 Lloyd's Rep. 337; [1998] C.L.C. 730 CA (Civ Div); [1998] 2 Lloyd's Rep. 337; [1998] C.L.C. 730 .... S20–117
Sojuzneftexport v JOC Oil Ltd (1990) XV YCA 384 CA (Bermuda) S20–17, S20–73
Sokofl Star Shipping Co Inc v GPVO Technopromexport (1998) XXIII YCA 742 District Ct (Moscow) S20–17
Soleh Boneh International v Uganda and National Housing Corp [1993] 2 Lloyd's Rep. 208 CA (Civ Div) S20–141, S20–146, R71–51, R71–52
Soleimany v Soleimany [1999] Q.B. 785, [1998] 3 W.L.R. 811; [1999] 3 All E.R. 847; [1998] C.L.C. 779 .... S4–18, S20–113, S20–114, R68–60
Sonatrach Petroleum Corp (BVI) v Ferrell International Ltd [2002] 1 All E.R. (Comm) 627 QBD (Comm) S20–29, R19–13
South Tyneside MBC v Wickes Building Supplies Ltd [2004] EWHC 2428 (Comm); [2004] N.P.C. 164 .... R26–14
Spencer v Wood (t/a Gordon's Tyres) [2004] EWCA Civ 352; [2004] 3 Costs L.R. 372; (2004) 148 S.J.L.B. 356 .... R59–12
SPP (Middle East) Ltd v Egypt (1985) X YCA 487 District Ct (Amsterdam) S20–86, S21–15
St Andrews Bay Development Ltd v HBG Management Ltd, 2003 S.L.T. 740; 2003 S.C.L.R. 526; 2003 G.W.D. 13-397 OH R51–61
Stinnes Interoil GmbH v A Halcoussis & Co (The Yanxilas); Yanxilas, The [1982] 2 Lloyd's Rep. 445 QBD (Comm Ct) R51–18
Studd v Cook (1883) 10 R. (HL) 53 .... R46–20
Succula & Pomona Shipping Co Ltd v Harland & Wolff Ltd [1980] 2 Lloyd's Rep. 381 QBD (Comm Ct) R12–18

Table of Cases

Suda v Czech Republic (1643/06) Unreported October 28, 2010 ECtHR S1–20, S1–21, S4–10, S16–04, S16–05, R26–05
Sulamerica Cia Nacional de Seguros SA v Enesa Engenharia SA; sub nom. Sul America Cia Nacional de Seguros SA v Enesa Engenharia SA [2012] EWCA Civ 638; [2013] 1 W.L.R. 102; [2012] 2 All E.R. (Comm) 795; [2012] 1 Lloyd's Rep. 671; [2012] 2 C.L.C. 216; [2012] Lloyd's Rep. I.R. 405 .... S6–11, S6–12
Sumitomo Heavy Industries v Oil and Natural Gas Commission [1994] 1 Lloyd's Rep. 45 QBD (Comm Ct) R19–13
Sumner v Costa Ltd [2013] EWHC 4116 (Ch) R71–30
Suovaniemi v Finland (31737/96) Unreported February 23, 1999 ECtHR S1–20, S1–21, S1–22, R26–03
Sutton (Deceased), Re; sub nom. Sutton v Sutton [2009] EWHC 2576 (Ch); [2010] W.T.L.R. 115; (2009-10) 12 I.T.E.L.R. 627 .... R4–05
Svenska Handelsbanken v India Charge Chrome Ltd (1996) XXI YCA 557 Sup Ct (Inda) S10–50
Svenska Petroleum Exploration AB v Lithuania (No.1) [2005] EWHC 9 (Comm); [2005] 1 All E.R. (Comm) 515; [2005] 1 Lloyd's Rep. 515 .... S19–02, S20–06
Svenska Petroleum Exploration AB v Lithuania (No.2) [2005] EWHC 2437 (Comm); [2006] 1 All E.R. (Comm) 731; [2006] 1 Lloyd's Rep. 181; [2005] 2 C.L.C. 965; (2005) 102(47) L.S.G. 26 .... S20–24
Switzerland Court decision (1979) IV YCA 309 .... S20–42
Switzerland Federal Tribunal in (1996) XXI YCA 172 .... S20–109
Syria v SIMER (1983) VIII YCA 386 .... S20–131

Tame Shipping Ltd v Easy Navigation Ltd (The Easy Rider); Easy Rider, The [2004] EWHC 1862 (Comm); [2004] 2 All E.R. (Comm) 521; [2004] 2 Lloyd's Rep. 626; [2004] 2 C.L.C. 1155 .... R51–45, R71–28
Tang Chung Wah vs Grant Thornton International Ltd [2012] EWHC 3198 (Ch); [2013] 1 All E.R. (Comm) 1226; [2013] 1 Lloyd's Rep. 11 .... R67–15
Tanning Research Laboratories Inc v O'Brien [1990] HCA 8 .... S10–40
Taylor Woodrow Construction Ltd v RMD Kwikform Ltd [2008] EWHC 825 (TCC); [2009] Bus. L.R. 292; [2009] 1 All E.R. (Comm) 770; [2008] 2 Lloyd's Rep. 345; [2008] 1 C.L.C. 793; [2008] B.L.R. 383; 118 Con. L.R. 57 .... R1–24
Taylor Woodrow Holdings Ltd v Barnes & Elliott Ltd [2006] EWHC 1693 (TCC); [2006] 2 All E.R. (Comm) 735; [2006] B.L.R. 377; 110 Con. L.R. 169; [2006] C.I.L.L. 2375 .... R41–09, R42–07
Television New Zealand Ltd v Langley Productions Ltd [2000] N.Z.L.R. 250 .... S15–08
Texaco Melbourne, The. See Attorney General of Ghana v Texaco Overseas Tankships Ltd (The Texaco Melbourne)
Thomson v Earl of Galloway (Expenses), 1919 S.C. 611; 1919 2 S.L.T. 80 IH (2 Div) R42–04, R46–71
Three Mile Inn Ltd (formerly Rivergrant Ltd) v Daley (Liquidator of New Northumbria Hotel Ltd) [2012] EWCA Civ 970 .... R24–29
Through Transport Mutual Insurance Association (Eurasia) Ltd v New India Assurance Co Ltd (The Hari Bhum) (No.2); Hari Bhum, The (No.2) [2005] EWHC 455 (Comm); [2005] 2 Lloyd's Rep. 378; [2005] 1 C.L.C. 376 .... S10–39
Thyssen Canada Ltd v Mariana Maritime SA [2005] EWHC 219 (Comm); [2005] 1 Lloyd's Rep. 640 .... R71–19
Ting Kang Chung John v Teo Hee Lai Building Constructions Pte Ltd [2010] SGHC 20 .... S9–03
Tiong Huat Rubber Factory Bhd v Wah Chang International Co Ltd (1992) XVII YCA 516 .... S20–78, S20–79
Tongyuan (USA) International Trading Group v Uni-Clan Ltd (2001) XXVI YCA 886 .... S20–11, S20–62, R68–49
Torch Offshore LLC v Cable Shipping Inc [2004] EWHC 787 (Comm); [2004] 2 All E.R. (Comm) 365; [2004] 2 Lloyd's Rep. 446; [2004] 2 C.L.C. 433 ..... R51–46, R51–51, R58–19, R71–06
Tournier v National Provincial and Union Bank of England [1924] 1 K.B. 461 CA S15–16, R26–14, R26–16

xxx

Table of Cases

Tracomin SA v Sudan Oil Seeds (No.1) [1983] 1 W.L.R. 1026; [1983] 3 All E.R. 137; [1983] 2 Lloyd's Rep. 384; [1983] Com. L.R. 269; [1984] E.C.C. 165 CA (Civ Div) S3–21
Trade Fortitude, The. *See* Food Corp of India v Marastro Cia Naviera SA (The Trade Fortitude) (No.1)
Trade Fortitude, The. *See* Exmar BV v National Iranian Tanker Co (The Trade Fortitude)
Trans Trust SPRL v Danubian Trading Co Ltd [1952] 2 Q.B. 297; [1952] 1 All E.R. 970; [1952] 1 Lloyd's Rep. 348; [1952] 1 T.L.R. 1066; (1952) 96 S.J. 312 CA R54–07
Trans World Film SpA v Film Polski Import and Export of Films (1993) XVIII YCA 433 Corte Suprema di Cassazione (Italy) S20–41
Transocean Shipping Agency (P) Ltd v Black Sea Shipping (1998) XXIII YCA 713 Sup Ct (India) S20–121
Tresor Public v Galakis, 1966 Revue de l'Arbitrage 99 Cour de Cassation (France) S20–18

UNICHIPS FINANZIARIA SPA v Gesnouin (1994) XIX YCA 658 Cour d'Appel (Paris) S20–36
Union de Cooperativas Agricolas Epis-Centre v La Palentina SA (2002) XXVII YCA 533 .... S20–37
United Mexican States v Karpa [2005] 74 O.R. 3d 180 CA (Ontario) S20–109
United Steelworkers of America v Enterprise Wheel & Car Corp, 363 U.S. 593 (1960) R51–38

VALERY, COUNT JOSEPH v John Scott (1876) 3 R. 965 IH (1 Div) S6–07, S6–08, S20–15
Van der Giessen-de Noord Shipbuilding Division BV v Imtech Marine & Offshore BV [2008] EWHC 2904 (Comm); [2009] 1 Lloyd's Rep. 273 .... R68–22, R68–37, R68–39
Van Hopplymus v Societe Coherent Inc (1997) XXII YCA 637 Comm Ct (Brussels) S30–19
Vee Networks Ltd v Econet Wireless International Ltd [2004] EWHC 2909 (Comm); [2005] 1 All E.R. (Comm) 303; [2005] 1 Lloyd's Rep. 192 .... R19–11, R67–25

W AND S v BB Unreported June 8, 2001 QBD (TCC) ... R12–09, R14–08, R24–54, R68–89, R73–08
WAC Ltd v Whillock, 1989 S.C. 397; 1990 S.L.T. 213; 1990 S.C.L.R. 193 IH (2 Div) R46–49
Walker v Rome; sub nom. Walker v Rowe [1999] 2 All E.R. (Comm) 961; [2000] 1 Lloyd's Rep. 116; [2000] C.L.C. 265 QBD (Comm Ct) S1–05, S12–18
Ward v Walker, 1920 S.C. 80; 1920 1 S.L.T. 2 IH (1 Div) R46–18
Watson v McEwan; Watson v Jones; sub nom. McEwan v Watson [1905] A.C. 480; (1905) 7 F. (H.L.) 109; (1905) 13 S.L.T. 340 .... R75–04
Wealands v CLC Contractors Ltd; sub nom. Wealand v CLC Contractors Ltd [2000] 1 All E.R. (Comm) 30; [1999] 2 Lloyd's Rep. 739; [1999] C.L.C. 1821; [1999] B.L.R. 401; (2000) 2 T.C.L.R. 367; 74 Con. L.R. 1 CA (Civ Div) R49–05
Weinstein International Corp v Nagtegaal NV (1980) V YCA 269 .... S21–07
Weldon Plant Ltd v Commission for the New Towns [2001] 1 All E.R. (Comm) 264; [2000] B.L.R. 496; (2000) 2 T.C.L.R. 785; 77 Con. L.R. 1 QBD (T&CC) R51–28
Welex AG v Rosa Maritime Ltd (The Epsilon Rosa) (No.2); Epsilon Rosa, The (No.2) [2003] EWCA Civ 938; [2003] 2 Lloyd's Rep. 509; [2003] 2 C.L.C. 207 .... R49–10
Westacre Investments Inc v Jugoimport SDPR Holding Co Ltd [2000] Q.B. 288; [1999] 3 W.L.R. 811; [1999] 3 All E.R. 864; [1999] 1 All E.R. (Comm) 865; [1999] 2 Lloyd's Rep. 65; [1999] C.L.C. 1176; [1999] B.L.R. 279 CA (Civ Div) S20–110, S20–113, S20–114, S20–116, S20–119, R68–68
Westdeutsche Landesbank Girozentrale v Islington LBC; Kleinwort Benson Ltd v Sandwell BC; sub nom. Islington LBC v Westdeutsche Landesbank Girozentrale [1996] A.C. 669; [1996] 2 W.L.R. 802; [1996] 2 All E.R. 961; [1996] 5 Bank. L.R. 341; [1996] C.L.C. 990; 95 L.G.R. 1; (1996) 160 J.P. Rep. 1130; (1996) 146 N.L.J. 877; (1996) 140 S.J.L.B. 136 HL R50–22
Westland Helicopters Ltd v Al-Hejailan [2004] EWHC 1625 (Comm); [2004] 2 Lloyd's Rep. 523 .... R50–24

Table of Cases

Whatlings (Foundations) Ltd v Shanks & McEwan (Contractors) Ltd, 1989 S.C. 253; 1989 S.L.T. 857; 1989 S.C.L.R. 552 IH (1 Div) R48–05

Whitworth Street Estates (Manchester) Ltd v James Miller & Partners Ltd; sub nom. James Miller & Partners Ltd v Whitworth Street Estates (Manchester) Ltd [1970] A.C. 583; [1970] 2 W.L.R. 728; [1970] 1 All E.R. 796; [1970] 1 Lloyd's Rep. 269; (1970) 114 S.J. 225 HL S3–18, S3–19, S6–10

William Co v Chiu Kong Agency Ltd [1995] 2 H.K.L.R. 139 .... S10–48

Wilson v Keen Unreported June 25, 1991 CA S25–13

Wm Dixon Ltd v Jones, Heard & Ingram (1884) 11 R. 739 .... R3–03

World Trade Corp Ltd v C Czarnikow Sugar Ltd [2004] EWHC 2332 (Comm); [2004] 2 All E.R. (Comm) 813; [2005] 1 Lloyd's Rep. 422 .... R58–18, R68–34

XL Insurance Ltd v Owens Corning [2001] 1 All E.R. (Comm) 530; [2000] 2 Lloyd's Rep. 500; [2001] C.P. Rep. 22; [2001] C.L.C. 914 .... S20–30

Younger v Caledonian Railway Co (1847) 10 D. 133 .... R59–09, R61–08, R61–15

Yukos Oil Co v Dardana Ltd. *See* Dardana Ltd v Yukos Oil Co (No.1)

Zaporozhye Production Aluminium Plan Open Shareholders Society v Ashly Ltd [2002] EWHC 1410 (Comm) S14–04

Zealander v Laing Homes Ltd (2000) 2 T.C.L.R. 724 .... A1–06

Zermalt Holdings SA v Nu-Life Upholstery Repairs Ltd [1985] 2 E.G.L.R. 14; (1985) 275 E.G. 1134 QBD (Comm) R24–32

Zheijiang Province Garment Import and Export Co v Siemssen & Co (Hong Kong) Trading Ltd [1993] A.D.R.L.J 183 .... S20–88

TABLE OF UK STATUTES

1843	Evidence by Commission Act (6 & 7 Vict. c.82)	R45–08, R45–10
1868	Titles to Land Consolidation (Scotland) Act (31 & 32 Vict. c.101)	
	s.155	R46–38
	s.159	R46–26
1894	Arbitration (Scotland) Act (57 & 58 Vict. c.13)	S29–01
1895	Court of Session Consignations (Scotland) Act (58 & 59 Vict. c.19)	R71–42, R71–58
1907	Sheriff Courts (Scotland) Act (7 Edw. 7 c.51)	S10–57, S14–08
	s.6	R43–09, R46–53
	Sch.1 Ch.15	S10–57
	r.16.3	S10–65
1924	Conveyancing (Scotland) Act (14 & 15 Geo. 5 c.27)	
	s.46	S27–01
1947	Crown Proceedings Act (10 & 11 Geo. 6 c.44)	
	s.21	R49–09, R49–12
	s.43	R49–09
1950	Arbitration Act (c.27)	S4–20, S20–63, S20–64, S29–01, R37–10, R52–05
	s.2(2)	R79–04
	s.9(1)	S20–63
	s.11	S25–02
	s.15	R49–13
	s.16	S11–03
	s.19	R56–03
	s.30	S34–01
1970	Administration of Justice Act (c.31)	
	s.4	S25–02, S25–09
1971	Banking and Financial Dealings Act (c.80)	
	Sch.1	R84–11
1972	Administration of Justice (Scotland) Act (c.59)	
	s.1	R26–27, R46–33, R46–34, R46–35, R46–36, R46–73, A2–16
	s.3	S29–01, S36–14, S36–15, S36–16, S36–17, R41–02, R41–04, R41–07, R42–01, R42–03, R55–06, R69–12, R69–17, R69–18, A2–17
	(1)	S36–14

1973	Prescription and Limitation (Scotland) Act (c.52)	S23–02, S23–03, S23–13
	s.1	S23–05
	s.2	S23–04
	s.3	S23–06
	s.4(1)	S23–07
	(2)	S23–07, S23–10
	(3)	S23–07, S23–08
	(4)	S23–08, S23–11
	ss.6–8	S23–09
	s.9(3)	S23–11
	(4)	S23–10, S23–11
	s.17	S23–13
	s.18	S23–13
	s.18B	S23–13
	s.18A	S23–13
	s.19D	S23–14
	s.22A	S23–09
	s.22C	S23–13
	s.22CA	S23–14
1975	Arbitration Act (c.3)	S10–19, S10–47, S12–03, S18–02, S18–04, S20–92, S20–144, S29–01, R37–10, R52–06, A2–19
	s.1	S10–03
	(1)	S10–44, S10–61
	s.3(2)	S19–02
	s.4	S21–02
	s.5	S20–02
	(1)	S20–10
	(d)	S20–71
	(f)	S20–85, S20–92
	(2)(a)	S20–13
	(b)	S20–27
	(c)	S20–32
	(e)	S20–55
	(3)	S20–104, S20–106
	(4)	S20–129
	(5)	S20–133, S20–144
	s.6	S22–01
	s.7(2)	S18–14
1975	Evidence (Proceedings in Other Jurisdictions) Act (c.34)	R45–10
1975	Industry Act (c.68)	
	Sch.3 para.18	S16–15
1977	Unfair Contract Terms Act (c.50)	
	s.27(2)	R47–21
	(3)	R47–21
1978	Interpretation Act (c.30)	R3–06
	s.5	R64
	s.7	R83–16, R83–18
	s.17(2)(a)	S18–15
	Sch.1	R44–16, R45–36, R64

Table of UK Statutes

1978	State Immunity Act (c.33)	
	s.9(1)	S20–24
1979	Arbitration Act (c.42)	R28–16, R42–11, R42–20, R52–05, R67–14, R68–12, R70–12
	s.1(4)	R70–15
	s.5	R39–03
1980	Law Reform (Miscellaneous Provisions) (Scotland) Act (c.55)	
	s.17	S25–01, S25–06, S29–01
	(2)	S25–14
1981	Senior Courts Act (c.54)	
	s.16	R70–48
1982	Civil Jurisdiction and Judgments Act (c.27)	
	s.18	S12–07, S12–34
	s.19	S3–21
	s.21(1)(a)	R43–09
	s.32	S3–21
	s.41	S12–10, S14–06, S19–04, R44–10, R45–19, R46–65
	s.42	S12–10, S14–06, S19–04, R44–10, R45–19, R46–65
	Sch.6	S12–07, S12–34
	Sch.7	S12–07, S12–34
	Sch.8	S3–24, R43–09
1985	Law Reform (Miscellaneous Provisions) (Scotland) Act (c.40)	
	s.8	S11–09, R49–18
	s.9	S11–10, R49–18
1987	Debtors (Scotland) Act (c.18)	
	s.15D	R46–65
	s.15E(2)	R46–41
	s.15F(3)	R46–41
	s.15G	R46–30, R46–43
	s.15K	R46–44
	s.15L	R46–44
1987	Consumer Protection Act (c.43)	S23–09
1988	Civil Evidence (Scotland) Act (c.32)	R28–58
1988	Court of Session Act (c.36)	R69–05, R70–49
	s.10	R46–55
	s.18	R70–32, R70–49
	s.40	R67–36, R68–89, R70–51
	s.46	R46–55
	s.47(2)	R46–55
1990	Contracts (Applicable Law) Act (c.36)	R47–16
1990	Law Reform (Miscellaneous Provisions) (Scotland) Act (c.40)	
	s.66	S29–01, S36–10
	Sch.7	S29–01, S36–10
1990	Courts and Legal Services Act (c.41)	S29–01
	s.58	R59–11
	s.93	S25–02
1991	Age of Legal Capacity (Scotland) Act (c.50)	
	s.1	R4–03
	s.3	R4–04
	(2)(f)	R4–04
	s.9	R4–03
1991	Coal Mining Subsidence Act (c.45)	
	s.19	R70–28
1991	Agricultural Holdings (Scotland) Act (c.55)	R69–04
	s.61	S16–09, S16–10
	s.61A	S16–10
1992	Trade Union and Labour Relations (Consolidation) Act (c.52)	
	s.212A	S30–09
1995	Requirements of Writing (Scotland) Act (c.7)	
	s.1(1)	S4–15
	(2)	S4–15
1996	Employment Rights Act (c.18)	S30–08
	s.203	S30–08
1996	Arbitration Act (c.23)	S2–01, S3–03, S3–16, S4–09, S4–14, S5–03, S6–05, S8–01, S9–02, S10–26, S10–31, S10–66, S14–11, S17–01, S17–03, S18–02, S20–92, S25–07, S25–09, S25–12, S25–12, S26–03, S32–01, S36–02, R1–20, R10–06, R20–18, R20–21, R20–28, R23–21, R24–07, R27–04, R28–16, R29–04, R30–08, R39–03, R39–04, R46–16, R47–07, R47–20, R47–32, R47–35, R48–10, R49–10, R51–09, R51–12, R51–33, R51–39, R51–58, R56–20, R57–25, R57–27, R58–19, R58–25, R58–28, R58–29, R58–36, R60–12, R60–15, R64–08, R65–08, R67–14, R68–12, R68–72, R69–02, R69–16, R70–12, R70–48, R71–06, R71–30, R78–05
	s.1	S1–03, S1–04, S1–05, S1–09
	(b)	S2–13
	(c)	S1–09, S1–10, S14–11, R7–04
	s.2(2)	R29–06
	(3)	R29–06
	(3)–(5)	R46–07
	(4)	R29–06
	s.3	S3–16, S3–17, S18–13

xxxiv

Table of UK Statutes

(a)–(c)	S3–07
(b)	S3–08
(c)	S3–09
s.4	S9–02
(1)	S8–01
(3)	S9–04
(5)	S3–10, S9–09
s.5	S18–09, S18–10
(1)	S4–14
s.6(2)	S4–12
s.7	S4–08, S5–06, S5–10, R19–04
s.9	S10–03, S10–47
(3)	S10–59, S10–63, S10–65
(4)	S1–05, S10–26
(a)(iii)	R47–32
(5)	S10–70
ss.9–11	R29–06
s.10(1)(d)	S2–13, S10–66, S10–67
s.13	S1–10
s.14	R1–15, R1–19, R1–20
(4)	R1–14, R1–22, R1–23
s.17	R6–06
s.18	R7–03
s.21(4)	R30–08
s.23(3)	R11–08
s.24	R10–06, R12–04, R12–16, R28–41, R73–08
(1)(c)	R12–03, R12–18
(4)	R78–05
s.25	R16–13, R78–05
(5)	R16–20
s.26	R79–04
(1)	R3–07, R79–05
s.28(5)	R60–12
s.29	R68–88, R73–08
s.30	S18–08
(1)	R19–08
s.31	R20–03, R20–05, R20–06
(4)	R20–24
(5)	R23–17
s.32	R22–01, R25–03
(1)	R23–04
(2)	R23–07
(a)	R23–06
(d)	R28–34
(4)	R22–01
(5)	R23–21
s.33	R28–40, R28–47
(1)(a)	R12–10, R24–16
s.34	R28–13
(2)(b)	R28–57
(c)	R28–24
(e)	R28–38
(f)	R28–16, R28–60
(h)	R28–47
s.36	R33–05
s.37	R34–02
s.38(5)	R36–03
s.39	R53–12, R53–13
(4)	R53–12
s.40(1)	R25–03, R25–05
(2)	R25–03
s.41	R25–05
(3)	R37–03, R37–09
(5)	R12–09, R39–01, R39–03
(7)	R39–12
s.42	R46–15
s.43	R29–06
s.44	R29–06
(2)	R46–21
(4)	R46–09
s.45	R25–03, R41–14, R41–08
(2)(b)(i)	R42–10
(5)	R50–10
s.46	R47–07
(1)(b)	R47–29
(2)	R47–15
(3)	R47–22
s.48	R48–03, R49–05
(4)	R48–12
(5)(b)	R49–13
s.49	R50–03, R50–06
(3)(a)	R50–10
(6)	R50–25
s.51	R57–12
(2)	R57–18
(5)	R57–28
s.52	R51–01
(4)	R51–49
(5)	R51–22
s.53	R52–02, R52–04, R52–06
s.54(1)	R51–26
(2)	R51–27
s.56	R56–03, R56–05
(2)	R56–15
(4)	R56–23
(5)	R56–09
(7)	R56–24
s.57	R51–46, R58–07, R58–08, R58–36
(3)	R58–11
(a)	R58–18, R58–21
(b)	R58–03
(5)	R58–33
s.58	S11–03
(1)	S11–04, S11–05
(2)	S11–11
ss.59–65	R59–13
s.60	R63–03, R63–04
s.63(4)	R61–06
(5)	R59–12
(b)	R61–16
s.65	R65–04, R65–06, R65–07, R65–17
s.66	S12–07, S12–18, R29–06
s.67	S20–19, R47–17, R67–26
(3)	R68–77

Table of UK Statutes

s.68 ...	R12–16, R24–42, R47–06, R47–17, R47–28, R59–12, R62–08, R68–12, R68–28, R68–35, R68–44, R68–77
(2)	R12–10, R28–47
s.69 ...	R28–16, R47–06, R62–09, R68–44, R69–22, R69–24, R70–11, R70–12, R70–17, R70–22
(3)	R28–16, R70–12
(7)	R68–77
s.70(2)	R51–46
(4)	R51–49, R71–27
(7)	R71–54
s.72	S14–01, S14–04, S14–15, S14–09, S14–12, S14–13
s.73	R20–17, R76–11
s.79	R58–30, R71–17
s.81(1)	R1–19
s.82(2)	S10–37
ss.89–91	R24–37, A1–01, A1–03, A1–04, A1–10
s.90	S4–22, A1–08
s.93	S25–02
(1)–(2)	S25–08
ss.94–97	S16–01
s.96	S25–07, R28–16
(2)	R19–17
(3)	S16–19
(c)	R28–16
s.98(1)	S17–01
ss.100–104	S18–02, S18–04
s.101(1)	S19–02
s.102	S21–02
(2)(a)	S18–09
(b)	S18–12
s.103	S20–02, S20–101, S20–139
(1)	S20–10
(2)(a)	S20–13
(b)	S20–27
(c)	S20–32
(d)	S20–71
(e)	S20–55
(f)	S20–101
(5)	S20–101, S20–133, S20–139, S20–144
s.104	A1–10
s.106	S34–01
Sch.1	S8–01
Sch.2	S25–03, S25–16
para.2(1)	S25–16
1996 Housing Grants, Regeneration and Construction Act (c.53)	S2–07, S2–11
1998 Human Rights Act (c.42) ...	S1–12, S1–13, S1–14, S1–18, R24–06
s.3(1)	S1–15, S1–16, S16–05, R24–08, R24–12, R24–25, R26–05
s.6(1)	S1–12, S1–18
(2)	S1–18
(3)	S1–13
s.9(1)	R70–48
s.21(1)	S1–18
Sch.1	S1–15
1998 Scotland Act (c.46)	S1–11, S1–14, A1–02
s.29(1)	S1–17
(2)(d)	S1–17
s.100(2)	R24–08, R24–12
s.101	S1–16
s.104	A1–10
s.127	S16–07
s.126(1)	S16–07
1999 Access to Justice Act (c.22)	
s.27	R59–11
1999 Contracts (Rights of Third Parties) Act (c.31)	
s.8	S10–42
2002 Proceeds of Crime Act (c.29)	R57–16
2006 Companies (c.46)	
s.994	S10–17
2010 Equality Act (c.15)	R50–05

TABLE OF SCOTTISH STATUTES

2000 Adults with Incapacity (Scotland) Act (asp 4) R4–04, R4–06
    s.1(6) R4–06
    s.328 .... R4–07
2002 Debt Arrangement and Attachment (Scotland) Act (asp 17)
    s.9C R46–65
    s.9D(2) R46–28
    s.9E(3) R46–28
    s.9G R46–30
    s.9M R46–31
    s.9N R46–31
2003 Agricultural Holdings (Scotland) Act (asp 11) R69–04
    s.78 .... S16–09, S16–10
    s.79 .... S16–10
2003 Mental Health (Care and Treatment) (Scotland) Act (asp 13) ... R4–07
2007 Bankruptcy and Diligence etc. (Scotland) Act (asp 3) S12–09, R46–41
    s.149 .... R46–38
2010 Arbitration (Scotland) Act (asp 1) S1–09, S1–17, S1–18, S2–14, S3–03, S3–25, S4–09, S4–14, S5–06, S10–14, S10–19, S10–20, S10–31, S10–67, S13–03, S14–11, S15–01, S16–02, S16–09, S16–10, S17–03, S18–02, S18–09, S18–11, S18–13, S20–13, S20–93, S20–144, S23–03, S25–08, S25–09, S29–01, S36–07, S36–10, S36–17, R15–06, R20–19, R20–28, R24, R24–16, R24–53, R28–43, R28–60, R56–24, R58–28, R66–05, R67–17, R68–12, R68–59, R71–31, A2–15, A2–16, A2–17, A2–18, A2–19, A2–21, A2–22, A2–23, A2–25, A2–26, A2–27, A2–28, A2–37
    s.1 ... **S1**, S3–11, S10–16, S10–28, R8–03, R9–02, R10–04, **R16–05**, R16–11, R16–13, R24–04, R24–23, R24–43, R26–05, R45–15, R70–31, R71–49, A2–16
    (a) S12–29, R10–09, R14–13, R15–13, R17–07, R19–04, R21–10, R21–12, R23–10, R23–15, R23–19, R28–24, R28–46, R28–48, R28–51, R28–56, R31–03, R31–05, R33–04, R37–12, R38–04, R39–07, R44–16, R45–36, R58–24, R68–17, R70–13, R70–30
    (b) R48–07
    (c) S13–05, R10–06, R14–12, R16–20, R19–07, R21–09, R23–12, R44–16, R45–06, R45–36, R46–17, R55–09, R60–14, R67–16, R68–11, R69–03, R69–05, R70–13, R71–04, R71–13, R71–25
    s.2 ...... **S2**, S4–03, S6, S7, S8, S9, S10–36, S12, S16, S28–02, R1, R2, R5, R6, R7, R10, R31, R32, R33, R34, R35, R36, R38, R39, R76, R77, R78, R80, R81, R82, R83
    (1) ... S1, S2–01, S2–15, S2–18, S3, S4, S5, S6, S7, S8, S9, S10, S11, S12, S13, S14, S15, S16, S17, S20, S23, S25, S26, S28, S30, S34, S36, R19, R20, R21, R22, R23, R24, R25, R26, R27, R28, R29, R30, R31, R32, R33, R34, R35, R36, R37, R38, R39, R40, R41, R42, R43, R44, R46–07, R47, R48, R49, R50, R51, R53, R54, R55, R56, R57, R58, R59, R60, R61, R62, R63, R64, R65, R67, R68, R69, R70, R71, R72, R73, R74, R75, R76, R77, R78, R79, R81, R82, R83, R84
    (2) ... S1, S2–19, S3, S4, S6, S7, S8, S9, S10, S12, S13, S14, S15, S16, S17, S20, S23, S26, S28, S34, S36, R19, R20, R21, R23, R25, R26, R40, R45, R46, R50, R54, R57
    (3) S2–20
    s.3 ...... S2–14, **S3**, S3–04, S3–17, S3–20, S6–01, S10–49, S18–13, R29–04, R51–20, R51–23, R52–08
    (1) S3–07
    (a) S3–07, S3–09, S3–11
    (b) S3–15, S16–15
    (2) S3–25
    s.4 ...... **S4**, S4–03, S4–12, S4–14, S5, S5–12, S6, S8, S9, S10, S10–32, S10–36, S12–30, S14,

Table of Scottish Statutes

	S16, S16–11, S18, S20, S21, S30–10, S36, R1, R2, R3, R4, R5, R6, R7, R8, R9, R10, R11, R12, R13, R14, R15, R16, R17, R18, R19, R19–13, R39, R43, R67–06, R68, R76, R80, R81, R83
s.5	**S5**, S5–06, S10–36, R1–09, R19–03, R19–04, R67–06, R82
(1)	S5–07, S5–09
(2)	S5–09, S5–11
(3)	S5–06, S5–11
s.6	S4–03, S4–20, **S6**, S6–01, S6–06, S10–36, S10–45, S20–28, R19–14, R19–16, R19–20, R80–02
s.7	S3–05, **S7**, S8, S9, S11, S13, S14, S16, S17, S24, S26, R16–13, R51, R51–19, R52–04, R57
s.8	**S8**, S13–09, R3–01, R4–01, R7–01, R8–01, R12–01, R13–01, R14–01, R15–01, R16–01, R24–01, R25–01, R26–01, R28–05, R60–01, R60–02, R60–08, R82–05
s.9	**S9,** R1–01, R2–01, R6–01, R9–01, R9–04, R10–01, R11–01, R17–01, R17–04, R18–01, R22–01, R26–01, R27–01, R28–01, R29–01, R30–01, R31–01, R32–01, R33–01, R34–04, R35–01, R36–01, R37–01, R38–01, R39–01, R40–01, R41–01, R43–01, R46–01, R47–01, R49–01, R51–01, R53–01, R55–01, R57–01, R58–01, R59–01, R61–01, R62–01, R64–01, R65–01, R66–01, R67–16, R69–01, R69–03, R78–01, R80–01, R81–01, R83–01, R84–01, A2–15, A2–18
(1)	S7, S9–01
(2)	S9–01, S13–08, R64–03
(3)	S9–02, S9–01, S9–04, S13–08
(b)	R83–03
(4)	S9–02, S16–12
(a)	S9–03, S9–04, S9–08, S13–08, R19–04, R49–04, R49–21
(b)	S3–10, S3–25, S9–07, S9–09, R49–19, R51–38
s.10	**S10**, S10–03, S10–04, S10–05, S10–10, S10–14, S10–15, S10–16, S10–22, S10–28, S10–44, S10–72, S14–10, S29–01, S30–25, R19–05, R19–06
(1)(a)	S10–30, S10–35
(b)	S10–30, S10–35, S11–03
(c)	S10–57
(d)	S10–13, S10–59, S10–62, S10–63, S10–67, S10–68
(e)	S4–05, S4–20, S10–30, S10–35, S10–45, S10–47, S10–50, S10–52, R19–13
(2)	S10–69
(3)	S10–04, S10–72
s.11	**S11**, S11–03
(1)	S11–04, S11–06, S11–07, S11–08, S11–10
(2)	S11–06, S11–08, S11–09, S11–10, R49–22
(3)	S11–06
(4)	S11–12
s.12	**S12**, S12–04, S12–05, S12–06, S12–07, S12–08, S12–19, S12–20, S12–26, S12–34, S15–08, S18–06, S22–03, S27–01, S30–25, A2–18, A2–41
(1)	S12–14, S12–23, S12–24, S19–08, S22–03
(2)	S12–22, S12–24, S12–28, R20–17
(3)	S12–28, S12–29, S13–02, R20–17
(4)	S12–29
(5)	S12–32, S22–03
s.13	S12–33, **S13**, S13–02, R12–20, R15–06, R20–15, R68–11, R69–05, A2–17
(1)	A2–17
(b)	S13–06, R46–13
(2)	S12–20, A2–17
(3)	S13–07
(a)	S13–02
(4)	S13–08, S13–09
s.14	**S14**, S14–03, S14–07, S14–10, S14–12, S30–25, R20–07
(1)	S14–12
(a)–(c)	S14–03
s.15	**S15**, S15–02, S15–03, S15–08, S15–10, S15–11, S15–11, R26–05, A2–37, A2–38, A2–40
(1)	S15–04, S15–05
(2)	S15–14
(a)	S15–15
(b)	S15–17
(c)	S15–18, S15–19
(d)	S15–21
(3)	S15–22
s.16	**S16**, S19, S35–01, R26–05
(1)	S10, S14, S16–06,

Table of Scottish Statutes

	S16–08, S16–13, S17, R19, R69–04
(2)	S10–70, S16–11
(3)	S16–12
(4)	S3–06, S16–13
(5)	S16–16
(6)	S16–19
s.17	**S17**, S17–03
s.18	**S18**, S20, S21, S22, S22–02
(1)	S18–05
(2)	S18–12, R52–04
(3)	S18–15
ss.18–21	S18–06
ss.18–22	S18–02, S18–03, S18–04, S29–01
s.19	S15–08, **S19**, S21–03, A2–18, A2–41
(1)	S19–02
(2)	S12–05, S12–06, S12–19, S12–34
ss.19–21	S12–05
s.20	S12–05, S12–21, S12–34, **S20**, S20–01, S20–02, S20–11, S22–02, R46–04, R68–71
(1)	S20–09
(2)	S20–03, S20–08, S20–12
(a)	S20–13, S20–25, S20–26
(b)	S20–27, S20–32, S20–77, S20–104, S30–24
(c)	S20–32, S20–37, S20–39, S20–44, S20–47
(d)	S20–51, S20–55, S20–56, S20–63, S20–67
(3)	S20–03, S20–08
(a)	S20–71
(b)	S20–82, S20–104, S20–129
(c)	S20–85, S20–101
(d)	S20–57, S20–85, S20–92, S20–94, S20–101, S20–104
(4)	S20–03, S20–08, S20–102
(a)	S20–104, S20–105
(b)	S20–38, S20–104, S20–105, S20–106, S30–25, R68–56, R68–57
(6)	S20–133
(a)	S20–90, S20–101, S20–134, S20–139
(b)	S12–25, S20–144, R71–50, R71–51
s.21	S12–05, **S21**, S21–01, S21–02, S22–02
(1)	S21–04
(a)	S21–07
(b)	S21–13
(2)	S21–14
s.22	S12–05, S18–06, **S22,** R7, R11–07, R59, R60, R74, R74–03
s.23	**S23**
(3)	S23–09
(5)	S23–09
(4)	S23–13, S23–14
(6)	S23–13, S23–14
s.24	**S24**
(1)(b)	R38–09
(c)	R38–09
(2)	S24–05, S36–12
(b)	S24–07
(3)	S24–08
s.25	**S25, S29–01,** R21–21
(1)	S25–08, S25–10, S25–11
(2)	S25–14
(3)	S25–15
s.26	**S26**, S26–03, R68–53
(1)	S26–04, R26–23
(2)	S26–05
s.27	**S27**, S27–01
s.28	**S28**
s.29	**S29**
s.30	S4–18, S10–16, S20–08, S20–105, **S30**, S30–02, R19–07, R19–16, R49–21, R68–71
s.31	**S31**, R59
(1)	S1, S3, S3–20, S4, S5, S6, S7, S8, S9, S10–15, S11, S12, S13, S14, S15, S15–22, S16, S17, S18, S19, S20, S21, S22, S23, S24, S25, S26, S27, S28, S30, S31–01, S32, S33, S34, S36, R1, R2, R3, R4, R5, R6, R7, R8, R9, R10, R11, R12, R13, R14, R15, R16, R17, R18, R19, R20, R21, R22, R23, R25, R26, R27, R30, R31, R32, R33, R34, R35, R36, R37, R38, R39, R40, R41, R42, R43, R44, R45, R46, R47, R48, R49, R50, R51, R53, R54, R55, R56, R57, R58, R59, R60, R61, R62, R63, R64, R65, R66, R67, R68, R69, R70, R71, R72, R73, R74, R75, R76, R77, R78, R79, R80, R81, R82, R83, R84
(2)	S1, S3, S6, R7, S7, S8, S9, S10, S11, S12, S13, S14, S15, S16, S20, S23, S31–02, S34, S36, R6, R20, R21, R22, R23, R25, R26, R27, R31, R32, R33, R34, R35, R36, R37, R38, R39, R41, R42, R43, R44, R45, R46, R47, R49, R51, R55, R56, R57, R58, R59, R60, R61, R62, R63, R64, R65, R67, R68,

Table of Scottish Statutes

	R69, R70, R71, R76, R77, R78, R80, R81, R82, R83
s.32	**S32**, S32–01, S32–02, S32–03, R23–17
(1)	S32–01
(2)	S32–04
(4)	R23–16
s.33	S17–03, **S33**
s.34	**S34**
s.35	**S35**
(2)	S36, S36–18
s.36	**S36**, S36–01
(1)	S36–06
(2)	S36–07
(3)	S36–07, S36–09, S36–11
(4)	S36–09, S36–11
(5)	S36–09
(6)	S36, S36–13
(7)	S36–13
(8)	S36–14, S36–16, R41–02, R69–12
(9)	S36–19
s.37	**S37**
Sch.1	S7–01, S9–09, R26–21, R46–53, A2–15, A2–16, A2–18
r.1	S36–01, S36–06, **R1**, R1–09, R1–10, R1–26, R46–16, R46–75, R83–22
r.2	S29–01, **R2**, R2–02, R2–04
rr.2–7	R17–05, R67–06
r.3	**R3**, R3–02, R3–07, R6, R79–03
r.4	**R4**, R4–02, R4–03, R4–06, R4–08, R6, R12–18, R16–03, R76–08
r.5	**R5**, R5–07
rr.5–7	S4–20
r.6	S9–03, R2–03, **R6**, R6–04, R6–06, R6–18, R17–06, R43–06
(b)	R6–08, R6–09, R6–16, R11–05, R30–04, R30–06
r.7	S4–19, S15–09, S29–01, R2–03, R6–06, R6–08, R6–18, **R7**, R7–08, R17–06, R43–06, R59, R60, R74–03
(1)	R7–07
(2)	R7–08
(3)	R7–09
(5)	R7–10
(6)	R7–02, R7–08, R7–11
(7)	R7–02, R7–11
(8)	R6–02, R7–08, R7–10, R7–11, R8–05
r.8	**R8**, R8–08, R12–11, R24–03, R30–07, R78–04, R78–05, R82–04
(2)	R8–08, R77–04
r.9	R4–03, **R9**, R10–03, R16, R16–03, R17, R18, R57–08
(a)	R4–09, R12–18
r.10	R8–05, **R10**, R10–01, R10–04, R10–08, R10–10, R14–11, R15–12, R16–03, R53–03
(1)	R10–05
(2)	R10–02, R10–10, R10–12, R10–13, R12–03, R12–19, R68–73, R77–04, R81–03
(3)	R10–17
(4)	R10–17, R10–20
rr.10–11	R82–04
r.11	**R11**, R11–02, R11–03, R16–03, R24–51
(1)	R11–08, R11–09
rr.11–14	S13–06
r.12	S15–09, R10–04, R10–18, **R12**, R12–02, R12–03, R12–04, R13–05, R15–12, R16–03, R24–20, R24–34, R53–19
(a)	R6–09, R10–11, R12–13, R12–14, R24–20, R24–54, R57–19, R77–04
(b)	R10–14, R12–17, R24–41
(c)	R4–09, R10–15, R12–17, R24–50, R68–73
(d)	R10–13, R12–19, R68–73
(e)	R12–19, R12–20, R28–05
rr.12–14	R82–04
r.13	S15–09, **R13**, R13–02, R13–03, R13–04, R16–03
r.14	R12–03, R13–03, **R14**, R14–02, R14–03
(1)	R10–04, R14–11, R15–21, R16–17
(2)	R14–12
(3)	R14–13
r.15	**R15**, R15–02, R15–03, R15–06, R15–07, R16, R16–03, R16–13, R73–14
(1)	R12–18, R15–03, R15–04, R15–08, R15–10, R15–12, R15–14, R15–17, R16–11, R16–13, R57–20
(2)	R15–17, R57–20
r.16	S15–10, R4–09, R10–17, R11–04, R12–03, R13–04, R15–07, R15–08, R15–10, R15–12, R15–13, R15–17, **R16**, R16–03, R16–04, R16–05, R16–08, R16–13, R16–20, R24–51, R56–09, R73–14, R78–07

Table of Scottish Statutes

(1)	R15–03, R16–04, R16–05, R16–08, R16–11, R16–14, R78–03
(2)	R15–06, R16–08
(3)	R16–20
r.17	**R17**, R17–06
(1)	R17–04, R17–05, R17–06
(2)	R17–07
(3)	R17–09
r.18	**R18**
r.19 ...	S10–20, S10–26, R1–25, **R19**, R19–01, R19–03, R19–04, R19–05, R19–07, R19–08, R20–04, R67–05, R67–06, R67–07, R67–20
(a)	R19–08, R19–10, R19–17
(b)	R19–08, R19–18
(c)	R19–08, R19–19
rr.19–23	R1–06
r.20	S30–25, R1–25, **R20**, R20–01, R20–06, R20–07, R20–08, R20–09, R58–23, R67–22, R68–26, R68–31
(1)	R20–03, R20–08
(2)	R20–04, R20–06, R20–14
(3)	R20–21, R20–22, R57–10, R76–08
(4)	R20–24, R20–29, R21–08, R21–15, R67–18, R67–22
rr.20–22	R67–21
r.21	S10–21, S13–07, S15–09, S30–25, R20–27, **R21**, R21–01, R21–03, R21–12, R21–13, R21–15, R21–16, R67–23
(1)	R21–04, R21–09, R57–10, R67–21
(3)	R21–11, R23–18, R67–23
r.22	S10–21, S10–30, S13–07, S15–09, S30–25, R19–17, R20–03, **R22**, R22–01, R22–02, R22–04, R22–06, R23–03, R23–14, R23–16, R23–19, R23–20, R23–21, R41–10, R41–11, R68–26, R68–31, A2–25, A2–31
r.23 ...	S8–01, S10–21, R22–04, R22–06, **R23**, R23–01, R23–03, R23–04, R23–16, R23–17, R23–19, R23–20, R23–21, R41–10, R42–08
(1)	R6–09, R23–03
(2)	R23–05, R23–05, R42–11
(3)	R23–13, R23–16
(4)	R23–18, R67–21
r.24	R8–04, R10, R10–09, R10–11, R12, R12–20, R15–13, S1–21, S2–05, S2–07, S3–04, **R24**, R24–02, R24–12, R28–07, R28–15, R28–19, R28–34, R28–36, R28–40, R28–42, R28–46, R30–07, R37–12, R39–07, R42–19, R45–35, R46–72, R47–39, R53–19, R55–09, R61–06, R61–09, R65–05, R65–11, R65–14, R68–06, R68–23, R68–27, R68–28, R68–73, R71–23, R82–04, R83–21
(1)	S3–13, R7–11, R8–03, R10–11, R24–29, R24–33, R24–34, R24–37, R24–40, R24–43, R24–44, R24–49, R24–54, R8–14, R12–12, R12–13, R12–20, R15–12, R17–07, R20–26, R21–09, R21–10, R23–09, R23–15, R23–17, R24–02, R24–04, R24–07, R24–16, R24–20, R24–22, R24–23, R24–25, R24–26, R28–46, R28–48, R28–51, R28–56, R31–03, R31–05, R33–04, R34–05, R34–06, R38–04, R42–09, R44–12, R45–33, R46–10, R46–72, R54–08, R55–04, R55–07, R55–13, R58–26, R76–08, R77–01, R77–04, R77–05
(2)	S3–13, R12–17, R24–23, R24–25, R24–27, R24–28, R28–15, R28–37, R34–05
r.25	R10–09, R15–13, R17–07, **R25**, R25–03, R25–04, R31–05, R37–06
(a)	R31–03
r.26	S15–01, S15–17, **R26**, R26–02, R26–04, R26–05, R26–21, R26–24, R26–26, R28–24, R28–32, R40–10, R68–27, R82–04, A2–37
(1)	S15–03, S15–15, R26–17, R26–23
r.27	**R27**, R27–03, R27–04, R27–06
(1)	R27–05, R27–06, R27–09
(2)	R27–08, R27–10, R28–35, R28–36, R51–11
r.28	R24–49, R25–04, **R28**, R28–01, R28–04, R45–06, R65–11

xli

Table of Scottish Statutes

(1) R28–06, R28–07, R28–12, R28–13, R28–38	R41–14, R41–15, R42–01, R42–05, R55–06, R69–18, R69–42, A2–25, A2–31
(2) R28–18, R28–19, R28–21, R28–25, R28–26, R28–38, R28–40, R28–44, R28–50, R28–54, R28–57, R28–58, R29–04, R45–15, R45–16	rr.41–46 .... S10–08
	r.42 .... R23–13, R41–01, R41–06, R41–10, **R42**, R42–01, R42–03, R42–05, R46–53, R55–07, S8–01, S29–01
r.29 ...... S18–13, R28–19, **R29**, R29–04, R29–05	(1) R42–06, R42–12, R70–05
r.30 .... **R30**, R51–08, R82–03	(2) R23–11, R41–09, R42–06, R42–10, R42–12, R42–13, R42–14, R42–16, R67–10, R68–09, R70–05
(1) R30–03	
(2) R5–06, R30–02, R30–04, R30–05, R30–06, R30–07, R30–08	
	(3) R42–19
r.31 .... **R31**, R45–15	(4) R42–20
(1) R31–03	r.43 ...... S16–17, R37–07, **R43**, R43–01, R43–05, R43–06, R43–07, R43–09, R44–03
(2) R31–05	
r.32 .... R3–14, **R32**, R32–05	
(1) R32–03	r.44 .... S8–01, R43–01, R43–09, **R44**, R58–24
(2) R23–11, R32–20	
r.33 ..... **R33**, R33–02, R33–05, R42–05	(1)–(3) R44–03
	(2) R44–05
(1) R33–09	(4) R44–12
r.34 ...... R15–16, R28–55, **R34**, R34–02, R34–03	(5) R44–15, R44–16
	r.45 ...... R28–25, R28–38, **R45**, R45–05, R45–06, R45–15, R45–18, R45–35, R46–35, A2–30
(1) R34–04, R42–09	
(2) R32–13, R34–05, R34–09, R34–11, R34–12	
	(1) R45–06, R45–14, R45–16, R45–19, R45–20
r.35 .... R6–60, R28–25, **R35**, R35–02, R35–03, R35–04, R35–05, R35–06, R35–08, R45–15, R46–12	
	(2) R28–28, R45–27, R64–10
	(3) R45–33
r.36 .... **R36**	(4) R45–36
r.37 .... S14–03, R31–05, **R37**, R37–05, R37–06, R37–08, R37–09, R38–04, R38–08, R43–04, R57–10	r.46 ..... R35–05, **R46**, R46–07, R46–08, R46–12, R46–17, R46–65, R46–72, R46–74
	(1) S12–27, R35–05, R46–09, R46–16, R46–18, R46–21, R46–22, R46–27, R46–33, R46–34, R46–36, R46–37, R46–46, R46–47, R46–55, R46–56, R46–57, R46–60, R46–61, R46–62, R64–10, R64–10
(1) R23–11, R37–08, R37–09, R39–03	
(2) R37–12	
rr.37–39 .... R25–05	
r.38 .... **R38**, R43–04	
(a) R38–05	
r.39 .... R24–33, R31–05, R31–06, R37–05, **R39**, R39–05, R39–08, R39–11, R39–17, R43–04	
	(2) R46–09, R46–64
	(3) R46–43, R46–72
(1) R39–05, R39–06, R39–07, R39–09, R39–10	(4) R46–08, R46–16, R46–30, R46–34, R46–36, R46–48, R46–55, R46–73
(2) R39–05, R39–10, R39–12, R39–13, R39–14, R39–15, R39–16, R39–18	r.47 .... S3–25, **R47**, R47–01, R47–02, R47–08, R47–11, R47–15, R47–18, R69–14
r.40 .... **R40**, R40–04	(1) R47–04, R47–12, R47–13, R47–16, R47–19, R47–26, R47–27, R47–28, R47–29, R47–42
(2) R40–12	
r.41 .... S29–01, S36–14, S36–15, S36–17, R22–04, **R41**, R41–01, R41–06, R41–02, R41–10, R41–11,	

xlii

Table of Scottish Statutes

(2)	R47–05, R47–08, R47–11, R47–29, R47–30, R47–34	r.55	**R55**, R55–01, R55–04, R55–08, R56–01
(3)	R47–07, R47–35, R47–37, R47–39, R47–40, R47–41, R47–42, R47–43, R63–05	(a)	R55–01
		(b)	R55–11
		r.56	R51–60, R51–62, **R56**, R56–04, R56–05, R56–06, R56–07, R56–09, R56–13, R56–22, R56–24, R57–25
r.48	**R48**, R48–01, R48–03, R48–05, R48–06, R48–07	(1)	R56–03, R56–13
(1)	R48–04	(2)	R56–13, R56–15, R56–19, R56–20
(2)(c)	R68–42		
r.49	R48–03, **R49**, R49–01, R49–03, R49–13	(3)	R56–23
(a)	R49–07	(4)	R56–24
(b)	R46–47, R46–48, R46–49, R49–08	r.57	R54–04, **R57**, R57–01, R57–02, R57–05, R57–07, R57–19, R57–27, R57–28
(c)	S11–09, R49–17, R49–20, R49–21, R49–22	(1)	R57–04, R57–10, R57–11, R62–15
r.50	**R50**, R50–01, R50–04, R50–06, R50–07, R50–09, R50–18, R50–24, R51–25	(2)	R57–10
		(3)	R57–11
(1)	R50–04, R50–10, R50–14, R50–15, R50–16	(4)	R51–35, R57–12, R57–14, R57–18, R57–26
(2)	R50–17	(5)	R57–28, R68–80
(3)	R50–17	r.58	S3–14, S12–22, R51–21, R51–46, R55–04, R55–07, R57–06, **R58**, R58–01, R58–05, R58–06, R58–07, R58–08, R58–14, R58–17, R58–22, R58–29, R67–09, R68–09, R68–46, R68–48, R68–78, R68–80, R71–05, R71–06, R71–09, R71–10, R71–13, R71–14, R71–15
(4)	R50–04, R50–18		
(5)	R50–25		
r.51	S3–14, R20–29, R51–13, **R51**, R51–01, R51–02, R51–07, R51–19, R51–32, R53–18, R58–38		
(1)	R51–05, R51–49, R54–06		
(2)	R51–19, R51–24, R51–26, R51–29, R51–32, R51–33, R51–40, R51–57, R51–59, R52–08, R54–11, R56–04, R57–24, R69–13, R69–30, R71–24, R71–25, R71–31	(1)	R51–28, R58–11, R58–12, R58–18, R68–46, R71–09, R71–25
		(2)	R58–19, R68–46
		(3)	R58–22
		(4)	R51–25, R58–21, R58–23, R58–24, R71–06
(3)	R21–08, R51–25, R51–29, R51–60, R51–61, R51–63, R56–04, R56–06, R56–13, R58–23, R58–34, R71–10	(5)	R58–26
		(6)	R51–25, R58–31, R58–33
		(7)	R58–36, R58–37
		(8)	R58–38
r.52	R29–05, **R52**, R52–01, R52–02, R52–04, R52–05, R52–06	r.59	R14–07, R15–22, R16, R16–19, R42–04, R44–11, R46–71, R56–04, **R59**, R59–04, R59–05, R61, R61–04, R61–06, R62, R63, R64–07, R65, R65–03, R66–02, R82–04
r.53	R39–18, R46–48, R49–10, **R53**, R53–01, R53–03, R53–05, R53–06, R53–11, R53–12, R53–13, R53–14, R53–18, R53–21, R54–09, R71, R71–08, S11–12		
		(c)	R59–07, R61–04
		rr.59–66	R66–05
r.54	R53–05, R53–06, **R54**, R54–01, R54–02, R54–09, R62–10	r.60	R16, R16–05, R32–18, R32–20, R34–07, R46–71, **R60**, R60–02, R60–06, R60–07, R60–08, R60–09, R62–08, R62–26, R82–04
(1)	R54–04		
(2)	R51–56, R54–04		
(3)	R54–11		

xliii

Table of Scottish Statutes

(1)	R34–07, R56–07, R60–09, R62–26, R68–91
(2)	R56–07, R60–09
(3)	R16–05, R16–18, R34–07, R56–17, R56–19, R56–21, R60–11, R60–12
(4)	R16–05, R16–18, R34–07, R60–13, R60–14
(5)	R16–05, R56–19, R60–13, R60–14
r.61	R59–01, **R61**, R61–02, R61–04, R61–21, R62–05, R62–08, R62–10, R65–14
(1)	R61–04, R61–06, R61–10, R82–04
(2)	R61–06, R61–07, R61–08, R61–09, R61–17
(3)	R24–55, R61–12, R61–16
r.62	R16–05, R42–04, R56–14, R59–01, R61–04, **R62**, R62–02, R62–06, R62–08, R62–10, R68–43
(1)	R60–09, R60–10, R62–10, R62–13, R62–15
(2)	R62–17, R62–19, R63–05
(3)	R56–07, R60–09, R62–26, R62–27
(4)	R62–26
r.63	**R63**, R63–03, R63–04, R63–05
r.64	R46–61, R46–62, **R64**, R64–02, R64–03, R64–10, R64–11, R71–39, R71–46
(1)(a)	R46–32
(2)	R46–61, R64–12
rr.64–66	R59–01
r.65	R61–05, **R65**, R65–02, R65–08, R65–09, R65–10, R65–11, R65–13, R65–15, R65–16
r.66	R62–12, **R66**, R66–03, R66–05
(2)(c)	R68–38
Pt 8 (rr.67–72)	R68–11
r.67	S9–06, S10–21, S12–29, S13–02, S13–07, S14–14, S30–25, R1–25, R20–07, R20–15, R20–20, R20–27, R21–12, R21–13, R21–14, R21–15, R23–19, R23–20, R23–21, R47–27, R51–53, R54–04, R56–24, R60–14, R61–11, R65–08, **R67**, R67–01, R67–03, R67–04, R67–07, R67–11, R67–14, R67–16, R67–17, R67–18, R67–19, R67–20, R67–21, R67–22, R67–23, R67–24, R67–25, R67–31, R67–32, R68–04, R68–05, R68–14, R68–26, R68–31, R69–06, R69–07, R71–01, R76–04, A2–25, A2–31
(1)	R67–19, R71
(2)	R67–32, R67–33, R68–77
(3)	R67–32, R67–34
(4)–(6)	R67–35
(5)	R21–13, R23–20, R67–24, R67–35
(7)	R67–36
rr.67–69	R50–24, R58–29
rr.67–71	S3–24
r.68	S9–06, S14–14, R20–15, R21–14, R23–21, R24–34, R24–49, R24–54, R28–14, R38–06, R42–20, R44–14, R45–35, R46–72, R51–20, R51–28, R51–53, R53–18, R54–04, R56–24, R60–14, R61–11, R61–12, R62–06, R62–08, R65–08, R66–05, R67–03, R67–04, R67–16, R67–17, R67–18, R67–19, **R68**, R68–01, R68–03, R68–04, R68–05, R68–06, R68–11, R68–12, R68–13, R68–17, R68–22, R68–47, R68–77, R69–06, R69–07, R71–01, R71–26, R71–31, R72–01, R76–04, R82–04, A2–25, A2–31
(1)	R68–13, R71, R72
(2)	A2–04, R7–06, R12–03, R12–20, R20–15, R24–20, R24–40, R24–50, R28–05, R47–18, R47–26, R47–27, R47–28, R47–43, R50–13, R50–20, R50–23, R51–42, R51–55, R54–11, R55–13, R58–16, R58–17, R58–29, R61–21, R62–08, R62–15, R68–13, R68–15, R68–16, R68–24, R68–25, R68–26, R68–30, R68–31, R68–32, R68–33, R68–34, R68–42, R68–45, R68–46, R68–52, R68–54, R68–58, R68–68, R68–69, R68–73, R68–74, R68–75, R68–78, R68–86, R68–90, R68–91, R71–31, R71–32, R76–08
(3)	R58–15, R58–17, R68–51, R68–68, R68–76, R68–84
(4)	R68–25, R68–74, R68–89, R68–90, R68–92, R78–03

Table of Scottish Statutes

(5)	R68–93	(3)	R53–17, R65–15, R71–08
(6)	R68–93	(4)	S14–14, R51–25, R56–06, R58–30, R58–34, R67–08, R68–07, R69–26, R70–04, R71–09, R71–13, R71–16, R71–27
(7)	R68–93		
(8)	R68–93		
r.69	S9–06, S16–10, S29–01, S36–14, S36–15, S36–17, R21–14, R23–21, R28–14, R28–15, R42–11, R42–20, R47–27, R47–44, R48–11, R50–20, R51–41, R51–53, R54–04, R56–24, R60–14, R61–11, R61–21, R61–22, R62–08, R65–08, R67–04, R67–16, R67–17, R67–18, R67–19, R68–05, R68–07, R68–14, R68–51, **R69**, R69–01, R69–03, R69–04, R69–05, R69–06, R69–07, R69–08, R69–09, R69–10, R69–11, R69–12, R69–14, R69–15, R69–16, R69–17, R69–18, R69–22, R69–24, R70–01, R70–12, R70–17, R71–01, A2–23, A2–25, A2–31, A2–32	(5)	R67–37, R68–95, R69–26, R70–45, R71–09, R71–20
		(6)	R71–09, R71–22
		(7)	R68–39, R71–23
		(8)	S20–11, R51–49, R51–57, R57–06, R70–03, R71–24, R71–25, R71–27, R71–29, R71–31, R71–33, R71–34, R71–35, R71–36
		(9)	S16–18, R71–38
		(10)	S12–25, R71–39
		(10)–(12)	R69–21
		(11)	R71–39
		(12)	R67–24, R71–49, R71–50, R71–51, R71–53, S12–25
(1)	R69–25, R70, R71, R72, A2–18	r.72	R68–87, R70–37, **R72**, R72–01
(2)	R51–35, R69–30	(1)	R68–87, R70–42
r.70	S8–01, R47–44, R62–08, R67–04, R69–03, R69–05, R69–17, **R70**, R70–01, R70–04, R70–12, R71–01, R72–01	r.73	R12–09, R15–07, R16–06, R16–08, R16–11, R23–04, R24–54, R51–06, R71–35, **R73**, R73–01, R73–05, R74–05, R82–04
(1)–(6)	A2–23	(1)	R16–11, R73–06
(2)	R69–25, R70–03, A2–18, A2–32	(2)	R15–03, R15–09, R68–90, R71–36, R73–11, R73–12, R78–07
(3)	R28–14, R28–16, R28–45, R69–25, R70–11, R70–13, R70–15, R70–16, R70–17, R70–19, R70–21, R70–22, R70–31, A2–33	(3)	R73–14
		r.74	R73–15, **R74**, R74–01, R74–05, R74–08
		(1)	R74–10
		(2)	R74–10
(4)	R69–19, R70–03, A2–33	r.75	R34–08, **R75**, R75–01, R75–03
(5)	R70–29, A2–35	r.76	R10–15, R16–03, R20–04, R20–14, R20–16, R20–17, R20–20, R23–04, R24–22, R24–34, R24–40, R55–15, R67–20, R67–27, **R76**, R76–01, R76–03, R76–11, R82–04
(6)	R70–32, R70–43		
(7)	R70–09, R70–31		
(8)	R68–76, R68–80, R70–36, R70–40		
(9)	R67–39, R68–97, R70–43	(1)	R20–04, R68–26, R76–04, R76–08, A2–17
(10)	R67–39, R68–97, R70–43	(2)	R20–14, R67–20, R73–09, R76, R76–09, R76–12, A2–17
(11)	R67–39, R68–97, R70–43	(3)	R20–15
r.71	S12–23, R58–27, **R71**, R71–01, R71–03, R71–27	r.77	R8, R24, R24–07, R24–09, R24–16, **R77**, R77–01, R77–04, R78–03, R82–04
(1)	R71–03		
(2)	R51–46, R58–06, R67–09, R68–09, R68–47, R69–27, R71–04, R71–25		

Table of Scottish Statutes

r.78	**R78**, R78–01, R78–04, R78–07, R82–04
r.79	R9–04, **R79**, R79–01, R82–04
r.80	**R80**, R80–01, R80–04, R80–05, S16–18
(2)	R80–07
r.81	**R81**, R81–01, R81–03
r.82	R5–06, R30–07, R56–09, **R82**, R82–01
(1)	R82–04
(2)	R82–04, R82–05
r.83	R1, R1–09, R7–09, R11, R11–10, R15, R16, R21–08, R21–09, R51–29, R51–60, R51–63, R56–04, R56–06, R57–11, R58–33, R71, R71–10, R71–12, R71–13, **R83**, R83–01, R83–02, R83–03, R83–04, R83–05, R83–07, R83–08, R83–16, R83–18, R83–19, R83–20, R84–07
(1)	R51–13, R83–08
(2)	R51–13, R83–03, R83–08
(3) ...	R1–09, R1–10, R1–12, R23–11, R58–34, R83–11, R83–12, R83–16, R83–17, R83–18
(4)	R83–08, R83–09
(5)	R1–10, R58–33, R83–11, R83–15, R83–16, R83–18
(6)	R83–19, R83–21, R83–22
(7)	R83–07
r.84	**R84**, R84–01, R84–02, R84–05, R84–08
(b)	R84–03, R84–09
Sch.2	A2–17

TABLE OF ABBREVIATIONS

1695 Articles	Articles of Regulation 1695
1894 Act	Arbitration (Scotland) Act 1894 (57 and 58 Vict. c.13) (July 3, 1894)
1950 Act	Arbitration Act 1950 (14 Geo 6, c.27); repealed (as regards England & Wales and Northern Ireland but not Scotland) by the 1996 Act; repealed as regards Scotland by the 2010 Act
1966 Act	Arbitration (International Investment Disputes) Act 1966 (c.41); the 1966 Act implemented the International Convention on the Settlement of Investment Disputes between States and Nationals of Other States ("ICSID"; the "Washington Convention"); the 1966 Act applies in each of England & Wales, Scotland and Northern Ireland and is not affected by the 1996 Act or the 2010 Act
1972 Act	Administration of Justice (Scotland) Act 1972 (c.59)
1973 Act	Prescription and Limitation (Scotland) Act 1973 (c.52) (s.23 refers)
1975 Act	Arbitration Act 1975 (c.3); the 1975 Act implemented the New York Convention into the law of England & Wales, Scotland and Northern Ireland but was repealed, insofar as regards England & Wales and Northern Ireland, by the 1996 Act; repealed as regards Scotland by the 2010 Act
1979 Act	Arbitration Act 1979 (c.42); this made a number of important changes to the 1950 Act but did not recodify the law; not applicable in Scotland
1982 Act	Civil Jurisdiction and Judgments Act 1982 (c.27)
1990 Act	Law Reform (Miscellaneous Provisions) (Scotland) Act 1990 (c.40)
1996 Act	Arbitration Act 1996 (c.23); the 1996 Act applies in full in England & Wales and in Northern Ireland but only ss.89–91 (dealing with consumer arbitration) applied (and continues to apply) in Scotland
2009 Bill (or "the Bill")	Arbitration (Scotland) Bill 2009, laid before the Scottish Parliament on January 30, 2009 and finally passed on November 18, 2009

Table of Abbreviations

2010 Act (or "the Act")	Arbitration (Scotland) Act 2010 (asp 1) (January 5, 2010)
AAA	American Arbitration Association
AAA Appellate Rules	the AAA/ICDR Optional Appellate Arbitration Rules effective November 1, 2013
AAA Rules	the arbitration rules incorporated in the AAA's International Dispute Resolution Procedures (Including Mediation and Arbitration Rules), amended and effective June 1, 2009
AAR	arbitral appointments referee (s.24 and r.7 refer)
ABA	American Bar Association
ABA Code	The Code of Ethics for Arbitrators in Commercial Disputes Approved by the American Bar Association House of Delegates on February 9, 2004, approved by the Executive Committee of the Board of Directors of the AAA, annotated and updated 2011
ACICA	the Australian Centre for International Commercial Arbitration
ADR	Alternative Dispute Resolution, comprising all form of private dispute resolution outwith the courts and, in particular, including arbitration
Auditor	the Auditor of the Court of Session
BAC	Beijing Arbitration Commission, one of approximately 200 arbitration commissions in the PRC
Bell on Arbitration	J.M. Bell, *Treatise on the Law of Arbitration in Scotland*, 2nd edn (Edinburgh: T. & T. Clark, 1877)
BGH	[Deutsches] Bundesgerichtshof, the German Supreme Court
Chartered Arbitrator	the highest level of qualification in the CIArb, broadly equivalent to QC
CIArb	Chartered Institute of Arbitrators, a worldwide organisation with >12,000 members in approximately 120 countries
CIArb Code of Ethics	"Code of Professional and Ethical Conduct"—The Chartered Institute Of Arbitrators (October 2009)

Table of Abbreviations

CIArb Practice Guidelines	CIArb Practice Guidelines, available at: *http://www.ciarb.org/information-and-resources/practice-guidelines-and-protocols/list-of-guidelines-and-protocols/* [Accessed January 7, 2014]
CIArb Protocols	CIArb Protocols, available at: *http://www.ciarb.org/information-and-resources/practice-guidelines-and-protocols/list-of-guidelines-and-protocols/* [Accessed January 7, 2014]
CIArb SSFARs	CIArb Scottish Short Form Arbitration Rules (effective November 15, 2012)
CIETAC	China International Economic Trade Arbitration Commission, the leading such body in the PRC
CIMAR	Construction Industry Model Arbitration Rules (effective February 1, 1998)
Convention	(also the "New York Convention") Convention on the Recognition and Enforcement of Foreign Arbitral Awards done in New York on June 10, 1958; the Convention came into force on June 7, 1959
CPR	Civil Procedure Rules
DAC	Departmental Advisory Committee on Arbitration Law; it produced a Report (February 1996) and a Supplementary Report (January 1997) on the Arbitration Act 1996, both of which are considered highly persuasive in interpreting the 1996 Act
Dervaird Bill	the Arbitration (Scotland) Bill 2002, a privately-drafted Bill prepared by a joint working group of the CIArb, SCIA and RICS
Dervaird Committee	The Scottish Advisory Committee on Arbitration Law chaired by Lord Dervaird—it produced a *Report to the Lord Advocate on the UNCITRAL Model Law* (1989), *The Operation of Arbitration in Scotland in light of the UNCITRAL Model Law* (1990), and a *Report on Legislation for Domestic Arbitration in Scotland* (1996)
ECHR	the European Convention on Human Rights
ECJ	The Court of Justice, being one of the courts forming the Court of Justice of the European Union
ECtHR	European Court of Human Rights

Table of Abbreviations

FCIArb/MCIArb/ACIArb	Fellow/Member/Associate of the CIArb
FINRA	Financial Industry Regulatory Authority, the largest independent regulator for all securities firms doing business in the USA
FLAGS	Scottish branch of the CIArb Family Law Arbitration Group Scotland
FOSFA Rules	Rules of Arbitration and Appeal of the Federation of Oils, Seeds and Fats Associations (effective January 1, 2012)
GAFTA Rules	Arbitration Rules No.125 of the Grain and Feed Trade Association (effective April 1, 2012)
HGCRA	Housing Grants, Construction and Regeneration Act 1996 (colloquially known as "the Construction Act") of which ss.107–113 provides for adjudication of disputes in the UK construction industry; it applies (separately) in each of England & Wales, Scotland and Northern Ireland
HKIAC	the Hong Kong International Arbitration Centre
HKIAC Rules	the Administered Arbitration Rules of the HKIAC (effective November 1, 2013)
HRA	Human Rights Act 1998 (c.42)
IBA	International Bar Association
IBA Conflict Guidelines	IBA Guidelines on Conflicts of Interest in International Arbitration (approved on May 22, 2004 by the Council of the IBA)
IBA Evidence Rules	IBA Rules on the Taking of Evidence in International Arbitration, adopted by a Resolution of the IBA Council on May 29, 2010
IBA Representation Guidelines	the IBA "Guidelines on Party Representation in International Arbitration" (as adopted by a Resolution of the IBA Council on May 25, 2013); these are accessible via *http://www.ibanet.org/Search/Default.aspx?q=guidelines%20party%20representation* [Accessed June 11, 2014]

Table of Abbreviations

ICAC Rules	the Arbitration Rules of the International Commercial Arbitration Court at the Chamber of Commerce and Industry of the Russian Federation (the "Chamber"), as approved by Order No.76 of the Chamber dated October 18, 2005 as amended by Order No.28 of the Chamber on June 23, 2010
ICC	International Court of Arbitration of the International Chamber of Commerce
ICC Rules	the Arbitration and ADR Rules of the ICC (effective January 1, 2012)
ICC Expertise Rules	[ICC] Rules for Expertise (effective January 1, 2003)
ICDR Rules	International Arbitration Rules of the International Centre for Dispute Resolution, the Dublin-based international arm of the AAA (effective June 1, 2009)
ICE	Institution of Civil Engineers
ICSID	International Centre for the Settlement of Investment Disputes, established under the Washington Convention
Interpretation Order	The Scotland Act 1998 (Transitory and Transitional Provisions) (Publication and Interpretation etc. of Acts of the Scottish Parliament) Order 1999 (SI 1999/1379)
Irons and Melville on Arbitration	J.C. Irons and R.D. Melville, *Treatise on the Law of Arbitration in Scotland* (Edinburgh: W. Green, 1903)
KLRCA	Kuala Lumpur Regional Centre for Arbitration
LCIA	London Court of International Arbitration
LCIA Rules	The LCIA Arbitration Rules 2014 as published on July 25, 2014 and effective October 1, 2014.
LMAA	the London Maritime Arbitrators Association
LMAA Terms	the LMAA Terms (2012) effective January 1, 2012
LMAA SCP	the LMAA Small Claims Procedure, an accelerated/simplified arbitration scheme on a documents-only basis with a fixed arbitrator fee and a maximum cost recovery; there is an indicative maximum claim of $50,000
Merkin & Flannery	Robert Merkin and Louis Flannery, *Arbitration Act 1996*, 5th edn (Abingdon: Informa Law, 2014)

Table of Abbreviations

Model Law	UNCITRAL Model Law on International Commercial Arbitration; United Nations document A/40/17, Annex I, dated December 1, 1985 as adopted by the UN by General Assembly Resolution 40/72 on December 11, 1985 and as amended by General Assembly Resolution 61/33 dated December 4, 2006
New York Convention	(also "the Convention") Convention on the Recognition and Enforcement of Foreign Arbitral Awards done in New York on June 10, 1958; the Convention came into force on June 7, 1959
OCR	the Ordinary Cause Rules of the Sheriff Courts (Scotland) Act 1907
ÖZPO	Österreichische Zivilprozeßordnung, the Austrian Code of Civil Procedure
PAE	a party-appointed expert
PCA	Permanent Court of Arbitration, based in The Hague
PRC	the People's Republic of China
RCS	Act of Sederunt (Rules of the Court of Session) 1994 (SI 1994/1443) Sch.2 (as amended)
RIBA	Royal Institute of British Architects
RICS	Royal Institution of Chartered Surveyors
SAAVA	the Scottish Agricultural Arbiters & Valuers Association
SAC07	Scottish Arbitration Code 2007
SAR	the Scottish Arbitration Rules as set out in Sch.1 to the 2010 Act
SASAR	Act of Sederunt (Summary Applications, Statutory Applications and Appeals etc. Rules) 1999 (SI 1999/929) (as amended)
SCC	Arbitration Institute of the Stockholm Chamber of Commerce
SCC Rules	Arbitration Rules of the SCC, adopted by the SCC and in force from April 1, 1999
SCIA	Scottish Council for International Arbitration
Scotland Act	Scotland Act 1998 (c.46)
SIAC	Singapore International Arbitration Centre

Table of Abbreviations

Swiss Rules	Swiss Rules of International Arbitration (effective June 1, 2012)
TAE	a tribunal-appointed expert (r.34(1) refers)
TCC	Technology and Construction Court, a division of the English High Court
UK	the United Kingdom of Great Britain and Northern Ireland
UKSC	UK Supreme Court, successor (w.e.f. October 1, 2009) to the Appellate Committee of the House of Lords, the latter colloquially referred to as the "House of Lords" in legal circles
UN	the United Nations
UNCITRAL	the United Nations Commission on International Trade Law, an arm of the United Nations based in Vienna
UNCITRAL Rules	the Arbitration Rules of UNCITRAL adopted by UN General Assembly Resolution 31/98 on August 15, 2010
Unfair Terms Regulations	the Unfair Terms in Consumer Contracts Regulations 1999 (SI 1999/2083)
VIAC	Vienna International Arbitration Centre
Washington Convention	International Convention on the Settlement of Investment Disputes between States and Nationals of Other States, done in Washington DC on March 18, 1965
WIPO Rules	the Arbitration Rules of the World Intellectual Property Organisation (effective October 1, 2002)
ZpO	Zivilprozeßordnung, the German Code of Civil Procedure

INTRODUCTION

The Arbitration (Scotland) Act 2010 represents the most significant step in the history of the Scots law of arbitration. Scotland moved from a regime largely based on common law (much of it antiquated) to one substantially based on statute. Its importance, therefore, cannot be overestimated. A draft Bill was created in June 2008 and, after extensive consultation leading to substantial redrafting, a Bill was presented to the Scottish Parliament in January 2009. Further amendments were made during its passage through the parliamentary process. The Bill was formally approved by the Scottish Parliament on November 18, 2009 and Royal Assent was granted on January 5, 2010.

The final outcome is a very comprehensive and modern arbitration statute with numerous innovations which undoubtedly puts the Scots law of arbitration on a very firm footing, not only providing effective support for the arbitral process but also remedying the many inadequacies and lacunae of the previous common law.

HISTORICAL BACKGROUND

The common law of arbitration had been built up over the course of several centuries but, long ago, had become antiquated with key aspects being dictated by 19th century case law, much of which bore no relevance to the modern commercial world. The common law was not only silent or, if not, often obscure, uncertain and sometimes plainly contradictory on key aspects of arbitration. Worse still, where the law was clear, the answers which it provided were often unhelpful and sometimes even in contradiction to the norms of modern arbitration.

While, over the centuries, fragmentary legislation dealing with particular issues had been created (Acts of 1598, 1695, 1894 etc.), these were often not entirely satisfactory. Typically, art.25 of the 1695 Articles (endeavouring to deal with the reduction (annulment) of an arbitral award) was expressed in archaic and somewhat opaque language which was not entirely elucidated by subsequent judicial pronouncements thereon.

While England had had arbitration statutes since 1697 (also enacting comprehensive statutes in 1856, 1889, 1934, 1950 and 1996), the 1894 Act was no such comprehensive measure, containing only seven sections correcting certain minor anomalies in the common law.

The next statute affecting arbitration was the 1972 Act, whose s.3 sought to introduce the stated case procedure into the Scots law of arbitration, despite no domestic support ever having been expressed for such a development. Indicative of the undesirability of such a provision is that the 1979 Act repealed the highly unpopular "stated case" in England. While one of the aims of the provision had been to create a right of appeal against an arbitral award on a point of law, because of a drafting mishap s.3 not only failed to achieve this objective but also enabled such delay to and obstruction of the arbitral process that its repeal was advocated by many including the judiciary. In *ERDC Construction Ltd v HM Love & Co Ltd (No. 2)*, 1997 S.L.T. 175, Lord Hope said that:

> "Excessive use of this procedure is liable to bring the whole process of arbitration into disrepute", and "If arbiters are to have the confidence which they require to simplify and accelerate procedure in such cases, they ought not to be exposed to the risk of challenge to their decisions by means of the cumbersome and time consuming procedure of a stated case."

THE ROAD TO REFORM

Much emphasis has been laid above on the deficiencies of the pre-2010 Scots law of arbitration but it would be wholly inaccurate and unfair to infer that those involved in seeking to develop the law have been unaware of its deficiencies. In 1990, the Scottish Advisory Committee on Arbitration Law highlighted the weaknesses of domestic arbitration law in its report *The Operation of Arbitration in Scotland in light of the UNCITRAL Model Law* (Edinburgh: Scottish Courts Administration, 1990). Its 1996 consultation paper, *Report to the Lord Advocate on Legislation for Domestic Arbitration in Scotland* (Edinburgh: Scottish Courts Administration, 1996) then contained a draft Arbitration Bill. If that measure had been enacted, it would certainly have achieved a considerable improvement in the law, albeit that there were suggestions that it could have gone further than it did.

However, the appearance of radical, modern arbitration legislation in a variety of other jurisdictions, in particular the 1996 Act in England & Wales (and Northern Ireland), then inspired a number of private parties (principally the Scottish Branch of the Chartered Institute of Arbitrators ("CIArb") and the Scottish Council for International Arbitration under the chairmanship of Lord Dervaird who had chaired the Scottish Advisory Committee on Arbitration Law) to produce a much more ambitious and wide-ranging Arbitration Bill in 2002. Regrettably, the then Scottish Executive failed to take that Bill forward.

Legislative reform of arbitration in Scotland thus seemed unlikely until, in 2007, both the Scottish National Party and the Labour Party adopted the manifesto goal of encouraging arbitration in Scotland.

A draft Arbitration (Scotland) Bill and accompanying consultation document were therefore produced in June 2008 and were followed by a lengthy consultation process. The 2008 Bill drew heavily on the 2002 Bill (and therefore, like that Bill, on the Model Law and the 1996 Act), but covered a number of matters not addressed in that Bill. Some, but not all, of these provisions survived the consultation process and appear in the 2010 Act. The consultation document also sought to canvass opinion on whether certain matters not addressed in the Bill should be the subject of statutory provision. In the end, many of these additional matters were not addressed by the Act but one issue—confidentiality—is now the subject of a specific statutory provision (see the commentary to r.26 below).

THE MODEL LAW AND ITS INFLUENCE

Potentially the most significant piece of legislation in the pre-2010 history of the Scots law of arbitration was s.66 and Sch.7 of the 1990 Act, which introduced the Model Law into Scotland.

Starting in the 1970s, there grew wide international consensus that

> "it would be in the interest of international commercial arbitration if UNCITRAL would initiate steps leading to the establishment of uniform standards of arbitral procedure",

and that the preparation of a model law on arbitration would be "the most appropriate way to achieve the desired uniformity" (see *Note by the Secretariat: further work in respect of international commercial arbitration*, UN A/CN.9/169, para.6, found at *http://www.uncitral.org* [Accessed February 6, 2014]).

A Model Law was then developed by UNCITRAL, the process taking several years and a number of drafts and involving many states and a number of international organisations. The final version of the Model Law was promulgated in 1985 (it was subsequently revised in 2006) and has (as at January 3, 2014) been adopted by 97 jurisdictions in 67 sovereign states. It was given force in Scotland (in a slightly amended form) by the 1990 Act, following the recommendations of the Scottish Advisory Committee on Arbitration Law's *Report to the Lord Advocate on the UNCITRAL Model Law* (Edinburgh: Scottish Courts Administration, 1989).

Unfortunately, the 1990 legislation was fatally flawed since the Model Law, being a compromise among many divergent legal cultures, is by no means comprehensive (e.g. it nowhere mentions expenses (costs) or interest) and, given that the legislation applied only to international commercial arbitration (albeit with an opt-in for domestic arbitration) seated in Scotland, it left all the serious deficiencies of the Scots common law of arbitration, and s.3 of the 1972 Act, in place. Unsurprisingly, the Model Law was applied in Scotland in only a tiny handful of arbitrations over the next 20 years and, in addition, the authors are unaware of any instance of the domestic opt-in.

Many states which included major arbitration centres (e.g. France, Sweden, Switzerland, England & Wales) were prompted to reform their arbitration law in the wake of the Model Law and on a basis highly consistent with it since it was seen as capturing much of the best practice in the law of international commercial arbitration. The most remarkable conversion to the principles of the Model Law was, of course, England & Wales which had, in 1989, rejected adoption but where the 1996 Act's wholesale reform of its law of arbitration followed "wherever possible the structure, language and spirit of the Model Law".

Given the stature and influence of the Model Law then, it is one of the most striking features of the 2010 Act that it appears, prima facie, to discard the Model Law by repealing the 1990 legislation (which, to repeat, was fatally flawed from the outset). However, prima facie appearances are misleading in this regard in that, while the exact form of the Model Law is not retained, all the principles which underpin the Model Law are to be found in the Act; further, the Scottish Government's Justice Department prepared a "reconciliation" showing where in the 2010 Act the components of the Model Law are to be found, so UNCITRAL continues to list Scotland as a Model Law jurisdiction

There were a variety of reasons for this approach.

First, not only was it awkward to have separate systems governing international domestic arbitration (as was the case in Scotland after 1990), but also HM Government was advised, in respect of ss.85–88 of the 1996 Act which would have applied only to domestic arbitration, that to have separate international/domestic regimes was likely to breach EU law.

Secondly, particularly in common law countries and given that the Model Law was incomplete and dealt only with those issues on which the various drafting parties could reach general agreement (either because they proved too controversial or because it was felt that they could be more appropriately dealt with by domestic law), a Part II of the arbitration law was required filling in the gaps where, in some cases, the Part II was longer than the Model Law itself, e.g. the word count of New Zealand's 1996 Act is 250 per cent of the count for the Model Law which it incorporates and Bermuda's Arbitration Act 1993 is 191 per cent. One example of the contortions certain jurisdictions have been forced into is s.18C of Australia's International Arbitration Act 1974 (as revised in 2010):

> "For the purposes of Article 18 of the Model Law, a party to arbitral proceedings is taken to have been given a full opportunity to present the party's case if the party is given a reasonable opportunity to present the party's case."

Thirdly, while it might be expected that in those civil law jurisdictions which have adopted the Model Law, the gaps are filled by the Civil Code, even this is not the case, e.g. neither the ZpO (Germany) nor the ÖZpO (Austria) expressly empower an arbitral tribunal to award interest.

Taking all these (and other) considerations into account, the best way forward for the Bill was clear, i.e. to incorporate the principles (and much of the language) of the Model Law and to construct a single, integrated and fully-comprehensive statute covering all relevant matters. The 1996 Act was, of course, drafted on a very similar basis. Further, reinforcing the 2010 Act's strong relationship to, and incorporation of the spirit of, the Model Law, s.26 (see commentary below) allows the Scottish Ministers to modify any provision of the Act in consequence of any amendment made to the Model Law; the same applies to the UNCITRAL Rules and the possibility of a s.26 revision is being considered in order to take into account the UNCITRAL Rules (which post-dated the 2010 Act by five weeks). It is clear that Scotland is determined to remain at the forefront of improvements to the legislation and rules governing international arbitration.

THE RELATIONSHIP OF THE 2010 ACT TO THE 1996 ACT

Scotland decided not to adopt the 1996 Act, for four main reasons. First, the Scottish and English legal systems are distinct and there are several key differences, as will be seen later in this book. Secondly, the 1996 Act would have been insufficient to have cured all of the deficiencies in the pre-2010 common law. Thirdly, while there is no pressing necessity to amend the 1996 Act, English case law and 13 years of experience in practice had revealed several areas for improvement (e.g. (a) s.6 of the 2010 Act rules out potential litigation in an area not addressed in the 1996 Act where English jurisprudence is contradictory; (b) s.24 and r.7 of the 2010 Act present a significant improvement over s.18 of the 1996 Act; (c) by 2009, case law had developed to the point (not at all the case in 1995/96) that a confidentiality rule (r.26) could be drafted in a simple yet precise form; and (d) r.46(4)(b) and r.58(7) address lacunae in the 1996 Act papered over by judicial decisions). Fourthly, the decision was taken to place the involvement of the courts on a much more restricted basis than under the 1996 Act (e.g. an application to the court under s.45 of the 1996 Act could go all the way to the UKSC whereas the equivalent rr.41/42 in the 2010 Act allow for no appeal whatsoever from a first instance decision (and, in addition, the SAR allow no appeal whatsoever to the UKSC)).

As Lord Glennie noted in the first ever case under the 2010 Act (*Arbitration Application No.3 of 2011* [2011] CSOH 164):

> "Since the Act was closely and unashamedly modelled on the English Act, and reflects the same underlying philosophy, authorities on the Act (and its predecessor, the Arbitration Act 1979) in relation to questions of interpretation and approach will obviously be of relevance. There is no point in re-inventing the (arbitration) wheel. In the written submissions relating to this application, both parties have helpfully referred to authorities on the approach to granting leave to appeal under the English Act."

Following the 1996 Act-based approach taken in developing the Bill, as endorsed by Lord Glennie, the authors of this book have considered English jurisprudence thoroughly as readers will see. Having said that, the value of that jurisprudence depends on its persuasive quality and Scottish courts are not bound by it.

THE APPROACH OF THE 2010 ACT

A detailed analysis of the provisions of the Act appears below; however, certain features of the Act are worthy of separate comment here.

Although much of the Act will strike a chord with those who are familiar with the Model Law and with the 1996 Act, one major feature of the Act is unique: its main substance is divided into the Act proper (consisting of 37 sections) and Sch.1 which contains the 84 rules comprising the SAR. A main reason why this novel approach has been adopted is the fact that those provisions regarding the conduct of the arbitral process are to be found in the SAR and the policy memorandum accompanying the Bill stated (at para.78) that the "intention is that the rules will guide the parties and the arbitrator through various stages of the arbitral process".

The drafters considered that it was more user-friendly for those provisions which will govern how the arbitration is carried on to take the form of rules. This mirrors the many sets of institutional rules which are available in both domestic and international arbitration for parties to invoke by means of agreement to govern their arbitration; in fact, the policy memorandum continued (para.79) that they can be compared with such institutional rules. The advantage of this is that parties can decide whether they would prefer institutional rules to govern their arbitration rather than those SAR which are default rules (i.e. open to being excluded, modified or replaced by the parties). The policy memorandum added that some consultees were pleased that "arbitrators would not have to search for the rules in the middle of the legalese of the main body of the legislation". Nevertheless, the definitions of important concepts in the SAR (e.g. "arbitration agreement") are set out in the main body of the Act and the SAR must be read as part thereof.

Experience to date has demonstrated that the hopes the drafters had for the legislative structure were indeed well-founded.

THE RELATIONSHIP OF THE 2010 ACT TO OTHER LEGISLATION

The Act relates to, or impacts on, other legislation, first and foremost in repealing both the 1894 Act and s.3 of the 1972 Act (the stated case procedure).

However, some legislation remains intact or is re-enacted by the Act, particularly that UK (i.e. not Scottish) legislation which gives effect to international treaties on arbitration ratified by the UK; in particular, the

Introduction

1966 Act, which gave effect to the Washington Convention, continues in force at least so long as Scotland remains part of the UK. In contrast, the 1975 Act, which gave effect to the New York Convention, is repealed by, and its provisions re-enacted in, ss.18–22 of the 2010 Act. In this the Act follows the example of the 1996 Act, which had repealed the 1975 Act as regards England (but not Scotland) and reproduced its provisions in ss.100–104 of the later Act.

Further, ss.89–91 of the 1996 Act, the only sections of that Act which ever applied in Scotland, dealing with consumer arbitration, continue in force since the 2010 Act made no change thereto. Consumer arbitration is dealt with in Appendix 1 towards the end of this book.

The law is stated as at July 1, 2014.

ARBITRATION (SCOTLAND) ACT 2010

(asp 1)

CONTENTS

Introductory

1. Founding principles
2. Key terms
3. Seat of arbitration

Arbitration agreements

4. Arbitration agreement
5. Separability
6. Law governing arbitration agreement

Scottish Arbitration Rules

7. Scottish Arbitration Rules
8. Mandatory rules
9. Default rules

Suspension of legal proceedings

10. Suspension of legal proceedings

Enforcing and challenging arbitral awards etc.

11. Arbitral award to be final and binding on parties
12. Enforcement of arbitral awards
13. Court intervention in arbitrations
14. Persons who take no part in arbitral proceedings
15. Anonymity in legal proceedings

Statutory arbitration

16. Statutory arbitration: special provisions
17. Power to adapt enactments providing for statutory arbitration

Recognition and enforcement of New York Convention awards

18. New York Convention awards
19. Recognition and enforcement of New York Convention awards

20. Refusal of recognition or enforcement
21. Evidence to be produced when seeking recognition or enforcement
22. Saving for other bases of recognition or enforcement

Supplementary

23. Prescription and limitation
24. Arbitral appointments referee
25. Power of judge to act as arbitrator or umpire
26. Amendments to UNCITRAL Model Law or Rules or New York Convention
27. Amendment of Conveyancing (Scotland) Act 1924 (c. 27)
28. Articles of Regulation 1695
29. Repeals
30. Arbitrability of disputes

Final provisions

31. Interpretation
32. Ancillary provision
33. Orders
34. Crown application
35. Commencement
36. Transitional provisions
37. Short title

SCHEDULE 1—SCOTTISH ARBITRATION RULES

PART 1

COMMENCEMENT AND CONSTITUTION OF TRIBUNAL ETC.

Rule 1. Commencement of arbitration D
Rule 2. Appointment of tribunal D
Rule 3. Arbitrator to be an individual M
Rule 4. Eligibility to act as arbitrator M
Rule 5. Number of arbitrators D
Rule 6. Method of appointment D
Rule 7. Failure of appointment procedure M
Rule 8. Duty to disclose any conflict of interests M
Rule 9. Arbitrator's tenure D
Rule 10. Challenge to appointment of arbitrator D
Rule 11. Removal of arbitrator by parties D
Rule 12. Removal of arbitrator by court M
Rule 13. Dismissal of tribunal by court M
Rule 14. Removal and dismissal by court: supplementary M

Rule 15. Resignation of arbitrator M
Rule 16. Liability etc. of arbitrator when tenure ends M
Rule 17. Reconstitution of tribunal D
Rule 18. Arbitrators nominated in arbitration agreements D

PART 2

JURISDICTION OF TRIBUNAL

Rule 19. Power of tribunal to rule on own jurisdiction M
Rule 20. Objections to tribunal's jurisdiction M
Rule 21. Appeal against tribunal's ruling on jurisdictional objection M
Rule 22. Referral of point of jurisdiction D
Rule 23. Jurisdiction referral: procedure etc. M

PART 3

GENERAL DUTIES

Rule 24. General duty of the tribunal M
Rule 25. General duty of the parties M
Rule 26. Confidentiality D
Rule 27. Tribunal deliberations D

PART 4

ARBITRAL PROCEEDINGS

Rule 28. Procedure and evidence D
Rule 29. Place of arbitration D
Rule 30. Tribunal decisions D
Rule 31. Tribunal directions D
Rule 32. Power to appoint clerk, agents or employees etc. D
Rule 33. Party representatives D
Rule 34. Experts D
Rule 35. Powers relating to property D
Rule 36. Oaths or affirmations D
Rule 37. Failure to submit claim or defence timeously D
Rule 38. Failure to attend hearing or provide evidence D
Rule 39. Failure to comply with tribunal direction or arbitration agreement D
Rule 40. Consolidation of proceedings D

PART 5

POWERS OF COURT IN RELATION TO ARBITRAL PROCEEDINGS

Rule 41. Referral of point of law D
Rule 42. Point of law referral: procedure etc. M
Rule 43. Variation of time limits set by parties D

Rule 44. Time limit variation: procedure etc. M
Rule 45. Court's power to order attendance of witnesses and disclosure of evidence M
Rule 46. Court's other powers in relation to arbitration D

PART 6

AWARDS

Rule 47. Rules applicable to the substance of the dispute D
Rule 48. Power to award payment and damages M
Rule 49. Other remedies available to tribunal D
Rule 50. Interest M
Rule 51. Form of award D
Rule 52. Award treated as made in Scotland D
Rule 53. Provisional awards D
Rule 54. Part awards M
Rule 55. Draft awards D
Rule 56. Power to withhold award on non-payment of fees or expenses M
Rule 57. Arbitration to end on last award or early settlement D
Rule 58. Correcting an award D

PART 7

ARBITRATION EXPENSES

Rule 59. Arbitration expenses D
Rule 60. Arbitrators' fees and expenses M
Rule 61. Recoverable arbitration expenses D
Rule 62. Liability for recoverable arbitration expenses D
Rule 63. Ban on pre-dispute agreements about liability for arbitration expenses M
Rule 64. Security for expenses D
Rule 65. Limitation of recoverable arbitration expenses D
Rule 66. Awards on recoverable arbitration expenses D

PART 8

CHALLENGING AWARDS

Rule 67. Challenging an award: substantive jurisdiction M
Rule 68. Challenging an award: serious irregularity M
Rule 69. Challenging an award: legal error D
Rule 70. Legal error appeals: procedure etc. M
Rule 71. Challenging an award: supplementary M
Rule 72. Reconsideration by tribunal M

Part 9
Miscellaneous

Rule 73. Immunity of tribunal etc. M
Rule 74. Immunity of appointing arbitral institution etc. M
Rule 75. Immunity of experts, witnesses and legal representatives M
Rule 76. Loss of right to object M
Rule 77. Independence of arbitrator M
Rule 78. Consideration where arbitrator judged not to be impartial and independent D
Rule 79. Death of arbitrator M
Rule 80. Death of party D
Rule 81. Unfair treatment D
Rule 82. Rules applicable to umpires M
Rule 83. Formal communications D
Rule 84. Periods of time D
Index

SCHEDULE 2—REPEALS

The Bill for this Act of the Scottish Parliament was passed by the Parliament on 18th November 2009 and received Royal Assent on 5th January 2010
An Act of the Scottish Parliament to make provision about arbitration.

Introductory

Founding principles

1. The founding principles of this Act are—
    (a) that the object of arbitration is to resolve disputes fairly, impartially and without unnecessary delay or expense,
    (b) that parties should be free to agree how to resolve disputes subject only to such safeguards as are necessary in the public interest,
    (c) that the court should not intervene in an arbitration except as provided by this Act.

Anyone construing this Act must have regard to the founding principles when doing so.

DEFINITIONS

"arbitration": ss.2(1), (2), 31(1)
"court": s.31(1)
"party": ss.2(1), 31(1), (2)

MODEL LAW

S1–01 Article 2A (adopted in 2006) provides:

> "(2) Questions concerning matters governed by this Law which are not expressly settled in it are to be settled in conformity with the general principles on which this Law is based."

S1–02 Article 5 provides:

> "In matters governed by this Law, no court shall intervene except where so provided in this Law."

COMMENTARY

Introductory

S1–03 The inspiration of this provision is clearly the "general principles" to be found in s.1 of the 1996 Act. The drafters of that Act were persuaded to include the statement of general principles therein, partly because of a "significant number of submissions" which called for this, and partly because they saw the value in such an exercise, given the fact that the Act marked the dawn of a new approach to arbitration in England—see the DAC Report, paras 18–22.

S1–04 Section 1 stresses the principle of party autonomy which lies at the heart of practically all modern arbitration regimes. It is useful in emphasising the principle of limited court intervention which is a key aspect of arbitration. The principles underpin most of the SAR and the appropriate balance between the principles is struck in particular contexts by the detailed provisions of the rules.

S1–05 The principles are to be borne in mind by anyone seeking to interpret or apply the Act—whether arbitrators, parties, the courts or any others. The courts in England have on occasion found s.1 of the 1996 Act useful in indicating the approach they should take to particular questions, e.g. whether s.9(4) of the 1996 Act excluded the court remedy of summary judgment (see Henry L.J. in *Halki Shipping Corp v Sopex Oils Ltd* [1998] 1 W.L.R. 726 at 750), the interaction between the parties' agreement and the statutory time limits for appointing arbitrators (see Rix J. in *Federal Insurance Co v Transamerica Occidental Life Insurance Co* [1999] 2 Lloyd's Rep. 286 at 290), whether a court could add interest to that awarded by the tribunal (see Aikens J. in *Walker v Rome* [2000] 1 Lloyd's Rep. 116 at 121; followed in *Martrade Shipping and Transport Gmbh v United Enterprises Corp* [2014] EWHC 1884 (Comm)), whether the right to appeal an award as to jurisdiction prevented parties from making an ad hoc agreement that an arbitrator should decide whether they were party to another arbitration agreement (see Lord Phillips M.R. in *LG Caltex Gas Co Ltd v China*

National Petroleum Co [2001] 1 W.L.R. 1892 at [49]), and whether the court might refuse an oral hearing to a party seeking to appeal against an award (see Arden L.J. in *BLCT (13096) Ltd v J Sainsbury Plc* [2004] 1 C.L.C. 24 at [43]).

Principle (a)—Object of arbitration

It cannot rationally be argued that arbitration should aim to do other than seek to resolve disputes fairly and impartially, and a number of specific rules seek to achieve that object. Leaving aside the advantages over court judgments in respect of enforcement, if arbitration is to offer advantages over court litigation it must avoid unnecessary delay or expense. This principle gives express effect to that essential requirement of arbitration. It means that where any issue arises over the meaning of a particular rule, the meaning which gives best effect to the object of arbitration should be preferred. **S1–06**

In *G1 Venues Ltd* [2013] CSOH 202, Lord Malcolm made an observation (at [18]) with which the authors respectfully and strongly concur: **S1–07**

> "Those acting as arbitrators should keep in mind that the founding principles of the 2010 Act include that arbitrations should be resolved without unnecessary delay."

Principle (b)—Party autonomy

Party autonomy is at the root of all modern arbitration legislation across the world, including the Model Law (see DAC Report, para.19). It is useful to advertise this fact, and the principle receives practical expression in the fact that the majority of rules under the Act are default rules, which may be excluded or varied by the parties. Of course, party autonomy cannot be insisted upon if this would mean that fairness or justice is denied. Accordingly, a number of rules are mandatory. **S1–08**

Principle (c)—Limited court intervention

Another key aspect of modern arbitration legislation is that court intervention in the arbitral process is limited to the extent laid down by that legislation. Thus the principle is expressed in art.5 of the Model Law and echoed in the 1996 Act s.1(c). The drafters of the Model Law were driven by the fact that the Model Law was originally designed to be adopted in jurisdictions which had no great profile as arbitral forums, or which indeed had a reputation for inappropriate court intervention in the arbitral process. Thus the drafters wished to signal that such intervention was to be limited to that laid down by the Model Law (see *Report of the UNCITRAL on the work of its 18th session*, UN A/40/17, paras 61–63). The drafters of the 1996 Act were sensitive to the fact that, internationally, English courts were **S1–09** regarded as having a tendency to intervene in arbitrations more than was appropriate (DAC Report, para.21). Thus the 1996 Act was intended to signal a departure from the traditional English approach. The background of the 2010 Act is rather different but s.1(c) is nonetheless welcome, first, because it articulates a key principle, and secondly, because it might indeed help curb any tendency towards intervention on the part of the Scottish courts.

S1–10 Principle (c) extends to intervention in an "arbitration" and this is reflected in the wording used, in contrast to that in s.1(c) of the 1996 Act and art.5 of the Model Law both of which apply the principle to "matters governed by this Part" or "matters governed by this law", respectively. The clearest example of the application of principle (c) is in s.13 which restricts legal proceedings in a Scottish court in respect of the tribunal's award and any other act or omission by a tribunal when conducting an arbitration.

European Convention of Human Rights

S1–11 Arbitrators and courts should also be aware of the effect on the Act of the ECHR. The ECHR affects the Act through (1) the HRA; and (2) the Scotland Act 1998. It affects the work of both Scottish arbitrators and Scottish courts in relation to arbitration.

S1–12 Arbitral tribunals are private bodies and not emanations of the state. The authors submit that arbitrators, at least when acting under voluntary arbitration agreements, are not "public authorities" with the express duties imposed on such bodies in the HRA (e.g. the duty in s.6(1) not to act incompatibly with an ECHR right).

S1–13 The HRA defines "public authority" as "any court or tribunal" and "any person certain of whose functions are public in nature" but excludes the acts of such a person that are private in nature (HRA s.6(3)). It defines a "tribunal' as "any tribunal in which legal proceedings may be brought". Arbitrations are not proceedings that are brought "in" an arbitral tribunal. An arbitral tribunal, unlike a statutory tribunal, does not exist independently of its proceedings. Furthermore, its functions are not public in nature since privacy is one of the essential features of arbitration.

S1–14 However, arbitrators must conform to the law of Scotland in their procedures and, if those are governed by Scots law and are not to be decided on general considerations of justice, fairness and equity, in deciding the merits of the dispute. This means that in interpreting Scots law, both in relation to procedure and the merits, they must take account of the rules of interpretation (or construction) within the HRA and the Scotland Act.

S1–15 Section 3(1) of the HRA provides:

> "So far as it is possible to do so, primary legislation and subordinate legislation must be read and given effect to in a way that is compatible with the Convention rights".

This provision must be applied to the Act by arbitrators and courts alike. The rights are those rights in the ECHR that are set out in Sch.1 to the HRA.

There is a provision similar to s.3(1) in s.101 of the Scotland Act but it has **S1–16** been held on high authority that in interpreting Acts of the Scottish Parliament in relation to the effect on them of the ECHR, s.3(1) of the HRA should be applied (*DS v HM Advocate,* 2007 S.C. (P.C.) 1 at [23]–[24], per Lord Hope of Craighead).

In *DS v HM Advocate,* 2007 S.C. (P.C.) 1 the obligation in s.3(1) was **S1–17** described as a "strong" one. In the very unlikely event that a provision of the 2010 Act cannot be read and given effect to compatibly with an ECHR right, that provision is beyond the competence of the Scottish Parliament (Scotland Act s.29(2)(d)) and will be void (Scotland Act s.29(1)).

In contrast to arbitral tribunals, courts are "public authorities" under the **S1–18** HRA and it is unlawful for a court to act in a way incompatible with a "Convention right" (HRA s.6(1)). But if the court acts to give effect to or enforce a provision of the 2010 Act which cannot be read and given effect to in a way that is compatible with a Convention right, it does not act unlawfully (HRA ss.6(2) and 21(1)). As noted above, given the effect of the interpretative obligation in s.3(1) it is unlikely that a court would act unlawfully when applying the 2010 Act.

The main issue for courts and arbitral tribunals in connection with **S1–19** arbitration may concern the effect on the Act of art.6(1) of the ECHR which provides:

> "In the determination of his civil rights and obligations ... everyone is entitled to a fair and public hearing within a reasonable time by an independent and impartial tribunal established by law. Judgment shall be pronounced publicly ... "

The right to have a dispute determined by a tribunal "established by law", **S1–20** typically a court, is seen as being of great significance. However nothing in art.6 prevents the parties to a dispute waiving their right to determination of their civil rights and obligations by a tribunal established by law provided that it is done with the free, admissible and unequivocal consent of the parties (*Suda v Czech Republic* (1643/06) Unreported October 28, 2010 ECtHR at [42]; *Suovaniemi v Finland* (31737/96) Unreported February 23, 1999 ECtHR).

Arbitration agreements are seen as waivers of the right to a public hearing **S1–21** and judgment and a determination by a tribunal established by law (*Suda v Czech Republic* (1643/06) Unreported October 28, 2010 ECtHR) but statutory arbitration does not involve such waiver. In contrast, the right to a fair hearing within a reasonable time will not be waived merely through an arbitration agreement (*Suovaniemi v Finland* (31737/96) Unreported February 23, 1999 ECtHR). Rule 24 of the SAR, however, provides sufficient guarantees of this aspect of the art.6(1) right.

S1–22 Impartiality of an arbitral tribunal under art.6(1) can be waived. In *Suovaniemi v Finland* (31737/96) Unreported February 23, 1999 ECtHR, it was argued that a Finnish court had violated art.6(1) in refusing to set aside an award on the grounds of an arbitrator's lack of apparent impartiality because the appellant had waived his right of challenge. The ECtHR rejected the claim, finding that the art.6(1) right to impartiality had been waived, and observing:

> "The Court considers that the Contracting States enjoy considerable discretion in regulating the question on which grounds an arbitral award should be quashed, since the quashing of an already rendered award will often mean that a long and costly arbitral procedure will become useless and that considerable work and expense must be invested in new proceedings (see also ... *Nordström-Janzon v. the Netherlands*, Dec. 27 November 1996, D.R. 87-A, at 116). In view of this the finding of the Finnish court based on Finnish law that by approving M. as an arbitrator despite the doubt, of which the applicants were aware, about his objective impartiality within the meaning of the relevant Finnish legislation does not appear arbitrary or unreasonable. Moreover, considering that throughout the arbitration the applicants were represented by counsel, the waiver was accompanied by sufficient guarantees commensurate to its importance."

Key terms

2.—(1) In this Act, unless the contrary intention appears—
"arbitration" includes—
   (a) domestic arbitration,
   (b) arbitration between parties residing, or carrying on business, anywhere in the United Kingdom, and
   (c) international arbitration,
"arbitrator" means a sole arbitrator or a member of a tribunal,
"dispute" includes—
   (a) any refusal to accept a claim, and
   (b) any other difference (whether contractual or not),
"party" means a party to an arbitration,
"rules" means the Scottish Arbitration Rules (see section 7), and
"tribunal" means a sole arbitrator or panel of arbitrators.

(2) References in this Act to "an arbitration", "the arbitration" or "arbitrations" are references to a particular arbitration process or, as the case may be, to particular arbitration processes.

(3) References in this Act to a tribunal conducting an arbitration are references to the tribunal doing anything in relation to the arbitration, including—
   (a) making a decision about procedure or evidence, and
   (b) making an award.

COMMENTARY

Section 2(1)—"Arbitration"

S2–01 Subsection (1) does not define the concept of arbitration. Most laws and international conventions follow this line, while the DAC Report (para.18) suggested that any attempt to do so in the 1996 Act would be fraught with difficulties and would serve no useful purpose. Rather, the Act leaves it to the courts to determine in the circumstances of each case whether the process with which they are concerned amounts to arbitration or some other form of dispute resolution.

S2–02 Arbitration is one form of what is commonly described as "alternative dispute resolution" or "ADR". "Alternative" means alternative to resolution by a court. Arbitration must be distinguished from other types of ADR. These include expert determination, valuation, mediation, construction adjudication and judicial reference.

S2–03 The distinction between arbitration and valuation or other forms of expert determination is sometimes unclear. Where the parties agree to refer any dispute or difference to a person who is to act as an expert and not as an arbitrator (or arbiter, to use the pre-Act term), prima facie the dispute resolution mechanism will be expert determination and not arbitration, even if the process adopted by the expert resembles that in an arbitration (*AGE Ltd v Kwik Save Stores Ltd*, 2001 S.C. 144). Difficulties can arise where in their agreement the parties refer the dispute or difference to a third party but do not require expressly that he either act or not act as an arbitrator. Such a case was *MacDonald Estates Plc v National Car Parks Ltd*, 2010 S.C. 250 where the Inner House of the Court of Session said:

> "Expert determination ... can be broadly distinguished from arbitration in not being judicial in character ... A person who sits in a judicial or quasi-judicial capacity, as an arbiter ordinarily does decides matters on the basis of submissions and evidence put before him, whereas an expert, subject to the provisions of his remit, is entitled to carry out his own investigations and come to his own conclusion regardless of any submissions or evidence adduced by the parties themselves." (at [21], per Extra Division)

S2–04 See Hew R. Dundas, "Arbitrator or Expert Determiner? That is the Question: A Scottish Case Note: MacDonald Estates Plc v National Car Parks Ltd" (2010) 76 *Arbitration* 21–31.

In *MacDonald Estates Plc v National Car Parks Ltd*, 2010 S.C. 250 at [21] the court noted that Scottish legal terminology had developed over the previous 100 years and that the concept of arbitration has become distinct from other forms of dispute resolution agreed by the parties such as mediation, conciliation, early neutral evaluation, adjudication and expert determination.

Arbitration (Scotland) Act 2010

S2–05 One of the characteristics which distinguishes arbitration from expert determination is that, unlike an arbitrator, an expert determiner is not required to adjudicate as between rival contentions (*Holland House Property Investments Ltd v Crabbe*, 2008 S.C. 619 at [22], per First Division). In effect an expert determiner is not bound by the mandatory requirement of r.24 to give each party a reasonable opportunity to put its case and to deal with the other party's case whereas an arbitrator is.

S2–06 This critical distinction between arbitration and expert determination (whether by a valuer or other expert), is reflected in English law also (*David Wilson Homes Ltd v Survey Services Ltd* [2001] B.L.R. 267 at [13], per Longmore L.J.). In that case it was held that a clause referring any dispute or difference to a Queen's Counsel of the English Bar to be appointed in the event of disagreement by the Chairman of the Bar Council but which did not identify the dispute resolution mechanism was to be seen as a reference to arbitration. The reasoning was that normally such references were to be carried out with quasi-judicial procedure and that the aim of the reference was finality which was best served by arbitration. "Finality" in relation to issues of fact, such as typically, valuation, is something that can be achieved through expert determination. The position is less clear in relation to expert determination in relation to issues of law where in England it has been suggested that the court may retain some residual jurisdiction to set aside the decision of the expert on a pure point of law (see *Barclays Bank Plc v Nylon Capital LLP* [2011] 2 Lloyd's Rep. 347 and Hew R. Dundas, "*Barclays Bank v Nylon*: Expert Determination—ADR Stays and the Jurisdiction of the Expert" (2012) 78 *Arbitration* 194–202).

S2–07 A distinction must also be drawn between arbitration and mediation. Mediation not only does not involve the third party deciding the dispute between the parties but also, conventionally, does not involve the making of any recommendation to the parties. The mediator's role is rather to facilitate the parties reaching a compromise settlement agreement between themselves. In the course of mediation the mediator may become party to information given to him in confidence by either party, thereby enabling the mediator to identify a potential "zone of settlement". However, being party to such confidential information may be incompatible with the obligation of an arbitrator under r.24 to be impartial. Such a conclusion was reached in relation to the similar obligation of a construction adjudicator under the HGCRA (*Glencot Development and Design Co Ltd v Ben Barrett & Son (Contractors) Ltd* [2001] B.L.R. 207 at [21] to [27]).

S2–08 In some foreign jurisdictions such as the PRC, Germany and Switzerland, the divide between arbitration and mediation is very different to the position in the UK. In the PRC, it is routine for a tribunal to act as conciliator (i.e. mediator) and to revert to being the arbitral tribunal if the conciliation fails; see e.g. art.39 of the BAC Rules and the discussion at paras S20–122 to S20–125 below of *Gao v Keeneye Holdings Ltd* [2011] HKCA 459. Further, under §278 ZpO a German judge, while not acting as "mediator" as understood in the UK, is statutorily obliged to try to engineer a settlement between litigating parties and German arbitrators, by analogy, adopt that same objective.

Further, there are various hybrid processes such as Med-Arb and Arb-Med which, in different ways, combine elements of arbitration with some of mediation. Such matters are beyond the scope of this book. **S2–09**

An agreement merely to refer a dispute arising under a commercial services agreement to a body which did not arbitrate such disputes and which mentioned a party "prevailing" in mediation was held not to be a reference to arbitration (*Flight Training International v International Fire Training Equipment Ltd* [2004] EWHC 721 (Comm)). **S2–10**

Mention should also be made of adjudication in construction matters under the HGCRA. This a form of preliminary dispute resolution which parties have agreed in their contract or which is imposed directly under the HGCRA and its regulations. The decision of a construction adjudicator is, however, provisional in the sense that the dispute may be litigated or arbitrated afresh and a new decision substituted by the court or arbitral tribunal. For this reason it has been held that adjudication under the HGCRA is not a form of arbitration (*Diamond v PJW Enterprises Ltd*, 2004 S.C. 30). **S2–11**

Finally, arbitration must also be distinguished from the Scottish "judicial reference". A "judicial reference" in this context is where parties have begun litigation with no arbitration agreement and have then agreed to have the dispute, or aspects of the dispute being litigated, decided by a named third party known as a "referee". The agreement must be set out in a joint minute signed by the parties or their representatives and must have the approval of the court. Equally, the referee is an officer of the court. He has the powers of an arbiter at common law and he must make an award in the same way. However, in order for the award to take effect, the referee must report it to the court and the court must, on the application of a party, grant authority to it. If authority is granted to the referee's award it is transformed into a court decree (judgment). It is at the stage of applying for authority that challenges to the award can be made in the same way as challenges could have been made to a final award under the old common law. These were restricted to matters of jurisdiction and procedure such as not dealing with all the issues referred and acting beyond the scope of the reference, or specific allegations of irregularity in the proceedings, e.g. unfair conduct. (See *Mackenzie v Girvan* (1840) 3 D. 318; *Brakinrig v Menzies* (1841) 4 D. 474; *Campbell v Campbell* (1843) 5 D. 530; and *Irons and Melville on Arbitration*, pp.93–110). **S2–12**

Judicial reference was popular as a device of avoiding a civil jury trial of non-personal injury disputes but, after the restriction of civil jury trials, has become obsolete. The authors submit that there is no rule of Scots law preventing parties during the course of litigation from agreeing to submit their dispute to arbitration under the 2010 Act. If they so agree and make a **S2–13**

Arbitration (Scotland) Act 2010

joint application to the court to sist the proceedings, it is submitted that the court should exercise its discretion, having regard to s.1(b) and notwithstanding s.10(1)(d), to grant the application to allow the arbitral process to take effect.

S2–14　Arbitration is expressed to include domestic arbitration, international arbitration and arbitration between parties residing or carrying on business anywhere in the UK. This is intended to underline that the 2010 Act applies to all arbitrations where Scotland is the juridical seat of the arbitration under s.3, regardless of the location of the parties. This represented a change to the previous law which had a separate legal regime for international commercial arbitrations and other arbitrations.

Section 2(1)—"Dispute"

S2–15　There is English authority to the effect that "difference" is a term of potentially wider meaning than "dispute", so that by indicating that a "dispute" includes a "difference", the Act seeks to cover arbitration agreements which remit to arbitration any "difference" between the parties and to prevent arguments over whether matters have escalated into a "dispute". In England, an arbitration clause which provided that,

> "if any difference shall arise between the parties as regards ... the meaning or effect of this agreement or in relation to any matters incidental thereto such differences shall be referred to arbitration"

was held to allow the arbitrator to decide how many goods should be supplied where the parties had not agreed that issue and to prevent the agreement from being void for uncertainty (*F & G Sykes (Wessex) Ltd v Fine Fare Ltd* [1967] 1 Lloyd's Rep. 53).

S2–16　In England it has been held that a dispute exists where it is clear that one party is refusing to entertain the other's claim, and this idea no doubt inspires the other leg of the definition of that term. It, of course, largely depends on the circumstances as to whether a party can actually be taken to refuse a claim (see the guidance given by Jackson J. in *Amec Civil Engineering Ltd v Secretary of State for Transport* [2005] 1 W.L.R. 2339 at [68], approved by the Court of Appeal in *Collins v Baltic Quay Management (1994) Ltd* [2005] 1 B.L.R. 63). English case law also suggests that a dispute exists between the parties even if it is clear that a party has no real basis for making a claim or no arguable defence (see *Halki Shipping Corp v Sopex Oils Ltd* [1998] 1 W.L.R. 726). As Saville J. noted in *Hayter v Nelson* [1990] 2 Lloyd's Rep. 265 at 268:

> "Because one man can be said to be indisputably right and the other indisputably wrong does not entail that there was never therefore any dispute between them."

By contrast, in a pre-Act Scottish case *Norwest Holst Ltd v Carfin Developments Ltd* [2009] 1 B.L.R. 167, the Outer House followed older case law in stating: S2–17

> "The jurisidiction of the arbiter should only be ousted by the Court if there is no basis upon which a two sided dispute can be identified."

That is consistent with Saville J. in *Hayter v Nelson* [1990] 2 Lloyd's Rep. 265. However, in *Norwest Holst* the parties had an agreement whereby "any dispute or difference" should be referred to an engineer for expert determination. The contractors commenced litigation for payment in terms of an engineer's certificate. The employers defended this claiming that the certificate was invalid for a number of reasons and that in any event they were entitled to retain payment pending resolution of a counterclaim for damages. They sought a sist for expert determination. It was agreed that the application for a sist should be determined as if it was for arbitration. The Outer House rejected the employers' arguments as manifestly wrong and thereafter refused to sist. It is submitted that (notwithstanding the erroneous nature of the employers' arguments) it could not be said that there was no basis for identification of a two sided dispute or indeed difference and therefore the court should have respected the parties' dispute resolution clause.

Section 2(1)—Other terms

The definitions of the terms "arbitrator", "party", "rules" and "tribunal" serve to avoid doubt. S2–18

Section 2(2)

The meaning and purpose of this provision appears to be to avoid "arbitration" being construed as arbitrations in general rather than a particular arbitration. S2–19

Section 2(3)—Conduct of arbitration

This perhaps serves slightly more purpose than subs.(2), above, in that it makes the (possibly obvious) point that the conduct of the proceedings encompasses the making of the award (r.68(2)(a) refers). S2–20

Seat of arbitration

3.—(1) An arbitration is "seated in Scotland" if—
    (a) Scotland is designated as the juridical seat of the arbitration—
        (i) by the parties,
        (ii) by any third party to whom the parties give power to so designate, or

(iii) **where the parties fail to designate or so authorise a third party, by the tribunal, or**
(b) **in the absence of any such designation, the court determines that Scotland is to be the juridical seat of the arbitration.**
(2) **The fact that an arbitration is seated in Scotland does not affect the substantive law to be used to decide the dispute.**

DEFINITIONS

"arbitration": ss.2(1), (2), 31(1)
"court": s.31(1)
"dispute": ss.2(1), 31(1)
"party": ss.2(1), 31(1), (2)
"tribunal": ss.2(1), 31(1)

MODEL LAW

S3–01　Article 20(1) of the Model Law provides that the parties are free to agree on the place of arbitration and that failing such agreement the place shall be determined by the arbitral tribunal having regard to the circumstances of the case, including the convenience of the parties. Article 20(2) of the Model Law provides that notwithstanding the place of the arbitration, the arbitral tribunal may, unless otherwise agreed by the parties, meet at any place it considers appropriate. This makes it clear that "place of arbitration" in art.20(1) means the juridical "place" or "seat" of the arbitration.

COMMENTARY

Introductory

S3–02　The purpose of the juridical seat is to determine the curial law or *lex arbitri* which governs the procedure in an arbitration. The old Scots common law did not contain any clear rules on the determination of the curial law. It did, however, recognise that the parties could choose, either expressly or by implication, a curial law that differed from the law to be used to determine the merits of the dispute (*Hamlyn & Co v The Talisker Distillery* (1894) 21 R. (HL) 21). While common law precedents did not say so in terms, the choice by the parties of the geographical location of the arbitration was seen as a clear indicator of the curial law chosen. The idea that an arbitration could take place in one location but be governed by a curial law of a country other than of that location was not something which the common law required to consider.

S3–03　By contrast, modern international arbitration law is quite familiar with the mechanism of the juridical seat of an arbitration determining the applicability of a particular national law, and that the juridical seat is not necessarily the same place as the physical location of the arbitral proceedings, which proceedings indeed may be held in more than one state. The idea of the juridical seat is particularly useful in terms of supplying a governing law for arbitrations which are peripatetic, or which have no obvious location, as in the case of online arbitrations. Sometimes the "seat" of an arbitration is referred to as the "place" of an arbitration, as in art.20 of the Model Law. It is also recognised by the New York Convention and well established in national legislation, being central to both the 1996 Act and the Model Law. Therefore, in adopting the concept the 2010 Act is simply bringing Scotland into line with contemporary thinking.

The principal purpose of s.3 is to provide a means for arbitral tribunals and Scottish courts to identify whether an arbitration is seated in Scotland and thus governed by the SAR. **S3–04**

The effect of the provision is that if parties designate Scotland as the seat of the arbitration, the SAR will apply to that arbitration (s.7 refers), even if it has no connection with Scotland, and even if none of the proceedings are held in Scotland. If, for example, the parties were to designate England as the seat of the arbitration, but agreed that the procedural law was that of Scotland, the issue for the Scottish court would be whether the reference to "seat" was merely to the geographical or physical location rather than a designation of the juridical seat (*Braes of Doune Wind Farm (Scotland) Ltd v Alfred McAlpine Business Services Ltd* [2008] EWHC 426 (TCC); [2008] 1 Lloyd's Rep. 608; see para.S3–16 below). **S3–05**

It should also be borne in mind that under s.16(4) all statutory arbitrations are seated in Scotland. **S3–06**

Section 3(1)(a)—Designation of seat by parties, third party or tribunal

As in art.20(1) of the Model Law, the agreement of the parties is the primary determinant of where the seat might be. However, s.3(1) requires "designation" of Scotland as the seat. "Designation" is also the approach used by s.3(a)–(c) of the 1996 Act. Can designation of the seat be implied through conduct? It is suggested that it cannot. "Designated" has been held to mean "pointed out with particularity" and not merely incidentally referred to (*Newton v Marylebone BC* (1915) 84 L.J.K.B. 1721 at 1725 per Swinfen Eady L.J.). There must, therefore, be some express pointing to Scotland as the seat by some means. Typically, arbitration agreements provide for the arbitration to be seated in a city rather than a country. If the city or other location was in Scotland, that might be seen as designation of Scotland by the parties, but this must be seen in the context of other provisions of the arbitration agreement which might suggest that "seat" is meant in the sense of venue only and not juridical seat. **S3–07**

As an alternative to designating the seat themselves, as under s.3(b) of the 1996 Act, the parties may entrust that designation to a third party. A third party here would include but not be limited to an institution. Thus if the parties have agreed to arbitrate under the ICC Rules but have not agreed on **S3–08**

Arbitration (Scotland) Act 2010

a seat, the ICC Rules art.18 indicates that the ICC Court will determine the place (seat) of arbitration. This example also serves to illustrate that, while the parties may explicitly empower a third party to designate the seat, they may also do so implicitly by adopting arbitral rules which confer that power.

S3–09   If the parties neither designate the seat nor authorise a third party to designate the seat, then the tribunal is automatically entitled to do so. This contrasts with s.3(c) of the 1996 Act under which the tribunal may only designate the seat if authorised to do so by the parties. In this the Act is much closer to art.20(1) of the Model Law which provides that, failing agreement by the parties, the place (seat) of arbitration shall be determined by the tribunal. Section 3(1)(a)(iii) assumes that the tribunal has already been constituted *de facto* even though as a matter of law there is no arbitration agreement (*Arab National Bank v El Sharif Saoud Bin Masoud Bin Haza'a El-Abdali* [2004] EWHC 2381 (Comm) at [14]).

S3–10   Again, while as under s.9(4)(b) of the 2010 Act, s.4(5) of the 1996 Act allows the parties to an arbitration seated in England to apply a foreign procedural law to govern issues not covered by mandatory provisions of that Act, the English courts have taken the view that an agreement that an arbitration is to be governed by a particular procedural law yields a strong inference that it is agreed that the state in question should also be the seat (see *A v B* [2007] 1 Lloyd's Rep. 237).

S3–11   Where the decision devolves on the tribunal in terms of s.3(1)(a)(iii), the Act does not give any guidance as to what considerations it should take into account in determining what the seat is to be. Under art.20(1) of the Model Law, where the decision devolves on the tribunal it must have "regard to the circumstances of the case, including the convenience of the parties". Section 3(1)(a)(iii) does not express any such guidance. However, guidance can be found in founding principle (a) in s.1 of the 2010 Act which provides that the object of arbitration is "to resolve disputes fairly, impartially and without unnecessary delay or expense". It is suggested that, in designating the seat, the tribunal should be guided by these criteria as a minimum, inter alia since they accord with the approaches of arbitral institutions. A tribunal may also wish to take account of other factors, e.g. the *UNCITRAL Notes on Organizing Arbitral Proceedings* state at para.22:

> "Various factual and legal factors influence the choice of the place of arbitration, and their relative importance varies from case to case. Among the more prominent factors are:
>
> *(a)* suitability of the law on arbitral procedure of the place [seat] of arbitration;
> *(b)* whether there is a multilateral or bilateral treaty on enforcement of arbitral awards between the State where the arbitration takes place and the State or States where the award may have to be enforced;

(c) convenience of the parties and the arbitrators, including the travel distances;
(d) availability and cost of support services needed; and
(e) location of the subject-matter in dispute and proximity of evidence."

Another important factor may be the neutrality of a proposed seat. Scotland is a mixed civil law and common law jurisdiction incorporating features of both types of legal system. In the not uncommon situation of a dispute between a party from a civil law state and a party from a common law state, Scotland would appear to be ideally placed to be a neutral seat for such an arbitration. Its arbitral law reflects the best modern principles, it is accessible by air from most international centres and has a high level of support services available at a competitive cost substantially below that of London. S3–12

The tribunal would also appear to have a duty to give each party a reasonable opportunity to present its case on the designation of the seat: see r.24(1)(b) and (2) which will apply should the tribunal decide in favour of a Scottish seat. S3–13

There is also the question of the stage at which the seat might be designated. Presumably, designation could happen at any time, perhaps even after the award was made, if as a result of an omission it was not stated therein (rr.51 and 58 refer). However, as a practical matter one would expect a tribunal, if no designation had already been made, to raise the issue with the parties at the earliest opportunity since it would wish to know the procedural (curial) law which should govern its conduct. S3–14

Section 3(1)(b)—Court decides seat

If no designation is made by the parties, by an empowered third party or by the arbitral tribunal, then the question of what the seat is to be devolves on the court. It might be thought that this is an unlikely scenario, since if the parties do not designate the seat, then the tribunal surely will, and indeed the framers of the Model Law made no provision for what might happen if the tribunal did not do so. Yet such an eventuality is not impossible, as the few English cases that exist demonstrate. In that case, presumably any party or the tribunal might apply to the court to decide the issue. S3–15

Equally, a seeming designation may, on a proper interpretation, not be a designation at all. In *Braes of Doune Wind Farm (Scotland) Ltd v Alfred McAlpine Business Services Ltd* [2008] 1 Lloyd's Rep. 608, the seat of an arbitration was stated to be Glasgow, Scotland. Equally, a seeming designation may, on a proper interpretation, not be a designation at all. In *Braes of Doune Wind Farm (Scotland) Ltd v Alfred McAlpine Business Services Ltd* [2008] EWHC 426 (TCC); [2008] 1 Lloyd's Rep. 608, the seat of an arbitration was stated to be Glasgow, Scotland. However, the arbitration agreement between the parties (i) expressed itself to be subject to English S3–16 law, (ii) provided that references to arbitration should be deemed to refer to arbitration under the 1996 Act, and (iii) provided that the arbitration would be subject to CIMAR (which apply only where England and Wales is the seat and which also invoke the 1996 Act). Further, the contract also stated that the English courts had exclusive jurisdiction to settle any dispute. The TCC held (applying the similarly worded s.3 of the 1996 Act) that (i) the parties had intended England to be the seat in a juridical sense and (ii) the clause specifying Glasgow to be the seat was merely a reference to the agreed physical venue of the arbitration.

S3–17   Section 3 does not give the court any guidance on how it should determine whether the seat is to be Scotland. By contrast, s.3 of the 1996 Act provides that the court should have regard to the parties' agreement and all the relevant circumstances. That would appear to be appropriate for s.3 of the 2010 Act also. In *Dubai Islamic Bank PJSC v Paymentech Merchant Services Inc* [2001] 1 Lloyd's Rep. 65, Aikens J. observed at [52]:

> "[All the relevant circumstances] must mean that a court has to have regard to any connections with one or more particular countries that can be identified in relation to (i) the parties; (ii) the dispute which will be the subject of the arbitration; (iii) the proposed procedures in the arbitration, including (if known) the place of interlocutory and final hearings; (iv) the issue of the award or awards."

S3–18   It was also held in *Dubai Islamic Bank PJSC v Paymentech Merchant Services Inc* [2001] 1 Lloyd's Rep. 65 at [48]–[49] that in determining the seat the court must look only at the circumstances at the time that the arbitration begins. Such an approach appears unduly restrictive as it could leave out important and arguably relevant matters such as the qualifications and location of the arbitrator, his initial procedural steps and the parties' attitude towards them. These were significant factors in *James Miller & Partners Ltd v Whitworth Street Estates (Manchester) Ltd* [1970] A.C. 583. In that case, despite the contract being in a form commonly used in England and despite one of the parties applying to RIBA for appointment of an arbitrator pursuant to English legislation, the appointment of a Scottish arbiter who indicated at the outset that he would follow Scottish procedure, to which neither party objected, was held by the House of Lords to indicate that the parties had chosen Scots law as the curial law.

S3–19   While *James Miller & Partners Ltd v Whitworth Street Estates (Manchester) Ltd* [1970] A.C. 583 was not concerned with the "seat" as such, the authors submit that there is no good reason why its reasoning cannot be applied by a court determining the seat should that issue arise once significant procedural steps have been taken in the arbitration. A similar approach was followed in *Arab National Bank v El Sharif Saoud Bin Masoud Bin Haza'a El-Abdali* [2004] EWHC 2381 (Comm) at [14] where the court considered the arbitrator's procedures.

In s.3 the decision of the "court" is not restricted to the Court of Session **S3–20**
or sheriff court: see s.31(1) below. Could this include a court outside Scotland so that, if such a foreign court decides that Scotland is the seat, then a Scottish court will recognise that decision as binding on it? As in *Braes of Doune* (above), one party might apply to a foreign court to decide the question of the seat. If the other party prefers a Scottish court to decide the question there is nothing to prevent it applying thereto. In the event of such an application, if there is a concurrent application to, or a decision by, a foreign court, the party seeking to uphold the latter's decision will have to persuade the Scottish court either to recognise that decision (if it has been made) or to find that it, i.e. the Scottish court, is forum non conveniens (*Argyllshire Weavers Ltd v A. Macaulay (Tweeds) Ltd*, 1962 S.C. 388; 1962 S.L.T. 310).

It might happen that, as in *Braes of Doune*, a foreign court had already **S3–21**
made a final decision as to the seat without any application having been made to any Scottish court; in such circumstances, the latter is likely to recognise the foreign decision. It would not do so if it can be shown either that the foreign court had had no jurisdiction over the defender in the foreign proceedings or that there had been a serious procedural irregularity in the foreign proceedings (e.g. a failure to give notice of the proceedings) or that, in relation to non-UK foreign courts, s.32 of the 1982 Act applies. Section 19 of the 1982 Act excludes the "no jurisdiction over defender" objection to recognition by providing that a judgment from another part of the UK is not to be refused recognition solely on the grounds that the court was not competent under Scots private international law rules. Section 32 of the 1982 Act provides further grounds for refusal of recognition if there was an arbitration agreement and the person against whom judgment was given did not raise the foreign proceedings nor agree to them or otherwise submit to the jurisdiction of the court (see *Tracomin SA v Sudan Oil Seeds Ltd* [1983] 1 W.L.R. 1026).

Neither Council Regulation (EC) No 44/2001 of 22 December 2000 on **S3 22**
jurisdiction and the recognition and enforcement of judgments in civil and commercial matters, nor its successor Regulation (EU) No 1215/2012 of the European Parliament and of the Council of 12 December 2012 on jurisdiction and the recognition and enforcement of judgments in civil and commercial matters, nor the Lugano Convention of 2007, apply to proceedings the purpose of which is concerned with arbitration (art.1(2)(d) of both Regulations and the Lugano Convention; *Allianz SpA v West Tankers Inc (The Front Comor)* [2009] 1 A.C. 1138 at [22]–[23] per ECJ, and see, in particular, the preamble to the 2012 Regulation at [12]).

When the English courts believe that a dispute is most closely connected **S3–23**
to England, so that they should most appropriately rule on the issue of the seat, they have certainly been prepared to issue injunctions restraining parties from seeking to ask foreign courts to rule on the matter. While the decision in *Allianz SpA v West Tankers Inc (The Front Comor)* [2009] 1 A.C.

1138 prevents them issuing such injunctions as regards proceedings within the EU and EFTA areas which are concerned with the merits of a claim, they have continued to issue injunctions to restrain other proceedings (see, e.g. *Shashoua v Sharma* [2009] EWHC 957 (Comm); *Midgulf International Ltd v Group Chimiche Tunisien* [2009] EWHC 963 (Comm)). There is no recorded instance of a Scots court acting in a similar way. One reason for this may be that Scots law has never viewed the raising of proceedings for a court order on the merits as being in breach of an arbitration agreement and therefore liable to be restrained through an interdict (Scottish injunction). It is therefore suggested that if a party wishes a Scottish court to determine the seat it should not hesitate to make the application to the Scottish court and contest, if possible, the jurisdiction of the foreign court to make the decision.

S3–24   Applications to the Court of Session are made by petition (RCS r.100.5) or to the sheriff court of the appropriate sheriffdom determined by Sch.8 to the 1982 Act by summary application (SASAR r.2.4). Whether either court has jurisdiction over the respondent party will be determined by Sch.8. For details of the procedure for an application, reference should be made to *Greens Annotated Rules of the Court of Session* (Edinburgh: W. Green). Often the issue of the seat arises in the context of an appeal against an award. In that case, the procedure is as for an appeal (see rr.67–71 and the commentary thereon).

Section 3(2)—Seat not affecting law governing the substance of the dispute

S3–25   This provision makes the point that the fact that Scotland is the seat of the arbitration does not mean that Scots law will govern the substance of the dispute—see r.47, below. The fact that Scotland is the seat means only that the procedural law of the arbitration will be governed by Scots law in the form of the 2010 Act including the SAR and, presumably, the common law in areas not addressed by the Act or Rules. Indeed, by virtue of s.9(4)(b) a foreign law can even apply to the arbitral procedure with the exception of the mandatory rules of the SAR.

Arbitration agreements

Arbitration agreement

4. An "arbitration agreement" is an agreement to submit a present or future dispute to arbitration (including any agreement which provides for arbitration in accordance with arbitration provisions contained in a separate document).

DEFINITIONS

"arbitration": ss.2(1), (2), 31(1)
"dispute": ss.2(1), 31(1)

MODEL LAW

Article 7 of the Model Law (as amended in 2006) has two "options" for the definition of an arbitration agreement. Option I is: **S4–01**

"(1) 'Arbitration agreement' is an agreement by the parties to submit to arbitration all or certain disputes which have arisen or which may arise between them in respect of a defined legal relationship, whether contractual or not. An arbitration agreement may be in the form of an arbitration clause in a contract or in the form of a separate agreement.
(2) The arbitration agreement shall be in writing.
(3) An arbitration agreement is in writing if its content is recorded in any form, whether or not the arbitration agreement or contract has been concluded orally, by conduct, or by other means.
(4) The requirement that an arbitration agreement be in writing is met by an electronic communication if the information contained therein is accessible so as to be useable for subsequent reference; 'electronic communication' means any communication that the parties make by means of data messages; 'data message' means information generated, sent, received or stored by electronic, magnetic, optical or similar means, including, but not limited to, electronic data interchange (EDI), electronic mail, telegram, telex or telecopy.
(5) Furthermore, an arbitration agreement is in writing if it is contained in an exchange of statements of claim and defence in which the existence of an agreement is alleged by one party and not denied by the other.
(6) The reference in a contract to any document containing an arbitration clause constitutes an arbitration agreement in writing, provided that the reference is such as to make that clause part of the contract."

Option II is: **S4–02**

"'Arbitration agreement' is an agreement by the parties to submit to arbitration all or certain disputes which have arisen or which may arise between them in respect of a defined legal relationship, whether contractual or not."

COMMENTARY

Introductory

Section 4 points out that an arbitration agreement may be an agreement to submit an existing dispute to arbitration or an agreement that the parties will submit any dispute which arises between them in the future to **S4–03** arbitration. For the meanings of "arbitration" and "dispute" see the commentary on s.2. For what law is to apply to questions on the form and substance of an arbitration agreement, see the commentary on s.6.

S4–04 An "agreement" exists where the parties are bound to submit the dispute to arbitration. In *Halifax Financial Services Ltd v Intuitive Systems Ltd* [1999] 1 All E.R. (Comm) 303; (2000) 2 T.C.L.R. 35, the parties had entered into a dispute resolution clause which provided, in the event of a dispute, (i) for a party to serve a notice to the other requiring attendance at a meeting to attempt to resolve the dispute, then (ii) for a party to serve a notice that structured negotiations be entered into with the advice of a mediator. If, following these steps, there was still no settlement then any dispute might be referred to the court "unless ... the parties agree to arbitration in accordance with the procedure set out below". The court found that this was an "agreement to agree" and did not amount to an arbitration agreement, merely providing for the parties to negotiate and possibly refer the dispute to arbitration. Drafters of dispute resolution clauses should take careful note.

S4–05 Equally a dispute resolution clause which provided for parties to "endeavour to first resolve the matter through Swiss arbitration" and that, should resolution not be forthcoming, to give the English courts non-exclusive jurisdiction was held not to be an arbitration agreement (*Kruppa v Benedetti* [2014] EWHC 1877 (Comm)). Not only was the obligation merely to "endeavour" to go to arbitration but the presence of one binding tier followed by another binding tier in the event of the first tier not being binding was inconsistent with the parties being bound to go to arbitration.

S4–06 However, the situations in each of *Halifax* or *Kruppa* must be distinguished from an agreement that in the event of a dispute either party has an option, or "may" refer the dispute to arbitration (e.g. as in *Lobb Partnership Ltd v Aintree Racecourse Co Ltd* [2000] C.L.C. 431). That is an agreement where the parties are bound to go to arbitration if either one exercises the option to do so. That was consistent with the general position for all arbitration agreements in that if neither party commences the arbitration the dispute must be resolved by the court. See also the commentary at paras S10–45 to S10–56 below on s.10(1)(e) ("void" agreements).

Interpretation (construction) of arbitration agreements

S4–07 In the 1760s, the Scottish institutional writer John Erskine wrote:

> "Yet submissions [to arbiters], being intended for a most favourable purpose, the amicable composing of differences ought to receive the most ample interpretation of which such words are capable. A submission, therefore, drawn in general terms, of all controversies and questions between the parties, is understood to authorise the arbiters to decide upon questions, not only of moveable, but of heritable [immoveable]

bonds; *Durie* Dec.15, 1631, *Kincaid* (Mor. 5064). This, however, ought not to be stretched, as to include rights that cannot be presumed to have fallen under the view of the submitters ... " (Erskine, 4.3.32).

In *Fiona Trust and Holding Corp v Privalov* [2007] 4 All E.R. 951, Lord **S4–08** Hoffmann agreed with Longmore L.J.'s view (expressed in the Court of Appeal) that the time had come for the traditional English authorities on the construction of arbitration clauses to be set to one side:

"In my opinion the construction of an arbitration clause should start from the assumption that the parties, as rational businessmen, are likely to have intended any dispute arising out of the relationship into which they have entered or purported to enter to be decided by the same tribunal. The clause should be construed in accordance with this presumption unless the language makes it clear that certain questions were intended to be excluded from the arbitrator's jurisdiction. As Longmore LJ remarked, at para.17: 'if any businessman did want to exclude disputes about the validity of a contract, it would be comparatively easy to say so'" at [13].

The authors submit that in construing an arbitration agreement governed by **S4–09** Scots law, the approaches of Erskine and Lord Hoffmann should be followed. The justification given for the setting aside of the old precedents was the new start to English arbitration law given by the reforms in the 1996 Act, including s.7. The same justification should apply to the old Scottish precedents given the reforms of the 2010 Act. Fine distinctions based on wording should be avoided. Where, however, the arbitration agreement covers only a limited scope of disputes arising out of a main contract and leaves other disputes for litigation or other forms of dispute resolution the assumption in *Fiona Trust* (above) will not apply and standard principles of contractual interpretation will apply (*Guidance Investments Ltd v Guidance Investments Hotel Co BSC (Closed)* [2013] EWIIC 3413 (Comm)).

An arbitration agreement governed by Scots law which is part of a main **S4–10** contract which confers a *jus quaesitum tertio* (right conferred to a third party) will not bind the third party to arbitration, not least because its mere existence will not amount to a waiver by the third party of its right under art.6(1) of the ECHR to have its right determined by a tribunal established by law, i.e. court or statutory tribunal (*Suda v Czech Republic* (1643/06) Unreported October 28, 2010 ECtHR).

Categories of arbitration clause

Traditionally, arbitration clauses were categorised into executry and **S4–11** general or universal clauses (*Sanderson v Armour*, 1922 S.C. (HL) 117 at 125, per Lord Dunedin). Executry clauses were limited to disputes arising during the course of the performance of the contract, particularly a contract to perform works (e.g. a construction contract). General clauses were wide enough to embrace both disputes arising during and after the performance of the contract. Whether the clause is of one type or the other is a matter of interpretation or construction. The significance of this distinction is no longer relevant given that, subject to the observations in *Fiona Trust* (above), arbitration agreements have to be interpreted according to the ordinary rules of construction (interpretation) applicable to all contracts (*ERDC Construction Ltd v HM Love & Co*, 1994 S.C. 620 at 625E per Lord Justice-Clerk Ross).

Incorporation or importation of arbitration agreement

S4–12   The reference to "any agreement which provides for arbitration in accordance with arbitration provisions contained in a separate document" is clearly an attempt to make clear that an arbitration agreement includes an arbitration agreement incorporated by reference. This might arise where, for example, parties agree to be bound by the terms of a contract which is standard in a particular industry, and contains an arbitration clause. What it does not do is provide any guidance as to when incorporation by reference might occur. However, this is also true of s.6(2) of the 1996 Act and art.7(6) of the Model Law, both of which deal with the matter.

S4–13   The Scottish courts have not been persuaded that, in every instance of incorporation of the terms of another contract by reference, the parties must have intended to be bound by an arbitration clause in that contract. In *Babcock Rosyth Defence Ltd v Grootcon (UK) Ltd*, 1998 S.L.T. 1143, the question was whether a sub-contract had incorporated cl.66 of the ICE Conditions of Contract (5th edn) which included an arbitration clause. Lord Hamilton, in holding that it did not, said (at 1150–1):

> "the proper approach under Scots law [to a question whether an arbitration clause in one contract has been incorporated into another] is, while not requiring an express reference to an arbitration clause as a prerequisite to its incorporation, to hold it to have been incorporated only where it is in all the circumstances clear that the parties intended to embrace that clause within the scope of the clauses to be incorporated. Any difficulty or impracticability in adapting such a clause [in a main contract] to the circumstances of the subcontract is also ... a relevant consideration."

While that was a pre-Act case, the authors submit that it continues to apply in respect of s.4 of the Act.

Oral agreements

Given the significance of the fact that the parties are giving up the right to litigate and to reduce the scope for argument as to whether such an agreement has been entered into, both s.5(1) of the 1996 Act and art.7(2) of the Model Law adopt the approach that arbitration agreements must be in writing. However, art.7(3) of the Model Law makes it clear that "writing" comprehends any form of record of the agreement, including an oral agreement, and indeed certain situations in which the parties have acted as if they have an arbitration agreement. Oral agreements are not invalid under the 1996 Act (s.81(1)(b) refers) but Part I of that Act does not apply to them (s.5(1)); s.81(1)(b) preserves the common law as applicable to such agreements. The 2010 Act does not follow that approach. Section 4 covers oral arbitration agreements unless they are invalidated by other provisions of Scots law. S4–14

Since they do not appear in the list of agreements which require to be in writing in terms of s.1(1) and (2) of the Requirements of Writing (Scotland) Act 1995, there is nothing in principle to prevent oral arbitration agreements being effective under Scots law. Oral arbitration agreements will be extremely rare in any case and, if there is a dispute as to whether such an oral agreement has been reached or its terms (and therefore over the jurisdiction of a potential tribunal), it may be difficult to arrange for the appointment of a tribunal. S4–15

Awards deriving from an oral arbitration agreement will not be enforceable abroad under the New York Convention; arts II and IV(1)(b) refer. S4–16

Writing for foreign enforcement

The form of an arbitration agreement is also important from the point of view of enforcement of any award originating from the agreement. As part of the enforcement procedure in a foreign state under the New York Convention, the "agreement in writing" submitting the differences to arbitration must be produced to the competent authority of the state of enforcement (art.IV(1)(b)). S4–17

Article II(2) of the Convention provides that the "agreement in writing" shall S4–18

> "include an arbitral clause in a contract or an arbitration agreement, signed by the parties or contained in an exchange of letters or telegrams".

This indicates that if the arbitration agreement is in one document, it must be signed by the parties. The New York Convention was drafted in 1958 when letters and telegrams were the predominant means for the conclusion of contracts where parties did not sign one document. The purpose of the

Convention is to enable the enforcement of arbitral awards among countries which have adopted the Convention. Applying a purposive interpretation of "letters", exchange of electronic documents whether in the form of e-mail or other format should be sufficient to amount to an "agreement in writing" for the purposes of the Convention, although a few signatory states have not accepted this. The requirements for signature do not apply to an exchange of letters (properly interpreted) and telegrams.

Voidness or unenforceability for public policy

S4–19   If there was a contract for drug smuggling or other illegal or legally unenforceable activity and a dispute arose out of it that was covered by an arbitration clause in it, the arbitration clause itself, having been conceived in connection with an illegal activity, might be open to challenge on the grounds of illegality or being *contra bonos mores* or contrary to the public policy of Scots law. The same would apply to free-standing arbitration agreements covering such disputes. For a detailed treatment of contracts which are invalid or unenforceable on the grounds of *contra bonos mores* or public policy, see W.W. McBryde, *The Law of Contract in Scotland*, 3rd edn (Edinburgh: W. Green, 2007), Ch.19. In *O'Callaghan v Coral Racing Ltd* Unreported November 19, 1998 CA (Civ Div), Hirst L.J. observed that a hallmark of the arbitration process is a procedure that determines rights and obligations with binding effect and enforceable in law. On that basis the court concluded that an arbitration clause relating to a dispute arising out of a bet established a procedure devoid of legal consequences and could not be regarded as an arbitration agreement at all. It is suggested that the Scottish courts would adopt a similar approach. See also *Soleimany v Soleimany* [1999] Q.B. 785 and the commentary on s.30 (arbitrability of disputes).

Voidness for uncertainty

S4–20   In theory an arbitration agreement could be found to be void for uncertainty. Thus, in relation to a free-standing submission to arbitration created through the exchange of letters, there was found to be no *consensus in idem* in relation to the nature of the dispute to be submitted and the identity of the parties to that dispute (*Fronta Oceanica Brasileira v Steamship Underwriting Association (Bermuda) Ltd (The Frontanorte)* [1996] 2 Lloyd's Rep. 461). Cases under the old Scots common law such as *Bruce v Kordula,* 2001 S.L.T. 983 where there was voidness for uncertainty over the procedure for the appointment of the tribunal would now be decided differently in the light of the default r.7 in the SAR. Given the provisions for the appointment of an arbitrator in the 1950 Act (SAR rr.5–7 refer), it has been held that a clause in a contract which stated merely "Suitable Arbitration Clause" was a valid and enforceable arbitration agreement (*Hobbs Padgett & Co (Reinsurance) Ltd v J.C. Kirkland Ltd* [1969] 2 Lloyd's Rep. 547).

For the law which governs an arbitration agreement and would determine **S4–21** whether the agreement was void for uncertainty, see the commentary on s.6. For an international perspective see also the commentary on s.10(1)(e).

Unenforceability for unfairness in respect of consumers

In terms of the Unfair Terms Regulations, any unfair term in a contract **S4–22** concluded with a "consumer" by a "seller or supplier" is not binding on the consumer.

A "seller or supplier" is any natural or legal person who, in the agree- **S4–23** ment, is acting for purposes relating to his trade, business or profession, whether publicly owned or privately owned (Unfair Terms Regulations reg.3(1)). A "consumer" is any natural or legal person who, in the agreement, is acting for purposes which are outside his trade, business or profession (Unfair Terms Regulations reg.3(1), as extended by the 1996 Act s.90).

Where there is an arbitration agreement between (1) a seller or supplier; **S4–24** and (2) a consumer, the arbitration agreement is automatically "unfair" (and thus not binding on the consumer) in so far as it relates to a claim for a sum not exceeding £5,000 (Unfair Arbitration Agreements (Specified Amount) Order 1999 (SI 1999/2167) art.3).

An arbitration agreement between such persons will also be "unfair" (and **S4–25** thus not binding on the consumer) if it has not been individually negotiated and, contrary to the requirement of good faith, it causes a significant imbalance in the parties' rights and obligations arising under the main contract, to the detriment of the consumer (Unfair Terms Regulations reg.5(1)). An arbitration agreement is not individually negotiated if it has been drafted in advance and the consumer has therefore not been able to influence its substance of the term (Unfair Terms Regulations reg.5(2)).

For an unsuccessful attempt by a consumer to have an arbitration **S4–26** agreement found unfair, see *Heifer International Inc v Christiansen* [2008] 2 All E.R. (Comm) 831.

See Appendix 1 to this book for commentary concerning consumer **S4–27** arbitration

Separability

5.—(1) An arbitration agreement which forms (or was intended to form) part only of an agreement is to be treated as a distinct agreement.

(2) An arbitration agreement is not void, voidable or otherwise unenforceable only because the agreement of which it forms part is void, voidable or otherwise unenforceable.

(3) A dispute about the validity of an agreement which includes an arbitration agreement may be arbitrated in accordance with that arbitration agreement.

DEFINITIONS

"arbitration agreement": ss.4, 31(1)
"dispute": ss.2(1), 31(1)

MODEL LAW

S5–01   Article 7(1) of the Model Law (as amended in 2006) provides:

"An arbitration agreement may be in the form of an arbitration clause in a contract or in the form of a separate agreement."

S5–02   Article 16(1) provides:

"For that purpose [the arbitral tribunal ruling on its own jurisdiction] an arbitration clause which forms part of a contract shall be treated as an agreement independent of the other terms of the contract. A decision by the arbitral tribunal that the contract is null and void shall not entail ipso jure the invalidity of the arbitration clause."

COMMENTARY

S5–03   This section adopts the principle of separability, which is well established in most major arbitration regimes, including the 1996 Act and the Model Law.

S5–04   There is usually no difficulty in parties agreeing to arbitrate a dispute as to the meaning of their contract. But suppose the parties have entered into a contract which contains an arbitration clause and a dispute then arises as to the validity of that contract. Is it the case that the invalidity of the contract necessitates the invalidity of the arbitration clause? The old common law tended to support that proposition (see, e.g. *Ransohoff and Wissler v Burrell* (1897) 25 R. 284) but was out of line with modern practice and the Model Law.

S5–05   Alternatively, suppose the parties have entered into a contract with an arbitration clause and one party repudiates the contract and the repudiation is accepted by the other party who seeks damages. Does the arbitration clause survive the repudiation or termination of the contract to allow any dispute over the repudiation or the damages to be decided by arbitration? Under the old Scots common law, the arbitration clause did survive provided that its terms were wide enough to cover the dispute (*Sanderson v Armour*, 1922 S.C. (HL) 117).

S5–06   The 2010 Act has sought to bring clarity to both scenarios through s.5. In particular, s.5(3) has overturned the old common law as given by *Ransohoff and Wissler v Burrell* (1897) 25 R. 284 and has brought Scots law into line with modern international practice. Section 5(3) is helpfully more explicit than either s.7 of the 1996 Act or art.16 of the Model Law in providing that a dispute concerning the validity of the main agreement may be arbitrated in accordance with an arbitration clause within that agreement.

Section 5(1) and (2)

Section 5(1) requires an arbitration agreement which forms a clause in a contract dealing with other matters to be treated as if it was a distinct freestanding agreement. Thus challenges to the arbitration clause must be separated from challenges to the contract of which it forms part (*Fiona Trust and Holding Corp v Privalov* [2007] 4 All E.R. 951; 2007 UKHL 40 at [35] per Lord Hope of Craighead). This means that any challenge to the validity or enforceability of the arbitration clause must be made on grounds relating to that clause, although there may be cases (e.g. forgery) where the grounds of challenge to the clause will be identical with the challenge to the main contract (*Fiona Trust and Holding Corp v Privalov* [2007] 4 All E.R. 951; 2007 UKHL 40 at [17] per Lord Hoffmann). S5–07

Thus where a party sought to set aside an agreement which contained an arbitration clause on the grounds of duress (force and fear), it was held that this did not amount to a challenge to the arbitration clause and the litigation should be stayed (sisted) pending the challenge to the main agreement being arbitrated (*El Nasharty v J Sainsbury Plc* [2008] 1 Lloyd's Rep. 360). S5–08

Section 5(2) follows on from s.5(1) in providing that a finding that the main contract is void, voidable or otherwise unenforceable does not of itself render the arbitration clause equally void, voidable or otherwise unenforceable. Both the main contract and the arbitration clause must be treated separately. S5–09

It is also important to note that, like art.16 of the Model Law but unlike s.7 of the 1996 Act, parties cannot agree to have the arbitration agreement and the main contract treated as an *unum quid*. S5–10

Section 5(3)

As noted above, s.5(3) has overturned the old common law and brought it into line with modern international practice. While subs.(3), unlike subs.(2), does not refer to "enforceability" of the main contract, if that is something which is covered by the arbitration clause in question, it must be something which can be arbitrated under that clause. In *Fiona Trust and Holding Corp v Privalov* [2007] 4 All E.R. 951, the House of Lords held inter alia that a clause which referred "any dispute arising under this charter" to arbitration included a dispute as to whether the contract was invalid as having been procured by bribery. Lord Hoffmann held at [13] that such a clause should be interpreted on the presumption that the parties, as rational businessmen, were likely to have intended that any dispute arising out of the relationship they entered or purported to enter to be decided by arbitration unless the language made it clear that certain questions were excluded (see also Lord S5–11

S5–12　All of this assumes that the arbitration clause relates to a dispute that is arbitrable. As noted in the commentary on s.4, if the dispute is not of itself arbitrable, an arbitration agreement will not have the status of an arbitration agreement. See also commentary on s.30.

Hope at [26]). The same approach must apply to issues of whether the main contract was actually concluded and *consensus in idem* reached.

Law governing arbitration agreement

6. Where—
  (a) the parties to an arbitration agreement agree that an arbitration under that agreement is to be seated in Scotland, but
  (b) the arbitration agreement does not specify the law which is to govern it,
then, unless the parties otherwise agree, the arbitration agreement is to be governed by Scots law.

DEFINITIONS

"arbitration": ss.2(1), (2), 31(1)
"arbitration agreement": ss.4, 31(1)
"party": ss.2(1), 31(1), (2)
"seated in Scotland": ss.2, 31(1)

COMMENTARY

S6–01　The thrust of s.6 is that if the parties "agree" Scotland as the seat of their arbitration but the arbitration agreement does not specify the law governing the arbitration agreement, then that agreement will be governed by Scots law. However, the parties may agree to the contrary. While s.6 refers to the parties "agreeing" the seat, given that s.6 appears to be subsidiary to s.3, "agreement" of the seat should be interpreted as "designation" of the seat under s.3.

S6–02　Such agreement to the contrary will usually arise after the conclusion of the arbitration agreement, as and when the parties decide that, despite agreeing on Scotland as the seat, they would prefer a law other than that of Scotland to govern the arbitration agreement. Nonetheless, it is always possible for the arbitration agreement to designate Scotland as the seat but to declare that Scots law will not govern the agreement, leaving that issue to be decided in the traditional way.

S6–03　Given that the provision refers to the *arbitration agreement* not specifying the governing law thereof, it must be assumed that if a contract containing an arbitration clause features a provision designating the law which is to govern the main agreement, that will not amount to a specification of a law to govern the arbitration agreement.

S6–04　Institutional rules will play no role in this context, since the only set of rules known to the authors which features a choice of law provision is art.6

LMAA Terms which lay down the default rule that London is the seat of the arbitration and English law governs the agreement to arbitrate.

The issue of the law to govern the arbitration agreement is addressed by neither the 1996 Act nor the Model Law—at least not directly. Indeed, it is rarely directly addressed by arbitration statutes. The Swiss Private International Law Act 1987 art.178(2) and the Spanish Arbitration Act art.9(6) both provide that the arbitration agreement will be regarded as valid if it conforms with the law chosen by the parties, or the law governing the main agreement, or Swiss/Spanish law, but that is a long way removed from an actual choice of law provision. The only actual choice of law provision of which the authors are aware is s.48 of the Swedish Arbitration Act 1999, which indicates that international arbitration agreements shall be governed, in the absence of an express choice, by the law of the "country in which by virtue of the [arbitration agreement] the proceedings have taken place or shall take place". **S6–05**

Section 6 only applies where the Scottish seat has been designated by the agreement of the parties. Thus it does not apply where Scotland is designated as the seat by a third party, by the arbitral tribunal or by the court. This was an unfortunate oversight in drafting the Act. For this reason a tribunal or Scots court must still turn to Scots common law for the determination of the law to govern an arbitration agreement where s.6 does not apply. Arbitration agreements are excluded from the Rome I Regulation (Regulation (EC) No 593/2008 of the European Parliament and of the Council of 17 June 2008 on the law applicable to contractual obligations reg.1(2)(e)) and the Rome Convention (art.1(2)(d)) so the governing law falls to be decided under Scots common law using its rules of international private law for contracts in general. What is that Scots common law? Under the residual Scots common law rules of international private law a distinction is drawn between the rules applicable to: **S6–06**

(1) (i) the capacity of the parties;
    (ii) the formal validity of the contract, and
    (iii) the legality of the contract, and

(2) the interpretation, operation and substantive validity of the substantive provisions of the contract.

With regard to the rules relating to the formation of the agreement, capacity of the parties is to be determined by the *lex loci contractus* (*McFeetridge v Stewarts & Lloyds*, 1913 S.C. 773). In Scots law *lex loci contractus* in general means the law of the locality of the contract as ascertained from the nature of the contract and the place of performance or, if it is more important than performance, of the place where the contract was signed (*Valery v Scott* (1876) 3 R. 965 at 967). **S6–07**

For formal validity it is sufficient that the contract complies with either **S6–08** meaning of *lex loci contractus* (*Valery v Scott* (1876) 3 R. 965 and *Hamilton v Wakefield*, 1993 S.L.T. (Sh. Ct) 30).

S6–09   With regard to the legality of the arbitration agreement, which will be linked closely to the arbitrability of the dispute, the agreement must not be unlawful or contrary to essential public policy under both Scots law as the *lex arbitri* (*lex fori*) and the law governing the substantive validity, interpretation and operation of the contract (*English v Donnelly*, 1958 S.C. 494; *Hamlyn & Co v The Talisker Distillery* (1894) 21 R. (HL) 21 at 27, per Lord Watson; *Kahler v Midland Bank* [1950] A.C. 24).

S6–10   The interpretation and operation of the agreement is governed by the law chosen expressly or impliedly by the parties. If that does not determine the issue, the law would be that most closely connected with the agreement, taking account of various factors including the form of the agreement and the place of performance of the characteristic of the agreement (*James Miller & Partners Ltd v Whitworth Street Estates (Manchester) Ltd* [1970] A.C. 583). This law (whether chosen or not), known as the "proper law", will also govern questions relating to the formation of the contract such as the creation of *consensus in idem* other than matters of capacity or formal validity (A.E. Anton with P.R. Beaumont, *Private International Law*, 2nd edn (Edinburgh: W. Green, 1990), pp.282–283). In this respect, Scots common law reflects the common law of England and Wales.

S6–11   The approach to selecting the "proper law" of an arbitration agreement was considered by the English Court of Appeal in *Sulamerica CIA Nacional de Seguros S.A. v Enesa Engenharia S.A.* [2012] EWCA Civ 638 to be as follows:

> " ... the proper law is to be determined by undertaking a three-stage enquiry into (i) express choice, (ii) implied choice and (iii) closest and most real connection. As a principle those three stages ought to be embarked on separately and in that order, since any choice made by the parties ought to be respected, but it has been said on many occasions that in practice stage (ii) often merges into stage (iii), because identification of the system of law with which the agreement has its closest and most real connection is likely to be an important factor in deciding whether the parties have made an implied choice of proper law: see *Dicey, Morris & Collins, The Conflict of Laws 14th Ed* paragraph 32-006. Much attention has been paid in past cases to the closest and most real connection, but ... it is important not to overlook the question of implied choice of proper law, particularly when the parties have expressly chosen a system of law to govern the substantive contract of which the arbitration agreement forms part" at [25] per Moore-Bick L.J.

S6–12   In *Sulamerica*, the main contract stated that it was to be governed by Brazilian law. The arbitration clause provided for the seat to be London, England. The court, finding that in the circumstances the choice of Brazilian law was insufficient to indicate an implied choice for the arbitration clause, held at stage (iii) that the arbitration clause was governed by English law. This was in line with *C v D* [2008] 1 Lloyd's Rep. 239 at [22], where Longmore L.J. opined that:

> "if there is no express law of the arbitration agreement, the law with which the agreement has its closest and most real connection is more likely to be the law of the seat of the arbitration than the law of the underlying contract."

C v D was considered in Hew R. Dundas, "*C v D*: The USA Conquers England—or Does it? The Law of the Arbitration Agreement, Challenges to Awards and Abuse of Process" (2007) 73 *Arbitration* 431–440.

Courts elsewhere have also taken such an approach (e.g. *Ledee v Ceramich Ragno*, 684 F.2d 184 (1982); *Matermaco SA v PPM Cranes Inc* (2000) XXV YCA 653 Brussels Commercial Court; *Bulgarian Foreign Trade Bank Ltd v Al Trade Finance Inc* (2001) XXVI YCA 291 Swedish Supreme Court; compare the approach of the French Cour de Cassation which considers that the scope and validity of international arbitration agreements depends only on the intention of the parties, divorced from any national law—*Municipalite de Khoms El Megreb v Societe Dalico*, 1994 Revue de l'Arbitrage 116 at 117). **S6–13**

Indirect support for the view that the law of the forum should be the default choice of law to govern the arbitration agreement is also provided by art.V(1)(b) of the New York Convention which indicates that it is a ground for refusing enforcement of an arbitral award that the arbitration agreement is invalid under the law chosen by the parties, or, in the absence of any indication thereon, under the law of the place where the award was made. This is echoed by art.36(1)(a)(i) of the Model Law. **S6–14**

The governing law must be a law of a country and not some other non-state based set of rules. In this respect Scotland differs from e.g. France where the Cour de Cassation has considered that the scope and validity of international arbitration agreements depends only on the intention of the parties, divorced from any national law—*Municipalite de Khoms El Megreb v Societe Dalico*, 1994 Revue de l'Arbitrage 116 at 117. **S6–15**

Scottish Arbitration Rules

Scottish Arbitration Rules

7. The Scottish Arbitration Rules set out in schedule 1 are to govern every arbitration seated in Scotland (unless, in the case of a default rule, the parties otherwise agree).

DEFINITIONS

"arbitration": ss.2(1), (2), 31(1)
"default rule": ss.9(1), 31(1)
"party": ss.2(1), 31(1), (2)
"seated in Scotland": ss.2, 31(1)

COMMENTARY

S7–01 As indicated in the introduction to this commentary, the structure of the Act is strikingly unusual in dividing its main substance into the Act proper and Sch.1, which contains the SAR. That introduction also considers the juridical basis of the application of these rules. Suffice to say here then, that, prima facie, every arbitration seated in Scotland is to be governed by these rules, although as will be seen presently, the parties may contract out of certain of them.

Mandatory rules

8. The following rules, called "mandatory rules", cannot be modified or disapplied (by an arbitration agreement, by any other agreement between the parties or by any other means) in relation to any arbitration seated in Scotland—
   rule 3 (arbitrator to be an individual)
   rule 4 (eligibility to act as an arbitrator)
   rule 7 (failure of appointment procedure)
   rule 8 (duty to disclose any conflict of interests)
   rules 12 to 16 (removal or resignation of arbitrator or dismissal of tribunal)
   rules 19 to 21 and 23 (jurisdiction of tribunal)
   rules 24 and 25 (general duties of tribunal and parties)
   rule 42 (point of law referral: procedure etc.)
   rule 44 (time limit variation: procedure etc.)
   rule 45 (securing attendance of witnesses and disclosure of evidence)
   rule 48 (power to award payment and damages)
   rule 50 (interest)
   rule 54 (part awards)
   rule 56 (power to withhold award if fees or expenses not paid)
   rule 60 (arbitrators' fees and expenses)
   rule 63 (ban on pre-dispute agreements about liability for arbitration expenses)
   rules 67, 68, 70, 71 and 72 (challenging awards)
   rules 73 to 75 (immunity)
   rule 76 (loss of right to object)
   rule 77 (independence of arbitrator)
   rule 79 (death of arbitrator)
   rule 82 (rules applicable to umpires)

DEFINITIONS

"arbitration": ss.2(1), (2), 31(1)
"arbitration agreement": ss.4, 31(1)
"arbitrator": ss.2(1), 31(1)
"dispute": ss.2(1), 31(1)
"party": ss.2(1), 31(1), (2)
"rules": ss.7, 31(1)
"seated in Scotland": ss.2, 31(1)
"tribunal": ss.2(1), 31(1)

COMMENTARY

Certain of the SAR are mandatory rules of law, which apply irrespective of the will of the parties, and the Act sensibly follows s.4(1) and Sch.1 of the 1996 Act in stipulating which rules are mandatory and therefore which can be disapplied or varied by the agreement of the parties. The status of each rule is indicated by the appearance alongside it of the letter "D" (default) or "M" (mandatory). That approach is subject to the limitation that, unlike provisions in the 1996 Act, a rule cannot be mandatory only in part. That has led to certain provisions having to be split into two separate rules, one default and the other mandatory, when it has been realised that that the objectives of the Act could not be achieved if the rule were wholly default. This necessitated the creation of rr.23, 42, 44 and 70.   S8–01

The explanatory notes (para.29) observe that failure to conduct the proceedings in accordance with mandatory rules may make the arbitrator liable to removal (r.12(e) refers) and any award open to challenge (r.68(2)(a)(ii) refers).   S8–02

The question of which rules should be mandatory is very much a policy decision striking a balance between party autonomy and quality control in the public interest. The policy memorandum notes (para.85) that an attempt has been made to keep mandatory rules to a minimum, while reference is also made to ensuring "the fairness and impartiality of the process" (para.82), and the smooth and efficient running of the arbitration, as well as reducing the prospect of delay (para.83). The matters covered by the mandatory rules have been seen by the Scottish Parliament as of such general importance that they cannot be left to variation or exclusion by the particular parties in an arbitration.   S8–03

Default rules

9.—(1) The non-mandatory rules are called the "default rules".

(2) A default rule applies in relation to an arbitration seated in Scotland only in so far as the parties have not agreed to modify or disapply that rule (or any part of it) in relation to that arbitration.

(3) Parties may so agree—
  (a) in the arbitration agreement, or

(b) by any other means at any time before or after the arbitration begins.

(4) Parties are to be treated as having agreed to modify or disapply a default rule—

   (a) if or to the extent that the rule is inconsistent with or disapplied by—
      (i) the arbitration agreement,
      (ii) any arbitration rules or other document (for example, the UNCITRAL Model Law, the UNCITRAL Arbitration Rules or other institutional rules) which the parties agree are to govern the arbitration, or
      (iii) anything done with the agreement of the parties, or
   (b) if they choose a law other than Scots law as the applicable law in respect of the rule's subject matter.

This subsection does not affect the generality of subsections (2) and (3).

DEFINITIONS

"arbitration": ss.2(1), (2), 31(1)
"arbitration agreement": ss.4, 31(1)
"arbitrator": ss.2(1), 31(1)
"party": ss.2(1), 31(1), (2)
"rules": ss.7, 31(1)
"seated in Scotland": ss.2, 31(1)
"UNCITRAL Arbitration Rules": s.31(1)

COMMENTARY

Section 9(1), (2) and (3)—When rules may be modified or disapplied

S9–01 The majority of the rules are default rules which may be modified or disapplied, whether in whole or in part, by the agreement of the parties. This ensures maximum party autonomy and flexibility. The default rules ensure a ready made procedural framework on which the parties can (and, in fact, are recommended to) rely if they so choose, or indeed on which they can fall back if they prove unable to agree how to proceed (see policy memorandum, paras 86–88).

S9–02 Section 9(3) goes further than s.4 of the 1996 Act in making it plain that the parties may reach agreement to modify or disapply any non-mandatory rules even after the arbitration has begun. Moreover, while any such agreement under the 1996 Act would require to be in writing, under s.9(3) there is no need for the agreement to take any particular form. However, s.9(3) contemplates express agreement. Implicit modification or disapplication arises under s.9(4).

Section 9(4)(a)(i)—How rules may be modified or disapplied

The arbitration agreement need not explicitly exclude particular default rules. If, for example, it specifies a method of appointing the tribunal which is at odds with r.6, that rule will be excluded to the extent that it is inconsistent with the agreement. **S9–03**

Section 9(4)(a)(ii)—Arbitration rules

This provision to some degree echoes s.4(3) of the 1996 Act. A number of sets of arbitration rules have been developed to govern domestic and/or international arbitration or arbitrations dealing with particular types of dispute or within given industries. Many of these rules are very comprehensive and, if adopted by the parties, would cover most if not all of the matters dealt with by the default rules. **S9–04**

The Act makes it clear that, if the parties agree that such rules should apply, they will prevail over the default rules to the extent that the latter are inconsistent with the chosen rules. Of course the chosen rules will have no effect to the extent that they are inconsistent with any mandatory rule. **S9–05**

For example, if the parties agree to arbitrate under the ICC Rules, art.34.6 of which excludes recourse to the court, that will constitute a valid exclusion of a challenge on the basis of error of law, since r.69 is a default rule, but cannot exclude challenges on the basis of serious procedural irregularity or lack of jurisdiction, since rr.67 and 68 are mandatory. The provision takes the interesting step of citing the UNCITRAL Rules as an example of a set of institutional rules. This reflects the underlying policy drive to emphasise that the Act is friendly to international arbitrations and the international recognition of those Rules as providing a model for arbitral rules. **S9–06**

The reference to the default rules being inconsistent with another document, such as the UNCITRAL Model Law, which the parties have adopted is clearly a concession to the body of opinion which argued for the direct wording of the Model Law to be adopted against the replacement of the Model Law by the new legislative regime. The parties could always attempt to achieve this effect under s.9(4)(b) (which allows the parties to disapply the default rules by choosing a foreign procedural law) by choosing a foreign procedural law based on the Model Law, albeit that it would then be uncertain whether the Scots courts would be prepared to support that arbitration—see s.13(4) below. **S9–07**

Section 9(4)(a)(iii)—Conduct with parties' agreement

The tribunal may take steps in an arbitration which are not in accordance with a default rule. However, if such steps are done with the agreement of the parties, the taking of such steps will be seen as a modification or disapplication of the default rule. **S9–08**

Section 9(4)(b)—Choice of foreign procedural law

S9–09 Like s.4(5) of the 1996 Act, this provision indicates that agreement to disapply non-mandatory rules may take the form of invoking a law other than the law of Scotland. Thus if the parties agree that Scotland should be the seat of the arbitration, but that French law should govern the arbitration, French law will prevail over the default rules but not the mandatory rules of Sch.1. A choice of French law to govern the substance of the dispute (as opposed to governing the arbitration) will not exclude any default rules (see *C v D* [2007] 2 Lloyd's Rep. 367).

S9–10 An arbitration seated in Scotland but subject to a foreign procedural law opens up all sorts of possibilities for mishaps and confusion; such arbitrations should be strongly discouraged. For example, if court intervention is sought, in most cases a foreign court will decline to become involved in an arbitration seated outwith its jurisdiction (see *Naviera Amazonica Peruans SA v Cia Internacional de Seguros del Peru* [1988] 1 Lloyd's Rep. 116 at 120), while it is by no means certain that the Scottish courts will be willing to act as contemplated by that foreign procedural law. Thus it is not surprising that English experience suggests that the courts will strive to interpret the parties' agreement as not making this election (see, e.g. *ABB Lummus Global Ltd v Keppel Fels Ltd* [1999] 2 Lloyd's Rep. 24 at 35 per Clarke J.)

Suspension of legal proceedings

Suspension of legal proceedings

10.—(1) The court must, on an application by a party to legal proceedings concerning any matter under dispute, sist those proceedings in so far as they concern that matter if—

 (a) **an arbitration agreement provides that a dispute on the matter is to be resolved by arbitration (immediately or after the exhaustion of other dispute resolution procedures),**
 (b) **the applicant is a party to the arbitration agreement (or is claiming through or under such a party),**
 (c) **notice of the application has been given to the other parties to the legal proceedings,**
 (d) **the applicant has not—**
   (i) **taken any step in the legal proceedings to answer any substantive claim against the applicant, or**
   (ii) **otherwise acted since bringing the legal proceedings in a manner indicating a desire to have the dispute resolved by the legal proceedings rather than by arbitration, and**
 (e) **nothing has caused the court to be satisfied that the arbitration agreement concerned is void, inoperative or incapable of being performed.**

(2) Any provision in an arbitration agreement which prevents the bringing of

the legal proceedings is void in relation to any proceedings which the court refuses to sist.

This subsection does not apply to statutory arbitrations.

(3) This section applies regardless of whether the arbitration concerned is to be seated in Scotland.

DEFINITIONS

"arbitration": ss.2(1), (2), 31(1)
"arbitration agreement": ss.4, 31(1)
"court": s.31(1)
"dispute": ss.2(1), 31(1)
"party": ss.2(1), 31(1), (2)
"statutory arbitrations": ss.16(1), 31(1)

MODEL LAW

The Model Law provides, in art.8:   S10–01

"(1) A court before which an action is brought in a matter which is the subject of an arbitration agreement shall, if a party so requests not later than when submitting his first statement on the substance of the dispute, refer the parties to arbitration unless it finds that the agreement is null and void, inoperative or incapable of being performed.
(2) Where an action referred to in paragraph (1) of this article has been brought, arbitral proceedings may nevertheless be commenced or continued, and an award may be made, while the issue is pending before the court."

Article 8 of the Model Law is based on art.II(3) of the New York Convention but with the additional provision that the court's duty to refer appropriate cases to arbitration arises no later than submission by the party seeking referral of his first statement on the substance of the dispute.

COMMENTARY

Introductory

Scots common law, in contrast to English common law, traditionally   S10–02
respected the right of the parties to have an arbitrable dispute determined by an arbiter (arbitrator), rather than by the court. Thus in *Hamlyn & Co v Talisker Distillery* (1894) 21 R. (HL) 21, Lord Watson observed at 27:

"The law of Scotland has, from the earliest times, permitted private parties to exclude the merits of any dispute between them from the consideration of the court by simply naming their arbiter."

This included the resolution of disputes by foreign (e.g. English) arbitrators as in the *Hamlyn* case itself, and disputes under foreign arbitration agreements. The means by which courts gave effect to this right at common law was to sist (stay) any court proceedings in relation to the dispute pending the determination of the dispute by arbitration. In contrast to the position in England, the court was obliged to sist if a party pointed to a binding arbitration agreement in respect of the subject-matter of the proceedings (see Lord Dunedin in *Sanderson v Armour*, 1922 S.C. (HL) 117 at 120 and 126).

S10–03 After the UK adopted the New York Convention, s.1 of the 1975 Act was enacted to give effect to art.II of the Convention across the Unoted Kingdom. Section 1 of the 1975 Act did not innovate on the common law position. Section 10 seeks to place the matter on a statutory footing as regards both domestic and non-domestic arbitration agreements, much as s.9 of the 1996 Act does in England. The common law is thus supplanted. Again, the provision carries distinct echoes of art.8 of the Model Law. There are some similarities with s.9 of the 1996 Act but also some differences to take account of the traditionally different approaches to sists (stays) and the use of judicial proceedings in support of arbitration under Scots and English law respectively.

S10–04 Section 10 applies to arbitration agreements whether or not the arbitrations in them are seated in Scotland: see s.10(3).

Obligation to sist (stay)

S10–05 The court is, subject to a variety of conditions, obliged to sist (stay) any legal proceedings if it is satisfied that it has been agreed that the matter under dispute is to be settled by arbitration. It is for the party making the application to satisfy the court in this regard. It can be seen that proceedings may only be sisted in part if other aspects of the proceedings concern issues which are not the subject of an arbitration agreement. Thus a court must grant a sist if a party can point to an arbitration agreement or, for example, to an agreement which insists that a dispute must be referred to mediation and then to arbitration if no settlement is reached. Under Scots (but not English) common law, once the court was satisfied that the arbitration agreement covered the matter under dispute before it, the court was obliged to sist the proceedings pending the outcome of the arbitration and did not have a discretion to refuse to sist (*Roxburgh v Dinardo*, 1981 S.L.T. 291 following Lord Dunedin in *Sanderson v Armour*, 1922 S.C. (HL) 117 at 126). This absence of discretion has been preserved in s.10.

Effect of sist

S10–06 Article 8 of the Model Law sees the court in such a context actually referring the parties to arbitration but that would not be the effect of a sist, which merely suspends the judicial proceedings (see Lord Watson in *Hamlyn*

& Co v Talisker Distillery (1894) 21 R. (HL) 21 at 25 and 27; *Channel Tunnel Group Ltd v Balfour Beatty Construction Ltd* [1993] A.C. 334 per Lord Mustill at 345H–346A). This might seem to run contrary to the terms of art.II(3) of the New York Convention, which does appear to require that the parties be referred to arbitration. However, there is an argument that such is not the intention of the Convention, which fact is clear from reading the original French version of art.II(3) (see Claude Reymond, "The Channel Tunnel Case and the Law of International Arbitration" (1993) 109 L.Q.R. 337).

Should the arbitration for any reason prove abortive, for example if there was unreasonable delay in securing the appointment of a tribunal or pursuant to an award of no jurisdiction, any party can apply to the court to recall the sist and determine the merits of the dispute. In that situation the full jurisdiction of the court would revive (*Hamlyn & Co v Talisker Distillery* (1894) 21 R. (HL) 21 at 25). **S10–07**

The sist can also be recalled temporarily during the arbitration to allow the court to take steps to support the arbitration under rr.41–46. **S10–08**

Once an award is made on the merits the sist can be recalled and the court invited to grant decree (issue judgment) in accordance with the award. **S10–09**

Necessity and form of application

Given that the court retains jurisdiction even where the parties have agreed to have the dispute arbitrated, the court will not sist court proceedings for arbitration unless a party applies for a sist. This is reflected in s.10, the Model Law and the New York Convention. **S10–10**

How a party applies for a sist will depend on which party seeks the sist and when a sist is sought. A pursuer who wishes to have the dispute resolved by arbitration may nevertheless have raised court proceedings in order to obtain interim measures such as diligence on the dependence or interim interdict (*McDougall v Argyll & Bute DC*, 1987 S.L.T. 7). In that event the pursuer should include in the summons or initial writ the arbitration agreement together with a plea along the lines: **S10–11**

> "The parties having agreed to arbitration upon the subject-matter of the action, the action should be sisted pending such arbitration" (*Inverclyde (Mearns) Housing Association Ltd v Lawrence Construction Co Ltd*, 1989 S.L.T. 815 at 821F).

The pursuer should apply for a sist after the request for the interim measure has been disposed of. This is to avoid any possible argument that he is barred by s.10(1)(d)(ii) from seeking a sist. **S10–12**

A defender who wishes to go to arbitration should apply for a sist before lodging defences (s.10(1)(d)(i)). Failure to do so may bar either the pursuer or defender, or both, from thereafter having the dispute arbitrated. **S10–13**

S10–14 Aside from the necessity to aver the arbitration agreement and insert a plea-in-law in any pleadings that have been lodged with the court, there is some doubt as to the form of an application for a sist. A common law application would be made by motion in the court proceedings. This continues to apply for s.10 applications in the sheriff and other courts. In the Court of Session, doubt has been caused by RCS r.100.5 which provides, without excluding s.10, that applications under the 2010 Act in the Court of Session are to be made by petition in fresh proceedings under the 2010 Act. On the face of it, until RCS r.100.5 is modified, an application to the Court of Session will have to be made by a separate petition process unless it can be argued successfully that an application for sist is not "under" the 2010 Act in that s.10 does not give power to make the application but rather sets out what the court is to do upon such an application being made. The delay and expense caused by such a separate petition process is clearly undesirable.

Court granting sist

S10–15 In s.10, the decision of the "court" is not restricted to the Court of Session or sheriff court (see s.31(1), below). What other courts could be covered? The only other court in Scotland is the Scottish Land Court.

S10–16 On an ordinary meaning of "court", s.10 does not extend to tribunals. Nevertheless, various tribunals have jurisdictions over claims which could be resolved through the agreement of the parties and are prima facie arbitrable (see commentary on s.30). It is conceivable that the reference to "any court" in the context of s.10 was intended to cover any non-arbitral tribunal with jurisdiction in Scotland to resolve in legal proceedings any dispute that parties agreed to be resolved by arbitration. Furthermore, such an interpretation of "any court" for the purposes of s.10 would be supported by founding principle (b) in s.1.

Legal proceedings subject to sist

S10–17 The obligation to sist relates to "legal proceedings concerning any matter under dispute". It will cover a petition for relief from unfairly prejudicial conduct under s.994 of the Companies Act 2006 (*Fulham Football Club (1987) Ltd v Richards* [2012] Ch. 333).

S10–18 The legal proceedings must seek to determine the merits of the dispute. Thus a pre-action petition or summary application for recovery of documents or information under s.1 of the 1972 Act will not be capable of being sisted as that does not determine the merits of the dispute (*EDO Corp v Ultra Electronics Ltd* [2009] EWHC 682 (Ch)), nor will a statutory demand for payment which is not a legal proceeding at all (*Shalson v DF Keane Ltd* [2003] EWHC 599 (Ch)).

Approach to opposed application

Suppose a party in the litigation denies that there is an arbitration agreement? How should the court deal with such an opposition to a sist? Before the 2010 Act the matter was straightforward since Scottish arbitrators (arbiters) did not have the competence to rule on their own jurisdiction, the court would decide the argument either on the motion roll or at a legal debate or at a proof (civil trial). So far as the authors are aware, there have been no reported Scottish cases under s.1 of the 1975 Act. S10–19

The 2010 Act changed the common law by giving a Scottish arbitral tribunal a power, at least in the first instance, to rule on inter alia whether there is a valid arbitration agreement and what matters have been submitted to arbitration in accordance with the agreement (r.19). S10–20

The tribunal's ruling can be appealed to the Outer House either under r.21 or r.67. In the case of an appeal under r.67, there is the possibility of leave to appeal to the Inner House. Alternatively, there is the possibility of a direct referral from the tribunal to the Outer House under rr.22 and 23 unless default r.22 has been excluded. Both an appeal under r.21 or a direct referral under r.22 allow the arbitration to continue pending the determination by the Outer House if that is appropriate. S10–21

In contrast, the court's ruling under s.10 is appealable from the Outer House without leave and from the sheriff with leave against the refusal of a sist, up the court hierarchy in theory to the UKSC. Refusal to sist can also leave open the possibility of ongoing parallel proceedings before the court and arbitral tribunal respectively. S10–22

It is suggested that there are a number of possible approaches that the court could take. The most obvious are: first, to hold a full scale legal debate or proof (civil trial) on the issue; or secondly, to decide the argument on a prima facie basis, possibly taking into account the convenience to all parties. S10–23

The arbitral regimes of some countries (e.g. France) entail the court deferring to the arbitral tribunal except if an arbitral tribunal has not yet been seized of the dispute and if the arbitration agreement is manifestly void or manifestly not applicable (French Code of Civil Procedure art.1448). S10–24

In Hong Kong (see Kaplan J. in *Fun Sang Trading Ltd v Kui Sun Sea Products & Food Co Ltd* [1992] A.D.R.L.J. 93 at 101); Canada (*Dalimpex Ltd v Janicki* [2003] 172 O.A.C. 321) and India (*Shin-Etsu Chemical Co v Aksh Opticfibre Ltd* (2006) XXXI YCA 747) the second approach is followed. Switzerland also broadly adopts the approach outlined above (*Fondation M v Banque X*, ATF 122 III 139, ASA Bulletin 527, Swiss Fed. Trib. Apr. 29 1996) but only where the arbitral agreement provides for a Swiss seat. The reasoning is that where the tribunal has a Swiss seat, the court will have the final say in an appeal against the award, whereas if it has a foreign seat, it will not. S10–25

Under the 1996 Act a court considers, first, whether it can decide in a summary fashion on the written evidence before it that the applicant has S10–26 satisfied the court that the matter being litigated is covered by a concluded arbitration agreement. Secondly, if it cannot make such a summary decision, it has a choice whether to hold a civil trial on the issue or to sist the proceedings leaving the matter to the tribunal to decide the issue under the equivalent of r.19 (*JSC Aeroflot-Russian Airlines v Berezovsky* [2013] EWCA Civ 784 at [73] per Aikens L.J. following *Al-Naimi v Islamic Press Agency* [2000] 1 Lloyd's Rep. 522). The various factors bearing on the choice were discussed at length in *Al-Naimi* in the context of English procedure. The same approach applies in relation to any issue as to the arbitration agreement being "void, inoperative or incapable of being performed". In relation to that aspect in *JSC Aeroflot-Russian Airlines v Berezovsky* [2013] EWCA Civ 784, Aikens L.J. observed at [79]:

> "In theory I suppose the court could order that there be a trial of an issue to determine whether the arbitration agreement was "null and void" or "inoperative". But if the evidence and possible findings going to the issue of whether the arbitration agreement is "null and void" or "inoperative" also impinge on the substantive rights and obligations of the parties the court is unlikely to do so unless such a trial can be confined to "a relatively circumscribed area of "investigation" (*A. v. B.* [2006] EWHC 2006 (Comm), [2007] 1 Lloyd's Rep. 237 at [137] per Colman J.), Otherwise, in such a case, where the court is satisfied of the existence of the arbitration agreement and that the matters in dispute are within its scope, then logically it must be for the arbitral tribunal finally to decide the 'section 9(4) matters', ["null and void" etc.] assuming it has *compétence-compétence* to do so."

S10–27 *A v B* (above) was a case of a foreign arbitration agreement with a foreign-seated arbitration where it was alleged that the arbitration agreement was "null and void" due to fraudulent misrepresentation and duress. Colman J. observed (at [138]) that if the foreign curial law allowed the arbitral tribunal to determine whether the agreement was void for such reasons, the English court should be slow to displace the arbitral regime that the parties had decided to apply to such matters; this was because the emphasis in modern international arbitration law is to maximise the arbitrators' opportunity to determine their own jurisdiction.

S10–28 In relation to Scots law, it must be borne in mind that s.10 must be construed in accordance with founding principles (a) and (b) in s.1 of the Act (see the commentary on s.1). Put shortly, those principles are that parties should be free to agree to resolve disputes subject only to safeguards which are necessary in the public interest and that the object of arbitration is to resolve disputes without unnecessary delay or expense.

S10–29 "Denial" of an arbitration agreement under s.10(1)(a), (b) or (e) can take a number of forms. Mainly it involves (i) a claim that there is no such agreement or the applicant is not a party thereto (see above), or that the agreement is invalid for some reason (see below); or (ii) a concession that there is some arbitration agreement between the parties but that the matter under dispute in the court proceedings is not within the scope of the arbitration agreement.

Looking at a type (i) objection, the authors suggest that a court should take a prima facie approach in making its decision under s.10(1)(a) and (b) and a "manifestly satisfied" approach under s.10(1)(e). Such a construction of those provisions is consistent with the founding principles of the Act that have been mentioned. To allow a full assessment of the validity of the arbitration clause would risk undue delay and expense in the resolution of the dispute as a whole when the arbitral tribunal has ample powers to make the full assessment itself and is (or will be) best placed to assess whether it should be carried out prior to or at the same time as the merits. If r.22 has not been disapplied or modified, there is also the possibility of a direct reference to the Outer House. **S10–30**

A full assessment approach by the court could, certainly for domestic arbitration agreements, render the resolution of the dispute slower than it would have been without any arbitration agreement. In addition, it could lead to an appeal as to jurisdiction to be taken to the UKSC, at least in theory. That cannot have been the purpose of the 2010 Act, which in contrast to the 1996 Act, does not allow an appeal against an award on jurisdiction to be taken to the UKSC. If the issue is to be decided under a foreign law then that would be a further factor in support of a prima facie or manifestly satisfied assessment. **S10–31**

A type (ii) objection to a sist involves the interpretation of the arbitration agreement (see commentary on s.4). Often, but not always, this can be done without the leading of evidence. Sometimes evidence is necessary to establish the factual context in which the agreement was entered into. While there may be more scope to argue for a full assessment to be carried out by the court, the authors submit that a prima facie approach would be appropriate here also for the same reasons as discussed above. **S10–32**

It is of note that, under the common law, when the court was faced with an application to interdict an existing arbitration on the basis of a type (ii) objection, the court would consider whether the objection was plainly well founded and, only if it was, would they interdict the arbitrators from deciding the issue (*Dumbarton Water Commissioners v Lord Blantyre* (1884) 12 R. 115 at 119; *McCosh v Moore* (1905) 5 F. 946). This is entirely consistent with the prima facie approach and if anything is more consistent with the French approach set out above. **S10–33**

In apparent contrast to English procedure it is not usual Scottish practice for affidavits to be used in connection with applications to sist. **S10–34**

Arbitration (Scotland) Act 2010

Section 10(1)(a),(b) and (e)

S10–35 The basic requirements for an obligation on the court to sist the proceedings are (i) that the arbitration agreement provides that a dispute on the matter in dispute is to be resolved by arbitration, (ii) that the applicant seeking the sist is party to the arbitration agreement and (iii) that nothing has caused the court to be satisfied that the arbitration agreement concerned is void, inoperative or incapable of being performed. These requirements are specified in more detail in paras (a), (b), and (e) of subs.(1). The requirements in paras (a) and (b) are for the applicant to satisfy. By contrast, under para.(e) the opponent of a sist must satisfy the court that the arbitration agreement concerned is void etc. although the court can also raise the matter on its own initiative.

Arbitration agreement covering litigated dispute

S10–36 The matter under dispute in the court action must be a matter that an arbitration agreement provides must be resolved by arbitration. Whether the litigated matter falls within the arbitration agreement will depend on the interpretation or construction of the arbitration agreement: see commentaries on ss.4, 2, 5 and 6.

Party to arbitration agreement or claiming through or under such party

S10–37 An applicant must be a party to the arbitration agreement or at least be claiming "through or under any such party". This reflects s.82(2) of the 1996 Act and s.7(2) and (4) of the Australian International Arbitration Act 1974.

S10–38 Singular successors of landlords (i.e. purchasers) under a lease will themselves be parties to the arbitration agreement contained within a commercial lease (*Montgomerie v Carrick* (1848) 10 D. 1387) and the same principle will apply to assignees of an original party's rights under a contract which may include an arbitration agreement. Where the contract and arbitration agreement are governed by Scots law, intimation of the assignation to the creditor is required in order to make the assignee step into the shoes of the assignor (cedent) and become a party to the contract and arbitration agreement.

S10–39 However, even where an assignee has not become a party to the arbitration agreement, he may be a person claiming "through or under" the assignor who is still party to the agreement (*Schiffahrtsgesellschaft Detlev von Appen GmbH v Voest Alpine Intertrading GmbH (The Jay Bola)* [1997] C.L.C. 993 at 1000 per Hobhouse L.J., followed in relation to an insurer claiming under a statutory right of subrogation in *Through Transport Mutual Insurance Association (Eurasia) Ltd v New India Assurance Co Ltd* [2005] 1 C.L.C. 376 at [20] to [28] per Moore-Bick J.)

S10–40 In the Australian case *Tanning Research Laboratories Inc v O'Brien* [1990] HCA 8, Brennan and Dawson JJ. held at [11] that a liquidator may be a person claiming through or under a company in liquidation if the causes of action or grounds of defence on which he relies are vested in or exercisable by the company and a trustee in bankruptcy may be such a person on the same basis because the causes of action or grounds of defence on which he relies were vested in or exercisable by the bankrupt. It was observed in *Tanning* that the essence of a person claiming through or under a party was that the claim was derived from the party. This would appear to admit claims by agents of parties to arbitration agreements.

Where a parent company is party to an agreement, it has been held in England that a claim by a subsidiary is not per se a claim "through or under a party" to the agreement (*City of London v Sancheti* [2008] 2 C.L.C. 730). In the USA, a different view has been reached where claims are brought against both companies based on the same facts (*J.J. Ryan & Sons v Rhone Poulenc Textile, S.A.* [1988] USCA4 2036). **S10–41**

The holder of a *jus quaesitum tertio* (right conferred by contract to a third party) by virtue of a contract which also contains an arbitration agreement governed by Scots law will not be bound by and therefore not be a party to the arbitration agreement, given the absence of a Scottish equivalent of s.8 of the Contracts (Rights of Third Parties) Act 1999. **S10–42**

A party to the legal proceedings who is neither a party nor a claimant through or under a party to the arbitration agreement cannot seek a sist (for a consideration of the Australian authorities see *BHPB Freight Pty Ltd v Cosco Oceania Chartering Pty Ltd* [2008] F.C.A. 551, where a party claiming the benefit of the English equivalent of a *jus quaesitum tertio* was held not to be claiming through or under a party to the agreement). **S10–43**

Arbitration agreement not "void, inoperative or incapable of being performed"—General

These words originate from s.1(1) of the 1975 Act which in turn took them from art.II(3) of the New York Convention. The words are also used in art.8(1) of the Model Law. The meaning of these terms are individually considered below but it should be borne in mind that, reflecting civil law practice, neither the Convention nor the Model Law was drafted with the terminological exactitude of a UK statute and both employ expressions which require to make sense in a variety of languages. Thus it has been held that the three grounds tend to overlap (see, e.g. *Jean Charbonneau v Les Industries AC Davie Inc* Unreported March 14, 1989 Supreme Court of Quebec), and should be read together. Although s.1(1) of the 1975 Act introduced these grounds only in relation to sists arising out of non-UK jurisdiction seated arbitrations, the effect of their use in s.10 of the 2010 Act is to apply them in relation to sists arising out of arbitrations anywhere in the world, wherever seated. **S10–44**

Application of s.10(1)(e)

S10–45 On the face of it, "void, inoperative or incapable of being performed" should be assessed by reference to the law governing the arbitration agreement (s.6 refers). Should the international origin of the wording in s.10(1)(e) affect its application in any way? In France, the Paris Cour d'Appel in *Gatoil v National Iranian Oil Co* (1993) Revue de l'Arbitrage 281, even suggested that validity should be assessed not according to any national law but "solely in light of the requirements of international public policy". This has proved rather too bold an approach for some (e.g. the Genoa Court of Appeal in *Della Sanara Kustvaart v Fallimento Cap Giovanni Coppola Srl* (1992) XVII YCA 542). However, echoes of that approach are to be found in the statement of the US Court of Appeals in *Ledee v Ceramiche Ragno*, 684 F.2d 184 (1981) at 187:

> "The goal of the Convention ... was to encourage the recognition and enforcement of commercial arbitration agreements in international contracts and to unify the standards by which agreements to arbitrate are observed ... in signatory countries. The parochial interests of ... any state cannot be the measure of how the 'null and void' clause is interpreted ... Rather, the clause must be interpreted to encompass only those situations—such as fraud, mistake, duress and waiver—that can be applied neutrally on an international scale."

S10–46 In *JSC Aeroflot-Russian Airlines v Berezovsky* [2013] EWCA Civ 784 at [73] it was noted that an English court should not interpret the phrase in an "anglo-centric" way but in a broad, international sense. The authors respectfully commend that view to the Scottish courts.

Section 10(1)(e)—"Void"

S10–47 The Convention, the Model Law and the 1975 Act each refer to the agreement being null and void, as indeed does s.9 of the 1996 Act, but it must be assumed that the omission of the former term makes no difference, since the French version simply refers to the agreement being "caduque", and the Spanish version, "to nulo". There is authority in England that, since courts there have to make a full assessment of whether the arbitration agreement has been entered into, this category cannot mean to cover opposition to a stay on the grounds that there was no arbitration agreement at all, for example because a party's signature to the agreement was forged but rather covers agreements admittedly entered into but subject to an internationally recognised defence such as duress, mistake, fraud or waiver (*Albon v Naza Motor Trading SDN BHD* [2007] EWHC 665 (Ch); relying on the US case *Rhone Mediterranee v Achille Lauro*, 712 F.2d 50 (1983)).

S10–48 There is also considerable international case law under both the Convention and the Model Law, e.g. courts outside the UK have held that an agreement, providing for arbitration in and under the law of a "3rd country" under specified procedural rules which did not exist, was not void (*Lucky-Goldstar International (HK) Ltd v Ng Moo Kee Engineering Ltd* [1994] A.D.R.L.J. 49; see also *Laboratorios Grossman v Forest Laboratories*, 295 N.Y. Supp. (2d) 756 (1985)). Further, an agreement is not void for uncertainty where it is based on mutual (common) error as to the applicable provisions of the law of the seat (*China Resources Metal Ltd v Anada Non-Ferrous Metals Ltd* [1994] 3 H.K.C. 526). Further, it is not void where it provides that a dispute "may" be referred to arbitration (*China State Construction Engineering Corp Guandong Branch v Madiford Ltd* [1992] 1 H.K.C. 320). In addition, it is not void where it provides that the matter may be decided by litigation or arbitration (*William Co v Chiu Kong Agency Ltd* [1995] 2 H.K.L.R. 139) since there will be a valid arbitration agreement at the point when a party elects to arbitrate.

The authors submit that the approach in *Lovelock Ltd v Exportles* [1968] 1 Lloyd's Rep. 163, where an agreement containing a clause referring "any dispute" to arbitration in England was followed by a clause referring "any other dispute" to arbitration in Russia was held to be void for uncertainty, is inconsistent with developments in modern arbitration law which seek to give effect to the parties' choice of arbitration. Issues as to the juridical seat of the arbitration can be resolved: see commentary on s.3. If the party opposing a sist was induced to agree to arbitration by fraud that could render it void (*Riley v Kingsley Underwriting Agencies*, 969 F.2d 953 (1992)).

S10–49

Section 10(1)(e)—"Inoperative"

"Inoperative" seems to denote an agreement which was initially valid, but which for some reason no longer carries legal force (see Max Bonnell, "When is an Arbitration Agreement 'Inoperative'?" (2008) 11 Int. A.L.R. 111). An arbitration agreement has been held to be inoperative where the subject matter of the dispute was arbitrable under the governing law (see *Aguna v Smith Industries* (1983) VIII YCA 360) and where the agreement allowed a party to elect either to arbitrate or to bring proceedings before a US regulatory authority and the latter choice had clearly been made (*Fowler v Merrill Lynch Pierce and Smith Inc* (1985) X YCA 499. In another case, an arbitration agreement was held not to be inoperative where the agreement provided for a reference to arbitration if, within a certain time limit, one party gave a notice of arbitration and that time limit was not adhered to (*China Merchant Heavy Industry Co Ltd v JGC Corp* (2003) XXVIII YCA 267)); where parties have waived the right to arbitrate (see, e.g. *ACD Tridon Inc v Tridon Australia Pty Ltd* (2004) XIX YCA 533). Further, an arbitration agreement was held not to be inoperative in both (i) *Halvanon Insurance Co Ltd v Companhia de Seguros do Estado de Sao Paolo* [1995] L.R.L.R 403, where a party was estopped (i.e. personally barred) from seeking to arbitrate

S10–50

and (ii) in *Corcoran v Adra Insurance Company Ltd* (1989) XIV YCA 733 where the agreement had been impliedly revoked.

S10-51 But an arbitration agreement is not inoperative simply because arbitration may produce an unenforceable award (*Molino e Pacifico Ponte San Giovanni Spa v Anrde & Cie SA* (1983) VIII YCA 378 Italian Supreme Court), or may involve multiple arbitral proceedings (*Svenska Handelsbanken v India Charge Chrome Ltd* (1996) XXI YCA 557 at 566 Indian Supreme Court).

Section 10(1)(e)—"Incapable of being performed"

S10-52 The idea that the agreement may be incapable of being performed suggests that the agreement is entirely valid. In *Gatoil International Plc v National Iranian Oil Company* Unreported February 22, 1990 CA (Civ Div), Bingham L.J. said:

> "The words "incapable of being performed" are a strong expression, in my judgment denoting impossibility, or practical impossibility, and certainly not mere inconvenience or difficulty. A mere change of circumstances rendering arbitration a less attractive mode of resolving a dispute or rendering the forum or the procedural rules chosen for any reason unattractive, could never be enough. For a party who has agreed to resolve any dispute by arbitration to be freed from his obligation under section 1(1) [of the 1975 Act] it is, in my judgment, necessary for him to show that the arbitration agreement simply cannot, with the best will in the world, be performed. I am satisfied that the words of exception should be strictly construed so as to reflect the intention of the Convention and the Act."

S10-53 English cases suggest that an agreement is not incapable of being performed merely because it is suggested that a party lacks the financial resources to meet any award (see *The Rena K* [1979] Q.B. 377), or to pay an obligatory deposit in the arbitration (see *Haendler v Paczy* [1981] 1 Lloyd's Rep. 302) or that the arbitrator lacks the power to grant a particular remedy (*Société Commerciale de Réassurance v Eras (International) Ltd (formerly Eras (UK))* [1992] 1 Lloyd's Rep. 570 at 611, per Mustill L.J.).

S10-54 In contrast, in a German case (*A v B*; III ZR 33/00 9th April 2000), A commenced arbitration but subsequently terminated the arbitration agreement on the basis that B was unable to afford the arbitration, suing for damages for breach of contract. The BGH reversed the appellate court's decision in A's favour since §1032(1) ZpO (i.e. Model Law art.8(1)) provided that the court must decline jurisdiction in favour of arbitration except "where the arbitration agreement is null & void, inoperative, or incapable of being performed". The BGH held that the subject arbitration agreement was indeed incapable of being performed because of B's inability to pay the costs whereas B could obtain legal aid to defend the action in court. Furthermore, B's right of access to the courts would be excluded only if it had acted in bad faith. The authors consider that this must be wrong in principle since one party's inability to pay its costs cannot amount to the arbitration agreement being incapable of being performed; as a practical solution, given the legal aid twist, this decision may have some merit but that is insufficient to overcome the "wrongness" of the decision.

However, stays have been refused where the courts of the system which governed the contract would not have regarded the agreement as excluding the right to litigate, albeit not expressly on this ground (*Abu Dhabi Investment Co v H Clarkson & Co Ltd* [2006] 2 Lloyd's Rep. 381). **S10–55**

Elsewhere, it has been held that an agreement is not incapable of being performed merely because it may not be performed immediately (see *Hip Hing Construction Co Ltd v Hope Lee Iron Work Co* [2002] 633 H.K.C.U. 1, where arbitration could not be commenced until the completion of the contract works), or because there are doubts about the enforceability of the award (*Rhone Mediterranee v Achille Lauro*, 712 F.2d 50 (1983)). However, a sist has been denied on this basis where the nominated arbitration institution no longer existed (*Pierreux NV v Transportmaschinen Handelshaus GmbH* (1997) XXII YCA 631), although sometimes a court will still grant a sist in such cases (see, e.g. *Dalimpex v Janicki* [2003] 172 O.A.C. 321). **S10–56**

Section 10(1)(c)—Notice of application to sist

Notice of the application must be given to the other parties to the legal proceedings. For further details see Ch.23 of the RCS (motions) for the Court of Session and see Ch.15 of the OCR for the sheriff court. **S10–57**

Equally, if in the Court of Session a petition or note is required, the petitioner or noter must enrol a motion for intimation and service, if this is not ordered automatically by the court. An application cannot be granted if notice has not been given. **S10–58**

Section 10(1)(d)(i)—Timing of application: Lodging of defences or answers

The court need not grant a sist if the applicant has taken any step in the proceedings to answer the substantive claim against them. This formulation is drawn from s.9(3) of the 1996 Act. Like s.9(3), s.10(1)(d)(i) creates a bar to a defender seeking a sist of the litigation. Article 8 of the Model Law would have allowed a party to request a sist, "not later than when submitting his first statement on the substance of the dispute". **S10–59**

Under the old common law, an application for a sist (by means of plea-in-law and motion) could be made at any time up to and shortly after the "closure of the record", that is to say the settlement of the written pleadings. Typically a number of months can elapse before the pleadings in the form of a summons (or initial writ) and the defences are settled and much time and **S10–60** expense can be incurred in the drafting of defences and their subsequent adjustment before the closure of the record.

S10–61 At the same time, s.1(1) of the Arbitration Act 1975 (repealed by the 2010 Act), which implemented the New York Convention into Scots, English/Welsh and Northern Irish law, indicated that a party who sought a sist in respect of a non-domestic arbitration agreement had to do so before delivering any pleadings or taking any other step in the proceedings. It was clear that a purely defensive act by a defender could not amount to a "step" (see *Roussel-UCLAF v G D Searle & Co Ltd* [1978] 1 Lloyd's Rep. 225), and in *Eagle Star Insurance Co Ltd v Yuval Insurance Co Ltd* [1978] 1 Lloyd's Rep. 357 at 361, Lord Denning M.R. suggested that a "step" must be one which "impliedly affirms the correctness of the proceedings".

S10–62 It was thought undesirable that the question of whether a dispute should be litigated or arbitrated should remain for such a significant period of time. For that reason, s.10(1)(d) introduced forms of statutory personal bar (estoppel) to speed up and unify the court's decision-making as to dispute resolution.

S10–63 In s.10(1)(d)(i) the decision was taken to import the second part of s.9(3) of the 1996 Act. Looking to Scottish litigation procedure, the first opportunity that a defender has to answer any substantive claim is through the lodging of defences (or answers). This stage is known as "*litis contestatio*". It follows that defences or answers which purport to answer any substantive claim in the proceedings will bar any subsequent application by the defender for a sist.

S10–64 Where a defender's advisers have not had sufficient opportunity to put in a substantive response in the defences it is common practice for the defences to contain a series of bare denials. Would the lodging of such skeletal defences be a step in the proceedings answering any substantive claim? The English case law is not entirely helpful as much of it (e.g. *Baker Hughes Ltd v Steadfast Engineering* [2009] EWHC 3123 (QB)) is based on the pre-1996 Act English legislation which was not concerned with whether the step in proceedings sought to "answer any substantive claim". Only in *Patel v Patel* [2000] Q.B. 551 is there any acknowledgment that s.9(3) of the 1996 Act improved upon previous law by requiring the "step" to "answer any substantive claim". Although skeletal defences are often simply a provisional measure before the substantive defence is introduced by adjustment, they can amount to a substantive defence (*Gray v Boyd,* 1996 S.L.T. 60) and the safer view would be that a defender is barred from seeking a sist after lodging skeletal defences.

S10–65 If a defender or respondent seeks more time to decide whether to seek arbitration he should seek prorogation (extension) of time for the lodging of defences in the sheriff court (OCR r.16.3) or answers to a petition in the Court of Session (RCS r.4.9(2)). The RCS do not allow prorogation of time for lodging defences in the Court of Session. In that event, the only possible means for preserving the position, while complying with the time limit for defences in the RCS, is to intimate the defences under express reservation of the entitlement to seek a sist. That means has been held to be effective in England and Wales in *Bilta (UK) Ltd v Nazir* [2010] 2 Lloyd's Rep. 29, although the court did not explain how such a reservation could be reconciled with the wording of s.9(3) of the 1996 Act.

Section 10(1)(d)(ii)—Timing of application: Other action barring sist

The applicant must not have acted since bringing the legal proceedings in a manner which indicates a desire to have the dispute resolved by litigation rather than arbitration. This provision has no counterpart in either the 1996 Act or the Model Law. **S10–66**

The purpose of s.10(1)(d)(ii) is to reflect the decision under the pre-Act common law in *Inverclyde (Mearns) Housing Ltd v Lawrence Construction Co Ltd*, 1989 S.L.T. 815. That case (approved by the Inner House in *Presslie v Cochrane McGregor Group Ltd*, 1996 S.C. 289 at 292) is one of many which recognise that there may be an implied waiver of the right to arbitrate—in that instance by significant delay in applying for a sist. That case involved an application by a defender who under the 2010 Act would, in any event, be barred under subs.(1)(d)(i). However, Lord McCluskey (at 821) applied the following test: **S10–67**

> "In the light of that consideration of the facts the court must consider whether the actings (including failure to act) of a party must be construed as being inconsistent with an intention to insist upon his contractual right to go to arbitration. I agree with the learned Dean of Faculty that, although there might in certain cases be particular actings which of themselves were decisively inconsistent with any intention to continue to exercise the waivable right, the proper course, in the absence of any such decisive acting, is to look at the whole actings."

This approach is reflected in s.10(1)(d)(ii) which, unlike s.10(1)(d)(i), applies to pursuers as well as defenders. A further difference from subs.(1)(d)(i) is that it allows regard to be had to conduct other than the taking of steps in legal proceedings. **S10–68**

Section 10(2)—Scott v Avery clauses

In *Caledonian Insurance Co v Gilmour* (1892) 20 R. (HL) 13, an insurance policy provided that where a difference arose between insurers and insured as to the amount payable under the policy it should be referred to arbitration and that no court proceedings could be commenced under the policy until the arbitral tribunal's award and then only in respect of the award. After the Outer House had refused the insurers' application for a sist, it found the insured entitled to payment and the matter was appealed to the House of Lords. The House of Lords held, following the English case *Scott* **S10–69** *v Avery* (1856) 5 H.L. Cas. 811, that the insured had no entitlement to payment under the policy until the making of the award. Such conditions precedent are known as "*Scott v Avery* clauses".

S10–70 The DAC Report (para.57) recommended that if a court refused to stay proceedings, a *Scott v Avery* clause should cease to have effect. This was implemented in s.9(5) of the 1996 Act. Section 10(2) seeks to achieve the same result and reverse the outcome in *Caledonian Insurance Co v Gilmour* (1892) 20 R. (HL) 13. The effect is, however, limited since without an application to sist which has been refused, *Scott v Avery* clauses will continue to be valid.

S10–71 The provision indicates that it does not apply to statutory arbitrations. This is because s.16(2) provides that any reference to the arbitration agreement shall, in the case of statutory arbitrations, be taken to be a reference to the relevant enactment. Consequently, were it not for this saving, subs.(2) could be interpreted as nullifying *Scott v Avery* clauses contained in statutory provisions.

Section 10 (3)—Sisting for non-Scots arbitrations

S10–72 Section 10 applies whether or not the arbitration in terms of the arbitration agreement is seated in Scotland. In respect of non-UK seated arbitrations, s.10 implements in Scotland the UK's obligation to give effect to art.II of the New York Convention.

Enforcing and challenging arbitral awards etc.

Arbitral award to be final and binding on parties

11.—(1) A tribunal's award is final and binding on the parties and any person claiming through or under them (but does not of itself bind any third party).

(2) In particular, an award ordering the rectification or reduction of a deed or other document is of no effect in so far as it would adversely affect the interests of any third party acting in good faith.

(3) This section does not affect the right of any person to challenge the award—
    (a) under Part 8 of the Scottish Arbitration Rules, or
    (b) by any available arbitral process of appeal or review.

(4) This section does not apply in relation to a provisional award (see rule 53), such an award not being final and being binding only—
    (a) to the extent specified in the award, or
    (b) until it is superseded by a subsequent award.

DEFINITIONS

"party": ss.2(1), 31(1), (2)
"rules": ss.7, 31(1)

"tribunal": ss.2(1), 31(1)

MODEL LAW

There is no equivalent provision in the Model Law. S11–01

COMMENTARY

Introductory

At common law an arbitral award was seen as part of an express agreement of the parties. In other words, any obligation or other order in the award was seen as a contractual obligation superseding any underlying obligation given effect to in the award. An award refusing a claim was seen as rendering any such underlying obligation as unenforceable. Arbitral awards were therefore binding as contractual obligations and enforceable as such. S11–02

Section 11 makes it plain that Scots law and Scottish courts will regard an arbitral award from whatever jurisdiction as final and binding on the parties to it and on persons claiming "through or under" the parties, provided that the award is not provisional and subject to any rights of appeal or challenge. For a consideration of "through and under", see the commentary on s.10(1)(b). Section 11 is clearly inspired (at least in part) by s.58 of the 1996 Act, which in turn was based on s.16 of the 1950 Act. Unlike s.58 it is mandatory in form, so that an agreement, for example on particular arbitral rules, that an award will only become binding when promulgated by some institution or third party, will itself be of no effect before the Scottish courts or a Scottish arbitral tribunal. S11–03

Section 11(1)

Section 11(1) differs from s.58(1) of the 1996 Act in that it makes clear that the award does not bind third parties. This is again axiomatic, the jurisdiction of an arbitral tribunal being created by an agreement between two private parties and cannot extend beyond those limits. This overrides the old common law under which a cautioner (guarantor) was bound by an award in an arbitration between the creditor and the principal debtor to which he was not a party (*Anderson v Wood* (1821) 1 S. 31). S11–04

Interestingly, the DAC Report, para.263, having noted the suggestion that the "other side" of s.58(1) be spelt out, S11–05

> "i.e. whatever the parties may or may not agree, the award is of no substantive or evidential effect against anyone who is neither a party nor claiming through or under a party"

concluded (at para.264):

"Such a provision would, of course, have to be mandatory. It would have to confine itself to the cases exclusively concerned with the laws of this country, for otherwise it could impinge on other applicable laws which have a different rule. Even where the situation was wholly domestic, it would have to deal with all those cases (e.g. insurers) who are not parties to the arbitration but whose rights and obligations may well be affected by awards (agreed or otherwise) in one way or another. In our view it would be very difficult to construct an acceptable provision and we are not persuaded it is needed."

S11–06 Section 11(1) is mandatory. It does not confine itself expressly to awards by Scottish tribunals. However, the references in s.11(2) to the Scottish remedies of rectification and reduction and in s.11(3) to challenges under the SAR suggest that s.11(1) is limited to awards by Scottish tribunals. Given that it could not have been intended to impinge on the awards of foreign tribunals, such an interpretation of s.11(1) makes practical sense also.

Section 11(2)

S11–07 This directs Scots courts (and tribunals) as to the "effect" in Scots law of awards ordering the rectification or reduction (annulment or setting aside) of documents. It is a fundamental principle of arbitration that, since the foundation of the tribunal's jurisdiction is the agreement to arbitrate, only the rights of the parties to the arbitral proceedings may be determined and the rights of third parties cannot be affected. That principle is expressed in s.11(1).

S11–08 Thus where there is a document containing a sale agreement with one seller and two joint purchasers containing an arbitration clause, and where one purchaser commences arbitration against the seller seeking reduction of the document, the award of the tribunal reducing the document would not "bind" the second purchaser as he was never party to the arbitral proceedings. There is, however, an argument that reduction renders the document null and void and that therefore the second purchaser could not, for example, have any right of relief in respect of half of the purchase price against the first purchaser. This is excluded by the provision in s.11(2) which is expressed as a "particular" example of the principle relating to third parties mentioned in s.11(1). By "good faith" is presumably meant lack of actual knowledge by the third party of the cause of the reduction or the rectification.

S11–09 Turning first to the effect of s.11(2) on Scottish awards, the power of a Scottish tribunal (unless excluded by the parties) is to rectify a document only to the extent permitted by the law governing the document. If the law governing the document is Scots law the circumstances in which that law allows rectification is set out in s.8 of the Law Reform (Miscellaneous Provisions) (Scotland) Act 1985: see the commentary to r.49(c).

Given that the tribunal would have to follow s.9 of the Law Reform **S11–10**
(Miscellaneous Provisions) (Scotland) Act 1985, which provides detailed
protection for the interests of third parties who have acted in good faith in
reliance on the document, it is unclear why s.11(2) was thought necessary in
order to provide any further protection to third parties. Perhaps the clue to
the thinking behind s.11(2) is the use of the words "In particular" at the
beginning of the subsection. These words appear to indicate that the provision of subs.(2) as to ineffectiveness is given merely as an example of the
principle expressed in subs.(1), namely that an award cannot bind, and
therefore cannot affect, a third party. If that was so, it remains unclear why
the example was necessary at all, given s.9 of the 1985 Act. When applied to
Scottish awards, s.11(2) is arguably unfortunate as it does tend at the very
least to cast doubt on their effectiveness.

Section 11(3)

To some extent echoing s.58(2) of the 1996 Act, this provides that the **S11–11**
finality and binding nature of an award is qualified by the availability of any
process of arbitral appeal or review, and by the rights of appeal under the
2010 Act. Certain arbitral rules permit institutional scrutiny of an award,
e.g. the ICC Rules; additional examples of arbitral appeal or review include
the ICSID Rules (which allow for a different tribunal to consider and decide
an application for annulment (only)) and the various GAFTA/FOSFA/
other commodity trade association rules (which provide for a full rehearing
(under different procedures) by a new tribunal).

Section 11(4)

A provisional award is an award which deals with a particular issue or set **S11–12**
of issues but on an interim basis pending subsequent final resolution. The
power to make such awards is conferred by r.53: see commentary on r.53.

Enforcement of arbitral awards

12.—(1) The court may, on an application by any party, order that a tribunal's award may be enforced as if it were an extract registered decree bearing a warrant for execution granted by the court.

(2) No such order may be made if the court is satisfied that the award is the subject of—
  (a) an appeal under Part 8 of the Scottish Arbitration Rules,
  (b) an arbitral process of appeal or review, or
  (c) a process of correction under rule 58 of the Scottish Arbitration Rules,
which has not been finally determined.

(3) No such order may be made if the court is satisfied that the tribunal which made the award did not have jurisdiction to do so (and the court may

restrict the extent of its order if satisfied that the tribunal did not have jurisdiction to make a part of the award).

(4) But a party may not object on the ground that the tribunal did not have jurisdiction if the party has lost the right to raise that objection by virtue of the Scottish Arbitration Rules (see rule 76).

(5) Unless the parties otherwise agree, a tribunal's award may be registered for execution in the Books of Council and Session or in the sheriff court books (provided that the arbitration agreement is itself so registered).

(6) This section applies regardless of whether the arbitration concerned was seated in Scotland.

(7) Nothing in this section or in section 13 affects any other right to rely on or enforce an award in pursuance of—

(a) sections 19 to 21, or

(b) any other enactment or rule of law.

(8) In this section, "court" means the sheriff or the Court of Session.

DEFINITIONS

"arbitration": ss.2(1), (2), 31(1)
"court": s.31(1)
"party": ss.2(1), 31(1), (2)
"seated in Scotland": ss.2, 31(1)
"tribunal": ss.2(1), 31(1)

MODEL LAW

S12–01   The Model Law provides, in art.35:

> "(1) An arbitral award, irrespective of the country in which it was made, shall be recognised as binding and upon application in writing to the competent court, shall be enforced subject to the provisions of this article and of article 36.
>
> (2) The party relying on an award or applying for its enforcement shall supply the original award or a copy thereof. If the award is not made in an official language of this State, the court may request the party to supply a translation thereof into such language."

Article 36 of the Model Law provides for the refusal of enforcement only on grounds which reflect those in s.20 of the Act or if it is found that the subject-matter of the dispute was not arbitrable under the law of its state or recognition or enforcement of the award would be contrary to the public policy of that state.

COMMENTARY

Introductory

At common law, enforcement of an arbitral award was by means of an action for payment or other remedy reflecting the terms of the award. The only exception was where the parties agreed that the tribunal could grant a warrant for the registration of the award in the Books of Council and Session (or sheriff court books) for execution. If such a warrant was granted and the award was subsequently registered, the registered award acquired the status of a Scottish court decree and could be enforced (executed) immediately. **S12–02**

In terms of the 1975 Act, enforcement of a New York Convention award required to be carried out in the same way. At the end of the litigation, if enforcement was upheld the court would grant decree (judgment) in terms of the award and the decree would fall to be enforced in the same way as any other decree of a Scottish court. **S12–03**

The common law action and the possibility of enforcement through registration remain competent both for non-Convention (including Scottish) and Convention awards. However, enforcement procedure by action could be lengthy. Accordingly, the principal purpose of s.12 is to provide an expedited procedure for enforcement by means of an "application" to the court. In the Court of Session this takes the form of a petition and in the sheriff court in the form of a summary application. **S12–04**

Enforcement under the s.12 procedure applies to awards from Scotland, other parts of the UK and non-UK countries, including those relatively few countries or territories not covered by the New York Convention (e.g. Taiwan, Iraq, Yemen (both North and South) and Libya). Section 12 does not exclude Convention awards from its ambit. Section 22 in turn specifies that nothing in ss.19 to 21 affects any other right to enforce a Convention award in pursuance of any other enactment. The word "enactment" would include s.12. This would seem to suggest that a Convention award can be enforced by the court making an order under either s.12 or s.19(2). What is clear is that whether an applicant proceeds under s.12 or s.19(2), an applicant seeking enforcement of a Convention award must comply with s.21 (evidence to be produced) and the court may refuse recognition of a Convention award only in accordance with s.20. **S12–05**

In respect of Convention awards, it is suggested that an application for enforcement be made under s.19(2) rather than s.12 as the procedure under s.19(2) is swifter. **S12–06**

Section 12 provides a route for the enforcement of an award from another UK jurisdiction alternative to the existing route under s.18 of and Schs 6 and 7 to the 1982 Act. Under the 1982 Act route, a judgment in terms of the award must first be obtained from the English, Welsh or Northern Irish court under s.66 of the 1996 Act and application for registration of that judgment must then be made to the Outer House. That route does not offer **S12–07** enforcement of any part of a judgment that incorporates a provisional (or interim) measure other than the payment of money and so would not include an interim injunction. By contrast, s.12 might allow the enforcement of such an injunctive award, subject to the general restrictions and discretion in the section.

S12–08 The authors submit that it is possible under s.12 to enforce an arbitral award which does not claim to have a seat.

Section 12(1) and (8)

Application to enforce

S12–09 On application by a party, the Outer House or the sheriff court may order the award to be enforced as if it were a Scottish court decree (judgment) bearing a warrant for execution. Enforcement of a court decree in Scotland is known as "diligence". This includes attachment (the seizure of corporeal (tangible) moveable assets in the hands of the debtor), arrestment and furthcoming (the seizure of corporeal (tangible) or incorporeal assets (i.e. debts or obligations including future and contingent obligations owed to the debtor)), inhibition (the freezing of voluntary transfers of or mortgaging) of heritable (immoveable) property, and adjudication (seizure) of heritable property. Adjudication is due to be replaced by the process of land attachment in terms of the Bankruptcy and Diligence etc. (Scotland) Act 2007 but this new process is not yet in force. Sequestration (individual bankruptcy) or liquidation (corporate bankruptcy) of the debtor is also available.

S12–10 An application may be made to either the Outer House or to a sheriff court of the sheriffdom where the respondent in the application is domiciled in terms of ss.41 or 42 of the 1982 Act.

S12–11 If the application is made to the Outer House it is made by petition in the style contained in RCS Form 14.4 (RCS rr.100.5(1), 14.4) or, if there are undisposed of Outer House petitions in relation to the same arbitration process, by note (RCS r.100.5). The requirements for the petition are set out in RCS r.14.4 and Ch.100 (r.15.2 for notes). The petition should crave service or intimation on the other parties to the arbitration, and to the members of the tribunal.

S12–12 If a shorter period of notice is required, then this should also be craved in the petition and the reasons averred in the body of the petition.

S12–13 Together with the petition the applicant should lodge with the Court of Session:

(i) as a production, any written arbitration agreement;
(ii) the original award (or a copy certified to be a true copy by the tribunal);
(iii) any other document founded on or adopted as incorporated in the petition;

(iv) the bundle of court documents known as the process (see RCS rr.4.3, 4.4).

Inventories of any productions should be intimated to the other parties and members of the tribunal.

After the end of the period for answers, whether answers have been lodged or not, the petitioner should enrol a motion to have the court grant the s.12(1) order with or without a hearing as may be appropriate in the circumstances. The motion should seek the expenses of the application process from the court. **S12–14**

If the application is made to the sheriff court it is made by summary application in the style contained in SASAR Sch.1 Form 1 (SASAR r.2.4). The requirements for the summary application are broadly the same as for the petition described above. Detailed reference should be made to the SASAR. **S12–15**

Court discretion

There are situations in which the court cannot enforce the award. This explains the use of the word "may". Cases where the court might decline to enforce the award might include the situation where the award deals with issues which are not arbitrable, or where enforcement appears to be illegal or otherwise to offend against public policy (see *Hamlyn & Co v Talisker Distillery* (1894) 21 R. (HL) 21 at 27, per Lord Watson; DAC Report, paras 371 to 377). **S12–16**

Another ground for non-enforcement would be where the award was a nullity under the law of its seat (the *lex arbitri*) (*Earl of Hopetoun v Scots Mines Co* (1856) 18 D. 739 where the court enforced an award made in England by an English arbitrator pursuant to a Scottish arbitration agreement on the basis that by appointing an English arbitrator the parties had opted for an English *lex arbitri* or curial law under which the award was not a nullity). If a non-Scottish, non-Convention award has been set aside under the law of its seat or even if it is being appealed or otherwise challenged under that law, that might cause a court to exercise its discretion to refuse to enforce the award, either permanently or at least until the outcome of the challenge is known. **S12–17**

Authority under s.66 of the 1996 Act indicates that it is the award as it stands which can be ordered to be enforced, and the court at this stage has no power to correct it or otherwise remedy deficiencies (see, e.g. *Walker v Rome* [1999] 2 All E.R. (Comm) 961). **S12–18**

However, authority in relation to Convention awards under the English equivalent of s.19(2) also suggests that it is open to the court to enforce an award in part (*ASM Shipping Ltd of India v TTMI Ltd* [2009] 1 Lloyd's Rep. 293; see also *Nigerian National Petroleum Corp v IPCO (Nigeria) Ltd* [2008] EWCA Civ 1157, and the commentary by Hew R. Dundas—"Partial **S12–19**

Enforcement of Arbitral Awards" (2008) 74 *Arbitration* 330 and "*IPCO v NPPC* on Appeal" (2009) 75 *Arbitration* 126), and the Scottish courts might also decide that this is within their discretion under s.12 as well as under s.19(2).

Setting aside by exception excluded

S12–20 Finally, it is not competent for a party to oppose a s.12 application by seeking to have a Scottish award reduced by exception (*ope exceptionis*): s.13(2). This would now appear to apply equally to a common law action of enforcement although, given the existence of the s.12 procedure, it is unclear why anyone would still wish to resort to it.

Section 12(2)—No enforcement pending appeal, review or correction

S12–21 In a number of situations the court cannot enforce an award. Where the award is a Convention award the circumstances in which enforcement might be refused are addressed by s.20: see commentary on s.20. Where the award is a non-Scottish non-Convention award (e.g. an award from a non-Scottish UK jurisdiction), the court has the discretion to refuse enforcement under subs.(1).

S12–22 Section 12(2) is concerned with Scottish awards. Thus the award may not be enforced where the court is satisfied that the award "is the subject of":

- an appeal to the Outer House under any of the grounds laid down by Part 8 of the rules (lack of jurisdiction, serious irregularity, legal error);
- an arbitral process of appeal or review, e.g. an appeal to a second arbitral tribunal (e.g. as in GAFTA/FOSFA arbitrations) or other body;
- an application to have the award corrected by the tribunal under r.58;

and that process has not been determined. It must be presumed that it is for the other party to satisfy the court under any of these grounds, although this should be fairly straightforward, since an award is either the "subject of" an ongoing process of appeal, etc. or it is not. The court has no discretion under subs.(2).

S12–23 Where the time limits for appeal in r.71, including leave to appeal, have not expired, and the party resisting enforcement submits that he will be appealing or seeking leave to appeal, the word "may" in s.12(1) gives the court a discretion not to grant the order pending the appeal being made or the time limits expiring without an appeal having been made. Unless there are circumstances indicating that the appeal is not to be made it is anticipated that, instead of granting the application at the outset, the court will continue the application to the first available day after the expiry of the time limits to see if an appeal has been made.

In deciding whether an appeal etc. was likely to be made, the court may expect the party resisting enforcement to put forward some grounds for the course of action contemplated in order to satisfy itself that an appeal etc. is likely to be brought. However, it must be borne in mind that, if an appeal has actually been made, enforcement is prevented by subs.(2) regardless of the merits of the appeal. To allow enforcement before the determination of an appeal etc. which is likely to be made could pre-empt the effectiveness of the appeal etc. which would be inappropriate. In these circumstances the authors submit that only grounds which are unintelligible or plainly unfounded on their face should allow the exercise of a discretion to grant a s.12(1) order at the pre-appeal stage. **S12–24**

With regard to an appeal against a Scottish award, it must be borne in mind that the court can grant an order against the appellant (or applicant for leave to appeal) to provide security for the sum awarded in the award and the expenses of the appeal: r.71(10) and (12). The court has a similar power in relation to challenges made outside the UK to Convention awards sought to be enforced in Scotland: s.20(6)(b). **S12–25**

An applicant under s.12 would be well advised to keep a close eye on the time limits for the making of an appeal or application for leave with a view to a possible application for security. **S12–26**

In addition, the appellant may already have been subjected to security in the form of diligence on the dependence or caution for expenses during the arbitration up to the issue of the award (see rr.46(1)(c) and (e) and 64). **S12–27**

In Scotland, in contrast to England and Wales, a court does not have an inherent common law power to suspend the enforcement of an award pending an appeal. Suspension of enforcement of non-Convention awards is limited to the grounds set out in s.12(2) and (3). **S12–28**

Section 12(3) and (4)—No enforcement where tribunal lacked jurisdiction

At first sight, s.12(3) and (4) appear to allow the issue of jurisdiction to be (re)argued where no r.67 appeal has been made or one has and it has been unsuccessful. However, this is not the case for two reasons: first, s.12(3) confines court involvement in this regard to two specific instances and, secondly, such an interpretation of s.12(3) would be contrary to the founding principle in s.1(a) that the object of arbitration is to resolve disputes without unnecessary delay or expense. Therefore, s.12(3) must be interpreted as meaning that a court will be satisfied as to lack of jurisdiction of a Scottish tribunal only if there has been a successful r.67 appeal. **S12–29**

If the award is a foreign non-Convention one, the court may require to consider the issue of jurisdiction in the light of the law which governs the arbitration agreement. See also the commentary on s.4. **S12–30**

Section 12(5)—Registration for execution

S12–31   At common law, if the arbitration agreement is registered for execution in the books of a sheriff court or the Books of Council and Session, then provided the parties agreed to its registration, the award itself could also be registered for execution (see *Baillie v Pollock* (1829) 7 S. 619). This then allowed the award to be enforced as if it was a court decree without the need for any application or other proceedings before the court.

S12–32   Section 12(5) removes the need for both parties to consent to registration of the award, and instead allows either party to register an award for execution provided that the arbitration agreement is itself registered for execution. Many leases containing arbitration agreements are registered in the Books of Council and Session for execution. The authors submit that in such a case it is sufficient for the creditor of an award deriving from such an agreement to register it in the Books of Council and Session and proceed to enforce it as if it was a court decree.

S12–33   If the award creditor attempted to execute diligence (including sequestration (bankruptcy)) in reliance on the award before the period for appealing had expired or any appeal had been disposed of, an appellant could apply to the Court of Session for suspension of any enforcement steps (e.g. the service of a charge for payment) and interim interdict of future enforcement steps until the days had expired or the appeal had been determined. Such an application for suspension would be legal proceedings in respect of enforcement of an award rather than in respect of the award and so is not covered by s.13.

Section 12(6) and (7)

S12–34   These subsections make it clear that a s.12 order may be made in respect of awards made outside Scotland. As stated above, enforcement of a Convention award can be made either under s.12 or s.19(2) but the grounds for resisting enforcement in s.20 and the evidential requirements in s.21 apply to both types of application. If enforcement of a Convention award is sought in the Court of Session, then the RCS has expedited rules for s.19(2) applications. Indirect enforcement of a non-Scottish UK award already exists by means of an application to the Outer House under s.18 of and Schs 6 and 7 to the 1982 Act.

Court intervention in arbitrations

13.—(1) Legal proceedings are competent in respect of—
   (a) a tribunal's award, or
   (b) any other act or omission by a tribunal when conducting an arbitration,
only as provided for in the Scottish Arbitration Rules (in so far as they apply to that arbitration) or in any other provision of this Act.
   (2) In particular, a tribunal's award is not subject to review or appeal in any

legal proceedings except as provided for in Part 8 of the Scottish Arbitration Rules.

(3) It is not competent for a party to raise the question of a tribunal's jurisdiction with the court except—
  (a) where objecting to an order being made under section 12, or
  (b) as provided for in the Scottish Arbitration Rules (see rules 21, 22 and 67).

(4) Where the parties agree that the UNCITRAL Model Law is to apply to an arbitration, articles 6 and 11(2) to (5) of that Law are to have the force of law in Scotland in relation to that arbitration (as if article 6 specified the Court of Session and any sheriff court having jurisdiction).

DEFINITIONS

"arbitration": ss.2(1), (2), 31(1)
"court": s.31(1)
"party": ss.2(1), 31(1), (2)
"rules": ss.7, 31(1)
"tribunal": ss.2(1), 31(1)

MODEL LAW

The Model Law provides, in art.5: S13–01

"In matters governed by this Law, no court shall intervene except where so provided in this Law."

COMMENTARY

Introductory

Section 13 is directed towards Scottish arbitral awards. While it is not S13–02 restricted expressly to such awards, this is implicit in its provisions. The principal purpose of s.13 is to create a single exclusive method of challenge to a Scottish arbitral award, or anything done or proposed to be done by a tribunal, namely the exercise of rights of appeal under the SAR. Section 13(3)(a) does not allow for the possibility of a re-hearing of a challenge to jurisdiction under s.12(3) of the Act or the hearing of such a challenge when there was no appeal under r.67; see the commentary on s.12(3) at paras R12–29 and R12–30.

Section 13(1) and (2)—Court intervention regarding awards

The Act takes particular care to emphasise that the award may only be S13–03 challenged in the way and on the grounds it prescribes. The aim is to exclude the process of judicial review of arbitral awards and arbitral conduct which existed under the pre-2010 Act law and to create a unified form of challenge under the 2010 Act.

S13–04 Instead, all questions relating to the arbitration, whether about the composition or jurisdiction of the tribunal, its conduct of the arbitration or its award are governed by the Act and the SAR (*Arbitration Application No. 3 of 2011*, 2012 S.L.T. 150 at [3] per Lord Glennie).

S13–05 The Court of Session has traditionally been reluctant to accept that its jurisdiction has been excluded, Lord Fraser asserting in *Brown v Hamilton DC*, 1983 S.L.T. 397 at 414 that it exists "even in cases where appeal is expressly excluded by statute". That approach is excluded by s.1(c) and to allow judicial review to remain as a means of recourse would be contrary to the spirit and policy of the Act and lead to procedural and administrative confusion.

S13–06 Under the pre-Act judicial review regime, parties could seek interim orders from the court against the tribunal, e.g. in respect of apprehended natural justice or other procedural breaches. These are no longer competent by virtue of s.13(1)(b). Instead, such fears of serious irregularity must be expressed to the tribunal. If the tribunal does not respond appropriately, the immediate remedy is for a party to seek the removal of the arbitrator or dismissal of the tribunal under rr.11 to 14.

Section 13(3)—Court intervention regarding jurisdiction

S13–07 The Act also stresses that the tribunal's jurisdiction cannot be challenged by a court except as it contemplates under:

- r.21 when a party appeals against the tribunal's own jurisdictional ruling;
- r.22 when the issue of jurisdiction has been referred to the Outer House; and
- r.67 when the award is challenged on the basis of lack of jurisdiction.

It has been shown above, however, that a court may effectively determine an issue of jurisdiction if it refuses a sist on the basis that the arbitration agreement is invalid.

Section 13(4)

S13–08 It was shown earlier how default (but not mandatory) rules can be overridden by the parties in terms of s.9(2) and (3), and how s.9(4)(a)(ii) made it clear that one of the ways of doing so would be through agreeing that the Model Law should govern the arbitration. If the parties do this, then subs.(4) provides that it is a mandatory rule of law that for the purposes of art.6 of the Model Law the courts that are to perform the functions set out in art.6 are to be the Court of Session and the sheriff court which has jurisdiction.

There is a drafting tension/inconsistency between (i) s.13(4), the effect of which appears to be that, in such a case, art.11(2) to (5) of the Model Law (which relate to the appointment of the tribunal) prevail over rr.6 and 7 of the SAR, despite r.7 being a mandatory rule and (ii) s.8 which applies all mandatory rules to all arbitrations in Scotland. The only possible resolution of this tension/inconsistency is that s.8, given its express and clear terms, must override s.13(4) in this regard. **S13–09**

Persons who take no part in arbitral proceedings

14.—(1) A person alleged to be a party to an arbitration but who takes no part in the arbitration may, by court proceedings, question—
   (a) **whether there is a valid arbitration agreement (or, in the case of a statutory arbitration, whether the enactment providing for arbitration applies to the dispute),**
   (b) **whether the tribunal is properly constituted, or**
   (c) **what matters have been submitted to arbitration in accordance with the arbitration agreement,**
and the court may determine such a question by making such declaration, or by granting such interdict or other remedy, as it thinks appropriate.

(2) Such a person has the same right as a party who participates in the arbitration to appeal against any award made in the arbitration under rule 67 or 68 (jurisdictional and serious irregularity appeals) and rule 71(2) does not apply to such an appeal.

DEFINITIONS

"arbitration": ss.2(1), (2), 31(1)
"arbitration agreement": ss.4, 31(1)
"court": s.31(1)
"dispute": ss.2(1), 31(1)
"party": ss.2(1), 31(1), (2)
"rules": ss.7, 31(1)
"statutory arbitrations": ss.16(1), 31(1)
"tribunal": ss.2(1), 31(1)

COMMENTARY

Introductory

This is essentially a Scottish version of s.72 of the 1996 Act, and deals with a situation not fully addressed by the Model Law. While it is not limited expressly to Scottish seated arbitrations, such a limitation is implicit in the provisions relating to appeal which are the same as for such arbitrations. **S14–01**

Section 14(1)

S14–02 A person who is sought to be made a party to arbitral proceedings, but who contests the tribunal's jurisdiction, may obviously participate in those proceedings in the sense of challenging the tribunal or its jurisdiction under r.20. However, the Act recognises a second possibility—that a party may simply refuse to have anything to do with the proceedings.

S14–03 Under art.25 of the Model Law, such a course of action would mean that the party risked having an enforceable arbitral award made against him. That risk exists under the Act also (see r.37), but under the Act such a party may ask the court to consider the questions mentioned in s.14(1)(a)–(c). This position has the merit that a person who contends that the tribunal has no jurisdiction is not effectively forced to participate in arbitral proceedings in order to defend his position (see DAC Report, para.295). An application may be made by petition to the Outer House (see RCS r.100.5 and the commentary thereon; Appendix 2 paras A2–22 to A2–28 refer) or, it is suggested, by summary application to the sheriff court holding jurisdiction. However, it is possible in the absence of any sheriff court rules dealing with s.14 that an ordinary action of declarator or interdict may be raised.

S14–04 A declarator as to the correct legal position may be the usual remedy, but there may be situations where it may be appropriate for the court to interdict the arbitrator(s) and the other party from proceeding. If interim interdict is sought to prevent an arbitration from proceeding, it should be brought in good time before any hearing for which the claimant has prepared, otherwise the balance of convenience will tend to favour the claimant in the arbitration and the arbitration proceeding (see, e.g. in relation to s.72 of the 1996 Act *Zaporozhye Production Aluminium Plan Open Shareholders Society v Ashly Ltd* [2002] EWHC 1410 (Comm)).

S14–05 *Arab National Bank v El Sharif Saoud Bin Masoud Bin Haza'a El-Abdali* [2005] 1 Lloyd's Rep. 541 is an example of where an award had been issued against a bank which had never agreed to submit a dispute to arbitration, and the bank obtained a declaration under s.72 of the 1996 Act that the award was invalid.

S14–06 Court proceedings may be raised either in the Outer House or in a sheriff court of the sheriffdom where the respondent is domiciled in terms of ss.41 or 42 of the 1982 Act.

S14–07 While s.14 does not refer to an "application" being made, s.14 proceedings appear to be covered by the provisions of RCS r.100.5 and so require to be made by petition in the style contained in RCS Form 14.4 (RCS rr.100.5(1), 14.4) or, if there is an undisposed of Outer House petition by note (RCS r.100.5(2)). The requirements for the petition are set out in RCS r.14.4 and Ch.100 (r.15.2 for notes). The petition should crave service or intimation on the other parties founding on the alleged arbitration agreement, and to the members of any arbitral tribunal that has been appointed. For further details see the RCS.

S14-08 The procedure in the sheriff court is even more unclear. Given the absence of sheriff court rules it would appear that proceedings could be by either ordinary action or summary application. A summary application would require to comply with the style contained in SASAR Sch.1 Form 1 (SASAR r.2.4). The pleading requirements for either form of process are broadly the same as for the petition described above. Detailed reference should be made to the OCR in Sch.1 to the Sheriff Courts (Scotland) Act 1907 or to SASAR.

"[T]akes no part in the arbitration"

S14-09 In relation to s.72, where a person wrote to an arbitral institution rejecting a request or notice of arbitration and questioning the jurisdiction of the tribunal, such a rejection and questioning was held not to amount to "taking part" in the arbitration (*Caparo Group Ltd v Fagor Arrasate Sociedad Cooperative* [2000] A.D.R.L.J. 254 (Clarke J.).

Section 14 application and s.10 application

S14-10 A question can arise as to the relationship between a s.14 application by the party resisting arbitration and an opposed s.10 application for a sist by the party seeking arbitration. The equivalent occurred in *Fiona Trust and Holding Corp v Privalov* [2007] 1 All E.R. (Comm) 891 where the party resisting the arbitration applied to the court for an injunction against the arbitration proceeding on the basis that that arbitration agreement was invalid through bribery, followed by the party seeking arbitration applying to the court for a stay of court proceedings. The Court of Appeal observed at [36]:

" ... if the party who denies the existence of a valid arbitration agreement has himself ... instituted court proceedings and the party who relies on the arbitration clause has applied for a stay, the application for a stay is the primary matter which needs to be decided. It would only be if a stay were never applied for or were refused, but for some reason the party relying on the arbitration clause insisted on continuing with the arbitration, that any question of an injunction should arise. Of course s.72 might well be applicable if the party denying the existence of an arbitration agreement had not started English proceedings and did not wish to do so. Such a party would then be entitled to apply under s.72 for a declaration that there was no valid arbitration agreement; even then an injunction would usually only be necessary only if there was some indication that the other party was intending not to comply with any declaration which the court might make."

The authors submit that the observations on s.72 of the 1996 Act apply equally to s.14.

S14-11 The Court of Appeal in *Fiona Trust* (above) also commented on the relationship of the equivalent of a s.14 application to the arbitral tribunal's power to determine its own jurisdiction and the remedies available in respect of an award on jurisdiction. It noted at [36] that the combined effect of the various provisions in the 1996 Act in relation to jurisdiction and the principle of non-intervention by the court was that, in general, it should be right for the arbitrators to be the first tribunal to determine jurisdiction. In addition, the court should, in light of the founding principle in s.1(c) of the 1996 Act, be "very cautious" about agreeing that its s.72 process be utilised as the first means of determining jurisdiction. The founding principle in s.1(c) is the same in the 2010 Act and the authors submit that the observations of the Court of Appeal apply equally to the s.14 process.

S14-12 Section 14(1) provides that the court "may" determine such a question which indicates that it has a discretion whether to determine the application or to leave it to the arbitral tribunal. Whether it would exercise the discretion one way or the other might depend on the stage reached in the arbitral proceedings and the remedy sought under s.14. If the court rules against a s.14 applicant, such party should seek to participate in the arbitration. In *Hackwood v Areen Design Services Ltd* [2005] EWHC 2322 (TCC) the court rejected the absurd contention that a party who sought relief under s.72 unsuccessfully was not entitled to take part in subsequent arbitral proceedings but held that it was for the arbitral tribunal to decide whether to allow the unsuccessful s.72 applicant to participate in the arbitration.

S14-13 In *London Steam Ship Owners' Mutual Insurance Association Ltd v Kingdom of Spain* [2013] EWHC 2840 (Comm) Walker J. held, at [83]–[84], that at the stage of enforcement, after the expiry of the period for appeal, a non-participant could still apply under s.72 of the 1996 Act for a declaration that the arbitration agreement was of no effect.

Section 14(2)

S14-14 A non-participant party in the arbitration against whom an award is made is given a right of appeal against the award under rr.67 and 68 and, given his non-participation, is excused from having to exhaust any available arbitral process of appeal or review, including recourse under r.58. However, he still has to comply with the time limits under r.71(4) (see *London Steam Ship Owners' Mutual Insurance Association Ltd v Kingdom of Spain* [2013] EWHC 2840 (Comm) at [84] per Walker J.).

Arbitration (Scotland) Act 2010 (s.15)

Anonymity in legal proceedings

15.—(1) A party to any civil proceedings relating to an arbitration (other than proceedings under section 12) may apply to the court for an order prohibiting the disclosure of the identity of a party to the arbitration in any report of the proceedings.

(2) On such an application, the court must grant the order unless satisfied that disclosure—
- (a) is required—
  - (i) for the proper performance of the discloser's public functions, or
  - (ii) in order to enable any public body or office-holder to perform public functions properly,
- (b) can reasonably be considered as being needed to protect a party's lawful interests,
- (c) would be in the public interest, or
- (d) would be necessary in the interests of justice.

(3) The court's determination of an application for an order is final.

DEFINITIONS

"arbitration": ss.2(1), (2), 31(1)
"court": s.31(1)
"party": ss.2(1), 31(1), (2)

COMMENTARY

Introductory

One of the many innovative aspects of the 2010 Act was the introduction, **S15–01** as a default rule, of an express duty of confidentiality in Scottish arbitrations on arbitrators and parties. That duty prohibits the disclosure of any information relating to the dispute, the arbitral proceedings and any award which is not and has never been in the public domain (see r.26 and the commentary thereon).

Information relating to the dispute includes the identity of the parties. **S15–02** That could be readily undermined if the identity of the parties was automatically disclosed upon any court proceedings relating to the arbitration taking place, whether they were a challenge to the award, a reference for an opinion of the court or other applications to the court for orders supportive of the arbitration. To deal with that situation, s.15 was enacted to allow the parties to keep their identities confidential. However, s.15 has broader application in that it is not restricted to applications to the court from Scottish arbitrations but may, e.g. cover applications in relation to foreign arbitrations.

Given the existence of s.15, the authors submit that the exception to the **S15–03** duty of confidentiality in r.26(1)(c)(i), requiring compliance with any enactment or rule of law, will operate to excuse disclosure at any hearing before the court only if an application has been made under s.15 and refused.

Section 15(1)

S15–04 The provision places the burden on a party to civil proceedings to apply to the court for an order prohibiting disclosure of the identity of a party to the proceedings in any report of the proceedings. RCS r.100.9 (Appendix 2 paras A2–36 to A2–39 refer) requires that the application must be made no later than the hearing of a motion by the petitioner (or noter) for further procedure under RCS r.100.5(5). Until that time, there is only a petition (or note), the petition is not available for inspection except by the court staff and parties, and any court proceedings must be held in private (RCS r.100.9(2); and *Arbitration Application No. 3 of 2011*, 2012 S.L.T. 150 at 155A, [22] per Lord Glennie).

S15–05 There might, however, not be a hearing on the petitioner's motion so the authors submit that any application to the Outer House under s.15(1) be made as part of the motion for further procedure.

S15–06 There is, as yet, no equivalent rule for the sheriff court. In these circumstances the authors submit that a motion should be made to the sheriff at the earliest opportunity as any material delay in making the application could result in the sheriff deciding that anonymity cannot reasonably be considered as being needed to protect a party's lawful interests.

S15–07 The order will prohibit disclosure of the identity of any party to the arbitration in any report of the proceedings. Giving the word "report" its ordinary English meaning, if an order is made, any account of the proceedings, even if oral, even if given only to a single individual, would be prohibited.

"Civil proceedings"

S15–08 An applicant under s.15 must be a party to civil proceedings relating to an arbitration. Thus, if an arbitration leads to criminal proceedings, e.g. as regards an attempt to bribe an arbitrator, no such order may be sought. Civil proceedings relate to an arbitration where a court is invited to exercise its powers under Part 5 of the rules, or where an award is under challenge in terms of Part 8, or where a court is invited to enforce an award under ss.12 or 19 (but a s.12 application is expressly excluded from anonymity; and see *Associated Electric & Gas Insurance Services Ltd v European Reinsurance Co of Zurich* [2003] 1 W.L.R. 1041; *Television New Zealand Ltd v Langley Productions Ltd* [2000] N.Z.L.R. 250). It is unclear whether court proceedings under r.26 (breach of confidentiality) would be covered.

S15–09 The same applies where the court is involved in appointing an arbitrator under r.7 or removing an arbitrator under r.12, or dismissing the tribunal under r.13, or in deciding on a jurisdictional objection under rr.21 and 22—even if it decides that the tribunal does not have jurisdiction.

A court may have to make a decision under r.16 on an arbitrator's **S15–10** entitlements or liabilities when his tenure ends or a party may seek to sue an arbitrator in respect of something done in bad faith. The authors submit that such proceedings fall within s.15 since the object is the protection of the identity of the parties to the arbitration.

The matter is less clear regarding court proceedings which have been **S15–11** raised in respect of matters covered by an arbitration agreement. On one view, such proceedings do not "relate to an arbitration" as they relate to the merits of the claim itself, regardless of any arbitration agreement. On another view, if they have been raised solely to obtain protective measures pending an arbitration, it could be said that they relate to an arbitration. If a party applies validly for a sist for arbitration and at the same time there is an application under s.15, the authors submit that a court that granted the sist would be entitled to grant the application under s.15.

It is noteworthy that, in England, such matters are dealt with via rules of **S15–12** court. The presumption is that applications to determine a preliminary point of law or to set aside an award on the basis of error of law will be heard in public, while all other arbitration claims will be heard in private, although the court has discretion to hold any hearing in public or private and thus may be persuaded by either party to hold a hearing in private (CPR r.62.10).

Any judgment is then presumed to be a public document, although the **S15–13** English courts have asserted an inherent power to declare the judgment unavailable for publication, albeit that they will only exercise that power if a party makes a persuasive case against publication. They have made it clear that the presumptions in the rules of court are mere starting points which apply in the event that neither party raises the issue but if the issue of privacy or publication is raised, the court must in each case weigh up the factors for maintaining or moving from the private or public starting point (see Mance L.J. in *Department of Economics Policy and Development of the City of Moscow v Bankers Trust Co* [2005] Q.B. 207 at [42]; this case is discussed in Hew R. Dundas, "Confidentiality in Arbitration: the Court of Appeal Decides: *Department of Economic Policy & Development, City of Moscow v (1) Bankers Trust Company and (2) International Industrial Bank*" [2004] 70 *Arbitration* 3, 218–228).

Section 15(2)—Exceptions to anonymity

The court must make the order unless it is satisfied that disclosure meets **S15–14** any one of a number of exceptions. It is for the party opposing the application to satisfy the court that an exception applies, unless the court decides on its own initiative that that is the case.

Section 15(2)(a)—Discloser's public functions

S15–15 The exception in question appears to address situations where there is a public duty to disclose. This exception exists also for the duty of confidentiality in r.26(1)(c)(ii).

S15–16 The duty appears to be drawn from the attempt by Potter L.J. in *Ali Shipping Corp v Shipyard Trogir* [1999] 1 W.L.R. 314 at 326–327 to devise a list of exceptions to a duty of confidentiality based on the exceptions to the banker's duty of confidentiality elaborated by Bankes L.J. in *Tournier v National Provincial and Union Bank of England* [1924] 1 K.B. 461 at 472–473. One of Potter L.J.'s examples was compliance with an order of the court which would involve a duty to disclose.

Section 15(2)(b)—Protection of party's lawful interests

S15–17 This exception appears also to be drawn from Potter L.J.'s exceptions in *Ali Shipping Corp v Shipyard Trogir* [1999] 1 W.L.R. 314 at 327B. The authors have difficulty in envisaging circumstances where disclosure of a party's identity in a report of the court proceedings might be necessary in order to protect the discloser's lawful interests. It is much easier to think of examples of situations where this exception might apply in the context of confidentiality of the award: see commentary on r.26. However, one example which might operate in the current context is where the fact that a company has succeeded in an arbitration has to be revealed in order to defend its share price or reassure its shareholders.

Section 15(2)(c)—Public interest

S15–18 The question under this head is whether it is in the public interest that the identity of a party to the arbitration be disclosed in any report of the civil proceedings. It is therefore a narrower question than that which arose, e.g. in the *City of Moscow* case (above) where one of the questions for the English court was whether its judgment as a whole should be published and reported. It is also narrower than that which arose in *Ali Shipping Corp* (above) where the exception was first elucidated by Potter L.J. at 327G in connection with an expert witness giving an opinion in an earlier arbitration contrary to that to be expressed in the current arbitration.

S15–19 The concern under subs.(2)(c) is whether the identity of a party should be disclosed. Thus matters such as the public interest in the fairness of an arbitral process are not significant here given that an anonymised judgment can be given in public (see *Department of Economics Policy and Development of the City of Moscow v Bankers Trust Co* [2005] Q.B. 207 at [39]). It might perhaps be in the public interest to reveal that a party which has failed in a challenge of an award of £500 million against it is a publicly quoted construction company, even if such revelation is very damaging to the company. Equally, if there was something in the conduct of the parties which affected the public as a whole, it might be in the public interest that the party in question be "named and shamed".

English courts have been unclear whether there is a public interest exception to the principle of confidentiality which is separate from the interests of justice exception (compare Potter L.J. in *Ali Shipping Corp v Shipyard Trogir* [1998] 2 All E.R. 136 at 148 with Lawrence Collins L.J. and Carnwath L.J. in *Emmott v Michael Wilson & Partners Ltd* [2008] 1 Lloyd's Rep. 616 at [99], [100], [134]), although such an exception has been mooted by the Australian courts (see *Esso Australia Resources v Plowman* (1995) 128 A.L.R. 391; *Commonwealth of Australia v Cockatoo Dockyard Pty Ltd* (1995) 36 N.S.W.L.R. 662).

Section 15(2)(d)—Interests of justice

This may overlap with the "public interest" exception. Again, there are examples where it is clearly in the interests of justice that the principle of confidentiality should not be maintained, such as where a witness gives evidence which is materially different to that which he gave in an earlier arbitration (see Mance J. in *London and Leeds Estates Ltd v Paribas Ltd (No.2)* [1995] 1 E.G.L.R. 102 at 109; and see *Ali Shipping Corp v Shipyard Trogir* [1999] 1 W.L.R. 314 at 328A–B).

Section 15(3)

The ruling of the court on this matter is not subject to appeal. The court in this context means any court rather than merely the sheriff court or Outer House—see s.31(1).

Statutory arbitration

Statutory arbitration: special provisions

16.—(1) "Statutory arbitration" is arbitration pursuant to an enactment which provides for a dispute to be submitted to arbitration.

(2) References in the Scottish Arbitration Rules (or in any other provision of this Act) to an arbitration agreement are, in the case of a statutory arbitration, references to the enactment which provides for a dispute to be resolved by arbitration.

(3) None of the Scottish Arbitration Rules (or other provisions of this Act) apply to a statutory arbitration if or to the extent that they are excluded by, or are inconsistent with, any provision made by virtue of any other enactment relating to the arbitration.

(4) Every statutory arbitration is to be taken to be seated in Scotland.

(5) The following rules do not apply in relation to statutory arbitration—
rule 43 (extension of time limits)
rule 71(9) (power to declare provision of arbitration agreement void)
rule 80 (death of party)

Arbitration (Scotland) Act 2010

(6) Despite rule 40, parties to a statutory arbitration may not agree to—
  (a) consolidate the arbitration with another arbitration,
  (b) hold concurrent hearings, or
  (c) authorise the tribunal to order such consolidation or the holding of concurrent hearings,
unless the arbitrations or hearings are to be conducted under the same enactment.

DEFINITIONS

"arbitration": ss.2(1), (2), 31(1)
"arbitration agreement": ss.4, 31(1)
"dispute": ss.2(1), 31(1)
"party": ss.2(1), 31(1), (2)
"rules": ss.7, 31(1)
"seated in Scotland": ss.2, 31(1)
"tribunal": ss.2(1), 31(1)

COMMENTARY

Introductory

S16–01 The Act looks to extend its provisions to statutory arbitrations where those provisions might appropriately apply to such arbitrations. Much the same ground is covered by ss.94–97 of the 1996 Act.

S16–02 For reasons that are unclear, the substantive provisions of the Act have not been brought into force for statutory provisions (The Arbitration (Scotland) Act 2010 (Commencement No.1 and Transitional Provisions) Order 2010 (SSI 2010/195) art.2). Until this occurs, statutory arbitrations will continue to be governed by the pre-2010 Act law.

S16–03 Article 6(1) of the ECHR (see commentary on s.1 at paras S1–11 to S1–22) gives a right to a fair trial of civil rights and obligations by a tribunal "established by law". Typically, arbitral tribunals are not "established by law" but by the consent of the parties in the choice of arbitrator or mechanism for choice of arbitrators. This means that, in the absence of a clear and unequivocal waiver by the parties of this part of art.6(1), a statutory (and therefore compulsory) arbitration will be incompatible with art.6(1) unless in the circumstances of the statutory provision in question, the imposition of arbitration was in pursuit of a legitimate aim and was a proportionate means of pursuing that aim (*Lithgow v United Kingdom* (1986) 8 E.H.R.R. 329 at [194]).

S16–04 In *Suda v The Czech Republic* (1643/06) Unreported October 28, 2010 ECtHR, it was held that a provision which referred a dispute over compensation for compulsory purchase of shares to arbitrators chosen by the disputing parties from a list kept by a company limited by guarantee would not involve determination of rights by a tribunal "established by law".

The authors submit that, in the light of *Lithgow* and *Suda*, any statutory provision that imposes arbitration for the resolution of a dispute (which is not a proportional means of pursuing a legitimate aim) must be read as being subject to the proviso that the parties consent thereto (HRA s.3(1)). On that interpretation, if the parties do not consent thereto the arbitral tribunal will lack jurisdiction. In any statutory arbitration this matter should be dealt with by the tribunal at the outset of the arbitration. **S16–05**

Section 16(1)—Scope of "statutory arbitration"

A "statutory arbitration" is one that is pursuant to an enactment which "provides for a dispute to be submitted to arbitration". **S16–06**

"Enactment" in this context includes Acts of (the UK) Parliament, Acts of the Scottish Parliament and subordinate legislation under either, provided that they are part of Scots law (Interpretation Order art.6(3) and Scotland Act 1998 ss.127 and 126(1)). **S16–07**

If the enactment makes arbitration mandatory, it is plainly a statutory arbitration in terms of s.16(1). If the wording of the enactment merely permits arbitration, the authors submit that the subsequent arbitration is not a "statutory arbitration" in terms of s.16(1) but is an ordinary arbitration founded on a voluntary arbitration agreement which may incorporate some elements of the statute. **S16–08**

SAAVA has taken the view that the 2010 Act is in force for arbitrations voluntarily agreed by the parties under s.61 of the Agricultural Holdings (Scotland) Act 1991 and s.78 of the Agricultural Holdings (Scotland) Act 2003 (notwithstanding that the 2010 Act is not in force for "statutory arbitrations") and, by implication, agree with the view of the authors expressed above. SAAVA has produced a set of arbitral rules for such disputes. It is available on *http://www.saava.org.uk/dispute-resolution.php* [Accessed January 28, 2014]. **S16–09**

Section 61 of the Agricultural Holdings (Scotland) Act 1991 provides that various matters may be resolved by arbitration "if the landlord and tenant so agree at or after the time when the matter arises". Section 61A contains various provisions as to procedure for such a voluntarily agreed arbitration, which includes a right of appeal on a "question of law" to the Scottish Land Court. In effect, s.61A forms part of the parties' own arbitral rules and the right of appeal to the Land Court must be seen as an arbitral process of review that cannot supersede or affect the restricted right of appeal under r.69 (see also commentary on r.69). Sections 78 and 79 of the Agricultural Holdings (Scotland) Act 2003 contain similar provisions. The authors submit that such arbitrations are not "statutory arbitrations" in terms of s.16(1) and that nothing in ss.61A or 79 affects the application of the 2010 Act to such arbitrations. **S16 10**

Section 16(2)

S16–11 The Act is clearly designed to apply to consensual arbitrations. Accordingly, in order to ensure that the Act (including the rules) applies to non-consensual statutory arbitrations, it is necessary to treat the relevant statute as if it were an arbitration agreement.

Section 16(2) should be read as extending the definition of "arbitration agreement" in s.4 and elsewhere in the Act.

Section 16(3)

S16–12 This echoes s.9(4) of the Act. In effect it makes the statutory provisions applicable to statutory arbitrations equivalent to institutional arbitral rules, with the difference that the statutory arbitral provisions override even inconsistent mandatory rules of the SAR.

Section 16(4)

S16–13 Section 16(4) follows on from subs.(1) in that it takes an arbitration pursuant to legislation in force in Scotland as being seated in Scotland. There are a number of aims behind this.

S16–14 First, it avoids, from the viewpoint of the Scottish courts, any question of whether a statutory arbitration involving, for example, one party resident in Scotland and the other in England is seated in Scotland or England or indeed anywhere else.

S16–15 Secondly, it ensures that the parties cannot agree to have a statutory arbitration under Scottish legislation decided by a non-Scottish arbitral procedure. There is of course the possibility, unlikely in the context of a statutory arbitration, that a non-Scottish court might decide that the arbitration is seated in its own jurisdiction. If that *Braes of Doune*-type scenario should arise (see commentary at para.S3–16 above), a Scottish court will have to consider whether it should recognise the foreign judgment: see the commentary on s.3(1)(b). Sometimes the statute itself will specify the criteria which will determine whether arbitration is to be Scottish (see, e.g. Industry Act 1975 Sch.3 para.18).

Section 16(5)

S16–16 Certain SAR are excluded entirely from statutory arbitrations.
S16–17 Rule 43 allows any party to apply to the court to extend time limits in the arbitration agreement or as otherwise agreed by the parties.
S16–18 The wish not to derogate from the statutory arbitration agreement is evident in the exclusions of rr.71(9) and 80.

Section 16(6)

Like s.96(3) of the 1996 Act, this makes it clear that in the statutory context the power to agree to the consolidation of other proceedings or to the holding of concurrent hearings only applies to proceedings held under the same enactment, thus avoiding the potential difficulties of the consolidation of proceedings held under inconsistent statutory codes or indeed of the consolidation of statutory and consensual arbitrations.

S16–19

Power to adapt enactments providing for statutory arbitration

17. Ministers may by order—
  (a) modify any of the Scottish Arbitration Rules, or any other provisions of this Act, in so far as they apply to statutory arbitrations (or to particular statutory arbitrations),
  (b) make such modifications of enactments which provide for disputes to be submitted to arbitration as they consider appropriate in consequence of, or in order to give full effect to, any of the Scottish Arbitration Rules or any other provisions of this Act.

DEFINITIONS

"arbitration": ss.2(1), (2), 31(1)
"dispute": ss.2(1), 31(1)
"Ministers": s.31(1)
"party": ss.2(1), 31(1), (2)
"rules": ss.7, 31(1)
"statutory arbitrations": ss.16(1), 31(1)

COMMENTARY

Paragraph (a) is the equivalent of s.98(1) of the 1996 Act, albeit that the latter provision also confers power to exclude any provision of that Act in relation to statutory arbitrations. No orders have as yet been made under the 1996 Act.

S17–01

Section 17 requires to be read with s.33.

It may be that these provisions could be used to give effect to art.6(1) of the ECHR, insofar as it applies to statutory arbitrations.

S17–02

The power in para.(b) to modify other enactments to give full effect to the 2010 Act is not similar to anything in the 1996 Act, and seems rather bold. It is, of course, beyond the competence of the Scottish Parliament to empower Ministers to modify an enactment of the UK Parliament.

S17–03

Recognition and enforcement of New York Convention awards

New York Convention awards

18.—(1) A "Convention award" is an award made in pursuance of a written arbitration agreement in the territory of a state (other than the United Kingdom) which is a party to the New York Convention.

(2) An award is to be treated for the purposes of this section as having been made at the seat of the arbitration.

(3) A declaration by Her Majesty by Order in Council that a state is a party to the Convention (or is a party in respect of any territory) is conclusive evidence of that fact.

DEFINITIONS

"arbitration agreement": ss.4, 31(1)
"New York Convention": s.31(1)

COMMENTARY

Introductory

S18–01 On June 24, 1975, the UK (belatedly) ratified the New York Convention which ensures both the international recognition of arbitration agreements (see s.10 above) and, more importantly, the recognition and enforcement, in contracting states, of arbitral awards made in other contracting states. It was enacted into law by the 1975 Act, applicable in each of England and Wales, Northern Ireland and Scotland, and it entered into force in respect of the UK on December 23, 1975 pursuant to SI 1975/1662.

S18–02 The 1996 Act repealed the 1975 Act as regards England and Wales (and Northern Ireland) and re-enacted its provisions in ss.100–104, but the 1975 Act remained in force in Scotland. The 2010 Act has repealed the 1975 Act as regards Scotland and has re-enacted its provisions in ss.18–22 with certain modifications. This repeal and re-enactment was necessary because of the importance of making the 2010 Act as comprehensive as possible (however, see Appendix 1 concerning arbitrations involving consumers).

S18–03 Sections 18–22 differ from the rest of the Act in that they do not address arbitral proceedings seated in Scotland but instead address the recognition and/or enforcement in Scotland of arbitration agreements and awards made outwith the UK. Such recognition or enforcement in Scotland is thought to be very rare (the authors know of only a single relevant reported case of recognition—*La Pantofola D'Oro SpA v Blane Leisure Ltd*, 2000 S.L.T. 105—where the right to arbitrate was waived) and anecdotal evidence from the authors' colleagues reveals no others.

S18–04 It is important to note that the 1975 Act and, therefore, ss.18–22 of the 2010 Act reflect (at least until (if ever) Scotland achieves full independence and becomes party to the New York Convention in its own right) the UK's, not Scotland's, obligations under an international treaty. It follows that decisions of the English courts interpreting ss.100–104 of the 1996 Act must, in Scotland, be considered highly persuasive and those of the House of Lords/UKSC virtually binding.

Section 18(1)—Convention awards

Sections 18–21 provide for the recognition and enforcement in Scotland of arbitral awards made in non-UK states which are parties to the Convention, hence the concept of a "Convention award". S18–05

This does not mean that foreign awards which are not Convention awards may not be enforced in Scotland—see ss.22 and 12—but they cannot be enforced under the regime created by ss.18–21. This restriction is provided for by art.I(3) of the Convention and, as at June 17, 2014, it was applicable in 73 of the 150 contracting states (on June 23, 2014, Burundi acceded to the Convention thereby becoming the 150th party thereto, including practically every significant trading nation—see *http://www.uncitral.org/uncitral/en/uncitral_texts/arbitration/NYConvention_status.html* [Accessed July 10, 2014]). S18–06

Article I(3) also allows contracting states to apply the Convention only to legal relationships which are considered commercial (the "commercial reservation"). As at June 17, 2014, this reservation applied in respect of 45 states but not the UK. S18–07

Whereas under the law of certain states, procedural and jurisdictional rulings and suchlike may take the form of awards (see, e.g. s.30 of the 1996 Act), the Convention is aimed at the recognition and enforcement of final awards in the sense of an award which deals conclusively with a substantive issue between the parties. It follows that part awards (see r.54 and paras R54–04 to R54–11) can be enforced under the Convention (see *Resort Condominiums International Inc v Bolwell* (1994) XX YCA 628; *Nigerian National Petroleum Corp v IPCO (Nigeria) Ltd* [2008] EWCA Civ 1157; in respect of *NNPC v IPCO*, see (i) "Partial Enforcement of Arbitral Awards" (2008) 74 *Arbitration* at 330–337 and (ii) "*IPCO v NPPC* on Appeal" (2009) 75 *Arbitration* at 126–127, both by Hew R. Dundas). S18–08

In pursuance of a written arbitration agreement

Convention awards can be made only "in pursuance of a written arbitration agreement", echoing s.102(2)(a) of the 1996 Act. However, while an agreement in writing is particularly widely defined by art.7(2) of the Model Law and by s.5 of the 1996 Act, the 2010 Act does not offer any definition. However, a definition is provided by the Scotland Act 1998 (Transitory and Transitional Provisions) (Publication and Interpretation etc. of Acts of the Scottish Parliament) Order 1999 (SI 1999/1379), by virtue of para.6(2) and Sch.2, which provides that "writing includes any means of representing or reproducing words in a visible form". Although this is not how "writing" is S18–09 defined in art.II(2) of the Convention, it is no doubt sufficiently widely defined to accord with the UK's Convention obligations.

S18–10 However, the 1999 definition is not as wide as s.5 of the 1996 Act under which there is a written arbitration agreement where the agreement is made by an exchange of communications in writing, where it is evidenced in writing, where the parties agree otherwise than in writing by reference to written terms, and where there is an exchange of submissions in legal or arbitral proceedings where the existence of an unwritten arbitration agreement is alleged by one party and not denied by the other. It is also provided that the idea of writing includes an agreement being recorded by any means. Thus s.5 of the 1996 Act covers, for example, Lloyds Open Form ("LOF"), the worldwide salvage industry's standard contract which includes an arbitration clause. LOF envisages the Master of a salvage tug asking, by radio, the Master of a stricken vessel "do you accept Lloyds Open Form?" and, on the latter's responding "yes", a contract is deemed entered into including a (written) arbitration agreement.

S18–11 Even if a wide, purposive interpretation is given to the idea of a written arbitration agreement under the 2010 Act, it might not stretch to covering all of the above situations. This could, in theory, lead to the anomalous result that, while the UK is a party to the Convention, certain awards (e.g. LOF ones) might be enforced in England but might not be enforceable in Scotland or at least not enforceable under the regime laid down by s.18.

Section 18(2)—Award made at seat of arbitration

S18–12 This mirrors s.100(2)(b) of the 1996 Act in making it clear that an award is to be regarded as made at the seat of the arbitration. This negates the effect of the remarkable decision of the House of Lords in *Hiscox v Outhwaite* [1992] 1 A.C. 562 that an award in an arbitration between two English parties, conducted in London by an English arbitrator under English substantive and procedural law, was to be treated as a French award because the arbitrator indicated that he had signed it while in Paris. The question of where an arbitrator (or the last arbitrator to sign) happens to be when he signs the award is now irrelevant; see paras R52–02, R52–05 and R52–06.

S18–13 The concept of the (juridical) seat ("place" in Model Law terminology) of the arbitration appears in s.3 which determines when Scotland is to be treated as the seat of the arbitration; importantly, the physical location of the arbitration may not be, and need not be, the same as the seat (see commentary on r.29). However, the 2010 Act omits any equivalent to s.3 of the 1996 Act actually defining that concept.

Section 18(3)

This, like s.100(3) of the 1996 Act, represents an advance on s.7(2) of the 1975 Act by recognising the possibility, contemplated by art.X(1) of the Convention, that a state may extend the Convention to any territory for the international relations of which it is responsible. Certain states have extended the Convention in that manner, e.g. in respect of the PRC, Hong Kong and Macao, in respect of the UK, Gibraltar, the Isle of Man, Bermuda, the Cayman Islands, Guernsey and Jersey. For an up-to-date list of states party to the Convention and territories to which the Convention has been extended, see *http://www.uncitral.org/uncitral/en/uncitral_texts/arbitration/NYConvention_status.html* [Accessed June 17, 2014]. **S18–14**

The purpose of s.18(3) is to remove any question of whether a state or territory is covered by the Convention where the state or territory is declared in the Order. The only order that has been made is the Arbitration (Foreign Awards) Order 1984 (SI 1984/1168) which declares a number of states to be parties to the Convention in respect of territories for whose international relations they are responsible (e.g. France in respect of all the territories of the French Republic and USA in respect of all territories for whose international relations they are (respectively) responsible). It also covers the Byelorussian and Ukrainian Soviet Socialist Republics which were state parties to the Convention even before the dissolution of the Soviet Union and are now independent. The 1984 Order remains in force and has to be interpreted as having been made under s.18(3) (Intepretation Act 1978 s.17(2)(a)). **S18–15**

Recognition and enforcement of New York Convention awards

19.—(1) A Convention award is to be recognised as binding on the persons as between whom it was made (and may accordingly be relied on by those persons in any legal proceedings in Scotland).

(2) The court may order that a Convention award may be enforced as if it were an extract registered decree bearing a warrant for execution granted by the court.

DEFINITIONS

"Convention award": ss.16, 31(1)
"court": s.31(1)

MODEL LAW

Article 35 of the Model Law (as amended in 2006) is quoted at para.S12–01 above. **S19–01**

Arbitration (Scotland) Act 2010

COMMENTARY

Section 19(1)—Recognition

S19–02 This provides for the recognition of a Convention award and derives from s.3(2) of the 1975 Act, which provided that the award could be "relied on by way of defence, set off or otherwise in any legal proceedings" in the UK. Section 101(1) of the 1996 Act is in similar terms. Although s.19(1) uses different language, the wider language gives an indication of what its effect might be. Thus if litigation is sought to be commenced in Scotland, the award can be used to support a plea of res judicata. In one English case, it was held that an award might be recognised as barring litigation but might still not be enforced since appeal proceedings remained open at the seat of the arbitration (*Svenska Petroleum Exploration AB v Republic of Lithuania* [2005] 1 Lloyd's Rep. 515).

S19–03 The award may also justify a plea of compensation, so that if one party is suing the other for, say, £1,000,000, the respondent can argue that he is due £500,000 from the other under an arbitral award. It has also been held in England that it is possible to seek a declaration that an award is binding (*Irvani v Irvani* [2000] 1 Lloyd's Rep. 412).

Section 19(2)—Enforcement

S19–04 An application for enforcement may be made either to the Outer House or to a sheriff court of the sheriffdom where the respondent in the application is domiciled in terms of ss.41 or 42 of the 1982 Act.

S19–05 If the application is made to the Outer House, it is made by petition in the style contained in RCS Form 14.4 (RCS rr.62.57, 14.4) or, if there are undisposed of Outer House proceedings, by note (RCS r.62.57). The requirements for the petition are set out in RCS r.14.4 and r.15.2 for notes.

S19–06 Together with the petition, the applicant should lodge the following documents with the Court of Session:

(i) the documents listed in s.21 and RCS r.62.57(2);
(ii) the bundle of court documents known as the process (see RCS rr.4.3, 4.4).

Inventories of any productions should be intimated to the other parties and members of the tribunal.

S19–07 If the application is made to the sheriff court, it is made by summary application in the style contained in SASAR Sch.1 Form 1 (SASAR r.2.4). The requirements for the summary application are broadly the same as for the petition described above. Detailed reference should be made to the SASAR. Unlike the Court of Session procedure, the sheriff court application will require to be served on the respondent party at the outset.

S19–08 On granting the application, the Outer House or the sheriff court will grant a warrant for registration (RCS r.62.58) which, when lodged with the documents in r.62.58(4) with the Keeper of the Registers of Scotland, will enable registration in the Books of Council and Session for execution. Such registration will enable the extract of the registered award to be enforced as if it were a Scottish court decree (judgment): for types of enforcement see commentary on s.12(1).

S19–09 Upon registration of the Court of Session warrant the applicant must serve on the respondent party a statutory notice of the granting of the warrant (RCS r.62.59) and before the Keeper will issue an extract of the registered award, the applicant must lodge the certificate of service of the notice of the warrant on the respondent party (RCS r.62.58(5)).

S19–10 If this certificate has been served, it may trigger an application for refusal of enforcement under r.62.60 of the RCS and art.V of the New York Convention under which the respondent can seek to establish a defence to the enforcement and recall any warrant granted (see RCS r.62.60).

S19–11 In *IPCO (Nigeria) Ltd v Nigerian National Petroleum Corp (No.2)* [2009] 1 Lloyd's Rep. 89 CA the Court of Appeal granted partial enforcement (as distinct from enforcement of a part award) in circumstances where the award was being challenged at the seat but where certain sums were undoubtedly due to the claimant; see "Partial Enforcement Of Arbitral Awards" (2008) 74 *Arbitration* 330–337 and "*IPCO v NNPC* On Appeal" (2009) 75 *Arbitration* 126–127, both by Hew R. Dundas.

S19–12 An application under s.19 for enforcement under the New York Convention is a proceeding in relation to which a respondent can apply for caution (security) (pronounced "*kayshon*") for the expenses (costs) of that proceeding. For further information the reader is referred to the commentary in Ch.33 of *Greens' Annotated Rules of the Court of Session* (Edinburgh: W. Green). While for the purposes of an application for caution an applicant under s.19 will be treated as a pursuer rather than a defender (*Diag Human SA v Czech Republic* [2014] 1 All E.R. (Comm) 605; [2013] EWHC 3190 (Comm) at [35]), if the award gives the s.19 applicant on any view a claim well in excess of the likely expenses of the enforcement proceedings, that will suggest that an application for caution should be refused (*Diag Human SA* (above) at [48] per Burton J.). The authors submit that the Scottish courts should adopt the same approach as in *Diag Human*.

Refusal of recognition or enforcement

20.—(1) Recognition or enforcement of a Convention award may be refused only in accordance with this section.

(2) Recognition or enforcement of a Convention award may be refused if the person against whom it is invoked proves—
- **(a) that a party was under some incapacity under the law applicable to the party,**
- **(b) that the arbitration agreement was invalid under the law which the**

parties agree should govern it (or, failing any indication of that law, under the law of the country where the award was made),
- (c) that the person—
  - (i) was not given proper notice of the arbitral process or of the appointment of the tribunal, or
  - (ii) was otherwise unable to present the person's case,
- (d) that the tribunal was constituted, or the arbitration was conducted, otherwise than in accordance with—
  - (i) the agreement of the parties, or
  - (ii) failing such agreement, the law of the country where the arbitration took place.

(3) Recognition or enforcement of a Convention award may also be refused if the person against whom it is invoked proves that the award—
- (a) deals with a dispute not contemplated by or not falling within the submission to arbitration,
- (b) contains decisions on matters beyond the scope of that submission,
- (c) is not yet binding on the person, or
- (d) has been set aside or suspended by a competent authority.

(4) Recognition or enforcement of a Convention award may also be refused if—
- (a) the award relates to a matter which is not capable of being settled by arbitration, or
- (b) to do so would be contrary to public policy.

(5) A Convention award containing decisions on matters not submitted to arbitration may be recognised or enforced to the extent that it contains decisions on matters which were so submitted which are separable from decisions on matters not so submitted.

(6) The court before which a Convention award is sought to be relied on may, if an application for the setting aside or suspension of the award is made to a competent authority—
- (a) sist the decision on recognition or enforcement of the award,
- (b) on the application of the party claiming recognition or enforcement, order the other party to give suitable security.

(7) In this section "competent authority" means a person who has authority to set aside or suspend the Convention award concerned in the country in which (or under the law of which) the Convention award concerned was made.

DEFINITIONS

"arbitration": ss.2(1), (2), 31(1)
"arbitration agreement": ss.4, 31(1)
"Convention award": ss.18, 31(1)
"court": s.31(1)
"dispute": ss.2(1), 31(1)
"party": ss.2(1), 31(1), (2)

"tribunal": ss.2(1), 31(1)

MODEL LAW

Article 36 of the Model Law (as amended in 2006) follows closely arts V **S20–01** and VI of the New York Convention upon which s.20 is based.

COMMENTARY

Introductory

No court faced with a request for recognition or enforcement of a Con- **S20–02** vention award is obliged to grant it in all cases. There will be situations where it will be appropriate to decline recognition or enforcement (see paras S20–17, S20–18 and S20–23) and these are addressed by s.20, which is a revised version of s.5 of the 1975 Act and which in turn was based on arts V and VI of the Convention (see also s.103 of the 1996 Act).

The grounds on which recognition or enforcement may be denied fall into **S20–03** two categories. The first, given in s.20(2) and (3), defines the grounds which have to be established by the party resisting recognition or enforcement. That party bears the burden of proof (see *Corporacion Transnacional de Inversiones SA de CV v STET International SpA* (2000) O.R. 414), by contrast to the position taken by the 1927 Geneva Convention. The second, given in s.20(4), consists of two grounds which merely have to be perceived by the court as existing. Even if a party appears to have no defence to an enforcement application, or if a defence tendered under s.20(2) or (3) is found to have no substance, then should the court find, for example, that the award deals with a matter which may not, under the law of Scotland, be arbitrated, then it will almost certainly refuse enforcement whether or not the issue is raised by any party.

The primary role of the Convention in practice is in ensuring the enfor- **S20–04** cement of arbitral awards rather than to find grounds upon which enforcement may be denied. Most developed legal jurisdictions apply a "pro-enforcement bias" (e.g. see Gross J. in *IPCO (Nigeria) Ltd v Nigerian National Petroleum Corp* [2005] 2 Lloyd's Rep. 326 at 328). It follows that the grounds in s.20(2) and (3) afford a basis on which the recognition or enforcement of an award "may" be denied, allowing for the possibility that an award might yet be enforced even if a ground is made out. As Kaplan J. noted in the Hong Kong Supreme Court in *China Nanhai Oil Joint Service Corp v Gee Tai Holdings Ltd* [1995] A.D.R.L.J 127 at 132:

> "Even if a ground of opposition is proved, there is still a residual discretion left in the enforcing court to enforce nonetheless. This shows that the grounds of opposition are not to be inflexibly applied. The residual discretion enables the enforcing court to achieve a just result in all the circumstances."

S20–05 There are numerous examples of situations where a Convention award has been enforced despite the respondent's establishing an apparent defence. This might arise where, for example, although a ground might technically exist, it is not regarded as having sufficient substance to prevent enforcement. It is also recognised that the doctrine of personal bar or estoppel may be invoked to prevent a party relying on a ground of which he must have been aware throughout most of the arbitral proceedings, but which he chose not to raise before the stage of enforcement; as Kaplan J. observed in *China Nanhai Oil* [1995] A.D.R.L.J 127 at 131:

> "If the doctrine of estoppel can apply to arguments of the written form of the arbitration agreement then I fail to see why it cannot also apply to the grounds in Art. V. It strikes me as quite unfair for a party to appreciate that there might be something wrong with the composition of the tribunal yet not to make any formal submission whatsoever to the tribunal about its own jurisdiction and then to proceed to fight the case on its merits and then two years after the award to attempt to nullify the whole proceedings".

S20–06 Analogously, courts are often reluctant to deny enforcement on the basis of an issue which might have been raised before the courts of the seat, but which was not (see *Minmetals Germany GmbH v Ferco Steel Ltd* [1999] 1 All E.R. (Comm) 315; *Svenska Petroleum AB v Lithuania* [2005] 1 Lloyd's Rep. 515). In *China Agribusiness Development Corp v Balli Trading* [1998] 2 Lloyd's Rep. 76 at 80 (see also *Karaha Bodas Co LLC v Perusahaan Pertambangan Minyak Dan Gas Bumi Negara-Pertamina* (2003) XXVIII YCA 752) Longmore J. said:

> "A party who, only at the door of the enforcing court, dreams up a reason for suggesting that a Convention award should not be enforced is unlikely to have the Court's sympathy exercised in his favour."

S20–07 The Court of Appeal has, however, in recent years made it clear that the discretion to enforce despite a ground being made out should not be exercised lightly: if a party establishes a substantial ground of objection, the court should decline to enforce the award unless estoppel appears to have arisen (see *Yukos Oil Ltd v Dardana Ltd* [2002] 2 Lloyd's Rep. 326 at [8] and [18] per Mance L.J.; *Kanoria v Guinness* [2006] 1 Lloyd's Rep. 701). See also *Dallah Real Estate & Tourism Holding Co v Ministry of Religious Affairs of the Government of Pakistan* [2011] 1 A.C. 763 at 843, [127] per Lord Collins of Mapesbury J.S.C.).

S20–08 However, this approach tends to be adopted only in relation to the grounds mentioned in s.20(2) and (3), dealing with issues relating to the parties or to the proceedings in question. The grounds which appear in s.20(4) are more fundamental, going to the heart of Scots law, e.g. it is all but inconceivable that a Scottish court would enforce an award on an issue not arbitrable under the law of Scotland. See commentary on s.30.

Section 20(1)—Exclusive grounds for refusing recognition or enforcement

It is clear from the text of art.V of the Convention that recognition or enforcement may be refused *only* on the basis of the grounds therein and that contracting states may not seek to add to these. This principle has also been widely accepted in Convention jurisprudence (see e.g. *Parsons & Whittemore Overseas Co Inc Societe Generale de l'Industrie du Papier (RAKTA)*, 508 F.2d 969 (2nd Cir. 1974); *Karaha Bodas Co LLC v Perusahaan Pertambangan Minyak Dan Gas Bumi Negara-Pertamina* (2003) XXVIII YCA 752). **S20–09**

Both s.5(1) of the 1975 Act, which this provision replaces, and s.103(1) of the 1996 Act are in different language, indicating that enforcement "of a Convention award shall not be refused except in the cases mentioned in this section". The authors submit, however, that the effect is identical. **S20–10**

Note that, as a practical matter, enforcement might not be granted where it is unclear what the award has ordered (see *Tongyuan (USA) International Trading Group v Uni-Clan Ltd* (2001) XXVI YCA 886). As regards "unclear", r.71(8) (see below) does not assist since s.20 is, by definition, concerned only with Convention awards to which r.71(8) cannot apply. **S20–11**

Section 20(2)—Defences to recognition or enforcement

This subsection allows, but does not oblige, the court to refuse recognition or enforcement if the party resisting recognition or enforcement can establish any one or more of a number of grounds. **S20–12**

Section 20(2)(a)—Incapacity

Section 20(2)(a) re-enacts (in slightly different language) s.5(2)(a) of the 1975 Act (see also s.103(2)(a) of the 1996 Act). Article V(1)(a) of the Convention refers to the parties to the arbitration agreement being "under the law applicable to them, under some incapacity" but the language of the 2010 Act captures the intended meaning more precisely, since it cannot have been envisaged that *both* parties had to lack capacity before art.V(1)(a) was triggered, particularly given that the respective capacities of the parties may be governed by different laws. **S20–13**

The wording of art.V(1)(a) was criticised by the framers of the Model Law, since: **S20–14**

> "they appeared to contain a conflict of law rule which in fact was either incomplete or misleading in that the rule might be understood as referring to the law of the nationality, domicile or residence of the

parties" (*Report of UNCITRAL on the work of its eighteenth session*, UN A/40/17, para.280).

Yet the framers of the Model Law offered no practical solution to this problem, and nor does the current provision.

S20–15 It is therefore necessary to refer to the Scots conflict of law rules to determine the law to be used to judge capacity: the capacity of any party is to be determined by the *lex loci contractus* (*McFeetridge v Stewarts & Lloyds*, 1913 S.C. 773) which in Scots law means the law of the locality of the contract as ascertained from the nature of the contract and the place of performance, or, if it is more important than performance, the place in which the contract was signed (*Valery v Scott* (1876) 3 R. 965 at 967).

S20–16 In the modern world, the capacity of a legal person is generally determined by the law of the state in which the entity in question is incorporated or, if different, possibly (in certain exceptional circumstances) the place of its central management and control (e.g. a recent highly-publicised instance of a Delaware-incorporated corporation which had reportedly transferred its domicile, and the place of its central management and control, to Switzerland).

S20–17 There have been cases where an award has been refused enforcement because the act of entering into the agreement was ultra vires a corporate party (compare the approaches of the BGH in (1999) XXIV YCA 928; and the Bermuda Court of Appeal in *Sojuzneftexport v JOC Oil Ltd* (1990) XV YCA 384), or because such a party was not properly incorporated (see *Sokofl Star Shipping Co Inc v GPVO Technopromexport* (1998) XXIII YCA 742 Moscow District Court).

S20–18 A number of awards have also been denied enforcement on this ground on the basis that the individual seeking to bind the corporation to the arbitration agreement lacked the power or authority to do so (see, e.g. the Italian Corte Suprema di Cassazione in *Dalmine SpA v M & M Sheet Metal Forming Machinery* (1999) XXIV YCA 709). It can be argued that this is a matter affecting either the validity of the arbitration agreement or the jurisdiction of the tribunal and not an issue of capacity at all, a view taken by the French Cour de Cassation in *Tresor Public v Galakis*, 1966 *Revue de l'Arbitrage* 99.

S20–19 There is no UK authority on the issue, but then there is no UK authority on any aspect of art.V(1)(a); however, in *Continental Enterprises Ltd v Shandong Zhucheng Foreign Trade Group Co* [2005] EWHC 92 (Comm), a challenge under s.67 of the 1996 Act, the court upheld the decision by the tribunal that it had no jurisdiction over the respondent on the ground that the latter had had no capacity to have entered into the contract or the arbitration agreement. David Steel J. concluded (at [72]):

> "A Chinese court would thus conclude that a Chinese party without a foreign trade permit would not be entitled to enter into a GAFTA arbitration agreement. The issues of policy are the same: see *Harbour*

Assurance v. Kansa [1993] 1 Lloyd's Rep 455 per Lord Hoffman at p. 469."

Public bodies have been known to claim that, under the laws of the state which created them, they have no capacity to enter into an arbitration agreement, or that such capacity is dependent on receiving certain official approval or permission which has not been obtained in the case in question. Certain states (e.g. Spain, Switzerland but not the UK) have enacted legislation preventing such bodies relying on their own law to seek to evade their obligations under arbitral awards where they freely agreed to arbitrate in the first place. However, certain courts have decided that, by agreeing to arbitrate, such bodies have impliedly waived the right to rely on their alleged incapacity, e.g. in *Societe Arabe des Engrais Phosphates v Gemanco Srl* (1997) XXII YCA 737 at 742, the Italian Corte Suprema di Cassazione said: **S20–20**

"Under the law applicable to international commercial arbitration, which necessarily governs the arbitration clause in the present case, legal persons of public law may undoubtedly agree to arbitration, independent of domestic prohibitions, by expressing their consent."

Other courts have held that, while such restrictions may be pleaded in domestic arbitrations, they may not be relied upon to seek to prevent the enforcement of awards in international arbitration (see the decision of a Tunisian court in *Societe Tunisienne d'Electricitee et de Gaz v Societe Entrepose* (1978) III YCA 283; and the Paris Cour d'Appel in *Ministere Tunisien de l'Equipment v Bec Freres* (1997) XXII YCA 682). **S20–21**

Where a foreign public body claims that it did not have the capacity to enter into the arbitration agreement, there may be scope for the exercise of the overriding discretion to allow enforcement as discussed in the introductory commentary above. **S20–22**

State entities may sometimes seek to invoke the doctrine of state or sovereign immunity to resist enforcement of arbitral awards. This has sometimes been done successfully (e.g. *Egypt v SPP Ltd* (1985) X YCA 113), while on other occasions courts have decided that an arbitration agreement operates as a waiver of immunity (e.g. *American Oil Co v Libya* (1981) 20 I.L.M. 893). **S20–23**

In Scotland, the position is governed by s.9(1) of the State Immunity Act 1978 which indicates that a state which agrees to arbitrate is not immune as respects proceedings in the courts of the UK which relate to the arbitration (see, e.g. *Svenska Petroleum AB v Republic of Lithuania (No.2)* [2006] 1 Lloyd's Rep. 181). Concerning *Svenska*, vide (i) Hew R. Dundas, "Non-Party Disclosure and Witnesses, Enforcement of Foreign Awards and Costs: Recent Decisions in the English Courts" (2005) 71 *Arbitration* 172–178 and (ii) Hew Dundas' Newsletter #12 (entries dated October 13, 2005 and November 16, 2005) available at *http://www.dundasarbitrator.com* [Accessed **S20–24**

June 17, 2014]. The court may also decline to enforce under s.20(4)(a) (art.V(2)(a) of the Convention) on the basis that the dispute is not arbitrable under Scots law (see paras S20–102 to S20–105).

S20–25 The case law demonstrates that, subject to issues such as waiver, the party seeking to resist enforcement may found either on its own incapacity or that of the other party. Further, the language of s.20(2)(a) allows it to found on the incapacity of any party to the arbitration agreement, whether or not the latter is party to enforcement proceedings, or indeed participated in the arbitration. The authors are unaware of any authority on this point and they seriously doubt whether a court would accept such a tangential defence as a bar to enforcement.

S20–26 Reference to "was" in s.20(2)(a) should, as a matter of language, be interpreted to mean that the relevant point should be the date of entry into the arbitration agreement, i.e. that any incapacity arising after that point is irrelevant; this was the view taken by one New York decision (*Corcoran v AIG Multi-line Syndicate Inc* (1990) XV YCA 586). However, a later decision from the same jurisdiction insists that supervening incapacity is a good ground for refusing enforcement (*Corcoran v Ardra Insurance Co Ltd* (1991) XVI YCA 663).

Section 20(2)(b)—Arbitration agreement invalid

S20–27 This re-enacts s.5(2)(b) of the 1975 Act (see also s.103(2)(b) of the 1996 Act) and is based on the second part of art.V(1)(a) of the Convention.

S20–28 A party can seek to resist enforcement if it can establish that the arbitration agreement was invalid under the law agreed as governing it or, in the absence of such agreement, under the law of the seat. The law of the seat therefore becomes of importance only if there is no indication of the law governing the arbitration agreement (see commentary on s.6, above). The parties may, of course, have expressly specified that law.

S20–29 If they have not so established, then the fact that the parties have chosen a particular law to govern the contract between them has in the past been regarded as an implied choice of the law governing the arbitration agreement, in the absence of strong indications to the contrary. In *Sonatrach Corporation (BVI) v Ferrell International Ltd* [2002] 1 All E.R. (Comm) 627, Colman J. said at [32]:

> " ... Where the substantive contract contains an express choice of law, but the agreement to arbitrate contains no separate express choice of law, the latter agreement will normally be governed by the body of law expressly chosen to govern the substantive contract ..."

Further, in *Deutsche Schachtbau v Shell Petroleum International Co Ltd* [1990] 1 A.C. 295, the House of Lords decided that the circumstances suggested that the parties must have intended that the arbitration agreement be governed by Swiss law, despite the contract being governed by English law.

Recently, however, the English courts have held in several cases that the choice of a particular arbitral seat amounts to an implied choice of the law of that state to govern the arbitration agreement, even though the contract between the parties is explicitly subject to a different law (see, e.g. *Sulamerica CIA Nacional Seguros SA v Enesa Enghenharia SA* [2012] EWCA Civ 638 and *C v D* [2008] 1 Lloyds Rep. 239; in the latter regard, see Hew R. Dundas, *"C v D*: The USA Conquers England—or Does it? The Law of the Arbitration Agreement, Challenges to Awards and Abuse of Process" (2007) 73 *Arbitration* 431–440). S20–30

That approach was recently followed in *Dallah Real Estate and Tourism Holding Co v Pakistan* [2011] 1 A.C. 763 where the UKSC upheld the Court of Appeal (which, in turn, had upheld Aikens J. at first instance) in refusing enforcement of a French-seated award. The essence of those prior decisions concerned the application of French law (given the French seat) to the issue of the validity of the arbitration agreement. Since, at least in the unanimous view of all nine UKSC Justices (one was Scots), French law led to the conclusion that Pakistan was not a party to the agreement (perhaps unsurprisingly, the Paris Cour d'Appel disagreed—forcefully), it could not be valid, so that the award—an ICC award—was refused enforcement. S20–31

Section 20(2)(c)—Party not able to present its case (failure of "due process")

Section 20(2)(b) largely re-enacts s.5(2)(c) of the 1975 Act (see also s.103(2)(c) of the 1996 Act), and is based on art.V(1)(b) of the Convention. Both measures refer to the arbitral proceedings rather than the arbitral process whereas the latter is a wider term, inter alia making it clear that a party might complain about being given proper notice of parts of the arbitral process which are not "proceedings", e.g. in respect of certain interlocutory steps or interim measures. S20–32

The internationally-used shorthand phrase "due process" encapsulates a party's entitlement to be given proper notice of the arbitral process and of the appointment of the tribunal and to be able to present its case and to deal with its opponent's. Any failure of due process, if established, is a ground for seeking to resist enforcement. S20–33

A challenge founded on this ground will likely be rejected (and, the authors submit, should be) if what is involved is essentially an attack on the correctness of the award (see, e.g. *Inter-Arab Investment Guarantee Corp v Banque Arabe et Internationale d'Investissements* (2001) XXVI YCA 207 (French) Cour de Cassation). In a considerable number of decisions, albeit on appeals as opposed to enforcement actions, the Swiss Federal Tribunal (i.e. the Supreme Court) has developed a comprehensive jurisprudence on S20–34

Arbitration (Scotland) Act 2010

"failure of due process" with the overall general outcome that it has established a high threshold that applicants must meet.

S20–35 The party resisting enforcement could lose its right to object if the enforcing court considers that that party should have raised the matter before the tribunal and/or before a court of the seat but had failed to do so (see, e.g. *La Societe National des Hydrocarbures v Shaheen National Resources Inc*, 585 F.Supp. 57 (1983)).

S20–36 When the matter has been raised before a court of the seat and the award has been upheld, the authorities are divided as to whether the issue can be raised again at the enforcement stage. In *Unichips Finanziaria SpA v Gesnouin* (1994) XIX YCA 658, the Paris Cour d'Appel held that it can, while in *International Investor KCSC v Sanghi Polyesters Ltd* (2005) XXX YCA 577, the Indian High Court held that the matter should be regarded as res judicata.

Relationship of due process with public policy—s.20(2)(c) and (4)(b)

S20–37 There has been a growing tendency to raise the due process question as an issue of public policy under art.V(2)(b) (see commentary on s.20(4)(b) at paras S20–106 to S20–128). That is generally regarded as acceptable, since the enforcement of an award following failure of due process, or the rules of natural justice, would be regarded as contrary to public policy in most jurisdictions. The Spanish Corte Suprema has described due process as "procedural public policy" in *Union de Cooperativas Agricolas Epis-Centre v La Palentina SA* (2002) XXVII YCA 533 at 538.

S20–38 However, there may be a tactical advantage in raising such a matter under the public policy ground, since ordinarily a party who founds on this ground does not bear the burden of proof, by contrast to the position should he raise the matter under art.V(1)(b). This led Mason J., in the Hong Kong Court of Appeal in *Hebei Import & Export Corp v Politek Engineering Co Ltd* (1998) XXIV YCA 652 at 667, to suggest that a party who raises, as a matter of public policy under art.V(2)(b), a specific issue which might appropriately fall under art.V(1)(b) might still bear the burden of proof. As regards "public policy", see the commentary on s.20(4)(b) at paras S20–106 to S20–128 below.

Section 20(2)(c)(i)—Lack of proper notice

S20–39 As regards lack of notice, in *Sesostris v Transportes Navales*, 727 F.Supp. 737 (1989) a US District Court denied enforcement when the first proper notice a party received of the proceedings was the award, an earlier indication that proceedings had commenced "in Madrid, Spain" being insufficient. Further, the Oberlandesgericht of Bavaria (i.e. its Court of Appeal) decided that, when a party's address was different from that laid down in the contract, the other party should make a genuine attempt to discover its business or mailing address. If that is done, then notice sent to the last known address will be sufficient but if, as in the case in question, no such attempt was made, then notice was not properly sent and the award should be denied enforcement ((2002) XXVII YCA 445).

However, if proper notice is given, the fact that the relevant notice **S20–40** employed the wrong name will not suffice to prevent enforcement if the party in question received it and should have realised that it referred to him (*LKT Industrial Berhad (Malaysia) v Chun* [2004] N.S.W.S.C. 820). If notice is served, it will not avail a party simply to seek to reject the notice (see *Cominco France SA v Soquiber SL* (1983) VIII YCA 408 Spanish Corte Suprema).

The burden of proof lies on the party seeking to contend that the means of **S20–41** giving notice were unsuitable (*Trans World Film SpA v Film Polski Import and Export of Films* (1993) XVIII YCA 433 Italian Corte Suprema di Cassazione), while it has been held that, if it is clear that a party was not prejudiced despite receiving seemingly inadequate notice, e.g. where it is unable to submit a defence in any case, enforcement will not be denied (see *Guandong New Technology Import and Export Corp v Chiu Sing* (1993) XVIII YCA 385; Hong Kong High Court).

The idea that "proper" notice must be given implies that sufficient time **S20–42** must be given for the party to respond to the notice but this can sometimes be consistent with fairly tight time limits being imposed in relation to certain aspects of the process. Thus the Swiss courts (see (1979) IV YCA 309) ultimately enforced a Dutch award where the tribunal had refused to extend a seven day time limit provided in the applicable arbitral rules for a party to appoint its arbitrator; this decision was clearly correct since the complainant party, in agreeing to the rules to be applied, must be deemed to have waived any right of objection

The concept of proper notice is not necessarily dependent on the standard **S20–43** procedural formalities of the enforcing state: in *Malden Mills Inc (US) v Hilaturas Lourdes SA* (1979) IV YCA 302, the Mexican Court of Appeal overturned a first instance decision that the service of notices in accordance with the AAA International Arbitration Rules, by which the parties had agreed to be bound, did not amount to proper notice since it did not adhere to what was required by Mexican law. More dubiously, the Oberlandesgericht of Schleswig (Germany) has decided that even when a party can establish that it was denied the right to present its case, then, before enforcement could be refused, it must establish that it had a case to present ((2004) XXIX YCA 687).

Enforcement may also be refused under s.20(2)(c) where the identity of **S20–44** the arbitrators is unknown to the parties. This occurred in a case where, under the rules of a commodity trade association, parties were allowed to veto names from a list of potential arbitrators put forward by the association, but were not permitted to know the eventual composition of the tribunal lest they should seek to influence its members. The award was signed only by the chairman. The Oberlandesgericht Cologne ((1979) IV YCA 258) declined to enforce the award.

S20–45 An example of lack of notification occurred in *Lenmorniiproekt OAO v Arne Larsson & Partner Leasing AB* (case Ö 13-09; April 16, 2010 Swedish Supreme Court) where enforcement was refused. The first intimation that ALPL had of any arbitration involving LMP was when the latter sought to enforce a 2004 ICAC award in Sweden. Although the two companies had had prior dealings, ALPL had moved its office address prior to the commencement of the present arbitration and, it appears, had not made forwarding arrangements. LMP was aware of this in that a subpoena it sent to ALPL's former address had been returned "gone away". LMP argued that ALPL must be deemed to have received the notice of arbitration, inter alia because it had been obliged to have notified, but did not notify, LMP of its change of address. The Supreme Court upheld the Court of Appeal's decision to refuse enforcement on the ground that the general requirement to notify the arbitration rested on LMP and had not been satisfied. New York Convention art.V(1)(b) refers.

S20–46 To one of the authors, this appears to have been incompetence on LMP's part in not making it a contractual obligation on ALPL either (i) to advise any change of address, or (ii) to advise an address (e.g. a law firm's) for service. Further, the ICAC tribunal appears to have failed to have taken the obvious and elementary precautions necessary when one party to an arbitration fails to appear.

Section 20(2)(c)(ii)—Other inability to present case

S20–47 The fact that a party chooses not to present his case, e.g. where it declines to participate in the proceedings altogether (e.g. *Pasrederiet m/v Jytte Dania v Mas SA* (1989) XIV YCA 704 Spanish Corte Suprema), or fails to submit evidence (e.g. *Nanjing Cereals, Oils and Foodstuffs Import and Export Corp v Luckmate Commodities Trading Ltd* (1999) XXI YCA 542 Hong Kong Court of Final Appeal), or does not present its case as fully as possible (see, e.g. *Inter-Arab Investment Guarantee Corp v Banque Arabe et Internationale d'Investissements* (1997) XXII YCA 643 Brussels Court of First Instance), does not mean that it was unable to present its case. As Colman J. said in *Minmetals Germany GmbH v Ferco Steel Ltd* [1999] 1 All E.R. (Comm.) 315 at 318:

> "Inability to present a case ... contemplates at least that the enforcee has been prevented from presenting his case by matters outside his control. Where, however, the enforcee has, due to matters within his control, not provided himself with the means of taking advantage of an opportunity to present his case, he does not bring himself within that exception."

S20–48 Further, arguments based on language difficulties, either in terms of a failure of the arbitrator to comprehend the proceedings (see *Bargues Agro Industrie SA v Young Pecan Ltd* (2005) XXX YCA 499 Paris Court of Appeal), or in terms of the problems which the applicable language had caused the party in question (see *Fashion Ribbon Co Inc v Iberband SL* (2005) XXX YCA 627 Spanish Corte Suprema), have also received short shrift. Further, a party's fear of arrest at the seat does not mean that he was unable to present his case (see *National Development Co v Khashoggi* (1993) XVIII YCA 506 New York District Court).

S20–49 Moreover, if a party is aggrieved about the way in which it was allowed to present its case, that will usually not prevent enforcement because the tribunal is usually regarded as the master of procedure including what evidence is or is not relevant (see, e.g. *Laminoires-Trefileries-Cableries de Lens SA v Southwire Co*, 484 F.Supp. 1065 (1981) US Court of Appeals), and is not necessarily expected to follow the sorts of procedures one would see in court (see, e.g. *Generica Ltd v Pharmaceuticals Basics Inc*, 125 F.3d 1123 (1997) US Court of Appeals).

S20–50 The tribunal is, in particular, generally entitled to decide whether requests for adjournments and the like are justified (*Parsons & Whittemore Overseas Co Inc v Societe Generale de l'Industrie du Papier (RAKTA)* (1976) I YCA 205 US Court of Appeals), and to set time limits in relation to such matters as the presentation of evidence, so long as these are not unreasonably short (see *Carters (Merchants) Ltd v Ferraro* (1979) IV YCA 275 Naples Court of Appeal).

S20–51 The tribunal may decide whether oral hearings are required (see *O'Donoghue v Enterprise Inns Ltd* [2008] EWHC B15 (Ch) and also *Overseas Cosmos Inc v NR Vessel Corp* (1998) XXIII YCA 1096 New York District Court), although the law of the seat may also bear on this issue—see commentary on s.20(2)(d) at paras S20–55 to S20–81.

S20–52 The party seeking to resist enforcement will face an uphill task if what was done was proper in terms of the procedural law of the seat (see *Karaha Bodas Co LLC v Perusahaan Pertambangan Minyak Dan Gas Bumi Negara-Pertamina* (2003) XXVIII YCA 752). As was said in *Parsons & Whittemore Overseas Co Inc* (1976) I YCA 205 at 215: "The Convention essentially sanctions the forum state's notions of due process."

S20–53 To succeed under this ground, a respondent will generally have to show that the tribunal had proceeded on the basis of evidence that it had had no opportunity to counter, whether because it was not made aware of that evidence (see, e.g. *Kanoria v Guinness* [2006] EWCA Civ 222), or was not permitted to challenge it (see *Paklito Investment Ltd v Klockner (East Asia) Ltd* [1995] A.D.R.L.J 127 High Court of Hong Kong). This might happen where the tribunal considers evidence tendered by one party but not made available to the other (see, e.g. *GWL Kersten & Co BV v Societe Commerciale Raoul-Duval & Cie* (1994) XIX YCA 708 Amsterdam Court of Appeal).

S20–54   The same result has followed when the tribunal has misled the party as to the type of evidence required (*Iran Aircraft Ind v Avco Corp* (1993) XVIII YCA 599 US Court of Appeals).

Section 20(2)(d)—Arbitration improperly conducted

S20–55   A party can seek to resist enforcement if it can establish that the tribunal was constituted, or the arbitration was conducted, contrary to the agreement of the parties or, if the agreement did not address those issues, contrary to the law of the seat. This re-enacts s.5(2)(e) of the 1975 Act (see also s.103(2)(e) of the 1996 Act), and is based on art.V(1)(d) of the Convention, although the language of those provisions differs slightly.

S20–56   The logic of subs.(2)(d) is clear: the enforcement court must first look to see whether the parties have reached agreement on the issues concerned and only if they have not need it concern itself with the law of the seat. However, this creates a potential practical problem: if the agreement of the parties runs contrary to mandatory provisions of the law of the seat, a tribunal which follows the former runs the serious risk that a court of the seat is likely to set the award aside if invited to do so by a party.

S20–57   Under art.V(1)(d) of the Convention, mirrored in s.20(2)(d) of the 2010 Act, the fact that the court at the seat has set the award aside is itself a ground for refusing enforcement. Such situations will undoubtedly occur, due deference necessarily being paid by any enforcement court to the decisions of the supervising court. However, this is of no direct concern to the tribunal which is not responsible for enforcement and which, having issued the award, is *functus officio*.

S20–58   However, as a general but not immutable policy, enforcing courts worldwide normally exercise their discretion in favour of enforcing awards. On certain occasions this means enforcing an award when what has been done is in accordance with the law of the seat, albeit running contrary to what the parties agreed (see, e.g. *Al Haddad Bros Enterprises v M/S Agapi* (1987) XII YCA 549), while in others it means enforcing an award when the tribunal followed the will of the parties, even though it conflicted with mandatory norms of the law of the seat (see, e.g. *Joseph Muller AG v Bergesen* (1986) IX YCA 437).

S20–59   As always, the burden of proof lies on the party resisting enforcement (see, e.g. *Grow Biz International v DLT Holdings Inc* (2005) XXX YCA 450 at 457); however, that party could have lost its right to object since courts are generally unimpressed where this issue is raised for the first time at the enforcement proceedings, when it should have been raised before either the tribunal or a court of the seat (see Longmore J. in *China Agribusiness Development Corp v Balli Trading* [1998] 2 Lloyd's Rep. 76 at 80).

S20–60   In *China Nanhai Oil Joint Service Corp v Gee Tai Holdings Ltd* [1995] A.D.R.L.J 127 (see Kaplan J. at 132), the Hong Kong Court of Final Appeal enforced an award despite the arbitrators not being chosen from the

Not every procedural breach automatically leads to refusal of enforcement. Thus a US District Court said in *Compagnie des Bauxites de Guinee v Hammermills Inc* (1993) XVIII YCA 566 at 571: **S20–61**

> "The Court does not believe that Art.V(1)(d) was intended to permit courts to police every procedural ruling by the arbitrator, and to refuse to enforce the award if any procedural violation is found. Such an interpretation would directly conflict with the 'pro-enforcement bias' of the Convention and its intention to remove obstacles to confirmation of arbitral awards. The Court believes that a more appropriate standard of review would be to refuse to enforce an award based on a procedural violation only if such violation worked substantial prejudice to the complaining party."

In *Tongyuan (USA) International Trading Group v Uni-Clan Ltd* (2001) XXVI YCA 886, Moore-Bick J. rejected the argument that, because an arbitration had been held in Beijing rather than in Shanghai or Shenzhen as stipulated in the arbitration clause, that was a ground for refusing enforcement. That case also emphasised the fact that it will be difficult for a party to persuade a court that it had been prejudiced by an irregularity when he opted not to participate in the arbitral proceedings. **S20–62**

Section 20(2)(d)—Tribunal not in agreed form

Cases where enforcement has been refused on the basis that the tribunal did not take the form agreed by the parties include *Rederi Aktiebolaget Sally v Srl Termarea* (1979) IV YCA 294 in the Florence Court of Appeal, where, in a 1950 Act London arbitration, the party-appointed arbitrators had decided the case without appointing a third arbitrator as required by the arbitration agreement. This course of action was validated by the now-repealed s.9(1) of the 1950 Act under which the third arbitrator was not so but was deemed to be an umpire, so that this is a rare instance of a court allowing the agreement of the parties to override the law of the seat **S20–63**

However, where a party declines or fails to act as contemplated by the arbitration agreement, so that the tribunal cannot be constituted as agreed, enforcing courts tend to take the view that it is proper for the other party to fall back on the law of the seat. That was what occurred in *Al Haddad Bros Enterprises v M/S Agapi* (1987) XII YCA 549 where a party-appointed arbitrator was asked to serve as sole arbitrator when the other party failed to nominate an arbitrator, this being acceptable in terms of the 1950 Act. A US District Court was prepared to enforce the award, noting (at 551) that: **S20–64**

> "The Convention allows recognition of an award, which although not in accord with the parties' agreement, complied with the law of the country where the arbitration occurred."

S20–65 The courts in certain jurisdictions have granted enforcement of awards where the composition of the tribunal was as agreed by the parties, despite that composition contravening mandatory rules of the law of the seat (see *SEEE v Yugoslavia* (1986) XI YCA 491 Rouen Court of Appeal; but the same award had been earlier denied enforcement by the Dutch Hoge Raad (Supreme Court) (1976) I YCA 195).

S20–66 One situation where one might expect the plea to arise is where two or more arbitrations have been compulsorily consolidated, a power historically asserted by the courts in certain jurisdictions and conferred on them by legislation in others. In such situations the tribunal is very clearly not composed in the way agreed by at least one of the parties. The counter argument is that, by agreeing to arbitrate in such jurisdictions, the parties have impliedly accepted this possibility. The authors have not found any reported decision on this issue under the Convention.

Section 20(2)(d)—Procedural irregularity

S20–67 It is difficult to find consistency in the authorities regarding the position where it is alleged that there has been procedural irregularity. Thus while in *Dubois & Vanderwalle v Boots Frites BV* (1999) XXIV YCA 640 the Paris Cour d'Appel refused to enforce an award where the tribunal had failed to observe an agreed time limit for making it, the Bavarian Oberlandsgericht (Court of Appeal) in *K Trading v Bayerische Motoren Werke AG* (2005) XXX YCA 568, enforced an award in the same circumstances, stating (at 572–573):

> "In order to prevent the setting aside of an award on purely formal grounds and the carrying out of a new arbitration necessarily leading to the same result as the annulled arbitral award, a distinction must be made between essential and non-essential procedural defects even if such distinction is not made in the text of Art. V(1)(d) of the Convention A procedural defect is deemed essential to the arbitral award when it is causal to it or when the arbitral tribunal would have decided differently had it not been for the procedural violation."

S20–68 A similar approach was seen in *Food Services of America Inc v Pan Pacific Specialities Ltd* (2004) XXIX YCA 581, where the British Columbian Supreme Court enforced an award despite its not containing reasons as stipulated by the then applicable AAA Rules which had been agreed by the parties. The court said (at 587) that the failure to have given reasons had affected neither the fairness of the hearing nor the decision-making process.

Of course, such a failure would render an award subject to being set aside by the courts of the seat in many jurisdictions, which would itself afford a basis for refusing enforcement.

Finally, in *Inter-Arab Investment Guarantee Corp v Banque Arabe et Internationale d'Investissements* (1999) XXIV YCA 603, a Belgian court rejected an objection that the tribunal had improperly acted as *amiables compositeurs* on the basis that the tribunal had in fact done no such thing. However, the interesting aspect is that the court clearly considered that the question of the powers the tribunal had to decide the dispute was a matter of procedure rather than of substantive law, thus allowing a challenge to enforcement to be considered in the first place **S20–69**

By analogy, the question of whether the tribunal has applied the appropriate substantive law to the dispute might also permit a challenge to enforcemen; in *Osuuskunta METEX Anderlag VS v Turkiye Electric Kurumu Genel Mudurlugu General Directorate* (1997) XXII YCA 807, the Ankara Court of Appeal held that an award might be denied enforcement on the basis of the tribunal's erroneous choice of procedural law. **S20–70**

Section 20(3)

This subsection identifies a number of grounds for resisting enforcement which relate to the award and derives from art.V(1) of the Convention, just as those in s.20(2). Importantly, taking s.20(2), (3) and (4) together, the combined list is exhaustive. **S20–71**

Section 20(3)(a)—Lack of jurisdiction

Section 20(3)(a) and (b) together replace s.5(1)(d) of the 1975 Act and give effect to art.V(1)(c) of the Convention. Dispute includes "difference": see s.2(1). Section 5(1)(d) of the 1975 Act employed the term "difference" rather than "dispute", as indeed does s.103(2)(d) of the 1996 Act, but this is not material. **S20–72**

As in all applications to resist Convention enforcement, the burden of proof lies on the resisting party (see Donaldson M.R. in *Deutsche Schachtbau und Tiefbohrgesellschaft v Ras Al Khaimah National Oil Co* [1987] 2 Lloyd's Rep. 522 at 529), while it has even been said that there is a presumption that the tribunal has acted within the scope of its authority (see the Bermuda Court of Appeal in *Sojuzneftexport v Joc Oil Ltd* (1990) XV YCA 384 at 390). **S20–73**

The House of Lords has confirmed that art.V(1)(c) is to be construed narrowly (see Lord Steyn in *Lesotho Highlands Authority v Impregilo SpA* [2006] 1 A.C. 221 at [30]), e.g. matters of procedural impropriety, such as where the tribunal relies on evidence not placed before it, are insufficient (*Minmetals Germany GmbH v Ferco Steel Ltd* [1999] 1 All E.R. (Comm) 315). **S20–74**

The same applies where the tribunal fails to apply the chosen law to the **S20–75** substance of the dispute (*Karaha Bodas Co LLC v Perusahaan Pertambangan Minyak Dan Gas Bumi Negara-Pertamina* (2003) XXVIII YCA 752), even if the argument is that the tribunal has improperly applied a-national norms to the subject matter of the dispute. Thus, in *Ministry of Defence of the Republic of Iran v Cubic Defense Systems, Inc*, 29 F.Supp. 2d 1168 (1998) at 1173 a US District Court said that an arbitral tribunal's:

> "... reference to an application of the UNIDROIT Principles (i.e. the Principles of International Commercial Contracts) and principles of good faith and fair dealing do not violate Art. V(1)(c). The Tribunal applied these principles to differences falling within the terms of the submission to arbitration and therefore the Award does not violate Art. V(1)(c)."

If the tribunal has been asked to deal with the matter, a complaint about how it does so may not be raised under art.V(1)(c).

S20–76 A party can, however, resist enforcement if he can prove that the award deals with a dispute not contemplated by or not falling within the scope of the submission to arbitration, a ground sometimes known as *extra petita* and arising when the tribunal deals with an issue it was not asked to address.

S20–77 One very fundamental respect in which the tribunal may lack jurisdiction is where it is alleged that there is no valid arbitration agreement. However, this would be a plea to be raised under s.20(2)(b), giving effect to art.V(1)(a) of the Convention. There have indeed been cases where it has been pleaded that there is no valid arbitration agreement but that, if there is, the tribunal has exercised powers not conferred by that agreement. The courts have tended to deal first with the former question and then, only if it is decided that there is a valid arbitration agreement, will they proceed to deal with the issue of jurisdiction (see (1979) IV YCA 305 Hague Court of First Instance).

S20–78 An award was refused enforcement under this head in *Tiong Huat Rubber Factory Bhd v Wah Chang International Co Ltd* (1992) XVII YCA 516 where a contract for the supply of rubber provided that all disputes regarding "the quality or condition of rubber or other dispute" should be settled by arbitration. The contract also provided that payment was to be made via a Letter of Credit and, when this was not provided, the seller went to arbitration and obtained an award in his favour. The buyer sought to resist enforcement on the basis that the contract provided only for the arbitration of disputes relating to the "quality or condition". The High Court of Hong Kong held that it could not be imagined that the arbitration clause intended to exclude claims for payment from its scope, but the Court of Appeal agreed with the buyer and held that the matter did indeed lie outwith the tribunal's jurisdiction.

S20–79 The decision in the House of Lords in *Fiona Trust v Privalov* [2007] 2 All E.R. (Comm) 1053 flatly contradicts *Tiong Huat Rubber Factory Bhd v Wah Chang International Co Ltd* (1992) XVII YCA 516. Lord Hoffmann said:

"6. In approaching the question of construction, it is therefore necessary to inquire into the purpose of the arbitration clause. As to this, I think there can be no doubt. The parties have entered into a relationship, an agreement or what is alleged to be an agreement or what appears on its face to be an agreement, which may give rise to disputes. They want those disputes decided by a tribunal which they have chosen, commonly on the grounds of such matters as its neutrality, expertise and privacy, the availability of legal services at the seat of the arbitration and the unobtrusive efficiency of its supervisory law. Particularly in the case of international contracts, they want a quick and efficient adjudication and do not want to take the risks of delay and, in too many cases, partiality, in proceedings before a national jurisdiction.

7. If one accepts that this is the purpose of an arbitration clause, its construction must be influenced by whether the parties, as rational businessmen, were likely to have intended that only some of the questions arising out of their relationship were to be submitted to arbitration and others were to be decided by national courts. Could they have intended that the question of whether the contract was repudiated should be decided by arbitration but the question of whether it was induced by misrepresentation should be decided by a court? If, as appears to be generally accepted, there is no rational basis upon which businessmen would be likely to wish to have questions of the validity or enforceability of the contract decided by one tribunal and questions about its performance decided by another, one would need to find very clear language before deciding that they must have had such an intention."

Similarly, in *AAMCO Transmissions Inc v Kunz* [1996] A.D.R.L.J 32, the Saskatchewan Court of Appeal held that where an arbitration clause formed part of a standard form contract, its terms should be construed *contra proferentem* when deciding what matters lay within its scope. **S20–80**

Such decisions are rare, however, and this defence generally fails, mainly because the tribunal is usually regarded as best placed to determine the scope of the arbitration agreement and the law which governs that issue (see, e.g. *Fiona Trust v Privalov* [2007] 2 All E.R. (Comm) 1053). **S20–81**

Section 20(3)(b)—Excess of jurisdiction

A party can also resist enforcement of an award if he can prove that it contains decisions on matters beyond the scope of the submission to arbitration (*ultra petita*). However, as stated above, courts other than English courts (e.g. see *AES Ust-Kamenogorsk Hydropower Plant LLP v Ust-Kamenogorsk Hydropower Plant JSC* [2011] EWCA Civ 647 per Rix L.J. at **S20–82**

[78]–[82]) are generally reluctant to question a tribunal's view as to the scope of its jurisdiction.

S20–83 There are cases where enforcement has been granted despite the tribunal awarding remedies not claimed by a party (e.g. price reductions, *AB Gotaverken v General National Maritime Transport Co* (1981) VI YCA 237 Swedish Supreme Court; interest, (2000) XXV YCA 714 Hamburg Court of Appeal; and expenses, *Aasma v American Steamship Owners Mutual Protection and Indemnity* (2003) XXVIII YCA 1140 US District Court), or which even appear to be expressly excluded by the agreement of the parties (see *Fertilizer Corp of India v IDI Management Inc* (1982) VII YCA 382 US District Court—damages for consequential loss).

S20–84 Further, the fact that an award fails to exhaust the submission is not a good ground for resisting enforcement. As the Luxembourg Court of Appeal pointed out in *Kersa Holding Co v Infancourtage* (1996) XXI YCA 617 at 625:

> "This ground, even if established, could not hinder the enforcement of the awards, as an *infra petita* decision is not sanctioned by the New York Convention."

See also paras S20–129 to S20–132 below for discussion of partial enforcement.

Section 20(3)(c)—Award not yet binding

S20–85 Section 20(3)(c) and (d) together replace s.5(1)(f) of the 1975 Act and give effect to art.V(1)(e) of the Convention. A court may refuse enforcement if the party resisting enforcement can show that the award is not yet binding on him. The use of the term "binding" was deliberately chosen (see *Summary Record of the 17th meeting of the United Nations Conference on International Commercial Arbitration*, UN E/CONF.26/SR.17). Thus, the Swedish Supreme Court said in *AB Gotaverken v General National Maritime Transport Co* (1981) VI YCA 237 at 240:

> "The possibility of an action for setting aside the award shall not mean that the award is considered as not being binding. A case in which a foreign award is not binding is when its merits are open to appeal. The choice of the term binding was [intended] to avoid the necessity of a double *exequatur*, or the need for the party relying on the award to prove that the award is enforceable according to the authorities of the country in which it was rendered."

S20–86 Awards are normally binding as soon as they are made (see *SPP (Middle East) Ltd v Egypt* (1985) X YCA 487 District Court of Amsterdam) and have been enforced even though some formality is missing which would be necessary to make them enforceable at the seat (*Resort Condominiums International Inc v Bolwell* (1994) XX YCA 628 Supreme Court of Queensland), e.g. confirmation by (*Fertilizer Corp of India v IDI Management Inc* (1982) VII YCA 382 US District Court) or deposit with (*Compagnie de Saint Gobain-Pont a Mousson v Fertilizer Corp of India Ltd* (1976) I YCA 184) a court at the seat.

In addition, where a court confirms an award, it remains enforceable under the Convention but is not necessarily converted into a judgment (*Schreter v Gasmac Inc* (1992) 89 D.L.R. (4th) 365). However, in *Rosseel NV v Oriental Commercial Shipping Co Ltd* [1991] 2 Lloyd's Rep. 625 at 628, Steyn J. suggested that an award cannot be considered binding if the parties agreed that it could not be enforced without authorisation from a particular court. **S20–87**

In contrast, the Hong Kong High Court held in *Zheijiang Province Garment Import and Export Co v Siemssen & Co (Hong Kong) Trading Ltd* [1993] A.D.R.L.J 183 per Kaplan J. at 187, that an award is still binding although a party argues that a condition precedent to its operation has not been fulfilled. The fact that an award has ceased to be binding is not specified as a ground for refusing enforcement, yet where the parties agreed to ignore an award and arbitrated the matter anew, reaching a different result, enforcement was refused (*Dutco (Pvt) Ltd v Dajen (Pvt) Ltd* [1997] 2 Zimbabwe L.R. 199). **S20–88**

The *AB Gotaverken* dicta (see para.S20–83 above) suggest, however, that an award cannot be considered binding if it can be challenged on the merits. The parties may provide for such a mechanism themselves, and will do so implicitly if they arbitrate under certain arbitral rules. Alternatively, the law of the seat may allow an award to be challenged on the basis of an error of law. An award which may not be issued until it has undergone some form of scrutiny, such as that by the ICC Court under art.33 of the ICC Rules, does not fall to be regarded as an award at all until that process is complete. **S20–89**

It should also be noted that, while an award may be enforced despite there being a possibility of challenge, the fact that it is actually being challenged may cause a court to take a different attitude to enforcement—see the commentary to s.20(6)(a) (paras S20–134 to S20–143). **S20–90**

The issue of whether "awards" made via informal dispute resolution processes, such as the Italian *arbitrato irrituale*, are binding is not relevant here since the real issue is whether such awards are to be recognised under the Convention at all. The Italian Corte Suprema di Cassazione effectively said "yes" in *Butera v Pagnan* (1979) IV YCA 296, while the BGH effectively said "no" in *COMITAS v SOVAG* (1983) VIII YCA 366. "Awards" (usually called "determinations") in expert determination are clearly not enforceable under the Convention but the authors know of no reported case where such has been attempted. **S20–91**

Section 20(3)(d)—Award set aside or suspended

S20–92 Section 20(3)(d) replaces s.5(1)(f) of the 1975 Act and seeks to give effect to the second ground under art.V(1)(e) of the Convention. A court may refuse enforcement if the party resisting enforcement can show that the award has been set aside by a competent authority. Section 20(7) defines the term "competent authority" as a "person" who has the authority to set aside or suspend the award in the country in which (or under the law of which) the award was made. No attempt was made to define that term in the 1975 and 1996 Acts, nor indeed in the Convention itself. All the authorities under the Convention suggest that a competent authority means a court.

S20–93 There is a theoretical argument that, by referring to "person", the 2010 Act permits an award to be refused enforcement because it has been "set aside" by an individual or institution which is contractually empowered to do so. The authors submit that this cannot have been intended by the drafters of the Convention since its focus is on ensuring the enforcement of foreign arbitral awards, subject only to the limited exceptions it lays down, and does not envisage any attempt to extend the grounds on which enforcement may be denied. A preferable view is that an award which has been set aside under some contractual appeal process should be regarded as a nullity.

So far as the authors are aware, instances of an institution other than a court being empowered to set an award aside are rare, e.g. the two-tier arbitral processes of the international commodity trade associations such as GAFTA, FOSFA et al, and the Rules of none of the ICC, LCIA, VIAC, SIAC, HKIAC, KLRCA, ACICA, CIETAC or BAC provide for this. However, readers' attention is drawn to the AAA Appellate Rules under which the underlying award is deemed not final and the running of time for any appeal to the courts is suspended. In its decision, the Appeal Tribunal may adopt the underlying award or may substitute its own, in the latter event incorporating such parts of the underlying award as it considers appropriate. For purposes of s.20(3)(d), in each of AAA/GAFTA/FOSFA et al, the underlying/first-tier award is effectively suspended until confirmed or superseded and is not "set aside".

S20–94 Section 20(3)(d)'s focus is that enforcement may be denied if the award has been set aside at the seat of arbitration but the setting aside of an award by some other court is not a ground for denying enforcement; in *Karaha Bodas Co LLC v Perusahaan Pertambangan Minyak Dan Gas Bumi Negara-Pertamina* [2003] 380 H.K.C.U. 1, an award made in Switzerland was set aside in Indonesia on the basis that the contract was governed by Indonesian law. The Hong Kong High Court held that this was not a ground for refusing enforcement.

S20–95 Certain Conventions (e.g. the 1961 Geneva Convention, to which the UK is not a party) characterise the setting aside of an award at the seat as a ground for resisting enforcement provided that the award has been set aside only on certain limited grounds, so that the award should not be denied enforcement if it is set aside on any other ground. Thus the Austrian Supreme Court, in *Kajo-Erzeugnisse Essenzen GmbH v DO Zdravilisce Radenska* (1995) XX YCA 1051, enforced an award set aside in Slovenia on the basis of contravention of public policy since that was not a ground recognised by the Convention. In addition, a US District Court observed in *International Standard Electric Corp v Bridas Sociedad Anonima Petrolera* (1992) XVII YCA 639 at 645:

> "Art. V(1)(e) refers exclusively to procedural and not substantive law, and more precisely the regimen of arbitral procedural law under which the arbitration was conducted."

However, there is otherwise no restriction on the grounds upon which an award has been set aside at the seat.

S20–96 It does not follow, however, that an award set aside by the courts of the seat can never be enforced. As will be seen later (see paras 22–01 to 22–03), the fact that it cannot be enforced under the New York Convention is no bar to it being enforced under any other applicable Convention or under any other rule of law.

S20–97 More importantly, however, courts have exercised their discretion under the Convention in favour of enforcing such awards, e.g. in *Chromalloy Aeroservices Inc v Arab Republic of Egypt*, 939 F.Supp. 907 (1996) a US District Court enforced an award set aside by an Egyptian court on the ground that the tribunal had applied the wrong substantive law. However, while countries like France reasonably routinely enforce awards set aside by the courts of the seat, *Chromalloy* is rather atypical of the US approach (see, e.g. *Baker Marine (Nigeria) Ltd v Chevron (Nigeria) Ltd*, 191 F.3d 194 (1999) at 197) and courts are generally reluctant to enforce such awards.

S20–98 A high profile example of enforcement of awards despite their having been set aside by the courts at the seat occurred in *OAO Rosneft v Yukos Capital SARL* (Case 09/02565 Hoge Raad (First Chamber); judgment June 25, 2010). Four arbitral awards issued in Moscow in 2006 in Yukos' favour were set aside by the Russian courts in 2007 but the Hoge Raad refused to disturb an Amsterdam Court of Appeal decision of April 28, 2009 (case reference 200.005.269/01) which had reversed, notwithstanding the set-aside in Russia, the decision of the first instance court (case reference 365094/KG RK 07-7 50; judgment dated February 28, 2008) to refuse enforcement pursuant to New York Convention art.V(1)(e). The basis of the Court of Appeal's decision was that it had to be assumed that the decisions of the Russian courts had been partial and politically motivated.

S20–99 In the authors' opinion, while a reading of UK newspapers might lead an individual to forming that view, it is far from obvious on what grounds a court should do so; no doubt Counsel for Yukos presented very cogent arguments supported by extensive evidence, but none of this is visible in the judgment.

S20–100 On one view, it is in line with the pro-enforcement bias of the Convention that awards, especially international awards where the parties may have no real connection with the seat, should not be denied enforcement because of some peculiarity of the law of the seat. The alternative view is that such awards only gain legal force because they are part of the legal fabric of the law of the seat, so that they are in effect deprived of legal authority if set aside at the seat. Even if one does not accept this argument, however, the authors submit that the Scottish courts should be slow to enforce awards set aside at the seat, given that the Convention expressly contemplates the courts of the seat having the power to do so.

S20–101 In *Continental Transfert Technique Ltd v Nigeria* [2010] EWHC 780 (Comm) the defendants submitted that, since the award was one which should not be recognised or enforced, it followed that the English judgment based on that award should be set aside. However, the court rejected this argument since it was clear that s.103(2)(f) of the 1996 Act (the equivalent of s.20(3)(c) and (d) combined) was inapplicable in this case. It only applied where the award "has been set aside or suspended" and the fact that there was an application on foot to set it aside does not mean that it has been set aside. The position where there is an application to set aside is dealt with under s.103(5) of the 1996 Act (equivalent to s.20(6)(a)). Authority to support that conclusion based on the clear wording of s.103 can be found in the judgment of Gross J. in *IPCO v NNPC* [2005] 2 Lloyd's Rep. 326 in which he said at [12]:

> "Secondly, s.103(2)(f) is only applicable when there has been an order or decision suspending the award by the court in the country of origin of the award ('the country of origin'). S.103(2)(f) is not triggered automatically by a challenge brought before the court in the country of origin. This conclusion flows from the wording of s.103(2)(f) itself, it is supported by leading commentators (*Van den Berg, The New York Convention of 1958* (1981), at p.352, *Fouchard, Gaillard, Goldman on International Commercial Arbitration* (1999), at pp. 980-1) and it is consistent with the provisions of s.103(5) of the Act—which would be otiose, or at least curious, if an application to the court in the country of origin automatically resulted in the award being suspended",

and at [21]:

> "... NNPC contended that by virtue of its application to the Federal High Court in Lagos to set aside the award, the award had been 'suspended'; accordingly, s.103(2)(f) of the Act was applicable and NNPC was entitled on this ground to have the order set aside. For the reasons already set out, this ground is misconceived; s.103(2)(f) is not triggered merely by an application before the court in the country of origin."

Section 20(4)—New York Convention art.V(2)

The final two grounds on which recognition or enforcement may be refused are of a quite different character to the preceding ones which were largely particular to the parties, their agreement or the arbitral proceedings. The grounds addressed by s.20(4) relate to arbitral awards which a Scottish court should consider refusing to enforce reflecting the fact that, while in relation to the previous grounds the party resisting enforcement had to establish the existence of the ground in question, no such burden is imposed under s.20(4). S20–102

If a Scottish court recognises that an award deals with a matter which is not arbitrable in Scotland, it should refuse to enforce it even if that plea is not raised by any party. Of course, a party may make such a plea and may in certain situations even be compelled in practice to tender evidence to establish that the ground exists, e.g. when it is contended that to enforce the award would be contrary to public policy due to the way in which the award was allegedly procured. S20–103

Section 20(4)(a)—Matter not arbitrable under Scots law

Recognition or enforcement may be refused when the award relates to a matter which is not capable of being settled by arbitration under Scots law. Section 20(4)(a) and (b) replace s.5(3) of the 1975 Act and the provision seeks to give effect to art.V(2)(a) of the Convention. This states that arbitrability is to be judged according to the law of the place of enforcement and, while the current provision, as with s.5(3) of the 1975 Act, omits that reference, it is the only sensible way to interpret the provision. The fact that a dispute is not arbitrable in terms of the law governing the substance of the dispute or the law of the seat may of course have consequences, since in the former situation enforcement might be resisted under s.20(2)(b), while in the latter situation the award might be set aside in the seat so that enforcement might be resisted under s.20(3)(d). However, in the current context the question is whether the dispute is arbitrable under Scots law. S20–104

The question of arbitrability is discussed in the commentary on s.30 below. For present purposes, there is a limited range of matters that are not arbitrable under Scots law. Since arbitrability is reflective of public policy, there may sometimes be an overlap between s.20(4)(a) and (b). S20–105

Section 20(4)(b)—Public policy

Recognition or enforcement may be refused when to do so would be contrary to public policy. This provision seeks to give effect to art.V(2)(b) of the Convention. As above, the Convention makes it clear that the public policy referred to is that of the place of enforcement and, while the current provision, as with s.5(3) of the 1975 Act, omits that reference, this is how the English courts have interpreted the provision. S20–106

S20–107   Courts in certain jurisdictions have decided that, where only part of an award offends against public policy, the remainder of the award might be enforced if it is properly separable (see *Laminoires-Trefileries-Cableries de Lens SA v Southwire Co*, 484 F.Supp. 1065 (1981); *Agro Industries (P) Ltd v Texuna International Ltd* [1994] 1 H.K.L.R. 89).

International public policy

S20–108   In this context, courts will normally treat foreign awards differently to domestic awards, e.g. the US Court of Appeals (2nd Circuit) said in *Parsons & Whittemore Overseas Co Inc v Societe Generale de l'Industrie du Papier (RAKTA)*, 508 F.2d 969 (2nd Cir. 1974) at 973:

> "Enforcement should only be denied on the basis of public policy where enforcement would violate the forum state's most basic notions of morality and justice."

S20–109   This approach is often described on the basis that an award must run contrary to international public policy for enforcement to be denied. Some states indeed have enshrined the idea of international public policy in legislation (see, e.g. the French Code of Civil Procedure art.1520(5) (as revised January 13, 2011)). While the Swiss Federal Tribunal in (1996) XXI YCA 172 speaks of:

> "a universal conception of public policy, under which an award will be incompatible with public policy if it is contrary to the fundamental moral or legal principles recognised in all civilised countries",

as the *Parsons* quotation suggests, the concept does not properly relate to a core of public policy which is uniform in every state, but to each individual state's fundamental concepts of justice (numerous examples might be cited but see, e.g. the BGH in *Manufacturer v Exclusive Distributor* (2004) XIX YCA 687 at 696; and Armstrong J.A. in the Ontario Court of Appeal in *United Mexican States v Karpa* [2005] 74 O.R. 3d 180 at [116]).

S20–110   Such a doctrine is also recognised by the English courts, e.g. in *Westacre Investments Inc v Jugiimport-SPDR Holding Co Ltd* [1998] 2 Lloyd's Rep. 65 at 74, Waller L.J. noted that:

> "while there are some rules of public policy which, if infringed, will lead to non-enforcement whatever their proper law and wherever their place of performance,"

other rules did not fall into that category. Westacre's contract related to the "purchase of influence" (i.e. not bribery), legal under the applicable law (Swiss), but would not be enforceable on public policy grounds if the award was Scottish, English or Northern Irish-seated. However, the contract was not so fundamentally repugnant to English law's notions of justice that it offended against international public policy. Waller L.J. added that, even if an award offended against the domestic public policy of the forum state, it could still be enforced if it did not contravene the English standard of international public policy.

With reference to para.S18–04 above, the authors submit that, if the English courts have embraced the idea of international public policy in interpreting legislation giving effect to the UK's international treaty obligations, the Scottish courts should be reluctant in the extreme to take a different approach. **S20–111**

National public policy

With reference to the quotation in S20–108 above, an interesting example occurred in *Mosstroyekonombank Joint Stock Commercial Bank CJSC v Kalinka-Stockmann CJSC* (Federal Arbitrazh Court of the Moscow Circuit; Resolution No. KG-A40/9254-08; judgment of October 13, 2008; Case No.40-30560/08-25-257). In a dispute over commercial leases, an award was issued in April 2008 in favour of Kalinka-Stockmann (a subsidiary of a Finnish company) under the auspices of ICAC, but was set aside in the Moscow City Arbitrazh Court in August 2008. This was on two grounds: **S20–112**

(i) the subject-matter of the dispute, real property, was not arbitrable under Russian Law but instead fell (by statute) within the exclusive competence of the state courts; and
(ii) ICAC had failed to have guaranteed the tribunal's impartiality in permitting Kalinka-Stockmann to appoint the same (a Swedish national, bilingual in Russian) arbitrator in repeated cases involving the two companies where he had (allegedly) repeatedly sided with his appointor.

Illegality

While public policy is clearly an extremely broad concept, certain broad headings may be identified. Thus the fundamental immorality or illegality of the contract between the parties may preclude the enforcement of an award; Waller L.J. said in *Soleimany v Soleimany* [1998] 3 W.L.R. 811 at 821G that: **S20–113**

> "There may be illegal or immoral dealings which are, from an English law perspective, incapable of being arbitrated, because an agreement to arbitrate them would itself be contrary to public policy."

This was a case decided at common law but, in the context of the Convention, Colman J. noted in *Westacre Investments Inc v Jugimport-SPDR Holding Co Ltd* [1998] 2 Lloyd's Rep. 111 at 127, that if a contract was:

"indisputably illegal at common law, the award would not be enforced for it would be contrary to public policy that the arbitrator should be able to ignore palpable and indisputable illegality."

S20–114 That said, it is increasingly commonplace for jurisdictions to permit arbitrators themselves to rule, at least in the first instance, on the issue of illegality under the related principles of separability and Kompetenz-Kompetenz. Thus Colman J. observed in *Westacre Investments Inc v Jugimport-SPDR Holding Co Ltd* [1998] 2 Lloyd's Rep. 111 that, in such a situation, the court would have to consider whether the illegality was of such a nature for it to be in line with public policy to allow it to be considered in an arbitration. If such was the case, and the arbitrator had decided that the contract was not illegal then (contrast the view of Waller L.J. in *Soleimany* [1998] 3 W.L.R. 811 at 821D–G):

"the enforcement court would have to consider whether the public policy against the enforcement of illegal contracts outweighed the countervailing public policy in support of the finality of awards."

S20–115 Colman J. concluded (*Westacre Investments* [1998] 2 Lloyd's Rep. 111 at 131) that:

"an English court would give predominant weight to the public policy of sustaining the parties' agreement to submit the particular issue of illegality and initial invalidity to arbitration rather than of sustaining the non-enforcement of contracts illegal at common law."

S20–116 A similar view was expressed regarding allegations that the contract had been illegally procured, e.g. by bribery (*Westacre Investments* [1998] 2 Lloyd's Rep. 111 at 129, where the decision was upheld by a majority of the Court of Appeal at [1999] 1 All E.R. (Comm) 865; but contrast *Corvetina Technology Ltd v Clough Engineering Ltd* [2004] N.S.W.S.C. 700). Thus as long as a contract is not blatantly illegal, the fact that an arbitrator has treated it as legal in his award will count heavily against the award being refused enforcement.

S20–117 Enforcement is commonly granted even if the contract between the parties is admittedly illegal in the place of performance, and indeed even if it has been judicially declared to be so, as long as it is not illegal under the law chosen by the parties to govern the contract (*Omnium SA v Hilmarton Ltd* [1998] 2 Lloyd's Rep. 222; *R v V* [2008] EWHC 1531 (Comm)). As Waller L.J. stated in *Soinco Saci v Novokuznetsk Aluminium Plant* [1998] 2 Lloyd's Rep. 337 at 340:

"[I]t is the award with which the English Court is concerned and not the underlying contract. The question of illegality having been raised and dealt with by the arbitrators, and there being no requirement as a result to perform some act which English law would regard as illegal or contrary to the recognised morals of this country, the public policy is if anything in favour of abiding by the terms of the Convention and enforcing the award."

For a full discussion of *Soinco* and related cases, see the article by Hew R. Dundas, "Сибирский вклад в английское право: пувличный порядок, незаконность и пяинудительное исполнение режений международных арвитражей. Дело Soinco S.A.C.I. против Новокузнецкого алюминиевого забода и последующие дела"("A Siberian Contribution to English Law: Public Policy, Illegality and the Enforcement of International Arbitration Awards: Soinco S.A.C.I. v Novokuznetsk Aluminium Plant and Subsequent Cases"), Международный Коммерческий Арбитраж ("International Commercial Arbitration") (Moscow) 2004/3, pp.53–79).

Improperly obtained awards

Public policy is often seen as being bound up with the substance of an award, but the phrase is the translation of the French *ordre publique*, which undoubtedly has a procedural dimension (see K.H. Nadelmann and A.T. Von Mehren, "Equivalences in Treaties in the Conflicts Fields" (1966) 15 Am. J. Comp. L. 195). See also the excellent discussion in J.F. Poudret and S. Besson, *Comparative Law of International Arbitration*, 2nd edn (London: Sweet and Maxwell, 2007), para.933ff, in particular para.940. **S20–118**

Consequently, where it is suggested that the award had been improperly obtained, e.g. on the basis of perjury or fraud, enforcement may be resisted on the grounds of public policy (see Lord Keith in *Masimport v SMLI Ltd*, 1976 S.C. 102 at 109; *Gater Assets Ltd v Nak Naftogaz Ukrainiy (No.2)* [2008] 2 Lloyd's Rep. 295). However, the court will wish to know why the award has not been challenged in the forum. Moreover, if such a challenge has already failed, enforcement is unlikely to be denied. As Colman J. pointed out in *Westacre Investments* [1998] 2 Lloyd's Rep. 111 at 139: **S20–119**

> "Where a party to a foreign New York Convention award alleges at the enforcement stage that it has been obtained by perjured evidence, that party will not normally be permitted to adduce in the English courts additional evidence to make good that allegation unless it is established that:
>
> (i) the evidence sought to be adduced is of sufficient cogency and weight to be likely to have materially influenced the arbitrators' conclusion had it been advanced at the hearing and,

(ii) the evidence was not available or reasonably obtainable either,

   (a) at the time of the hearing of the arbitration; or
   (b) at such time as would have enabled the party concerned to have adduced it in the Court of supervisory jurisdiction to support an application to reverse the award if such procedure were available.

Where the additional evidence has already been deployed before the Court of supervisory jurisdiction for the purpose of an application for the setting aside of the award but the application has failed, the public policy of finality would normally require that the English Courts should not permit further evidence to be adduced at the enforcement stage."

S20–120 As regards bias on the part of an arbitrator, mere potential for bias is not enough. An enforcing court will wish to know why the aggrieved party did not challenge an apparently biased arbitrator at the appropriate time (see *Hebei Import and Export Corp v Polytek Engineering Co Ltd* (1999) XXIV YCA 652 Hong Kong Court of Final Appeal). Moreover, in (2004) XXIX YCA 700 at 704, the BGH said that:

"the participation of a biased arbitrator must have had a concrete impact on the arbitration. It must be proven that the biased arbitrator was prejudiced against a party and that this prejudice influenced the decision."

S20–121 For examples of cases where enforcement has been refused see (i) the decision of a French Court of First Instance in *Excelsior Film TV Srl v UGC-PH* (1999) XXIV YCA 643 and (ii) the decision of the Indian Supreme Court in *Transocean Shipping Agency (P) Ltd v Black Sea Shipping* (1998) XXIII YCA 713.

S20–122 An interesting issue of public policy arose in the Hong Kong Court of Appeal in the case *Gao v Keeneye Holdings Ltd* [2011] HKCA 459 on appeal from [2011] HKCFI 240. The case also raises a major issue concerning the interface between arbitration and mediation.

S20–123 Mr and Mrs Gao had obtained an award issued by the Xi'an Arbitration Commission ("XAC") dated June 3, 2010. The award annulled an agreement transferring shares in a Hong Kong company to Keeneye. The facts were rather murky but, in brief, art.37 of the XAC's Rules (as in all such rules of major PRC Arbitration Commissions including CIETAC and BAC) authorised either the tribunal, or its president, or a third party appointed by the tribunal to act as mediator and XAC's General Secretary had had dinner with Mr and Mrs Gao, apparently in the capacity of a mediator. While this would be wholly unacceptable in the UK (and many other jurisdictions), such conduct is wholly normal in the PRC and, consequently, the Xi'an

People's Court (i.e. the supervisory court) had previously dismissed Keeneye's challenge to the award as groundless.

Mr and Mrs Gao obtained an order from a Hong Kong court to enforce the award. Keeneye applied in Hong Kong to set the order aside complaining, inter alia, of collusion between Mr and Mrs Gao, the tribunal and the General Secretary, and the first instance judge did so saying (at [102]):

> "... as a matter of public policy [pursuant to section 40E(3) of the Arbitration Ordinance (Cap. 341)]. I should refuse enforcement of the Award here."

The judge also said (at [99]):

> "Second, it would, however, be wrong to uphold an award tainted by an appearance of bias. Upholding such an award will have the consequence that justice would not be seen to be done. Enforcement of such award would be an affront to this Court's sense of justice. See generally *A v. R* HCCT No. 54 of 2008 (30 April 2009) on when the public policy ground may be invoked."

The Hong Kong Court of Appeal reinstated the enforcement order effectively on the basis that Keeneye had agreed to the XAC Rules so could not complain when they were duly applied; the Court of Appeal considered that the Xi'An People's Court had been better able to consider the basis of Keeneye's challenge than itself. Further it stated (at [105]):

> "It is clear from the observations in the judgments of Sir Anthony Mason NPJ and Litton PJ quoted in [*Hebei Import & Export Corp v. Polytek Engineering Co Ltd* (1999) 2 HKCFAR 111 at 139 and 118] enforcement of an award should only be refused if to enforce it 'would be contrary to the fundamental conceptions of morality and justice' of the forum'. It does not mean, for example, if it is common for mediation to be conducted over dinner at a hotel in Xian, an award would not be enforced in Hong Kong, because, in Hong Kong, such conduct, might give rise to an appearance of apparent bias."

Procedural irregularity

It might be expected that enforcement might be denied on the basis of public policy when the arbitration had been conducted in flagrant breach of the rules of natural justice. However, deference must be paid to the procedural rules of the forum, to the tribunal's right to conduct the proceedings, and to the fact that arbitral proceedings cannot be expected to be conducted with the same level of formality as court proceedings (see Kerr J. in *Dalmia Dairy Industries Ltd v National Bank of Pakistan* [1978] 2 Lloyd's Rep. 223

at 270). Any such challenge might be expected to be made under art.V(1)(b) of the Convention

S20–127   Further, Colman J. said, in *Minmetals Germany GmbH v Ferco Steel Ltd* [1999] 1 All E.R. (Comm) 315, that the English courts would be unlikely to consider denying enforcement where the enforcee has unreasonably failed to invoke the supervisory jurisdiction of the courts of the forum or, a fortiori, where such a court has declined to set aside the award (see also the decision of the Hong Kong Court of Final Appeal in *Hebei Import and Export Corp v Polytek Engineering Co Ltd* (1999) XXIV YCA 652). Accordingly, while it remains a theoretical possibility that enforcement might be denied because of how the arbitration was conducted, there is no reported English case where this has actually happened.

Breach of EU law

S20–128   In *EcoSwiss China Time Ltd v Benetton International* [1999] ECR I-3055, the ECJ said that infringement of a fundamental provision of EU law such as art.101 relating to unfair competition may be regarded as being contrary to public policy under art.V(2)(b) of the New York Convention. However, the Bavarian Landsgericht (High Court) has adopted the approach that it does not itself have to consider the the parties' agreement in order to decide whether it is anti-competitive, instead it is sufficient that the tribunal appears to have considered the issue—see the decision of August 25, 2004 reported in (2006) *Cahiers de l'Arbitrage* 441.

Section 20(5)—Partial enforcement

S20–129   This replaces s.5(4) of the 1975 Act and giving effect to a proviso to art.V(1)(c) of the Convention; the context in which it operates is s.20(3)(a) and (b): if the award only partly exceeds a tribunal's jurisdiction, then the court may decide to enforce the remainder of the award.

S20–130   An authoritative commentator on the Convention suggests that a court should exercise this discretion only when the excess of authority "is of a very incidental nature and the refusal of enforcement would lead to unjustified hardship for the party seeking enforcement" (Albert Jan van den Berg, *The New York Arbitration Convention of 1958: Towards a Uniform Judicial Interpretation* (Boston: Kluwer Law and Taxation, 1981), p.319).

S20–131   However, this appears to be contrary to the general thrust of the Convention, and such limited case law as exists on this issue would not seem to support such an approach. An example of the provision in action is provided by *Syria v SIMER* (1983) VIII YCA 386, where a contract provided that non-technical disputes should be settled by local arbitration, while technical disputes should be referred to ICC arbitration. A series of issues were referred to local arbitration and an award made. In enforcement proceedings, the Court of Appeal of Trento held that some of the issues which the award purported to determine were technical and it therefore granted enforcement only of that part of the award which addressed non-technical issues.

Another example is the decision of a US District Court in *FIAT SpA v Suriname* (1998) XXIII YCA 880, that an award made against both a party to the arbitration agreement and a non-party could be enforced only against the former. S20–132

Section 20(6)

This reflects s.5(5) of the 1975 Act which derives from art.VI of the Convention (see also s.103(5) of the 1996 Act). S20–133

Section 20(6)(a)—Sisting decision on recognition or enforcement

Since the fact that the award has been set aside by a court at the seat is a ground for refusing enforcement, it is logical that a Scottish court which has been asked to enforce an award should be able to sist (i.e. stay) its decision pending the outcome of the set-aside proceedings. S20–134

Further, given that the provision refers to an application having been made, the court does not have the power to sist if the party resisting enforcement indicates that it is contemplating embarking on such proceedings. S20–135

The authors submit that the court can exercise this power on an application by the party resisting enforcement or on its own motion, although in the latter case it would, of course, have to have been made aware of the set-aside proceedings. The English Court of Appeal held, in *Yukos Oil Ltd v Dardana Ltd* [2002] 1 Lloyd's Rep. 326, that it was not open to the party seeking enforcement to apply for a stay under this provision. S20–136

It might appear that, where the conditions for the application of this subsection are met, a sist will be routinely granted in order to avoid the possibility of inconsistency (see, e.g. *Europcar Italia SpA v Maiellano Tours International Inc*, 156 F.3d 310 (1998) US Court of Appeals at 317). However, it frequently happens that an award is enforced despite the fact that such proceedings are ongoing (see W. Michael Tupman, "Staying Enforcement of Arbitral Awards under the New York Convention" (1987) 3 Arbitration Int. 209). This may be because it is thought that the proceedings have been raised simply as a device to delay enforcement, or that they have no reasonable prospect of success, or that the grounds on which the award might be set aside are not such as should prevent its enforcement. S20–137

In *IPCO (Nigeria) Ltd v Nigerian National Petroleum Corp* [2005] 2 Lloyd's Rep. 326, the English High Court (subsequently upheld by the Court of Appeal; see *Nigerian National Petroleum Corp v IPCO (Nigeria) Ltd* [2008] EWCA Civ 1157) considered that a certain sum awarded was certainly due but that there was an arguable case that the remainder of the award might be set aside at the seat. It consequently ordered partial enforcement, staying the proceedings in respect of the remaining sum but S20–138 ordering very substantial security ($450 million). See Hew R. Dundas, "Partial Enforcement of Arbitral Awards" (2008) 74 *Arbitration* 330–337 and "*IPCO v NNPC* On Appeal" (2009) 75 *Arbitration* 126–127.

S20–139 With regard to the court's discretion in s.20(6)(a), the relevant principles under the equivalent s.103(5) of the 1996 Act were set out in the judgment of Gross J. in *IPCO* [2005] 2 Lloyd's Rep. 326. The relevant principles are as follows:

> (i) s.103 embodied a pre-disposition to favour enforcement of New York Convention Awards—see para.11;
> (ii) s.103(5) was a compromise between
>> (1) the concern that enforcement should not be frustrated merely by the making of an application in the country of origin; and
>> (2) the concern that, pending proceedings in the country of origin, it should not necessarily be pre-empted by rapid enforcement of the award in another jurisdiction;
>
> (iii) the court is unfettered when considering the exercise of its discretion and, ordinarily, relevant considerations will include:
>> (a) whether the application before the court in the country of origin is brought bona fide and not simply by way of delaying tactics;
>> (b) whether that application has at least a real (i.e. realistic) prospect of success; and
>> (c) the extent of the delay occasioned by an adjournment and any resulting prejudice—see para.15.

S20–140 Gross J. also observed as follows (at para.16):

> "... the fact that the arbitration was domestic in the country of origin must generally be likely to enhance the deference due to the court exercising supervisory jurisdiction in that country. Comity and common sense are likely to require no less; pre-empting the decision on a challenge to an award before the court exercising supervisory jurisdiction in the country of origin would be a strong thing in a case where all parties were domiciled or incorporated in that country."

S20–141 Gross J. also quoted and referred to the judgment of the Court of Appeal in the case of *Soleh Boneh International Ltd v The Government and the Republic of Uganda* [1993] 2 Lloyd's Rep. 208. He said as follows:

> "As it seems to me, the right approach is that of a sliding scale, in any event embodied in the decision of the Court of Appeal in *Soleh Boneh v Uganda Govt.* [1993] 2 Lloyd's Rep 208 in the context of the question of security".

Gross J. then sets out a quotation from the judgment of Staughton L.J. as follows:

> "... two important factors must be considered on such an application, although I do not mean to say that there may not be others. The first is the strength of the argument that the award is invalid, as perceived on a brief consideration by the Court which is asked to enforce the award while proceedings to set it aside are pending elsewhere. If the award is manifestly invalid, there should be an adjournment and no order for security; if it is manifestly valid, there should either be an order for immediate enforcement, or else an order for substantial security. In between there will be various degrees of plausibility in the argument for invalidity; and the Judge must be guided by his preliminary conclusion on the point.
>
> The second point is that the Court must consider the ease or difficulty of enforcement of the award, and whether it will be rendered more difficult if enforcement is delayed. If that is likely to occur, the case for security is stronger; if, on the other hand, there are and always will be insufficient assets within the jurisdiction, the case for security must necessarily be weakened."

So the Court of Appeal was stressing here the importance of the court's considering, on the material before it, the strength of the case for invalidity of the award.

S20–142 The English courts have also held that it is possible to reconsider a decision on staying enforcement proceedings if it can be shown that circumstances have changed (see *IPCO (Nigeria) Ltd v Nigerian National Petroleum Corp (No.2)* [2008] EWHC 797 (Comm)).

S20–143 The Convention does not address the adjournment of enforcement proceedings except in this context, and its logic might seem to be that such proceedings should not be sisted except on this basis. From time to time the English courts have asserted a general discretion to stay enforcement proceedings (see *Far Eastern Shipping Co v AKP Sovconflot* [1995] 1 Lloyd's Rep. 520; *Air India v Caribjet Inc* [2002] 1 Lloyd's Rep. 314; but compare *Arab Business Consortium International Finance & Investment Co v Banque Franco-Tunisienne* [1995] 1 Lloyd's Rep. 485), but the authors submit that the Scottish courts should not follow them in this regard.

Section 20(6)(b)—Ordering the provision of security

S20–144 In both art.VI of the Convention and s.5(5) of the 1975 Act (as well as s.103(5) of the 1996 Act) the question of security and adjournment are treated as linked, i.e. that if there is an adjournment, the provision regarding security is triggered. The apparent separation of these provisions in the 2010 Act prima facie raises the possibility that security might be ordered absent an adjournment, but that cannot be the case since that differs from what the Convention and, previously, the 1975 Act, requires (see para.S18–04 above and see also *Yukos Oil Ltd v Dardana Ltd* [2002] 1 Lloyd's Rep. 326).

S20–145 If the court does decide to adjourn enforcement proceedings pending the outcome of set-aside proceedings, then there may be a risk that the ultimate enforceability of the award may be imperilled. This may be because the enforcee may seek to thwart enforcement, whether by moving its assets out of Scotland or otherwise, but may also arise in other ways, e.g. the continuing deterioration of the enforcee's financial situation. Accordingly, the party seeking enforcement may ask the court to order the other party to provide security for the enforcement of the award.

S20–146 In respect of the exercise of this power, Staughton L.J., delivering the judgment of the Court of Appeal in *Soleh Boneh International Ltd v Uganda* [1993] 2 Lloyd's Rep. 208 at 212, offered the following guidance:

> "If the award is manifestly invalid, there should be an adjournment and no order for security; if it is manifestly valid, there should be either an order for immediate enforcement, or else an order for substantial security. In between there will be various degrees of plausibility in the argument for invalidity; and the Judge must be guided by his preliminary conclusion on the point.
>
> [T]he court must consider the ease or difficulty of enforcement of the award, and whether it will be rendered more difficult, for example, by movement of assets or by improvident trading, if enforcement is delayed. If that is likely to occur, the case for security is stronger; if, on the other hand, there are and always will be insufficient assets within the jurisdiction, the case for security must necessarily be weakened."

S20–147 The fact that the party resisting enforcement has been unduly dilatory in raising set-aside proceedings enhances the case for ordering security (*Yukos Oil Ltd v Dardana Ltd* [2002] 1 Lloyd's Rep. 326). The amount for which security should be ordered and how and where it should be provided lies in the discretion of the court, taking into account all the circumstances (see *IPCO (Nigeria) Ltd v Nigerian National Petroleum Corp* [2005] 2 Lloyd's Rep. 326).

S20–148 Where the proceedings are adjourned, the English courts have asserted a power to order the party seeking enforcement to provide security for the cost of the enforcement proceedings, on the basis that the party might seek to abandon the proceedings if the award is in fact set aside at the seat (*Dardana Ltd v Yukos Oil Ltd (No.2)* [2002] 2 Lloyd's Rep. 261). However, it would appear that they will not otherwise order that party to provide security (*Gater Assets Ltd v Nak Naftogaz Ukrainiy* [2007] EWCA Civ 988).

S20–149 In regard to the quantum of security, see para.S20–138 above.

Section 20(7)

This is discussed in the context of s.20(3)(d) above.　　　　　　　　　　S20–150

Evidence to be produced when seeking recognition or enforcement

21.—(1) A person seeking recognition or enforcement of a Convention award must produce—
　(a) the duly authenticated original award (or a duly certified copy of it), and
　(b) the original arbitration agreement (or a duly certified copy of it).

(2) Such a person must also produce a translation of any award or agreement which is in a language other than English (certified by an official or sworn translator or by a diplomatic or consular agent).

DEFINITIONS

"arbitration agreement": ss.4, 31(1)
"Convention award": ss.18, 31(1)

MODEL LAW

Article 35(2) of the Model Law (as amended in 2006) follows closely art.IV of the New York Convention upon which s.21 is based.　　S21–01

COMMENTARY

Section 21 re-enacts s.4 of the 1975 Act, which in turn derived from art.IV of the Convention. It is in almost identical terms to s.102 of the 1996 Act.　　S21–02

Unless a party can produce the documentation required, the court cannot recognise or enforce the award under s.19, although that would not preclude that party from finding some other basis on which the court might be persuaded to recognise or enforce the award.　　S21–03

The question arises as to who should perform the authentication or certification demanded by s.21(1); the authorities are contradictory. First, the Austrian Bundesgerichtshof (Supreme Court) ((1977) I YCA 232) has said that the Convention does not make it clear whether it should be done in terms of the law of the seat or that of the enforcing state, saying further that either would usually be acceptable, but recommending the latter. Secondly, the Italian Corte Suprema di Cassazione held in *SODIME v Schuurmans & Van Ginneken BV* (1996) XXI YCA 607 that it was the law of the seat which prevailed and, thirdly, the Bulgarian Supreme Court held in *ECONERG Ltd v National Electricity Company AD* (2000) XXV YCA 678 that the requirements of the seat and the enforcing state must both be satisfied.　　S21–04

While art.4(1) of the Geneva Convention had provided that these issues be determined by the law of the seat, the drafters of the New York Convention had deliberately omitted this requirement in order to confer discretion on the enforcing court (see A.J. van den Berg, *The New York*　　S21–05

Arbitration Convention of 1958 (Kluwer Law International, 1981), p.252). The authors respectfully submit that this latter approach is, save possibly in exceptional circumstances, the correct one.

S21–06 The authors submit that, should the issue ever arise in Scotland, the courts should favour the position adopted by the Austrian Supreme Court (see para.S21–04 above). Note that art.III of the Convention directs that an enforcing state must not impose conditions on recognition and enforcement which are substantially more onerous than those imposed on parties seeking recognition or enforcement of domestic awards.

Section 21(1)(a)—Duly authenticated original award

S21–07 A party must produce the duly authenticated original award or a duly certified copy, and courts in various jurisdictions have declined to enforce an award where this has not been done (see, e.g. *Weinstein International Corp v Nagtegaal NV* (1980) V YCA 269 (Holland); (1994) XIX YCA 700 (Italy)). Yet this is a curable defect in that enforcement will be granted if the party returns to the court with the proper documentation (see *Sea Traders SA v Participaciones, Proyectos y Estudios SA* (1996) XXI YCA 676 (Spain)).

S21–08 Where the original document appears to have been tendered, the onus will then lie on the party disputing authenticity. The BGH observed in (2001) XXVI YCA 771 at 773 that it

> "would be a hollow formality to require that the claimant prove the existence and authenticity of the arbitral award, whose copy is supplied."

S21–09 This was also the approach taken by the English Court of Appeal (*Yukos Oil Ltd v Dardana Ltd* [2002] 1 Lloyd's Rep. 326). Authentication means that the signatures of the arbitrators are confirmed as genuine, while certification means that a copy is attested as a true copy of the original (see van den Berg, *The New York Arbitration Convention of 1958* (1981), p.648). It follows that if a duly certified copy of the award is produced, then there is no need to prove that the signatures thereon are genuine (see (2000) XXV YCA 717 Rostock Court of Appeal). One practical solution to demonstrate genuineness is that the arbitrators' signatures be witnessed.

S21–10 Certification of a copy under Scots law requires authentication by the person responsible for the making of the copy (Civil Evidence (Scotland) Act 1988 s.6). One of the authors is aware of real difficulties in certain jurisdictions with certified copies hence, in practice, always prepares 3–6 additional signed/witnessed originals in case they are needed. Although not an arbitration case, an extradition warrant presented by HM Government in Country X was refused since local law required that four originals be presented to the court and while the four had, self-evidently, original signatures, stamps and seals, the judge ascertained that, of the four, one had been printed and then three copies run off on a photocopier. The judge held that these three documents were not "original". While no English or Scottish court could conceivably take such a view, the context of enforcement of awards can be "Big Foreign Company is trying to bankrupt Little Local Company" and it is not difficult to understand local judges trying to find any way to refuse enforcement.

Aside from legal theory, in a practical case the award creditor will necessarily take all possible steps to minimise enforcement difficulties, e.g. in a Latin American country, domestic awards presented to court have to be printed and bound in a particular way before the court will even consider them. Whether or not that stipulation would be applied to a Convention award is unclear but, to avoid tripping up, the award creditor is strongly advised to play safe. **S21–11**

It is the responsibility of the claimant, not of the tribunal, to anticipate difficulties such as exemplified at paras S21–10/11. Sensible tribunals should, at the conclusion of the arbitration, ask the parties whether or not there are any special considerations to be taken into account. **S21–12**

Section 21(1)(b)—Original arbitration agreement

A party must also produce the original arbitration agreement or a duly certified copy. Again, while a party who produces the award but not the agreement cannot be granted enforcement, this can be cured if he returns to the court with the agreement at a later stage (see *Ethiopia v Baruch Foster Corp* (1977) II YCA 252). This requirement has sometimes caused difficulties where parties have been joined to arbitral proceedings (see, e.g. *Javor v Francoeur* (2004) XXIX YCA 596), although on other occasions courts have been willing to treat a party as the representative or alter ego of the party to the agreement (see, e.g. *Pan Liberty Navigation Co Ltd v World Link (HK) Resources Ltd* (2005) B.C.C.A. 206). **S21–13**

Section 21(2)—Translation

If the award or agreement is not in English (the authors reserve comment about Gaelic), the party seeking recognition or enforcement must also produce a translation thereof certified by an official or sworn translator or by a diplomatic or consular agent. This means that the translation can be conducted by anyone, so long as it is appropriately certified **S21–14**

Again, this certification can be carried out in terms of either the law of the seat or the place of enforcement (see Van den Berg, *The New York Arbitration Convention of 1958* (1981), pp.259–262). Even though this appears to be a mandatory requirement, an Amsterdam court in *SPP (Middle East) Ltd v Egypt* (1985) X YCA 487 enforced an untranslated award because it was in English and understood by the court. Rather more surprisingly, in *RSA v A Ltd* (2001) XXVI YCA 863 a court in Geneva recognised an award **S21–15**

S21–16　Analogous to paras S21–10/12, this area is fraught with local complications but it is for the claimant to find a way through. English speakers need only to compare "eats shoots and leaves" with "eats, shoots and leaves" to begin to see how complicated such matters can get. "My translator is better than your translator" is a common theme.

Saving for other bases of recognition or enforcement

22. Nothing in sections 19 to 21 affects any other right to rely on or enforce a Convention award in pursuance of any other enactment or rule of law.

DEFINITIONS

"Convention award": ss.18, 31(1)

COMMENTARY

S22–01　This replaces s.6 of the 1975 Act, and gives effect to art.VII(1) of the Convention.

S22–02　If it would be more straightforward to enforce a Convention award at common law, or under another treaty or under another set of statutory provisions, then that is permissible so a party might seek to enforce an award at common law which would not be enforceable under s.18 because he was unable to meet the requirements of s.21 (see *Hamlyn & Co v Talisker Distillery* (1894) 21 R. (HL) 21). It must be doubted, however, whether a party could seek to enforce an award at common law where enforcement was refused under s.20, since the authors submit Scots law would generally accept those grounds for resisting enforcement.

S22–03　Could a party seek to rely on s.12 as a basis for enforcement? There seems to be no reason why he could not, since, as noted above, s.12(5) makes it clear that the section applies to foreign as well as domestic awards. There might indeed be an advantage in doing so, since s.12 only appears to contemplate one ground for resisting enforcement—lack of jurisdiction. Nevertheless, since s.12(1) gives courts a discretion whether or not to enforce an award, that advantage may be more apparent than real.

Supplementary

Prescription and limitation

23.—(1) The Prescription and Limitation (Scotland) Act 1973 (c. 52) is amended as follows.

　　(2) In section 4 (positive prescription: interruption)—

　　　　(a) in subsection (2)(b), after "Scotland" insert "in respect of which an arbitrator (or panel of arbitrators) has been appointed",

(b) in subsection (3)(a), for the words from "and" to "served" substitute ", the date when the arbitration begins",

(c) for subsection (4) substitute—

"(4) An arbitration begins for the purposes of this section—

(a) when the parties to the arbitration agree that it begins, or

(b) in the absence of such agreement, in accordance with rule 1 of the Scottish Arbitration Rules (see section 7 of, and schedule 1 to, the Arbitration (Scotland) Act 2010 (asp 1)).".

(3) In section 9 (negative prescription: interruption)—

(a) in subsection (3), for the words from "and" to "served" substitute "the date when the arbitration begins",

(b) in subsection (4), for "preliminary notice" substitute "the date when the arbitration begins".

(4) After section 19C, insert—

"19D Interruption of limitation period: arbitration

(1) Any period during which an arbitration is ongoing in relation to a matter is to be disregarded in any computation of the period specified in section 17(2), 18(2), 18A(1) or 18B(2) of this Act in relation to that matter.

(2) In this section, "arbitration" means—

(a) any arbitration in Scotland,

(b) any arbitration in a country other than Scotland, being an arbitration an award in which would be enforceable in Scotland.".

(5) In section 22A(4), for the words from "and" to "served" substitute "the date when the arbitration begins (within the meaning of section 4(4) of this Act)".

(6) After section 22C, insert—

"22CA Interruption of limitation period for 1987 Act actions: arbitration

(1) Any period during which an arbitration is ongoing in relation to a matter is to be disregarded in any computation of the period specified in section 22B(2) or 22C(2) of this Act in relation to that matter.

(2) In this section, "arbitration" means—

(a) any arbitration in Scotland,

(b) any arbitration in a country other than Scotland, being an arbitration an award in which would be enforceable in Scotland.".

DEFINITIONS

"arbitration": ss.2(1), (2), 31(1)
"party": ss.2(1), 31(1), (2)

COMMENTARY

Introductory

S23–01 Scots law operates systems of positive prescription, negative prescription and limitation of actions. Under positive prescription, ownership of heritable (immoveable) property and lesser rights over heritable property are acquired through the passage of time. Under negative prescription, personal obligations (and their correlative rights) expire and disappear. Under limitation the right to bring an action in a Scottish court to enforce a right becomes barred, although the underlying obligation and right continue to exist until they negatively prescribe. This co-existence of prescription and limitation reflects the nature of Scots law as a mixed system derived in part from Roman law principles and English common law practice.

S23–02 All three systems are codified in the 1973 Act. Arbitration can interrupt a prescriptive period and prevent obligations and rights from becoming time-barred in the same way as litigation. However, the 1973 Act has special provisions for the termination of prescription and limitation through the commencement of arbitration.

S23–03 Given the changes in the law effected by the 2010 Act, consequential amendments to the 1973 Act in relation to the interruption of periods of prescription and limitation were necessary.

Section 23(2)—Effect on positive prescription

S23–04 Positive prescription allows the fortification and acquisition of ownership of heritable (immoveable) property, the acquisition of positive servitudes over heritable property (e.g. rights of access and aqueduct), and the acquisition of public rights of way. The acquisition of rights by positive prescription brings with it automatically loss of ownership or rights. In certain restricted cases, the real rights of a tenant under a long lease can also be fortified (see s.2 of the 1973 Act).

S23–05 The acquisition of ownership of heritable (immoveable) property requires the registration of a title deed in the General Register of Sasines or, if state indemnity has been excluded, in the Land Register of Scotland, and possession by the grantee of the deed or his successors possession openly, peaceably and "without any judicial interruption" for a continuous period of 10 years (see s.1 of the 1973 Act).

S23–06 The acquisition of positive (private) servitudes over heritable property or public rights of way requires the exercise of the access etc. for a continuous period of 20 years openly, peaceably and "without any judicial interruption" (see s.3 of the 1973 Act).

S23–07 Section 4(1) of the 1973 Act provides that "judicial interruption" means the making in "appropriate proceedings" of a claim by any person having an interest, challenging the possession in question. Section 4(2) defines "appropriate proceedings" to include,

"   ... (b) any arbitration in Scotland in respect of which an arbitrator (or panel of arbitrators) has been appointed;
   (c) any arbitration in a country other than Scotland, being an arbitration an award in which would be enforceable in Scotland."

It seems to be a resolutive condition of judicial interruption by means of arbitration that the tribunal is appointed, although if it is appointed, the date of interruption will be as set out in s.4(3).

Critically, s.4(3) of the 1973 Act provides that the date of judicial interruption where a claim is made in an arbitration is the date when the arbitration "begins" and s.4(4) provides that it "begins" when the parties agree, or more pertinently in accordance with r.1 of the SAR. See commentary on r.1.   **S23–08**

Section 23(3) and (5)—Effect on negative prescription

In most arbitrations, negative prescription of the obligation being relied on by the claimant will be the most important form of time bar. Under ss.6–8 of the 1973 Act, the making of a "relevant claim" interrupts the running of the standard periods of negative prescription—either 5 or 20 years. Under s.22A of the 1973 Act, the making of a "relevant claim" interrupts the running of the 10 year period of negative prescription for obligations to pay damages arising out of defective products under the Consumer Protection Act 1987.   **S23–09**

A "relevant claim" means a claim made by or on behalf of the creditor for implement of the obligation in "appropriate proceedings". "Appropriate proceedings" has the meaning given in s.4(2) quoted above (s.9(4) of the 1973 Act) and therefore includes arbitration.   **S23–10**

A "relevant claim" is made in an arbitration on the date when the arbitration "begins" (s.9(3) of the 1973 Act) and that is the date of commencement agreed by the parties, failing which the date ascertained in accordance with rr.1 and 83 of the SAR (ss.9(4) and 4(4) of the 1973 Act). A lot will depend on the content of the notice of submission to arbitration, to whom it was given and when. See commentary on r.1.   **S23–11**

Once a relevant claim has been made, the period of negative prescription ceases to run for the duration of the arbitration (*GA Estates Ltd v Caviapen Trustees Ltd (No.2)*, 1993 S.L.T. 1051).   **S23–12**

Section 23(4) and (6)—Effect on statutory limitation period

The 1973 Act imposes a three year period for the bringing of various actions: s.17, solatium or other damages in respect of personal injury; s.18, damages in respect of personal injury leading to death; s.18A, damages in respect of defamation; s.18B, damages in respect of harassment; s.22B, damages in respect of a defective product; and s.22C, damages in respect death caused by a defective product.   **S23–13**

S23–14 Subsections (4) and (6) insert ss.19D and 22CA into the 1973 Act, which provide that any period during which the arbitration is "ongoing" will be disregarded in the computation of the three year period. An arbitration is "ongoing" if it has begun.

S23–15 It can be seen that the arbitration in question need not be seated in Scotland if the award would be enforceable in Scotland.

Arbitral appointments referee

24.—(1) Ministers may, by order, authorise persons or types of person who may act as an arbitral appointments referee for the purposes of the Scottish Arbitration Rules.

(2) Ministers must, when making such an order, have regard to the desirability of ensuring that arbitral appointments referees—
  (a) have experience relevant to making arbitral appointments, and
  (b) are able to provide training, and to operate disciplinary procedures, designed to ensure that arbitrators conduct themselves appropriately.

(3) Despite subsection (2)(b), an arbitral appointments referee is not obliged to appoint arbitrators in respect of whom the referee provides training or operates disciplinary procedures.

DEFINITIONS

"arbitral appointments referee": s.31(1)
"Ministers": s.31(1)
"rules": ss.7, 31(1)

COMMENTARY

S24–01 One of the most striking of the innovative features of the 2010 Act is that under r.7 the default position when procedures for appointing arbitrators fail is that any appointment is to be made not by the court, as is traditional, but by an arbitral appointments referee ("AAR"), a concept unknown in any other legal system.

S24–02 The underlying principle is simple: the leading private institutions in the UK make, in total, 15–20,000 arbitral appointments per annum and some such institutions have departments dedicated to such work, utilising large databases of potential appointees. The English courts are understood to make no more than 5–10 appointments per annum and do not possess any such database. It is therefore self-evident that the AARs are vastly better equipped to make such appointments.

S24–03 Ministers are empowered to authorise persons or types of person so to act. In terms of the Scotland Act 1998 (Transitory and Transitional Provisions) (Publication and Interpretation etc. of Acts of the Scottish Parliament) Order 1999 (SI 1999/1379) para.6(2) and Sch., a person would include a body of persons.

S24–04 The Arbitral Appointments Referee (Scotland) Order 2010 (SSI 2010/196) has authorised the CIArb, the Dean of the Faculty of Advocates, the Institution of Civil Engineers, the Law Society of Scotland, the Royal Incorporation of Architects in Scotland, RICS and SAAVA to act as arbitral appointments referees under r.7.

The policy memorandum, para.111, suggested that any body which can satisfy the requirements of s.24(2) might apply to be an arbitral appointments referee. Those requirements are a track record of past appointments, plus an ability to provide appropriate training and operate suitable disciplinary procedures, both designed to ensure that arbitrators conduct themselves appropriately. S24–05

The consultation paper, para.39, mentioned a further criterion, that the body had regularly to assess the procedures of arbitrators. That criterion was omitted from s.24 because it was realised that only two of the 8–10 candidate bodies were in a position to meet it. S24–06

Section 24(2)(b) lists matters for consideration by Ministers whereas its provisions could conceivably have been made mandatory. The reason for this is that not all AARs operate disciplinary procedures in respect of their members acting as arbitrators as opposed to acting in their primary profession S24–07

Section 24(3) did not form part of the Bill as presented to the Scottish Parliament in January 2009 and was added to maximise the size of the pool of arbitrators available to any individual AAR. S24–08

Power of judge to act as arbitrator or umpire

25.—(1) **A judge may act as an arbitrator or umpire only where—**
   (a) **the dispute being arbitrated appears to the judge to be of commercial character, and**
   (b) **the Lord President, having considered the state of Court of Session business, has authorised the judge to so act.**

(2) **A fee of such amount as Ministers may by order prescribe is payable in the Court of Session for the services of a judge acting as an arbitrator or umpire.**

(3) **Any jurisdiction exercisable by the Outer House under the Scottish Arbitration Rules (or any other provision of this Act) in relation to—**
   (a) **a judge acting as a sole arbitrator or umpire, or**
   (b) **a tribunal which the judge forms part of,**
is to be exercisable instead by the Inner House (and the Inner House's decision on any matter is final).

(4) **In this section—**
"judge" means a judge of the Court of Session, and
"Lord President" means the Lord President of the Court of Session.

DEFINITIONS

"arbitrator": ss.2(1), 31(1)

"dispute": ss.2(1), 31(1)
"Inner House": s.31(1)
"Outer House": s.31(1)
"tribunal": ss.2(1), 31(1)

COMMENTARY

Introductory

S25–01   This largely re-enacts s.17 of the Law Reform (Miscellaneous Provisions) (Scotland) Act 1980 by virtue of which it was already possible for a judge of the Court of Session who considered that a dispute is of a commercial character to accept appointment as an arbitrator, as long as the Lord President authorised him so to act, having regard to the state of Court of Session business.

S25–02   It may appear strange that sitting judges should sit as arbitrators and the concept is unknown in some jurisdictions, and indeed prohibited in others, but it is certainly known in England where it is currently authorised by s.93 of the 1996 Act and was previously authorised by s.4 of the Administration of Justice Act 1970 and s.99 of the Courts and Legal Services Act 1990 (and before that by s.11 of the 1950 Act.)

S25–03   Why might parties consider appointing a judge as arbitrator? In England there appear to be five main reasons:

> (i) simple economics: there is an appointment fee of £2,390 for a High Court judge, £1,860 for a TCC judge, with day rates in the same (respective) amounts and the use of the courtroom is included in the dayrate;
> (ii) particular expertise: TCC judges are expert in dealing with construction cases, particularly large, complex ones. It is understood that approximately 15–20 cases a year are heard by TCC judge-arbitrators;
> (iii) where the key to the arbitration is a particular point of law and the judge chosen is a noted authority in that area of law. For example, Sir Christopher Staughton, while a sitting judge, sat as sole arbitrator in *Owners of the Bamburi v Compton (The Bamburi)* [1982] 1 Lloyd's Rep. 312. The case concerned the question whether a vessel trapped in the Shatt-al-Arab waterway during the 1979 Iraq/Iran war was a constructive total loss for the purposes of the applicable insurance policy. Many other vessels were similarly trapped and Sir Christopher's award, containing an elegant and comprehensive restatement of the law, was considered sufficiently important to be published, thus providing authoritative guidance on the issue;
> (iv) national security, where a judge is preferred to a "civilian" arbitrator on such grounds;

(v) the fact that, by virtue of Sch.2 of the 1996 Act, a number of powers that are normally only exercisable by the court can be exercised by a judge-arbitrator, while any appeal against the award would be heard by the Court of Appeal, rather limiting the risk of an appeal.

As is discussed more fully below, not all of these reasons would resonate in Scotland. Currently, there appears to be no recourse to judge-arbitrators, and the policy memorandum, para.115, notes that in light of pressures on the Court of Session there is, at present, no scope for a judge to be used in this way.

It speculates that this may change as a result of the recommendations following the Scottish Civil Courts Review (*Report of the Scottish Civil Courts Review* (Scottish Civil Courts Review, 2009), so the possibility of recourse to a judge-arbitrator was retained in the Act. While those recommendations, if implemented, may reduce some of the pressure on the Court of Session, given that Court of Session judges also sit as judges of the High Court of Justiciary in criminal cases, this may prove a rather optimistic view.

The last known recourse to a judge-arbitrator in Scotland was in 1986 when Lord Jauncey (then a Court of Session judge) sat as sole arbiter pursuant to s.17 of the 1980 Act in an arbitration which eventually saw him stating a case for the opinion of the Court of Session on two issues. He was upheld on one issue but not the other in *Scott Lithgow Ltd v Secretary of State for Defence*, 1988 S.L.T. 697. However, the House of Lords (1989 S.L.T. 236) ultimately upheld him on neither issue.

There has only been one recorded challenge to a judge-arbitrator's award under the 1996 Act—*Henry Boot Construction Ltd v Alstom Combined Cycles Ltd* [2005] EWCA Civ 814. Of particular interest is that the judge-arbitrator's award was substantially overturned on an appeal under s.69 (appeal on a point of law) of the 1996 Act.

Section 25(1)—When judge may act as arbitrator

Section 25(1) is the equivalent of s.93(1)–(2) of the 1996 Act by virtue of which a judge can only act if the Lord Chief Justice has informed him that he can be made available. Under the 2010 Act, the Lord President must authorise them to act. However, under both Acts, subject to this authorisation, it is for the judge in question to decide whether he wishes to act.

Under the 2010 Act, a judge must consider a dispute to be of a commercial character in order to be able to act. That condition need not apply under the 1996 Act (compare Administration of Justice Act 1970 s.4), but only a Commercial Court judge or a TCC judge is allowed to act as a judge-arbitrator under that Act, although the DAC Report, para.390 (see also paras 341–343) recommended that all judges should be allowed so to act.

Arbitration (Scotland) Act 2010

S25–10 The restrictions set out in s.25(1) alter the common law in *Fisher v Colquhoun* (1844) 6 D. 1286 where it was held that an appointment of Lord Wood as an arbiter before he became a judge continued notwithstanding his judicial appointment and it was observed (obiter) that while it was to be discouraged there was nothing to prevent a judge on the bench accepting a fresh appointment.

S25–11 While s.25(1) uses the words "may act as an arbitrator" the authors submit that the elevation of an arbitrator to judicial office does not terminate his appointment and that the outcome of *Fisher* would remain unaltered under the Act. The arbitrator has a contract with the parties to fulfil his functions and such contract continues unless there is resignation, incapacity or death. If the arbitration has just begun it may be prudent for the arbitrator to consider resignation but the position will be different once parties have spent significant resources in the arbitration.

S25–12 Under the 1996 Act a judge may only act as a sole arbitrator or umpire, whereas under the 2010 Act a judge-arbitrator may also be a member of an arbitral tribunal. Whether it would be sensible for the Lord President to authorise scarce judicial resources to be deployed in this way is open to serious doubt, and it might be guessed that few judges would be prepared to act except as a sole arbitrator, since the point of having a judge-arbitrator is otherwise largely lost.

S25–13 In England, an application that a judge should sit simultaneously as both judge and arbitrator was rejected on the basis that an individual cannot discharge both functions at the same time (*Wilson v Keen* Unreported June 25, 1991 CA).

Section 25(2)—Fees

S25–14 This re-enacts s.17(2) of the 1980 Act under which the Appointment of Judges as Arbiters (Fees) Order 1993 (SI 1993/3125) was made. That Order, which is still in force, provides for the payment of £1,350 on appointment and £1,350 per day or part thereof (after the first day) of the hearing of the reference.

Section 25(3)

S25–15 Most of the powers exercisable by the court under the SAR are invested in the Outer House. It would be highly inappropriate for certain powers, e.g. in relation to appeals, to be exercisable by a single Outer House judge when the arbitrator is a Senator of the College of Justice, so that jurisdiction is invested in the Inner House, whose decision is final. However, there is no reason why a single Outer House judge could not provide assistance to the arbitrator, e.g. under rr.45 and 46. Nevertheless, s.25(3) appears to prevent this.

S25–16 This provision is the equivalent of Sch.2 para.2(1) of the 1996 Act where references to the High Court are generally treated as reference to the Court of Appeal in cases of judge-arbitrators. However, Sch.2 then goes on to enumerate the various powers which are ordinarily exercisable by the court, but which may be exercised by a judge-arbitrator.

Amendments to UNCITRAL Model Law or Rules or New York Convention

26.—(1) Ministers may by order modify—
- (a) the Scottish Arbitration Rules,
- (b) any other provision of this Act, or
- (c) any enactment which provides for disputes to be resolved by arbitration,

in such manner as they consider appropriate in consequence of any amendment made to the UNCITRAL Model Law, the UNCITRAL Arbitration Rules or the New York Convention.

(2) Before making such an order, Ministers must consult such persons appearing to them to have an interest in the law of arbitration as they think fit.

DEFINITIONS

"arbitration": ss.2(1), (2), 31(1)
"dispute": ss.2(1), 31(1)
"Ministers": s.31(1)
"New York Convention": s.31(1)
"rules": ss.7, 31(1)
"UNCITRAL Arbitration Rules ": s.31(1)
"UNCITRAL Model Law": s.31(1)

COMMENTARY

This section allows the Scottish Ministers, subject to affirmative procedure in the Scottish Parliament, to modify the Act or any other statutory provision to reflect changes in the Model Law, the New York Convention, or the UNCITRAL Rules. This is a particularly noteworthy provision. S26–01

The New York Convention is now rather venerable, and there have been calls for certain of its provisions to be updated (see K.H. Böckstiegel, "Future Perspectives" in Emmanuel Gaillard and Domenico Di Pietro (eds), *Enforcement of Arbitral Agreements and International Arbitral Awards* (London: Cameron May, 2008)). It is therefore possible (albeit highly unlikely) that it may be amended at some point in the future, and one might expect that the UK would ultimately ratify any amended version. S26–02

Section 26 treats any such ratification as irrelevant. The Scottish Ministers may act regardless of ratification which would, in any event, not be applicable for the UNCITRAL Rules. No corresponding provision is to be found in the 1996 Act. The policy memorandum, para.117, comments that this will permit Scots arbitration law to keep up-to-date with international arbitral practice, and that Scotland will have an arbitration law which is S26–03 based on Model Law principles. The international arbitration community may regard Scotland as having stolen a march on the rest of the world in this respect.

S26–04   The Bill was drafted in the full light of the 2006 revisions to the Model Law and was being drafted while the 2010 revision of the UNCITRAL Rules was being prepared, the latter being promulgated one month after the Act came into force. While it might be possible to find minor improvements to the Act in the detail of the new UNCITRAL Rules, the authors consider that no application of s.26(1) is necessary.

Section 26(2)

S26–05   In practice any amendment is likely to arise as a result of lobbying from interested parties. However, the legislation now imposes an actual duty to consult. Ministers must consult such persons appearing to have an interest in arbitration as they think fit, which gives some degree of protection against challenges from marginal groups who believe they should have been consulted.

Amendment of Conveyancing (Scotland) Act 1924 (c. 27)

27. In section 46 of the Conveyancing (Scotland) Act 1924—
  (a) in subsection (2), for "This section" substitute "Subsection (1)", and
  (b) after subsection (2) insert—
    "(3) Where—
      (a) an arbitral award orders the reduction of a deed or other document recorded in the Register of Sasines (or forming a midcouple or link of title in a title recorded in that Register), and
      (b) the court orders that the award may be enforced in accordance with section 12 of the Arbitration (Scotland) Act 2010 (asp 1),
    subsection (1) applies to the arbitral award as it applies to a decree of reduction of a deed recorded in the Register of Sasines.".

DEFINITIONS

"court": s.31(1)

COMMENTARY

S27–01   Section 46 of the Conveyancing (Scotland) Act 1924 provides for the recording in the Register of Sasines of the extract of a court decree reducing (annulling) or rectifying a deed or other document registered in that register. Under r.49(d) of the SAR, unless the parties have agreed otherwise, the arbitral tribunal itself has the power to reduce or rectify a deed or other document, and its award may then be enforced by the court under s.12. The amendments introduced by s.27 permit the arbitral award to be recorded in the Register of Sasines. Such an award is of no effect in so far as it would adversely affect the interests of any third party acting in good faith (s.12).

Articles of Regulation 1695
28. The 25th Act of the Articles of Regulation 1695 does not apply in relation to arbitration.

DEFINITIONS

"arbitration": ss.2(1), 2(2), 31(1)

COMMENTARY

The 25th Act of the Articles of Regulation provides that the Court of Session will not reduce a "decreet arbitral" unless on the grounds of "corruption, bribery or falsehood to be alleged against the judges arbitrators". This provision, which was introduced to prevent the court's undue interference with 17th century arbitral awards, is now disapplied in relation to arbitration, and the exclusive grounds for challenging awards are now laid down in Part 8 of the SAR. The removal of this archaic provision from arbitration, which in practice was not exhaustive of the grounds of challenge, is to be commended. S28–01

The 25th Act still appears to apply in relation to judicial reference (see commentary on s.2). S28–02

Repeals
29. The repeals of the enactments specified in column 1 of schedule 2 have effect to the extent specified in column 2.

COMMENTARY

A number of other statutes and statutory provisions are repealed. Aside from Part II of the 1950 Act, the following are repealed: S29–01

- 1894 Act. This disapplied the common law rule whereby an arbitration agreement was invalid unless it named an arbitrator. See now r.2 below. It also laid down procedures whereby the court could appoint an arbitrator or oversman (umpire) where conventional appointments procedures failed. However, the court could act only in a limited range of circumstances, and in a variety of situations was powerless to assist the parties (see the commentary to r.7 below). Rule 7 now contains a much more comprehensive set of provisions to deal with failure of appointments procedures.
- 1972 Act s.3. This introduced the notorious stated case procedure into Scotland on the model of the old English special case procedure. There had been no particular call for this to happen from

within Scotland, and the provision was even then widely regarded as an unnecessary and unwelcome English transplant (see Robert L.C. Hunter, "Stated Cases in Contractual Arbitration in Scotland" (1972) 17 J.L.S.S. 168). It was, moreover, a provision which, due to inept drafting, failed in one of its main objectives of permitting appeals against arbitral awards on questions of law (see Lord President Emslie in *Fairlie Yacht Slip v Lumsden*, 1977 S.L.T. (Notes) 41 at 42). Repeal of s.3 was advocated by the Scottish Advisory Committee on Arbitration Law at para.5.22 of its *Report on Legislation for Domestic Arbitration in Scotland* (1996), and the stated case procedure was roundly criticised by Lord President Hope in *ERDC Construction Ltd v H M Love & Co (No.2)*, 1997 S.L.T. 175 at 178. It was replaced by the rather more limited procedure in rr.41 and 42 for referring questions of law for the opinion of the Outer House, while r.69 creates a right of appeal against an award on the basis of legal error in certain circumstances. Both rr.41 and 69 are default rules.
- 1975 Act. This gave effect to the New York Convention, and is now replaced by ss.10 and 18–22 of the 2010 Act.
- The Law Reform (Miscellaneous Provisions) (Scotland) Act 1980 s.17. This allows a judge of the Court of Session to accept appointment as an arbitrator. It is re-enacted by s.25.
- 1990 Act s.66 and Sch.7. This gave effect to the Model Law in Scotland for international commercial arbitration only with an opt-in (understood by the authors never to have been exercised) for domestic arbitrations. The 2010 Act unifies the domestic and international commercial arbitration regimes and does so paying close attention to the Model Law.

Arbitrability of disputes

30. Nothing in this Act makes any dispute capable of being arbitrated if, because of its subject-matter, it would not otherwise be capable of being arbitrated.

DEFINITIONS

"dispute": ss.2(1), 31(1)

MODEL LAW

S30–01 Article 1(5) provides that:

"This Law shall not affect any other law of this State by virtue of which certain disputes may not be submitted to arbitration ... ".

COMMENTARY

Introductory

Like art.1(5) of the Model Law, s.30 makes it clear that the Act does not render any dispute capable of being arbitrated if it was not previously capable of being arbitrated. Whether a dispute is capable of being arbitrated is the issue of "arbitrability".   S30–02

In some jurisdictions there are statutory provisions which list the matters which may not be referred to arbitration (see, e.g. French Civil Code art.2060). In others, legislation provides that matters which are of a pecuniary nature (e.g. Swiss Private International Law Act art.177(1)) or are capable of being settled by the parties may be arbitrated, while it is increasingly common to combine these two approaches (as in the Austrian Code of Civil Procedure art.582(1)).   S30–03

What is arbitrable under the Scottish law of arbitration is found in the common law. The 18th century statement of the institutional writer, Lord Bankton (*Institute* I, 23, 17), still represents the basic principle of the common law: "Whatever can be transacted may be determined by arbitrament".   S30–04

Particular instances of non-arbitrability

The interest of the general members of the public cannot as such be transacted with. Thus matters of status or criminal liability cannot be settled by arbitration. Issues such as parentage, marriage, legitimacy, the holding of honours or titles are not arbitrable. A dispute over who was to be the guardian for a minor was held not to be arbitrable (*Ramsay v Hay* (1624) Mor. 16245).   S30–05

Equally, an arbitrator may not wind up a company and a declarator as to the existence of a public right of way over private property is not arbitrable.   S30–06

Social security claims will not be arbitrable, given that neither the First-tier nor the Upper Tribunals are bound by agreements reached between the claimant and the Secretary of State.   S30–07

In certain jurisdictions (e.g. the USA) employment disputes are arbitrable but while in Scotland contractual rights arising from employment contracts are arbitrable, most disputes relating to statutory employment rights must be referred to an employment tribunal. By virtue of the Employment Rights Act 1996 s.203, the general rule is that arbitration agreements which purport to exclude or limit the operation of any provision of the 1996 Act, or to preclude a person from bringing any proceedings under the Act before an employment tribunal, are void. However, s.203 does have exceptions to the general rule of non-arbitrability: see *Clyde & Co LLP v Bates van Winkelhof* [2011] EWHC 668 (QB).   S30–08

However, the Trade Union and Labour Relations (Consolidation) Act 1992 s.212A also allowed the Advisory, Conciliation and Arbitration   S30–09

Service to create a mechanism whereby unfair dismissal claims disputes may be referred to arbitration (see ACAS Arbitration Scheme (Great Britain) Order 2004 (SI 2004/753)).

Contra bonos mores

S30–10 Disputes over matters that are *contra bonos mores* are not arbitrable (s.4 refers). Thus, if a dispute arose out of a contract for drug smuggling or other illegal or even legally unenforceable activity (e.g. gambling, prostitution) which was covered by an arbitration clause in it, the arbitration clause itself, having been conceived in connection with an illegal activity, might be open to challenge on the grounds of illegality or being *contra bonos mores* or contrary to the public policy of Scots law. The same would apply to free-standing arbitration agreements covering such disputes.

Particular instances of arbitrability

S30–11 Applying Bankton's general principle, the civil consequences of an alleged fraud may be referred to arbitration (*Earl of Kintore v Union Bank of Scotland* (1863) 4 Macq. 465), as may the question of who counts as a dependant of a deceased individual for the purposes of a contractual compensation scheme (*Brown v EE Caledonia Ltd*, 1993 G.W.D. 24–1478).

S30–12 An arbitrator may be empowered to dissolve a partnership (*Roxburgh v Dinardo*, 1981 S.L.T. 291 (not empowered); *Hackston v Hackston*, 1956 S.L.T. (Notes) 38 (empowered)), since a partnership can be wound up by the partners' agreement. And while arbitrators cannot directly confer real rights in immoveable property they can decide a dispute between two parties as to whether one has infringed the other's real rights.

S30–13 Disputes over financial provision on divorce or aliment between spouses and parent and child are arbitrable as are disputes over residence (custody) of and contact between parents and children. FLAGS lists various family law disputes that may be arbitrable: see *http://www.flagscotland.com/faq* [Accessed February 3, 2014].

Particular instances of non-arbitrability in other jurisdictions

S30–14 While matters *contra bonos mores* can be assumed to be non-arbitrable in all jurisdictions (although attitudes to *bonos mores* may differ), the matters in the following non-exhaustive list are non-arbitrable in certain ones:

- Criminal matters;
- Issues relating to fraud/bribery;
- Exclusive distributorships (Belgium);
- Matrimonial (arbitrable in Beth Din, Shari'a);
- Testamentary matters (arbitrable in Beth Din);
- Real property;

- Technology transfer (India/Egypt);
- Arbitrations where one party is a State-owned enterprise (many examples).

Certain jurisdictions may reserve disputes on certain issues to the court. In the United Arab Emirates, the law generally excluded arbitration except in relation to certain issues and the making of a misrepresentation inducing a contract was not one of them (*Abu Dhabi Investment Co v H Clarkson & Co. Ltd* [2006] 2 Lloyd's Rep. 381). **S30–15**

Foreign arbitration agreement or foreign law governing merits

If the issue of arbitrability arose in relation to an international arbitration which chose Scotland as its seat, which law should decide the issue (see P. Bernadini, "The Problem of Arbitrability" in Gaillard and Di Pietro (eds), *Enforcement of Arbitral Agreements and International Arbitral Awards* (2008))? The most straightforward and perhaps the most appealing answer is that Scots law deals with the matter. This is the approach taken in a variety of jurisdictions (see *Matermaco SA v PPM Cranes Inc* (2000) XXV YCA 673 (Belgium); *G SpA v V SpA* (1993) XVIII YCA 143 (Switzerland)). Thus in *Fincantieri-Cantieri Navali Italiani SpA v Ministry of Defence of Iraq* (1996) XXI YCA 594 at 599 the Court of Appeal of Genoa insisted that: **S30–16**

> "[W]hen an objection for foreign arbitration is raised the arbitrability of the dispute must be ascertained according to Italian law, as the court can only deny jurisdiction on the basis of its own legal system. This also corresponds to the principles expressed in Articles II and V of the New York Convention."

Article II(1) of the New York Convention provides for recognition of an arbitration agreement "concerning a subject matter capable of settlement by arbitration". This provision supports the view that Scots law, as the law of the seat, should decide the issue. **S30–17**

There is however an argument that in international arbitration the forum state should seek to be more accommodating and should not automatically apply domestic standards of arbitrability. As the British Columbia Court of Appeal observes in *Quintette Coal Ltd v Nippon Steel Corp* (1993) XVIII YCA 159 at 161:, **S30–18**

> "it will be necessary for courts to subordinate domestic notions of arbitrability to the international policy favouring commercial arbitration".

(See also the US Supreme Court in *Mitsubishi Motors Corp v Soler Chrysler-Plymouth, Inc*, 473 U.S. 614 (1985) at 639).

S30–19 Alternative approaches see the matter as being governed by the law which governs the arbitration agreement (see *Societe Van Hopplymus v Societe Coherent Inc* (1997) XXII YCA 637 Brussels Commercial Court), or the law chosen to apply to the substance of the dispute (*JSC Surgutneftegaz v Harvard College*, 2005 WL 1863676 US District Court), should that be different, and there is an argument that a tribunal should decline jurisdiction if the dispute is not arbitrable under any of these laws (see Bernard Hanotiau, "What Law Governs the Issue of Arbitrability?" (1996) 12 Arbitration Int. 391).

S30–20 In certain states particular sorts of bodies may not arbitrate, or require special authorisation to do so, or require special authorisation to arbitrate certain types of disputes. This may be more a matter of capacity rather than arbitrability, but is treated as an issue of arbitrability (subjective rather than objective arbitrability) in certain jurisdictions (see, e.g. the Swiss Private International Law Act art.177(2), and the approach of the Swiss Federal Tribunal in *Fincantieri-Cantieri navali italiani SpA v M* (1995) XX YCA 76).

S30–21 Instances exist in other jurisdictions where courts have declined to apply a foreign governing law under which the dispute would be non-arbitrable (see *Ledee v Ceramiche Ragno* (1984) IX YCA 471 US Court of Appeals).

S30–22 Where the decision on arbitrability is being made in the context of undetermined arbitral proceedings, the authors submit that if the dispute is not arbitrable under Scots law but arbitrable under the foreign law the tribunal or court should consider whether a finding of arbitrability would be *contra bonos mores*. Unless it was *contra bonos mores* and thus against fundamental aspects of Scottish public policy, the authors submit that the tribunal should find the dispute arbitrable.

S30–23 If the dispute is arbitrable under Scots law but not under the foreign law, the tribunal should find the dispute arbitrable. Such arbitrability may lie behind the choice of the Scottish seat. The award may be enforceable in countries other than that of the foreign law (which might find it to be contrary to their public policy).

S30–24 When the stage of enforcing an award is reached, a court is entitled to decline to enforce an award under s.20(2)(b) (art.V(1)(a) of the New York Convention) on the basis that the dispute in question is not arbitrable under the law which the parties agreed should govern the arbitration agreement or failing any indication of that law, the law of the seat (see the commentary on s.20(2)(b). It may also decline to enforce under s.20(4)(a) (art.V(1)(a) of the Convention) on the basis that the dispute is not arbitrable under Scots law (see paras S20–102 to S20–105).

Effect of non-arbitrability

Issues of non-arbitrability may arise in various situations including upon an application to the court for a sist (s.10), an application to the court by a non-participant (s.14), objection to the tribunal in respect of its jurisdiction (r.20), in a referral to the court on jurisdiction (r.22), in appeals to the court (rr.21, 67 and 68(2)(f)), and in enforcement of foreign award proceedings (ss.12 and 20(4)(b)). S30–25

A finding of non-arbitrability will result in the court not sisting the litigation, the tribunal or court ending the arbitration or the court not enforcing the award. S30–26

Final provisions

Interpretation

31.—(1) In this Act, unless the contrary intention appears—
"arbitral appointments referee" means a person authorised under section 24,
"arbitration" has the meaning given by section 2,
"arbitration agreement" has the meaning given by section 4,
"arbitrator" has the meaning given by section 2,
"claim" includes counterclaim,
"Convention award" has the meaning given by section 18,
"court" means the Outer House or the sheriff (except in sections 1, 3, 10, 13 and 15, where it means any court),
"default rule" has the meaning given by section 9(1),
"dispute" has the meaning given by section 2,
"Inner House" means the Inner House of the Court of Session,
"mandatory rule" has the meaning given by section 8,
"Ministers" means the Scottish Ministers,
"New York Convention" means the Convention on the Recognition and Enforcement of Foreign Arbitral Awards adopted by the United Nations Conference on International Commercial Arbitration on 10 June 1958,
"Outer House" means the Outer House of the Court of Session,
"party" is to be construed in accordance with section 2 and subsection (2) below,
"rule" means one of the Scottish Arbitration Rules,
"Scottish Arbitration Rules" means the rules set out in schedule 1,
"seated in Scotland" has the meaning given by section 3,
"statutory arbitration" has the meaning given by section 16(1),
"tribunal" has the meaning given by section 2,
"UNCITRAL Arbitration Rules" means the arbitration rules adopted by UNCITRAL on 28 April 1976, and
"UNCITRAL Model Law" means the UNCITRAL Model Law on International Commercial Arbitration as adopted by the United Nations

Commission on International Trade Law on 21 June 1985 (as amended in 2006).

(2) This Act applies in relation to arbitrations and disputes between three or more parties as it applies in relation to arbitrations and disputes between two parties (with references to both parties being read in such cases as references to all the parties).

COMMENTARY

Section 31(1)

S31–01 These rules of interpretation apply to the SAR as well as the Act proper, especially since terms such as "claim" appear in the SAR but not elsewhere in the Act.

Section 31(2)

S31–02 This provision reflects the fact that although normally an arbitration will involve two parties, multi-party arbitration is not uncommon. The provision ensures that where a section or rule speaks of a party taking certain action in relation to "the other party", it is to be interpreted as if it means all other parties. Equally, where a section or rule speaks of "either" party being entitled to take certain action, it is to be interpreted as if it means "any" party.

Ancillary provision

32.—(1) Ministers may by order make any supplementary, incidental, consequential, transitional, transitory or saving provision which they consider appropriate for the purposes of, or in connection with, or for the purposes of giving full effect to, any provision of this Act.

(2) Such an order may modify any enactment, instrument or document.

DEFINITIONS

"Ministers": s.31(1)

COMMENTARY

Section 32(1)

S32–01 The Scottish Ministers may make any order they consider necessary to give full effect to any provision of the Act. This is clearly a saving provision should it transpire that, whether because of unfortunate drafting, unanticipated judicial interpretation or otherwise, any provision of the Act is found to fall short of its intended effect. It is not a provision which allows Ministers to fill gaps in the Act, or to add provisions which might later be deemed desirable. There is nothing comparable to s.32 in either the 1996 Act or the Model Law.

The origins of s.32 lie in two Singaporean cases. In the first, *John Holland Pty Ltd v Toyo Engineering Corp* (Japan) [2001] SGHC 48 the parties' choice of ICC Rules was held by the court to exclude the Model Law in its entirety, never remotely the intention of the legislators. A very prompt amendment to the legislation corrected the anomaly. In the second, *Dermajaya Properties Sdn Bhd v Premium Properties Sdn Bhd* (2002) 2 S.L.R. 164, the Singapore High Court surprisingly treated as ineffective the parties' agreement that the UNCITRAL Rules (then the 1976 version) should be applied rather than the default provisions of the Singapore Arbitration Act. This was rectified by primary legislation, processed at spectacular speed.

If a similar situation arose in Scotland, it could be addressed under s.32.

Section 32(2)

Such an order may go so far as to modify any enactment, including primary legislation and indeed the Act itself.

Orders

33.—(1) Any power of Ministers to make orders under this Act—
  (a) is exercisable by statutory instrument, and
  (b) includes power to make—
    (i) any supplementary, incidental, consequential, transitional, transitory or saving provision which Ministers consider appropriate,
    (ii) different provision for different purposes.

(2) A statutory instrument containing such an order (or an Order in Council made under section 18) is subject to annulment in pursuance of a resolution of the Scottish Parliament.

This subsection does not apply—
  (a) to orders made under section 35(2) (commencement orders), or
  (b) where subsection (3) makes contrary provision.

(3) An order
  (a) under section 17 or 32 which adds to, replaces or omits any text in this or any other Act,
  (b) under section 26, or
  (c) under section 36(4),

may be made only if a draft of the statutory instrument containing the order has been laid before, and approved by resolution of, the Scottish Parliament.

DEFINITIONS

"Ministers": s.31(1)

COMMENTARY

S33–01　Any orders made by the Scottish Ministers will take the form of statutory instrument. These are to be promulgated using the negative procedure, whereby the statutory instrument will stand unless annulled by a resolution of the Scottish Parliament.

S33–02　The exceptions are any order which brings a provision into force, or amends primary legislation, or which seeks to bring the Act into line with future amendments of the Model Law or the New York Convention, or which seeks to remove the right of parties to arbitration agreements made before the commencement of the Act to opt out of the Act. Any such order would require to be approved by a positive resolution of the Scottish Parliament.

Crown application

34.—(1) This Act binds the Crown.

(2) Her Majesty may be represented in any arbitration to which she is a party otherwise than in right of the Crown by such person as she may appoint in writing under the Royal Sign Manual.

(3) The Prince and Steward of Scotland may be represented in any arbitration to which he is a party by such person as he may appoint.

(4) References in this Act to a party to an arbitration are, where subsection (2) or (3) applies, to be read as references to the appointed representative.

DEFINITIONS

"arbitration": ss.2(1), (2), 31(1)
"party": ss.2(1), 31(1), (2)

COMMENTARY

S34–01　This provision is the equivalent of s.106 of the 1996 Act, which in turn largely re-enacts s.30 of the 1950 Act. It makes it clear not only that the Crown may be a party to an arbitration, but also that Her Majesty The Queen and HRH the Prince of Wales may equally be a party to an arbitration in their personal capacities, and may be represented therein by such person as she or he may appoint. The Act applies to the Crown or to any such representative as it would apply to any other party

Commencement

35.—(1) The following provisions come into force on Royal Assent—
　section 2
　sections 31 to 34
　this section
　section 37

(2) Other provisions come into force on the day Ministers by order appoint.

COMMENTARY

Only the ancillary and definitional provisions came into force on the day S35–01
of Royal Assent (January 5, 2010). The remainder of the provisions came
into force (except for the purposes of statutory arbitrations) on June 7, 2010
(The Arbitration (Scotland) Act 2010 (Commencement No.1 and Transitional Provisions) Order 2010 (SSI 2010/195)). The provisions are not yet in
force in respect of statutory arbitrations: see s.16.

Transitional provisions

36.—(1) This Act does not apply to an arbitration begun before commencement.

(2) This Act otherwise applies to an arbitration agreement whether made on, before or after commencement.

(3) Despite subsection (2), this Act does not apply to an arbitration arising under an arbitration agreement (other than an enactment) made before commencement if the parties agree that this Act is not to apply to that arbitration.

(4) Ministers may by order specify any day falling at least 5 years after commencement as the day on which subsection (3) is to cease to have effect.

(5) Before making such an order, Ministers must consult such persons appearing to them to have an interest in the law of arbitration as they think fit.

(6) Any reference to an arbiter in an arbitration agreement made before commencement is to be treated as being a reference to an arbitrator.

(7) Any reference in an enactment to a decree arbitral is to be treated for the purposes of section 12 as being a reference to a tribunal's award.

(8) An express provision in an arbitration agreement made before commencement which disapplies section 3 of the Administration of Justice (Scotland) Act 1972 (c. 59) in relation to an arbitration arising under that agreement is, unless the parties otherwise agree, to be treated as being an agreement to disapply rules 41 and 69 in relation to such an arbitration.

(9) In this section, "commencement" means the day on which this section comes into force.

DEFINITIONS

"arbitration": ss.2(1), (2), 31(1)
"arbitration agreement": ss.4, 31(1)
"commencement" : ss.36(9) and 35(2)
"party": ss.2(1), 31(1), (2)
"rule": s.31(1)

COMMENTARY

Introductory

S36–01 The default position is that the Act applies prospectively to all arbitral matters where rights have not been accrued under the old law. That default position is modified by the transitional provisions of s.36.

S36–02 The Act provides that arbitrations "begun" (r.1 refers) before commencement of the Act (June 7, 2010) will continue to operate under the pre-Act law. This is the approach which successive Arbitration Acts in England, including the 1996 Act (see DAC, *Supplementary Report on the Arbitration Act 1996* (Stationery Office, 1996), paras 70–74), have taken since at least 1889.

S36–03 Arbitrations which begin following the commencement of the Act, but under arbitration agreements which were entered into prior to that commencement, operate under the new Act except where the parties have agreed to opt out of the new Act. It had been suggested in some quarters that the new law should only apply to arbitrations under agreements entered into after the date of commencement. The downside of this approach is that it perpetuates the existence of parallel regimes and keeps in place an outdated and inefficient domestic arbitral law.

S36–04 If, as was plainly the case, the legislature had decided that the law was in need of reform, then it seemed appropriate that parties to all arbitrations which begin after the measure was passed should obtain the benefit of the new provisions.

S36–05 Enforcement of awards is something different from an arbitration process. It is submitted that the Act applies to all enforcement proceedings (including those of foreign awards) from June 7, 2010 whether or not the award being enforced was made in an arbitration process to which the Act applies.

Section 36(1)

S36–06 This seems straightforward, but when does an arbitration begin? Rule 1 of the SAR provides the answer.

Section 36(2)

S36–07 As noted in the introduction to this section, subject to s.36(3) which provides an opt-out from the 2010 Act, if the arbitration has not itself begun at the date of commencement, then it does not matter when the arbitration agreement was entered into. Even if it were entered into 100 or more years previously, any such arbitration under it is subject to the 2010 Act.

S36–08 Obviously, the Act also governs all future arbitration agreements.

Section 36(3), (4), and (5)

If the arbitration has not itself begun at the date of commencement, but **S36–09** the arbitration agreement was nonetheless made before commencement, the parties may nevertheless agree that the Act is not to apply to the arbitral process. This will then mean that the previous law will apply to that process. It does not appear possible for the parties to choose for the process to be governed partly by the Act while invoking aspects of the previous regime.

The authors cannot imagine any credible reasons why any party should **S36–10** wish their arbitration to be governed by the pre-2010 Act law, except possibly for an international commercial arbitration agreement concluded on the basis that the arbitration would be governed by the Model Law under s.66 of and Sch.7 to the 1990 Act.

Under subs.(4), Ministers have power to deprive subs.(3) of effect at any **S36–11** time at least 5 years after commencement. The power remains to be exercised.

Once more the Ministers must consult as envisaged by s.24(2). While there **S36–12** were a few adherents of the old order when the Act was passed, it is difficult to see why any continuing objection into the future could prevent an order being made.

Section 36(6) and (7)

Arbitrators have traditionally been known as arbiters in Scotland and are **S36–13** so designated in both contracts and legislation. Similarly, statute tends to speak of decrees (or decreets) arbitral when referring to an award. It is extremely unlikely that such references would have been interpreted otherwise under the new regime, but these provisions remove any doubt.

Section 36(8)

The parties were entitled to contract out of the stated case procedure **S36–14** under the 1972 Act s.3(1), and many contracts routinely did so. There are two default rules under the Act which occupy the same broad territory as s.3—the power of a party to refer a point of law to the court under r.41 and the power to challenge an award on the basis of legal error under r.69.

The Act operates on the assumption that if the parties had decided to **S36–15** exclude s.3 they will similarly reject rr.41 and 69. It is doubtful whether that assumption would be well founded in every case, but this provision has the commendable merit of clarity. Parties who nevertheless decide they do want the benefit of these rules may agree to contract into rr.41 and 69. If only one party takes this view, then he will be disappointed.

Unfortunately, subs.(8) applies only to arbitration agreements made **S36–16** before commencement (June 7, 2010) and not agreements on and after commencement. Non-litigators and drafters of legal documents habitually use styles which take time to be modified to reflect changes in legislation

S36–17 such as the repeal of s.3. It can be expected that there will be post-commencement agreements which refer to s.3.

Whether the references to s.3 in such a document should be treated as referring to rr.41 and 69 depends on a construction (interpretation) of the agreement. While all of the wording of the document will have to be taken into account, it may be easier to construe an exclusion of s.3 as excluding r.41 than r.69 which is a process not in existence in Scots law before the 2010 Act.

Section 36(9)—Commencement

S36–18 See s.35(2) and the commentary thereon.

Short title
37. This Act is called the Arbitration (Scotland) Act 2010.

SCHEDULE 1

SCOTTISH ARBITRATION RULES

(introduced by section 7)

Mandatory rules are marked "**M**".
Default rules are marked "**D**".

Part 1

Commencement and Constitution of Tribunal etc.

Rule 1: Commencement of arbitration **D**

1. An arbitration begins when a party to an arbitration agreement (or any person claiming through or under such a party) gives the other party notice submitting a dispute to arbitration in accordance with the agreement.

DEFINITIONS

"arbitration": ss.2, 31(1)
"arbitration agreement": ss.4, 31(1)
"dispute": ss.2, 31(1)
"notice": r.83

STATUS

This is a default rule so it is open to the parties to modify it, agree something different or disapply it completely (see s.9). **R1–01**

All sets of arbitral rules known to the authors contain an equivalent provision; see below. **R1–02**

MODEL LAW

Article 21 "Commencement of arbitral proceedings" provides that: **R1–03**

"Unless otherwise agreed by the parties, the arbitral proceedings in respect of a particular dispute commence on the date on which a request for that dispute to be referred to arbitration is received by the respondent."

It will be noted that this refers to "receipt" by the respondent but the Model Law provides no definition of what "receipt" requires, inter alia because practice varies around the world (see below regarding rules applicable in litigation). **R1–04**

COMMENTARY

Introduction

R1–05 The principle is straightforward, i.e. that an arbitration is commenced by a notice of arbitration, but practical difficulties have arisen in deciding what constitutes a valid notice, particularly where the purported notice appears to be conditional on some other event occurring or when it is not expressed with legal precision.

R1–06 In addition, there is a critical threshold question of whether or not there is any arbitration agreement at all and this will be addressed under Part 2 (rr.19–23) below. For the present, "a party to an arbitration agreement" should, in practical terms, be interpreted as "a party believing itself to be party to an arbitration agreement".

R1–07 This is a default rule so it is open to the parties to agree some different approach to when an arbitration begins. There are three general aspects to the rule, namely (1) the person to whom the notice should be given, (2) the date when the notice becomes effective to begin the arbitration, and (3) the content of the document which purports to be the notice.

The giving/receipt of notice

R1–08 The various sets of arbitral rules differ in who is to be the recipient of the notice; the rules of institutions which administer arbitrations normally require that the notice be sent to the institution and the date of receipt thereby is the date of commencement (LCIA Rules art.1.4; ICC Rules art.4(2)). Where there is no administering institution (e.g. as in SAC 07 and UNCITRAL Rules), the notice will normally be sent to the other party as in r.1.

R1–09 Rule 1 provides that the arbitration commences when the notice is given. The giving of notice is further defined in r.83(3): see the commentary on r.83, below. Given that in terms of s.5 of the Act an arbitration agreement is to be treated as separate from any contract of which it may form part, it is suggested that the provisions of r.83(3) prevail over any general provisions for the giving of notice in such a contract.

R1–10 As already noticed, many arbitral rules, such as the ones mentioned above, provide that the arbitration is to begin when the notice is "received" by the institution or other party. Do such provisions prevail over the "giving" provisions of rr.1 and 83(3) and (5)? The authors submit that such provisions do prevail over those rules. The focus of r.83(3) is on the "making, giving or serving" of the document. If the parties have agreed that the arbitration is to begin on the "receipt" of the notice, that indicates an agreement to tie commencement to actual receipt and to disapply r.83(3) and (5). In such circumstances the date of receipt thereby becomes the date of commencement. This can, of course, give rise to practical difficulties in establishing what constitutes "receipt".

Typically, in *Bernuth Lines Ltd v High Seas Shipping Ltd (The Eastern Navigator)* [2005] EWHC 3020 (Comm), Christopher Clarke J. dismissed a challenge to an arbitral award where the entire arbitration had been conducted by email (the final award was also sent by courier) including the service of the notice of arbitration. The judge said at [28]: **R1–11**

> "I do not regard the provisions of CPR Part 6 [which allowed limited service by e-mail in court proceedings] as an appropriate benchmark by which to judge whether or not service by e-mail is effective in the context of an arbitration. The CPR cater for litigants of all kinds from major corporations represented by the most accomplished firms of solicitors to individuals represented by more modest firms and those who are not represented at all. By contrast arbitrations are usually conducted by businessmen represented by, or with ready access to, lawyers. Section 76(3), when providing that a notice could be served on a person by any effective means was, in my judgment, purposely wide. It contemplates that any means of service will suffice provided that it is a recognized means of communication effective to deliver the document to the party to whom it is sent at his address for the purpose of that means of communication (eg post, fax or e-mail). *There is no reason why, in this context, delivery of a document by e-mail — a method habitually used by businessmen, lawyers and civil servants — should be regarded as essentially different from communication by post, fax or telex*" (authors' emphasis added).

It is submitted that this is, in general, the correct, modern approach, consistent with one of the objectives of arbitration being to appeal to, and be useable by, business people. It is reflected in r.83(3)(c). **R1–12**

What is a valid notice?

Problems can arise where the intentions of the party serving the notice or alleged notice are unclear, particularly when the intention to proceed to arbitration can be read as conditional on some other event occurring, e.g. the expiry of a time period, or is a mere threat of arbitration. This issue has arisen in several English cases, of which three are particularly relevant. **R1–13**

In *Seabridge Shipping AB v AC Orssleff's Eftf's A/S (The MV Fjellvang)* [1999] 2 Lloyd's Rep. 685, two relevant issues arose for determination by Thomas J.: the first (for the second issue see R1–19 below) was whether the charterers' notice, addressed to the proposed arbitrator but copied to the owners and given just before the expiry of the applicable one year time limit, "been served on the owners" in terms of s.14(4) of the 1996 Act? **R1–14**

If not, could an arbitration be commenced in a manner other than that expressly permitted by s.14? The purported notice, a fax by the charterers to an LMAA arbitrator, Mr O (cc the owners), said, inter alia: **R1–15**

> "Pursuant to the arbitration agreement charterers are to appoint their arbitrator and we would be grateful if you could indicate your acceptance of your appointment as charterers' arbitrator in this reference. Would owners who read in copy please indicate if they are prepared to accept you [as] sole arbitrator, alternatively, attend to the appointment of their arbitrator within 7 days of this fax, failing which charterers will seek to have you appointed as sole arbitrator."

R1–16 The following day the arbitrator confirmed by telephone his acceptance of the appointment and the charterers replied by fax (cc the owners) stating:

> "We refer to your today's telephone conversation with our [Mr A] when you confirmed your appointment as arbitrator on behalf of [charterers]."

R1–17 The owners did not respond to either fax and charterers then took steps to have Mr O appointed sole arbitrator. Several weeks later the owners challenged the validity of Mr O's appointment and he decided that the purported notice had not been valid.

R1–18 The owners accepted that the words, "Would owners ... ", required them to appoint an arbitrator, or to agree to Mr O's appointment but contended that the fax was not a proper notice because it was not addressed to them but merely copied to them. The judge considered

> " ... that section 14 should be interpreted broadly and flexibly and that a strict and technical approach to this section had no place in the scheme of the 1996 Act. Notices are given by international traders and businessmen who often use shorthand expressions, or ways of doing things, which are objectively clear in giving notice to the other party of a reference and of the requirement to appoint an arbitrator."

In the judge's view the charterers' notice was objectively clear, requiring the owners to appoint an arbitrator or to agree the appointment of Mr O and it was sent by an effective means and received by owners.

R1–19 The second issue addressed by Thomas J. was whether an arbitration could be commenced in a manner other than that expressly permitted by s.14. The charterers had argued in the alternative that the arbitration had been commenced on the day when Mr O had accepted the appointment and when the owners had been given notice thereof. This argument, however, involved the contention that s.14 was not a complete code for the commencement of arbitration proceedings and that it was permissible to commence an arbitration in another manner (see s.81(1) of the 1996 Act).

R1–20 Thomas J. considered that, in cases where a party had given an objectively clear notice, it was likely that these would be met by a construction of s.14 which was broad enough to include an implied request to appoint an arbitrator. If there were circumstances which could not properly be met in this way, then the question must remain open as to whether an arbitration could be commenced in a way not expressly set out in s.14. While it was not necessary for the judge to decide that question, he considered that given the fact that the 1996 Act was intended for use by laymen and was written in "user-friendly language" capable of application by international traders and businessmen, it was difficult to see why it should have been intended that methods for commencing an arbitration other than those set out in s.14 were to be permitted. The section was very clearly expressed, easy to follow and apply and provided for certainty and, from it, the requirements of the law of England and Wales were readily ascertainable without resort to pre-Act authorities. Since, in the judge's view, the section should be construed broadly, it was difficult to envisage an apparent justification for providing for other means outside the Act which would only make for complexity and uncertainty and diminish the easy ascertainability of the law of arbitration where the Act, as in this case, expressly dealt with this subject matter.

Similarly, in *Atlanska Plovidba v Consignaciones Asturianas SA (The Lapad)* [2004] EWHC 1273 (Comm), Moore-Bick J. stated at [17]: **R1–21**

> "Arbitration is widely used by commercial parties, often acting without the benefit of legal advice, and there are good reasons, therefore, for concentrating on the substance of their communications rather than the form. *If a notice of arbitration is to be effective, it must identify the dispute to which it relates with sufficient particularity and must also make it clear that the person giving it is intending to refer the dispute to arbitration, not merely threatening to do so if his demands are not met.* Apart from that, however, I see no need for any further requirements. Whether any particular document meets those requirements will depend on its terms which must be understood in the context in which it was written. The weight of authority supports a broad and flexible approach to this question" (authors' emphasis added).

In *Bulk & Metal Transport (UK) LLP v VOC Bulk Ultra Handymax Pool LLC (The VOC Gallant)* [2009] EWHC 288 (Comm) a similar issue arose and H.H. Judge Mackie QC (sitting as a Deputy Judge of the High Court) quoted with approval from the skeleton argument of counsel for the charterers, stating that it was common ground that: **R1–22**

> "(1) A broad and flexible approach must be adopted with respect to the effect of s.14(4).
> (2) The requirements of that section will be satisfied provided that it is objectively clear that a communication is intended to refer a dispute to arbitration and to require the necessary steps in that regard to be taken. In that regard the communication must be viewed in its context and not taken in isolation.

(3) A communication will satisfy that test if, by its wording (construed in a matter which is not unduly strict, scrutinous, technical, legalistic or formulaic, and which focuses upon its substance rather than its form) that intention is objectively express or implied.

(4) That intention will be implied from a communication which simply demonstrates that an arbitration clause is being invoked, or which intimates that a dispute is to be submitted to arbitration or that an arbitration is to be resorted to, or which states to the effect that 'I demand the right to have this dispute decided by arbitration as we agreed and require your co-operation in bringing about' or 'I require the difference between us to be submitted to arbitration' or 'unless you are prepared to make proposals for settlement, you must take this letter as requiring you to appoint your arbitrators'.

(5) A communication which makes the invocation of the arbitration clause conditional upon the failure to accept an offer of settlement will also suffice, provided that the time of commencement is made clear (by way of a time limit for acceptance of any proposal). Thus, a communication to the effect of 'Unless you are prepared to settle the matter amicably, we must ask you to agree to the appointment of an arbitrator' will suffice to commence proceedings as from the expiry of the stated time limit for acceptance."

R1–23 H.H. Judge Mackie QC made a separate but important point: it was important not to confuse commencing arbitration under s.14(4) with taking a step towards constituting the tribunal. These principles have been applied subsequently as in *Finmoon Ltd v Baltic Reefers Management Ltd* [2012] EWHC 920 (Comm) where a notice stated that arbitration was to be commenced in respect of loss or damage of a cargo of bananas during a voyage of a vessel from Ecuador to Russia but did not refer to the contract with the arbitration agreement. It was held by Eder J. that, applying the principles in the above cases, the notice should be construed as commencing arbitration under whatever was the relevant contract governing the particular identified voyage.

R1–24 In contrast to these decisions, in distinguishable circumstances Ramsey J. reached a different conclusion in *Taylor Woodrow Construction v RMD Kwikform Ltd* [2008] EWHC 825 (TCC) in which solicitors for Taylor Woodrow had written as follows:

> "We have tried to avoid the need to litigate, but our approaches have been rebuffed. We therefore enclose a draft Particulars of Claim, which will be served in due course. Kindly advise us [concerning communications] ... [TW]'s Standard Conditions of Sub-Contract were incorporated into the contract and Paragraph 26 provides that disputes should be referred to Arbitration. Please confirm whether you wish to

rely on Paragraph 26 and insist on proceedings by way of arbitration, or would be agreeable to the matter being litigated."

Ramsey J. agreed with RMD's submission that that letter was not objectively clear in giving notice to the other party of a reference to arbitration and of the requirement to appoint an arbitrator, rather that it gave notice that TW was preparing to litigate and was seeking to find out whether RMD would insist on arbitration. The emphasised passage in *The Lapad* [2004] 2 Lloyd's Rep. 109 was applicable: the notice

> "must also make it clear that the person giving it is intending to refer the dispute to arbitration, not merely threatening to do so if his demands are not met."

The case raised a separate issue which can arise in practice: Taylor Woodrow had applied to the President of the CIArb for the appointment of an arbitrator and he had duly made one, in the full knowledge of RMD's objections. Ramsey J. (wholly correctly) set that appointment aside: where did that leave the appointment system? As a general rule (on a worldwide basis, e.g. see Model Law art.16) it is for the arbitrator(s), not the appointing body or person, to become involved in, and decide, issues of jurisdiction subject to any available rights of challenge (refer rr.19, 20, 67). Irrespective of whether the appointing body is an administering one with a full time secretariat (e.g. ICC, LCIA, SIAC et al) or a non-administering appointing body (e.g. CIArb, LMAA), the correct response to such circumstances is to appoint and leave the arbitrator(s) to deal with the jurisdictional issue.

Summarising, the authors submit that the English jurisprudence in this area offers persuasive assistance in the application of r.1, inter alia giving a wide construction of any notice of arbitration and applying commercial common sense in strong preference to over-attention to form requirements.

Submissions to arbitration

Where there is no prior arbitration agreement and parties become involved in a dispute they can enter into an agreement to submit that dispute to arbitration. Traditionally in Scots law such an agreement was known as a "submission". Such a "submission" becomes an arbitration agreement and also comprises notice under r.1 (unless r.1 had been modified).

Rule 2: *Appointment of tribunal* D

2. An arbitration agreement need not appoint (or provide for appointment of) the tribunal, but if it does so provide it may—
    (a) specify who is to form the tribunal,
    (b) require the parties to appoint the tribunal,

(c) **permit another person to appoint the tribunal, or**
(d) **provide for the tribunal to be appointed in any other way.**

DEFINITIONS

"arbitration agreement": ss.4, 31(1)
"tribunal": ss.2, 31(1)

STATUS

R2–01 This is a default rule so it is open to the parties to modify it, agree something different or disapply it completely (see s.9).

MODEL LAW

R2–02 There is no equivalent of r.2 in the Model Law.

COMMENTARY

R2–03 Rules 6 and 7 below provide a mechanism for appointing the arbitrator, absent any contrary agreement by the parties. It is expected that the majority of such contrary agreements will be in the form of the parties' agreement, normally incorporated in their arbitration agreement by reference to a set of rules such as SAC 07 (whose art.3 addresses these matters); arts 7–10 of the UNCITRAL Rules, arts 11–15 ICC Rules, arts 5–9 LCIA Rules and arts 5–8 of the Swiss Rules which contain equivalent provisions.

R2–04 It may appear that r.2 is otiose but the draftsman appears to have considered it important, given that these rules are to be user-friendly in the context of commercial and individual parties, to set out the main options at the outset for the benefit of commercial parties perhaps unfamiliar with the various options.

Rule 3: Arbitrator to be an individual M
3. Only an individual may act as an arbitrator.

DEFINITIONS

"arbitrator": ss.4, 31(1)

STATUS

R3–01 This is a mandatory rule so the parties cannot disapply or vary it (see s.8).

MODEL LAW

R3–02 There is no equivalent of r.3 in the Model Law.

COMMENTARY

To some this rule may appear otiose but it is in fact necessary since under the common law it was competent to appoint an unincorporated body as arbiter (*Bremner v Elder* (1875) 2 R. (HL) 136) or a firm (*Wm Dixon Ltd v Jones, Heard & Ingram* (1884) 11 R. 739) and that possibility had to be eliminated. **R3–03**

The question of whether or not an arbitrator can be a legal person, whether corporate entity, partnership or otherwise, proves a surprisingly difficult one to answer as a worldwide survey by one of the authors in late 2009 demonstrated. **R3–04**

The Model Law provides at art.11(1) that, "No person shall be precluded by reason of his nationality from acting as an arbitrator, unless otherwise agreed by the parties", and that might appear strong support for the proposition that the arbitrator must be an individual. That proposition fails, however, since art.3(1)(a) provides that, **R3–05**

> "any written communication is deemed to have been received if it is delivered to the addressee personally or if it is delivered at his place of business, habitual residence or mailing address ...",

and it is clear from that reference that "person" includes legal persons.

Further, the Interpretation Act 1978 states that "person" includes a body of persons, corporate or unincorporate. That approach is common in common law countries and not only provides no support for the proposition that an arbitrator must be an individual, but in fact points in the other direction. **R3–06**

Section 26(1) of the 1996 Act provides that, "[t]he authority of an arbitrator is personal and ceases on his death", and the authors submit that that has the same effect as r.3 since a legal person cannot "die". **R3–07**

Surprisingly, few of the leading English law texts even consider the issue at all: Sir Michael J. Mustill and Stewart C. Boyd, *The Law and Practice of Commercial Arbitration in England*, 2nd edn (London: Butterworths, 1989), state at p.247: **R3–08**

> " ... the person appointed as arbitrator must be a natural person. A limited company, possessing only corporate personality, cannot validly be appointed [fn.]. Nor can a group of people, such as a partnership firm, be nominated to act as an arbitrator."
>
> Footnote: "We can cite no authority for this proposition, but it must surely be correct."

In some states in the USA, a law firm, i.e. a limited liability partnership, can be appointed arbitrator but in practice it will nominate one partner to fulfil the role. There appears to be no express statutory or other requirement to that effect. **R3–09**

R3–10 The position in civil law jurisdictions varies between (a) the crystal clarity of the French Code of Civil Procedure which at art.1450 expressly requires that the arbitrator under a French arbitration agreement be an individual and if a legal person is designated such person shall only have power to administer the arbitration; (b) the equally clear position in Italy, where Corte Suprema di Cassazione case law provides that an arbitration agreement providing for a corporate entity as arbitrator is void (case no.123365 (November 1999); ditto case no.258717 (August 1962)); and (c) the lack of precision in Belgium where para.1680 of the Code of Civil Procedure provides that:

> "[A]nyone who has the capacity to conclude a contract, can be an arbitrator, with the exception of minors, persons who have a legal tutor, and those who have lost their right to vote."

Since legal persons can conclude contracts, one might conclude that they can also be arbitrators. However, since paras 1687 and 1688 refer to the death of an arbitrator it appears that the legislators had probably only natural persons in mind.

R3–11 More confusingly still, in Germany there appears to be not only no applicable statute or case law but there is conflicting academic authority on the point. The leading English-language commentary, K. Böckstiegel, S. Kröll and P. Nacimiento (eds), *Arbitration in Germany*, 1st edn (Kluwer, 2007) formulates in its annotation 9 to para.1035 Zivilprozeßordnung (corresponding to art.11 of the Model Law) as follows:

> " ... only natural persons can be arbitrators. If a legal person is specified in the arbitration agreement as being responsible for the arbitration, it is to be ascertained by interpretation which natural person according to the law, statute or the intention of the parties is meant".

R3–12 However, K.H. Schwab and G. Walter, *Schiedsgerichtsbarkeit*, 7th edn (Munich: CHBeck, 2005), at Ch.9, note 1, argue that, since there is no rule in German law which would regulate this question, both natural and legal persons can be arbitrators.

R3–13 In conclusion, therefore, while few jurisdictions address this surprisingly complicated issue head on, Scotland has.

R3–14 The concept of personal appointment has a second and important implication in that arbitrators may be obliged to carry out their main duties and fulfil their main responsibilities themselves; see the commentary to r.32 below.

Rule 4: Eligibility to act as arbitrator M

4. An individual is ineligible to act as an arbitrator if the individual is—
(a) aged under 16, or

(b) an incapable adult (within the meaning of section 1(6) of the Adults with Incapacity (Scotland) Act 2000 (asp 4)).

DEFINITIONS

"arbitrator": ss.4, 31(1)

STATUS

This is a mandatory rule so the parties cannot disapply or vary it (see s.8). **R4–01**

MODEL LAW

There is no equivalent of r.4 in the Model Law. **R4–02**

COMMENTARY

Rule 4 introduces two sources of ineligibility namely (1) under age; and **R4–03** (2) adult incapacity. It applies both to the initial appointment of an arbitrator and the subsequent performance of his duties: see r.9. Before the Act, the position as regards incapacity due to age was governed by ss.1 and 9 of the Age of Legal Capacity (Scotland) Act 1991 in terms of which a person under the age of 16 years has no legal capacity to enter into any transaction involving him acting as arbiter. Rule 4 makes no change to that.

While a person aged 16 or over is not ineligible by virtue of age, s.3 of the **R4–04** 1991 Act provides that a person under the age of 21 years may apply to the court to set aside a transaction involving him acting as arbiter while he was of or over the age of 16 years but under the age of 18 years which an adult, exercising prudence, would not have entered into in the circumstances of the applicant at the time of entering into the transaction, which has caused or is likely to cause substantial prejudice to the applicant. One theoretically relevant exception is where the transaction was in the course of the applicant's trade or business: s.3(2)(f) of the 1991 Act. While it would be unlikely that parties would wish to entrust a dispute to resolution by a 16 or 17 year old person, the practical effect of s.3 of the 1991 Act is that it would be particularly unwise to do so, given the possibility of the arbitrator seeking to have his appointment set aside in the event of difficulties.

With regard to adult incapacity, before the Adults with Incapacity **R4–05** (Scotland) Act 2000, the position was governed by the common law governing capacity to enter into contracts. That common law was unsophisticated. It distinguished between "furiosity", which was concerned with a permanent condition and "idiocy" which was concerned with a condition with lucid intervals (Bell, *Principles*, s.2105). If the former was established, there could be no question of the person having capacity to act as arbitrator (*McKenzie v Inverness and Ross-shire Railway Co* (1861) 24 D. 251 at 254). The case of the latter condition was more complex as a deed executed during a lucid interval could still nevertheless be valid. Ultimately, whether a person has capacity to contract during a lucid interval depends on whether he could understand (i) what he was doing and (ii) the effect of any contract entered into (cf. *Re Sutton* [2009] EWHC 2576 (Ch)). The effect of incapacity is to render the contract void (*Gall v Bird* (1855) 17 D. 1027) rather than voidable.

R4–06 Rule 4 seeks to introduce some clarity by providing that an adult (a person over the age of 16 years) is ineligible to act as arbitrator if he or she is "incapable" within the meaning of s.1(6) of the Adults with Incapacity (Scotland) Act 2000. Section 1(6) provides that "incapable means:

"incapable of—
(a) acting; or
(b) making decisions; or
(c) communicating decisions; or
(d) understanding decisions; or
(e) retaining the memory of decisions

as mentioned in any provision of [the 2000 Act] by reason of mental disorder or of inability to communicate because of physical disability; but ... not ... by reason only of a lack of deficiency in a faculty of communication if that lack or deficiency can be made good by human or mechanical aid (whether of an interpretative nature or otherwise)".

R4–07 "Mental disorder" is itself defined for the purposes of the Adults with Incapacity (Scotland) Act 2000 by s.328 of the Mental Health (Care and Treatment) (Scotland) Act 2003. That provides that "mental disorder" means any mental illness, personality disorder or learning disability however caused or manifested but that mere sexual orientation, sexual deviancy, transsexualism, transvestism, dependence on, or use of alcohol, or drugs, behaviour that causes or is likely to cause harassment, alarm or distress to any other person or acting as no prudent person would act does not amount to "mental disorder".

R4–08 It can be seen that for an adult arbitrator to become ineligible to act under r.4, he or she must suffer from a mental illness, personality disorder or learning disability which results in a lack of capability to act, make decisions etc.

R4–09 The effect of such incapability is that the tenure of the arbitrator ends automatically (r.9(a)). There is no need to have an arbitrator removed by the court. However, if there are justifiable doubts about the arbitrator's "ability to act" (by which is meant, presumably, lack of capability as a result of the causes set out above), the court has power to remove the arbitrator: see r.12(c) and the commentary thereon. For the effect of the cessation of tenure on the arbitrator's entitlement to fees and expenses see r.16.

Rule 5: *Number of arbitrators* D

5. Where there is no agreement as to the number of arbitrators, the tribunal is to consist of a sole arbitrator.

DEFINITIONS

"arbitrator": ss.4, 31(1)
"tribunal": ss.2, 31(1)

STATUS

This is a default rule so it is open to the parties to modify it, agree something different or disapply it completely (see s.9). **R5–01**

The LCIA Rules art.5.8 and the ICC Rules art.12(2) both default to a sole arbitrator, "save where it appears to the Court that the dispute is such as to warrant the appointment of three arbitrators". The UNCITRAL Rules (art.7(1)) default to a tribunal of three. The Swiss Rules (art.6.1) empower the Arbitration Court of the Swiss Chambers of Arbitration to decide, taking account of all relevant circumstances, with a slight push towards a sole arbitrator (art.6.2) **R5–02**

MODEL LAW

Article 10 provides for a default to a tribunal of three in accordance with international practice. **R5–03**

COMMENTARY

Since this is a default rule, the parties may agree otherwise; in domestic arbitrations a sole arbitrator is the norm (a main reason being to limit costs) while in international arbitrations a tribunal of three is almost always chosen. **R5–04**

In international arbitration, three is preferred for the following reasons: (a) to allow each party to select one, thereby giving effect to the "party autonomy" principle; (b) to achieve a constructive and balanced mix of some or all of nationalities, skill sets, professional disciplines and languages; and (c) the key role played by tribunal deliberations in the decision-making process where discussion of key issues can lead to a fuller understanding of them. In addition, in some cases, e.g. large ones, the tribunal workload, particularly drafting the award, can helpfully be shared between the three arbitrators. It is sometimes asserted that three person tribunals are an unnecessary expense but an ICC study showed that approximately only 16 per cent of the costs of arbitration were the costs of the tribunal (plus ICC 2 per cent, parties' legal and other costs 82 per cent) (an earlier ICC study had reported 12 per cent/8 per cent/80 per cent). **R5–05**

There are some classes of London arbitration which proceed with two **R5–06** arbitrators and an umpire (formerly "oversman" in Scotland); concerning umpires, see below under r.30(2)(b)(ii) and r.82.

R5–07 Rule 5 is important as it counters any argument that a simple agreement to "arbitrate" certain matters without specification as to by whom, from being void for uncertainty.

Rule 6: Method of appointment D

6. The tribunal is to be appointed as follows—
   (a) where there is to be a sole arbitrator, the parties must appoint an eligible individual jointly (and must do so within 28 days of either party requesting the other to do so),
   (b) where there is to be a tribunal consisting of two or more arbitrators—
      (i) each party must appoint an eligible individual as an arbitrator (and must do so within 28 days of the other party requesting it to do so), and
      (ii) where more arbitrators are to be appointed, the arbitrators appointed by the parties must appoint eligible individuals as the remaining arbitrators.

DEFINITIONS

"arbitrator": ss.4, 31(1)
"eligible": r.4
"individual": r.3
"party": ss.4, 31(1), (2)
"tribunal": ss.2, 31(1)

STATUS

R6–01 This is a default rule so it is open to the parties to modify it, agree something different or disapply it completely (see s.9). Many arbitration clauses provide for a method of appointment that will vary or disapply this rule.

R6–02 If an arbitration clause provides for appointment by a sheriff or sheriff principal or indeed any other person, then while he or she is not bound to do so, the authors submit that he or she should apply the approach in r.7(8) below.

R6–03 All LCIA appointments are made by the LCIA Court (refer art.5.7 of the LCIA Rules) even where a party has purported to nominate an arbitrator (the LCIA will, of course, take careful account of any party's stated preference).

R6–04 Like r.6, the UNCITRAL Rules have different provisions for appointment depending on whether the parties have agreed that a sole arbitrator be appointed or three arbitrators appointed (the default UNCITRAL position). If there is agreement on a sole arbitrator, art.8 of the UNCITRAL

Rules provides that the appointment be made by an appointing authority following a list-procedure set out in the article.

MODEL LAW

Article 11 provides a similar mechanism, including that the two arbitrators appoint the third (see below). The Model Law also provides (on an opt-otherwise basis) that nationality shall not be a bar to appointment.

R6–05

COMMENTARY

Section 17 of the 1996 Act provides that, absent contrary agreement of the parties, where each of them is to appoint an arbitrator and one party refuses or fails timeously to do so, the other party may, having complied with applicable procedural requirements, convert its arbitrator into a sole arbitrator. There is no equivalent in r.6 and r.7 will apply in the event of such refusal or failure.

R6–06

In many instances in practice, the parties' relationship will be such that they will not agree anything in this regard, in which case r.7 will apply.

R6–07

Conventionally, the third arbitrator, whether chosen by the two co-arbitrators or by the administering institution, shall chair the tribunal—refer art.9.1 of the UNCITRAL Rules and art.12.5 of the ICC Rules; in any event, a chairman is appointed whereas r.6(b) does not so provide; in the view of the authors, this is a curious and unnecessary lacuna. A multi-member tribunal should check with the parties at the outset about whom they wish to chair the tribunal.

R6–08

Party-appointed arbitrators ("PAAs")

Despite appointment under r.6(b)(i), the PAAs are obliged to be wholly neutral in relation to the parties, with r.24(1)(a) requiring all arbitrators' impartiality and independence (refer also para.7.1 of the CIArb Code of Ethics which provides that a CIArb member shall not be influenced by outside pressure or self-interest) and r.12(a) providing for an application to the court to remove an arbitrator who fails to be both impartial and independent.

R6–09

While in some US domestic arbitrations the PAAs may, by prior agreement, be partisan (refer to Canon X of the ABA Code), this is not the case elsewhere; it is a reasonably popular misconception that the PAA owes some obligation to their appointor (but see below regarding appointment of the third arbitrator).

R6–10

A party's choice of its PAA is a very important stage in the process, arguably even critically so, but it can be a difficult task with attendant complications. In an article by Doak Bishop and Lucy Reed, "Practical Guidelines for Interviewing, Selecting and Challenging Party-appointed

R6–11

Arbitrators in International Commercial Arbitration" (1998) 14 Arbitration Int. 395, the authors state:

> "The ability to appoint one of the decision-makers is a defining aspect of the arbitral system and provides a powerful instrument when used wisely by a party. It is also a truism that a party will strive to select an arbitrator who has some inclination or predisposition to favour that party's side of the case such as by sharing the appointing party's legal or cultural background or by holding doctrinal views that, fortuitously, coincide with a party's case. Provided the arbitrator does not 'allow this shared outlook to override his conscience and professional judgment' (Redfern & Hunter) this need carry no suggestion of disqualifying partiality. This is a natural and unexceptional aspect of the party appointment system in international arbitration. There is a distinction to be drawn, however, between a general sympathy or predisposition and a positive bias or prejudice. Bias in favour of, or prejudice against, the party or its case encompasses a willingness to decide a case in favour of the appointing party regardless of the merits or without critical examination of the merits."

R6–12 The PAA, while remaining impartial and independent, has a vital contribution to play in the effective conduct of the proceedings and the determination of the merits of the case, not because the PAA advocates his appointing party's case but because the two PAAs (i) choose the third, presiding, arbitrator (see below), and (ii) play a role in ensuring that both parties' cases are given appropriate consideration during the procedural stages of the arbitration and when the merits are discussed.

Interviewing of prospective arbitrators

R6–13 Given the right of each party to choose its PAA, it is generally accepted internationally that a party need not make such choice based solely on CVs, websites or word-of-mouth recommendations since these might not give a complete picture of the appointee. It is therefore common practice, in some jurisdictions but not in others, that the appointor interviews a list of prospective PAAs prior to making the appointment. Such a practice undoubtedly carries certain risks but practical experience shows that a comprehensive interview can be conducted without jeopardising the PAA's neutrality, independence or impartiality. In *Redfern and Hunter on International Arbitration*, edited by N. Blackaby et al., 5th edn (Oxford: Oxford University Press, 2009), the authors state at para.4–69:

> "However, it is hard to perceive the practice [i.e. of interviews] as being objectionable in principle, provided that it is not done in a secretive way and that the scope of the discussion is appropriately restricted."

Certain information must, in any event, be disclosed by the prospective **R6–14**
appointor before the arbitrator can contemplate accepting the appointment:
the names of the parties in the dispute and any third parties involved must
be disclosed in order for the arbitrator to assess his position with regard to
conflicts and it may be necessary for the prospective appointor to disclose
the names of other *dramatis personae*. Some information about the nature of
the dispute must be disclosed: for example, there is a substantial difference
between expertise in building (i) offshore oil and gas production platforms,
(ii) LNG carriers, and (iii) petrochemical refineries, although all three might
be seen as "oil and gas construction". It is also reasonable that the location
of the project be disclosed since the conduct of business varies in different
parts of the world and the US business environment is not the same as that
in South Asia, West Africa or England.

The CIArb has published a Practice Guideline on "The Interviewing of **R6–15**
Prospective Arbitrators" which explains and delineates the interview process
including the danger and the no-go areas (available at *http://www.ciarb.org/
resources/practice-guidelines-and-protocols/list-of-guidelines-and-protocols/*
[Accessed June 17, 2014]).

Appointment of third or additional arbitrators gives rise to some practical **R6–16**
difficulties concerning the role of the parties in this part of the process. On
the one hand, the arbitration "belongs to the parties" and the principle of
party autonomy would appear to require that the parties are involved in the
selection of a third arbitrator; on the other hand, r.6(b)(ii) requires that the
two PAAs select the third. Article 3.6 of SAC 07 also requires the two PAAs
to appoint the third, failing which the Chairman, CIArb Scottish Branch
will make the appointment; art.9 of the UNCITRAL Rules is the same, save
that the appointing authority is to make the appointment if the PAAs do not
do so.

Questions therefore arise as to (i) how to balance these conflicting **R6–17**
requirements and (ii) to what extent, and how, the parties can become
involved in the selection process. It is standard practice that the third
arbitrator should not be appointed without the consent of (or, at least, not
over the objection of) the parties but practice varies as to (i) whether the
parties should be given a shortlist of prospective third arbitrators or be given
a single name, (ii) whether the parties agree a shortlist between themselves
and present this to the two PAAs for consideration, and (iii) whether there
can be any consultation between the parties and their respective PAAs
concerning the appointment. It is generally accepted that such consultation
is permissible (subject to obvious limits) and that this is an exception to the
general rule prohibiting communication between each party and its PAA.
The CIArb Practice Guideline (para.R6–15 above) also addresses the
question of the parties' interviewing prospective third arbitrators. A suggestion has been made to the relevant CIArb committee that the guideline
should be extended to cover the foregoing issues relating to selection of a
third arbitrator.

Multi-party arbitrations

R6–18 Rules 6 and 7 provide for multi-party arbitrations involving more than two parties. This is clear from the definition of "party". Rule 6, read with r.7, ensures equality between parties in such a multi-party arbitration and that the situation in *Siemens AG and BKMI Industrienlagen GmbH v Dutco Construction Co*, French Cass. Civ. 1ere, January 7, 1992 (1992) 1 Bull Civ. is avoided.

R6–19 In *Dutco* there was a contract with two parties on one side (B and S) and one party (D) on the other side. The contract provided for disputes to be resolved by a tribunal of three arbitrators and under the then ICC Rules. The ICC Rules contemplated that there would be no more than three arbitrators in the tribunal but that parties would each appoint an arbitrator and that the third arbitrator would be appointed by the ICC Court failing agreement between the parties. When D sought to claim in an arbitration against B and S, the latter parties did not agree on a joint arbitrator. The ICC requested B and S to make a joint nomination which they did under protest. B and S then applied to the tribunal objecting to its jurisdiction. The tribunal made a provisional award finding it to have jurisdiction which was eventually successfully set aside by the French Cour de Cassation on the grounds that the tribunal had not been properly constituted because the ICC's intervention was contrary to French public policy that there should be equality between the parties in the appointment of the tribunal.

Emergency arbitrator

R6–20 See commentary at paras R35–07 and R35–08 concerning the role of an emergency arbitrator; the mechanism for the appointment of such is dealt with in the various institutional rules referred to in that commentary.

Rule 7: Failure of appointment procedure M

7.—(1) This rule applies where a tribunal (or any arbitrator who is to form part of a tribunal) is not, or cannot be, appointed in accordance with—

    (a) any appointment procedure set out in the arbitration agreement (or otherwise agreed between the parties), or

    (b) rule 6.

(2) Unless the parties otherwise agree, either party may refer the matter to an arbitral appointments referee.

(3) The referring party must give notice of the reference to the other party.

(4) That other party may object to the reference within 7 days of notice of reference being given by making an objection to—

    (a) the referring party, and

    (b) the arbitral appointments referee.

(5) If—

    (a) no such objection is made within that 7 day period, or

(b) the other party waives the right to object before the end of that period,

the arbitral appointments referee may make the necessary appointment.

(6) Where—
 (a) a party objects to the arbitral appointments referee making an appointment,
 (b) an arbitral appointments referee fails to make an appointment within 21 days of the matter being referred, or
 (c) the parties agree not to refer the matter to an arbitral appointments referee,

the court may, on an application by any party, make the necessary appointment.

(7) The court's decision on whom to appoint is final.

(8) Before making an appointment under this rule, the arbitral appointments referee or, as the case may be, the court must have regard to—
 (a) the nature and subject-matter of the dispute,
 (b) the terms of the arbitration agreement (including, in particular, any terms relating to appointment of arbitrators), and
 (c) the skills, qualifications, knowledge and experience which would make an individual suitable to determine the dispute.

(9) Where an arbitral appointments referee or the court makes an appointment under this rule, the arbitration agreement has effect as if it required that appointment.

DEFINITIONS

"arbitrator": ss.4, 31(1)
"arbitration agreement": ss.4, 31(1)
"arbitral appointments referee": s.22
"court": s.31(1)
"party": ss.2, 31(1), (2)

STATUS

This is a mandatory rule so the parties cannot disapply or vary it (see s.8). **R7–01**

MODEL LAW

Article 11 provides a similar mechanism; r.7(6) and (7) substantially replicate Model Law art.11(5). **R7–02**

COMMENTARY

Introductory

R7–03 Section 18 of the 1996 Act provides that, absent contrary agreement of the parties, in the event of any failure in the appointment process, any party to the arbitration agreement may (upon notice to the other parties) apply to the court to rectify that failure by exercising its powers under the section.

R7–04 In contrast, the Scottish draftsmen took the view that (i) the court is not in the business of, and has little experience of, either appointing arbitrators or rectifying failures in the appointment process; and (ii) s.1(c) of this Act (reflecting art.5 of the Model Law) seeks to minimise the involvement of the court in the arbitral process. In consequence, as envisaged by arts 6 and 11(3) of the Model Law, an arbitral appointments referee ("AAR") will, at first instance, deal with such matters unless one of the parties objects to using the specified procedure. Only if there is such an objection or the AAR fails to make a timeous appointment is the court empowered to choose an arbitrator under this default rule.

R7–05 To put this in context, it is understood that the Commercial Court in England makes fewer than 10 appointments per annum; the CIArb makes 2,000–2,500, the RICS 8,000–12,000 and several other UK-based bodies more than 1,000. Such bodies not only have detailed appointment processes and procedures but also specialised departments handling them.

R7–06 It should be noted that if an AAR acts outwith its powers then any subsequent award may be rendered appealable under r.68(2)(d).

Rule 7(1)

R7–07 The CIArb, Agricultural Industries Confederation Ltd, the Dean of the Faculty of Advocates, the Institution of Civil Engineers, the Law Society of Scotland, the Royal Incorporation of Architects in Scotland, RICS and SAAVA have all been authorised to act as AARs (Arbitral Appointments Referee (Scotland) Order 2010 (SSI 2010/196)).

Rule 7(2)

R7–08 The parties may agree to exclude the referral to an AAR, in which case the only means of appointment under r.7 will be by application to the court (r.7(6)(c)). However, they cannot exclude the applicability of the criteria for appointment in r.7(8).

Rule 7(3)

R7–09 For the giving of notice see r.83 and the commentary thereon.

Rule 7(5)

Before making the appointment, the AAR must have regard to the criteria **R7–10**
for appointment set out in r.7(8). Given that an AAR has been authorised to make appointments on the basis that it has a track record of making appointments plus an ability to provide appropriate training and disciplinary procedures, this should be a task that an AAR is well prepared for.

Rule 7(6) and (7)

The issue here is the selection of an arbitrator who is obliged to be both **R7–11**
impartial and independent (see r.24(1)(a) below). Before making the appointment, the court must have regard to the criteria set out in r.7(8) and it therefore follows that there must be an early close to argument over the appointment so there is no right of appeal.

Rule 8: Duty to disclose any conflict of interests M

8.—(1) This rule applies to—
  (a) arbitrators, and
  (b) individuals who have been asked to be an arbitrator but who have not yet been appointed.
(2) An individual to whom this rule applies must, without delay disclose—
  (a) to the parties, and
  (b) in the case of an individual not yet appointed as an arbitrator, to any arbitral appointments referee, other third party or court considering whether to appoint the individual as an arbitrator,
any circumstances known to the individual (or which become known to the individual before the arbitration ends) which might reasonably be considered relevant when considering whether the individual is impartial and independent.

DEFINITIONS

"arbitrator": ss.4, 31(1)

Note that neither "impartial" nor "independent" is defined in the Act (nor in the Model Law) but the absence of "independence" is defined in r.77.

STATUS

This is a mandatory rule so the parties cannot disapply or vary it (see s.8). **R8–01**
They can, however, agree to provide additional requirements for intimation: see, e.g. the ICC rules below.

MODEL LAW

Article 12(1) of the Model Law provides that: **R8–02**

"When a person is approached in connection with his possible appointment as an arbitrator, he shall disclose any circumstances likely to give rise to justifiable doubts as to his impartiality or independence. An arbitrator, from the time of his appointment and throughout the arbitral proceedings, shall without delay disclose any such circumstances to the parties unless they have already been informed of them by him."

COMMENTARY

Introductory

R8–03 The necessity for arbitrators to be impartial and independent is fundamental, as is recognised in s.1 of this Act:

"The founding principles of this Act are: (a) that the object of arbitration is to resolve disputes fairly [and] impartially ... "

and in r.24(1)(a).

R8–04 These provisions are consistent with art.6(1) of the ECHR: >

"In the determination of his civil rights and obligations ... everyone is entitled to a fair ... hearing within a reasonable time by an independent and impartial tribunal established by law."

The various issues arising from this fundamental principle are addressed below under r.24, in particular the questions of what is impartiality and what is independence.

R8–05 The key principle underlying r.8 is that each party is entitled to know all "relevant" facts of an arbitrator's involvement with one or other of them so that it can either choose another arbitrator or can challenge one already appointed (see r.10 below); for the parties to be put in a state of knowledge, there must be disclosure.

R8–06 Article 11 of the UNCITRAL Rules is substantially identical to the Model Law. Article 11 of the ICC Rules provides that:

"(2) Before appointment or confirmation, a prospective arbitrator shall sign a statement of acceptance, availability, impartiality and independence. The prospective arbitrator shall disclose in writing to the Secretariat any facts or circumstances which might be of such a nature as to call into question the arbitrator's independence in the eyes of the parties, as well as any circumstances that could give rise to reasonable doubts as to the arbitrator's impartiality. The Secretariat shall provide such information to the parties in writing and fix a time limit for any comments from them.

(3) An arbitrator shall immediately disclose in writing to the

Secretariat and to the parties any facts or circumstances of a similar nature to those referred to in Article 11(2) concerning the arbitrator's impartiality or independence which may arise during the arbitration."

Similarly, the CIArb's Code of Ethics provides in Part 2 that: R8–07

"3.1 Both before and throughout the dispute resolution process, a member shall disclose all interests, relationships and matters likely to affect the member's independence or impartiality or which might reasonably be perceived as likely to do so.

3.2 Where a member is or becomes aware that he or she is incapable of maintaining the required degree of independence or impartiality, the member shall promptly take such steps as may be required in the circumstances, which may include resignation or withdrawal from the process."

The disclosure obligation is expressly made a continuing one (r.8(2)). Where R8–08 the rule concerns a person who has been asked to be but has not yet been appointed arbitrator, it requires disclosure to both the parties and the AAR or other third party considering whether to appoint the person as arbitrator. It follows from the mandatory nature of r.8 that if the parties have adopted rules such as the UNCITRAL Rules which do not require intimation to an AAR or other third party, such intimation is still required under r.8(2)(b).

The difficult questions here, and these are major ones, include: R8–09

(i) how does an arbitrator (or prospective arbitrator) determine what might reasonably be considered "relevant" to impartiality or independence in order to effect disclosure?
(ii) who determines what is reasonably relevant?
(iii) to what extent is the arbitrator obliged to search for disclosable facts?
(iv) how do individuals disclosing facts do so on a common basis?

What is reasonably *relevant?*

As regards the first question, there are no UK, or Scottish, standards in R8–10 this regard and domestic arbitrators have to rely on the CIArb's Code of Ethics, Part 2, para.3.1 (para.R8–07 above) (and equivalent obligations contained in the respective ethical codes of similar institutions) and extensive coverage of the issue in (non-Scottish) case law.

However, valuable assistance is available from the IBA Conflict Guide- R8–11 lines, and although not universally accepted either in England (e.g. they were summarily dismissed by Morison J. in *ASM Shipping Ltd of India v TTMI Ltd of England* [2005] EWHC 2238 (Comm) at [39(4)], a judgment regarded by many commentators as controversial, even wrong) or internationally, they have attracted widespread support as being the best current solution to the difficult problem of trying to establish standards.

R8–12   The IBA Conflict Guidelines class conflicts of interest into three categories, red, orange and green, where (i) red ones are serious and normally require the arbitrator to decline the appointment (e.g. the arbitrator owns a significant shareholding in one of the parties); (ii) orange ones require disclosure (e.g. the arbitrator has within the past three years served as counsel in a case against one of the parties or an affiliate of one of the parties in an unrelated matter) but do not normally require the arbitrator to decline; and (iii) green ones are minor matters which do not require disclosure (e.g. the arbitrator has a relationship with another arbitrator or with the counsel for one of the parties through membership in the same professional association or social organisation or the arbitrator and counsel for one of the parties or another arbitrator have previously served together as arbitrators or as co-counsel).

R8–13   The IBA Conflict Guidelines take the view that unnecessary disclosure sometimes raises an incorrect implication in the minds of the parties that the disclosed circumstances would affect the arbitrator's impartiality or independence. Excessive disclosures can thus unnecessarily undermine the parties' confidence in the process.

R8–14   Despite lacking unanimous international acceptance, the IBA Conflict Guidelines are the most comprehensive, most balanced, guidelines available and provide a well-tried baseline against which to measure disclosure both for domestic and international arbitrations. See also the commentary at paras R24–04 to R24–22 on r.24(1)(a) (duty to be independent and impartial).

Who determines what is reasonably relevant?

R8–15   This is, perhaps, the "easiest" of the four questions to answer: it will be the court.

Extent of obligation to search for disclosable facts

R8–16   This question is also not fully addressed in literature, standards or guidelines. It is clearly implicit that the arbitrator must make a reasonable endeavour to ascertain such facts and, for example, law firms' standard anti-conflict systems in place for their legal advisory work will reveal conflicts which might affect a solicitor considering an arbitral appointment. Sole practitioner arbitrators can, for example, run a search of their laptop easily and quickly.

Common basis for disclosure

This question is in part covered by the discussion above but where each **R8–17** arbitrator makes their own decision concerning disclosure, no system can regulate to such a high degree of precision. This gives rise to a consequent and very difficult practical question: if there are two shortlisted arbitrators and both possess the same factual matrix but one discloses certain facts and the other does not, what then ensues? These and related questions have been, and continue to be, hotly debated, particularly recently in the USA with the "Draft Arbitrator Disclosure Guidelines" promulgated by the ABA's Dispute Resolution Subcommittee (these are considered further, below).

Some US courts have taken disclosure to an extraordinary level, e.g. as in **R8–18** *Positive Software Solutions Inc v New Century Mortgage Corp Inc*[1] where, subsequent to the issue of the arbitrator's award, it was discovered (see para.R76–03) that S (the arbitrator) had, seven years previously, been a partner in a law firm (LF1) which had handled part of a multi-company six lawsuit litigation involving a large corporate group, Intel, (which had no relation to the present parties). Intel was represented by seven separate law firms and a total of 34 attorneys. Upon losing in the arbitration, Positive Software conducted a detailed investigation of S's background and discovered that, seven years earlier, he and his former law firm LF1 had represented the same party as New Century's law firm (LF2) had in the present arbitration and one of the latter's attorneys in the arbitration, C, who had been involved in the earlier litigation. C had participated in representing Intel in three of its lawsuits from August 1991 until July 1992, although her name remained on the pleadings in one of the cases until June 1993. In September 1992, S along with 12 other attorneys from LF1 had entered an appearance in two of the three cases on which C had worked. Although their names appeared together on pleadings, S and C never attended or participated in any meetings, telephone calls, hearings, depositions, or trials together.

On these facts the District Court vacated the arbitrator's award for his **R8–19** failure to disclose the "prior professional relationship"; this decision was subsequently upheld by the five judge Fifth Circuit Court of Appeals but, thereafter, the full 16 judge court sat "en banc" and overruled the earlier decision 11–5, concluding that the Federal Arbitration Act ("FAA") did not

---

[1] Refer to the "en banc" decision *Positive Software Solutions, Inc v New Century Mortgage Corp*, 476 F.3d 278 (5th Cir. 2007) (en banc), cert. den. 551 U.S. 1114 (2007); the initial Fifth Circuit Court of Appeals decision was *Positive Software Solutions, Inc v New Century Mortgage Corp*, 436 F.3d 495 (5th Cir. 2006), rehearing en banc granted, 449 F.3d 616 (5th Cir. 2006), revised 476 F.3d 278 (5th Cir. 2007) (en banc), cert. den. 551 U.S. 1114 (2007); the District Court decision was *Positive Software Solutions, Inc v New Century Mortgage Corp*, 337 F.Supp. 2d 862 (N.D. Tex. 2004), affirmed 436 F.3d 495 (5th Cir. 2006), rehearing en banc granted, 449 F.3d 616 (5th Cir. 2006), revised 476 F.3d 278 (5th Cir. 2007) (en banc), cert. den. 551 U.S. 1114 (2007).

mandate the extreme remedy of *vacatur* for non-disclosure of a trivial past association.

R8–20 In 2008/09 the ABA proposed disclosure guidelines ("Best Practices for Meeting Disclosure Requirements Under the RUAA and Similar Arbitrator Disclosure Standards"), which were withdrawn following waves of heavy criticism; these required, inter alia, that the arbitrator should investigate and disclose common membership in professional groups and committees, common membership in a church, social group, country club, etc. attendance at the same college or graduate school, that one of the counsel, co-arbitrators or party representatives is an "acquaintance" or a "neighbour", and that the arbitrator has had a "life interest pertinent to the matter" (see K.B. Reisenfeld, "ABA Dispute Resolution Section Rejects Proposed Arbitrator Disclosure Guidelines" in *Transnational Dispute Management* (May 2009)). It is submitted that, as a matter of English law and of the IBA Conflict Guidelines, this is a wholly unnecessary imposition. The authors submit, further, that the ABA's excessive proposal has no place whatsoever in Scotland.

Rule 9: Arbitrator's tenure D

9. An arbitrator's tenure ends if—
  (a) **the arbitrator becomes ineligible to act as an arbitrator (see rule 4),**
  (b) **the tribunal revokes the arbitrator's appointment (see rule 10),**
  (c) **the arbitrator is removed by the parties, a third party or the Outer House (see rules 11 and 12),**
  (d) **the Outer House dismisses the tribunal of which the arbitrator forms part (see rule 13), or**
  (e) **the arbitrator resigns (see rule 15) or dies (see rule 79).**

DEFINITIONS

"arbitrator": ss.4, 31(1)

STATUS

R9–01 This is a default rule so it is open to the parties to modify it, agree something different or disapply it completely (see s.9); that said, it is not open to the parties to disapply mandatory rules 4, 13, 15, or 79.

R9–02 At common law, if an arbitrator was required to make his award within a specified time limit his tenure ceased with the expiry of the time limit if his award had not been made by that time and it had not been extended (prorogated) (*Cunninghame v Drummond* (1491) Mor. 635; *Earl of Linlithgow v Hamilton* (1610) Mor. 636). While the matter is not beyond argument, the authors submit that, on a proper construction of r.9 and having regard to the founding principles in s.1, r.9 did not supersede the common law rule and that the two rules co-exist.

R9–03 In many cases in practice, this potentially drastic common law rule could operate to the detriment of the parties' better interests, e.g. where a lengthy arbitration collapses because the award is one day late. If there is any danger of such an outcome there are several solutions. These include (i) the parties agreeing a revised deadline; and (ii) failing such agreement, either party or the tribunal itself applying to the court under r.43 for an extension of the time limit. In such an application the factors in the Singaporean case *Ting Kang Chung John v Teo Hee Lai Building Constructions Pte Ltd* [2010] SGHC 20 at [42] might then come into play. These include illness, fire causing destruction of arbitral documents, unexpected complexity as well as one party adopting obstructive tactics productive of delay. If there is any danger of the award failing to comply with a time limit, the tribunal should raise this with the parties, and if no agreement can be reached, apply under r.43. Of course, where an arbitrator is genuinely recalcitrant, the automatic falling away of his jurisdiction precludes any necessity for an application to the court under r.12(e).

MODEL LAW

There is no equivalent in the Model Law; see next paragraph.   R9–04

COMMENTARY

This rule does no more than collect together, for ease of reference, the   R9–05
various relevant circumstances for termination of tenure which are addressed individually under the respective rules. It is exhaustive unless the parties have modified it under s.9 by adding to it.

Rule 10: Challenge to appointment of arbitrator D

10.—(1) A party may object to the tribunal about the appointment of an arbitrator.

(2) An objection is competent only if—
  (a) it is made on the ground that the arbitrator—
    (i) is not impartial and independent,
    (ii) has not treated the parties fairly, or
    (iii) does not have a qualification which the parties agreed (before the arbitrator's appointment) that the arbitrator must have,
  (b) it states the facts on which it is based,
  (c) it is made within 14 days of the objector becoming aware of those facts, and
  (d) notice of it is given to the other party.

(3) The tribunal may deal with an objection by confirming or revoking the appointment.

(4) If the tribunal fails to make a decision within 14 days of a competent objection being made, the appointment is revoked.

DEFINITIONS

"arbitrator": ss.4, 31(1)
"tribunal": ss.2, 31(1)

Note that neither "impartial" nor "independent" is defined in the Act (nor in the Model Law) but see the commentary to r.24 below.

STATUS

R10–01 This is a default rule so it is open to the parties to modify it, agree something different or disapply it completely (see s.9). This contrasts with the Model Law art.12(2) which does not allow modification. Adoption of some well-known arbitral rules will result in modification of r.10.

MODEL LAW

R10–02 Articles 12(2) and 13 have substantially the same effect as r.10(2)(a)(i) and (iii); the Model Law's challenge procedure (but not the grounds in art.12(2)) is also open to contrary agreement by the parties (art.13(1)).

COMMENTARY

R10–03 A challenge may be made at any time prior to the arbitrator's tenure ending; see r.9.

R10–04 Rule 10 allows a challenge to the appointment of an arbitrator to be made to the tribunal itself, including a sole arbitrator. Compliance with r.10 (if applicable) is a necessary prerequisite to any removal by the court under r.12 (r.14(1)(b)(i)). This is consistent with the founding principle in s.1(c) of the Act that the court should not intervene in an arbitration except as provided for in the Act.

Rule 10(1)

R10–05 This gives a right to object, which is not the same as a right to remove. This is in contrast to the very different world of jury trial-based systems widespread in the USA, e.g. Florida, where the parties can strike out, e.g. three members of the proposed jury without showing cause. This is mirrored in US arbitration practice (e.g. the AAA and FINRA) where the parties are presented with lists of, e.g. 10 ranked arbitrators and can strike out whomsoever they wish without needing to show cause; the highest-ranked remaining arbitrators form the tribunal; if all 10 names are struck out, then either (i) another 10 names are produced and so on, or (ii) the institution will appoint the arbitrators, i.e. the parties will have ceded control of the appointment process.

R10–06 The challenge is to be made to the tribunal. United Kingdom and international practice varies in this regard; in the remainder of the UK, s.24 of the 1996 Act provides that the challenge is made to the court (the 2010 Act has sought to minimise the involvement of the court (see s.1(c)) even in comparison to the 1996 Act) but SAC 07 has the more imaginative mechanism of an appeal to a panel specially established by the Chairman, CIArb Scottish Branch, and that panel's decision is final.

The UNCITRAL Rules provide for the appointing authority to determine the challenge (art.13.4) whereas the LCIA Rules (refer art.10.6) and ICC Rules (refer art.14) and Swiss Rules (refer art.11(2)) provide for the respective courts of the ICC and the Swiss Chambers to determine the challenge. Interestingly, the LCIA now publishes its decisions on challenges whereas, in contrast, the ICC does not. **R10–07**

Natural justice requires that the challenged arbitrator be given the opportunity to respond; this is implicit in r.10 since the tribunal deals with the challenge. The ICC Rules art.14(3) and the LCIA Rules art.10.4 expressly provide for the arbitrator to be given the opportunity to respond but the Swiss Rules do not; absent an express provision, there must be an implied one pursuant to ECHR art.6. **R10–08**

As a general rule, unmeritorious challenges to arbitrators are to be discouraged since otherwise a party might use the challenge procedure to delay or even derail the arbitral proceedings and this is not acceptable and cannot be tolerated (inter alia s.1(a) and rr.24 and 25 apply). **R10–09**

Rule 10(2)(a)

The list is exhaustive; there is no provision for groundless objection (in contrast to the very different world of those US jury-based systems where challenge without cause is permitted). The LCIA and the Swiss Rules limit the scope for challenge in a manner similar to r.10 but, anomalously, the ICC Rules do not place any limit on the grounds of challenge (art.14(1)), stating: "A challenge of an arbitrator, whether for an alleged lack of impartiality or independence or otherwise, shall be made ... ". **R10–10**

See discussion of "impartial and independent" under rr.12(a) and 24. For a discussion of the arbitrator's duty to treat the parties fairly, see discussion under r.24(1)(b). **R10–11**

Rule 10(2)(a)(iii)

A far from uncommon scenario in recruitment is to discover, after the appointment commences, that the appointee has claimed qualifications which he/she does not in fact possess and, e.g. professorships have been achieved on the basis of deliberate inclusion of false information in CVs. **R10–12**

Separate from the implications of any code of ethics (e.g. the CIArb's Code of Ethics at Part 2, rr.1, 4.1 and 4.2 will establish a prima facie charge of professional misconduct in such circumstances), an arbitrator in such circumstances is open to immediate challenge. However, a relatively common scenario is where the arbitrator is appointed by agreement based on his (accurate) CV but, later, one of the parties (looking for a ground of **R10–13** challenge) discovers that he is not precisely what they thought he was, e.g. a Professor of Civil Engineering, appointed as arbitrator on that ground, might in fact prove not to be a Chartered Civil Engineer as stated in the arbitration agreement; alternatively, a brilliant young QC might be appointed as arbitrator whereas many arbitration agreements refer to a barrister/advocate of not less than 15 years' call. In many such cases r.10(2)(c) will operate so as to extinguish the right to challenge. See also r.12(d) below.

Rule 10(2)(b)

R10–14 This refers to "facts" as opposed to allegations but in practice it will often be difficult, even impossible, to distinguish them.

Rule 10(2)(c)

R10–15 The time limit is deliberately short in order to limit the derailing of the arbitration by the objection. It applies to an objection to the appointment of the arbitrator but does not apply where a party does not challenge the appointment. Where a party does not challenge the appointment, the objection must be timeous in terms of r.76 (see the commentary to r.76 below). It is, however, difficult to see circumstances in practice where there would be an objection on the grounds of impartiality, independence or the holding of a qualification which did not at the time seek removal of the arbitrator.

R10–16 The time period for the making of a challenge will begin with the day on which the objector became aware of the "facts" on which it is based, even if the challenging party was unaware that the facts could give rise to a challenge.

Rule 10(3)

R10–17 The tribunal is not obliged to deal with the challenge but see r.10(4) below for the consequences of not doing so. For the effect of revocation on the arbitrator's entitlement to fees and expenses, see r.16.

R10–18 As in the Model Law art.13(2), the challenge is heard first by the tribunal, irrespective of whether the tribunal is of one or three arbitrators. If there is a sole arbitrator, then while it might appear that that arbitrator is being made a judge in his/her own cause, r.12 (a mandatory rule) gives the challenger a right of application to the court. In any event, an important practical requirement for an arbitrator is to maintain the trust and the confidence of the parties so, should that be lost by reason of whatever ground gave rise to the challenge, the arbitrator might well, in a finely-balanced circumstance, choose to resign (e.g. as happened in *ASM Shipping Ltd of India v TTMI Ltd of England* [2005] EWHC 2238 (Comm)), or revoke his own appointment rather than continue in a negative (or hostile) atmosphere. In *ASM*

Shipping Ltd v Harris [2007] EWHC 1513 (Comm) there was a secondary challenge to the two remaining arbitrators on the ground that they had become "infected" by the perceived bias on the part of the now-resigned third arbitrator. Very properly, this absurd challenge was robustly dismissed by Andrew Smith J.

Where the challenge is to one member of a tribunal of three, there is no requirement for the challenged arbitrator to stand aside from determining the challenge but many arbitrators will choose to do so in practice—"no man shall be a judge in his own cause". **R10–19**

Rule 10(4)

The time limit is deliberately short in order (i) not to permit the arbitration to be derailed by the objection, and (ii) to force the tribunal to an early decision, failing which the challenge will be successful. **R10–20**

Rule 11: *Removal of arbitrator by parties* D

11.—(1) An arbitrator may be removed—
  (a) by the parties acting jointly, or
  (b) by any third party to whom the parties give power to remove an arbitrator.
(2) A removal is effected by notifying the arbitrator.

DEFINITIONS

"arbitrator": ss.4, 31(1)
"notification": r.83

STATUS

This is a default rule so it is open to the parties to modify it, agree something different or disapply it completely (see s.9). **R11–01**

MODEL LAW

The Model Law has no direct equivalent of r.11 but art.14 deals with the circumstances where the arbitrator(s) fail(s) to act without undue delay, or are unable to act, in which event the parties may jointly remove him/her/them. **R11–02**

COMMENTARY

Arbitration is a consensual process so it is logical that the parties can agree both (a) whether or not to adopt r.11 at all and, if so, (b) whether and when to operate it. Circumstances do arise, albeit in the UK very rarely, where an arbitrator has lost the confidence of the parties, for whatever reason, and they jointly agree to remove him. **R11–03**

R11–04   Whereas in most circumstances the principles of natural justice would apply so that the arbitrator would be given the opportunity to make representations, in this circumstance such principles are irrelevant—the parties want rid of him and, despite his fulfilling a judicial function, he is, in one sense, merely a contracted service provider and such contract may be summarily terminated. The consequences for the arbitrator's fees and expenses are dealt with under r.16. In addition, the parties will, in practice, have to consider the impact on their own legal and other expenses consequent on removing the arbitrator, particularly if he is a sole arbitrator.

R11–05   If the arbitration agreement calls for a three person tribunal, the question then arises of whether, and if so how, to replace an arbitrator; in agreeing to remove an arbitrator, the parties may (and should) agree on this or, alternatively, the applicable institutional rules may cover the point. Under the ICC Rules art.15(5) the court may decide, but only if the removal is after the close of proceedings, that the two remaining arbitrators continue as a truncated tribunal; the LCIA Rules have no equivalent provision. Both LCIA Rules (art.11(1)) and ICC Rules (art.15(4)) give the institution the discretion whether or not to follow the same appointment process as originally; if they do not, r.6(b) (or agreed alternative) applies to appoint a replacement arbitrator.

R11–06   The question may arise as to whether the truncated two person tribunal can continue with the arbitration, pending replacement of the removed arbitrator; the SAR make no such provision expressly but if the arbitration agreement calls for a three person tribunal, a two person one is evidently not in accordance with that agreement but the agreement to remove one of the arbitrators is arguably a variation to the original arbitration agreement.

R11–07   A different issue of a truncated tribunal arose in an arbitration *Himpurna California Energy Ltd v PT (Persero) Perusahaan Listruik Negara* (2000) XXV YCA 13 (PLN was a state owned electricity utility that supplied electricity to the Indonesian public). This was an ad hoc arbitration under UNCITRAL Rules (1976) concerning the cancellation of a power plant construction project and the tribunal, sitting in Jakarta, was interdicted by the Indonesian Courts (at the instigation of the Indonesian government) with a fine of $1 million/day if they continued with the arbitration. The tribunal immediately relocated to The Hague to continue proceedings but, on arrival at Schiphol Airport, the Indonesian arbitrator was "met" by staff from the Indonesian Embassy and "escorted away", never (so far as concerned the arbitration) to be seen again. The other two arbitrators continued on a truncated basis and rendered a final award (in Himpurna's favour).

Rule 11(1)

R11–08   This mirrors s.23(3) of the 1996 Act.

Arbitration (Scotland) Act 2010 (r.12)

Rule 11(1)(b)

Absent express agreement by the parties, no AAR (see s.22) can act here **R11–09** and the reference will in practice be to an administering institution such as the LCIA or ICC where the institution's court plays a central role. Typically, the LCIA Rules (art.10.1) and the ICC Rules (art.15(2): "An arbitrator shall also be replaced on the Court's own initiative when it decides that he is prevented de jure or de facto from fulfilling the arbitrator's functions, or that the arbitrator is not fulfilling his functions in accordance with the Rules or within the prescribed time limits") provide that the respective court may revoke their appointment, or remove an arbitrator. There is no difference in practice here between revocation and removal.

Rule 11(2)

The notification must be in writing—for the method of notification see **R11–10** r.83.

Rule 12: Removal of arbitrator by court M

12. The Outer House may remove an arbitrator if satisfied on the application by any party—
   (a) that the arbitrator is not impartial and independent,
   (b) that the arbitrator has not treated the parties fairly,
   (c) that the arbitrator is incapable of acting as an arbitrator in the arbitration (or that there are justifiable doubts about the arbitrator's ability to so act),
   (d) that the arbitrator does not have a qualification which the parties agreed (before the arbitrator's appointment) that the arbitrator must have,
   (e) that substantial injustice has been or will be caused to that party because the arbitrator has failed to conduct the arbitration in accordance with—
      (i) the arbitration agreement,
      (ii) these rules (in so far as they apply), or
      (iii) any other agreement by the parties relating to conduct of the arbitration.

DEFINITIONS

"arbitrator": ss.4, 31(1)
"Outer House": s.31(1)
Note that none of "impartial", "independent" or "substantial injustice" is defined in the Act (nor in the Model Law) but see the commentary on r.24, below.

STATUS

R12–01 This is a mandatory rule so the parties cannot disapply or vary it (see s.8).

MODEL LAW

R12–02 The Model Law has no direct equivalent of r.12 but art.13(3) provides for such an application to the court only after there has been an unsuccessful challenge lodged with the tribunal. Article 14(1) provides for an application to the court

> "if an arbitrator becomes *de jure* or *de facto* unable to perform his functions or for other reasons fails to act without undue delay".

COMMENTARY

R12–03 This list is exhaustive in that no other grounds for such removal are competent. Grounds for removal (a), (b), and (d) replicate r.10(2)(a)(i)–(iii) but ground (c) replicates s.24(1)(c) of the 1996 Act and ground (e) mirrors r.68(2)(a) on challenging the award. It is important to read r.12 with r.14 which provides restrictions on the court's power to remove an arbitrator under r.12. For the effect of removal on the arbitrator's entitlement to fees and expenses, see r.16. For the procedure in an application for removal see the commentary on r.14 below.

R12–04 None of SAC 07, UNCITRAL, LCIA or ICC Rules cover the issues addressed in r.12 since such institutional rules, being agreements between parties, cannot affect the functioning of the court system. There have been relatively few removals under s.24 of the 1996 Act, those that have occurred being anomalous cases; this experience matches that of the CIArb which sees a very small number of professional misconduct cases each year and most are dismissed, the majority being no more than an attack on the arbitrator by a disgruntled loser. Most of the English cases covering s.24 feature removal applications being rejected.

R12–05 The circumstances in which a court has to decide whether to remove an arbitrator will vary. An application can be made before any award has been made, after the making of a part award or after a successful appeal against an award, part or final, whereby the award is set aside. Thus in *AOOT Kalmneft v Glencore International A.G.* [2001] 1 All E.R. 76 there was an appeal against an award on jurisdiction on the grounds of inter alia serious irregularity on the basis that the arbitrator had wrongly decided to make his own preliminary award on jurisdiction and had not given adequate opportunity to Kalmneft to respond to Glencore's submission. The appeal was combined with an application for removal of the arbitrator on the grounds of the same alleged irregularity. After rejecting these grounds of appeal, Colman J. added at [96] and [97]:

"Indeed, even if it were established that serious irregularity had been made out on any other grounds relied upon, I should not have ordered the removal of the arbitrator. This is a step which should be taken only if the serious irregularity is such that it may reasonably be concluded that there is a serious risk that the arbitrator's future conduct of the proceedings will not be in accordance with his duties under section 33 [of the 1996 Act]... In the present case the evidence goes nowhere near showing that there would be a serious risk of the arbitrator failing to comply in future with his duties under section 33 or that substantial injustice would thereby be caused to Kalmneft."

R12–06 The removal of an arbitrator was described by H.H. Judge Bowsher QC (in *Groundshire v VHE Construction* [2001] B.L.R. 395) as a "most serious step" which would only be ordered if the arbitrator's misconduct was so serious that, in the judge's words, he could not be trusted

"to complete the arbitration fairly and properly even with the benefit of an examination of his conduct by the parties and their representatives and guidance from the court ...".

R12–07 Further, the mere fact that one party has lost confidence in an arbitrator will not without evidence of real and substantial injustice lead to an order removing the arbitrator (*Conder Structures v Kvaerner Construction Ltd* [1999] A.D.R.L.J. 305).

R12–08 A pre-1996 example of a case where the arbitrator was removed for misconduct is *Damond Lock Grabowski v Laing Investments (Bracknell) Ltd*, 60 B.L.R. 112, where even the party resisting the application to remove him described him as "eccentric, autocratic and obsessive". The judge concluded:

"Looking at the whole sorry history of the matter, it seems to me clear that the arbitrator has unquestionably pointed the finger at the Applicants and repeatedly accused them, in my judgment unfairly, of deliberate delay. Above all, he has not paid proper heed to their objections and has insisted that the hearing must start on the day he ordered, when they cannot be in a position to conduct their case properly. In my judgment he must be removed. I therefore grant the order asked in paragraph 1 of the notice of motion."

R12–09 Post-1996, there have been very few successful removal applications in the English courts but two merit mention. First, in *W and S v BB* Unreported June 8, 2001 TCC the arbitrator was removed inter alia because he appeared either to have had no comprehension of how to conduct the case, a £60,000 dispute concerning building works at a residential property, or had otherwise wholly lost control of it. Although the case had reached only the conclusion of the claimants' evidence, the arbitrator had issued 19 directions orders and had spent 170 hours on it; in consequence, the parties had, of course, incurred substantial legal and other costs far out of proportion to the sums in dispute. Further, he had issued a directions order which sought to impose on the parties certain matters that they should incorporate in a proposed settlement agreement. Further, he issued a purported peremptory order which (i) failed to follow s.41(5) and (ii) sought to secure 100 per cent of his fees from each party. In removing him, the judge said this:

> "Not only that, but the terms of the two sets of directions to which I have referred, demonstrate to my satisfaction that [the arbitrator] has a pitifully inadequate comprehension of the nature of his function as arbitrator, what powers he has and what is the appropriate way in which to exercise these powers. He seems to have no conception of the fact that these powers are to be exercised in accordance with law, or what the relevant principles of law are.
>
> That fact on its own means that if the arbitration proceeds with [him] as the arbitrator, it is likely that substantial injustice will be caused to the claimants, because it is likely that [he] will continue to demonstrate that wholly inadequate grasp of the nature of his functions and powers to which I have referred."

This (and other similar comment by the judge) appears to be the harshest criticism on record in any English case. This case also raised a serious issue concerning the extent of an arbitrator's liability from suit; this is discussed at para.R73–08 below.

R12–10 In *Norbrook Laboratories Ltd v Tank* [2006] EWHC 1055 (Comm), the arbitrator, an engineer, inter alia contacted witnesses directly and contacted one of the parties to the arbitration directly, bypassing its solicitors. He was removed on the grounds (i) that circumstances existed that had given rise to justifiable doubts as to his impartiality, and (ii) that he had failed properly to have conducted the proceedings, including in particular a failure to have acted in accordance with s.33(1)(a) of the 1996 Act (equivalent to r.24(1)(b)) and had conducted the proceedings in such a manner as to have amounted to a serious irregularity under s.68(2) of the Act. Colman J. concluded (authors' emphasis added):

> "153. I am not persuaded that the Arbitrator has by his conduct demonstrated any all-pervading bias or want of impartiality against Norbrook on the grounds relied upon. He has been attempting to impose an orderly and economical procedure on the parties in an effort to achieve a relatively speedy award ... Further, with one exception, those procedural irregularities in the course of the reference to which I have referred have not caused substantial injustice to either party ... *Although I am satisfied that a more experienced Arbitrator would*

probably have avoided some, if not all, of those irregularities, it is important to keep firmly in mind that, particularly where, as here, the parties have agreed to the appointment of a sole Arbitrator because of his technical skill and knowledge, his procedural responses to a case involving relatively complicated evidence might not necessarily reflect the kind of management regime that would be imposed by a Queen's Counsel fulfilling that function.

154. However, I take a very different view of the Arbitrator's direct contact with the witnesses. For the reasons given ... above I have come to the conclusion that by the Arbitrator's conduct in that respect he has or may have been exposed to information about the operation of the plant or the pre-contract laboratory testing which consciously or unconsciously could have influenced him in his decision under Rule 16.3 and which might well influence him in his future conduct of the reference and in particular his final award.

155. To this risk his stated determination to put matters 'out of his mind' is, as Porter v. McGill, supra, shows, no answer. The essential attribute of objective impartiality is not to be achieved by subjective self-discipline.

156. In the event, I have no doubt that the fair minded and informed observer, having considered all the facts in this case relating to contact with the three witnesses would conclude that there was a real possibility that the tribunal was biased. The consequence of this conclusion is that the Second Decision cannot stand and must be set aside under s.68, there having been a serious irregularity which has caused substantial injustice. Further, although I am quite sure that the Arbitrator is admirably qualified to resolve the technical issues between the parties, the fact remains that his impartiality has been apparently impaired. The fair-minded and informed observer would entertain great reservations as to whether the Arbitrator's judgment had been affected by what he had been told by at least one of the potential witnesses. Accordingly, although the removal of the Arbitrator at this stage in the proceedings would involve the parties in considerable additional expense in the further prosecution of this arbitration, I have reluctantly come to the conclusion that this is the correct course. Consequently, an order will be made under s.24 of the 1996 Act that the Arbitrator be removed. I shall hear such representations as the parties may wish to advance ancillary to s.24, in particular with regard to s.24(4) of the 1996 Act."

In *ASM Shipping Ltd of India v TTMI Ltd of England* [2005] EWHC 2238 **R12–11** (Comm) (see r.8) ASM had taken up an award and had, it was held, thereby waived its right to object to the chairman of the tribunal so he was not removed but the judge made it clear that, at least in his opinion, he should have been. The judgment was heavily criticised (see, inter alia, Hew R. Dundas, "Arbitration and the English Courts: Progress and Regress" [2006]

72 *Arbitration* 104) as misapplying the law to the facts. In brief, ASM (the owners) and TTMI (the charterers) were engaged in a London arbitration arising out of a charterparty where Mr X QC was appointed chairman of the tribunal. The owners' principal witness was Mr M, a shipbroker. In a wholly separate (but relatively recent) arbitration (the "other arbitration") between entirely unrelated parties, M had been a key witness for one of the parties and *the charterers'* solicitors in the present case, WH, had represented the other side and, for a short time and in respect of one preliminary issue only (which was settled), X had been instructed by WH and had drafted certain disclosure applications. Summarising a long story, X had had a brief and peripheral involvement in the other arbitration in respect of which M, so the latter alleged (but these allegations were never substantiated), had been the target of an attack by WH. X had no recollection of meeting M and had not conducted any part of any hearing or other proceeding involving M. M was not even a party to the present arbitration, merely a witness.

R12–12 Based on M's unsubstantiated allegations and a connection between X and M which can, at best, be described as tenuous, the judge concluded:

> "In my view, given the facts and conclusions I have stated, Mr X QC should not continue to act in this matter."

In reaching this conclusion, the judge appears to have accepted M's allegations without substantiation, dismissing X's clear counter-statements concerning the other arbitration made after consultation of his papers. In effect M and his perceptions, however spurious, have been substituted for those of the FMIO. Further, the decision in ASM *Shipping Ltd* is wholly incompatible with that in *Rustal Trading Ltd v Gill & Duffus SA* [2000] 1 Lloyd's Rep. 14, which has stood the test of time and has never been criticised or dissented from.

Rule 12(a)

R12–13 See discussion of "impartial" and "independence" under the mandatory r.24(1)(a).

R12–14 The case of *ASM Shipping Ltd of India v TTMI Ltd of England* [2005] EWHC 2238 (Comm) has already been mentioned in connection with this ground for removal. In *A v B, X* [2011] EWHC 2345 (Comm), the arbitrator Mr X QC had been instructed by one of the firms acting in the arbitration to represent their client in a litigation. Neither the client nor the subject matter of the litigation had any connection with the arbitration. In 2008 the litigation settled and was stayed for implementation of the settlement. In May 2009 Mr X QC began to act as arbitrator. In November 2009 the settlement broke down and the litigation revived with Mr X QC being instructed by the firm but not by anyone concerned with the arbitration. At the same time he conducted preliminary hearings as arbitrator and fixed an evidential hearing for September 2010 which took place. Before he had completed a part award the litigation went to trial at which point he disclosed to the parties the situation with the firm. He then completed the part award and after it had been received by the parties it was appealed and his removal was sought under the equivalent of r.12(a) on the grounds of a real possibility of unconscious bias. In rejecting both appeal and application for removal Flaux J. considered the authorities on apparent bias in detail and observed in particular:

> "60. I do not consider that the fair-minded and informed observer, who is presumed to know how the legal profession in this country works, would consider that, merely because the arbitrator acted as counsel for one of the firms of solicitors acting in the arbitration, whether in the past or simultaneously with the arbitration, there was a real possibility of apparent bias ...
>
> 61. Of course, if the arbitrator has an actual predisposition towards the particular firm of solicitors because he is actually considering his relationship with the firm and wishing to foster that relationship, that would amount to actual bias, but there is no suggestion of any such actual predisposition here, nor could such a serious allegation be advanced in the absence of any evidence.
>
> 62. What might be described as a difficult halfway house between such an actual predisposition and [Counsel for the applicant's] allegation of unconscious predisposition may be the case to which I adverted several times during the hearing, of the barrister arbitrator who receives a very substantial proportion of his instructions as counsel, say 60%, from one of the firms acting in the arbitration. It may well be, not just that that is a matter which would have to be disclosed by the arbitrator at the outset but that (at least where there was no waiver by the parties) there might be a real possibility of apparent bias."

This case is considered in Hew R. Dundas, "Conflicts of Interest and Arbitrator Disclosure Revisited: Barristers Acting as Counsel and as Arbitrator" (2012) 78 *Arbitration* 72.

In *AT&T Corp v Saudi Cable Co* [2000] 1 Lloyd's Rep. 22 the applicant **R12–15** sought to remove the chairman of an ICC tribunal on the basis of his possessing a small number of shares in, and being a non-executive director of, Nortel which was a competitor of AT&T and which had been the disappointed bidder for a major telecoms contract with Saudi Cable, which contract was the subject matter of the present arbitration. The Court of Appeal upheld Longmore J.'s rejection of the application, the arbitrator's connection with the parties and the contract being too remote.

In *Sinclair v Woods of Winchester Ltd* [2005] EWHC 1631 (QB) the **R12–16** claimants sought to remove the arbitrator in a dispute over a £300,000 domestic housebuilding project. They contended that there had been a number of serious irregularities in the arbitrator's conduct of the arbitration which had caused them substantial injustice including that he had failed (i) to have conducted the arbitration properly both before and during one hearing, and (ii) in his award to have addressed all the issues put to him or have dealt with the issues clearly and unambiguously. They applied (a) under s.68 of the 1996 Act for the award to be set aside, and (b) under s.24 for the removal of the arbitrator since the irregularities had been so serious and the injustice so substantial. H.H. Judge Coulson QC dealt trenchantly with the claimants' application:

> "41. The Claimants contend that the arbitrator was wrong to [have issued] the peremptory order of 24th March 2004 requiring them to serve a statement of case ...
>
> 42. ... [A]s part of an application under sections 24 or 68 of the 1996 Act, this complaint can fairly be categorised as risible. First, it is clear from the arbitrator's letter of 2nd January 2004 that from the outset he
>
> expected the Claimants 'to quantify their claim concurrently with the preparation of their Statement of Case.' The arbitrator's understanding was based on the fact that the Claimants had promised to do just that ... Thirdly, it is plain that the Claimants were in delay, even at this early stage, in complying with the arbitrator's orders because they had not provided all the documentation they relied on to accompany the pleading.
>
> 43. In those circumstances it was entirely appropriate for the arbitrator on 24th March 2004 to issue an order in peremptory terms to get the Claimants to do in April what they had promised to do by early February, namely to provide a quantified claim document together with all documents relied on. There was therefore not only
>
> no serious irregularity, there was instead an entirely appropriate order ...
>
> 45. [Counsel for the claimants] said that he really relied on the order as 'evidence of the arbitrator's inability to control the course of the arbitration'. In my judgment the order demonstrates precisely the opposite: an arbitrator having to come to grips, not for the last time, with Claimants who were not prepared to do what they said they would do.
>
> 46. This purported criticism of the arbitrator is therefore rejected. Not only was it a hopeless point, but it also revealed another all pervasive feature of the Claimants' application before me, namely a tendency to attack the arbitrator for an underlying situation, in this case delay, for which, on analysis, they themselves were responsible."

This case typifies the many robust rejections of s.24 and s.68 applications.

Rule 12(b)

This derives from the mandatory r.24(2), the concept being of the arbitrator being unfair on both parties; to be unfair on one is to fail the impartiality test. See the commentary on r.24(2) at paras R24–23 to R24–33 below.

R12–17

Rule 12(c)

While an arbitrator becoming an "incapable adult" within the meaning of r.4 ends his tenure automatically (r.9(a)), if he becomes incapable of acting for other reasons or there exists justifiable doubts about his ability to act, a party can apply to the court for his removal. This ground of removal is similar to that in s.24(1)(c) of the 1996 Act and art.14(1) of the Model Law. In *Succula & Pomona Shipping Co Ltd v Harland & Wolff Ltd* [1980] 2 Lloyd's Rep. 381, Mustill J. said:

R12–18

> "No doubt [the words 'refuses to act' and 'incapable of acting'] embrace situations where the refusal or the incapacity is not life-long. But the disability must be serious enough to put the arbitrator out of action altogether, so far as the arbitration is concerned."

See below at paras R15–14 to R15–16.

Rule 12(d)

See the commentary on r.10(2)(a)(iii) at paras R10–12 and R10–13.

R12–19

Rule 12(e)

This ground of removal has the same wording as the ground of appeal on the basis of serious irregularity set out in r.68(2)(a). It is necessarily qualified by reference to "substantial injustice" otherwise any minor complaint could trigger a removal application. However, in r.12(e) "substantial injustice" must be viewed in the context of circumstances where the arbitration has not ended. The situation at the end of an arbitration in a serious irregularity appeal may differ. It is suggested that for r.12(e) the focus should be on the ongoing and likely future effect of the arbitrator's breach on a party and whether it would be seriously prejudicial for that party to continue to have to bear the arbitrator to decide the dispute (see the comments in *Kalmneft* (para.R12–05) and *Groundshire* (para.R12–06)). An example of "substantial injustice" might occur, for example, where an arbitrator in breach of his duty under r.24(1)(c)(i) to conduct the arbitration without unnecessary delay, was unwilling to fix a final hearing. Under the old common law a court could ordain an arbitrator or umpire to proceed with the arbitration. This is no longer possible given the terms of s.13. Therefore, in the event of substantially prejudicial breach of the duties in r.24, the only remedy during

R12–20

the course of the arbitration must be to seek removal of the arbitrator. For further consideration of "substantial injustice" see the commentary on r.68(2) at paras R68–15 to R68–75.

Rule 13: Dismissal of tribunal by court M

13. The Outer House may dismiss the tribunal if satisfied on the application by a party that substantial injustice has been or will be caused to that party because the tribunal has failed to conduct the arbitration in accordance with—
    (a) the arbitration agreement,
    (b) these rules (in so far as they apply), or
    (c) any other agreement by the parties relating to conduct of the arbitration.

DEFINITIONS

"arbitration agreement": ss.4, 31(1)
"arbitrator": ss.4, 31(1)
"Outer House": s.31(1)
Note that "substantial injustice" is not defined in the Act (nor in the Model Law).

STATUS

R13–01 This is a mandatory rule so the parties cannot disapply or vary it (see s.8).

MODEL LAW

R13–02 The Model Law has no direct equivalent of r.13 but art.13(3) provides for such an application to the court only after there has been an unsuccessful challenge lodged with the tribunal.

COMMENTARY

R13–03 This list is exhaustive in that no other grounds for such removal are competent. It is important to read r.13 with r.14 which provides restrictions on the court's power to dismiss the tribunal under r.13. For the effect of the dismissal of the tribunal on an individual arbitrator's entitlement to fees and expenses see r.16.

R13–04 None of UNCITRAL, LCIA or ICC Rules cover the issues addressed in r.12 since such institutional rules, being agreements between parties, cannot affect the functioning of the court system. Rule 13 empowers the court to dismiss the entire tribunal as opposed to removing a single arbitrator.

R13–05 The controversial decision in *ASM Shipping Ltd of India v TTMI Ltd of England* [2005] EWHC 2238 (Comm) is discussed above under r.12 (see paras R12–11 and R12–12), where the judge held that the chairman of a three person tribunal should have been removed, or should have recused himself, for apparent bias but ASM had, by taking up an award, lost its right to object to that arbitrator. The arbitrator subsequently resigned. ASM then sought (see *ASM Shipping Ltd v Harris* [2007] EWHC 1513 (Comm)) to remove the other two arbitrators on the ground that "circumstances exist[ed] that give rise to justifiable doubts about [their] impartiality"; however, it was made clear that no suggestion had been made that either continuing arbitrator had been guilty of any sort of improper or unprofessional conduct or was to be the subject of any such criticism—in brief, it was alleged that they must have been infected by their departed colleague's alleged bias.

The judge was unable to accept that there was an invariable rule, or it was necessarily the case, that where one member of a tribunal was tainted by apparent bias the whole tribunal was affected second-hand by apparent bias, and therefore should recuse themselves, or should be excluded, from the proceedings. Further, any objection to the two arbitrators continuing with the reference because M (see para.R12–11 above) would be a witness would not be on the basis of any involvement that they themselves had had with M, but could only be made on the basis that there was a risk that they would be other than impartial because they have been influenced by discussions that they had with the departed chairman. The judge considered this suggestion to be fanciful. ASM's application was dismissed. **R13–06**

Rule 14: Removal and dismissal by court: supplementary M

14.—(1) The Outer House may remove an arbitrator, or dismiss the tribunal, only if—
   (a) the arbitrator or, as the case may be, tribunal has been—
       (i) notified of the application for removal or dismissal, and
       (ii) given the opportunity to make representations, and
   (b) the Outer House is satisfied—
       (i) that any recourse available under rule 10 has been exhausted, and
       (ii) that any available recourse to a third party who the parties have agreed is to have power to remove an arbitrator (or dismiss the tribunal) has been exhausted.

(2) A decision of the Outer House under rule 12 or 13 is final.

(3) The tribunal may continue with the arbitration pending the Outer House's decision under rule 12 or 13.

DEFINITIONS

"arbitration agreement": ss.4, 31(1)
"arbitrator": ss.4, 31(1)
"Outer House": s.31(1)
Note that "substantial injustice" is not defined in the Act (nor in the Model Law).

Arbitration (Scotland) Act 2010

STATUS

R14–01 This is a mandatory rule so the parties cannot disapply or vary it (see s.8).

MODEL LAW

R14–02 The Model Law has no direct equivalent of r.14 but art.13(3) provides for such an application to the court but only after there has been an unsuccessful challenge lodged with the tribunal.

COMMENTARY

R14–03 Rule 14 expresses a simple, yet fundamental, rule of natural justice.

R14–04 The application for removal of an arbitrator or dismissal of a tribunal is made to the Outer House by petition (or note) in the style contained in Form 14.4 of the RCS (RCS 100.5, 14.4 and 15.2). The requirements for the petition are set out in r.14.4 (or the note in r.15.2) of the RCS together with the need to:

  (i) aver why the order of removal or dismissal is necessary;
  (ii) aver the circumstances in which the prerequisites for an application in rr.12 or 13 are satisfied;
  (iii) aver the satisfaction of the requirements in r.14(1)(b);
  (iv) aver (if appropriate) on the matters in r.16 (fees etc.);
  (v) aver the reasons why the usual period of 21 days for answers should be dispensed with (if that is necessary);
  (vi) require service or intimation on the other parties to the arbitration, and members of the tribunal.

R14–05 If a shorter period of notice is required, then this should also be craved in the petition. Upon lodging the petition (or note) the applicant must enrol a motion for intimation and service of the petition or note (RCS r.100.5(3)).

R14–06 Together with the petition the applicant should lodge with the Court of Session:

  (i) as a production, any written arbitration agreement or other agreement or other document by virtue of which the time limit is imposed;
  (ii) the written statements of case and defence in the arbitration (the pleadings);
  (iii) the bundle of court documents known as the process (see RCS rr.4.3, 4.4).

Inventories of any supporting productions should be intimated to the other parties, including the members of the tribunal, on whom the petition is served.

On the lodging of the above and the enrolment of the motion, the court **R14–07**
will make a first order for service on the other party or parties to the
arbitration, and the members of the tribunal and anyone else who has an
interest to allow such persons to lodge answers opposing the petition if they
wish within a certain time (RCS r.100.5). Typically, this will be 21 days from
the date of service or intimation. Therefore it is advised that if a shorter
period is required the motion should make a specific request for that period.
The period for answers should be sufficient to enable the arbitrator or tribunal concerned to make representations in their answers.

After the end of the period for answers, whether answers have been **R14–08**
lodged or not, the petitioner should enrol a motion to have the court
determine the petition, with or without a hearing as may be appropriate in
the circumstances (RCS r.100.5(5)). If answers have been lodged there will
probably have to be a hearing.

The expenses of the application will not be included in the "arbitration **R14–09**
expenses" (see the commentary to r.59 below) but will fall to be dealt with
by the court rather than the tribunal.

If these procedures are followed, the situation in *W and S v BB* Unre- **R14–10**
ported June 8, 2001 TCC (see paras R12–09 and R73–08) where the arbitrator was, in the authors' submission, denied the benefits of natural justice,
appearing without legal representation in the court hearing the application
to remove him and where the judge failed to address the question of arbitrator immunity, should be avoided.

Rule 14(1)(b)

Note that (i) r.10 is a default rule and (ii) there may be no reference to any **R14–11**
third party in the arbitration agreement so r.14(1)(b)*(ii)* may not apply.

Rule 14(2)

This reflects a key policy underlying this Act of minimising the involve- **R14–12**
ment of the court; see s.1(c), reflecting art.5 of the Model Law.

Rule 14(3)

This can give rise to difficult considerations in practice; on the one hand, **R14–13**
the arbitrator or tribunal is obliged to proceed without unnecessary delay
(refer s.1(a) and mandatory r.24(1)(c)(i)) but, on the other hand, if one
member of a tribunal is removed or the sole arbitrator/entire tribunal is
dismissed, the question of the ongoing proceedings has to be considered, in
particular to what extent the existing proceedings have to be repeated (at
worst the entire arbitration started again ab initio) at consequent additional
expense (s.1(a) and r.24(1)(c)(ii)). At its simplest, proceedings should not be
halted merely because a challenge has been made, otherwise a party might
seek to derail the arbitration by making a series of unmeritorious challenges.

R14–14 The arbitrators will have to weigh all relevant factors very carefully but, as a very general indication, the "if in doubt" policy is to proceed inter alia because the English experience shows that only a small minority of challenges are successful.

Rule 15: Resignation of arbitrator M

15.—(1) An arbitrator may resign (by giving notice of resignation to the parties and any other arbitrators) if—
  (a) the parties consent to the resignation,
  (b) the arbitrator has a contractual right to resign in the circumstances,
  (c) the arbitrator's appointment is challenged under rule 10 or 12,
  (d) the parties disapply or modify rule 34(1) (expert opinions) after the arbitrator is appointed, or
  (e) the Outer House has authorised the resignation.

(2) The Outer House may authorise a resignation only if satisfied, on an application by the arbitrator, that it is reasonable for the arbitrator to resign.

(3) The Outer House's determination of an application for resignation is final.

DEFINITIONS

"arbitrator": ss.4, 31(1)
"Outer House": s.31(1)
"notice": r.83

STATUS

R15–01 This is a mandatory rule so the parties cannot disapply or vary it (see s.8).

MODEL LAW

R15–02 The Model Law has no direct equivalent of r.15 but addresses part of it in art.14.

COMMENTARY

R15–03 Rule 15 must be read with rr.16(1)(c) and 73(2)(b) which deal with the consequences of resignation, including the potential liability of an arbitrator to the parties in respect of having resigned. Given the potentially openended liability of the arbitrator in respect of having resigned, it is strongly recommended that an arbitrator does not resign without having either (a) agreed with the parties the exclusion of liability in respect of the resignation; or (b) obtained from the court authorisation to resign under the procedure in r.15(1)(e).

Rule 15(1)

Viewed purely as a matter of contract, in accepting an appointment the arbitrator has contracted (a tripartite contract) to provide a service to the parties and is therefore bound to do so, subject to the applicable provisions of the law of contract, e.g. concerning rescission, termination, etc. **R15–04**

However, under the old common law it was always accepted that an arbitrator was, owing to his quasi-judicial position, in a different position to a plumber who fails or refuses to carry out a repair. Thus an arbitrator was permitted to resign if he showed valid reasons beyond a mere wish to resign (described as "caprice") (*Marshall v Edinburgh & Glasgow Railway Co* (1853) 15 D. 603). What amounted to "valid" reasons remained unclear. The approach of the common law was coloured by the context in which the issue of resignation typically arose. The issue tended to arise where a party sought judicial review of an arbitrator's inaction and an order of implement requiring him to proceed under pain of civil imprisonment. This made the court reluctant to scrutinise too critically the reasons for resignation, with Lord President Inglis in *Forbes v Underwood* (1886) 13 R. 465 at 469–470 approving an observation in *Marshall*: **R15–05**

> "The Court will not probably scan the objections critically when they occur, as the leaning of the law must be to liberate a conscientious man from a duty which he feels, on reasons satisfactory to himself, he cannot discharge with propriety."

Under the 2010 Act, however, judicial review and imprisonment are no longer competent (s.13) and the context in which the above observations were made no longer applies. Instead the Act provides statutory grounds for resignation which are intended to be exclusive. Unless one or other of these grounds is satisfied, the authors submit that a resignation is invalid and ineffective. Four of the grounds require no court intervention while the fifth ground does require the authorisation of the court. While r.16(2) appears to envisage resignation other than under r.15, it is suggested that it would undermine the aim of r.15 and its apparently comprehensive nature if the common law relating to resignation was still thought to exist. See further the commentary on r.16(2) at paras R16–08 to R16–13. **R15–06**

The following comments on r.15 reflect the fact that there are two separate, albeit closely related, issues for consideration by the arbitrator and the parties: first, can or should the arbitrator be released from his obligations and responsibilities and, second, if so, what consequences should follow? The latter issue, which includes arbitrators' fees and expenses and liability is also dealt with in the commentary on rr.16 and 73. **R15–07**

Rule 15(1)(a)

R15–08 Given the tripartite relationship between the arbitrator and the parties, and given the fundamental principle of party autonomy, i.e. that the arbitration "belongs" to the parties, it is self-evident that if they consent to the resignation, the arbitrator can be released from his obligations (subject, of course, to the provisions of r.16 below).

R15–09 It is likely that, in practice, the institutional rules agreed by the parties, whether in their arbitration agreement or subsequently, will provide the necessary consent. Given that this ground does not require the intervention of the court and the consequent delay and expense, an arbitrator who wishes to resign should always consider obtaining the consent of the parties as a primary basis for resignation. In doing so, however, the arbitrator should be conscious of both his claim for fees and expenses and his potential liability for resignation under r.73(2)(b). An agreement with the parties should, ideally, deal with both of those matters so that there is a "clean break" between the parties and the arbitrator and no doubt as to where anyone stands on those matters.

Rule 15(1)(b)

R15–10 If the parties' agreement with the arbitrator provides for resignation in certain circumstances, then the arbitrator has a contractual right to resign (subject, of course, to the provisions of r.16 below). There is, arguably, an overlap with r.15(1)(a) in that such contractual provisions constitute advance consent. The agreement referred to here is likely to be found in the institutional rules agreed by the parties, whether in their arbitration agreement or subsequently.

R15–11 If an arbitrator has a duty to make his award within a specific time limit he should ensure that his terms and conditions allow him to resign on the grounds of injury or ill health that prevent him from carrying out his arbitral duties.

Rule 15(1)(c)

R15–12 Faced with a challenge to the arbitrator under rr.10 or 12, and taking appropriate account of r.24(1)(c), an arbitrator may choose to resign rather than prolonging the matter (subject, of course, to the provisions of r.16, below). This is a matter for that individual's judgment and often involves striking a difficult balance, even before r.16 is considered.

R15–13 As a general rule, unmeritorious challenges to arbitrators are to be discouraged since otherwise a party might use the challenge procedure to delay or even derail the arbitral proceedings and this is not acceptable and cannot be tolerated (inter alia s.1(a) and rr.24 and 25 apply); it follows that for an arbitrator to resign in a knee-jerk response to any challenge cannot be

Rule 15(1)(d)

This is necessary because the arbitrator might otherwise be forced into a position of deciding matters over which they have no professional competence, without the benefit of an expert opinion on such matters when they agreed to act on the basis that they could obtain such an opinion. **R15–14**

To expect an arbitrator to make a quasi-judicial decision in such circumstances is clearly unfair on that individual (as acknowledged at common law in *Forbes v Underwood* (1886) 13 R. 465) but, perhaps more importantly, is to undermine the entire process. While it has hitherto been the practice in Scotland for non-lawyer arbitrators to rely on outside legal advice on legal issues, in England and internationally arbitrators are, in general, expected to deal with all the issues before them; if they have doubts about their capability to accept the appointment, they should not do so. Anecdotal evidence in London suggests that the taking of external legal advice by arbitrators is rare, whereas the taking by legally-qualified arbitrators of expert advice on welding, concrete, sub-sea oilfield equipment, etc. is commonplace. **R15–15**

It is, however, possible (even relatively common) that the complexion of a case changes over time so what starts as a dispute over issue X becomes transmuted (e.g. after submissions of statement of claim and of defence) into a dispute over issue Y and it may well be that the arbitrator is eminently qualified and experienced to deal with issue X but is less so with issue Y and therefore might require expert advice as envisaged by r.34. **R15–16**

Rule 15(1)(e) and (2)

If the Outer House receives an application by the arbitrator, it follows that none of the requirements in r.15(1)(a)–(b) will have been met; in practice it will follow that one or both of the parties has refused or declined to accept the resignation or to grant immunity from liability arising out of the resignation. This gives rise to three principal considerations: **R15–17**

(i) if neither party accepts the resignation then the authors submit that the court must be loth, and must find exceptional circumstances, to authorise it; one obvious possibility is where the parties agree on some procedural matter(s) which the arbitrator finds wholly unacceptable but that is a rare occurrence since it is difficult to envisage circumstances where the difference of views as to procedure is sufficient to trigger resignation;

(ii) if one party accepts the resignation but the other does not, there is a significant practical difficulty in that whatever decision is made will upset one of the parties; however, if the arbitrator is not permitted to resign, the party willing to accept their resignation will be compelled to continue the arbitration with an arbitrator it wishes taken off the case. Conversely, if the court authorises the resignation, the replacement arbitrator will, prima facie, be unacceptable to neither party which might well prove the lesser of two evils;

(iii) the effect of r.16 will inevitably be critical.

R15–18 The DAC Report said this about circumstances where a resignation might be reasonable:

> "115. ... [T]he arbitrator may (reasonably) not be prepared to adopt a procedure agreed by the parties (i.e. under Clause 34) during the course of an arbitration, taking the view that his duty under Clause 33 [equivalent to r.24] conflicts with their suggestions (the relationship between the duty of arbitrators in Clause 33 and the freedom of the parties in Clause 34, is discussed in more detail below). Again, an arbitration may drag on for far longer than could reasonably have been expected when the appointment was accepted, resulting in an unfair burden on the arbitrator. In circumstances where the Court was persuaded that it was reasonable for the arbitrator to resign, it seems only right that the Court should be able to grant appropriate relief."

R15–19 The application for authorisation to resign is made to the Outer House by petition (or note) in the style contained in Form 14.4 of the RCS (RCS rr.100.5, 14.4 and 15.2). The requirements for the petition are set out in r.14.4 (or for the note in r.15.2) of the RCS together with the need to:

(i) aver why it is reasonable that his resignation should be authorised;
(ii) require service or intimation on the parties to the arbitration, and any other members of the tribunal.

R15–20 If a shorter period of notice is required, then this should also be craved in the petition and supported by averments in the petition. Together with the petition the applicant should lodge with the Court of Session:

(i) as a production, any written arbitration agreement or other agreement or other document by virtue of which the time limit is imposed;
(ii) the written statements of case and defence in the arbitration (the pleadings);
(iii) the bundle of court documents known as the process (see RCS rr.4.3, 4.4).

Inventories of any supporting productions should be intimated to the other parties, including the members of the tribunal, on whom the petition is served.

On the lodging of the above, and the enrolment of the motion, the court will make a first order for service on the other party or parties to the arbitration, and the members of the tribunal and anyone else who has an interest to allow such persons to lodge answers opposing the petition if they wish within a certain time (r.14(1)(a) and RCS r.100.5). Typically, this will be 21 days from the date of service or intimation. Therefore it is advised that if a shorter period is required the motion should make a specific request for that period. The period for answers should be sufficient to enable the arbitrator or tribunal concerned to make representations in their answers. **R15–21**

After the end of the period for answers, whether answers have been lodged or not, the petitioner should enrol a motion to have the court determine the petition, with or without a hearing as may be appropriate in the circumstances (RCS r.100.5(5)). If answers have been lodged there will *probably* have to be a hearing. **R15–22**

The expenses of the application will not be included in the "arbitration expenses" (see the commentary to r.59, below) but will fall to be dealt with by the court rather than the tribunal. **R15–23**

Rule 16: Liability etc. of arbitrator when tenure ends M

16.—(1) Where an arbitrator's tenure ends, the Outer House may, on an application by any party or the arbitrator concerned, make such order as it thinks fit—
  (a) about the arbitrator's entitlement (if any) to fees and expenses,
  (b) about the repaying of fees or expenses already paid to the arbitrator,
  (c) where the arbitrator has resigned, about the arbitrator's liability in respect of acting as an arbitrator.
(2) The Outer House must, when considering whether to make an order in relation to an arbitrator who has resigned, have particular regard to whether the resignation was made in accordance with rule 15.
(3) The Outer House's determination of an application for an order is final.

DEFINITIONS

"arbitrator": ss.4, 31(1)
"fees and expenses": rr.59, 60
"notice": r.83
"Outer House": s.31(1)
"resigned": r.15
"tenure": r.9

STATUS

This is a mandatory rule so the parties cannot disapply or vary it (see s.8). **R16–01**

MODEL LAW

R16–02 The Model Law makes no provision for the consequences of an arbitrator's tenure ceasing.

COMMENTARY

R16–03 As with r.15, r.16 is closely related to r.73 (immunity of tribunal). As stated above, r.9 is a summary of the five ways an arbitrator's tenure can end: (a) the arbitrator becomes ineligible to act as an arbitrator (r.4); (b) the tribunal revokes the arbitrator's appointment (r.10); (c) the arbitrator is removed by the parties, a third party or by the Outer House (rr.11, 12); (d) the Outer House dismisses the tribunal of which the arbitrator forms part (see r.13); or (e) the arbitrator resigns (see r.15) or dies (see r.76).

R16–04 If an arbitrator's tenure ends in one of the five ways described above, there will be consequential matters to be attended to. Rule 16(1) identifies two of these, namely (1) the arbitrator's entitlement to fees and expenses; and (2) the arbitrator's liability in damages in respect of acting as an arbitrator. While the word "damages" is not expressed in r.16, having regard to the distinction drawn in the rule between fees and expenses on the one hand and "liability" on the other hand, the latter must be taken as meaning a liability in damages. Rule 16 empowers the court to make orders about the arbitrator's entitlement to fees and expenses in respect of all five types of termination of tenure. Perhaps because of the unlikelihood of there being liability where termination occurs by means (a) to (d), the court's power to make orders about the arbitrator's liability occurs only where the arbitrator has resigned. There is also no appeal against the court's decision on the arbitrator's liability for damages. For the reasons set out in para.R16–20, the authors submit that the absence of a right of appeal in respect of a decision on liability of an arbitrator is incompatible with the ECHR.

Rule 16(1)(a) and (b)

R16–05 Rule 16 has a number of different purposes. The first relates to recovery of an arbitrator's fees and expenses. Where tenure has terminated by any of the five means, the usual route for the arbitrator to obtain payment of fees and expenses from the parties, namely withholding the tribunal's award on expenses under r.56, will not be available. To cater for this situation, r.16 allows the arbitrator to apply instead to the court to make an order as to their entitlement for fees and expenses and for payment of those fees and expenses by one or both of the parties. The arbitrator's entitlement to fees and expenses derives from r.60 and therefore it is suggested that in dealing with an application by an arbitrator the court applies r.60, paying particular attention to the provisions of r.60(3), (4) and (5). For further details on the provisions, see the commentary on r.60. This is consistent with the court's discretion under r.16 to "make such order as it thinks fit". While that is a broad discretion it is not, in the authors' view, unfettered. In particular it must be exercised having regard to the purposes of r.16 and the founding principles of s.1, namely:

"(a) that the object of arbitration is to resolve disputes, fairly, impartially and without unnecessary delay or expense,
(b) that parties should be free to agree how to resolve disputes subject only to such safeguards as are necessary in the public interest,
(c) that the court should not intervene in an arbitration except as provided by this Act."

The provisions of r.60 can be seen as giving effect to these founding principles in the area of arbitrators' fees and expenses. In addition, r.78 may require to be applied.

R16–06 The possibility of an arbitrator being ordered to make repayment may also cover, for example, the standard practice of the arbitrator taking in deposits by way of security against future fees but having to refund the parties to the extent that fees have not been earned. It is self-evident that the arbitrator should not profit from the cessation of his tenure.

R16–07 The taking of such security may not presently be common in Scotland but is standard practice elsewhere. Typically, the CIArb's Practice Guideline No.3 ("Guidelines for Arbitrators as to How to Formulate their Terms of Remuneration") states at para.5.6.2:

"The most appropriate form of security may be a cash sum to be lodged with a stakeholder, such as the arbitrators' solicitor(s), or in a special deposit account at the arbitrators' bank(s), on terms that it may be drawn upon on the arbitrators' signatures alone. The Institute provides facilities for the holding of cash security."

Rule 16(1)(c) and (2)

R16–08 A second purpose of r.16 relates to the arbitrator's liability for damages in respect of acting as an arbitrator. For reasons that are not clear, r.16 addresses this only where the arbitrator has resigned and not where he has been removed or the tribunal dismissed. This raises the issue of an arbitrator's immunity. There is a general principle (applicable in most (but not all) common law jurisdictions but in few civil law ones) that the arbitrator is immune from suit by the parties but this immunity is restricted in certain circumstances; see r.73 (mandatory), below. The restrictions in r.73 are where (a) the arbitrator's act or omission is shown to have been in bad faith; or (b) the liability arises from the arbitrator's resignation itself. The latter can involve significant liability of the arbitrator.

R16–09 Consider the position part-way through an arbitration where the arbitrator resigns. The parties will, at that point, have expended time and resources, possibly significant, in pursuing the case but, in effect, will have to start again, at least in part, with consequent inevitable delay and additional costs. Of course, much of the documentary materials could be reused and taken over by a replacement arbitrator but, even with a full transcript, any hearing that had taken place would be wasted. In any event, there will be inevitable costs as the replacement arbitrator is brought up-to-speed and there will also inevitably be some delay.

R16–10 The duration of delay and quantum of additional costs will differ according to when the tenure ends; in broad terms, if that end is immediately after appointment of the arbitrator, then it is likely that there will in fact be minimal delay and little, if any, additional costs. Conversely, the worst point would likely be after the close of proceedings (including a hearing) but before the arbitrator starts to draft his/her award; in such a case, the delay and additional costs could both be significant.

R16–11 As with the subparas (a) and (b), the broad discretion given to the court is not, in the authors' view, unfettered. In particular, it must be exercised having regard to the founding principles of s.1 set out above. A further clue to the proper approach under r.16(1)(c) is given in the Explanatory Notes to the Act for r.73, which state at para.240:

> "Rule 16(1)(c) on the resignation of the arbitrator provides protection for a resigning arbitrator by allowing the court to grant relief from liability if it is satisfied that in all the circumstances it was reasonable for the arbitrator to resign."

Therefore, if the arbitrator's conduct is covered by either the immunity from liability under r.73(1) or takes place with the consent of the parties under r.15(1)(a) including preferably, but not essentially, the agreement of the parties with the arbitrator to extend the immunity to liability arising from a resignation, it is suggested that the court must give effect to such statutory or impliedly or expressly agreed immunities.

R16–12 Alternatively, if the court is considering a situation where there is no immunity, then it must still apply the founding principles and the approach set out in the explanatory note.

R16–13 It is suggested that if a resignation has been authorised by the court under r.15(1)(e), and there was no material change of circumstances between the authorisation and the notice of resignation, then, the authors submit, the court must uphold immunity in respect of the resignation that it had itself authorised. Similarly, if for some reason the arbitrator has not applied for court authorisation and has purported to resign under r.15(1)(b), (c), or (d), then if the court finds those grounds of resignation to have been satisfied, again, the authors submit, it should uphold immunity in respect of the resignation. Rule 15 forms an aspect of the parties' arbitral agreement to which the parties agreed when they agreed to resolve their dispute by an arbitration seated in Scotland (s.7). That is something which the court must respect under the founding principles in s.1. It is difficult to envisage any situation where the court finds there to be grounds for resignation under r.15 where the arbitrator was not entitled to full immunity from liability for such a resignation. In this respect, the requirement of the court to respect the agreement of the parties concerning resignation applies to r.16 as much as s.25 of the 1996 Act.

Rule 16(1)—Procedure

An application by either arbitrator or party is made to the Outer House by petition (or note) in the style contained in Form 14.4 of the RCS (RCS rr.100.5, 14.4 and 15.2). The requirements for the petition are set out in r.14.4 (or the note in r.15.2) of the RCS together with the need to: **R16–14**

  (i) aver why the order is necessary;
 (ii) aver the circumstances in which the prerequisites for an application in r.16(1)(a), (b), or (c) are satisfied;
(iii) aver the satisfaction of those requirements;
(iv) aver the reasons why the usual period of 21 days for answers should be dispensed with (if that is necessary);
 (v) require service or intimation on the other parties to the arbitration, and members of the tribunal.

If a shorter period of notice is required, then this should also be craved in the petition. Upon lodging the petition (or note) the applicant must enrol a motion for intimation and service of the petition or note (RCS r.100.5(3)). **R16–15**

Together with the petition, the applicant should lodge with the Court of Session: **R16–16**

  (i) as a production, any written arbitration agreement or other agreement or other document by virtue of which, the time limit is imposed;
 (ii) the written statements of case and defence in the arbitration (the pleadings);
(iii) the bundle of court documents known as the process (see RCS rr.4.3, 4.4).

Inventories of any supporting productions should be intimated to the other parties, including the members of the tribunal, on whom the petition is served.

On the lodging of the above, and the enrolment of the motion, the court will make a first order for service on the other party or parties to the arbitration, and the members of the tribunal and anyone else who has an interest to allow such persons to lodge answers opposing the petition if they wish within a certain time (r.14(1)(a) (in respect of tribunal members) and **R16–17**

RCS r.100.5(3)). Typically, this will be 21 days from the date of service or intimation. Therefore, it is advised that if a shorter period is required the motion should make a specific request for that period. The period for answers should be sufficient to enable the arbitrator or tribunal concerned to make representations in their answers.

R16–18 After the end of the period for answers, whether answers have been lodged or not, the petitioner should enrol a motion. That may require the court to determine the petition (or note) with or without a hearing as may be appropriate in the circumstances (RCS r.100.5(5)). If the application is for an order for payment of fees and expenses, there may, depending on whether there is agreement by the parties and arbitrator, have to be a remit to the Auditor of the Court of Session: see r.60(3) and (4) and the commentary thereon.

R16–19 The expenses of the petition or note will not be included in the "arbitration expenses" (see the commentary to r.59 below) but will fall to be dealt with by the court rather than the tribunal.

Rule 16(3)

R16–20 Section 25(5) of the 1996 Act contemplates an appeal against the court's order but r.16 allows no such appeal. While a policy driver underlying this Act is the limiting of the grounds of appeal to the court (see s.1(c)), an issue of natural justice arises in that the arbitrator's livelihood, even solvency (consider a major arbitration where the parties have racked up substantial costs of which £1,000,000 will be wasted as a consequence of the arbitrator's resignation; if he is made liable for that amount, he could well face bankruptcy) may be at stake in a context where he has no avenue for appeal. We submit that the exclusion of any right of appeal by either party or by the arbitrator on the issue of liability of the arbitrator is not a legitimate aim or, even if it was, involves a disproportionate response and so falls foul of both art.6(1) ECHR and of art.1 of the First Protocol thereto. See para.S1–17.

Rule 17: Reconstitution of tribunal D

17.—(1) Where an arbitrator's tenure ends, the tribunal must be reconstituted—

    (a) in accordance with the procedure used to constitute the original tribunal, or

    (b) where that procedure fails, in accordance with rules 6 and 7.

(2) It is for the reconstituted tribunal to decide the extent, if any, to which previous proceedings (including any award made, appointment by or other act done by the previous tribunal) should stand.

(3) The reconstituted tribunal's decision does not affect a party's right to object or appeal on any ground which arose before the tribunal made its decision.

DEFINITIONS

"arbitration agreement": ss.4, 31(1)
"arbitrator": ss.4, 31(1)
"tenure": r.9

STATUS

This is a default rule so it is open to the parties to modify it, agree **R17–01**
something different or disapply it completely (see s.9).

MODEL LAW

The Model Law makes no equivalent provision. **R17–02**

COMMENTARY

Although this is a default rule, it is inconceivable that the parties should **R17–03**
agree to disapply it in its entirety without any alternative. Typically, LCIA
art.11 places the responsibility for replacing the arbitrator(s) on the LCIA
Court.

Rule 17(1)

If the parties have agreed to arbitrate then, absent clear agreement to the **R17–04**
contrary, they are under a binding contractual obligation to do so therefore
the tribunal must, as a matter of law, be reconstituted. Section 10 denies
(with exceptions) each party (individually) access to the court in respect of
the substance of the dispute.

Rule 17(1)(a)

This is wholly logical since the procedure forms part of a binding con- **R17–05**
tractual obligation irrespective of whether rr.2–7 apply or some alternative
rules apply. In contrast, LCIA art.11.1 gives the court discretion as to
whether to follow the original procedure or not.

Rule 17(1)(b)

This is also wholly logical; however, an apparent anomaly arises in that if **R17–06**
the parties have both (a) either agreed alternatives to, or have wholly disapplied, rr.6 and/or 7, and (b) have agreed, e.g. by failing to vary or disapply
it, that r.17 shall apply, then they are forced back in to rr.6 and 7 which they
had previously agreed not to apply. The anomaly resolves itself in that
agreeing to apply r.17 brings with it the agreement to apply rr.6 and 7 in the
specified circumstances.

Rule 17(2)

R17–07 This rule purports to gives a new tribunal wide discretion but that discretion is far less wide than first appears. While we might conceivably envisage the new tribunal starting the arbitration from the very beginning, s.1(a) and rr.24(1)(c) and 25 reflect, in this context, simple common sense in that the new tribunal must endeavour to make the transition as near to seamless as is practicable and, therefore, to re-use as much of what had gone before as possible. In practice, this will normally mean re-using all written submissions, correspondence, expert reports and the like but more difficulty arises in respect of (a) witnesses, and (b) oral argument:

> (a) If witnesses are not examined/cross-examined and reliance placed solely on witness statements, it is likely that these can be re-used but if there had been any actual appearance by witnesses there is no substitute, not even a full transcript, for their physical examination since their demeanour, particularly in responding to cross-examination or tribunal questioning, may be fundamental to assessing their credibility;
>
> (b) While oral argument can be transcribed, practical experience shows that such is not fully sufficient to appreciate the strengths of the oral presentations, the interplay between opposing counsel often being a key factor.

R17–08 Concerning assessment of credibility, in *Discain Project Services Ltd v Opecprime Developments Ltd* [2001] EWHC 450 (TCC), H.H. Judge Seymour QC said (at [50]):

> "As was obvious, Mr X's evidence was extremely economical as an account of what had actually happened to the extent of being positively misleading. Mr X was not, in my judgment, a very proficient purveyor of untruths. His tactic to deal with the unwelcome experience of cross-examination was to give his evidence *quite unnecessarily loudly. He was virtually shouting.* No explanation for such behaviour was offered or emerged" (authors' emphasis added).

No transcript can capture this degree of "flavour" of a witness.

Rule 17(3)

R17–09 This is, the authors submit, self-evident.

Rule 18: Arbitrators nominated in arbitration agreements **D**

18. Any provision in an arbitration agreement which specifies who is to be an arbitrator ceases to have effect in relation to an arbitration when the specified individual's tenure as an arbitrator for that arbitration ends.

DEFINITIONS

"arbitration agreement": ss.4, 31(1)
"arbitrator": ss.4, 31(1)
"tenure": r.9

STATUS

This is a default rule so it is open to the parties to modify it, agree **R18–01**
something different or disapply it completely (see s.9).

MODEL LAW

The Model Law makes no equivalent provision. **R18–02**

COMMENTARY

This is, the authors submit, self-evident. **R18–03**

Part 2

Jurisdiction of Tribunal

Rule 19: Power of tribunal to rule on own jurisdiction M

19. The tribunal may rule on—
   (a) whether there is a valid arbitration agreement (or, in the case of a statutory arbitration, whether the enactment providing for arbitration applies to the dispute),
   (b) whether the tribunal is properly constituted, and
   (c) what matters have been submitted to arbitration in accordance with the arbitration agreement.

DEFINITIONS

"arbitration": ss.2(1), (2), 31(1)
"arbitration agreement": ss.4, 31(1)
"statutory arbitration": ss.16(1), 31(1)
"tribunal": ss.2(1), 31(1)

STATUS

Rule 19 is mandatory so cannot be disapplied, or modified in any way, by **R19–01**
the parties

MODEL LAW

Article 16 of the Model Law is in substantially similar terms **R19–02**

COMMENTARY

Introductory

R19–03 The power of an arbitral tribunal to rule on questions relating to its jurisdiction is central to any modern arbitration regime. While an arbitrator could rule on his own jurisdiction at common law (*Dumbarton Water Commissioners v Lord Blantyre* (1884) 12 R. 115, 119; *Donaldson's Hospital Trustees v Esslemont*, 1925 S.C. 199, 205–206 per L.P. Clyde; and *McCosh v Moore* (1903) 5 F. 946), the explicit recognition of this principle in r.19 is necessary both to eliminate any doubt and to be consistent with art.16 of the Model Law which also addresses closely-related principle of separability (see s.5 above).

R19–04 In contrast to s.7 of the 1996 Act, allowing the parties to contract out of the separability principle, r.19 and s.5 follow the Model Law in making them mandatory. The present authors see the mandatory nature of r.19 as fundamental so that arbitration is not derailed by recalcitrant parties, whether by agreement or otherwise. The policy memorandum (at para.136) noted that discussions with stakeholders had suggested that r.19 introduced "an important new power for arbitrators which will save a great deal of time and therefore expense", i.e. consistent with the principle expressed in s.1(a). Since r.19 is mandatory it cannot be ousted by the parties purporting under s.9(4)(b) to choose a foreign procedural law, which does not recognise the principle of "competence-competence", to govern the arbitration.

R19–05 Rule 19 is consistent with s.10, which (following art.II(3) of the New York Convention) requires that a court must sist legal proceedings if a party can show that the dispute is covered by an arbitration agreement, unless the court is satisfied that the arbitration agreement is void, unenforceable or incapable of being performed. The commentary on s.10 notes that this principle is a key feature of the Act and, because party autonomy and limited court intervention are among the guiding principles on which the Act is based, it might be thought that if there is at least an arguable case that an arbitration agreement exists, the court should sist any proceedings and let the arbitral tribunal determine questions relating to whether the agreement exists and whether it is rendered void, etc. by any element set out in s.10.

R19–06 This is certainly the approach adopted by at least some courts in considering the interaction of arts 8 and 16 of the Model Law (see Kaplan J in the Hong Kong case of *Fung Sang Trading Ltd v Kai Sun Sea Products & Food Co Ltd* [1992] A.D.R.L.J. 93 at 101). It is also consistent with the approach of the pre-Act common law in relation to the now incompetent applications to interdict arbitrations on the grounds of lack of jurisdiction (see the commentary on s.10).

R19–07 What is significant is that r.19 is mandatory and s.30 of the 1996 Act is not. The present authors suggest that "mandatory" is the correct approach, preventing errant or inexperienced parties entrusting all such matters of jurisdiction to the court where such would be inconsistent with s.1(c).

Rule 19(a), (b) and (c) set out what issues of jurisdiction may be decided **R19–08** by the tribunal whereas art.16 of the Model Law omits any delineation of "jurisdiction". Rule 19 does not specify whether its 3 part list (a), (b) and (c) is exhaustive or not. However, s.30(1) of the 1996 Act was itself based on art.16(1) of the Model Law (DAC Report, para.139) which is not exhaustive. Given that origin, applying s.1(c), and by analogy, Lord Hoffmann's analysis in *Fiona Trust v Privalov* [2007] All E.R. 951; [2007] UKHL 40 at [5] to [8], the authors submit that on a proper interpretation r.19 is not exhaustive.

This means, for example, that the tribunal can decide issues of arbitr- **R19–09** ability even though on one interpretation "validity" of the arbitration agreement does not include whether the matters covered by it are arbitrable.

Rule 19(a)—Valid arbitration agreement

The tribunal may rule on the question of whether there is a valid arbi- **R19–10** tration agreement between the parties to the arbitration. This would include deciding whether the agreement is undermined by the invalidity of the main contract and whether a party is no longer bound by the arbitration agreement because it has been abandoned (see *Chimimport Plc v G D'Alesio SAS (The Paola d'Alesio)* [1994] 2 Lloyd's Rep. 366), or the other party has acted so as to repudiate it (see *ABB Lummus Global Ltd v Keppel Fels Ltd* [1999] 2 Lloyd's Rep. 24). Given that the Act embraces the principle of separability, it would be inconsistent for the invalidity of the main agreement to necessarily invalidate the arbitration clause.

However, the English courts have in the past suggested that, if the main **R19–11** agreement is so fundamentally void as to be incapable of legal recognition, an arbitration clause cannot be allowed to have a separate existence (*O'Callaghan v Coral Racing Ltd*, *The Times*, November 26, 1998). Yet, except in such rare cases, the invalidity of the main agreement will have no effect on the validity of the arbitration clause, so that the arbitral tribunal will have jurisdiction to rule as to whether the main agreement is or is not valid and to determine the dispute accordingly (*Vee Networks Ltd v Econet Wireless Ltd* [2005] 1 Lloyd's Rep. 192; see Hew R. Dundas, "Challenging Awards and Arbitrators: a Losing Game ?" (2005) 71 Arbitration 362 for a short discussion of this case). In *Fiona Trust v Privalov* [2007] All E.R. 951; [2007] UKHL 40 the issue of whether or not the main contracts had been procured by bribery was left to the determination of the arbitral tribunal appointed by the arbitration agreement in the main contracts.

Article 16 of the Model Law refers to the tribunal dealing with objections **R19–12** as to the "existence" of the arbitration agreement, and in certain jurisdictions that has been interpreted as meaning that the tribunal rather than the court should determine the question of jurisdiction even where a party contends that he never entered into the agreement in the first place (see Kaplan J in the Hong Kong case of *Fung Sang Trading Ltd v Kai Sun Sea*

Products & Food Co Ltd [1992] A.D.R.L.J. 93 at 101; and Henry J in *Rio Algom Ltd v Sammi Steel Co* (1991) 47 C.P.C. 251 at 256 (Ontario)).

R19–13 Arbitral tribunals can be expected to rule on such matters as whether an alleged agreement is void for uncertainty (*Mangistaumunaigaz Oil Production Association v United World Trading Inc* [1995] 1 Lloyd's Rep. 617); whether an individual can properly be regarded to be a party to it (*Hussmann (Europe) Ltd v Al Ameen Development Trade Co* [2000] 2 Lloyd's Rep. 83); whether its terms in fact oblige the parties to arbitrate (*Lobb Partnership Ltd v Aintree Racecourse Ltd* [2000] B.L.R. 65); whether the agreement has been frustrated (*Sumitomo Heavy Industries Ltd v Oil and Natural Gas Commission* [1994] 2 Lloyd's Rep. 45); and whether the conditions for the operation of an arbitration clause have been met (*Sonatrach Petroleum Corp (BVI) v Ferrell International Ltd* [2002] 1 All E.R. (Comm) 627). See the commentary on ss.4 and 10(1)(e).

R19–14 A question arises as to what law the tribunal should apply in determining the question of validity, including the capacity of a party. That will normally be the law applicable to the substance of the contract, which of course may not be Scots law; see the commentary on s.6.

R19–15 However, if it is asserted that the agreement is invalid because a party lacked capacity, some other law might govern that issue, quite possibly the law of the place of incorporation of that party or of the place where its central management and control is located.

R19–16 Equally, if the dispute is not arbitrable under Scots law, a tribunal might feel obliged to rule that the agreement is invalid even though it might be arbitrable under the law governing the agreement (see the commentary to ss.6 and 30 above). The English courts favour the tribunal having the power to find jurisdiction absent in such cases (see *Azov Shipping Co v Baltic Shipping Co (No.3)* [1999] 1 Lloyd's Rep. 68) and a similar approach has been taken under the Model Law (see *International Civil Aviation Organisation v Tripal Systems Ltd* (1998) XXIII YCA 226 Supreme Court of Quebec).

R19–17 Rule 19(a) provides that, in the case of a statutory arbitration, the tribunal may rule on whether the relevant enactment applies to the dispute, in this respect echoing s.96(2) of the 1996 Act and reversing the common law position in *Hiskett v G & G Wilson*, 2003 S.L.T. 58 and *Love v Montgomerie* 1982 S.L.T. (Sh. Ct) 60. While r.19(a) does not refer to the validity of the enactment, it would be odd, if faced with a submission that the enactment was invalid (e.g. Scottish agricultural lease legislation that could not be construed to be compatible with the ECHR), for the tribunal not to be able to deal with it. In such a situation, it might, however, be prudent for the tribunal to refer the issue to a court under r.22 so the court could make a binding final decision.

Rule 19(b)—Whether the tribunal has been properly constituted

The tribunal may rule as to whether it has been properly constituted. This **R19–18** would obviously include issues such as whether each arbitrator has been validly appointed and whether the tribunal takes the shape agreed by the parties, or stipulated by rules, contractual or statutory, which might apply in default of agreement. In *Minermet SpA Milan v Luckyfield Shipping Corp* [2004] 2 Lloyd's Rep. 348, while the arbitration clause provided that each party should appoint an arbitrator and that the two arbitrators should then appoint a third, it continued that if a party did not appoint an arbitrator within 14 days of being notified that the other party had appointed an arbitrator, the single arbitrator could then proceed with the reference alone. The latter scenario duly unfolded and the arbitrator ruled that that he had jurisdiction to determine the dispute.

Rule 19(c)—Extent of matters submitted to arbitration

This empowers the tribunal to determine the scope of the arbitration **R19–19** agreement, the scope of the disputed matter that has been submitted to it and whether the disputed matter falls within that scope.

This may involve the tribunal having to determine the law governing the **R19–20** arbitration agreement in order to assess its validity, e.g. apply the criteria set out in s.6.

Rule 20: Objections to tribunal's jurisdiction M

20.—(1) Any party may object to the tribunal on the ground that the tribunal does not have, or has exceeded, its jurisdiction in relation to any matter.

(2) An objection must be made—
- **(a) before, or as soon as is reasonably practicable after, the matter to which the objection relates is first raised in the arbitration, or**
- **(b) where the tribunal considers that circumstances justify a later objection, by such later time as it may allow,**

but, in any case, an objection may not be made after the tribunal makes its last award.

(3) If the tribunal upholds an objection it must—
- **(a) end the arbitration in so far as it relates to a matter over which the tribunal has ruled it does not have jurisdiction, and**
- **(b) set aside any provisional or part award already made in so far as the award relates to such a matter.**

(4) The tribunal may—
- **(a) rule on an objection independently from dealing with the subject-matter of the dispute, or**
- **(b) delay ruling on an objection until it makes its award on the merits of the dispute (and include its ruling in that award),**

but, where the parties agree which of these courses the tribunal should take, the tribunal must proceed accordingly.

DEFINITIONS

"arbitration": ss.2(1), (2), 31(1)
"dispute": ss.2(1), 31(1)
"party": ss.2(1), 31(1), (2)
"tribunal": ss.2(1), 31(1)

STATUS

R20–01 Rule 20 is mandatory so cannot be disapplied, or modified in any way, by the parties

MODEL LAW

R20–02 Article 16 of the Model Law is in broadly similar terms

COMMENTARY

Rule 20(1)

R20–03 While it would be theoretically possible for a tribunal, at its own instigation, to rule on jurisdictional matters, in practice it will do so upon a party raising the issue. Mirroring art.16(2) of the Model Law (itself mirrored by s.31 of the 1996 Act), the Act provides that a party may raise a jurisdictional objection, whether by claiming that the arbitral tribunal has no jurisdiction over a particular issue or that it has exceeded its jurisdiction. It should be borne in mind that it may be possible for a point of jurisdiction instead to be referred to the Outer House under r.22 (see the commentary below on that rule).

Rule 20(2)—Timing of an objection

R20–04 An objection must be made before or as soon as is reasonably practicable after the matter is first raised in the arbitration. If a party believes from the outset that the tribunal lacks jurisdiction in any of the senses set out in r.19 that objection should be made at that time. However, if that, or that the tribunal proposes to exceed its jurisdiction only during the course of the proceedings, then an objection must be made as soon as reasonably practicable thereafter. See also r.76 (in particular, r.76(1)(d)) which makes wide-ranging provisions of a similar nature.

R20–05 Article 16(2) of the Model Law draws, necessarily, a distinction between an initial objection to jurisdiction and a later plea that the tribunal is exceeding its jurisdiction; this is mirrored in s.31 of the 1996 Act. Under the latter, the former type of objection must be raised not later than the time the party in question takes the first step in the proceedings to contest the merits of any matter in relation to which it challenges the tribunal's jurisdiction. This contrasts with art.16(2)'s requirement that such an objection must be raised no later than the submission of the statement of defence. The DAC (DAC Report, para.140) deliberately avoided the use of such language in the 1996 Act, "since this might give the impression, which we are anxious to dispel, that every arbitration requires some formal pleading or the like".

Both art.6(2) and s.31 of the 1996 Act also provide that a party is not precluded from raising such an objection by the fact that he has appointed, or participated in the appointment of, an arbitrator, but this provision is, perhaps strangely absent from r.20 which is wholly silent on the matter. The authors submit that that absence has no effect since r.20(2) sets out deadlines for the raising of jurisdictional objections which are not affected by, and do not relate to, the appointment process. **R20–06**

An objecting party has two options: (i) to permit the tribunal to be constituted and lodge an immediate r.20 objection; or (ii) to ignore the arbitration until the award is rendered then to challenge it under s.14 and r.67. As a simple practical matter, in almost every case the former is to be preferred. **R20–07**

Given r.20(1)'s reference to a party objecting "to the tribunal", it is clear that no r.20 objection can be made prior to the constitution of the tribunal so any earlier objection cannot be a r.20 one. This does not, of course, prevent any party raising objections before such constitution and, in practice, such a party would be well-advised to do so, possibly even in every item of correspondence. **R20–08**

Even if a party was to approach an individual enquiring as to his availability to accept an appointment as sole arbitrator and, in doing so, stating that one party believed that the tribunal would lack jurisdiction, such would not constitute a r.20 objection either since the tribunal (of one) has not (as this point) been constituted. **R20–09**

Once the tribunal (whether one or three) is constituted, the objection should be raised no later than the point at which the tribunal first addresses the issue of jurisdiction, but it can, of course, be raised earlier. Extending the comment at R20–05 above, practical considerations strongly suggest raising the objection immediately and the authors have difficulty in envisaging circumstances which would suggest any delay. **R20–10**

Furthermore, the objecting party will very likely ask the tribunal to address the disputed jurisdictional question as an early priority. In certain circumstances, the matter might be raised in a preliminary meeting designed to address procedural rather than substantive matters; alternatively, it might be raised during discussions between a party and the tribunal (see *Athletic Union of Constantinople v National Basketball Association* [2002] 1 Lloyd's Rep. 305). Finally, it may be appropriate to deal with the objection as a preliminary issue, whether in correspondence or in a hearing **R20–11**

The foregoing comments would apply equally to the situation where either: (i) a party denies that the tribunal has any jurisdiction whatsoever; or **R20–12**

Arbitration (Scotland) Act 2010

(ii) it is claimed from the outset that the tribunal is being asked to exceed its jurisdiction.

R20–13 Where it becomes apparent that the tribunal might exceed its jurisdiction only after the proceedings get under way, such as where the other party raises in its submissions such matters or where the tribunal itself proposes to examine evidence not connected with the resolution of the dispute submitted to it (see *Report of the UNCITRAL on the work of its eighteenth session*, UN A/40/17, para.155), it is wholly logical to provide that a party must raise its objection as soon as is reasonably practicable after the ground of objection emerges.

R20–14 Rule 20(2)(b) empowers the tribunal to admit a later objection in appropriate circumstances and such an objection may be made by such later time as the tribunal may allow. This is the same power that exists under r.76(2)(c) (see commentary on r.76).

R20–15 No tribunal may entertain a late objection absent justification: is a decision on admission of a late objection capable of review by the court? The authors submit not since, prima facie, s.13 excludes any court involvement in this area unless a challenge could be made under r.67. However, in a r.67 appeal there might be a possibility of seeking to persuade the court that it should consider the appeal on the basis that the lateness was excusable through the circumstances set out in r.76(3).

R20–16 Rule 76 (see commentary below) provides that a party may lose its right to challenge an award if it fails to raise an objection timeously so that a party which is aware of a jurisdictional objection but chooses not to raise it, i.e. letting the arbitration proceed, cannot then challenge the award on the basis of lack of jurisdiction.

R20–17 Equally, while lack or excess of jurisdiction is a ground for refusal to enforce an award (in whole or in part) under s.12(2), s.12(3) makes it clear that the right to contest enforcement on this ground may be lost by virtue of r.76. The position is similar under s.73 of the 1996 Act, and in that context it has been held that even if a party has raised a jurisdictional objection at an appropriate point, he may not challenge the award on the basis of a new jurisdictional objection which it had failed to raise at an appropriate point (*Athletic Union of Constantinople v National Basketball Association* [2002] 1 Lloyd's Rep. 305).

R20–18 On the other hand, in *Primetrade AG v Ythan Ltd (The Ythan)* [2006] 1 Lloyd's Rep. 457, Aikens J. held that a party was not barred from challenging an award under the 1996 Act where a rather similar challenge had been raised before the arbitrator, even though the grounds of challenge in court were slightly different and rather broader.

R20–19 It has been argued that the Model Law is wholly unclear as to the effect of a failure to object on the power to mount a jurisdictional challenge to an award (see Fraser P. Davidson, *International Commercial Arbitration, Scotland and the UNCITRAL Model Law* (Edinburgh: W. Green, 1991) paras 5.6–5.8), and the 2010 Act gives much-needed precision in this regard.

No jurisdictional objection may be made after the final award has been made and, at that point, the objector's only option is to appeal the award under r.67, subject to any time bar imposed by r.76. It may be that the tribunal's exceeding its jurisdiction becomes apparent only when it makes an award. **R20–20**

Rule 20(3)—Effect of upholding an objection

Where a tribunal upholds an objection it must set aside any provisional or part award insofar as it has exceeded its jurisdiction and must end the arbitration insofar as it relates to any matter over which it lacks jurisdiction. There is no counterpart of this provision in either the 1996 Act or the Model Law. **R20–21**

Rule 20(3) envisages the arbitration continuing insofar as it relates to matters which lie within the tribunal's jurisdiction. This is unlikely to occur in practice since practical experience is of cases where there is no jurisdiction at all. **R20–22**

It is logical for the tribunal formally to set such awards aside both because it then becomes clear what the effect of the jurisdictional ruling has been and because that provides a defence to attempted enforcement of the earlier award. **R20–23**

Rule 20(4)—How tribunal may rule on objection

This provision derives from the equivalent art.16(3) of the Model Law (reflected in s.31(4) of the 1996 Act) with the difference that, unlike as in art.16(3), the tribunal must defer to the agreement of the parties on this issue; see also paras R67–23 to R67–24. **R20–24**

The DAC Report points out, at para.146, that, "in some cases it may be simply impracticable to rule on jurisdiction before determining merits". The framers of the Model Law also felt that the tribunal should have this discretion since it would allow it to continue the proceedings where it believed that the raising of an objection was without merit and being employed merely as a delaying tactic (see *Report of the UNCITRAL on the work of its eighteenth session*, UN A/40/17, para.155). **R20–25**

The authors submit that it would be very difficult to challenge the exercise of the tribunal's discretion in this context (see *AOOT Kalmneft v Glencore International AG* [2001] 2 All E.R. (Comm) 577). In exercising that discretion the tribunal will obviously have regard to its duty under r.24(1)(c) to conduct the arbitration without unnecessary delay or expense. **R20–26**

Where a separate ruling is issued, a party may appeal against it under r.21. Where it is made as part of the award on the merits, a party who disagrees with the ruling has to appeal the award under r.67. **R20–27**

The 2010 Act follows the Model Law in referring to a "ruling" in contrast to the 1996 Act which would generate an award on that issue. The DAC Report opined, at para.142, that it was, "unnecessary to introduce the new **R20–28** concept of a preliminary ruling which is somehow different from an award", continuing that this had, "the advantage that awards on jurisdiction will have the benefit of those provisions on awards generally and, if appropriate, may be enforced in the same way as any other award". This leads to the question of what the status of a jurisdictional ruling might be if it is not an award.

R20–29   Under art.16(3) of the Model Law, the tribunal may continue proceedings pending the determination of the appeal; however, that article expressly empowers the tribunal to make an award. While r.20(4) does not expressly provide for an award, (i) ending arbitral proceedings is typically marked by an award (see para.R37–10) and (ii) nowhere in the Act is such a step precluded. Practical considerations, such as the triggering of the period for appeal point strongly in the direction of making such a ruling in the form of an award. For the form and making of an award see r.51.

Rule 21: Appeal against tribunal's ruling on jurisdictional objection M

21.—(1) A party may, no later than 14 days after the tribunal's decision on an objection under rule 20, appeal to the Outer House against the decision.

(2) The tribunal may continue with the arbitration pending determination of the appeal.

(3) The Outer House's decision on the appeal is final.

DEFINITIONS

"arbitration": ss.2(1), (2), 31(1)
"Outer House": s.31(1)
"party": ss.2(1), 31(1), (2)
"tribunal": ss.2(1), 31(1)

STATUS

R21–01   Rule 21 is mandatory so cannot be disapplied, or modified in any way, by the parties

MODEL LAW

R21–02   Article 16(3) of the Model Law provides that if the arbitral tribunal rules as a preliminary question that it has jurisdiction, any party may request, within thirty days after having received notice of that ruling, the court specified in article 6 to decide the matter, which decision shall be subject to no appeal; while such a request is pending, the arbitral tribunal may continue the arbitral proceedings and make an award.

COMMENTARY

A party who disagrees with the tribunal's separate ruling on jurisdiction (i.e. one prior to an award on the merits) must appeal under r.21. **R21–03**

Rule 21(1)—Period for appeal

A party has 14 days from the tribunal's ruling on an objection to appeal to the Outer House. (If the tribunal consists of or contains a Court of Session judge, then the appeal would be to the Inner House—see s.25 above.) The authors submit that this right of appeal does not include any right of appeal against a tribunal's decision that it cannot rule on a jurisdictional objection because it was not timeously raised (see para.R20–15 above). **R21–04**

In the context of the 1996 Act it seems unclear whether there can be an appeal against a tribunal's ruling that it lacks jurisdiction (see *LG Caltex Gas Co Ltd v China National Petroleum Co* [2001] 1 W.L.R. 1892). However, the language of r.21(1) covers an appeal against a decision that the tribunal has no jurisdiction just as much as a decision that it has. Article 16(3) of the Model Law, comparable to r.21, permits an appeal only against a decision that the tribunal has jurisdiction since it was felt inappropriate to compel arbitrators who had ruled that they lacked jurisdiction to continue (see *Report of the UNCITRAL on the work of its eighteenth session*, UN A/40/17, para.163). **R21–05**

It appeared to the Dervaird Committee in 1987 that, if parties thereafter resorted to litigation, one of them might raise the issue of the arbitration agreement and the court might rule that it was binding, so that the parties would have to arbitrate after all (see joint consultative document, Departmental Advisory Committee on Arbitration Law and Scottish Advisory Committee on Arbitration Law, *The UNCITRAL Model Law on International Commercial Arbitration* (1987), p.57). **R21–06**

The period within which an appeal might be brought is very tight, a mere 14 days after the tribunal's decision. The objective is clearly to prevent this aspect of the process delaying the proceedings unduly, but it might be noted that the corresponding period under art.16(3) of the Model Law is 30 days, which was itself regarded as demanding. **R21–07**

The trigger point for the running of the time for appealing is the tribunal's "decision" under r.20(4)(b). If, as is suggested, the decision is in the form of an award, the trigger point will be the "making" of the award under rr.51(3) and 83. **R21–08**

If the decision is not in the form of an award, the trigger point should be the same. Given the emphasis in s.1(a) on fairness in arbitration, the House of Lords ruling on a decision being ineffective until it has been notified to a party (see *R (on the application of Anufrijeva) v Secretary of State for the Home Department* [2003] UKHL 36; [2004] 1 A.C. 604)) and the duty of the tribunal under r 24(1)(b) and (c)(i) to notify the parties of the decision, the **R21–09** authors submit that on a proper construction of r.21(1) the trigger point is the date of notification or service of the tribunal decision to the parties. The date of notification or service of the document would then be ascertained under r.83.

Rule 21(2)

R21-10 Continuation with the arbitration must lie within the tribunal's discretion, exercised in consideration of the fact that an adverse decision by the court would vitiate the award to the applicable extent. In deciding on the appropriate course of action, the tribunal will necessarily have regard to the fact that one of the objects of arbitration in terms of s.1(a) is to resolve disputes without unnecessary delay or expense and indeed to its duty under r.24(1)(c) to conduct the arbitration without unnecessary delay or expense.

Rule 21(3)

R21-11 In order that the matter should be dealt with expeditiously, and the tribunal should not have to proceed against the background of the possibility that the arbitration may be undermined by a further appeal or appeals, the Outer House's decision on the issue is declared to be final. This matches the many sections and rules in the Act providing for such finality.

R21-12 In the context of s.1(a) of the Act, it would be wholly illogical to permit a party who has made an unsuccessful r.21 appeal to get a second chance in respect of the same issue under r.67 or s.12(3); the issue is res judicata.

R21-13 This leads to the apparently anomalous position that a r.21 appeal is a one-stop one while a r.67 appeal may, in certain limited circumstances, be subject to a further appeal to the Inner House. No such anomaly arises under the 1996 Act, since the tribunal's decision on jurisdiction will always take the form of an award, and be subject to challenge under s.67, just like a final award. However, given the terms of r.67(5) that

> "[l]eave may be given by the Outer House only where it considers (a) that the proposed appeal would raise an important point of principle or practice, or (b) that there is another compelling reason for the Inner House to consider the appeal",

the "anomaly" will, in practice, be more apparent than real.

R21-14 It is worth noting that any arbitral matter which can be appealed to the English court can, albeit with appropriate leave, be appealed all the way to the UKSC whereas, in Scotland, other than in respect of r.67/68/69, no appeal lies from any first instance decision and, even in respect of r.67/68/69, there is no appeal to the UKSC at all.

R21-15 A r.21 appeal relates only to a tribunal decision made under r.20(4)(a) in contrast to a r.67 appeal which relates to an award covering both jurisdiction and merits (or an award where the tribunal has found jurisdiction to be absent on its own initiative)(see also para.R67–18).

The first reported case involving a r.21 appeal was *G1 Venues Ltd* [2013] **R21–16**
CSOH 202 (judgment dated December 27, 2013).

Rule 22: Referral of point of jurisdiction D

22. The Outer House may, on an application by any party, determine any question as to the tribunal's jurisdiction.

DEFINITIONS

"Outer House": s.31(1)
"party": ss.2(1), 31(1), (2)
"tribunal": ss.2(1), 31(1)

STATUS

Rule 22 is a default rule so can be disapplied in whole or in part, or **R22–01** modified in any way, by the parties (s.9 refers). In contrast s.32 of the 1996 Act is (apart from s.32(4)) mandatory.

If the parties have agreed to adopt institutional rules, those rules may **R22–02** vary r.22. Examples include art.23 of the LCIA Rules and art.6 of the ICC Rules.

MODEL LAW

The Model Law has, consistent with art.5, no equivalent of a direct **R22–03** application to the court on jurisdiction.

COMMENTARY

A party may seek to refer a jurisdictional question to the Outer House, **R22–04** subject to the conditions laid down in r.23. Note that r.22 is a default rule but, if it applies, r.23 (see commentary below) applies in full as a mandatory rule, a duality that occurs in several places in the Act. Rule 22 is akin to r.41.

This provision is one of the many improvements made to the Bill during **R22–05** the parliamentary process, done so because consultees indicated that such a power could be useful (policy memorandum, para.139). Sometimes a difficult and/or important issue of jurisdiction will arise in relation to which any tribunal ruling is bound to be challenged by the losing party (see, e.g. *Belgravia Property Co Ltd v S & R (London) Ltd* [2001] B.L.R. 424). In such circumstances it is wholly sensible that it should be possible to bypass the tribunal and go straight to the court for a jurisdictional ruling.

Rule 23 sets out the procedure to be followed in relation to a referral **R22–06** under r.22 and the restrictions on referral.

Rule 23: Jurisdiction referral: procedure etc. M

23.—(1) This rule applies only where an application is made under rule 22.

(2) Such an application is valid only if—
  (a) the parties have agreed that it may be made, or
  (b) the tribunal has consented to it being made and the court is satisfied—
     (i) that determining the question is likely to produce substantial savings in expenses,
     (ii) that the application was made without delay, and
     (iii) that there is a good reason why the question should be determined by the court.

(3) The tribunal may continue with the arbitration pending determination of an application.

(4) The Outer House's determination of the question is final (as is any decision by the Outer House as to whether an application is valid).

DEFINITIONS

"arbitration": ss.2(1), (2), 31(1)
"Outer House": s.31(1)
"party": ss.2(1), 31(1), (2)
"tribunal": ss.2(1), 31(1)

STATUS

R23–01   Rule 23 is mandatory so cannot be disapplied, or modified in any way, by the parties.

MODEL LAW

R23–02   The Model Law has, consistent with art.5, no equivalent of a direct application to the court on jurisdiction.

COMMENTARY

Rule 23(1)—Introductory

R23–03   Rule 23 was originally part of r.22 but it was decided that, while the parties should be permitted (e.g. see R22–01 and R22–04) to exclude such recourse to the courts, if they did not do so they should not be permitted to alter the basis on which a point should be referred.

R23–04   Whereas s.32(1) of the 1996 Act provides that a party may lose its right to apply to the court under s.73 if it fails to make objection to jurisdiction timeously, there is no such provision in r.23. However, in practice, r.76 (which is mandatory) will have the same effect.

Rule 23(2)—Conditions for valid application

While any party is entitled to make such an application, such can be done only if either of two conditions has been met, the first being that all other parties have agreed to it being made. **R23–05**

Rule 23(2)(a) does not require agreement in writing, in contrast to s.32(2)(a) of the 1996 Act. **R23–06**

Secondly, if the agreement of the other parties cannot be obtained, then the party making the application must obtain the consent of the tribunal, and the court must be satisfied on each and all of three criteria: (i) that determining the question is likely to produce substantial savings in expenses; (ii) that the application has been made without delay; and (iii) that there is a good reason why the question should be determined by the court. **R23–07**

The DAC Report, at para.147 (in relation to the identical provisions of s.32(2) of the 1996 Act) considered that in most cases it would still be most appropriate for a tribunal to consider its own jurisdiction in the first instance, and it "anticipated that the Courts will take care to prevent this exceptional provision from becoming the normal route for challenging jurisdiction". **R23–08**

In deciding whether to give consent, the tribunal will have to comply with its duty under r.24(1)(c) to conduct the arbitration without unnecessary delay and without incurring unnecessary expense. This suggests that a tribunal will not consent to a referral unless it takes the view that the application will promote overall speed and economy. A tribunal may well wish to consider whether criteria (i),(ii) and (ii) are satisfied as, if they are not, then that would suggest that consent should not be given. **R23–09**

One obvious circumstance where the court would very likely be satisfied on the three criteria is where a party makes an immediate jurisdictional objection which raises a point in relation to which the determination of the tribunal is practically certain to be appealed by the losing party, so that much time and expense can be saved if the court considered the matter at a preliminary stage rather than as an appeal from a tribunal decision. A decision by the court here could conceivably terminate the arbitration forthwith, clearly a far more cost-effective and time-saving option (s.1(a) refers) than proceeding all the way to the conclusion of the arbitral proceedings and setting aside the award for lack of jurisdiction. **R23–10**

The simple word "likely" (which also appears in rr.32(2), 37(1)(c)(i) and (ii), 42(2)(b)(i) and 83(3)) opens up the far from straightforward matter of what it actually means. In *Pacific Basin IHX Ltd v Bulkhandling Handymax AS* [2011] EWHC 2862 (Comm), in connection with the interpretation of a time charter of a vessel with a condition that without the consent of owners the vessel should not proceed where the vessel was "likely to be" exposed to acts of piracy which were "likely to be or become" dangerous, Teare J. said at [40]: **R23–11**

> "Given that the words to be construed are 'likely to be' I consider that the parties' intentions are best captured by the concept of a 'real like-

lihood' that the vessel will be exposed to acts of piracy. The adjective 'real' reflects the need for the likelihood to be based on evidence rather than to be a fanciful likelihood based on speculation. Whilst 'a real likelihood' includes an event that is more likely than not to happen it can also include an event which has a less than an even chance of happening. ('Likely' does not necessarily mean more likely than not as a matter of language. It can include a degree of probability considerably less than an even chance... The OED gives as one meaning of likelihood 'a good chance.') A bare possibility would not be included because the phrase 'likely to be' suggests a degree of probability rather greater than a bare possibility. The degree of probability inherent in a 'real likelihood' is or can be reflected in phrases such as 'real danger' or 'serious possibility.'"

R23–12 In terms of the above scheme, if the tribunal is not prepared to give consent to the application, then (absent agreement of the parties) the court cannot rule on the issue (s.1(c) refers).

Rule 23(3)—Tribunal discretion to continue proceedings

R23–13 For the form of an application and court procedure see the commentary on r.42

R23–14 The tribunal may continue proceedings pending the determination of the application in any direction in which it grants consent to the r.22 application.

R23–15 In practice, it will probably be the case that, if a point of jurisdiction is seen as being sufficiently doubtful to justify seeking a referral, the tribunal will be disinclined to continue the proceedings at all, far less make an award, while the decision is pending, unless it is possible for part of the proceedings to continue without reference to the disputed point. In deciding on the appropriate course of action the tribunal will necessarily have regard to the fact that one of the objects of arbitration in terms of s.1(a) is to resolve disputes without unnecessary delay or expense and indeed to its duty under r.24(1)(c), to conduct the arbitration without unnecessary delay or expense.

R23–16 When r.23 was part of r.22, the default status of that rule would have meant that the parties could agree that the tribunal should not be permitted to continue the arbitration in these circumstances, but, now that r.23 is standalone and mandatory, the power cannot be excluded by the parties. This makes an interesting contrast with s.32 of the 1996 Act which is mandatory (where r.22 is not), save that s.32(4) provides that the tribunal's power to continue is subject to the contrary agreement of the parties whereas r.23(3), if it applies, is mandatory.

R23–17 Rule 23 omits any provision equivalent to s.31(5) of the 1996 Act whereby the tribunal is allowed to stay the proceedings pending the determination of an application under s.32, and must stay them if the parties so agree. The authors submit that any such provision would be otiose since a discretion to continue the proceedings is equally a discretion not to continue. As above, s.1(a) and r.24(1)(c) will be relevant in this context.

Rule 23(4)—Decision of Outer House final

Rule 23(4) matches r.21(3) (and many others) in providing that the Outer House's determination, on application by a party, of any question as to the tribunal's jurisdiction is final. **R23–18**

In the context of s.1(a) of the Act, it would be wholly illogical to permit a party who has made an unsuccessful r.22/23 application to get a second chance in respect of the same issue under r.67 or s.12(3); the issue is res judicata. **R23–19**

This leads to the apparently anomalous position that a r.22/23 appeal is a one-stop one while a r.67 appeal may, in certain limited circumstances, be subject to a further appeal to the Inner House. However, given the terms of r.67(5), that **R23–20**

> "[l]eave may be given by the Outer House only where it considers (a) that the proposed appeal would raise an important point of principle or practice, or (b) that there is another compelling reason for the Inner House to consider the appeal",

the "anomaly" will, in practice, be more apparent than real.

Continuing the theme of "finality", the Outer House's determination of the validity of a r.22/23 application is final and the same considerations set out above apply. This contrasts (as with many other aspect of the Act) with the 1996 Act which provides (s.32(5) refers) for leave to appeal to be given. It is worth noting that any matter which can be appealed to the English court can, albeit with appropriate leave, be appealed all the way to the UK Supreme Court, whereas, in Scotland, other than in respect of rr.67, 68 and 69, no appeal lies from any first instance decision and, even in respect of rr.67, 68 and 69, there is no appeal to the UKSC at all. **R23–21**

Part 3

General Duties

Rule 24: General duty of the tribunal M
24.—(1) The tribunal must—
  (a) be impartial and independent,
  (b) treat the parties fairly, and
  (c) conduct the arbitration—
    (i) without unnecessary delay, and
    (ii) without incurring unnecessary expense.

Arbitration (Scotland) Act 2010

(2) Treating the parties fairly includes giving each party a reasonable opportunity to put its case and to deal with the other party's case.

DEFINITIONS

"arbitration": s.2(1)
"tribunal": s.2(1)
Neither "impartial" nor "independent" is defined in the 2010 Act (nor in the Model Law). However r.77 defines lack of independence.

STATUS

R24–01 This is a mandatory rule so it is not open to the parties to agree anything else or to disapply it completely (see s.8). It is difficult to conceive of a rule that is any more fundamental to and central to the arbitral process.

MODEL LAW

R24–02 There is no direct equivalent of r.24 in the Model Law, save that r.24(1)(b) is very similar to art.18 (equal treatment of parties):

"The parties shall be treated with equality and each party shall be given a full opportunity of presenting his case."

R24–03 As discussed above (see r.8) art.12(1) of the Model Law provides that:

"When a person is approached in connection with his possible appointment as an arbitrator, he shall disclose any circumstances likely to give rise to justifiable doubts as to his impartiality or independence. An arbitrator, from the time of his appointment and throughout the arbitral proceedings, shall without delay disclose any such circumstances to the parties unless they have already been informed of them by him."

COMMENTARY

Rule 24(1)(a)—Duty to be impartial and independent

R24–04 Section 1 provides that, "the founding principles of this Act are: (a) that the object of arbitration is to resolve disputes impartially". The fundamental necessity for arbitrators to be both impartial and independent is also recognised in r.24(1)(a).

R24–05 This is consistent with art.6(1) of the ECHR, which provides that:

"In the determination of his civil rights and obligations ... everyone is entitled to a fair and public hearing within a reasonable time by an independent and impartial tribunal established by law."

R24–06 In the view both of the drafters of the Act and of the present authors the two-part requirement (impartial and independent) is axiomatic; the same view is common, almost universal around the world, including many non-ECHR jurisdictions. England and Wales and Northern Ireland represent the major difference here, but we should bear in mind that the 1996 Act predates the HRA 1998.

R24–07 While r.24(1)(a) provides for both "independence" and "impartiality", the authors submit that they shade into each other. An arbitrator lacking independence from the parties may well appear to lack impartiality. Rule 77 has gone further by defining lack of independence (non-exclusively) by reference to justifiable doubts as to impartiality.

R24–08 "Independence" is not defined. Appreciating that the concept requires to be read and given effect to in a way compatible with art.6(1) of the ECHR (HRA 1998 s.3(1) and Scotland Act 1998 s.100(2)), the authors are nevertheless unable to indentify in the context of arbitrators a real-world situation where an arbitrator lacks independence but is impartial (without any justifiable doubt thereon) save perhaps the hypothetical type of situation where the arbitrator owns one share in each of the parties.

R24–09 Rule 77 provides that an arbitrator is not independent if anything gives rise to justifiable doubts as to his impartiality and gives examples of this. The "justifiable doubts" test originates in art.12 of the Model Law. It accords with the reasonable suspicion of bias test applied in respect of Scottish courts and tribunals. That test followed the seminal Scottish case *Bradford v McLeod*, 1986 S.L.T. 244 and its successor *Millar v Dickson*, 2001 S.C. (P.C.) 30 at [64] per Lord Hope of Craighead.

R24–10 The test for England and Wales is whether the fair-minded, informed observer, i.e. having considered all of the facts having a bearing on bias, would conclude that there was a real possibility that the tribunal was biased (*Porter v Magill* [2002] 2 A.C. 357 at [103] per Lord Hope of Craighead). The test in *Porter v Magill* was designed to remove the requirement of a "real danger of bias" and bring English law into line with that of Scotland and other Commonwealth jurisdictions as well as the case law relating to impartiality under art.6(1) of the ECHR.

R24–11 In *Hauschildt v Denmark* (1989) 12 E.H.R.R. 266, 279, [48] the ECtHR observed that, in considering whether there was a legitimate reason to fear that a judge lacks impartiality, the standpoint of the accused is important but not decisive: "What is decisive is whether this fear can be held objectively justified".

R24–12 Given that impartiality must be read and given effect to in a way compatible with art.6(1) of the ECHR (HRA 1998 s.3(1) and Scotland Act 1998 s.100(2)) the compatibility of r.24 and ECtHR case law is welcome.

R24–13 In *Gillies v Secretary of State for Work and Pensions*, 2006 S.C. (HL) 71, objection was taken by a social security claimant to the presence on a social security tribunal of a doctor who had to assess medical reports from the Department of Work and Pensions that had been prepared by doctors from a company for whom she herself prepared similar medical reports for the Department on a fee-paying basis when she was not sitting on tribunals. The House of Lords considered that this was not sufficient to give a reasonable man reasonable apprehension of bias, with Lord Hope of Craighead observing at [17]:

> "The fair-minded and informed observer can be assumed to have access to all the facts that are capable of being known by members of the public generally, bearing in mind that it is the appearance that these facts give rise to that matters, not what is in the mind of the particular judge or tribunal member who is under scrutiny. It is to be assumed, as Kirby J put it in *Johnson v Johnson* ([2000] H.C.A. 48 [53]), that the observer is neither complacent nor unduly sensitive or suspicious when he examines the facts that he can look at. It is to be assumed too that he is able to distinguish between what is relevant and what is irrelevant, and that he is able when exercising his judgment to decide what weight should be given to the facts that are relevant."

R24–14 While the matter of bias is worth an entire book on its own, we content ourselves with this clear statement of the law and the following cases as illustrating the situations that may arise; however, there is such a book: S. Luttrell, *Bias Challenges in International Arbitration: The Need for a "Real Danger" Test* (Netherlands: Kluwer, 2009).

R24–15 In *AT&T Corp v Saudi Cable Co* [2000] 2 Lloyd's Rep. 127 CA; [2000] EWCA Civ 154, the applicant sought to remove the chairman of an ICC tribunal on the basis of his possessing a small number of shares in, and being a non-executive director of, a third party company, Nortel, which was a competitor of AT&T and which had been the disappointed bidder for a major telecoms contract with Saudi Cable where that contract was the subject matter of the present arbitration. The Court of Appeal upheld Longmore J.'s rejection of the application, the arbitrator's connection with the parties and the contract being too remote to create a real danger of bias (that being the English law test at that time). The authors submit that the same outcome would have followed under the "justifiable doubt" test in r.77.

R24–16 The authors note that the stated facts of the case included that the chairman had also possessed a shareholding in AT&T; while s.33(1)(a) of the 1996 Act does not require "independence", r.24 does; therefore the decision in *AT&T*, if similar circumstances occurred under the 2010 Act, would have justified removal, save only if either a de minimis approach was applied or application of r.77 led to the conclusion that there was no justifiable doubt.

R24–17 In contrast, in *Smits Leslie v Roach* [2006] H.C.A. 36 (Australia), a judge declined to recuse himself in circumstances where, if Smits Leslie, a law firm, had won its action (optimistic at best and, in fact, it lost) to recover fees from Roach, the latter would have had grounds for action in professional negligence, albeit close to hopeless, against another law firm F, the chairman of which was a brother of the judge. F could only attract liability at all if both cases went massively against the odds. There were 80 partners in F. The potential liability of F was unclear although a figure of AUS$500,000 (before consideration of insurance recoveries) was mentioned. While five judges in the High Court of Australia (the Supreme Court, despite its anomalous name), expressing obiter views, took the view that the outcome of the action could have no more than a negligible (de minimis) effect on the brother's finances, and therefore there was no reasonable apprehension of bias on the part of the judge, the sixth, Kirby J., in a powerful and widely-admired judgment, rejected such an approach, emphasising the perception of the public of the judge's link to his brother and that it would not view the brother's potential share as de minimis.

More recently in *Goel v Amega Ltd* [2010] EWHC 2454 (TCC), a party **R24–18** objected to the arbitrator on the basis that, in a report to him of a preliminary hearing which had been attended by the other party's solicitor, Mr T, alone, the arbitrator had noted "Mr T and I noted" and "Mr T and I were satisfied". Coulson J. rejected the objection robustly, describing it as unfair to the non-legal arbitrator and observing at [50]:

> "A fair-minded and informed observer would not, I think, consider the wording of the arbitrator's note of the ... meeting as indicating bias or anything like it."

Other than in the USA (particularly in California), the IBA Conflict **R24–19** Guidelines, although not universally accepted either in England (e.g. they were summarily dismissed by Morison J. in *ASM Shipping Ltd of India v TTMI Ltd of England* [2005] EWHC 2238 (Comm) at [39](4), a judgment regarded by many commentators as controversial, even wrong) or internationally, have attracted widespread support as being the best current solution to the difficult problem of trying to establish standards of independence and impartiality. They provide useful guidance to potential arbitrators and arbitrators on how to avoid challenges in relation to those matters.

Rule 12 provides for the removal of an arbitrator for breach of the duty in **R24–20** r.24(1)(a) while r.68(2)(g) allows for a serious irregularity appeal against an award for such a breach but requires the challenger to show substantial injustice as well. Success in either can have a material impact on the arbitrator's entitlement to his fees and expenses quite apart from the delay and wasted expense caused to parties. See also the commentary on r.12(a) above.

Impartiality covers actual as well as apparent bias (already discussed **R24–21** under "independence") but cases where this can be established are likely to be rare.

If a party wishes to found on a breach of the duty in r.24(1)(a) it must do **R24–22** so timeously (r.76 refers).

Rule 24(1)(b) and (2)—Duty to treat parties fairly

R24–23 Section 1 of the 2010 Act provides that: "the founding principles of this Act are: (a) that the object of arbitration is to resolve disputes fairly". This is axiomatic since it goes deep into the roots of natural justice.

R24–24 Model Law art.18 provides the basic principle that the parties shall be treated with equality and each party shall be given a "full" opportunity of presenting his case. Supplementing this fundamental principle, art.24(1) provides that, absent contrary agreement by the parties, there shall be oral hearings at an appropriate stage and art.24(3) provides for all documents to be copied equally to each party.

R24–25 Rule 24(1)(b) and (2) must be also be read and given effect to so as to be compatible with the right in art.6(1) of the ECHR to a "fair hearing" (HRA 1998 s.3(1)).

R24–26 Rule 24(1)(b) implements the object of fair resolution in s.1 by imposing a duty on the tribunal to treat the parties "fairly". Fair treatment is difficult to define. It is understood better where it is found to be absent. If one party is permitted by the tribunal to be represented by a QC and the other denied even an advocate, then we have unfairness. Megarry V.C. famously said:

> "It may be that there are some who would decry the importance which the courts attach to the observance of the rules of natural justice. 'When something is obvious', they may say, 'why force everybody to go through the tiresome waste of time involved in framing charges and giving an opportunity to be heard? The result is obvious from the start'. Those who take this view do not, I think, do themselves justice. As everybody who has anything to do with the law well knows, the path of the law is strewn with examples of open and shut cases which, somehow, were not; of unanswerable charges which, in the event, were completely answered; of inexplicable conduct which was fully explained; of fixed and unalterable determinations that, by discussion, suffered a change. Nor are those with any knowledge of human nature who pause to think for a moment likely to underestimate the feelings of resentment of those who find that a decision against them has been made without their being offered any opportunity to influence the course of events" (*John v Rees* [1969] 2 All E.R. 274 at 309).

R24–27 Echoing Megarry V.C., r.24(2) provides that "fair treatment" must include "giving each party a reasonable opportunity to put its case and to deal with the other party's case". This does not mean that a tribunal must treat each party identically. Rather the aim is to ensure that each party is not prejudiced in any genuine sense in presenting its case to the tribunal (*Dombo Beheer B.V. v Netherlands* (1994) 18 E.H.R.R. 213 at [33]—where a refusal by a court to allow a key witness to give evidence was a violation of the right to a fair hearing).

While art.24 of the Model Law obliges a tribunal to allow a party a "full" opportunity to present his case, r.24(2) requires the giving of a "reasonable" opportunity to a party to put its case and to deal with that of the opponent. This originates in the DAC which expressed the view: **R24–28**

> "We prefer the word *'reasonable'* because it removes any suggestion that a party is entitled to take as long as he likes, however objectively unreasonable this may be. We are sure that this was not intended by those who framed the Model Law, for it would entail that a party is entitled to an unreasonable time, which justice can hardly require. Indeed the contrary is the case, for an unreasonable time would *ex hypothesi* mean unnecessary delay and expense, things which produce injustice and which accordingly would offend the first principle of Clause 1, as well as Clauses 33 and 40" at [165].

A tribunal can use modern technology for assistance in performing its r.24(1)(b) and (c) duties. In *Three Mile Inn Ltd (formerly Rivergrant Ltd)* [2012] EWCA Civ 970, a party who was also to be a witness at a hearing was too ill to travel to the hearing. It was held that it was incompatible with his art.6(1) right for the court to oblige him to participate in the hearing by video link, given that for effective participation he required to be present to observe the whole hearing. However, in that case there had been no danger of undue delay being caused through the (necessary) adjournment of the hearing. The decision might be different if delay becomes an issue and a balancing exercise between the duties in r.24(1)(b) and (c) becomes necessary. Note that the ratio of the court was based on the need to allow a *party* to participate effectively and does not apply to a mere witness. **R24–29**

The basic requirements of the r.24 duty include (i) ensuring that each party has an opportunity to comment on and counter the submissions and evidence of the other party and (ii) informing the parties beforehand of any hearing or meeting which is to take place between the tribunal and any of the parties (*Ruiz-Mateos v Spain* (1993) 16 E.H.R.R. 505 at [63]—submission not intimated; *Lobo Machado v Portugal* (1997) 23 E.H.R.R. 79 at [31] to [32]). **R24–30**

A party to the proceedings must have the possibility to familiarise itself with the documentary evidence before the tribunal, as well as the possibility to comment on its existence, contents and authenticity in an appropriate form and within an appropriate time, if need be, in a written form and in advance (*Krcmar v The Czech Republic* (2001) 31 E.H.R.R. 41 at [42]). **R24–31**

A further basic requirement of the duty is to ensure that parties have had an opportunity to comment not merely on the submissions and evidence put forward by the other party but also any knowledge or evidence put forward by the tribunal itself which would not reasonably be known to the parties. This is the distinction between special knowledge of facts held by an arbitrator and the general knowledge of an arbitrator (*Checkpoint Ltd v* **R24–32**

Strathclyde Pension Fund [2003] L.&T.R. 22 at [29] to [32] per Ward L.J.). Given that arbitrators are often selected for their expertise it is important that they heed the following words of Bingham J.:

> "I fully accept and understand the difficulties in which an expert finds himself when acting as an arbitrator. There is an unavoidable inclination to rely on one's own expertise and in respect of general matters that is not only not objectionable but is desirable and a very large part of the reason why an arbitrator with expert qualifications is chosen. Nevertheless, the rules of natural justice do require, even in an arbitration conducted by an expert, that matters which are likely to form the subject of decision, insofar as they are specific matters, should be exposed for the comments and submissions of the parties. If an arbitrator is impressed by a point that has never been raised by either side then it is his duty to put it to them so that they have an opportunity to comment. If he feels that the proper approach is one that has not been explored or advanced in evidence or submission then again it is his duty to give the parties a chance to comment. If he is to any extent relying on his own personal experience in a specific way then that again is something that he should mention so that it can be explored. It is not right that a decision should be based on specific matters which the parties have never had the chance to deal with, nor is it right that a party should first learn of adverse points in the decision against him." *Zermalt Holdings S.A. v Nu-Life Upholstery Repairs Ltd* [1985] 2 E.G.L.R. 14 approved as part of Scots law in *Fountain Forestry Ltd v Sparkes*, 1989 S.C. 224.

R24–33 The powers given to arbitral tribunals for the fulfilment of their duties under r.24 are provided by rr.28 to 39: see commentary on those rules. It follows that the tribunal's exercise of its various powers under those rules must always comply with r.24(1)(b) and (2).

Complaint of breach of r.24(1)(b) and (2)

R24–34 A party who believes that the tribunal has breached its duty of fair treatment should make a timeous objection to the tribunal. For what amounts to a timeous objection see r.76 and the commentary thereon. Failure to make such an objection will result in the party being barred from raising the objection either later before the tribunal, or before the court either as part of a serious irregularity appeal under r.68 or an application to remove an arbitrator under r.12. A party is not permitted to keep its complaint to itself and then use it to challenge the award itself or enforcement of the award at a later stage.

R24–35 For its part, if the tribunal is faced with such an objection, it must decide whether there is substance in its alleged unfair treatment. Such objections can be used to delay proceedings and tribunals should look out for any such possibility. On the other hand if there is a ready cure for the claimed prejudice it may be prudent to adopt it to cut off any possibility of a serious irregularity appeal against any subsequent award.

In a private arbitration conducted by one of the authors, one of the parties was very late in lodging a written submission just before the final half day hearing for closing oral submissions, causing real scheduling difficulties for the other side; this was redressed by the time in the closing hearing being split one and a half/two and a half hours, later adjusted (by agreement of the parties) to three quarters/two and a quarter hours. Curiously, the counsel with the longer allowance overran it and his opponent addressed the arbitrator for just over a half an hour. The arbitrator found the shorter address much more persuasive. **R24–36**

Rule 24(1)(b) and consumer arbitrations

There is one particular class of circumstances where "treating fairly" presents real difficulties in practice; arbitrations involving consumers and parties with significant differences of resources; see Appendix 1 for dicussion of arbitrations involving consumers. These can raise difficult issues of jurisdiction and of case management. We assume in this context that the arbitration agreement in the contract between a consumer and a business is not invalid under the Unfair Terms Regulations which are substantially applied to arbitration agreements in ss.89–91 of the 1996 Act which do apply in Scotland (the only part of that Act which does). For a useful survey of the law in this area see paras S4–21 to S4–24 and *Mylcrist Builders v Buck* [2008] EWHC 2172 (TCC) which is considered in Hew R. Dundas, "Recent Developments in English Arbitration Law: Arbitrations Involving Consumers" (2009) 75 *Arbitration* 115. **R24–37**

Returning to the main theme, the difficulties spring from circumstances where one party, e.g. an individual or a small business, may have difficulties affording professional help in presenting their claims and their case generally. The arbitrator has to decide how much help they can give without compromising either their neutrality or their appearance of neutrality. Where there are significant differences of resources, the arbitrator's primary duty is to do justice in the case and they must do this while ensuring that they shows no bias in favour of any party. They can achieve this by asking questions and suggesting amendments to claims and the way in which a case is presented where this is necessary to achieve the primary objective. **R24–38**

The CIArb's Practice Guideline No.17, "Guideline on Arbitrations Involving Consumers and Parties with Significant Differences Of Resources", provides detailed guidance in this difficult area; see *http://www.ciarb.org/information-and-resources/practice-guidelines-and-protocols/list-of-guidelines-and-protocols/* [Accessed June 17, 2014]. **R24–39**

Breach of r.24(1)(b) and (2)—Appeal and/or removal of arbitrator

R24-40 Rule 68(2)(h) allows for a serious irregularity appeal if the tribunal fails the fairness test but requires the challenger to show substantial injustice as well. This, together with the need for timeous objection under r.76 will filter out the great majority of minor complaints made, in practice, by disgruntled losers.

R24-41 Breach of the fairness duty can also result in an application to remove the remove an arbitrator under r.12. See also the commentary on r.12(b) above.

R24-42 Typically, in *Margulead Ltd v Exide Technologies* [2004] EWHC 1019 (Comm), a challenge under s.68 of the 1996 Act, Margulead claimed that the sole arbitrator had failed to permit its counsel to reply orally to closing submissions by counsel for Exide, i.e. the latter (as respondent in the arbitration) had had the last word. However, the arbitrator had made it clear in advance that that was to be his proposed course of action and Margulead had accepted that at the time. Further, although it may be conventional practice in common law courts that the claimant has the last word (since it must prove his claim), this is by no means an absolute rule in English, let alone international, arbitration. Colman J. held, inter alia, that there had been no substantial injustice.

Rule 24(1)(c)(i)—Duty to avoid unnecessary delay

R24-43 Section 1 of the Act provides that: "the founding principles of this Act are: (a) that the object of arbitration is to resolve disputes without unnecessary ... delay".

R24-44 Rule 24(1)(c)(i) imposes a positive duty on arbitrators to "conduct the arbitration without unnecessary delay". One of the advantages, or possible advantages, of arbitration over litigation is that a dispute can be decided without the delay caused by the onerous case load and other duties of a judge. However, that advantage can only exist if the tribunal acts expeditiously.

R24-45 It is interesting to note that under art.1463 of the French Code of Civil Procedure provides that if an arbitration agreement does not specify a time limit, the duration of the arbitral tribunal's mandate shall be limited to six months from the date on which the tribunal is seized of the dispute.

R24-46 There is nothing to prevent parties from agreeing with the tribunal that it should issue its final award within a particular timescale or date. In general terms the ICC Rules provide that the tribunal must render its final award within six months from the settling of the terms of reference drawn up after the parties' submission of the request for arbitration and answer (see art.30 of the ICC Rules). The Swiss Rules have a similar provision in relation to cases where the aggregate of a claim and counterclaim is up to one million Swiss francs (see art.42 of the Swiss Rules). Nearer to home the Scottish Arbitration Rules 2007 of the CIArb provide in art.11.5 that the arbitrator must make and issue the final award no later than six months from the date of appointment (as defined). The fixing of timescales, provided they are realistic, is something to be encouraged.

If the parties have agreed with the tribunal that the award requires to be issued by a certain time, then if the award is not issued by that time and the time limit is not extended (prorogated) by the parties, the jurisdiction of the tribunal to make the award will fall (*Cunninghame v Drummond* (1491) Mor. 635; *Earl of Linlithgow v Hamilton* (1610) Mor. 636). **R24–47**

There is often a difficult balance to be struck in practice between the time schedule and fairness, e.g. where a party asserts that it needs 90 days to prepare its submission, not the 30 allowed in the agreed rules. In the past, arbitrators tended to give in to the parties, whether because of fear of an unfairness challenge or otherwise, but in practice now arbitrators are taking a more proactive and robust approach and are driving cases forward—active case management is the "name of the modern game". In a recent case (non-arbitration) in the English courts, the judge cut the time allowances requested by the parties by between 40 and 60 per cent and they merely buckled down to work within the shorter timescale. At a seminar in London, that judge made it clear that any application to him complaining of an arbitrator shortening time scales in the interests of efficient case management would likely receive a distinctly negative response. **R24–48**

Taken together rr.24(1)(c) and 28 require the tribunal to pursue active case management. While r.28 is a default rule so can be varied by the agreement of the parties, the authors submit that in the unlikely event of a conflict between the parties' agreement and r.24(1)(c), the tribunal should, override the wishes of the parties, if the parties' agreement would leave the tribunal in breach of its duty under r.24(1)(c). An example would if the parties kept deciding repeatedly that a hearing of evidence should be postponed without any unfairness or prejudice to either side being alleged. In such a situation the authors submit that the tribunal would have not merely the right but the duty to query the basis of the agreement, intimate to parties that it was minded to fix a hearing in any event and unless the agreement to postpone could be justified on the basis of genuine prejudice in the resolution of the dispute (rather than the mere convenience of the parties), to fix a hearing regardless of the agreement. In such a situation any subsequent appeal under r.68 would fail, there being no substantial injustice caused to any party. **R24–49**

In contrast, while r.68(2) does not expressly refer to delay (as it does to impartiality, independence and fairness) delay can still constitute a serious irregularity via r.68(2)(a), "the tribunal failing to conduct the arbitration in accordance with (ii) these rules (in so far as they apply)", or r.68(2)(i), "there being justifiable doubts about an arbitrator's ability to so act". As above, the substantial injustice test must be met by the challenger. See also the commentary to r.12(c) above. **R24–50**

In the unlikely event that the parties sought to remove such a pro-active arbitrator under r.11 they would find themselves faced with an order from the court for payment of the arbitrator's fees (r.16 refers). **R24–51**

R24–52 In *G1 Venues Ltd* [2013] CSOH 202, Lord Malcolm made an observation (at [18]) with which the authors respectfully and strongly concur:

> "Over ten months elapsed between the debate and the arbitrator's decision. Those acting as arbitrators should keep in mind that the founding principles of the 2010 Act include that arbitrations should be resolved without unnecessary delay."

Rule 24(1)(c)(ii)

R24–53 Section 1 of the Act provides that: "the founding principles of this Act are: (a) that the object of arbitration is to resolve disputes without unnecessary ... expense".

R24–54 In contrast to r.24(1)(c)(i), there is no clear direct or indirect entry into rr.68 or 12 in the context of breach of this obligation and it is rare for a tribunal to be responsible, even in part, for high levels of expense, the fault here almost always being with the parties and their advisers. One such case is *W and S v BB* Unreported June 8, 2001 TCC (see paras R12–09 and R73–08).

R24–55 There are limits as to what a tribunal can achieve to control costs in the sense that if a party wishes to instruct 12 advocates, six law firms and 10 experts, that is for that party to decide. However, the arbitrator has two ways of minimising the effect of this, first by efficient case management so as to limit the usefulness of the excess manpower, and secondly, by being robust in awarding expenses (see r.61(3)) so, in this example, recoverability should be restricted.

R24–56 Guidance on means to achieve cost control can be found in the ICC Commission Report, *Controlling Time and Costs in Arbitration*, 2nd edn (International Chamber of Commerce, 2012) available at *http://www.iccwbo.org/advocacy-codes-and-rules/document-centre/* [Accessed June 17, 2014].

Rule 25: General duty of the parties M

25. The parties must ensure that the arbitration is conducted—
  (a) without unnecessary delay, and
  (b) without incurring unnecessary expense.

DEFINITIONS

"arbitration": ss.2(1), (2), 31(1)
"party": ss.2(1), 31(1), (2)

STATUS

R25–01 This is a mandatory rule so it is not open to the parties to agree anything else or to disapply it completely (see s.8).

MODEL LAW

There is no equivalent provision in the Model Law. R25–02

COMMENTARY

Rule 25 mirrors s.40(1) of the 1996 Act but the latter is augmented by s.40(2) providing that: R25–03

> "This includes (a) complying without delay with any determination of the tribunal as to procedural or evidential matters, or with any order or directions of the tribunal, and (b) where appropriate, taking without delay any necessary steps to obtain a decision of the court on a preliminary question of jurisdiction or law (see sections 32 and 45)."

There are two major difficulties in practice: first, applying the axiom that arbitration is a consensual process; if the parties have agreed on some course of action either by agreeing some alternative to r.28 (a default rule) or by agreeing some deviation therefrom, then the tribunal has to overcome substantial, even insuperable difficulty in seeking to change that agreement. Secondly, there is no immediate sanction available to force or persuade a party to comply with its r.25 obligation; however, there are other provisions in the Act or in the rules, e.g. establishing time limits or providing limits on recoverability of expenses, which will at least go part way to ensuring compliance. R25–04

Section 41 of the 1996 Act provides, absent contrary agreement by the parties, a procedural structure giving the tribunal certain powers in the event that a party breaches its obligation under s.40(1). See rr.37–39 for the equivalent. R25–05

Rule 26: Confidentiality D

26.—(1) Disclosure by the tribunal, any arbitrator or a party of confidential information relating to the arbitration is to be actionable as a breach of an obligation of confidence unless the disclosure—
- **(a) is authorised, expressly or impliedly, by the parties (or can reasonably be considered as having been so authorised),**
- **(b) is required by the tribunal or is otherwise made to assist or enable the tribunal to conduct the arbitration,**
- **(c) is required—**
  - **(i) in order to comply with any enactment or rule of law,**
  - **(ii) for the proper performance of the discloser's public functions, or**
  - **(iii) in order to enable any public body or office-holder to perform public functions properly,**
- **(d) can reasonably be considered as being needed to protect a party's lawful interests,**
- **(e) is in the public interest,**

(f) is necessary in the interests of justice, or
(g) is made in circumstances in which the discloser would have absolute privilege had the disclosed information been defamatory.

(2) The tribunal and the parties must take reasonable steps to prevent unauthorised disclosure of confidential information by any third party involved in the conduct of the arbitration.

(3) The tribunal must, at the outset of the arbitration, inform the parties of the obligations which this rule imposes on them.

(4) "Confidential information", in relation to an arbitration, means any information relating to—
   (a) the dispute,
   (b) the arbitral proceedings,
   (c) the award, or
   (d) any civil proceedings relating to the arbitration in respect of which an order has been granted under section 15 of this Act,
which is not, and has never been, in the public domain.

DEFINITIONS

"arbitration": ss.2(1), (2), 31(1)
"arbitrator": s.2(1)
"party": ss.2(1), 31(1), (2)
"tribunal": ss.2(1), 31(1)

STATUS

R26–01 This is a default rule so it is open to the parties to modify it, agree something different or disapply it completely (see s.9).

R26–02 The privacy of arbitration is almost universally recognised by institutional rules. Thus art.28(5) of the UNCITRAL Rules provides that "hearings shall be heard *in camera* unless the parties otherwise agree" and art.34(5) provides for the making public of an award with the consent of all parties or to the extent that disclosure is required of a party by legal duty, to protect or pursue a legal right or in relation to legal proceedings before a court or other competent authority. Article 22(3) of the ICC Rules allows a party to request the tribunal to make orders concerning confidentiality of the arbitral proceedings or of other matters in connection with the arbitration. The LCIA Rules art.30.1 provide for a duty to keep confidential all awards, materials created for the purpose of the arbitration and all documents produced by another party not otherwise in the public domain except where disclosure is required in certain limited circumstances. The Swiss Rules have a more comprehensive coverage of confidentiality in art.44 (although not as broad as r.26); the WIPO Rules arts 73–76 are very thorough.

R26–03 The authors submit that an arbitration agreement freely entered into amounts to the waiver of the right to a public hearing and judgment under art.6(1) of the ECHR (*Suovaniemi v Finland* Unreported February 23, 1999

ECtHR (waiver of right to impartial tribunal); cf. *Scarth v United Kingdom* (1999) 27 E.H.R.R. CD37, relating to a statutory arbitration where there was no such agreement).

In any event the authors submit that the existence of r.26 in relation to voluntary arbitrations is a proportional means of pursuing a legitimate aim, namely the encouragement of the private settlement of disputes by the keeping from the public eye of information and material mentioned in the private arbitral process, unless the parties should agree otherwise: see further below. **R26–04**

Where an arbitration is not founded on an arbitration agreement freely entered into (e.g. a statutory arbitration (s.16 refers)) the arbitration must, in the absence of free and unequivocal waiver by the parties, provide all of the guarantees in art.6(1) of the ECHR, including the right to a public hearing and public judgment (*Suda v Czech Republic* Unreported October 28, 2010 ECtHR). Applying s.3(1) of the HRA 1998, r.26 should be read as inapplicable for statutory arbitrations except with the parties' free and unequivocal waiver (see commentaries on ss.1 and 15). In any statutory arbitration the applicability of r.26 should be dealt with by the tribunal at the outset of the arbitration. **R26–05**

MODEL LAW

There is no equivalent in the Model Law. **R26–06**

COMMENTARY

Background

For at least the 120 years until 1995 the arbitral world had existed in the belief that arbitral proceedings were both private and confidential; although there were (until 1990) no authorities specifically in point, there was clear evidence of strong judicial support for this proposition, as Sir Patrick Neill QC (as he then was) showed in his 1995 Bernstein Lecture (published at (1996) 62 *Arbitration* 1), with an erudite and comprehensive historical survey dating back to the 17th century. The first English case directly in point was *Dolling-Baker v Merrett* [1990] 1 W.L.R. 1205 CA, in which the Court of Appeal recognised the existence of a confidentiality obligation arising out of the very nature of arbitration, binding the parties thereto and preventing them from voluntarily disclosing or using materials from the arbitration outside it. **R26–07**

This decision certainly appeared unremarkable at the time since it appeared, at least in England, to reflect in formal terms what had been the status quo for more than 120 years. However, a major international reconsideration began in 1995 with the decision in the High Court of Australia in *Esso Australia Resources Ltd v Plowman* (1995) 128 A.L.R. 391 (note that the High Court is the Supreme Court of Australia; the case was an appeal from the Supreme Court of Victoria) where, on a three to two **R26–08** majority, it was held that there was no inherent confidentiality (as distinct from privacy) in respect of arbitral proceedings in Australia. This decision was seen by some as cataclysmic, threatening the very foundations of the principles of arbitration but, in his 1995 Bernstein Lecture, Sir Patrick Neill QC meticulously analysed the Australian judgments in critical terms and concluded that while, as the Chief Justice had stated (at 400), *Esso* reflected the Australian position, its arguments had no effect on English law. In particular, it clearly turned on its own facts, not least a strong "freedom of information" theme and on the rather surprising expert evidence that details of arbitrations in Victoria were common knowledge. Sir Patrick's opinion was essentially upheld by the Court of Appeal in *Ali Shipping Corp v Shipyard Trogir* [1999] 1 W.L.R. 314, in 1998 where the previous line of English jurisprudence (*Dolling-Baker* [1990] 1 W.L.R. 1205; *Hassneh Insurance Co of Israel v Mew* [1993] 2 Lloyd's Rep. 243; *Insurance Co v Lloyds Syndicate* [1995] 1 Lloyd's Rep. 272) was confirmed.

R26–09 In 2000 the Swedish Supreme Court reached a conclusion in *Bulbank* effectively concurring with that in *Esso v Plowman* (1995) 128 A.L.R. 391, i.e. that there was no implied term of confidentiality in Swedish law (*AI Trade Finance v Bulgarian Trade Bank* (case 1881–99) Unreported October 27, 2000 Supreme Court), a decision widely considered to represent civil law thinking on the matter.

R26–10 So far as English law is concerned, the leading (and, in all likelihood, definitive) judgment is that in *Emmott v Michael Wilson & Partners Ltd* [2008] EWCA Civ 184 (Carnwath, Thomas and Lawrence Collins L.JJ.) in the Court of Appeal which not only refined and redefined the law but also developed it since this appeal raised questions of considerable practical importance relating to confidentiality in national and international arbitration. The article by Hew R. Dundas, "Confidentiality in English Arbitration: The Final Word?" (2008) 74 *Arbitration* 458, gives a detailed exposition of this case which is central to r.26.

R26–11 Per Lawrence Collins L.J., who gave the leading judgment in *Emmott* (above), the uncontroversial starting point was that, in English law, arbitration was a private process, e.g. in *Russell v Russell* (1880) 14 Ch. D. 471 at 474, Sir George Jessel M.R. had said:

> "As a rule, persons enter into [arbitration] contracts with the express view of keeping their quarrels from the public eyes, and of avoiding that discussion in public, which must be a painful one, and which might be an injury even to the successful party to the litigation, and most surely would be to the unsuccessful."

R26–12 Parties who arbitrated in England expected that the hearing would be in private and that was an important advantage for commercial people as compared with litigation in court (Lawrence Collins L.J.'s view here is borne out in the 2006 and 2008 Queen Mary University of London/

PriceWaterhouseCoopers studies of the attitudes of commercial users to arbitration, where confidentiality ranked second to enforceability as the principal reason for choosing arbitration.)

In *Emmott,* Lawrence Collins L.J. observed further at [66]: **R26–13**

> "In the last 20 years or so the English courts have had to consider, in several different contexts, the consequences of the privacy of the arbitral process and the scope of the obligation of confidentiality. It is apparent that the English jurisprudence on this subject (as distinct from the confidentiality of awards, which is much discussed in other countries) is much richer than that of any other important arbitration centre, and that it constitutes a major contribution to the development of the law of international arbitration (see ICC, *Report on Confidentiality as a Purported Obligation of the Parties in Arbitration* (ICC, 2002); *Fouchard, Gaillard and Goldman on International Commercial Arbitration*, edited by Emmanual Gaillard and John Savage, (London: Kluwer Law International, 1999), at para.1412; Julian D.M. Lew, Loukas A. Mistelis and Stefan M. Kröll, *Comparative International Commercial Arbitration* (London: Kluwer, 2003), at paras 24–99 to 24–104)."

In reviewing the authorities, Lawrence Collins L.J. noted that it was not **R26–14** always easy to distinguish confidentiality from privacy and that it was also important to bear in mind the context of the decisions because quite different considerations might apply in different contexts, which he set out as follows:

> "72. First, a party to litigation in the courts could seek discovery or disclosure of documents generated in an arbitration. Confidentiality of documents was, of course, not in itself a reason for withholding disclosure, but the court will compel disclosure only if it considered it necessary for the fair disposal of the case (*Science Research Council v Nassé* [1980] A.C. 1028).
>
> ... 73. In *Dolling–Baker* [1990] 1 W.L.R. 1205, Parker L.J. had said (at 1213):
>
>> 'It must be perfectly apparent that, for example, the fact that a document is used in an arbitration does not *confer* on it any confidentiality or privilege which can be availed of in subsequent proceedings. If it is a relevant document, its relevance remains. But that the obligation exists in some form appears to me to be abundantly apparent. It is not a question of immunity or public interest. It is a question of an implied obligation arising out of the nature of arbitration itself. When a question arises as to production of documents or indeed discovery by list or affidavit, the court

must, it appears to me, have regard to the existence of the implied obligation, whatever its precise limits may be. If it is satisfied that despite the implied obligation, disclosure and inspection is necessary for the fair disposal of the action, that consideration must prevail. But in reaching a conclusion, the court should consider, amongst other things, whether there are other and possibly less costly ways of obtaining the information which is sought which do not involve any breach of the implied undertaking.'

... 75. Nor is confidentiality an absolute bar in a second type of case where a party to an arbitration may seek the assistance of the court to obtain, through a witness summons, material deployed in another arbitration (*London and Leeds Estates Ltd v Paribas Ltd (No.2)* [1995] 1 E.G.L.R. 102 and *Council of the Borough of South Tyneside v Wickes Building Suppliers Ltd* [2004] EWHC 2428 (Comm) (Gross J.)). In such cases the court will take into account the strong policy in favour of confidentiality in arbitration.

76. Third, issues may arise about the disclosure of documents on the court file relating to an arbitration (*Glidepath BV v Thompson* [2005] EWHC 818 (Comm)) or whether the judgment of a court given in relation to an arbitration should be published (*City of Moscow v Bankers Trust Co* [2004] EWCA Civ 314). Here the privacy of arbitration will be an important but not a decisive factor.

77. In each of those three cases the court will exercise a discretion in which privacy or confidentiality is an important factor in the balance.

78. Fourthly (and most relevant to the present case), a party to an arbitration may have an interest (commercial or otherwise) in disclosing documents generated in an arbitration (including the award itself) to third parties (*Hassneh Insurance Co of Israel v Mew* [1993] 2 Lloyd's Rep. 243; *Insurance Co v Lloyd's Syndicate* [1995] 1 Lloyd's Rep. 272; *Ali Shipping Corp v Shipyard Trogir* [1999] 1 W.L.R. 314; *Associated Electric and Gas Insurance Services Ltd v European Reinsurance Co of Zurich* [2003] 1 W.L.R. 1041) and the other party to the arbitration may seek to restrain disclosure by injunction.

79. Three legal concepts or categories have been in play in these cases. The first is privacy, in the sense that because arbitration is private that privacy would be violated by the publication or dissemination of documents deployed in the arbitration. The second is confidentiality in the sense where it is used to refer to inherent confidentiality in the information in documents, such as trade secrets or other confidential information generated or deployed in an arbitration. The third is confidentiality in the sense of an implied agreement that documents disclosed or generated in arbitration can only be used for the purposes of the arbitration. The distinction between the second and third cases may be illustrated by the example of the relevant documents in the

arbitration (such as the defence) not containing anything in themselves which is confidential but nevertheless the parties are under an obligation not to use it for any purpose other than the arbitration, and that obligation is described in the authorities as an obligation of confidence.

80. Some of the authorities treat privacy and confidentiality as equivalent: *London and Leeds Estates Ltd v Paribas Ltd (No.2)* [1995] 1 E.G.L.R. 102 at 109; *Hassneh Insurance Co of Israel v Mew* [1993] 2 Lloyd's Rep. 243 at 246–247; others draw a distinction between privacy and confidentiality, e.g. *Dolling-Baker* [1990] 1 W.L.R. 1205 at 1213–1214. In *Ali Shipping Corp v Shipyard Trogir* [1999] 1 W.L.R. 314, Potter L.J. said at 326 that, "the obligation of confidentiality arises as an essential corollary of the privacy of arbitration proceedings".

81. Documents in arbitration may, as I have said, be inherently confidential, as where they contain trade secrets. But it is clear that what has emerged from the recent authorities in England is that there is, separate from confidentiality in that sense, an implied obligation (arising out of the nature of arbitration itself) on both parties not to disclose or use for any other purpose any documents prepared for and used in the arbitration, or disclosed or produced in the course of the arbitration, or transcripts or notes of the evidence in the arbitration or the award, and not to disclose in any other way what evidence has been given by any witness in the arbitration, save with the consent of the other party, or pursuant to an order or leave of the court. That obligation is not limited to documents which contain material which is confidential, such as trade secrets and it does not arise as a matter of business efficacy, but is implied as a matter of law (*Ali Shipping Corp v Shipyard Trogir* [1999] 1 W.L.R. 314 at 326, disapproving *Hassneh Insurance Co of Israel v Mew* [1993] 2 Lloyd's Rep. 243 on this point).

... 83. The formulation of the implied obligation in arbitration is plainly influenced by the English rule in court proceedings (CPR r.31.22; for the history thereof see *Home Office v Harman* [1983] 1 A.C. 280) that a party to whom a document has been disclosed may use the document only for the purpose of the proceedings in which it is disclosed. Breach of this rule of court is a contempt, but the court has a power to give permission for the document to be used, particularly when it is in the public interest ...

... 85. There are, of course, limits and exceptions to the confidentiality obligation: an award may fall to be enforced, or challenged, in a court and the existence and details of an arbitration claim may need to be disclosed to insurers or to shareholders or to regulatory authorities. What, then, are the limits of the obligation to use documents in an arbitration only for the purposes of that arbitration?

86. Two preliminary points should be stressed: (i) the applicable institutional rules may provide an answer; (ii) it is particularly important that what has been said about the possible exceptions to

confidentiality must be read in context. Consider two examples: first, if a court decides in the context of a witness summons (as it did in *London and Leeds Estates Ltd v Paribas Ltd (No.2)* [1995] 1 E.G.L.R. 102) that the "public interest" may outweigh the confidentiality of arbitration documents, it does not necessarily follow that a party may voluntarily disclose documents to third parties on the ground that it is in "the public interest"; secondly, the court has no general or unlimited jurisdiction to consider whether an exception to confidentiality existed and was applicable.

... 88. The English courts have been strongly influenced in the development of exceptions to the basic rule of confidentiality in arbitration by the principles of banking confidentiality in *Tournier v National Provincial and Union Bank of England* [1924] 1 K.B. 461 (CA), where in a famous passage, Bankes L.J. said:

'In my opinion it is necessary in a case like the present to direct the jury what are the limits and what are the qualifications of the contractual duty of secrecy implied in the relation of banker and customer. There appears to be no authority on the point. On principle I think that the qualifications can be classified under four heads: (a) where disclosure is under compulsion by law; (b) where there is a duty to the public to disclose; (c) where the interests of the bank require disclosure; (d) where the disclosure is made by the express or implied consent of the customer.'

89. ... it is plain that the exceptions (especially the cases of "duty to the public" and "interests of the bank") are potentially very wide indeed.

90. The application to arbitration of these banking principles started in *Dolling-Baker* [1990] 1 W.L.R. 1205, continued in *Hassneh Insurance Co of Israel v Mew* [1993] 2 Lloyd's Rep. 243 and culminated in *Ali Shipping Corp v Shipyard Trogir* [1999] 1 W.L.R. 314, where Potter L.J. formulated a series of exceptions closely modelled on *Tournier*."

R26–15 Lawrence Collins L.J. noted the Privy Council's reservations concerning the *Ali Shipping* approach as expressed in *Associated Electric & Gas Insurance Services Ltd v European Reinsurance Company of Zurich* [2003] 1 WLR 1041; [2003] 1 All E.R. (Comm) 253 (on appeal from Bermuda). In that case, which involved the rejection of a claim of confidentiality for an award which was sought to be used to found a res judicata argument in a subsequent arbitration, Lord Hobhouse, speaking for the Privy Council, expressed the view that, given the private nature of commercial arbitrations and that in them, unlike litigations, nothing is placed in the public domain, the restriction on use of material from arbitrations might have a greater impact than on material from litigations. The only exception to this was in the award which required to be used in litigation for enforcement or referred to for accounting processes.

Nevertheless Lawrence Collins L.J. continued: **R26–16**

> "105. ... case law of the last 20 years has established that there is an obligation, implied by law and arising out of the very nature of arbitration, on both parties not to disclose or use for any other purpose any documents prepared for and used in the arbitration, or disclosed or produced in the course of the arbitration, or transcripts or notes of the evidence in the arbitration or the award, and not to disclose in any other way what evidence has been given by any witness in the arbitration. The obligation is not limited to commercially confidential information in the traditional sense.
>
> 106. ... this is in reality a substantive rule of arbitration law reached through the device of an implied term but this approach has led to difficulties of formulation and reliance (perhaps, over-reliance) on the banking principles in *Tournier*.
>
> 107. In my judgment the content of the obligation may depend on the context in which it arises and on the nature of the information or documents at issue and the limits of that obligation are still in the process of development on a case-by-case basis. On the authorities as they now stand, the principal cases in which disclosure will be permissible are these: (i) where there is consent, express or implied; (ii) where there is an order, or leave of the court (but that does not mean that the court has a general discretion to lift the obligation of confidentiality); (iii) where it is reasonably necessary for the protection of the legitimate interests of an arbitrating party; and (iv) where the interests of justice require disclosure, and also (perhaps) where the public interest requires disclosure."

Emmott (above) was an application to the court by a party to an ongoing **R26–17** arbitration in effect for a declarator that it was entitled to disclose pleadings in the arbitration to courts outwith England and Wales where matters the same or similar to those being arbitrated were being litigated. Observing that in effect the remedy was the mirror image of an injunction, and being persuade that the interests of justice required disclosure (r.26(1)(f) refers) the court allowed the disclosure.

There is, of course, one apparently simple route for the parties to an **R26–18** arbitration to adopt if they wish to clarify what part of the arbitral proceedings (and, in practice, most importantly the documents generated in the arbitration) are to be confidential as opposed to merely the proceedings being private and that is to agree specific confidentiality provisions, either by choice of law or in contract or in selecting the rules to govern the arbitration. Both Australian and Swedish law will recognise and enforce an express contractual confidentiality obligation, the *Esso v Plowman* (1995) 128

A.L.R. 391 and *Bulbank* decisions rejecting the proposition (enshrined in English law—see paras R26–07 and R26–14) that such an obligation is an implied term of an arbitration agreement but not rejecting an express term of such an agreement.

R26–19 While the Model Law is silent as regards confidentiality, New Zealand, in adopting it, has augmented it (at considerable length) by a specific statutory confidentiality provision. Among the major international arbitration institutions, only the LCIA has an express confidentiality provision in its rules whereas the ICC, AAA and others are generally silent, typically including confidentiality obligations binding the tribunal but with none binding the parties. The LCIA Rules art.30.1 state:

> "The parties undertake as a general principle to keep confidential all awards in the arbitration, together with all materials in the arbitration created for the purpose of the arbitration and all other documents produced by another party in the proceedings not otherwise in the public domain, save and to the extent that disclosure may be required of a party by legal duty, to protect or pursue a legal right, or to enforce or challenge an award in legal proceedings before a state court or other legal authority."

The position in Scotland under the common law

R26–20 Like so much of pre–2010 arbitration law in Scotland, it was unclear to what extent there was any confidentiality in arbitration. The statement in first edition of this book that the judiciary would give close consideration to the views of their English brethren has been borne out in *Gray Construction Ltd v Harley Haddow Ltd*, 2012 S.L.T. 1035 where Lord Hodge referred to Parker L.J. in *Dolling-Baker* at 1213 and Lawrence Collins L.J. in *Emmott* at [81] and [105] above and said at [5]:

> "... absent express contractual provision, I see no difficulty in implying such an [implied] obligation in a contract to refer a dispute for determination by means of arbitration. One of the attractions of arbitration is its privacy and this benefit would be negated if a party to the arbitration were not bound to respect confidentiality. It seems to me that such an obligation should be implied unless the terms of the parties' agreement exclude such implication".

R26–21 Lord Hodge observed, further, at [6]:

> "I do not need to address in any detail the boundaries of an obligation of confidentiality in relation to arbitration or the nature of the documents which it covers in the context of this motion [for recovery of arbitral pleadings]. We are not concerned with documents that are

inherently confidential such as trade secrets but with an obligation of confidentiality arising out of the nature of the arbitration proceedings. While counsel did not engage in a detailed discussion of the issue, I can readily see that pre–existing documents, which were voluntarily produced in an arbitration but were not otherwise publicly available, and documents produced under compulsion may be protected by implied restrictions as to their use for any purpose other than the arbitral proceedings. Pleadings and other documents created for the purpose of the arbitration may also be subjected to such obligations of confidentiality. But there must be exceptions to those obligations, for example, where a party needs to use such documents to enforce his award or otherwise to protect his legitimate interests or where the disclosure is in the public interest. See, by way of illustration, the default rule set out in the modern statutory code, which is Rule 26 of the Scottish Arbitration Rules in Schedule 1 to the Arbitration (Scotland) Act 2010."

In *Gray Construction* the issue arose in a litigation where a builder sought damages for professional negligence from his professional advisers which included a claim for loss sustained in settling, in an arbitration, a claim by a third party. The advisers applied to the court for recovery of among other things the pleadings from the arbitration. It was accepted that the documents sought did not contain any commercially sensitive material that was confidential for any reason other than that it had been used in the arbitration. **R26–22**

In finding that disclosure was necessary in the interests of justice (s.26(1)(f) refers), Lord Hodge said: **R26–23**

"In my view the court should take account of a private obligation of confidentiality and seek to strike a balance between respect for the honouring of that obligation and the public interest in the fair administration of justice. Where it is necessary to recover documents which a party holds subject to an obligation of confidentiality in order to achieve the fair disposal of an action, the court will as a norm order the production of those documents. The test is not one of absolute necessity; the court, in deciding how to achieve a fair disposal of the action, may take into account how a party can reasonably prepare to present his case. If the documents are not essential to the action or if the information can be recovered elsewhere without breaching a confidence, the court may exercise its discretion to refuse to order recovery. Similarly, it may consider whether there are less costly ways of gaining the needed information. These considerations, which one finds in *Scientific Research Council* v *Nassé* [1980] A.C. 1028, Lord Wilberforce at 1065–1066 and in *Emmott* (above) Lawrence Collins L.J. at [107] and Thomas L.J. at [127], are consistent with Lord Hunter's decision in

Santa Fe International Corporation v Napier Shipping SA, 1985 S.L.T. 430."

R26–24 Notwithstanding the order for disclosure, *Gray Construction* illustrates the importance of the arbitral obligation of confidentiality. Standing Lord Hodge's obiter remarks concerning the disclosure of commercially sensitive confidential material used in an arbitration, it can be expected that if disclosure of such material is sought there will be a heavy onus on the party seeking disclosure to show that any of the grounds for disclosure in r.26 are met.

Practical considerations

R26–25 There are two main practical difficulties in enforcing any confidentiality obligation, whether expressly set out in an arbitration agreement or incorporated in the agreed set of rules. First, breaches are normally discovered too late to take any action (your arbitration is headline news in today's tabloids) and, secondly, it can be impossible to prove any loss caused thereby and, even if loss is proved, quantification will normally be very difficult.

R26–26 Nevertheless the following factors provided justification for r.26: (i) the Scottish business community's response to the consultation process overwhelmingly endorsed the principle of having a confidentiality obligation; (ii) the two Queen Mary University of London/PriceWaterhouseCoopers studies confirmed that the international market place also so endorsed; (iii) the drafters considered that, facing a clear obligation, the overwhelming majority of parties would comply with it; (iv) neither LCIA Rules r.30.1 nor the implied term in English law had given rise to any significant difficulties over the years (the *City of Moscow v Bankers Trust Co* [2005] Q.B. 207 case showing that a confidentiality obligation could work); (v) r.26 would give parties a tool which they could use as they saw fit and to the extent that they could so far as the courts would allow.

R26–27 Issues of "actionability" will arise before a Scottish court in a number of possible situations. These include:

- Interdict and interim interdict (injunction) against disclosure.
- Damages for breach of duty of confidentiality.
- Declarator of absence of duty of confidentiality.
- Recovery of documents or information under a common law application for commission and diligence in terms of a specification of documents or an application under s.1 of the 1972 Act.

Rule 27: Tribunal deliberations D

27.—(1) The tribunal's deliberations may be undertaken in private and accordingly need not be disclosed to the parties.

(2) But, where an arbitrator fails to participate in any of the tribunal's deliberations, the tribunal must disclose that fact (and the extent of the failure) to the parties.

DEFINITIONS

"arbitrator": s.2(1)
"party": ss.2(1), 31(1), (2)
"tribunal": ss.2(1), 31(1)

STATUS

This is a default rule so it is open to the parties to modify it, agree something different or disapply it completely (see s.9). Article 44(2) of the Swiss Rules provides that the deliberations of the tribunal are confidential. The LCIA provision is referred to below. R27–01

MODEL LAW

There is no equivalent in the Model Law. R27–02

COMMENTARY

The policy memorandum published with the Bill on January 30, 2009 stated as follows (at para.158): R27–03

> "Although the parties will normally receive the tribunal's reasons for an award as part of that award, they should not be entitled to know what the deliberations of the tribunal are prior to the award, which should be confidential to its members (unless of course the tribunal shows the parties a draft award prior to issuing the final award). This is the policy behind rule 27. The only exception to this is that it may be necessary to disclose an arbitrator's refusal to participate in the arbitration."

There is no equivalent to r.27 either in the 1996 Act or in the ICC Rules but there is in the LCIA Rules (see below) and in art.1479 of the French Code of Civil Procedure. R27–04

Rule 27(1) is important to prevent the disclosure of deliberations, for example in the context of any appeal. R27–05

Rule 27(1)

R27–06 While intuitively obvious, it is perhaps less than straightforward to pin down the reasons for r.27, the main one being the concern that if the tribunal was obliged to deliberate "in public" (in the sense of the involvement of the parties, not in the sense of "live on TV"), the process would run a serious risk of contamination, in several regards: (i) by the loss of the arbitrators' freedom to express themselves fully which they can do with each other in private but not in a hearing room full of party representatives and advisers; (ii) party-appointed arbitrators might sense pressure from their respective appointing party or might be tempted to "play to the gallery"; (iii) all three arbitrators might feel concern that whatever they might say or write in deliberating might lead to challenge to the award or, worse still, some challenge to them individually, e.g. on grounds of perceived bias; and (iv) judges normally deliberate in private.

R27–07 LCIA Rules r.30.2 states:

> "The deliberations of the Arbitral Tribunal are likewise confidential to its members, save and to the extent that disclosure of an arbitrator's refusal to participate in the arbitration is required of the other members of the Arbitral Tribunal under Articles 10, 12, 26 and 27."

R27–08 See r.27(2) below concerning LCIA Rules art.12.1.

R27–09 The authors submit that the effect of r.27(1) is to render the arbitrators' deliberations and their notes and working papers confidential to themselves and privileged.

Rule 27(2)

R27–10 There is no equivalent in this Act of LCIA Rules art.12.1 which states:

> "In exceptional circumstances, where an arbitrator without good cause refuses or persistently fails to participate in the deliberations of an Arbitral Tribunal, the remaining arbitrators jointly may decide (*after their written notice of such refusal or failure to the LCIA Court, the parties and the absent arbitrator*) to continue the arbitration (including the making of any decision, ruling or award), notwithstanding the absence of that other arbitrator, subject to the written approval of the LCIA Court" (authors' emphasis added).

R27–11 LCIA Rules art.12 goes on to deal with the two consequent options, either the tribunal continues as a truncated one or it stops the arbitration; in either case, this is a matter of very great significance hence the necessity for written notice.

Arbitration (Scotland) Act 2010 (r.28)

PART 4

ARBITRAL PROCEEDINGS

Rule 28: Procedure and evidence D

28.—(1) It is for the tribunal to determine—
  (a) the procedure to be followed in the arbitration, and
  (b) the admissibility, relevance, materiality and weight of any evidence.
(2) In particular, the tribunal may determine—
  (a) when and where the arbitration is to be conducted,
  (b) whether parties are to submit claims or defences and, if so, when they should do so and the extent to which claims or defences may be amended,
  (c) whether any documents or other evidence should be disclosed by or to any party and, if so, when such disclosures are to be made and to whom copies of disclosed documents and information are to be given,
  (d) whether any and, if so, what questions are to be put to and answered by the parties,
  (e) whether and, if so, to what extent the tribunal should take the initiative in ascertaining the facts and the law,
  (f) the extent to which the arbitration is to proceed by way of—
    (i) hearings for the questioning of parties,
    (ii) written or oral argument,
    (iii) presentation or inspection of documents or other evidence, or
    (iv) submission of documents or other evidence,
  (g) the language to be used in the arbitration (and whether a party is to supply translations of any document or other evidence),
  (h) whether to apply rules of evidence used in legal proceedings or any other rules of evidence.

DEFINITIONS

"arbitration": s.2(1)
"tribunal": s.2(1)

STATUS

This is a default rule so it is open to the parties to modify it, agree something different or disapply it completely (see s.9 and the commentary thereon). All sets of institutional arbitral rules known to the authors contain equivalent provisions. Examples include arts 22(2) and 23–27 of the ICC Rules, art.14 of the LCIA Rules, and arts 17–25 of the UNCITRAL Rules. In such situations the starting point will be to consider what the position is under r.28 and then to see the extent to which the provisions of r.28 or its relevant part are inconsistent with or disapplied by the arbitral rule in question.

R28–01

MODEL LAW

R28–02 Articles 19, 20(2) and 22–24 are similar in principle but marginally less detailed.

COMMENTARY

R28–03 It is a universal feature of modern arbitration laws around the world that the tribunal is (or, at least, should be) the master of procedure so that it can select procedural rules, techniques and processes appropriate to the case in hand. The arbitrators have complete power over all procedural and evidential matters and are the sole judges of the evidence, including the assessment of the probabilities and resolving issues of credibility (*Hashwani v Jivraj* [2011] UKSC 40, [2011] 1 W.L.R. 1872 at [62] per Lord Clarke of Stone-cum-Ebony JSC).

R28–04 However, the principle of party autonomy, as reflected in the default status of this rule, means that parties can agree to modify or exclude elements of the default procedure, whether expressly or through adopting arbitral rules which are inconsistent with parts of r.28.

R28–05 Once the procedure is fixed, a failure by the tribunal to follow the procedure opens up a potential removal application under r.12(e) and its counterpart, challenge to any subsequent award under r.68(2)(a). Similarly, the procedure must, axiomatically, comply with all the mandatory rules in the Act (see s.8), most importantly r.24 (see para.R28–07).

Rule 28(1)

R28–06 This rule tracks the language of art.19(2) of the Model Law closely and establishes the key principles. A key point is that the tribunal is not required to follow the practices and procedures in court litigation. Indeed it should not do so unless the parties insist. Even under the old common law it was observed in *EDRC Construction Ltd v HM Love & Co (No.2)*, 1996 S.C. 523; 1997 S.L.T. 175, that:

> "It is ... disappointing to see the extent to which the formalities of written pleading and its associated procedure, from which the Court of Session is now seeking to detach itself in commercial actions under chap 47 of the Rules of Court, have been resorted to here for the disposal of what is, by the normal standards of building and engineering contracts, a comparatively small claim" (at 528 per Lord President Hope).

Rule 28(1)(a)—Tribunals Masters of Procedure

R28–07 While the tribunal has the power and discretion to determine procedure, that power and discretion must be exercised consistently with the tribunal's mandatory duties under r.24. These include the duty to conduct the arbitration without unnecessary delay and without incurring unnecessary expense, as well as the duty to treat the parties fairly, including giving each party a reasonable opportunity to put its case and deal with the other party's case. The authors submit that the effect of r.24 is to impose on arbitrators an obligation to adopt a proactive approach. Thus it is not open for a tribunal to sit back and wait until the parties propose the next procedural step. It is suggested that the duty in r.24 imposes on the arbitrator a duty to propose and, failing agreement by the parties, to impose procedures which will enable a quick and cost-effective resolution of the dispute while maintaining fairness between the parties.

If the parties have adopted institutional or other arbitral rules, then these will have a framework for the procedure to be followed. If the parties have not adopted such rules it is open for them to do so and for the arbitrator to suggest their adoption. At the time of writing there are few sets of rules that have been devised specially for domestic arbitrations in Scotland following the Act (e.g. the SSFARs and those devised by FLAGS and SAAVA). **R28–08**

The authors suggest that the UNCITRAL Rules, while devised for use in international commercial disputes, could be adopted for use in domestic commercial or other disputes. **R28–09**

Arbitrators may also find assistance in determining procedure in the UNCITRAL *Notes on Organizing Arbitral Proceedings* (United Nations Commission on International Trade Law, 2012) available at *http://www.uncitral.org/uncitral/uncitral_texts/arbitration.html* [Accessed June 18, 2014]. **R28–10**

In addition the ICC Commission *Report on Controlling Time and Costs in Arbitration* contains useful advice for arbitrators and parties in relation to the procedure to be adopted. This is available at *http://www.iccwbo.org/Advocacy-Codes-and-Rules* [Accessed June 18, 2014]. **R28–11**

Rule 28(1)(b)—Evidential Powers

At common law it was recognised that it was for the arbitrator to decide the relevancy, suitability, materiality and weight of evidence, provided that he or she did not act unfairly to a party in doing so (*Alston v Chappell* (1839) 2 D 348; *Mowbray v Dickson* (1848) 10 D 1102 at 1110, 1114, 1122 and 1125). However, there were no comprehensive judicial statements to that effect. This had the effect of creating uncertainty for arbitrators and parties. **R28–12**

Rule 28(1)(b) brings Scots law into line with art.19(2) of the Model Law and s.34 of the 1996 Act. It should be read with the particular examples of its application in rr.28(2)(c),(d),(h). **R28–13**

The decision of a tribunal as to the materiality and weight of evidence is not subject to any appeal. This is because the effect of such a decision will be reflected in the findings in fact of the tribunal which are not open to a legal error appeal under r.69: see r.70(3)(b) and para.R70–15, nor would such a **R28–14** decision involve any irregularity under r.68 which could give rise to an appeal for serious irregularity.

R28–15 A decision as to the admissibility and relevance of evidence will also not be subject to any legal error appeal under r.69 for the same reasons. The only conceivable appeal in respect of a decision as to admissibility and relevance would arise if the decision of the tribunal involved it failing to comply with its duty under r.24 to treat the parties fairly, including giving each party a reasonable opportunity to put its case and to deal with the other party's case. An example of this might be where the arbitrator admitted evidence and made findings in fact of which no fair notice was given to the parties (see commentary on r.24(2)).

R28–16 This has been accepted as the position in the rest of the UK under the 1996 Act, s.69(3) of which is worded similarly to r.70(3). Thus in *Demco Investments & Commercial SA v SE Banken Forsakring Holding AB* [2005] EWHC 1398 (Comm); [2005] 2 Lloyd's Rep. 650, Cooke J. said this:

> "35. ... There is no room for any appeal under s.69 against the findings of fact in the Award itself since these have to be accepted for the purpose of any application for permission to appeal.
>
> 36. The legislative intent behind the form of words used in the Act was made clear in the DAC Report of 1996 at paragraph 286 (iii) in the following words:
>
>> 'There have been attempts, both before and after the enactment of the Arbitration Act 1979, to dress up questions of fact as questions of law and by that means to seek an appeal on the Tribunal's decision on the facts. Generally, these attempts have been resisted by the Courts but to make the position clear, we propose to state expressly that consideration by the Court of the suggested question of law is made on the basis of the findings of fact in the award.'
>
> 37. Furthermore, section 34 (2)(f) of the 1996 Act, under the heading of 'Procedural and Evidential Matters' provides that it is for the Tribunal to decide all procedural and evidential matters which include 'whether to apply strict rules of evidence (or any other rules) as to the admissibility, relevance or weight of any material (oral, written or other) sought to be tendered on any matters of fact or opinion and the time, manner and form in which such material should be exchanged and presented.' Although there is no suggestion that the arbitrators made any specific ruling in relation to relaxation of rules of evidence, and there is some insistence in the award on the need for convincing evidence if gross negligence is to be found, the DAC Report at paragraph 170 throws light on the provision in stating that 'Clause 34 (2)(f) helps to put an end to any arguments that it is a question of law whether there is material to support a fact'.

38. In *The Baleares* [1993] 1 Lloyd's Report 215 at page 232 column1, Steyn LJ stated that an appeal on the *Edwards v Bairstow* principle did not constitute an appeal on a point of law under the Arbitration Act of 1979. Whilst there was some debate about this position under the 1979 Act because of the decision of Millett J in *Capital & Counties PLC v Hawa* [1991] 2 EGLR 133, in my judgment it is clear from the terms of the 1996 Act itself that there is no room for an appeal on this basis under that Act.

39. The leading text books on Arbitration are unanimous in saying that it is not open to a party to an arbitration to appeal on the basis that the question whether the Tribunal was right to find a fact on the basis of the evidential material before it is a question of law. The parties have chosen the tribunal which is to decide the facts and its conclusions cannot be questioned.

... 43. I have been referred to *Guardcliffe Properties Limited v City & St James* [2003] 2 E.G.L.R. 16 in which Etherton J expressed the view, obiter, that an error of law within the *Edwards v Bairstow* principle [i.e. a finding in fact without evidence to support it] could be an error of law under s.69 of the 1996 Act. He relied upon the earlier decision of Millett J and considered a decision of Evans Lombe J in *Secretary of State for the Environment v Reed International* [1994] 1 E.G.L.R. 22 as decided per incuriam, in ignorance of Millett J's decision. I regret that I am unable to agree with him and respectfully note that the point does not appear to have been argued before him by reference to the opening words of s.69(3)(c), nor to the wording of the DAC report. The learned judge did not have, in the event, to consider the scope of s.69 because the challenge under section 68 succeeded, but he drew no distinction between the 1979 Act and the 1996 Act, whereas the terms of section 1(2) of the earlier Act do not include the words to which I have drawn attention with which s.69 (3)(c) commences. For the same reasons I disagree with the decision of HH Judge Thornton QC in *Fence Gate Ltd v NEL Construction Ltd* [2001] 82 Con LR 41.

44. Under the terms of the 1996 Act therefore Steyn LJ's dictum in relation to arbitrations under the 1979 Arbitration Act, with which Neill LJ was impressed, without agreeing, takes full force and effect.

45. In the same decision, Steyn LJ, at page 228 said:

'The Arbitrators are the masters of the facts. On an appeal the Court must decide any question of law arising from an Award on the basis of a full and unqualified acceptance of the findings of facts of the Arbitrators. It is irrelevant whether the Court considers those findings of fact to be right or wrong. It also does not matter how obvious a mistake by the Arbitrators on the issues of fact might be, or what the scale of the financial consequences of the mistake of fact might be. That is of course an unsurprising

Arbitration (Scotland) Act 2010

position. After all, the very reason why parties conclude an arbitration agreement is because they do not wish to litigate in the Courts. Parties who submit their disputes to arbitration bind themselves by agreement to honour the Arbitrator's Award on the facts. The principle of party autonomy decrees that a Court ought never to question the Arbitrator's findings of fact.'"

R28–17 *Demco* has since been followed in *London Underground Ltd v Citylink Telecommunications Ltd* [2007] EWHC 1749 (TCC) at [60] to [65] per Ramsey J. and in *House of Fraser Ltd v Scottish Widows plc* [2011] EWHC 2800 (Ch) at [25] per Peter Smith J.

Rule 28(2)

R28–18 In an arbitration without a pre-agreed set of applicable rules it will be necessary in practice to work through these and other items and most professional arbitrators have their own extensive checklist; that said, it is not the intention of the 2010 Act that the parties and the arbitrator treat r.28(2) (or for that matter, any of rr.28–40) on a "pick and choose" menu basis—the Rules have been constructed as a complete and harmonious whole (see Policy Memorandum, paras 87–88). Of course, the parties and the arbitrator are free to agree otherwise (of which the adoption of comprehensive rules is a prime example) but the intention remains. One of the authors was sole arbitrator in a highly complex arbitration in England with senior (i.e. QC) and junior counsel and a large team of solicitors on each side. The parties had agreed the procedural details and presented a draft procedural order for the arbitrator's approval; his response was "what about . . . " and he listed a further 14 items, some significant, that the parties' lawyers had overlooked.

Rule 28(2)(a)—Timing and location of arbitration

R28–19 This should be read with r.29. See also art.20(2) of the Model Law. Flexibility of venue is one of the advantages of arbitration over litigation. There is no requirement for the arbitration to be conducted at any particular venue or even in Scotland. The parties can agree that it or part of it should take place elsewhere in the world, albeit that its juridical seat will always remain in Scotland. If one of the parties or the tribunal wish the arbitration or part of it to take place outwith Scotland it is open for the tribunal to make such a decision provided that in doing so the tribunal complies with its duties under r.24 as to fair treatment and conducting the arbitration without unnecessary delay or incurring of unnecessary expense. The location of parties, their witnesses and representatives will be matters to be taken into account in any contested proposal which the tribunal has to decide in this regard.

There is a Scottish Arbitration Centre in Edinburgh which has been set up R28–20
for the hearing of arbitrations, including international arbitrations.

Rule 28(2)(b)—Pleadings

This follows art.23 of the Model Law. Neither art.23 nor r.28(2)(b) refer R28–21
to written claims. It is a common feature of all arbitral rules of which the
authors are aware that claims and defences be submitted in writing. While in
theory a claim and defence could be submitted orally at a hearing or
hearings before the tribunal, it is suggested that for the sake of clarity and to
avoid any misunderstanding all tribunals require that claims and defences be
put in writing.

Modern arbitration outwith Scotland has (with a few exceptions) moved R28–22
far away from the court-based style of submissions and pleadings, e.g. as
used in the past in Scottish arbitrations. A typical modern procedural order
states:

> "Claim & Defence
> Submissions in the form of comprehensive statements, including all
> relevant facts, evidence (including witness statements if applicable),
> citations and all documents relied upon shall be served by one Party on
> the other (copied to the Arbitrator) as follows:
> [schedule of dates]"

The intention is that each of the claimant and respondent has "one shot"
(with, where appropriate, a single reply each) so that the process of
exchanging claim and defence is completed quickly (e.g. LCIA Rules r.15
gives a maximum of 112 days), without the continual, time consuming (and
expensive) adjustment of statements (pleadings) derived from Scottish litigation procedure.

In smaller arbitrations, it is always possible (and may be expeditious) to R28–23
limit the size of submissions of claim and defence. Too often substantial
time and money is wasted preparing vast bundles of documentation which is
never referred to or otherwise used.

While it is axiomatic that parties have the opportunity to respond to their R28–24
opponent's case, this does not mean continual rounds of rebuttal. Typically,
the defence will respond to the claim and may introduce a counterclaim then
the claimant will respond (i) to the defence and (ii) to the counterclaim.
Response (i) should be limited to responding to the points made in the
defence and should not introduce any new claim or arguments; ditto
response (ii). The respondent will then respond only to the response to
counterclaim. In some forms of arbitration, e.g. rent review, the parties
conventionally make simultaneous submissions and, e.g. 20 working days
later, simultaneous responses. There are no fixed rules, save that the process

must be efficient (see s.1(a) and rr.24(1)(c), 25 above) by terminating quickly. See s.34(2)(c) of the 1996 Act.

Rule 28(2)(c)—Disclosure and recovery of documents or other evidence

R28–25 This rule gives the tribunal very wide powers which are wider than those of a Scottish court in relation to disclosure of evidence by a party in a litigation. The rule is limited to disclosure by a party in the arbitration and does not give the tribunal power in relation to disclosure by a person who is not such a party. If disclosure is sought from a person who is not a party in the arbitration, an application must be made to the court under r.45 (see commentary on r.45). The tribunal should also be aware of its related powers under r.35 to direct a party to preserve a document or other evidence that it possesses or controls or to direct a party in relation to non-documentary property (see commentary on r.35).

R28–26 How is a tribunal to exercise its powers? In the first place, the authors suggest that at an early stage in the arbitration the tribunal decide under r.28(2)(h) what rules of evidence it should apply in relation to the disclosure or recovery of evidence. Before doing so, it should invite the parties to address it on its proposals. The parties may have agreed the matter. Otherwise there are a number of options for the tribunal.

R28–27 In relation to the production by a party of documents that it founds upon, the tribunal should require any documents founded on by the parties which are within their possession or control be lodged with it with their statements of claim, defence or reply.

R28–28 In relation to recovery from another party, the tribunal could decide to apply the Scots common law rule for recoverability of documents (including those kept in electronic or other form). The Scots common law rule for recovery of evidence for Scottish litigations has been expressed as follows:

> "Subject to confidentiality and relevancy, a document is recoverable if it is a deed [document] granted by or on behalf of a party or his predecessor in title, or a communication sent to or by or on behalf of a party, or a written record kept by or on behalf of a party" (M. L. Ross and J. Chalmers (eds), *Walker and Walker on The Law of Evidence in Scotland*, 3rd edn (Hayward's Heath: Tottel Publishing, 2009), para.21.6.2.)

The reference to confidentiality is to privileged confidentiality for which see the commentary on r.45(2). The reference to relevancy is to the requirement that the document sought must be capable either of proving or making more specific a factual allegation (averment) already made by the recovering party in the written pleadings, or at least answering a factual allegation made by the non-recovering party in its pleadings (*Boyle v Glasgow Royal Infirmary*, 1969 S.C. 72).

Under Scots law recovery to enable the possible making of a factual **R28–29** allegation not already made is not allowed and is referred to as a "fishing diligence". As a result applications are typically made in the form of a written specification of documents in which the documents to be recovered are expressed as "showing or tending to show" the factual allegation in question (*Paterson v Paterson*, 1919 1 S.L.T. 12) or individually named. In addition, recovery for proof of a factual allegation is permitted only after the pleadings have been settled. The Scots common law on recovery of evidence is therefore significantly more restrictive than for typical common law jurisdictions. As a mixed jurisdiction, the Scots position sits between the traditional common law position of a liberal approach to recovery and the civilian position of a restrictive and exclusionary approach to recovery. It is no accident that the Scots lawyer uses the term "recovery" rather than "discovery".

Alternatively, the decision may be taken to adopt other rules, which may **R28–30** or may not be Scottish. It is important to remember that disclosure is very much an Anglo-American process, not mirrored (at least to the same degree) in non-Anglo-American common law jurisdictions such as Scotland, and considered almost alien in civil law jurisdictions.

Fortunately, an excellent and widely-used compromise between the **R28–31** Anglo-American approach and the civilian approach has been reached in the IBA Evidence Rules, which also serve as a useful and recommended approach in domestic arbitration. The relevant parts of the IBA Evidence Rules provide as follows:

"Article 3 Documents

1. Within the time ordered by the Arbitral Tribunal, each Party shall submit to the Arbitral Tribunal and to the other Parties all Documents available to it on which it relies, including public Documents and those in the public domain, except for any Documents that have already been submitted by another Party.
2. Within the time ordered by the Arbitral Tribunal, any Party may submit to the Arbitral Tribunal a Request to Produce.
3. A Request to Produce shall contain:
    (a) (i) a description of each requested document sufficient to identify it, or (ii) a description in sufficient detail (including subject matter) of a narrow and specific requested category of Documents that are reasonably believed to exist; in the case of Documents maintained in electronic form, the requesting party may, or the Arbitral Tribunal may order that it shall be required to, identify specific files, search terms, individuals or other means of searching for such Documents in an efficient and economical manner;

Arbitration (Scotland) Act 2010

    (b) a statement as to how the Documents requested are relevant to the case and material to its outcome; and

    (c) (i) a statement that the Documents requested are not in the possession, custody or control of the requesting Party, or a statement of the reasons why it would be unreasonably burdensome for the requesting Party to produce such Documents, and (ii) a statement of the reasons why the requesting Party assumes the Documents requested are in the possession, custody or control of another Party.

4. Within the time ordered by the Arbitral Tribunal, the Party to whom the Request to Produce is addressed shall produce to other Parties and, if the Arbitral Tribunal so orders, to it, all the Documents requested in its possession, custody or control as to which it makes no objection.

5. If the Party to whom the Request to Produce is addressed has an objection to some or all of the Documents requested, it shall state the objection in writing to the Arbitral Tribunal within the time ordered by the Arbitral Tribunal. The reasons for such objections shall be any of those set forth in Article 9.2, or a failure to satisfy any of the requirements of Article 3.3.

6. Upon receipt of any such objection, the Arbitral Tribunal may invite the relevant Parties to consult with each other with a view to resolving the objection.

7. Either party may, within the time ordered by the Arbitral Tribunal, request the Arbitral Tribunal to rule on the objection. The Arbitral Tribunal shall then in consultation with the Parties and in timely fashion, consider the Request to Produce and the objection. The Arbitral Tribunal may order the Party to whom such Request is addressed to produce any requested Document in its possession custody or control as to which the Arbitral Tribunal determines that (i) the issues that the requesting party wishes to prove are relevant to the case and material to its outcome; (ii) none of the reasons for objection set forth in Article 9.2 applies; and (iii) the requirements of Article 3.3 have been satisfied. Any such Document shall be produced to the other Parties and, if the Arbitral Tribunal so orders, to it.

8. In exceptional circumstances, if the propriety of an objection can be determined only by review of the Document, the Arbitral Tribunal may determine that it should not review the Document. In that event, the Arbitral Tribunal may, after consultation with the Parties, appoint an independent and impartial expert, bound to confidentiality, to review any such Document and to report on the objection. To the extent that the objection is upheld by the Arbitral Tribunal, the expert shall not disclose to the Arbitral Tribunal and to the other Parties the contents of the Document reviewed. ...

Arbitration (Scotland) Act 2010 (r.28)

... 10. At any time before the arbitration is concluded the Arbitral Tribunal may (i) request any Party to produce Documents, (ii) request any Party to use its best efforts to take or (iii) itself take, any step that it considers appropriate to obtain Documents from any person or organisation. A party to whom such a request for Documents is addressed may object to the request for any of the reasons set forth in Article 9.2. In such cases, Article 3.4 to Article 3.8 shall apply correspondingly.
11. Within the time ordered by the Arbitral Tribunal, the Parties may submit to the Arbitral Tribunal and to the other Parties any additional Documents on which they intend to rely or which they believe have become relevant to the case and material to its outcome as a consequence of the issues raised in Documents, Witness Statements or Expert Reports submitted or produced by another Party or in other submissions of the Parties.
12. With respect to the form of submission or production of Documents:

    (a) copies of Documents shall conform to the originals and, at the request of the Arbitral Tribunal, any original shall be presented for inspection;
    (b) Documents that a Party maintains in electronic form shall be submitted or produced in the form most convenient or economical to it that is reasonably usable by the recipients, unless the Parties agree otherwise or, in the absence of such agreement the Arbitral Tribunal decides otherwise;
    (c) a Party is not obligated to produce multiple copies of Documents which are essentially identical unless the Arbitral Tribunal decides otherwise; and
    (d) translations of Documents shall be submitted together with the originals and marked as translations with the original language identified.

13. Any Document submitted or produced by a Party or non-Party in the arbitration and not otherwise in the public domain shall be kept confidential by the Arbitral Tribunal and the other Parties, and shall be used only in connection with the arbitration. This requirement shall apply except and to the extent that disclosure may be required of a Party to fulfil a legal duty, protect or pursue a legal right, or enforce or challenge an award in bona fide legal proceedings before a state court or other judicial authority. The Arbitral Tribunal may issue orders to set forth the terms of this confidentiality. This requirement shall be without prejudice to all other obligations of confidentiality in the arbitration.
14. If the arbitration is organised into separate issues or phases (such as jurisdiction, preliminary determinations, liability or damages)

Arbitration (Scotland) Act 2010

the Arbitral Tribunal may, after consultation with the Parties, schedule the submission of Documents and Requests to Produce separately for each issue or phase."

The reasons for objection in art.9.2 of the IBA Evidence Rules are:

(a) lack of sufficient relevance to the case or materiality as to its outcome;
(b) legal impediment or privilege under the legal or ethical rules determined by the Arbitral Tribunal to be applicable;
(c) unreasonable burden to produce the requested evidence;
(d) loss or destruction of the Document that has been shown with reasonable likelihood to have occurred;
(e) grounds of commercial or technical confidentiality that the Arbitral Tribunal determines to be compelling;
(f) grounds of special political or institutional sensitivity (including evidence that has been classified as secret by a government or public international institution) that the Arbitral Tribunal determines to be compelling;
(g) considerations of procedural economy, proportionality, fairness or equality of the Parties that the Arbitral Tribunal determines to be compelling.

Article 9.3 provides further factors to be taken into account in the consideration of legal impediment or privilege under art.9.2(b).

R28–32 It should be noted that all such documents produced are covered by r.26 (confidentiality), provided that the parties have not agreed to disapply that rule.

R28–33 The CIArb Protocol for E-disclosure in Arbitration (available at *http://www.ciarb.org/information-and-resources* [Accessed June 18, 2014]) assists tribunals in the issue of disclosure of documents kept in electronic form. It can be adopted by parties or provide guidance to tribunals.

R28–34 In making a decision as to which rules to apply to disclosure, the tribunal should have regard to its mandatory duties under r.24. Once the tribunal has decided the rules applicable it can simply apply those rules consistently with those mandatory duties. Thus, for example, if a document is lodged at a late stage for no good reason and is objected to and cannot be adequately answered by the other party, the tribunal, having regard to its duties, may refuse to allow it to be used. See also s.34(2)(d) of the 1996 Act.

Rule 28(2)(d)—Questioning of Parties

This rule enables the tribunal to determine whether any questions are to be put to and answered by the parties and, if the tribunal determines that questions are to be put and answered, it enables the tribunal to decide what questions are to be put and answered. **R28–35**

The issue of whether any questions are to be put will depend firstly on whether the tribunal decides that there is to be a hearing of oral evidence (see commentary on r.28(2)(f)(i)). Secondly, it will depend on whether the parties will wish to call themselves or, if they are legal persons, their representatives as witnesses at such a hearing. If they do call themselves, the parties' decision to do so will inevitably involve questioning. If, however, for any reason a party decides not to call itself (or its representatives) as witnesses, this rule, together with r.28(2)(e), makes it clear that the tribunal can nevertheless decide to have the party (or its representatives) called and questioned. In making any such decision the tribunal must of course bear in mind its mandatory duties under r.24. However, there is nothing in principle to prevent a tribunal from calling and questioning a party if its evidence is relevant and material to the issue in the case. The parties must be given an opportunity to ask questions following on from the questioning by the tribunal. **R28–36**

The rule also enables a party to be questioned by the tribunal if it presents itself or its representatives as witnesses. Moreover, the questioning by the tribunal can be inquisitorial and is not restricted to clearing up matters of doubt raised in the questions of parties or their representatives. The rule therefore caters for both the traditional civilian and Anglo-American approaches to arbitration. Does the rule enable the tribunal to restrict questions asked of a party (or its representatives), as, for example, in cross-examination? It is suggested that it can do so. It may be that the cross-examination lacks apparent purpose or relevance or seeks to raise relevant matters of which prior notice should have been given. In these situations, and in others, the tribunal has a power to restrict the questioning provided always that it acts "fairly" in the sense of r.24(2) in particular. **R28–37**

The rule refers only to "parties" as the tribunal has no jurisdiction to determine and direct that non-party witnesses attend a hearing for questioning. For that, a witness attendance order must be obtained by the tribunal (or a party) from the court under r.45. However, once such a witness is present at a hearing to give oral evidence, the arbitrator, as master of the procedure in the arbitration (r.28(1)) and with wide inquisitorial powers (r.28(2)(e)), has the same powers of questioning as in relation to a party. See also s.34(2)(e) of the 1996 Act. **R28–38**

If the tribunal decides that oral evidence should be heard, it should at the same time decide whether and if so how the evidence is to be recorded. **R28–39**

Rule 28(2)(e)—Inquisitorial power of tribunal

R28–40   This was at one time considered controversial since it was perceived as a foreign (civil law) practice with no place in Scots (or English) law. The DAC Report addressed certain concerns as follows:

> "172. ... Once again it seems to us that provided the tribunal in exercising its powers follows its simple duty as set out in Clause 33 (and subsection (2) of this Clause tells the tribunal that this is what they must do) then in suitable cases an inquisitorial approach to all or some of the matters involved may well be the best way of proceeding. Clause 33, however, remains a control, such that, for example, if an arbitrator takes the initiative in procuring evidence, he must give all parties a reasonable opportunity of commenting on it."

This argument applies equally under this Act since r.24 and s.33 of the 1996 Act are based on common ground.

R28–41   In some civil law jurisdictions, e.g. Germany and Switzerland, the tribunal drives the proceedings and leads the questioning of witnesses with counsel contributing as and when necessary or appropriate, quite unlike the traditional Anglo-Saxon style. Further, some leading international arbitrators favour a more open style which can become close to a discussion. Whether or not such an approach appeals in Scotland remains to be seen, but it certainly offers a greater flexibility than the formal court-style alternation of submissions by counsel. The authors are confident that Scottish arbitrators will embrace this and other new approaches and avoid being trapped in the mire of pre-2010 arbitration practices derived from litigation.

R28–42   The inquisitorial approach has to be adopted with restraint; the arbitrator must bear in mind his r.24 duties and in particular the duty of fairness to the parties. In *Norbrook Laboratories Ltd v Tank* [2006] EWHC 1055 (Comm) the arbitrator, Mr Tank, took it upon himself to contact three potential witness directly and for this and other reasons he was removed under s.24 of the 1996 Act (one of the tiny handful of s.24 removals under that Act). Colman J. said:

> "138. There is however a further matter of procedural management which is of a more serious nature. That began to occur before 22 September 2004. It involved the Arbitrator making direct unilateral contact with three witnesses as described in paragraph 84 above. The Arbitrator explained his contact with Ms Mountford, Mr Colussi and Mr Hendrix in the passages in his first witness statement quoted at paragraph 78 above. His reference to Rule 7 is clearly to 7(e) [of the Short Procedure Rules of the Institution of Chemical Engineers]. That Rule provides:
>
>> 'whether and to what extent the Arbitrator should himself take the

initiative in ascertaining the facts and the law, and to rely upon his own knowledge and expertise to such extent as he thinks fit.' I interpreted this to give me wide powers to ascertain the facts by speaking to witnesses including in this case, Matthew Forde, particularly as I considered that non-payment would lead to the arbitration coming to a close if Moulson Chemplant so chose and this could potentially disadvantage Norbrook.'

139. That rule certainly provides a power to the Arbitrator to ascertain by his own initiative primary facts relevant to the substantive issues. That is to say he can cause to be injected into the arbitration evidence of facts from witnesses whom neither party is able or willing to call. However, this power is clearly subject to the component of fairness expressed as an objective of arbitration in Rule 1.1 in reflection of section 1(a) of the 1996 Act. Rule 7(e) therefore has to be operated with great care if an Arbitrator makes direct contact with a potential witness in the absence of either or both parties. Each party must be given the opportunity of questioning the witness. If the Arbitrator decides not to make use of the witness's evidence, or if the witness declines to give evidence at the hearing, the Arbitrator ought still to make an accurate record of the witness's remarks which he should then show to both parties. In this connection, it should be clearly appreciated by any competent Arbitrator operating these rules that fairness under rule 1 demands transparency under Rule 7(e). The reason for this is very clear. An Arbitrator in contact with a factual witness in the absence of one or both parties may be exposed to information which consciously or unconsciously influences his judgment on a matter in dispute. It is therefore absolutely axiomatic that the parties should at the very least have the opportunity of access to what the witness or potential witness has said to the Arbitrator so as to enable that party to refute any statement adverse to its case or to rely upon any statement supportive of its case. Whereas, it would in theory be possible for both parties to waive that requirement by an agreement to that effect, Rule 7(e) is not such an agreement. Nor does the reference to the 'economic' resolution of disputes in Rule 1 have the effect of causing the component of fairness to yield to economic expediency.

140. The need for this principled construction of Rule 7.4(e) could be no better illustrated than by two sentences in the Arbitrator's first witness statement quoted earlier in this judgment which I repeat here for convenience:

'Both Pia Mountford and Robert Colussi stated that they were not willing to assist or to provide witness statements and so I decided to disregard any comments that they had made to me ... They had both left Norbrook under difficult circumstances but I did not allow this to bias my view of Norbrook'.

141. This statement obviously raises the question what comments did they make and what was said which might have led the Arbitrator to be biased against Norbrook such that he needed to put it out of his mind. No record of these conversations has been provided to the parties and it must be inferred that no such record exists. The reference to the risk of bias, however, strongly suggests that whatever was said, if not put out of the mind of the Arbitrator, might influence his judgment on matters relevant to his decision.

142. The Arbitrator having directly contacted the witnesses, but having failed to make any exact record of what they said or to disclose such record to the parties, has thus both failed to conduct the proceedings fairly in accordance with s.33(1)(a) and (2) and therefore 'properly' within s.24(1)(d) and has, in this respect, therefore also created a procedural irregularity within s.68."

R28–43 One area where the tribunal can, does and must take the lead using an inquisitorial approach is in the two modern techniques of (i) "hot-tubbing", and (ii) witness conferencing where the witnesses from both parties are put together "on the stand" so it is obvious that neither party can lead the questioning. In brief:

(i) "hot-tubbing" involves putting the parties' respective expert witnesses of like discipline "on the stand" together to be examined by the tribunal;
(ii) "witness conferencing" involves putting all of each side's witnesses of fact on any particular issue "on the stand" together to be examined by the tribunal.

Rule 28(2)(f)(i)—Evidential hearings

R28–44 Some arbitrations can be, and are, conducted on a documents-only basis, e.g. where the role of witnesses is of lesser importance. There is an increasing trend in international arbitration for smaller cases to be dealt with this way since the costs of convening a hearing can significantly outweigh the advantages (if any) of holding one. If parties agree to this form of disposal, then clearly there is no need for any hearings for the questioning of parties or other witnesses.

R28–45 If the parties have not agreed to a documents-only procedure, the rule does give power to the tribunal to decide nevertheless that there should not be a hearing of oral evidence (known in Scotland as a "proof"). Under the old Scots common law before the 2010 Act it had been held that the tribunal was entitled to exercise its discretion not to hear oral evidence (*Mowbray v Dickson* (1848) 10 D 1102) if the hearing of that evidence was unnecessary to decide the claim (*Robert Brown & Son Ltd v Associated Fireclay Companies Ltd*, 1936 S.C. 690; affirmed 1937 S.C. (HL) 42). In *Robert Brown* the arbitrator decided that, as a matter of law (involving the construction or interpretation of the contract), the factual case put forward by the claimant, even if proved, could not succeed. He refused the claim without hearing oral evidence. It was held by the Court of Session and affirmed by the House of Lords that, given the arbitrator's decision on the point of law, it was unnecessary for him to hear oral evidence and that he was entitled to make his award without hearing it. It remains open for a tribunal to adopt such an approach under the 2010 Act. Indeed r.70(3)(b) expressly contemplates such an approach.

R28–46 Some arbitrations do not warrant an oral hearing and it would arguably be a breach of s.1(a) and r.24(1)(c) of the Act to grant a hearing for oral evidence where none was merited. Further, some common law lawyers appear to view the main purpose of hearings as being to destroy, in cross-examination, the other side's witnesses, hence see the hearing as essential for that purpose. The civil law approach can be a great deal more productive. The approach of Scots common law, as exemplified above, has always avoided any rigid requirement for the hearing of oral evidence. If, of course, it is essential for the resolution of the claim that a disputed issue of fact is resolved, then the tribunal must hear oral evidence, but the mere existence of any factual dispute does not oblige the tribunal to decide that there should be a hearing. If the tribunal is minded not to provide for a hearing it should give parties an opportunity to make representations on the appropriateness of that course, consistent with its duty under r.24.

R28–47 Any lingering presumption for a hearing in England was disposed of in *O'Donoghue v Enterprise Inns Plc* [2008] EWHC 2273 (Ch), a rent review case, where Mr O'Donoghue's claim (under s.68(2)(a) of the1996 Act, i.e. failure by the arbitrator to comply with the general duty under s.33 of the Act) was that the award should be set aside or the rent review remitted to the arbitrator for reconsideration after an oral hearing, during which Mr O'Donoghue should be able to cross-examine Enterprise's expert witness. A serious irregularity had, so he claimed, occurred by reason of the arbitrator's failure to have held an oral hearing and to have allowed cross-examination. Section 34(2)(h) of the 1996 Act (i.e. the direct equivalent of the present r.28(2)(f)(i)) gives the arbitrator discretion whether and to what extent there should be oral evidence and submissions. His Honour Judge Behrens, relying on the judgment of H.H. Judge Coulson QC in *Sinclair v Woods of Winchester* [2005] EWHC 1631, said this:

> "46. To my mind there are a number of answers to [the claimant's] submissions. First, the fact that the Arbitrator might have come to a different conclusion if there had been an oral hearing does not begin to establish that the Arbitrator was not acting fairly and impartially as between the parties. Second, as already noted, the Act expressly gives the Arbitrator a discretion on whether to hold an oral hearing. Third, the Arbitrator in his letter of 22nd November invited Mr O'Donoghue

to set out his case as to why he wanted an oral hearing. Mr O'Donoghue failed to do this. It is plain from the correspondence I have summarised above that the Arbitrator has been conspicuously fair in giving the parties the opportunity to put their case before coming to a decision. It is true, of course, that the Arbitrator had provisionally decided to hold an oral hearing in the form he set out in his letter of 31st July 2007. However this proposal was not accepted by Mr O'Donoghue and it was in any event open to the Arbitrator to change his mind after receiving Mr O'Donoghue's Counter-Submissions and

viewing the premises. Importantly he gave the parties an opportunity to make representations on the point before reaching his conclusion on 8th January 2008.

... 48. Fourth the Arbitrator gave reasons for his decision not to hold an oral hearing. Whether or not I would have exercised my discretion in that way is not a matter I need to decide. In my view the decision he made was one that was open to him on the material before him. He gave both sides the opportunity to make submissions before he made it. He gave reasons for the exercise of his discretion. In those circumstances it is, to my mind, difficult to see that there was any irregularity at all in the failure to hold an oral hearing.

... 51. It follows in my view that there was no serious irregularity on either the original or the amended basis of the claim and the claim accordingly fails. ..."

The authors submit that equivalent logic must apply in Scotland.

R28–48 However, arbitrators must be careful since prudence will normally dictate that, having taken all factors into account, if there is reasonable uncertainty about whether or not a hearing should be held, it is likely to be appropriate to hold one. Section 1(a) and r.24(1)(b) and (c) are paramount. Further, art.24(1) of the Model Law gives a presumption of a hearing:

"However, unless the parties have agreed that no hearings shall be held the arbitral tribunal shall hold such hearings at an appropriate stage of the proceedings, if so requested by a party."

R28–49 CIArb Practice Guideline 5, "Guidelines for Arbitrators regarding Documents Only Arbitrations" (available at *http://www.ciarb.org/information-and-resources* [Accessed June 18, 2014]) provides guidance to tribunals where a "documents only" procedure is adopted by agreement between the parties or by the exercise of the arbitrator's discretion.

Rule 28(2)(f)(ii)—Written or oral submissions

R28–50 See art.24(1) of the Model Law which gives less procedural discretion to the tribunal.

Section 1(a) and r.24(1)(b) and (c) are the key here: in each arbitration (treated individually on its merits) how can the various competing requirements be balanced? **R28–51**

In many civil law jurisdictions, arbitral proceedings are dominated by written submissions with only a short oral phase; the tribunal comes to the hearing having fully mastered the written submissions and the hearing is for the tribunal to ask any clarificatory questions (and, of course, to examine the witnesses). This has the advantage that hearings are generally very short (in Germany, few run more than one week) and the 10/12/16 week hearings seen in some common law jurisdictions are unknown. **R28–52**

For the tribunal, written submissions offer one very significant practical advantage in that the necessity (tedious, concentration-destroying, time-wasting and wholly inefficient) to take notes during oral submissions is removed. It is clearly undesirable for any tribunal both to listen to detailed oral submissions on complex matters, especially of law, and to take detailed notes. Although in many cases in practice a transcript is taken with the text usually available late on the same day, this can mean working far into the night. Written submissions are, the authors submit, greatly to be preferred. **R28–53**

Rule 28(2)(f)(iii) and (iv)—Presentation, inspection and submission of evidence

These are self-explanatory. How the evidence, documentary or oral, is to be presented is a matter for the tribunal. **R28–54**

One issue for a tribunal to decide will be as to how expert evidence is to be presented. Another issue will be whether the parties should present their own expert witnesses or whether the tribunal should appoint an expert (see r.34). Should the former route be followed, the CIArb Protocol for the use of Party-Appointed Expert Witnesses is available for use either to govern or to provide guidance in the giving of evidence by such witnesses. It is available at *http://www.ciarb.org/information-and-resources* [Accessed June 18, 2014]. **R28–55**

In the tribunal's deciding how to deal with these matters, it will necessarily give careful consideration to s.1(a) and r.24(1)(c)(i). **R28–56**

Rule 28(2)(g)—Language of arbitration

This accords with art.22 of the Model Law; the rule tracks s.34(2)(b) of the 1996 Act. **R28–57**

Rule 28(2)(h)—Law and rules of evidence

It was unclear under the common law to what extent, if at all, the rules of evidence applicable in Scottish litigations applied to arbitration. However, in at least one case the court upheld an award which was founded on evidence that would not have been permitted under the rules of evidence in **R28–58** litigations (*Alston v Chappell* (1839) 2 D 348). In addition, it was held that in a quality of goods arbitration it was not necessary for witnesses to be put on oath or formally examined (*Hope v Crookston Brothers* (1890) 17 R 868). This tended to suggest that the rules of evidence in Scottish litigation were not applicable in Scottish arbitrations unless the arbitrator so decided.

R28–59 While it is true that, for example, the Civil Evidence (Scotland) Act 1988, which relaxed the rules for admissibility of evidence in litigation, was extended to arbitration, it was equally extended to other tribunals where rules of evidence in litigation do not apply. It is apparent that in both instances this was done for the avoidance of any doubt should the evidential rules of litigation be otherwise applicable.

R28–60 The authors submit that the default position in an arbitration under the 2010 Act is that the rules of evidence applicable to Scottish litigation do not apply. See also s.34(2)(f) of the 1996 Act. This means, for example, that the common law rule (relaxed but not removed by the Civil Evidence (Scotland) Act 1988) that original documents be presented rather than copies does not apply. However this is one of a number of evidential matters which the tribunal must address at the outset of the arbitration.

Rule 29: Place of arbitration D

29. The tribunal may meet, and otherwise conduct the arbitration, anywhere it chooses (in or outwith Scotland).

DEFINITIONS

"arbitration": s.2(1)
"tribunal": s.2(1)

STATUS

R29–01 This is a default rule so it is open to the parties to modify it, agree something different or disapply it completely (see s.9). All sets of arbitral rules known to the authors contain equivalent provisions.

MODEL LAW

R29–02 Article 20 is similar in principle.

COMMENTARY

R29–03 While this may appear self-explanatory, it was unclear under the common law what the status was of a Scottish arbitration where part or all of the proceedings was held outside Scotland. While Ouagadougou, Wuhan, Nome, Easter Island, or even Paris might seem candidates sufficiently unlikely to be ignored, it is easily possible to envisage proceedings taking place in Berwick-upon-Tweed, Newcastle or Carlisle as half-way points between English and Scottish parties.

The words "seat", "venue", "place" and "location" are a source of confusion even among jurisdictions where English is the principal language. Under this Act, and the 1996 Act, "seat" means the juridical seat. "Place" is not used in the provisions of this Act. However, in some Model Law-related circumstances, the word "place" is used where the Act uses "seat". It is, therefore, essential to be clear what is in fact meant, particularly if the arbitration is international or involves Scottish subsidiaries of foreign companies. Rules 29 and 28(2)(a) are concerned with the venue or physical location. Section 3 is concerned with the "seat" (see the commentary on s.3). **R29–04**

Rule 52 provides that an award is to be treated as having been made in Scotland even if it is signed at, or delivered to or from, a place outwith Scotland. This is necessary to prevent recurrence of the anomalous decision by the House of Lords in *Hiscox v Outhwaite (No.1)* [1992] 1 A.C. 562, that an award executed in Paris in relation to a London arbitration between English parties and concerning liabilities arising in England was held to be a French award. The same principle as r.52 applies to this r.29, i.e. to prevent the arbitration becoming English (or Mauritanian, Chinese, etc.) by reason of some part of it being held outwith Scotland. **R29–05**

There is another significance of the location of arbitral proceedings in that certain aspects of the law of that location will apply, e.g. (i) if a crime is committed by one of those involved in the proceedings, the law applicable at that location will apply, not the law of Scotland; or (ii) if the location is in England, then s.2(2), (3) and (4) of the 1996 Act will or may apply, thereby importing ss.9–11 and 66 and, subject to the discretion of the English court, ss.43 and 44 of that Act. Many other jurisdictions (but, curiously, not this Act) have similar provisions, but it is, for obvious reasons, wholly impracticable to list them all here. **R29–06**

Rule 30: Tribunal decisions D

30.—(1) Where the tribunal is unable to make a decision unanimously (including any decision on an award), a decision made by the majority of the arbitrators is sufficient.

(2) Where there is neither unanimity nor a majority in favour of or opposed to making any decision—
    (a) the decision is to be made by the arbitrator nominated to chair the tribunal, or
    (b) where no person has been so nominated, the decision is to be made—
        (i) where the tribunal consists of 3 or more arbitrators, by the last arbitrator to be appointed, or
        (ii) where the tribunal consists of 2 arbitrators, by an umpire appointed by the tribunal or, where the tribunal fails to make an appointment within 14 days of being requested to do so by either party or any arbitrator, by an arbitral appointments referee (at the request of a party or an arbitrator).

DEFINITIONS

"arbitration": s.2(1)
"arbitrator": s.2(1)
"tribunal" : ss.2(1) and 31(1)

STATUS

R30–01 This is a default rule so it is open to the parties to modify it, agree something different or disapply it completely (see s.9). All sets of arbitral rules known to the authors contain equivalent provisions, e.g. art.31(1) of the ICC Rules, art.26(5) of the LCIA Rules and art.31(1) of the Swiss Rules.

MODEL LAW

R30–02 Article 29 refers but it does not address the circumstances envisaged by r.30(2) above.

COMMENTARY

Rule 30(1)

R30–03 This is self-explanatory.

Rule 30(2)(a)

R30–04 Conventionally, the third arbitrator, whether chosen by the two co-arbitrators or by the administering institution, shall chair the tribunal—see art.9.1 of the UNCITRAL Rules and art.12.5 of the ICC Rules; in any event, a chairman is appointed whereas r.6(b) does not so provide; in the view of the authors, this is a curious and unnecessary lacuna.

Rule 30(2)(b)

R30–05 This caters for the situation where no arbitrator has been nominated as chairman. If the parties have adopted arbitral rules which provide for the appointment of a chairman, or have otherwise appointed the chairman, r.30(2)(b) will be inapplicable. It is suggested that if parties have not adopted arbitral rules which provide for appointment of a chairman they agree on who the chairman should be or alternatively agree that the tribunal members should appoint him or her.

Rule 30(2)(b)(i)

R30–06 Provided that the appointment procedure in r.6(b) is followed, there will always be a last-appointed arbitrator, but, where, in any set of rules similar to the LCIA's the institution appoints all three arbitrators simultaneously, or the parties do so in any event, and no person is appointed to chair the tribunal, this provision will evidently not work.

Rule 30(2)(b)(ii)

Section 24 and r.82 apply. The LMAA Terms (r.8) provide that the two arbitrators may proceed with the preliminary stages of the reference, deferring the appointment of the third until a later date. **R30–07**

> "If the tribunal is to consist of three arbitrators: ... (b) ... (ii) the two so appointed may at any time thereafter appoint a third arbitrator so long as they do so before any substantive hearing or forthwith if they cannot agree on any matter relating to the arbitration, and if the two said arbitrators do not appoint a third within 14 days of one calling upon the other to do so, the President shall, on the application of either arbitrator or of a party, appoint the third arbitrator ..."

In contrast to r.30(2)(b)(ii) the 1996 Act is, in our view, inaccurately drafted in regard to the appointment of an umpire. The underlying concept is that (and this in fact occurs in many circumstances in practice) of the arbitration proceeding until the point where the two arbitrators fail to agree on the substantive decision at which point the umpire steps in and makes the decision. However, s.21(4) of the 1996 Act goes further and provides: **R30–08**

> "Decisions, orders and awards shall be made by the other arbitrators unless and until *they cannot agree on a matter* relating to the arbitration. In that event they shall forthwith give notice in writing to the parties and the umpire, whereupon the umpire shall replace them as the tribunal with power to make decisions, orders and awards as if he were sole arbitrator." (emphasis added)

A disagreement on some minor matter, e.g. a procedural one such as whether to allow 7, 14, 21 or 28 days for replies (or even on something as minor as the timing of the lunch break), strictly triggers the replacement of the two arbitrators by the umpire for the entirety of the remainder of the arbitration.

Rule 31: Tribunal directions D

31.—(1) The tribunal may give such directions to the parties as it considers appropriate for the purposes of conducting the arbitration.

(2) A party must comply with such a direction by such time as the tribunal specifies.

DEFINITIONS

"arbitration": s.2(1)
"party": ss.2, 31(1), (2)
"tribunal" : ss.2(1) and 31(1)

STATUS

R31–01 This is a default rule so it is open to the parties to modify it, agree something different or disapply it completely (see s.9).

MODEL LAW

R31–02 The Model Law does not have express provision for the issuing of directions.

COMMENTARY

Rule 31(1)

R31–03 This is self-explanatory since, if the tribunal does not tell the parties what to do, the arbitration can hardly make progress sufficient to meet the overriding obligations imposed by the trio of s.1(a) and rr.24(1)(c)(i) and 25(a). Modern arbitration relies on the tribunal adopting a proactive approach to case management and this in turn requires that appropriate directions be issued as and when applicable; leaving matters to drift along, relying on the initiative (or lack thereof) of the parties, is no longer an option. Directions are often designated as "Procedural Order No.1", etc. This does not prevent them from being in substance directions.

R31–04 Typically, one of the authors was sole arbitrator in an English arbitration but was travelling on business in South East Asia, i.e. at GMT + 7 hours (all times in this paragraph are GMT). A procedural issue arose at 08.30 requiring urgent resolution; the arbitrator issued a procedural order within an hour ordering party A to make any representations it wished on the issue by 11.00, with party B to respond, if it wished, by 17.00. Having considered both sets of representations overnight, the arbitrator issued a new procedural order (in fact, a clarificatory revision of an earlier one) by 09.00 the next day.

Rule 31(2)

R31–05 This is self-explanatory: s.1(a) and rr.24(1)(c)(i) and 25 apply. A competently-drafted direction will specify a time limit for anything that a party is directed to carry out. If a party does not comply with the time limit in the direction, the general remedy for the other party or the tribunal is provided for in r.39. If the failure to comply with a time limit is in the submission of a claim or defence, then there is a specific remedy in r.37. See the commentary on rr.37 and 39.

R31–06 See para.R39–03 in relation to differences between an order under r.31 and one under r.39.

Arbitration (Scotland) Act 2010 (r.32)

Rule 32: Power to appoint clerk, agents or employees etc. D

32.—(1) The tribunal may appoint a clerk (and such other agents, employees or other persons as it thinks fit) to assist it in conducting the arbitration.

(2) But the parties' consent is required for any appointment in respect of which significant expenses are likely to arise.

DEFINITIONS

"arbitration": s.2(1)
"party": ss.2, 31(1), (2)
"tribunal": ss.2(1) and 31(1)

STATUS

This is a default rule so it is open to the parties to modify it, agree something different or disapply it completely (see s.9).   **R32–01**

MODEL LAW

There is no equivalent in the Model Law.   **R32–02**

COMMENTARY

Rule 32(1)—Administrative support

Given the absence until 2010 of a modern codified arbitration law and the consequent difficulty of ascertaining what the law in fact was, Scottish arbitrators have in the past often sat with a qualified solicitor in attendance as clerk. This practice is seen by non-Scottish arbitrators as being not too far removed from David Beckham hiring someone to kick the football for him or Tiger Woods hiring someone to hit his golf ball for him. Further, such practice was at one time so much the norm that the authority for a clerk not requiring to be appointed (*Mowbray v Dickson* (1848) 10 D. 1102 at 1125) required to be cited by some commentators. Whether one attributes this to nervousness about the uncertain state of the law or to some other reason, the cost of a clerk was often cited as a deterrent to parties wishing to submit a dispute to arbitration. It is understood that the practice has become less common in recent years.   **R32–03**

The functions of the clerk are: to keep in order and secure the documents of the arbitration; to advise a non-legally qualified arbitrator in connection with the drafting of directions, orders or awards; to record all directions or orders of the arbitrator; and to assist with the administration of the arbitration. In the past such administration has extended to communicating the arbitrator's directions, orders or awards to the parties, organising venues and facilities for hearings, minuting hearings, and if no shorthand or other recording facilities for oral evidence were provided, for noting evidence. In respect of international arbitration see also paras R32–11 to R32–14 below.   **R32–04**

R32–05 Rule 32 does not address the issue of the extent of the assistance which an arbitrator is entitled to obtain from the clerk. Handing the entire case over to a clerk or an associate (or pupil-arbitrator) is clearly prohibited and, conversely, employing a secretary to type an award is, equally clearly, permitted, but there is a grey area in between where arbitrators must tread carefully, in the event of any doubt erring on the side of caution. In this context, r.7.3 of the CIArb Code of Ethics is relevant:

> "A Member shall not delegate any duty to decide to any other person unless permitted to do so by the parties or applicable law."

The authors submit that this accurately reflects the law of Scotland.

R32–06 Delegation of decision-making by a tribunal to its clerk would represent a serious irregularity in English law. In *Brandeis Brokers Ltd v Black* [2001] 2 Lloyd's Rep. 359, Toulson J. said at [68]:

> "To show that an expert witness said things which he would not have been permitted to say in a court of law comes nowhere near to establishing that there was irregularity, let alone serious irregularity, within the meaning of section 68. It would be a different matter if Brandeis could establish, as it asserts, that the arbitrators effectively delegated their decision making on important questions to [the expert]. That criticism, if substantiated, would amount to serious irregularity, but I reject it."

R32–07 An international internet debate in early 2009 focused on the question of delegation, particularly in the context of busy leading arbitrators with a significant caseload prima facie not capable of being 100 per cent handled by one individual. The consensus was broadly "market choice" in that the international arbitration market knows who are the sole practitioner arbitrators carrying out the entirety of their own work and those who have, and rely on, back office support.

R32–08 The question of delegation arose in *Agrimex Ltd v Tradigrain SA and Ors* [2003] EWHC 1656 (Comm) (the "others" were GAFTA itself and the five individual members of the tribunal) in the context of an application to reduce allegedly excessive fees but where Thomas J. had some pertinent observations concerning delegation. In that case, 48 per cent of the costs of the arbitration (excluding the parties' own legal and other costs) was represented by the fees charged by a qualified solicitor from an external law firm employed to draft the award, in part because GAFTA arbitrators are "commercial men" (i.e. usually commodity traders) and GAFTA normally excludes lawyers from its panels. The chairman of the tribunal had decided that he required the appointment of a legal draftsman "to ensure as far as possible that the award reflected the opinions of the [tribunal] members, produced an appropriate and clear legal explanation for the award and provided justice to the parties".

At the hearing the solicitor was introduced to the parties and it was explained that he would be the draftsman for the award. The evidence was that it was made clear to him that his role was to be restricted to that of a draftsman and he was not instructed to advise the tribunal on any legal issues. He understood his instructions to be to consider the documentation, attend the appeal hearings, write such notes as were necessary and prepare an award that reflected the tribunal's findings. He was also present when the board subsequently deliberated on the issues and, subsequently, he was provided with the further views of the tribunal members and produced a draft award. He did not comment on any findings, but, in his view, simply did his best to reproduce the findings made by the tribunal in the draft award that he prepared.

Thomas J. had this to say:

R32–09

R32–10

> "32. For some time, and certainly since the enactment of the Arbitration Act 1996, it has been part of the skill ordinarily to be expected of a competent arbitrator that he should produce his own reasoned award. It is commonplace for decision-makers to explain the reasoning for their decision; it is commonly acknowledged that the quality of decisions is improved by requiring the decision-maker to go through the process of expressing those reasons himself. There is no reason why in general a person who takes on the responsibility and duty of an arbitrator should not be able to discharge the function of providing a reasoned explanation for the decision he has reached; for example, awards made by arbitrators of the London Maritime Arbitrators Association who are not legally qualified set out in clear terms their reasoning in disputes that are often far more complex than the matters in this award. It is also clear from the evidence of GAFTA that they recognise that if a person is to sit as an arbitrator, he should be capable of drafting an award; that is one of the objectives of their training."

In international arbitration, it is relatively common practice for a tribunal to appoint a Tribunal Secretary, typically a young but qualified (and able) lawyer, in order to carry out the administration of the case efficiently without burdening the arbitrators themselves (often intensely busy people with diaries largely booked up to two years ahead). Potentially difficult questions arise as to the role of such a Tribunal Secretary, particularly as to where the boundaries lie. In a celebrated article "The Fourth Arbitrator? The Role of Secretaries to Tribunals in International Arbitration", *Arbitration International*, Vol.18 - N°2 (2002), pp.147–164, Constantine Partasides brilliantly highlighted some of these difficulties and the *Luzon* case (below) highlights others.

R32–11

Since 2002 a great deal of debate has occurred and there is broad consensus, but certainly no unanimity (one of the authors is a well-known sceptic of the tribunal secretary system, not only because of *Luzon*), on the

R32–12

main issues. The arbitral community is now greatly assisted by two publications: (i) the ICC's "Note on the Appointment, Duties and Remuneration of Administrative Secretaries" (August 1, 2012) and (ii) ICCA's "ICCA Young Arbitrators' Guide on Arbitral Secretaries", published on April 15, 2014 and available for free download from *http://www.arbitration-icca.org/media/2/13975817558900/aa_arbitral_sec_guide_composite_15_april_2014.pdf* [Accessed June 11, 2014].

R32–13 The sceptical author does, however, acknowledge the sentiment expressed in the Foreword to the Young ICCA Guide by Guillermo Aguilar-Alvarez who states:

> "Publication of the Guide should nonetheless be applauded for one additional important reason. Young ICCA's association with this project underscores the need to recognize the importance of secretarial appointments as an invaluable training tool. Like judicial clerkships, secretarial appointments provide young lawyers with a unique opportunity to discern where advocacy meets persuasion."

R32–14 On June 6, 2014, HKIAC announced the roll-out of its tribunal secretary service for arbitrations either administered by HKIAC or ad hoc arbitrations, as well as publishing a set of guidelines on the use of tribunal secretaries who will be provided from the staff of the HKIAC Secretariat. HKIC's Chairman stated:

> "The HKIAC's new tribunal secretary service should prove to be an attractive offering for arbitration users in Hong Kong. Tapping into the Secretariat's talent and experience pool, the scheme provides a mechanism to enhance efficiency and reduce overall costs. I think it is a very welcome initiative."

Further information about the HKIAC service and a copy of the Guidelines can be accessed at *http://www.hkiac.org/en/arbitration/tribunal-secretary-service* [Accessed June 11, 2014].

R32–15 A different, but highly controversial issue concerning a clerk arose in Singapore in *Luzon Hydro Corp v Transfield Philippines Inc* [2004] S.G.H.C. 204. The case concerns aspects of the role of a tribunal-appointed expert (a qualified engineer) in an ICC arbitration whose role was downgraded to that of administrative assistant. However, the engineer not only attended the hearing on liability, but questioned the parties' respective expert engineering witnesses during it. At the close of the hearing the tribunal indicated to the parties that they would be seeking assistance from him in relation to some administrative matters which were identified as going through the transcript of evidence and collating evidence on technical issues under appropriate heads, collating references in the witness statements to the issues for the tribunal and "perhaps other matters purely of an administrative nature".

No objection was made to this by the parties. Subsequently, the tribunal wrote to the parties stating inter alia (i) that it had decided not to seek any written expert's report from the engineer, and (ii) outlining the administrative assistance he had rendered. This included "identifying expert evidence, technical matters referred to by witnesses of fact, technical issues in submissions", "collating the above into appropriate categories and issues", "reminding the tribunal of technical terms and equations" and "responding to technical queries of the Tribunal". The engineer was also to review the draft award to ensure the correct use of technical terminology. Neither of the parties raised any objection to the engineer's proposed tasks.

However, post-hearing, the engineer expended 486 hours on the case and his timesheet descriptions of his activities, such as "review of closing submissions generally" on which he had spent 8 hours, led Luzon's solicitors to request copies of all correspondence between the engineer and the tribunal—this disclosure was refused. Luzon applied to set aside the tribunal's award (on liability) on the grounds, inter alia, that: (i) the proceedings had not accorded with the agreement of the parties; (ii) there had been a breach of the rules of natural justice in that the engineer had been permitted by the tribunal an involvement substantially beyond that agreed by the parties; (iii) the engineer had assumed the task of reviewing and determining the relevance of the evidence; and (iv) since it had not been provided with copies of the engineer/tribunal correspondence, it had been deprived of any opportunity to comment thereon, as required by both ICC Rules and the Model Law. **R32–16**

The court dismissed Luzon's application on the grounds that Luzon had not objected to the engineer's administrative role and that it could not be said that the time spent on review of closing submissions involved advice to the tribunal on what it should decide rather than explanations of technical terms and evidence to which no objection had been made. This case illustrates the importance of scrutinising carefully the extent of the assistance that is to be given by a clerk and of ensuring that a clerk does not occupy the role of an informal expert without the protection for the parties in r.34(2). **R32–17**

To summarise, there are issues, some serious, concerning the delegation, actual or apparent, of an arbitrator's responsibilities (as opposed to the non-delegable decision-making responsibility) and such delegation (other than the most basic) should be done with considerable care. This is particularly so given that if "significant expenses" are likely to be raised with the appointment and the parties' consent is not obtained, the arbitrator may end up having to bear the expenses personally without the parties being liable to relieve him under r.60. **R32–18**

While, in the authors' view, the justification hitherto at common law for employing a solicitor as clerk had ceased to be applicable given modern developments in arbitral training and communications with parties, we submit that there can be no justification under this Act. **R32–19**

Rule 32(2)—Expense of administrative support

R32–20 Given the concern over the expense of a clerk or other agent or employee being appointed by an arbitrator, r.32(2) provides that the parties' consent is required for any such appointment if "significant expenses are likely to arise" thereby. In practice arbitrators should obtain the express consent of the parties before making any such appointment. This will avoid any dispute over whether "significant expenses" were likely to arise in respect of such appointment and the consequent risk of the arbitrator being personally liable for expense of the clerk, etc. with the right of relief against the parties under r.60 being excluded by the Auditor of the Court of Session on the basis that the expense was not incurred "reasonably".

Rule 33: Party representatives D

33.—(1) A party may be represented in the arbitration by a lawyer or any other person.

(2) But the party must, before representation begins, give notice of the representative—

(a) **to the tribunal, and**
(b) **to the other party.**

DEFINITIONS

"arbitration": s.2(1)
"party": ss.2, 31(1), (2)
"tribunal": s.2(1) and 31(1)

STATUS

R33–01 This is a default rule so it is open to the parties to modify it, agree something different or disapply it completely (see s.9). Such a modification occurred at common law where the parties' agreement to refer to an engineer arbitrator to decide the issue "without the formalities of a legal arbitration, and with a view to an amicable settlement, so as to save legal and other expenses" was held to be an agreement to exclude representation by lawyers (*Paterson & Sons Ltd v Glasgow Corporation* (1901) 3 F (HL) 34).

R33–02 Article 5 of the UNCITRAL Rules is in equivalent terms to r.33 but with the addition of the requirement that, where a person is to act as a representative of a party, the arbitral tribunal, on its own initiative or at the request of any party, may at any time require proof of authority granted to the representative in such a form as the tribunal may determine. Article 18.2 of the LCIA Rules provides that, first, the Registrar and, following its formation, the Tribunal may require such proof. One of the authors has in fact had to use this power in a circumstance where it was unclear which of two law firms was in fact representing one party. Articles 4(3) and 5(1) of the ICC Rules require the parties to disclose the identity of their representatives

Arbitration (Scotland) Act 2010 (r.33)

in the request for arbitration and answer to a request, while art.17 allows the tribunal or secretariat to require proof of the authority of any of the representatives.

MODEL LAW

There is no equivalent in the Model Law. R33–03

COMMENTARY

The giving of notice is a consequence of the fairness obligation of s.1(a) and r.24(1)(b). There would be an obvious unfairness if, such as in a case *Small Business Ltd v Big Multinational Plc*, the former arrived at a hearing accompanied by a small-town solicitor to find itself confronted by a pair of QCs and an army of solicitors from a large law firm. R33–04

The DAC Report made some helpful observations in respect of the equivalent s.36 of the 1996 Act and these are relevant to the r.33. R33–05

> "184. In the draft produced in July we used the phrase 'a lawyer or other person of his choice'. We have changed this, because we felt that it might give the impression that a party could stubbornly insist on a particular lawyer or other person, in circumstances where that individual could not attend for a long time, thus giving a recalcitrant party a good means of delaying the arbitral process. This should not happen. 'A lawyer or other person chosen by him' does not give this impression: if a party's first choice is not available, his second choice will still be 'a lawyer or other person chosen by him'. The right to be represented exists but must not be abused. Furthermore the right must be read with the first principle of Clause 1, as well as Clauses 33 and 40. If this is done then we trust that attempts to abuse the right will fail.
>
> 185. It has been suggested to the DAC that there should be some provision requiring a party to give advance notice to all other parties if he intends to be represented at a hearing. Whilst in some ways an attractive proposal, this would be difficult to stipulate as a statutory provision, given that it may be impossible in some circumstances, or simply unnecessary in others. Further, different sanctions may be appropriate depending on the particular case. It is clearly desirable that, as a general rule, such notice be given. If it is not, one sanction may be for the tribunal to adjourn a hearing at the defaulting party's cost. In the end, however, this must be a matter for the tribunal's discretion in each particular case."

However, the requirement to give notice might have wider consequences than that example. In an ICSID arbitration in 2008, *Hrvatska Elektroprivreda dd v the Republic of Slovenia* (ICSID case No.ARB/05/24), the latter's legal representatives notified the tribunal 10 days before the hearing R33–06 that a Mr M QC would participate as part of their team. There were two issues: (i) Mr M QC was a barrister at E Chambers of which the Presiding Arbitrator was a door tenant; and (ii) the lateness of the notification. Further, solicitors representing Slovenia refused to disclose either when Mr M had been retained (it later became clear that he had been on the Slovenian team for at least two months) or what role he was expected to play at the hearing. Hrvatska relied on ICSID Arbitration Rules r.18(1) which obliges a party to notify the Secretary-General of the identity of counsel and for him to "promptly inform the Tribunal and the other party" and sought an order by the tribunal removing Mr M from the case.

R33–07 The tribunal considered that it was obliged, as guardian of the legitimacy of the arbitral process, to make every effort to ensure that the award was not affected by procedural imperfection. If the tribunal granted the order sought, Slovenia might later contend that there had been a serious departure from a fundamental rule of procedure, i.e. the right to representation (ICSID Arbitration Rules r.19) and the right of being given a full opportunity to present a case. Conversely, if the order were refused, Hrvatska might later assert unfairness. In a key passage ([31] of its ruling), the tribunal said this:

> "The justifiability of an apprehension of partiality depends on all relevant circumstances. Here, those circumstances include second, [Slovenia's] conscious decision *not* to inform the Claimant or the Tribunal of Mr M's involvement in the case, following his engagement [two months earlier]; third, the tardiness of [Slovenia's] announcement of Mr M's involvement and, finally, Slovenia's subsequent insistent refusal to disclose the scope of Mr M's involvement, a matter of days before the commencement of the hearing on the merits. The last three matters were errors of judgment on [Slovenia's] part and have created an atmosphere of apprehension and mistrust which it is important to dispel."

R33–08 The tribunal concluded that, in the light of the fundamental rule enshrined in art.56(1) of the ICSID Convention that a tribunal should remain unchanged once proceedings had begun and given its inherent procedural powers confirmed by art.44 to deal with matters not covered by the ICSID Arbitration Rules, it was inappropriate for the tribunal president to resign and instead Mr M should not be allowed to participate further as counsel for Slovenia.

R33–09 Rule 33(1) takes away the common law power of a tribunal to decide that there should be no legal representation regardless of the wishes of a party.

R33–10 Further to R32–08 above, it is interesting to note that both GAFTA and FOSFA, whose arbitrators are almost all non-lawyer trade men, operate a 2-tier system of arbitration; at the first tier, lawyers are excluded from any hearing (but, of course, not from drafting submissions).

In recent years there has been growing concerns over the diverse and potentially conflicting rules and norms governing, and practices adopted by, party representatives in international arbitration since application of different practices could undermine the fundamental fairness and integrity of international arbitral proceedings. Further, while all party representatives in domestic litigation will be subject to essentially the same (national) norms, (i) such norms may be ill-suited to international arbitral proceedings and (ii) the range of rules and norms applicable in international arbitration may include those of the party representative's home jurisdiction, the arbitral seat, and the place where hearings physically take place. For example, under his/her professional code a Scottish advocate (barrister) must avoid doing or saying anything which could have the effect of, or could be construed as, inducing a witness, including an expert witness, to "tailor" his evidence to suit the case. There are similar provisions for barristers in England and Wales. In contrast, a US attorney might be liable to disbarment if he/she *does not coach* them since such is so much standard practice in the USA that an attorney who fails to coach will not be representing his/her client to the best of his/her professional ability. **R33–11**

As in other areas in arbitration (e.g. see the IBA Evidence Guidelines and the IBA Disclosure Guidelines), the IBA has published the IBA Representation Guidelines. The essence of these Guidelines is that party representatives should act with integrity and honesty and should not engage in activities designed to produce unnecessary delay or expense, including tactics aimed at obstructing the arbitration proceedings. **R33–12**

However, these Guidelines are not intended to displace otherwise applicable mandatory laws, professional or disciplinary rules, or agreed arbitration rules that may be relevant or applicable to matters of party representation. They are also not intended to vest arbitral tribunals with powers otherwise reserved to bars or other professional bodies. **R33–13**

The parties may adopt these Guidelines or a portion thereof by agreement. Arbitral tribunals may also apply them in their discretion under r.28(1) having consulted with parties beforehand and subject to any applicable mandatory rules. **R33–14**

Guideline 24 provides: **R33–15**

> "A Party Representative may, consistent with the principle that the evidence given should reflect the Witness's own account of relevant facts, events or circumstances, or the Expert's own analysis or opinion, meet or interact with Witnesses and Experts in order to discuss and prepare their prospective testimony."

However this does not affect the professional or other obligations that may bind party representatives in connection with the discussion and preparation of prospective testimony. Nor, the authors submit, does it allow a party representative to do anything calculated to lead a witness as to fact to give anything other than his/her own account of the facts or an expert witness to give anything other than his/her own expert analysis or opinion.

Rule 34: Experts D

34.—(1) The tribunal may obtain an expert opinion on any matter arising in the arbitration.

(2) The parties must be given a reasonable opportunity—
  (a) to make representations about any written expert opinion, and
  (b) to hear any oral expert opinion and to ask questions of the expert giving it.

DEFINITIONS

"arbitration": s.2(1)
"party": ss.2, 31(1), (2)
"tribunal": s.2(1) and 31(1)

STATUS

R34–01 This is a default rule so it is open to the parties to modify it, agree something different or disapply it completely (see s.9).

R34–02 Section 37 of the 1996 Act, art.29 of the UNCITRAL Rules, art.25(4) of the ICC Rules, art.21 of the LCIA Rules and art.27 of the Swiss Rules are in similar terms to r.34. Note that none of this Act, the 1996 Act, the ICC Rules, the LCIA Rules or the Swiss Rules contain any express power for parties to appoint their own experts, but the language of relevant parts of the respective rules assumes that such a power exists.

MODEL LAW

R34–03 Article 26 of the Model Law is in equivalent terms except that it requires there to be a hearing to allow parties to ask questions of the expert and to present expert witnesses themselves to testify on the points in issue. By contrast r.34 requires a hearing only where the tribunal-appointed expert gives oral expert opinion evidence.

COMMENTARY

Rule 34(1)

R34–04 Under Scots common law it was always recognised that an arbitrator had power to obtain an expert opinion on relevant matters of fact where the arbitrator found it necessary to do so (*Caledonian Railway Co v Lockhart* (1860) 3 Macq 808 (HL) at 812–813 and 823). The concept of a tribunal-appointed expert (TAE) was relatively unknown elsewhere in the common law world until the Civil Procedure Rules introduced it into England and Wales in 1999 (Part 35) in an effort to reduce the costs of litigation by reducing the tendency, in some classes of litigation, for the proceedings to become a "battle of the experts".

In contrast, a court-appointed expert is the norm in civil law jurisdictions and some such do not permit the parties to employ their own experts. Scots common law allowed the expert to be questioned by the parties if this was sought (*Caledonian Railway Co* (above) at 813). This has been preserved by r.34(2). One of the advantages of arbitration over litigation is being able to choose arbitrators with relevant expertise so there should be less need for any TAE and, in some sectors, employment of such an expert is rare (the authors have never had any case in practice where a TAE was employed). However, such an arbitrator must take care not to make findings in fact based on any special information, not generally available, that he possesses without giving the parties an opportunity to make submissions on such information (see commentary on r.24(1)(b) and (2) at para.R24–32). **R34–05**

A tribunal which is considering the obtaining of an expert opinion should invite the views of the parties before it makes any appointment. In inviting parties' views, the tribunal should indicate the terms of the proposed remit and the identity of a possible expert or experts. In deciding whether to appoint a TAE and the terms of the remit, the tribunal should be conscious of its duties in r.24(1)(c), to conduct the arbitration without unnecessary delay and without incurring unnecessary expense. Practice Guideline 10 issued by the CIArb (available at *http://www.ciarb.org/information-and-resources* [Accessed June 18, 2014]) assists tribunals in the process of appointing TAEs. One of the issues may be the extent to which a TAE should allow or exclude parties from presenting other expert evidence from their chosen experts. **R34–06**

The tribunal should also be conscious of the need to provide for the payment of the TAE's fees. Prima facie the person instructing an expert is liable for his fees. It can be agreed that the parties should lodge a cash sum into an interest bearing account held in trust for the parties (see commentary on r.60). Alternatively, at least if the TAE is instructed under Scots law, the tribunal can agree with the parties prior to instruction that it can instruct the opinion on behalf of the parties as disclosed principals while requiring the TAE to provide it to the tribunal. On any view, the parties are liable to the tribunal for the fees and expenses of the TAE either as agreed between the parties and the tribunal or, failing which, as determined by the Auditor of the Court of Session (r.60(1)(b)(ii), (3), and (4)). That liability is (effectively—see paras R60–09 and R60–10) joint and several and cannot be excluded by agreement. **R34–07**

See also r.75 (below) concerning the immunity of experts including TAEs. **R34–08**

Rule 34(2)

R34-09 The requirement to give parties an opportunity to respond to the expert evidence of the TAE ensures both fairness to the parties and acts as a safeguard against any tendency of a tribunal to delegate the decision-making in a disputed issue to the TAE.

R34-10 The tribunal must not hear evidence, even expert evidence, in the absence of the parties. This was confirmed in *Hussmann (Europe) Ltd v Al Ameen Development & Trade Co* [2000] 2 Lloyd's Rep. 83 where, after receiving a draft report from the TAE, the tribunal, without giving any notice to the parties, met with him and discussed his evidence and Thomas J. commented at [45]:

> "I agree with the observation of Professor Merkin in his work [*Arbitration Law*] at paragraph 13.46(e):
>
> > 'consultation with the experts should not take place after the close of the hearing or otherwise in the absence of the parties as this deprives the parties of their right to comment'."

He continued at [46]:

> "It seems to me that on this occasion the conduct of the tribunal in holding this private meeting with the expert to discuss his draft report without obtaining the consent of the parties to such a course fell below the standards ordinarily to be expected of arbitrators. Their failure to inform the parties of the fact of the meeting immediately after was also, in my view, an irregularity. Mr Mark Cato in his " *Arbitration Practice and Procedure: Interlocutory and Hearing Problems* " at para 14.5.2 gives the sensible and highly practical advice that an arbitrator who finds himself in this position should tell the parties about what he has done and give them a full opportunity to test the evidence by way of cross examination or by calling evidence in rebuttal. They did not do so, but fortunately the fact of the meeting did emerge when [the expert] was examined [at a subsequent hearing]."

R34-11 It is implicit in r.34(2) that the tribunal must communicate a copy of the TAE report to the parties to allow them to make representations on it. The parties then have an opportunity to make representations to the tribunal about the TAE report. The tribunal's direction concerning the appointment of the TAE should have made clear the time limits for such representations and any responses thereto. In particular the direction should have addressed the question of whether parties are to be allowed to request a hearing at which the TAE and party appointed experts (PAEs) are to be allowed to give evidence on disputed points of the TAE's report. Rule 34(2) does not provide that there requires to be such a hearing if the TAE produces nothing more than a written report (which would be the usual situation). It is suggested that, if such a hearing is to be held, its ambit is strictly limited beforehand in order to save time and expense.

As an alternative to a written report, the TAE may give his opinion evidence orally at a hearing (r.34(2)(b)). If that is what occurs, then it is suggested that the tribunal direct that PAEs may give evidence at the same time. **R34–12**

Rule 35: Powers relating to property D

35. The tribunal may direct a party—
  (a) to allow the tribunal, an expert or another party—
      (i) to inspect, photograph, preserve or take custody of any property which that party owns or possesses which is the subject of the arbitration (or as to which any question arises in the arbitration), or
      (ii) to take samples from, or conduct an experiment on, any such property, or
  (b) to preserve any document or other evidence which the party possesses or controls.

DEFINITIONS

"arbitration": s.2(1)
"party": ss.2, 31(1), (2)
"tribunal": s.2(1) and 31(1)

STATUS

This is a default rule so it is open to the parties to modify it, agree something different or disapply it completely (see s.9). **R35–01**

Article 26(2)(d) of the UNCITRAL Rules mirrors art.17(2)(d) of the Model Law (see below). Article 28(1) of the ICC Rules provides, **R35–02**

> " ... the arbitral tribunal may, at the request of a party, order any interim or conservatory measure it deems appropriate. The arbitral tribunal may make the granting of any such measure subject to appropriate security being furnished by the requesting party."

Article 25 of the LCIA Rules provides wide powers in this regard and art.26 of the Swiss Rules follows the Model Law in being very broadly drafted to deal with "interim measures" without the specific references to property in r.35.

MODEL LAW

R35–03 Article 17(2)(d) of the Model Law covers the items listed in r.35. A direction of the type contemplated by r.35 is described as a type of "interim measure". Articles 17A–17J then describe the procedure for the obtaining of such and other "interim measures".

COMMENTARY

R35–04 Rule 35 gives an important power to tribunals in relation to the preservation of evidence and the obtaining of evidence through experimentation. During the course of an arbitration, the condition and state of goods which are in dispute may deteriorate or be threatened, the situation on the ground of a building may change, important documentation may require to be transferred to a location outwith Scottish jurisdiction or an expert may be required to carry out an inspection or an experiment so that he can give his opinion. For any of these reasons, and more, it may be necessary for a party to seek a direction under r.35. Alternatively, the tribunal itself can take the initiative in making such a direction.

R35–05 Action under r.35 may require to be taken rapidly. In those circumstances, if the action requires to take place urgently within Scotland, it is suggested that a party or the tribunal applies directly to the court under r.46. See also r.46(1)(d) and the commentary thereon at paras R46–33 to R46–36 below.

R35–06 Practice Guideline 2, "Guideline on Interim Measures of Protection", issued by the CIArb (available at *http://www.ciarb.org/information-and-resources* [Accessed June 18, 2014]) provides guidance to tribunals in relation to the exercise of their powers to make directions under r.35.

Emergency Arbitrator

R35–07 It sometimes happens in practice that a party needs urgent interim or conservatory measures that cannot await the constitution of a tribunal. In recent years, led by the ICDR through its 2010 Rules, several leading arbitral institutions have created the "Emergency Arbitrator" (see, e.g. art.37 ICDR Rules, art.29 and Sch.V ICC Rules, art.9B LCIA Rules and art.23 and Sch.4 HKIAC Rules). These various rules allow for an Emergency Arbitrator to be appointed to deal with relevant matters within one day (ICDR) or two days (ICC and HKIAC) or three (LCIA). The institutions maintain panels of specialist arbitrators who can be available at very short notice. The emergency arbitrator will normally issue an appropriate order and the parties are bound to comply with it. However, no such order is binding on the tribunal when constituted and it may modify, terminate or annul any such order by the emergency arbitrator.

R35–08 There will be no difficulty under the Act or the SAR for any arbitration in Scotland under institutional rules providing for an emergency arbitrator,

Rule 36: Oaths or affirmations D

36. The tribunal may—
   (a) direct that a party or witness is to be examined on oath or affirmation, and
   (b) administer an oath or affirmation for that purpose.

DEFINITIONS

"party": ss.2, 31(1), (2)
"tribunal": s.2(1) and 31(1)

STATUS

This is a default rule so it is open to the parties to modify it, agree **R36–01** something different or disapply it completely (see s.9).

MODEL LAW

There is no equivalent provision in the Model Law. **R36–02**

COMMENTARY

Section 38(5) of the 1996 Act is in equivalent terms. The tribunal has a **R36–03** discretion in the matter, but again must bear in mind that, in exercising it, it must ensure that a fair hearing is given to the parties. This means that a party should not be prejudiced, for example, if a witness cannot give evidence under oath. In many civil law jurisdictions, the administering of an oath by a mere arbitrator would either be ineffective or void or even an offence in law, such administering being restricted to notaries and the like.

As a practical matter, the administration of an oath is fraught with dif- **R36–04** ficulty given the several different arms of the Christian Church with different versions of the Bible, let alone all the complications of other religions and cultures; in particular, in certain religions it would be highly offensive to a believer to use the equivalent holy book to swear an oath and, in others, it would be offensive for a non-believer to hand the relevant holy book to a believer. One well-known English arbitrator used to travel with a briefcase full of different holy books, but that is no longer appropriate. Affirmation gives a far easier solution.

In any event, good practice requires that the tribunal establish at an early **R36–05** date, e.g. in a procedural direction, what is to be done in this context.

The standard oath is "I swear by Almighty God that I will tell the truth, **R36–06** the whole truth and nothing but the truth". The standard affirmation is "I solemnly, sincerely and truly declare and affirm that I will tell the truth the whole truth and nothing but the truth".

Rule 37: Failure to submit claim or defence timeously D

37.—(1) Where—
  (a) a party unnecessarily delays in submitting or in otherwise pursuing a claim,
  (b) the tribunal considers that there is no good reason for the delay, and
  (c) the tribunal is satisfied that the delay—
    (i) gives, or is likely to give, rise to a substantial risk that it will not be possible to resolve the issues in that claim fairly, or
    (ii) has caused, or is likely to cause, serious prejudice to the other party,
the tribunal must end the arbitration in so far as it relates to the subject-matter of the claim and may make such award (including an award on expenses) as it considers appropriate in consequence of the claim.

(2) Where—
  (a) a party unnecessarily delays in submitting a defence to the tribunal, and
  (b) the tribunal considers that there is no good reason for the delay,
the tribunal must proceed with the arbitration (but the delay is not, in itself, to be treated as an admission of anything).

DEFINITIONS

"arbitration": s.2(1)
"claim": s.31(1)
"party": ss.2, 31(1), (2)
"tribunal": s.2(1) and 31(1)

STATUS

R37–01 This is a default rule so it is open to the parties to modify it, agree something different or disapply it completely (see s.9).

R37–02 Article 30 of the UNCITRAL Rules, art.15.8 of the LCIA Rules and art.28 of the Swiss Rules are in equivalent terms as to principle.

R37–03 The ICC Rules provide in art.4 for the claim to be contained in the Request for Arbitration, which in turn commences the arbitration. There is therefore no need for any provision for default. With regard to the defence, art.5(2) of the ICC Rules provides that if an answer is not submitted timeously the secretariat may grant the respondent an extension of the time for submitting the answer provided the application for such an extension contains the respondent's observations or proposals concerning the number of arbitrators and their choice, and, where required by arts.12 and 13, the nomination of an arbitrator, but if the respondent fails to do so, the ICC International Court of Arbitration must proceed in accordance with the ICC Rules. These include, in particular, art.6(3) which is consistent with r.37(2) and also provides for a reference to the ICC Court.

MODEL LAW

Article 25 of the Model Law is in equivalent terms. R37–04

COMMENTARY

Rules 37 and 39 are designed to give arbitrators powers to enforce their directions and progress the arbitration. Rule 39 must be regarded as subject to r.37 in respect of the failures to comply set out in r.37. These powers, when they arise, are substantial. No doubt this is to encourage the speed and effectiveness of the arbitral process. R37–05

Rule 37 applies to failures to submit a claim timeously, to "otherwise pursue" a claim or to submit a defence timeously. Failure to submit a claim or defence timeously must include failure to comply with either the direction of a tribunal or arbitral rules agreed upon or other agreement of the parties. Failure to "otherwise pursue" a claim could include failures such as not responding to correspondence or taking an inordinate time to do so. It would not cover failure to appear at a hearing or to produce documents as those are specifically provided for in r.38. It is interesting to note that r.37 gives the tribunal more powers in respect of claimants (and counter-claimants) than respondents, presumably because the residual initiative for progressing with the arbitration lies traditionally with them, despite r.25 which imposes duties on all parties. R37–06

If a time limit is imposed by virtue of arbitral rules or in terms of an arbitration agreement, there may be scope for a party to seek an extension of a time limit through an application to the court under r.43, but not if the time limit is imposed by a direction of the tribunal. R37–07

Rule 37(1)—Claimant's delay

Two key points must be noted: first, all three legs of r.37 ((a), (b) and (c)) must be satisfied before the tribunal can act in this regard; and secondly, if so, then the tribunal is obliged to end the arbitration and it has no discretion in the matter. R37–08

Rule 37(1) is based on s.41(3) of the 1996 Act but is more stringent. Whereas under s.41(3) the tribunal has a discretion to make an award dismissing the claim, under r.37(1) the tribunal has no such discretion but "must end the arbitration". There is provision that the tribunal "may make such award (including an award on expenses) as it considers appropriate in consequence of the claim". The authors are unable to see how such an award can be anything other than a refusal of the claim. Since an arbitral tribunal and r.37 are creatures of the arbitration agreement and finality is one of the objects of arbitration, a tribunal does not have the power to end the arbitration but reserve to the claimant the right to re-refer the dispute to arbitration or to a court. R37–09

There is no doubt that an award may refuse a claim even though it does R37–10 not deal with the merits of the dispute. In *Charles M Willie & Co (Shipping) Ltd v Ocean Laser Shipping Ltd* [1999] 1 Lloyd's Rep 225 (a case arising under the 1950 and 1979 Acts), Rix J. said this:

> "There is no statutory or common law definition of what constitutes an 'award'. The matter was considered in *Cargill v Kadinopoulos* [1992] 1 Lloyd's Rep 1. The arbitration in that case was governed by a sophisticated code known as the GAFTA Arbitration Rules. Those Rules provided for a two tier arbitration procedure with a right of appeal to a Board of Appeal from any 'award' of the first tier arbitrator. The Rules also contained detailed limitation provisions together with an overriding discretion in the first tier arbitrator to allow a claim to proceed despite its lateness. A first tier arbitrator found that Kadinopoulos's claim was time-barred and refused in his discretion to allow it to proceed. It followed that the claim, in the words of the Rules, was 'deemed to have been withdrawn and abandoned'. The arbitrator wrote up his decision in the form of an 'interim award'. The House of Lords had to say whether that was an award properly so-called in terms of the Rules so as to permit appeal to the Board of Appeal, which had reversed the arbitrator's decision. Lord Goff of Chieveley, with whose speech the other members of the House agreed, pointed out that the arbitrator's decision had involved both findings of fact, as to whether circumstances had arisen as to whether he was called upon to exercise his discretion, and a decision as to how he should exercise that discretion. Lord Goff then continued (at 4/5):
>
> > 'Like the Judge and the Court of Appeal, I am of the opinion that this decision was properly made the subject of an award. It is enough for me to say (subject to any right of appeal) it conclusively determined that the arbitration was at an end and so finally disposed of the relevant matters which had been submitted to arbitration; such a determination is properly the subject matter of an award, carrying with it the usual consequences which flow from an award—in particular, it renders the arbitrator functus officio and prevents the unsuccessful claimant from rearbitrating or litigating the identical claim in the future (see generally *Mustill and Boyd on Commercial Arbitration*, 2nd ed., pp.404–405 and 409–413, and cases there cited). It is, in my opinion, unnecessary in the present case to attempt an exhaustive definition of the precise nature of an arbitration award, because I am in no doubt that in the present case the arbitrator's decision was properly made the subject matter of an award. Indeed, as Lord Justice Leggatt pointed out in the Court of Appeal, it would be unrealistic to hold otherwise.
> >
> > 'It was suggested by the buyers that, in the arbitration rules, the expression "award" was, as a matter of construction, to be

confined to decisions on jurisdiction or on the merits of a dispute. This would in the present context impose an artificial limit upon the meaning of the word "award", which I would be unwilling to accept without good reason. As it is, there is certainly no express provision to this effect, and I cannot discover an acceptable basis for an implication displacing the ordinary understanding of what is meant by an award. *In the present case the determination of the arbitrator, although it did not amount to a decision of the merits of the sellers' claim, nevertheless did finally dispose of the relevant matters in dispute because it finally determined that the sellers' claim was deemed to have been withdrawn and abandoned and so could no longer be pursued against the buyers. Such a determination is, in my opinion, properly made the subject matter of an award.* In reaching this conclusion, I draw comfort from the fact that the new s.13A of the Arbitration Act, 1950 will, when brought into force, confer upon an arbitrator or umpire the power to make an award dismissing the claim for what, in the context of litigation, is called want of prosecution (see s.102 of the Courts and Legal Services Act, 1990)'" (emphasis added by the authors).

Practice Guideline 4, "Guideline for arbitrators on proceeding and making awards in default of party participation", issued by the CIArb (available at *http://www.ciarb.org/information-and-resources* [Accessed June 19, 2014]) provides guidance to tribunals where there has been delay in pursuit of claims or submission of statements of defence. **R37–11**

Rule 37(2)

This rule substantially follows art.25(b) of the Model Law. There are two key points, first that the tribunal must proceed with the arbitration in the absence of a defence and, secondly, the delay is not, per se and in isolation, to be treated as an admission of anything. **R37–12**

Section 1(a) and r.24 are paramount.

Rule 38: Failure to attend hearing or provide evidence D
38. Where—
  (a) a party fails—
    (i) to attend a hearing which the tribunal requested the party to attend a reasonable period in advance of the hearing, or
    (ii) to produce any document or other evidence requested by the tribunal, and
  (b) the tribunal considers that there is no good reason for the failure,
the tribunal may proceed with the arbitration, and make its award, on the basis of the evidence (if any) before it.

DEFINITIONS

"arbitration": s.2(1)
"claim": s.31(1)
"party": ss.2, 31(1), (2)
"tribunal": s.2(1) and 31(1)

STATUS

R38–01 This is a default rule so it is open to the parties to modify it, agree something different or disapply it completely (see s.9).

R38–02 Articles 30(2) and (3) of the UNCITRAL Rules and arts 28(2) and (3) of the Swiss Rules are in equivalent terms; art.26(2) of the ICC Rules mirrors r.38(a)(i). The LCIA Rules do not contain any equivalent.

MODEL LAW

R38–03 Article 25(c) of the Model Law is in substantially equivalent terms.

COMMENTARY

R38–04 There is a key point, in distinction to r.37, in that the tribunal *may* proceed with the arbitration but is not *obliged* to do so. In practice, absent obvious reasons such as insuperable transport delays, death, incapacity or serious ill health of one of the parties, a tribunal should be cautious in finding "good reason" for a no-show inter alia because of its obligations under s.1(a) and r.24(1)(c)(i).

R38–05 The circumstances of r.38(a)(i) are common, especially in the maritime and commodity sectors where wholly uncontestable actions for payment occur frequently.

R38–06 However, before concluding proceedings by issuing an award, the tribunal will have to consider very carefully whether "due process" has been properly and fully observed. If not, the award is not only open to challenge under r.68, but also, in an international case, open to refusal of enforcement (refer art.V(1)(b) of the New York Convention). If the tribunal issues an award where a party has not appeared, it should take care to specify in the award the circumstances in which notice of the hearing was given, any response of the party to the notification and the exercise of a discretion to proceed in the absence of the party. "Response" can include e-mail read-receipts (see *Bernuth Lines Ltd v High Seas Shipping Ltd* [2006] 1 Lloyd's Rep. 537 and (2005) EWHC 3020 (Comm)).

R38–07 It is important to note that a no-show by the respondent is not, in isolation, a ground for accepting the claimant's claim. The latter still has to meet the ordinary burden of proof. One of the authors has sat in a hearing where the respondent did not appear and the tribunal (of three, the other two being civil lawyers well used to proactive judges) tested the claimant's case thoroughly in a very inquisitorial style.

If there is non-appearance, r.37 merely allows the tribunal to proceed. The tribunal should take care to inform the non-attending party of the outcome of the hearing, including the sending of a transcript if one is made. This is particularly important if issues are raised or matters discussed at the hearing of which the non-appearing party has not had fair notice. Failure to appear does not entail waiver of any right of appeal or right to resist enforcement. **R38–08**

If, before the tribunal has issued its final award, the non-appearing party wishes nevertheless to continue to participate in the process, the tribunal will have to decide the extent to which, if any, that it should allow this to take place. In making such a decision, the tribunal must pay particular attention to its s.24(1)(b) and (c) duties. It may be inappropriate to re-open anything discussed at the hearing, but still possible to accommodate the non-appearing party in relation to other matters. It may be possible, perhaps even necessary, to recognise the no-show by an appropriate awards of costs. **R38–09**

Practice Guideline 4, "Guideline for arbitrators on proceeding and making awards in default of party participation", issued by the CIArb (available at *http://www.ciarb.org/information-and-resources* [Accessed June 19, 2014]) provides useful guidance to tribunals in how to proceed where a party fails to attend a hearing. **R38–10**

Rule 39: Failure to comply with tribunal direction or arbitration agreement D

39.—(1) Where a party fails to comply with—
  (a) any direction made by the tribunal, or
  (b) any obligation imposed by—
    (i) the arbitration agreement,
    (ii) these rules (in so far as they apply), or
    (iii) any other agreement by the parties relating to conduct of the arbitration,
the tribunal may order the party to so comply.

(2) Where a party fails to comply with an order made under this rule, the tribunal may do any of the following—
  (a) direct that the party is not entitled to rely on any allegation or material which was the subject-matter of the order,
  (b) draw adverse inferences from the non-compliance,
  (c) proceed with the arbitration and make its award,
  (d) make such provisional award (including an award on expenses) as it considers appropriate in consequence of the non-compliance.

DEFINITIONS

"arbitration": s.2(1)
"arbitration agreement": s.4 and 31(1)
"claim": s.31(1)
"party": ss.2, 31(1), (2)

"rules": s.31(1)
"tribunal": s.2(1) and 31(1)

STATUS

R39–01 This is a default rule so it is open to the parties to modify it, agree something different or disapply it completely (see s.9). It is noteworthy that exclusion of the equivalent (non-mandatory) s.41(5) of the 1996 Act appears unknown in England.

MODEL LAW

R39–02 There is no equivalent in the Model Law.

COMMENTARY

R39–03 Scots arbitrators, until this Act, had no powers and, prior to the 1996 Act, English arbitrators had inadequate, if any, powers to ensure that a party complied with the procedures governing the arbitration or, in fact, prosecuted its claim with adequate vigour. This was partially rectified in England by s.5 of the 1979 Act, but in a manner which proved too complex. The 1996 Act recognises two distinct circumstances: (a) the dormant arbitration where the claimant has failed to pursue its claim; and (b) cases where one or other of the parties has failed to comply with orders or directions of the tribunal. The first issue is covered by r.37(1) and the second is the subject of this rule, the equivalent of which is termed a "peremptory order" in England (see s.41(5) of the 1996 Act). The exclusion from the 2010 Act of the term "peremptory order" was deliberate so we must call such orders "Rule 39 orders"; it should be noted that such orders may, prima facie, appear similar to orders issued under r.31 but that is not the case primarily because (i) a r.39 order follows the failure by a party to comply with a r.31 order and (ii) there are very different consequences of non-compliance with the two types of order.

R39–04 CIArb Practice Guideline 14, "Guidelines for Arbitrators on how to approach an application for a peremptory and "unless" orders and Related Matters" (available at *http://www.ciarb.org/information-and-resources* [Accessed June 19, 2014]), while addressing the 1996 Act, provides useful guidance and suggestions to Scots arbitrators.

R39–05 Rule 39 has two elements. Firstly, r.39(1) sets out the power of the tribunal to make orders of a peremptory nature and the circumstances in which the power arises. Secondly, r.39(2) sets out the powers of the tribunal upon non-compliance with such an order.

Rule 39(1)

As regards "fails to comply", the object of r.39(1) is to provide powers to the arbitrator where a party has not complied with an arbitral direction or an obligation of the type specified in r.39(1)(b). In these circumstances "fails to comply" means "does not comply" and there is no requirement for any moral "failing" to be present. **R39–06**

Given that a direction requires to be complied in full, if there is non-compliance with any part of it, there is "failure" to comply and the power and discretion to make the r.39(1) order arises. Note the use of "may order", not "shall order". The element of discretion inherent here is not capable of challenge, other than in extreme circumstances such as infringement of s.1(a) and r.24 obligations. **R39–07**

Rule 39 brings out the importance of clear deadlines in arbitral directions. Without a clear deadline, it will often be impossible to reach a position of non-compliance, e.g. "I order you to complete your tax return" can be met with, "tomorrow/next month/next year", but "I order you by midnight on October 31, 2009" cannot. A stated deadline should always be given "5pm on Friday 31 [Month] [Year]". As a practical measure, arbitrators should always wait a short time thereafter before taking further action—mail does go astray, fax machines can break down, emails can get temporarily mislaid in cyberspace, etc. **R39–08**

As regards, "any direction made ", a r.39(1) order is ineffective unless it follows an existing, earlier direction and therefore cannot introduce anything substantive and new. In practice the drafting should track the earlier direction carefully and one of the authors uses a style where the recitals to the r.39(1) order repeat the earlier direction so that the actual r.39(1) order becomes very short: **R39–09**

IT IS HEREBY ORDERED PURSUANT TO RULE 39(1) THAT:

1. Respondent [perform some act] in accordance with Procedural Direction [*or* Order] #XX on or before midday GMT on [date stated]
2. Save as expressly amended herein, the provisions of Procedural Direction [*or* Order] #XX shall continue in full force and effect.
3. The expenses of this Order shall be included in arbitration expenses.

The same approach can be applied to drafting a r.39(1) order following a breach of an obligation mentioned in r.39(1)(b). A well drafted r.39(1) order should make it clear that it is made under that rule and that non-compliance may result in the consequences set out in r.39(2). **R39–10**

Careful consideration must be given to the means of service of the r.39 order, particularly on non-UK parties. Note that there is no express power to withdraw a r.39 order failing compliance. **R39–11**

Rule 39(2)

R39–12 This mirrors s.41(7) of the 1996 Act with some drafting differences which, the authors submit, are inconsequential.

R39–13 As a matter of practical common sense, arbitrators should beware of overreaction to non-compliance and should not rush into r.39(2)—it would be easy to take (unconscious) umbrage at having one's magisterial orders ignored. The tribunal has four exhaustively-listed remedies open to it and these are expected to cover most eventualities.

Rule 39(2)(a)

R39–14 Proportionality and relevance are the keys, e.g. with a failure to disclose documents relating to a particular part of a case or to give further information of that part of the case, the tribunal might consider the weight (possibly zero in many practical instances) it places on the affected parts of the claim. Sometimes that can mean that in effect a claim must fail, or (if the respondent is the defaulter) that it must succeed, but usually only part of the overall case is affected. However, art.V(1)(b) of the New York Convention may be relevant here.

Rule 39(2)(b)

R39–15 The "adverse inferences" must be limited to whatever was the subject of the peremptory order and does not permit the tribunal any wider discretion.

Rule 39(2)(c)

R39–16 A final or part award includes possibly the upholding or refusal of all or part of the claim, but this is a drastic measure not to be imposed lightly. Common sense suggests issuing appropriate warnings in directions and taking in appropriate representations.

R39–17 A common order in these circumstances is for service of defence submissions, the sanction for non-compliance being that the tribunal will proceed to its award on the basis of the statement of claim, defence, submissions and documentary evidence then available. However, one particular problem that arises quite regularly is that the claimant has not in fact exhibited with its claim all the evidence on which it wished to rely with the consequence that, following the respondent's failure to comply with the Rule 39 order, the claimant then asks to put in further evidence, while expecting the tribunal simply to proceed with that new evidence without giving the respondent a chance to comment. The tribunal should, in these circumstances, give the respondent the chance to comment and, perhaps, a chance to put in further evidence itself.

Rule 39(2)(d)

The key phrase is "consequences of the non-compliance": inter alia, the costs consequences must also be limited to whatever was the subject of the r.39 order and do not permit the tribunal any wider discretion. For provisional awards, see r.53 and commentary thereon. **R39–18**

Rule 40: Consolidation of proceedings D

40.—(1) Parties may agree—
  (a) to consolidate the arbitration with another arbitration, or
  (b) to hold concurrent hearings.
(2) But the tribunal may not order such consolidation, or the holding of concurrent hearings, on its own initiative.

DEFINITIONS

"arbitration": ss.2(1), (2), 31(1)
"tribunal": ss.2(1), 31(1)

STATUS

This is a default rule so it is open to the parties to modify it, agree something different or disapply it completely (see s.9). **R40–01**

Article 10 of the ICC Rules provides for the consolidation of arbitrations with the decision concerning consolidation being made by the International Court of Arbitration of the ICC. The Swiss Rules also make provision (art.4(1)) with the curious feature that the decision concerning consolidation will made by the Arbitration Court of the Swiss Chambers' (i.e. the Chambers of Commerce of the six cantons) Arbitration Institution, not by the tribunal, after full consultation with all parties. In one of the more notable differences between the 1998 and 2014 LCIA Rules, while the former made no reference to consolidation, the latter provide, at art.22.1(ix), that the tribunal may **R40–02**

> "... order, with the approval of the LCIA Court, the consolidation of the arbitration with one or more other arbitrations into a single arbitration subject to the LCIA Rules where all the parties to the arbitrations to be consolidated so agree in writing."

The UNCITRAL Rules do not provide for consolidation.

MODEL LAW

The Model Law makes no reference to consolidation. **R40–03**

COMMENTARY

R40–04 Both the LCIA Rules (art.22.1(viii)) and the Swiss Rules (art.4(2)) provide for the joining of third parties to the arbitration, a separate matter from that covered by r.40. However, joinder is very rare in practice since it requires all parties to agree. The SAR do not address joinder at all, there having been no interest shown in the matter during the consultation process while the 2009 Bill was being developed.

R40–05 There are two main types of consolidation: (a) where an employer is in dispute with a main contractor and the latter is in dispute with a sub-contractor on a construction project and the subject matter of the dispute is the same; and (b) commodity "string" contracts where A sells a parcel of goods to B who sells it to C etc. and Y sells it to Z who takes delivery.

R40–06 In the first type, a single arbitration *Employer v Main Contractor v Sub Contractor* might appear logical so that there is one hearing with one roomful of witnesses and so on. However, in practice this almost never happens because the parties cannot agree to proceed this way, because the two disputes are not in fact identical, despite superficial appearances to the contrary and/or because MC might envisage itself being sandwiched between E and SC and losing out to both.

R40–07 In the second, the rules of the main commodity trading associations provide that, within certain limitations, the 25 arbitrations *A v B, B v C, Y v Z* shall be consolidated into one single arbitration, effectively *A v Z*.

R40–08 A highly impressive example of concurrent arbitrations was seen in a LMAA case (*Bunge SA v Adm Do Brasil Ltda* [2009] EWHC 845 (Comm)) where there were nine arbitrations arising out of the same shipment of soybean meal and the arbitrations were heard together, with, in the words of Tomlinson J., "sensible co-operation as to representation and evidence". Two arbitrators sat on all nine tribunals, a third sat on seven and the eighth and ninth arbitrations had different third arbitrators. The five arbitrators issued one set of reasons which were common to all nine references. It would, of course, have been simpler with three arbitrators, not five.

R40–09 When arbitrations cannot be consolidated or run concurrently, one alternative sometimes seen in practice is to run one arbitration in the morning, the other in the afternoon, with the intention of matching the two sets of proceedings. This can be assisted by having the same tribunal.

R40–10 In such cases, if the arbitrations are not to be consolidated or conducted concurrently, r.26 applies so that everything in each arbitration is strictly confidential from the other, which might present significant practical difficulties where one party is common to both and/or one or more arbitrators is common.

R40–11 Construction arbitrators preach the consolidation gospel energetically at conferences and the like, but they rarely happen in practice for the reasons given above (and others).

Rule 40 (2)

We submit that this is self-explanatory. R40–12

Part 5

Powers of Court in Relation to Arbitral Proceedings

Rule 41: *Referral of point of law* D

41. The Outer House may, on an application by any party, determine any point of Scots law arising in the arbitration.

DEFINITIONS

"arbitration": ss.2(1), 31(1)
"Outer House": s.31(1)
"party": ss.2(1), 31(1), (2)

STATUS

This is a default rule so it is open to the parties to modify it, agree something different or disapply it completely (see s.9). However, if r.41 applies, r.42 applies mandatorily. R41–01

An arbitration agreement made before the commencement of the Act which disapplied the now repealed default provision in s.3 of the 1972 Act is deemed to be an agreement to disapply r.41 unless the parties otherwise agree (s.36(8); see paras S36–14 to S36–17). Given that many arbitration clauses excluded the unpopular s.3, it is important to note that these clauses will still be effective to exclude r.41, unless the parties agree that r.41 should apply. Equally, art.18.5 of SAC07 will be effective to exclude r.41 unless disapplied. R41–02

MODEL LAW

There is no equivalent provision of the Model Law. R41 03

COMMENTARY

This rule replaces the existing stated case procedure under s.3 of the 1972 Act. Under that procedure a party could, at any time during the arbitration until the issue of the final award, request the tribunal to state a case to the Inner House of the Court of Session, requesting it to give a binding opinion on any question of law which had arisen. The tribunal could decline to do so only on very narrow grounds and any refusal by the tribunal to do so could be reviewed by the court. It was widely believed that the procedure was open to abuse through parties seeking referrals to the court on dubious points of law in order to delay a final award or put financial pressure on the other party (see *ERDC Construction Ltd v HM Love & Co (No.2)*, 1996 S.C. 523 R41–04 per Lord Hope at 528). The 1996 Dervaird Committee Report (para.5.22) had recommended the abolition of s.3.

R41–05　There can, however, be merit in obtaining from a court a binding opinion on a point of law of general importance (see DAC Report, para.218). Equally, a preliminary ruling on a point of law may prevent an appeal against the final award on the basis of that point of law, i.e. thereby saving the time and cost of the arbitration, e.g. where a case has a threshold issue as to whether the claim was brought within time—if not, then there is nothing to arbitrate.

R41–06　Accordingly the drafters of the Act decided to provide a mechanism to allow the parties to seek a binding opinion on a point of Scots law but with safeguards against the potential for abuse which previously existed. Those safeguards are contained in r.42 which is mandatory if parties have not excluded r.41.

R41–07　In contrast to the old s.3, an application is made to the Outer House and not to the Inner House. Given that it is quicker to secure the services of a single Outer House judge rather than a three judge Inner House court, this will speed up the procedure. It is envisaged that, if the application concerns a point of commercial law, the court will allocate the application to a commercial judge even though, strictly speaking, an application in a commercial matter would not be a "commercial action" in terms of the Rules of the Court of Session 1994.

R41–08　The use of the word "may" indicates that the court has a residual discretion to refuse to determine the point of law. That discretion might be exercised where, for example, the parties have agreed that an issue be referred, but the court regards the matter as unimportant or not properly arising in the arbitration (under s.45 of the 1996 Act the court must be satisfied that the question substantially affects the rights of one or more of the parties).

R41–09　It is, however, difficult to imagine the court declining to determine the point of law if the validity conditions in r.42(2) have been met. In *Taylor Woodrow Holdings Ltd v Barnes* [2006] 2 All E.R. (Comm) 735, the equivalent to the condition in r.42(2)(a) (consent of all parties) had been met, but it was argued by the claimants in the arbitration that the court should exercise its discretion to refuse to determine the point of law on the grounds that: (i) the point should be decided by the arbitrator who was very experienced and who had been chosen by the parties; (ii) the proposed question of law was entangled with the facts which were for him to determine; and (iii) that there would be no saving in cost as the evidential hearing was to take place four or five months later in any event. Jackson J. rejected these arguments, observing: (i) that in that case the parties had expressly consented to the making of the application; (ii) there was no dispute over the facts relevant to the question of law which was one of the interpretation of the contract; and (iii) if the respondents in the arbitration were correct on that point of law it would decide the whole arbitration and that this would save substantial sums of money in the evidential hearing.

Arbitration (Scotland) Act 2010 (r.41)

Only a point of Scots law may be determined under r.41/42 following **R41–10** from the general position under Scots law that foreign law is an issue of fact to be proved by expert evidence. The Court of Session would not presume to give a binding opinion on the content of a foreign law. With regard to Scots law, there is no reason why the point of law could not cover both substantive and procedural law, including the Scots law of arbitration and the meaning of the Act itself, apart from any question as to the tribunal's jurisdiction which is dealt with by rr.22 and 23.

On what is a "point of law" as opposed to a point of fact, the classic **R41–11** explanation is contained in *Edwards v Bairstow* [1956] A.C. 14 at 34–36. A "point of law" under r.41 will not include any points of law affecting the tribunal's jurisdiction, any referral for which falls to be dealt with under r.22.

The following have been recognised to be "points of law": **R41–12**

- the meaning of a rule of substantive law;
- the meaning of a contractual document (*Halfdan Grieg & Co A/S v Sterling Coal & Navigation Corp (The Lysland)* [1973] Q.B. 843 per Lord Denning M.R. at 863); and
- the meaning of a rule of procedural arbitral law, e.g. the duty to act fairly *ERDC Construction Ltd v HM Love & Co (No.2)*, 1996 S.C. 523 at 527–528.

The exercise or proposed exercise by the arbitrator of a discretion where it is **R41–13** not alleged that he has misunderstood any rule of law or contractual document or that he has exercised the discretion or proposes to exercise it in a way in which no reasonable arbitrator would exercise it is not a "question of law", e.g. in an award of expenses (*ERDC Construction Ltd v HM Love & Co (No.2)*, 1996 S.C. 523 at 531) or in making a procedural direction.

It was suggested, during discussions leading up to the finalisation of the **R41–14** Bill, that r.41 would "open the floodgates"; however, the authors are aware of only three cases under the equivalent s.45 of the 1996 Act in the 17½ years it has been in force.

Reference on point of EU law

While a court can, an arbitral tribunal, to whom parties have granted **R41–15** jurisdiction pursuant to an arbitration agreement cannot, make a request directly to the ECJ for a preliminary ruling on the interpretation or validity of EU law (*Nordsee Deutsche Hochseefischerei GmbH v Reederei Mond Hochseefischerei Nordestern A.G. & Co. KG* [1982] E.C.R. 1095 at [10]–[12]; and *Eco Swiss* [1999] ECR I–3055 at [34]). Given that EU law is part of Scots law, should such an issue arise an application would first require to be made under r.41. Where an arbitral tribunal has jurisdiction through a mandatory referral to it under statute (e.g. when s.16 applies), it may have power to make a direct request to the ECJ (*Merck Canada Inc v Accord Healthcare Ltd* Case (C-555/13) ECJ February 14, 2014).

Rule 42: Point of law referral: procedure etc. M

42.—(1) This rule applies only where an application is made under rule 41.

(2) Such an application is valid only if—
  (a) the parties have agreed that it may be made, or
  (b) the tribunal has consented to it being made and the court is satisfied—
    (i) that determining the question is likely to produce substantial savings in expenses,
    (ii) that the application was made without delay, and
    (iii) that there is a good reason why the question should be determined by the court.

(3) The tribunal may continue with the arbitration pending determination of the application.

(4) The Outer House's determination of the question is final (as is any decision by the Outer House as to whether an application is valid).

DEFINITIONS

"arbitration": ss.2(1), 31(1)
"court": s.31(1)
"Outer House": s.31(1)
"party": ss.2(1), 31(1), (2)

STATUS

R42–01 Rule 42 is a mandatory rule thereby ensuring that, if the parties have not excluded r.41, they cannot by agreement force the tribunal to effectively sist (or stay) the arbitral proceedings (although the tribunal has a discretion to do so). The objective is to ensure that the delays caused through s.3 of the 1972 Act can be substantially avoided.

MODEL LAW

R42–02 There is no equivalent provision of the Model Law; see below at para.R69–05 for comment on this.

COMMENTARY

Introductory

R42–03 In contrast to the old s.3 of the 1972 Act, r.42 has been designed to promote the speed and reduce the cost of arbitration. In particular:

- if only one party agrees to the reference, the consent of the tribunal is now essential and cannot be overruled by the court, whereas

under the old s.3 the refusal of the tribunal to make the stated case to the court could be the subject of an application to the court which could overrule the tribunal;
- a refusal by the tribunal to consent is no longer subject to judicial review which could further delay the arbitral process (s.13(1)(b));
- the rule expressly provides that the tribunal may continue with the arbitration pending resolution of the reference to the court;
- the application is made by a party using a straightforward petition rather than the clumsy and time-consuming stated case procedure which involved written input from both the arbitrator and the parties.

R42–04 Expenses of the application will not be included in the "arbitration expenses" (see commentary to r.59) but will fall to be dealt with by the court rather than the tribunal but, on an analogy with the preparation of the former stated case, the expenses of obtaining the consent of the tribunal fall to be dealt with by the tribunal in terms of r.62 (*Thomson v Earl of Galloway*, 1919 S.C. 611).

R42–05 While r.33, which relates to representation, does not apply to court proceedings under rr.41/42, it has been observed by the UKSC that the court might proceed analogously to r.33 where a corporate party is unable to pay for a lawyer to act for it in the court proceedings (*Apollo Engineering Ltd v James Scott Ltd* [2013] UKSC 37 at [30]).

Rules 42(1) and (2)

R42–06 The court can consider the application only if it is valid. Accordingly, before taking any steps to consider the merits of the application, the court must satisfy itself that the application meets the test of validity set out in r.42(2). There are two ways in which an application may be valid: (a) that all of the parties have consented to it being made; or (b) that the tribunal has consented to it being made and the court is satisfied on all three of the sub-criteria in r.42(2)(b).

R42–07 The consent to the application being made can exist in the arbitration agreement itself (*Taylor Woodrow Holdings Ltd v Barnes* [2006] 2 All E.R. (Comm) 725).

R42–08 The criteria are the same as those in r.23 which allows a similar application to be made in respect of jurisdiction. The sub-criteria are stringent and are intended to preserve a useful tool for the parties where a particular point of law is critical to the dispute and an early decision from the court would be determinative, while at the same time guarding against abuse by a party seeking to cause delay for its own interests.

R42–09 The requirement for the tribunal to consent serves as a safeguard against the abuse of delay and additional expense identified in *ERDC Construction Ltd v HM Love & Co (No.2)*, 1996 S.C. 523. In deciding whether to give consent the tribunal will have to comply with its duty under r.24(1)(c) to conduct the arbitration without unnecessary delay and without incurring unnecessary expense. This suggests that a tribunal will not consent to a referral unless it takes the view that the application will promote overall speed and economy. It will normally be inappropriate to grant consent merely because the tribunal considers itself out of its depth; r.34(1) is the correct solution here.

R42–10 Even if the tribunal consents, the court must still be satisfied on all three sub-criteria in r.42(2)(b). "Likely" for the purposes of r.42(2)(b)(i) echoes s.45(2)(b)(i) of the 1996 Act.

R42–11 The use of "likely" in the 1996 Act, as opposed to the use of "might" in the 1979 Act, was intended to raise the bar for the demonstration of "substantial savings" (see also commentary on r.23(2) at para.R23–11). Equally "substantial savings" must be taken as it stands. "Delay" for the purposes of r.42(2)(b)(ii) is likely to be measured from the point when the need to have the point of law determined became evident. In short, the court might be satisfied where it is clear that a contested point of law lies at the heart of the dispute, which, if it was not resolved at the outset, would result in the lengthening of any evidential hearing due to both legal propositions requiring to be considered and an appeal under r.69.

Rule 42(1) and (2)—Procedure

R42–12 The application is made by petition in the style contained in RCS Form 14.4 (RCS rr.100.5(1) and 14.4) or, if there is an undisposed of Outer House petition, by note (RCS r.100.5). If both parties consent to the application, it is sensible for them to agree, if possible, the terms of the petition, in order to save time and the expense of answers.

R42–13 The requirements for the petition are set out in RCS rr.14.4 and 100.7(3) (rr.15.2 and 100.7(3) for notes) together with the need to:

    (i) aver the giving of consent of the other party or parties to the making of the application;

    (ii) aver the consent of the arbitrators making up the tribunal to the application being made and the circumstances in which the pre-requisites for an application in r.42(2)(b) (i.e. the substantial savings in expense, etc.) are satisfied;

    (iii) identify the point of law to be determined; the Outer House will not have the power that the English High Court has of amending, on its own initiative, the wording of the point of law concerned (cf. *HOK Sport Ltd v Aintree Racecourse Co Ltd* [2003] B.L.R. 155 at [39]); or

    (iv) require service or intimation on any non–applicant parties to the arbitration and the members of the tribunal and anyone interested in the arbitration.

Together with the petition the applicant should lodge with the Court of Session: **R42–14**

(i) as productions, any written consent of the other party or parties to the making of the application, any written consent of the tribunal to the application being made, and any documentary evidence in support of the matters in r.42(2)(b) as averred in the petition;
(ii) as productions, any documents which are necessary for the determination of the point of law, including the written statements of claim and defence (the pleadings) and any documents lodged in the arbitration which are necessary for the determination of the point of law; and
(iii) the bundle of court documents known as the process (see RCS rr.4.3, 4.4).

Inventories of any productions should be intimated to the other parties and members of the tribunal. On the lodging of the above, the applicant must move for a first order for service on the other party or parties to the arbitration or their representatives in the arbitration, and the members of the tribunal and anyone else who has an interest to allow such persons to lodge answers opposing the petition if they wish (RCS r.100.5). **R42–15**

If the consent of the court is required in order to validate the petition, then after the end of the period for answers, whether answers have been lodged or not, the petitioner should enrol a motion to have the court determine the petition as valid under r.42(2)(b). It seems appropriate for that preliminary matter to be decided before the court and the parties devote themselves to the point of law in issue. **R42–16**

Once the petition is validated, then whether answers are lodged or not (and there may be scope for a joint petition), the petitioner must apply by motion for further procedure (RCS r.100.5(5)) to have the point of law determined. **R42–17**

If the petitioner is not proactive in pursuing the petition, the respondent can enrol a motion to have the case put out for a hearing to allow the petitioner to explain his delay. Typically a hearing will be required to resolve the point of law but it might not be necessary for the validation issue if the arguments are clear from the petition and any answers or documents. However, the court may make such order for further procedure as it thinks fit (RCS r.100.5(5)). What is written above applies to notes in the same way as it does to petitions. **R42–18**

Rule 42(3)

Notwithstanding the making of an application the tribunal is empowered to continue with the arbitration and this must be exercised in the light of the tribunal's duty under r.24. In this context, an issue for the tribunal may be **R42–19**

Arbitration (Scotland) Act 2010

whether there is an aspect of the case which can be dealt with without the need for the court's decision on the referral. If there is such an issue, then it might seem reasonable for the tribunal to dispose of that issue while the court is deciding the referral.

Rule 42(4)

R42–20   The tribunal is bound to follow and apply the decision of the court on the referral (*Mitchell-Gill v Buchan*, 1921 S.C. 390). Failure to do so would amount to serious irregularity in terms of r.68 and inevitably lead to an appeal on that ground. However, if the decision on the referral forms part of the reasoning for an award it may be possible to have the decision on the referral reviewed by means of an appeal under r.69 (see *Babanaft International Co SA v Avanti Petroleum Inc (The Oltenia)* [1982] 2 Lloyd's Rep. 99, per Donaldson L.J. at 107, in relation to the similar provisions in the 1979 Act).

Rule 43: Variation of time limits set by parties D

43. The court may, on an application by the tribunal or any party, vary any time limit relating to the arbitration which is imposed—
  (a) in the arbitration agreement, or
  (b) by virtue of any other agreement between the parties.

DEFINITIONS

"arbitration agreement": ss.4, 31(1)
"court": s.31(1)
"party": ss.2(1), 31(1), (2)
"tribunal": ss.2(1), 31(1)

STATUS

R43–01   This is a default rule so it is open to the parties to modify it, agree something different or disapply it completely (see s.9); however, if r.43 applies, r.44 applies mandatorily.

MODEL LAW

R43–02   This rule has no equivalent in the Model Law.

COMMENTARY

R43–03   This rule allows a party or the tribunal to seek variation of any time limit which is imposed either (a) in the arbitration agreement itself; or (b) "by virtue of" any other agreement between the parties. The time limits which are the subject of this rule are ones such as a limitation on the period for commencing an arbitration or a time limit in institutional rules that the parties have agreed to adopt. The purpose of the rule is to provide some leeway for the prevention of "substantial injustice" through the existence of a time limit that is too tight for the circumstances in question. The ability to seek variation of time limits exists in Scottish litigation and is known as the ability to seek "prorogation" of a time limit. This rule provides an equivalent in arbitration.

It is important to note that the rule does not apply to time limits for the **R43–04** taking of procedural steps imposed by the arbitrator himself; such time limits are mandatory and, if they are not complied with, rr.37, 38, and 39 apply as appropriate.

One example of the use of r.43 is where the agreement requires the tri- **R43–05** bunal to make a decision within a particular time and there are practical difficulties in achieving that time limit; see para.R9–03.

The variation permitted under r.43 is of any time limit relating to the **R43–06** arbitration which is imposed either (a) in the arbitration agreement; or (b) "by virtue of" any other agreement between the parties. The reference to "arbitration agreement" is straightforward enough (see s.4), but a question arises whether the time limits imposed under the rules themselves, e.g. in rr.6 and 7 in relation to the appointment of an arbitrator, are covered by this rule.

While it is possible to argue that such rules are not rules imposed in the **R43–07** arbitration agreement itself but are imposed in the rules so that they cannot be varied under r.43, this is not the case. The correct approach is that if, for example, the parties have agreed to arbitrate under the SAR or the ICC Rules, that forms part of the agreement between them. If ICC, then the parties' ability under r.43 to vary any time limits imposed by the ICC Rules is subject to any provision of those rules governing such variation since any such provision is an agreement of the parties, so r.43 is deemed varied accordingly. In simple terms, r.43 does not get around the ICC Rules.

An application should be made before the time limit has expired but the **R43–08** rule can be read as only permitting applications before the expiry of the time limit. However, a more flexible reading would allow an out–of–time application but, in such circumstances, a court will require to be persuaded that it was not possible for the application to be submitted in time.

An application may be made to either the Outer House (RCS r.14.2(h)) or **R43–09** to the sheriff court of the sheriffdom where a respondent is domiciled in terms of ss.41 and 42 of the 1982 Act. The test for a variation of time limit and details of procedure are set out in r.44 and its commentary.

Rule 44: Time limit variation: procedure etc. M

44.—(1) This rule applies only where an application for variation of time limit is made under rule 43.

(2) Such a variation may be made only if the court is satisfied—
  (a) that no arbitral process for varying the time limit is available, and
  (b) that someone would suffer a substantial injustice if no variation was made. Arbitration (Scotland) Act 2010 (r.44)

Arbitration (Scotland) Act 2010

(3) **It is for the court to determine the extent of any variation.**

(4) **The tribunal may continue with the arbitration pending determination of an application.**

(5) **The court's decision on whether to make a variation (and, if so, on the extent of the variation) is final.**

DEFINITIONS

"court": s.31(1)
"party": ss.2(1), 31(1), (2)
"rule": s.31(1)
"tribunal": ss.2(1), 31(1)

STATUS

R44–01 This is a mandatory rule.

MODEL LAW

R44–02 This rule has no equivalent in the Model Law.

COMMENTARY

Rule 44(1)–(3)

R44–03 The court will consider the application only if there is no arbitral process for varying the time limit, consistent with the approach running throughout the SAR that an approach to the court is a step of last resort. This is also reflected in the requirement that the non-making of the variation would result in "substantial injustice". That is a high requirement and it is set high because the underlying policy is that variation of the time limits covered by r.43 should be for the parties themselves or the parties and the tribunal to resolve by agreement.

R44–04 The court has a discretion to decide, not merely whether there should be a variation, but as to what the variation should be. It is therefore not restricted to either granting the variation sought or refusing the application.

R44–05 If the application is made to the Outer House it is made by petition in the style contained in RCS Form 14.4 (RCS rr.100.5(1) and 14.4) or, if there is an undisposed of Outer House petition, by note (RCS r.100.5(2)). The requirements for the petition are set out in RCS r.14.4 and Ch.100 (r.15.2 for notes), together with the need to:

(i) aver the time limit in question;
(ii) aver the circumstances in which the prerequisites for an application in r.44(2) are satisfied;
(iii) aver the reasons why the usual period of 21 days for answers should be dispensed with (if that is necessary); and

(iv) require service or intimation on the other parties to the arbitration and the members of the tribunal.

If a shorter period of notice is required, then this should also be craved in the petition. **R44–06**

Together with the petition the applicant should lodge with the Court of Session: **R44–07**

(i) as a production, any written arbitration agreement in which or other agreement or other document by virtue of which, the time limit is imposed; and
(ii) the bundle of court documents known as the process (see RCS rr.4.3, 4.4).

Inventories of any productions should be intimated to the other parties and members of the tribunal.

On the lodging of the above, the applicant must move for a first order for service on the other party or parties to the arbitration or their representatives in the arbitration, and the members of the tribunal and anyone else who has an interest, to allow such persons to lodge answers opposing the petition if they wish within 21 days (RCS r.100.5). Therefore it is advised that if a shorter period is required a motion for that shorter period should be sought. **R44–08**

After the end of the period for answers, whether answers have been lodged or not, the petitioner should enrol a motion to have the court determine the petition, with or without a hearing as may be appropriate in the circumstances. What is written above applies to notes in the same way as it does to petitions. **R44–09**

If the application is made to the sheriff court it must be to a sheriff court of the sheriffdom where a respondent in the application is domiciled in terms of ss.41 or 42 of the 1982 Act. Procedure is by summary application in the style contained in SASAR Sch.1 Form 1 (SASAR r.2.4). The requirements for the summary application are broadly the same as for the petition described above. Detailed reference should be made to the SASAR. **R44–10**

Expenses of the application will not be included in the "arbitration expenses" (see the commentary to r.59 below) but will fall to be dealt with by the court rather than the tribunal. **R44–11**

Rule 44(4)

The tribunal has a discretion to continue with the arbitration whilst the court is determining the application. The best resolution of this issue is to have the parties agree on the procedure whilst the application is ongoing. If the parties cannot agree then, whilst the tribunal has a duty to conduct the arbitration without unnecessary delay (under r.24(1)(c)(i)), it also has a duty to treat the parties fairly (under r.24(b)). **R44–12**

R44-13 If the conduct of the arbitration while a time limit variation application is pending could result in unfairness to the applicant, then the tribunal will have to be very cautious in continuing with the arbitration during what should be a fairly short period during which the court is considering the application.

R44-14 Of course, unfairness to the applicant will have to be weighed against unfairness to the respondent who will not wish to be prejudiced by any delay in the process, particularly if the application could reasonably have been made at an earlier stage. The matter will be for the tribunal which will necessarily seek to avoid any substantial injustice which could conceivably result in a challenge to the award for serious irregularity (see r.68 below).

Rule 44(5)

R44-15 The decision of the "court" is clearly final. Where the court is the Outer House, the position is clear.

R44-16 Where the court is the "sheriff" it is not so clear given that, in terms of Sch.1 to the Interpretation Act 1978, "sheriff" includes "sheriff principal" unless the contrary intention appears. There is, however, no appeal to the sheriff principal, for three reasons: first, with reference to s.1(c), since there is no provision in the Act for review by the sheriff principal, there can be no such review; second, r.44(5) in its terms contemplates only one decision, that being final, i.e. thereby excluding any possibility of a review; and third, the existence of a right of appeal on a procedural matter would be wholly inconsistent with s.1(a), requiring that the object of arbitration is to resolve disputes inter alia without unnecessary delay or expense.

Rule 45: Court's power to order attendance of witnesses and disclosure of evidence M

45.—(1) The court may, on an application by the tribunal or any party, order any person—

　　(a) to attend a hearing for the purposes of giving evidence to the tribunal, or

　　(b) to disclose documents or other material evidence to the tribunal.

(2) But the court may not order a person to give any evidence, or to disclose anything, which the person would be entitled to refuse to give or disclose in civil proceedings.

(3) The tribunal may continue with the arbitration pending determination of an application.

(4) The court's decision on whether to make an order is final.

DEFINITIONS

　"court": s.31(1)
　"party": ss.2(1), 31(1), (2)
　"tribunal": ss.2(1), 31(1)

STATUS

This rule is mandatory. Parties cannot exclude the ability of each other to obtain witness attendance or document or other tangible evidence production orders. **R45–01**

MODEL LAW

Article 27 of the Model Law provides: (i) that the arbitral tribunal, or a party with the approval of the arbitral tribunal, may request from a competent court assistance in taking evidence; and (ii) that the court may execute the request within its competence and according to its rules on taking evidence. **R45–02**

Rule 45 follows art.27, except that it adds that a party may seek assistance from the court even without the approval of the tribunal. In practice, however, as noted below, it will be advisable for parties to exhaust any arbitral remedies before seeking the assistance of the court. **R45–03**

COMMENTARY

Introductory

It is a party's responsibility both to secure the attendance of a witness or witnesses to a hearing which is concerned with the establishment of the facts of the dispute and to obtain whatever documents it may wish to rely upon in the presentation of its case to the tribunal. Rule 45 provides for either the Court of Session or the sheriff court to assist a party, or the tribunal, in ordering the attendance of witnesses and the disclosure of documents or other material evidence. **R45–04**

Rule 45 widens the scope of recovery to include tangible evidence other than documents. It also provides for the recovery of documents other than those merely written by or passing to and from the parties. Further, it expedites the recovery process by omitting any need for the initial application to be to the arbitrator and by omitting any need for the appointment of a commissioner to receive the documentary evidence on behalf of the tribunal. **R45–05**

However, in *SGL Carbon Fibres*, 2013 S.L.T. 307, the first ever r.45(1) case under the Act, the judge took a different view. The case was an ex parte application for an order for the disclosure of documents and other material evidence by third party havers and the question arose as to whether the arbitrator should approve the specification of documents before a party to the arbitration applied to the court for such an order. Counsel for SGL submitted that the structure of the Act and the relevant rule of court supported the view that the pre-Act practice of obtaining the arbitrator's approval of a specification of documents before seeking the authority of the court should remain the norm. **R45–06**

In the absence of any contrary argument by the absent party, the judge broadly accepted counsel's submissions, for four reasons. First, s.1(c) provides that the court should not intervene in an arbitration except as provided by the Act. Secondly, r.28 provides that:

"(1) It is for the tribunal to determine ... (b) the admissibility, relevance, materiality and weight of any evidence. ..... (2)(c) whether any documents or other evidence should be disclosed *by or to any party* and, if so, when such disclosures are to be made and to whom copies of disclosed documents and information are to be given" (judge's emphasis).

Thirdly, while r.45 gives the court a discretion whether to grant or refuse the request for disclosure, r.100.6 RCS provides, "[i]n relation to a petition or note lodged under [r.45], intimation and service of the petition or note is not required", thereby creating an exception from the general requirement for intimation and service under r.100.5. The judge considered that the assumption must be that the r.45 application was not controversial between the parties because the arbitrator had already considered the substance of the request for disclosure. Further, he expected the norm to be that the parties first obtain the arbitrator's approval of the specification of documents before applying to the court under r.45. Fourth, he considered that that norm was a practical arrangement since, in most circumstances, the arbitrator, through his or her knowledge of the details of the parties' claims, would be in a better position than the court to promptly form a view on the admissibility and relevance of the proposed disclosures.

The authors respectfully disagree with counsel's submissions as espoused by the learned judge. Responding to his four reasons: (i) since r.45 expressly provides for court intervention, reference to s.1(c) is irrelevant; (ii) r.28 creates a power for the arbitrator exercisable in respect of the parties while r.45, in no way dependent on r.28, creates one for the court exercisable in respect of third parties (in addition to the parties); (iii) this is wrong given the fact that a r.45 application can be made even if the arbitrator has refused to order disclosure, i.e. so that the application is controversial and it would not be appropriate for the principal legislation [r.45] to be construed by reference to the RCS; and (iv) while this was the pre–2010 norm in Scotland, it is not so in England and the authors have found no other jurisdiction with any equivalent "norm". Finally, the judge's decision introduces an additional procedural stage not contemplated by the Act.

R45–07 Under the pre-2010 common law, if there was any doubt about whether a witness would attend a hearing, a party could apply to the tribunal for a certificate that there was good reason for the witness to be ordered to be present at the hearing and then, armed with that certificate, apply to the Court of Session or sheriff for a warrant for citation of that witness before the arbitrator at the hearing. Failure by a cited witness to attend would then amount to contempt of court.

R45–08 A warrant for citation to attend cannot, however, be enforced outwith

Scotland. In *Highland Railway Co v Mitchell* (1868) 6 M. 896, the court refused to grant a warrant to cite a witness resident outwith Scotland and accepted an argument that the party requiring the witness should seek, from both the arbitrator and the Court of Session, the appointment of a commissioner to take the evidence of the witness which commission could be enforced under the now repealed Evidence by Commission Act 1843.

If the witness is outwith Scotland, then steps to bring him before the tribunal will have to be taken in the jurisdiction where the witness is located. Where the witness is outwith Scotland and is unwilling to travel to Scotland, another option under the common law was to apply to the arbitrator for a certificate of good reason for an order together with a recommendation of the appointment of a particular person to act as a commissioner of the arbitrator to take the evidence of the witness. Having obtained that certificate and recommendation, the party could then petition the Court of Session to grant warrant for the commissioner to take that witness's evidence and to report it to the arbitrator. However, the commission, like the warrant for citation, could not be enforced outwith Scotland. **R45–09**

Unfortunately the Evidence by Commission Act 1843 has not been re-enacted in relation to commissions for use in arbitrations by the Evidence (Proceedings in Other Jurisdictions) Act 1975 (*Commerce and Industry Insurance Co of Canada v Certain Underwriters of Lloyd's of London* [2001] 1 W.L.R. 1323). **R45–10**

Similarly, it is a party's responsibility to obtain the documents that it needs in order to establish its case. At common law, if a party was experiencing difficulties in recovering relevant documents, the remedy was similar to that relating to witnesses described above. The party had to draft a document known as a "specification of documents" setting out in paragraphs known as "calls" the documents whose recovery was being sought in reference to the issues of fact in its pleadings (statements of case) to which they were supposed to relate. The specification was then presented to the arbitrator with an application for a commissioner to be appointed to receive the documents set out in the specification from any person in possession of the documents, i.e. the "haver" of the documents. The arbitrator would then decide the application on the basis of the relevancy of the documents in relation to a party's existing case and matters such as privilege. **R45–11**

An application to recover documents tending to show a fact not already in issue in terms of the pleadings would be seen as a "fishing diligence" and would be refused. In this respect Scots law is more restrictive in relation to recovery than the law of England and Wales and many other "common law" jurisdictions. **R45–12**

If the arbitrator granted the application he would approve the specification of documents and appoint the commissioner to receive the documents within the scope of the approved specification of documents from any haver to whom he was directed by the recovering party. Once the commissioner became aware of the identity and address of the haver, he would then **R45–13** request the latter to produce the documents. If the haver refused, the party seeking recovery could apply to the court for a warrant for citation of the haver to produce the documents to the court's commissioner who might or might not be the same as that appointed by the arbitrator (as in *Crudens Ltd, Petitioners*, 1971 S.C. 64). The court could grant the warrant in relation to a haver even if he was outwith Scotland. However, as with the attendance of witnesses, the order of the court was not enforceable by a Scottish court against a haver who was outwith Scotland and the commissioner would have to apply to a court or appropriate authority of the jurisdiction where the haver was located (*John Nimmo & Son Ltd, Petitioners* (1905) 8 F. 173).

Rule 45(1)

R45–14 Rule 45(1) gives the court power to order any person (a) to attend a hearing for the purpose of giving evidence or (b) to disclose "documents or other material evidence" to the tribunal. These powers may be exercised on the application not only of a party, but also the tribunal itself. However, the authors submit that this rule must be interpreted in the light of two of the founding principles of the Act, i.e. that the object of arbitration is to resolve disputes fairly, impartially and without unnecessary delay or expense, and that the court should not intervene in an arbitration except as provided by the Act (refer s.1).

R45–15 Where the application is by a party, the authors submit that, wherever practicable, it should exhaust any available arbitral remedy before applying to the court. For example, where the tangible evidence is thought to be in the hands of the other party, the recovering party should, if possible, first seek a tribunal direction under rr.35, 31 and 28(2)(c) ordering disclosure. Rule 45 gives the court a discretion on whether to grant the order so, if a party has not first made an application to the arbitrator, then it is likely that the court would, absent particular urgency, refuse the application as unnecessary or refuse to award the expenses of the application to the successful applicant.

R45–16 Rule 45(1) also permits an application by the tribunal itself, e.g. where either the tribunal's orders were being disregarded and the tribunal wished to obtain the evidence rather than decide the case without it, or the tribunal decided to exercise an inquisitorial role as it may do under r.28(2)(e).

R45–17 An order requiring a person to attend a hearing to give evidence is directly effective on the witness once he becomes aware of it. A separate citation of the witness as under the former common law is not appropriate. There is no restriction on the order being made against a witness who is outwith Scotland although, as under the common law, enforcement will depend either on the witness entering Scotland or on the law of the jurisdiction where the witness is located.

R45–18 The order for disclosure is effective against any haver of the evidence named in the order and is not restricted to the parties. The order may cover not merely documents, but "other material evidence" regardless of who was the author. In these respects recovery under r.45 is wider than the common law rule for recovery of documents in an approved specification of documents, which was restricted to documents written or sent by or received by a party. The key issue in an application under r.45 will be whether the tangible evidence sought (whether documentary or otherwise) is "material" to the issues in dispute before the tribunal. This is intended to prevent the abuse of r.45 for the purpose of fishing for evidence to allow a case to be made which is not currently made.

Rule 45(1)—Procedure

An application may be made either to the Outer House or to a sheriff court where the witness or haver is domiciled in terms of ss.41 or 42 of the 1982 Act. **R45–19**

If the application is made to the Outer House, it is made by petition in the style contained in RCS Form 14.4 (RCS rr.100.5(1) and 14.4) or, if there are undisposed of Outer House proceedings, by note (RCS r.100.5(2)). The requirements for the petition are set out in RCS r.14.4 (r.15.2 for notes), together with the need to: **R45–20**

- (i) aver why the order against the witness or haver is necessary; and
- (ii) aver the circumstances in which the prerequisites for an application in r.45(1) are satisfied.

If a shorter (or no) period of notice is required, then this should also be craved in the petition. Any documents or material evidence to be disclosed in terms of the order should be listed in a schedule to the petition, preferably in the form of "calls" as one would find in a specification of documents. It may be helpful for the court if the applicant narrates in the schedule next to the evidence in question its relevancy to the issues in the arbitration. **R45–21**

Together with the petition the applicant should lodge with the Court of Session: **R45–22**

- (i) as a production, any written arbitration agreement in which or other agreement or other document by virtue of which, the time limit is imposed;
- (ii) the written statements of case and defence in the arbitration (the pleadings); and
- (iii) the bundle of court documents known as the process (see RCS r.4.3 and 4.4).

Inventories of any productions should be intimated to the other parties on whom the petition is served. **R45–23**

On lodging per above, the petitioner should enrol a motion for intimation **R45–24** and service (notwithstanding RCS100.6) so to give an opportunity for objection and to avoid satellite procedure in the form of a petition for suspension being presented by the witness or more probably, the haver. Once the period of notice has expired the petitioner should enrol a motion to have the court determine the petition, with or without a hearing as may be appropriate in the circumstances. What is written above applies to notes in the same way as it does to petitions.

R45–25 If the application is made to the sheriff court, it is made by summary application in the style contained in SASAR Sch.1 Form 1 (SASAR r.2.4). The requirements for the summary application are broadly the same as for the petition described above. Detailed reference should be made to the SASAR.

R45–26 Expenses of the application will not be included in the "arbitration expenses" (see the commentary to r.59 below) but will fall to be dealt with by the court rather than by the tribunal.

Rule 45(2)

R45–27 In considering whether to grant the order, the court must apply the rules of privileged confidentiality as they exist in the Scots law of evidence, whether under common law or statute. The reader is referred to the standard works on the law of evidence in Scotland. There is also a useful statement of the various categories in *Greens Annotated Rules of the Court of Session* (Edinburgh: W. Green), para.35.2.7.

R45–28 The recognised categories of communications which attract privileged confidentiality are:

> (1) solicitor (or other lawyer) and client;
> (2) communications *post litem motam* (for the purposes of or in anticipation of litigation);
> (3) communications with a view to achieving settlement ("without prejudice" communications);
> (4) public interest immunity;
> (5) communications between spouses;
> (6) self-incrimination; and
> (7) communications made as a matter of moral duty, e.g. complaints to an appropriate body.

R45–29 Confidentiality and privilege of a document or communication may be waived in whole or in part.

R45–30 Documents may be privileged and confidential or merely confidential. Thus, documents or communications which are confidential pursuant to a contractual duty not to disclose their content (e.g. commercially confidential documents), journalists' sources, pursuant to a delictual duty of non-disclosure (e.g. doctors), or pursuant to a moral duty of non-disclosure (e.g. clergymen) are not on that basis privileged and immune from disclosure.

For the document or communication to be immune from disclosure, it must be not merely confidential, but also fall acceptably within one of the above categories. In this context, if a document or communication falls within one of the above categories, it may still be liable to be disclosed if it forms part of the res gestae of the dispute, i.e. the communication is an integral part of the disputed issue for which its recovery is sought (*Kid v Bunyan* (1842) 5 D. 193). **R45–31**

If a haver or a party claims privileged confidentiality for a document, then it should be produced to the court in a sealed packet to allow the court to assess the validity of the claim. **R45–32**

Rule 45(3)

The tribunal may continue with the arbitration whilst the court is determining the application. The preferred approach is to have the parties agree on the procedure whilst the application is ongoing. If the parties cannot agree, then while the tribunal has a duty to conduct the arbitration without unnecessary delay (r.24(1)(c)(i)) it also has a duty to treat the parties fairly (r.24(1)(b)). Everything will depend on the subject matter of the application to the court, the stage which the arbitration has reached and the nature of any prejudice that might be caused through the delay in not progressing with the arbitration while, e.g. documents are sought to be recovered. **R45–33**

It is clearly in the interests of the arbitral process that any recovery of material documents take place as early as possible so their importance can be assessed at an early stage and there is no delay in any evidential hearing that might have to take place through, in particular, the process of recovery of documents. **R45–34**

Ultimately, the question of whether, to what extent and how the arbitration should proceed while an r.45 application is pending will be a matter for the tribunal to decide. In complying with its duties under r.24, the tribunal will necessarily seek to avoid any substantial injustice which might result in a challenge to the award for serious irregularity (see r.68). **R45–35**

Rule 45(4)

Where the court is the "sheriff", it is not so clear given that, in terms of Sch.1 to the Interpretation Act 1978, "sheriff" includes "sheriff principal" unless the contrary intention appears. There is, however, no appeal to the sheriff principal, for three reasons: first, with reference to s.1(c), since there is no provision in the Act for review by the sheriff principal, there can be no such review; second, r.45(4) in its terms contemplates only one decision, that being final, i.e. thereby excluding any possibility of a review; and third, the existence of a right of appeal on a procedural matter would be wholly inconsistent with s.1(a) requiring that the object of arbitration is to resolve disputes inter alia without unnecessary delay or expense. **R45–36**

Rule 46: Court's other powers in relation to arbitration **D**

46.—(1) The court has the same power in an arbitration as it has in civil proceedings—
- (a) to appoint a person to safeguard the interests of any party lacking capacity,
- (b) to order the sale of any property in dispute in the arbitration,
- (c) to make an order securing any amount in dispute in the arbitration,
- (d) to make an order under section 1 of the Administration of Justice (Scotland) Act 1972 (c. 59),
- (e) to grant warrant for arrestment or inhibition,
- (f) to grant interdict (or interim interdict), or
- (g) to grant any other interim or permanent order.

(2) But the court may take such action only—
- (a) on an application by any party, and
- (b) if the arbitration has begun—
    - (i) with the consent of the tribunal, or
    - (ii) where the court is satisfied that the case is one of urgency.

(3) The tribunal may continue with the arbitration pending determination of the application.

(4) This rule applies—
- (a) to arbitrations which have begun,
- (b) where the court is satisfied—
    - (i) that a dispute has arisen or might arise, and
    - (ii) that an arbitration agreement provides that such a dispute is to be resolved by arbitration.

(5) This rule does not affect—
- (a) any other powers which the court has under any enactment or rule of law in relation to arbitrations, or
- (b) the tribunal's powers.

DEFINITIONS

"arbitration": ss.2(1), 31(1)
"court": s.31(1)
"party": ss.2(1), 31(1), (2)
"tribunal": ss.2(1), 31(1)

STATUS

R46–01 This is a default rule so it is open to the parties to modify it, agree something different or disapply it completely (see s.9). An example was where a FOSFA *"Scott v. Avery"* clause, prohibiting the bringing of any legal proceedings "in respect of any dispute arising out of this contract" until the making of the award, was held to exclude a court's power to grant an interim injunction under the equivalent s.44 of the 1996 Act (*B v S* [2011] 2 Lloyd's Rep. 18).

MODEL LAW

The 2006 revisions to the Model Law substantially expanded art.17, **R46–02** providing for "interim measures" which are defined in art.17(2) as:

> "any temporary measure, whether in the form of an award or in another form, by which at any time prior to the issuance of the award by which the dispute is finally decided, the arbitral tribunal orders a party to:
> (a) maintain or restore the status quo pending determination of the dispute;
> (b) take action that would prevent, or refrain from taking action that is likely to cause, current or imminent harm or prejudice the arbitral process itself;
> (c) provide a means of preserving assets out of which a subsequent award may be satisfied; or
> (d) preserve evidence that may be relevant and material to the resolution of the dispute."

Under art.17(1), unless the parties otherwise agree, the tribunal is given **R46–03** power, at the request of a party, to grant such interim measures. Article 17E(1) provides that the tribunal may require the applicant for an interim measure to provide appropriate security in connection with that measure. Article 17F(2) gives power to the tribunal to require any party to promptly disclose any material change in the circumstances on the basis of which the measure was requested or granted.

Having provided power to the tribunal in relation to the interim mea- **R46–04** sures, in art.17H the Model Law provides for the recognition and enforcement of interim measures by a competent court, irrespective of the jurisdiction in which the interim measure was issued, subject to the provisions of art.17I which gives limited defences to the recognition and enforcement by a court of interim measures. These are essentially the same as in relation to the recognition and enforcement of foreign arbitral awards under the New York Convention and s.20 with the addition of the following:

- that the tribunal's decision with respect to the provision of security in connection with the interim measure has not been complied with;
- that the interim measure has been terminated or suspended by the tribunal or where so empowered by the court of the state where the arbitration takes place or where the measure was granted; and
- that the interim measure is incompatible with the powers conferred upon the court unless the court decides to reformulate the interim measure to the extent necessary to adapt it to its own powers and procedures for the purposes of enforcing it but without modifying its substance.

R46–05 As with the enforcement of foreign arbitral awards, art.17I(2) prohibits any review of the substance of the tribunal's decision on the interim measure.

R46–06 Finally, art.17J provides that the court should have the same power of issuing an interim measure in relation to arbitration proceedings within its state as it has in relation to litigation before it. Article 17J requires the court to "exercise such power in accordance with its own procedures in consideration of the specific feature of international arbitration."

R46–07 A number of these new features of the Model Law are reflected in r.46. However, because r.46 applies only to arbitrations seated in Scotland, it does not give power to the courts in relation to what is defined in s.2(1) as, "arbitration between parties residing, or carrying on business, anywhere in the United Kingdom" or, "international arbitration". By reason of an unfortunate oversight, the proposed (by the CIArb) inclusion in the Act of the equivalent of ss.2(3) to (5) of the 1996 Act was not followed through. The only remedy would appear to be to seek to raise court proceedings in Scotland seeking the same remedies as in the arbitration, then apply for the interim measures at the outset of those proceedings and then to apply for a sist of proceedings (*Mendok BV v Cumberland Maritime Corp*, 1989 S.L.T. 192). Jurisdiction would have to be established for such court proceedings.

COMMENTARY

Introductory

R46–08 Rule 46 provides important additional powers for the sheriff court and the Outer House to support Scottish-seated arbitrations. In addition, an innovative provision (r.46(4)(b); see paras R46–16, R46–30, R46–34 and R46–48 below) confers relevant powers to these courts where such arbitral proceedings have not begun but there is or there might become a dispute which in terms of an arbitration agreement is to be resolved by arbitration.

R46–09 In relation to continuing arbitrations, r.46(2)(b) provides that a court can exercise the powers mentioned in r.46(1) only with the consent of the tribunal unless the case is one of "urgency". This structure appears to originate from s.44(4) of the 1996 Act which itself implements the proposal of the DAC Report (para.215). This indicates that a party who wishes the powers to be exercised must first apply to the tribunal for its consent unless the case is one of urgency.

R46–10 It will be a matter for the tribunal's professional judgment in granting, or not granting, its consent. It will have to consider, with particular reference to rr.24(1)(b) and 24(1)(c)(ii), whether the court should grant the remedy for which the party seeks consent to apply. This approach is consistent with the principle, purpose and spirit of arbitration which is that if the parties have entrusted the resolution of their dispute to an arbitral tribunal rather than merely to litigate it in the courts, the tribunal should do so (see *Fiona Trust v Privalov* (2007) UKHL 40 per Lord Hoffmann at [6]–[8]). It follows that a court should pay careful attention to the tribunal's views.

This approach is also consistent with the DAC's insistence on the **R46–11** requirement *for the tribunal's* consent, "in order to prevent any suggestion that the court might be used to interfere with or usurp the arbitral process or indeed any attempt to do so" (para.215).

Further support is found in *Emmott v Michael Wilson & Partners Ltd* **R46–12** [2009] 1 Lloyd's Rep. 233, where, under the 1996 Act's equivalent of r.35, the tribunal directed that a shareholding which was the subject matter of the dispute be placed into its name pending the resolution of the dispute. When the tribunal's order was not complied with, an application was made to the court for an order requiring compliance and an order under the equivalent of r.46 for freezing the shareholding. The tribunal had consented to the freezing order and the court took the view that the freezing order should be granted in order to help the arbitral process operate effectively.

If a party is discontent with the tribunal's refusal to consent to the **R46–13** application, judicial review is excluded (s.13(1)(b)) and the only potential remedy is to apply to the court under r.41 in relation to a point of law which would require the consent of the other party.

If a party is discontent with the tribunal's consenting to the application, **R46–14** its remedy is to challenge the substance of the consent in the hearing before the court.

Section 42 of the 1996 Act, and *Emmott* (above), resurfaced in *Patley* **R46–15** *Wood Farm LLP v Brake* [2013] EWHC 4035 (Ch); December 18, 2013, unreported, where the sole arbitrator had awarded a dissolution of the partnership and a declaration that dissolution accounts be prepared, if necessary by himself with the assistance of an expert accountant, and had made a direction requiring the defendants to produce the partnership books and records to the partnership accountant. The claimants applied to the court under s.42 of the 1996 Act to enforce the direction as a peremptory order. Peter Smith J held that it would be wrong to see the court's discretion under s.42 as a "rubber stamping" exercise of the tribunal's order, but that the court had discretion whether or not to go into its merits.

Following a detailed review of the facts and of *Emmott*, the judge concluded (at [66]):

> "I should consider all the relevant facts and I have set them out above. It seems to me that the proper consideration of the power under s.42 is to accede to the Claimant's application. It is entitled to enforce the Award for the reasons I have set out above; the Defendants are in breach of their contractual duties and their duties in the Arbitration and in the Award itself. The fact that they are appealing the Award of the Arbitrator is one factor but the rights of the Claimant to have access to the records and the undoubted inevitability of accounts in one form or another justifies the making of the order. When balanced against those factors the appeal is not of great significance ... I am of the same view and that is why this arbitration should, given the

Defendants' stance, be continued by the court exercising its power under s.42 which I will do."

For a discussion of *Patley Bridge*, see Hew R. Dundas, "Two Rarities: Subpoenaing an Arbitrator for Cross-Examination and Court Enforcement of a Peremptory Order" [2014] 80 *Arbitration* 2 at 196–203.

R46–16 In addition, r.46(4)(b) also allows a party in a situation where a dispute has arisen or might arise and there is an arbitration agreement covering that dispute, but the arbitration has not yet begun (see r.1 above), to apply to the court for the exercise of a r.46(1) power. In practice this is what occurred at common law whereby, if a party to a contract required an interim interdict against the other party in a contract where there was an arbitration clause, the claimant would raise an action and seek interim interdict. The court would grant the interim interdict, quite possibly on an ex parte (without notice) basis, which order would then be served on the defender who might seek to have it recalled. After the court had disposed of the interim order, the action would be sisted to allow the arbitration to be begun. A similar outcome could ensue if a party required to obtain an interim order of specific implement, although this had to be sought in the Outer House.

R46–17 Curiously, r.46 omits the express provision seen throughout the SAR, that the decision of the court is to be final.

Rule 46(1)(a)—Appointment of safeguarder

R46–18 Both the Outer House and the sheriff court have power, if necessary on their own initiative, to appoint a guardian (or tutor or curator) *ad litem* to a party in a litigation who has no legal capacity and either has no guardian or whose guardian cannot act, e.g. because of a conflict of interest (*Ward v Walker*, 1920 S.C. 80, a workman's compensation arbitration, where it was held that the arbitrator had the power to appoint a tutor *ad litem* to a child claimant whose mother had died and to whom no guardian had yet been appointed). The role of the guardian *ad litem* is to ensure that the case on behalf of the party lacking capacity is properly conducted.

R46–19 The appointment can be made in relation to a pursuer or defender at any time after the litigation has been raised (*Drummond's Trustees v Peel's Trustees*, 1929 S.C. 484).

R46–20 A guardian *ad litem* cannot be liable for the expenses of the litigation (*Fraser v Pattie* (1847) 9 D. 303). Remuneration for his services may be recovered either from his ward's estate or the estate of the unsuccessful party to the litigation. Where the guardian *ad litem* requires funds to allow him to perform his duties, he is entitled to apply to the court to order an appropriate party to put him in funds and to sist the litigation until he is put in funds (*Studd v Cook* (1883) 10 R. (HL) 53).

Rule 46(1)(b)—Sale of property

The power is to order the sale of any property in dispute in the arbitration, following s.44(2)(d) of the 1996 Act, e.g. if the dispute concerns a cargo of perishable goods, it may be necessary to order them sold immediately otherwise their value might reduce to zero. **R46–21**

Rule 46(1)(c)—Order securing any amount in dispute

In court proceedings in Scotland, a court in general does not make an order securing any amount in dispute except where it orders a party, generally the pursuer (claimant) to provide caution (a guarantee; pronounced "kayshun") for the expenses of the defender (respondent). Only where it is clear from the pleadings that a sum (e.g. the price of goods) will ultimately be due to the pursuer (claimant) does the court have a discretionary power to order some or part of the amount claimed to be lodged (consigned) with it (*George Cohen Sons & Co Ltd v Jamieson & Paterson,* 1963 S.C. 289). **R46–22**

Instead, where a pursuer (claimant) fears that the defender (respondent) will dissipate assets or become insolvent in order to prevent effective enforcement of the decree (judgment) to be obtained in the proceedings, he will apply to the court for a warrant to enable him to execute "diligence on the dependence" which has the effect of freezing assets which could satisfy the court decree. Almost always the court's role is therefore not to make the order for the provision of security itself, but rather to grant a warrant to enable the pursuer to secure the assets himself. **R46–23**

The forms of diligence on the dependence differ depending on whether the amount in dispute is to be secured in the form of moveable or heritable (immoveable) property of the defender (respondent). The diligences on the dependence against moveable property of the defender are: **R46–24**

- arrestment on the dependence of moveable property (including incorporeal (intangible) property, e.g. debts) of the defender held, owed or to be owed by third parties; and
- interim attachment of the corporeal (tangible) moveable property of the defender held by him.

The principal diligence on the dependence against heritable (immoveable) property of the defender is inhibition on the dependence which gives the claimant a right to "reduce" or quash any transfer of, or the granting of, any real right (*jus in rem*) by the defender in the heritable property. **R46–25**

It is also possible to register a notice of litigiosity under s.159 of the Titles to Land Consolidation (Scotland) Act 1868 against heritable property where the pursuer (claimant) seeks reduction (annulment) of a deed transferring rights over heritable property. Strictly speaking, a notice of litigiosity does not require a warrant from the court and is not a "diligence on the dependence". However, it performs the function of preventing the disposal **R46–26** of heritable property while there is an ongoing action to recover it through court proceedings to reduce the deed of transfer (usually a disposition or standard security (mortgage)).

R46–27 Rule 46(1)(e) covers the granting of warrants for arrestment or inhibition on the dependence. If, therefore, r.46(1)(c) covers any diligence on the dependence at all, it covers interim attachment. The authors submit that interim attachment is covered by r.46(1)(c) but, if that is incorrect, the alternative basis for an application for a warrant for interim attachment would be r.46(1)(g).

R46–28 The test for the obtaining of a warrant for interim attachment is set out in ss.9D(2) (in relation to an urgent order without a hearing) and 9E(3) (in relation to an order at a hearing) of the Debt Arrangement and Attachment (Scotland) Act 2002 (as amended). The warrant will be granted where:

(a) the claimant has a prima facie case on the merits;
(b) there is a real and substantial risk enforcement of any award for the claimant would be defeated or prejudiced by reason of:

   (i) the respondent being insolvent or verging on insolvency; or
   (ii) the likelihood of the respondent removing, disposing of, burdening, concealing or otherwise dealing with some or all of his assets; and

(c) it is reasonable in all the circumstances, including the effect on any person interested.

R46–29 If the warrant is to be granted without notice to the respondent, then the court must be persuaded that the insolvency or verging on insolvency or the likelihood of removal, etc. arises immediately or would arise before a hearing could take place.

R46–30 Warrants can be granted before the raising of litigation provided that it is raised within a certain period of time (see s.15G of the 1987 Act (as amended) and s.9G of the Debt Arrangement and Attachment (Scotland) Act 2002 (as amended). This indicates that a similar process could be followed in relation to arbitration as anticipated by r.46(4)(b) where the court is satisfied that a dispute has arisen or might arise and an arbitration agreement provides that such a dispute is to be resolved by arbitration.

R46–31 Warrants for, and subsequent executions of interim attachment can be recalled or restricted by the court under s.9M of the 2002 Act (as amended). The court may recall the warrant and any subsequent execution (a) if the claimant does not satisfy the test for the diligence on the dependence in question—the onus of persuasion being on the claimant; or (b) the respondent offers suitable and sufficient alternative security, often in the form of caution (typically a bond from an appropriate insurance company) or consignation of sums with the court. In recalling or restricting the warrant to inhibit, the court may impose such conditions as it thinks fit, having regard to the interests of both parties. Section 9N of the 2002 Act provides for variation of orders to recall or restrict and their conditions.

The only power which a court has actually to order provision of security is to order a party, typically a pursuer (claimant), to find caution (a guarantee) for the payment of the defender's (respondent's) expenses in the event of the defender's success. However, that is a power which is unlikely to be invoked by parties to an arbitration given that the tribunal itself has the power under r.64(1)(a) to make such an order and the power to make an award dismissing the claim if the security for expenses was not given. **R46–32**

Rule 46(1)(d)—Order under s.1 of 1972 Act

Under s.1 of the 1972 Act a court has power, subject to the law of privileged documents or oral evidence and to recovery of documents from the Crown, to order: **R46–33**

(1) the inspection, photographing, preservation, custody and detention of documents and other property (including where appropriate, land) which appear to the court to be property as to which any question may relevantly arise in any existing civil proceedings before it or in civil proceedings likely to be brought;
(2) the production and recovery of any such property, the taking of samples thereof and the carrying out of any experiment thereon or therewith;
(3) any person to disclose such information as he has as to the identity of any persons who:
    (a) might be witnesses in any existing civil proceedings before it or which are likely to be brought; or
    (b) might be defenders in any civil proceedings likely to be brought.

The powers under s.1 of the 1972 Act can be used before civil proceedings are actually brought. In relation to their application under r.46, if the arbitration has not "begun" then the court must separately be satisfied in terms of r.46(4)(b) that a dispute has arisen or might arise and that an arbitration agreement provides that such a dispute is to be resolved by arbitration. It is worth noting, however that the phrase "civil proceedings" in terms of s.1 has already been interpreted in the Outer House as meaning proceedings of a civil character irrespective of the court or tribunal before which they may be raised and therefore including arbitral proceedings (*Anderson v Gibb*, 1993 S.L.T. 726 at 729). If *Anderson* is correct, then technically the petition or application can be made directly under s.1 without the need to use r.46(1)(d). **R46–34**

The procedure for obtaining orders under s.1 of the 1972 Act is similar to that for obtaining an order for recovery of documents in a specification of **R46–35** documents at common law. This is described in the general commentary to r.45 above.

R46–36 The powers under s.1 of the 1972 Act do not apply to the taking of oral evidence. The power of the court to allow the taking of oral evidence of a witness by a commissioner is covered in the commentary to r.46(1)(g). In extraordinary circumstances, the Inner House of the Court of Session may exercise its *nobile officium* to grant a commission to take evidence of a witness where there was no arbitration or action before it or an arbitration or action immediately pending (*Galloway Water Power Co v Carmichael*, 1937 S.C. 135 at 140)—see the commentary to r.46(4) below.

Rule 46(1)(e)—Warrant to arrest or inhibit on the dependence

R46–37 Arrestment on the dependence or inhibition on the dependence are means by which a claimant, fearing that the respondent will dissipate its assets, or become insolvent, in order to prevent effective enforcement of an award, freezes assets of the respondent which could satisfy the award. Arrestment on the dependence and inhibition on the dependence are known collectively as "diligence on the dependence". The forms of diligence on the dependence differ depending on the nature of the asset to be frozen. The diligences on the dependence against moveable property of the respondent are:

- arrestment on the dependence of moveable property (including incorporeal (intangible) property, e.g. debts) of the respondent held by, owed or to be owed by third parties; and
- interim attachment of the corporeal (tangible) moveable property of the respondent held by him.

Warrants for interim attachment are dealt with under r.46(1)(c) or 46(1)(g).

R46–38 The principal diligence on the dependence against heritable (immoveable) property of the respondent is inhibition on the dependence which gives the claimant a right to "reduce" or quash any transfer of or the granting of any real right (*jus in rem*) by the respondent in, the heritable property owned by him at the date of inhibition. The inhibition on the dependence takes effect generally upon registration of the executed "schedule on inhibition" and certificate of execution in the Register of Inhibitions, but if a preliminary notice of registration is registered before execution, the inhibition can, in certain circumstances, take effect from the date of the execution. The reader is referred to s.155 of the Titles to Land Consolidation (Scotland) Act 1868 (as introduced by s.149 of the Bankruptcy and Diligence etc. (Scotland) Act 2007).

R46–39 An inhibition on the dependence attaches to all heritable property of the respondent in Scotland regardless of its value. For this reason, if more than one item of heritable property is covered, respondents often apply to the court for restriction of the inhibition to the property sufficient to cover the sum sought by the claimant and a reasonable figure for expenses.

If only one item of heritable property is covered, and there is no ground of challenge to the inhibition in relation to whether the test for obtaining it was satisfied, a respondent may apply to the court for recall of the inhibition and instead offer security in some other form, e.g. through caution or the lodging of a sum with the court (known as "consignation"). **R46–40**

The test for the obtaining of a warrant for arrestment on the dependence or inhibition on the dependence is set out in ss.15E(2) (in relation to an urgent order without a hearing) and 15F(3) (in relation to an order at a hearing) of the Debtors (Scotland) Act 1987 (as amended by the Bankruptcy and Diligence etc. (Scotland) Act 2007). The warrant will be granted where: **R46–41**

(a) the claimant has a prima facie case on the merits;
(b) there is a real and substantial risk enforcement of any award for the claimant would be defeated or prejudiced by reason of:

   (i) the respondent being insolvent or verging on insolvency; or
   (ii) the likelihood of the respondent removing, disposing of, burdening, concealing or otherwise dealing with some or all of his assets; and

(c) it is reasonable in all the circumstances, including the effect on any person interested.

If the warrant is to be granted without notice to the respondent and therefore a "hearing", then the court must be persuaded that the insolvency or verging on insolvency or the likelihood of removal, etc. arises immediately or would arise before a hearing could take place. **R46–42**

Warrants can be granted before the raising of a litigation provided that the litigation is raised within a certain period of time (see s.15G of the 1987 Act (as amended)). This indicates that a similar process could be followed in relation to arbitration as anticipated by r.46(3) where the court is satisfied that a dispute has arisen or might arise and an arbitration agreement provides that such a dispute is to be resolved by arbitration. **R46–43**

Warrants for, and subsequent executions of arrestment and inhibition on the dependence, can be recalled or restricted by the court under s.15K of the Debtors (Scotland) Act 1987 (as amended). The court may recall the warrant and any subsequent execution (a) if the claimant does not satisfy the test for the diligence on the dependence in question—the onus of persuasion being on the claimant; or (b) the respondent offers suitable and sufficient alternative security, often in the form of caution (typically a bond from an appropriate insurance company) or consignation of sums with the court. In recalling or restricting the warrant to inhibit the court may impose such conditions as it thinks fit, having regard to the interests of both parties. Section 15L of the Debtors (Scotland) Act 1987 provides for variation of orders to recall or restrict and their conditions. **R46–44**

It is also possible to register a notice of litigiosity against heritable **R46–45** property where the pursuer (claimant) seeks reduction (annulment) of a deed transferring rights over heritable property. Strictly speaking, this does not require a warrant from the court and is not a "diligence on the dependence". However, it performs the function of preventing the disposal of heritable property while there is an ongoing action to recover it through court proceedings to reduce the deed of transfer (usually a disposition or standard security).

Rule 46(1)(f)—Interdict or interim interdict

R46–46 The court is given the same power in an arbitration as it has in civil proceedings to grant interdict (injunction in English legal parlance) or interim interdict. An interdict is an order restraining an ongoing or reasonably anticipated future breach of legal duty owed by the respondent to the claimant (*Inverurie Magistrates v Sorrie*, 1956 S.C. 175). It may be interim or permanent and an interim interdict preserves the status quo until the court decides whether to grant a permanent interdict in its final decree (judgment).

R46–47 Rule 49(b) (a default rule) provides that the tribunal may make an award ordering a party to refrain from doing something. Rule 46(1)(f) therefore envisages the court's possibly usurping the tribunal's jurisdiction by granting a permanent interdict in a dispute, governed by an arbitration agreement, in which an arbitration had begun. The utility of r.46(1)(f) would therefore appear to be twofold: (i) to permit an order of interim interdict to be made to preserve the status quo until the tribunal makes its award on the issue of permanent interdict; and (ii) to deal with the situation where r.49(b), for whatever reason, is insufficient. Awards of permanent interdict are dealt with in the commentary to r.49(b) infra (at paras R49–08 to R49–16).

R46–48 At common law, a tribunal had power to grant interim interdict (*Gray v Brown* (1833) 11 S. 353) and, by implication, permanent interdict. This is restated in r.49(b) as read with r.53. A claimant seeking interim interdict may be in a number of different situations. First, the arbitration may not have begun. If it has not begun, the claimant will have to satisfy the court that it may hear the application under r.46(4)(b). Second, the arbitration may have begun but the case is one of urgency where the consent of the tribunal is not necessary. Third, the arbitration may have begun but the case is not one of urgency, the claimant should first seek a provisional award of (interim) interdict from the tribunal. However, breach of that award will not allow the tribunal to hold the respondent in contempt of court as a breach of a court order would allow. For that reason there may be an advantage for a claimant holding a provisional award of interim interdict to seek the authority of the court to be added with the court's own order.

R46–49 In whichever of these situations interim interdict is sought, either the tribunal will make a provisional award thereof or the court will grant it only where the claimant seeks an award under r.49(b), ordering a party to refrain from doing something where the claimant can demonstrate (a) a prima facie case for such an order, and (b) that the balance of convenience favours him rather than the respondent (*WAC Ltd v Whillock*, 1989 S.C. 397 per Lord Justice-Clerk Ross at 410). At the stage of granting interim interdict, the tribunal or court is not concerned with whether the respondent disputes the facts put forward by the claimant provided that there is prima facie evidence of some kind to support the claimant's factual position.

In considering the balance of convenience, the tribunal or court must weigh the inconvenience to the pursuer if the interim order is not granted with the inconvenience to the defender if the interim order is granted. The factors in relation to balance of convenience include: **R46–50**

- irreparable nature of apprehended wrong;
- offering of caution, consignation or other security or an undertaking to the court by the respondent;
- weakness of the prima facie case;
- financial effect of an interim order on the respondent;
- ease of quantification of putative damages if the respondent breached his duty in the future;
- adequacy of putative damages;
- safety implications;
- public interest; and
- undue delay in making the application.

Further detail on balance of convenience with reference to illustrative case law can be obtained from the commentary to RCS r.60.3 in *Greens Annotated Rules of the Court of Session*, also contained in *The Parliament House Book* (Edinburgh: W. Green), Vol.2. **R46–51**

Interim interdict is often granted by a court ex parte, that is, without notice of the application, or indeed the commencement of legal proceedings themselves, being given to the defender. The only way in which a person who fears he may be sued for interdict can obtain notice is by lodging a document known as a "caveat" with the court where he thinks that the legal proceedings might be raised. Before hearing an applicant on an application for interim interdict where proceedings have not been raised, the court will check whether the defender has lodged a caveat and, if he has, will intimate the application to the defender. However, the defender may have little time to prepare for the hearing if the matter is particularly urgent. If the court grants interim interdict ex parte then the defender may apply for recall of the interim interdict on the grounds of the absence of a prima facie case or the balance of convenience favouring him. **R46–52**

There seems to be no good reason why an order of interim interdict could not be made ex parte on the beginning of the arbitration either in terms of r.1 or other agreement of the parties as to commencement. Unfortunately there are conflicting authorities on whether a sheriff court has jurisdiction **R46–53** under s.6 of the Sheriff Courts (Scotland) Act 1907 to grant interim interdict restraining conduct outwith its sheriffdom. This suggests that if there is any possibility of the conduct to be restrained taking place over more than one sheriffdom within Scotland, or even outwith Scotland, the application under r.46(2) should be made by petition to the Outer House.

R46–54 An order of interim interdict comes into operation when the defender becomes aware of its content (*Clark v Stirling* (1839) 1 D. 955) whether or not there has been formal service; knowledge by the defender's solicitor may raise a presumption of knowledge by the defender (*Henderson v Maclellan* (1874) 1 R. 920 per Lord President Inglis at 923).

Rule 46(1)(g)—Any other interim or permanent order

R46–55 Other interim orders which may be covered include:

(a) a permanent order of specific implement (an order *ad factum praestandum*) for the performance of a "positive" obligation to do something—see the commentary below at paras R49–08 to R49–16;

(b) an order under s.46 of the Court of Session Act 1988 for the performance of any act by the respondent necessary for reinstating the claimant in a possessory right or for granting other specific relief where the respondent has done any act which the court could have but did not prohibit by interdict;

(c) an order under s.47(2) of the Court of Session Act 1988 as the court thinks fit regarding interim possession of any property to which the cause relate or regarding the subject matter of the cause—this can involve the making of an interim order of specific implement. This is an important power which could have been used by the court had the situation in *Cetelem SA v Roust Holdings Ltd* [2005] 2 Lloyd's Rep. 494 arisen in Scotland; and

(d) an order under s.10 of the Court of Session Act 1988 to (a) take and report on the depositions of havers of documents; or (b) take and report in writing on the evidence of any witness who is resident beyond the jurisdiction of the court or who by reason of age, infirmity or sickness is unable to attend the proof or trial.

R46–56 It has already been noted that an application for a warrant for interim attachment could be covered by r.46(1)(g). Reference is made to the commentary for r.46(1)(c) in relation to applications for warrants for interim attachment.

R46–57 It is unclear whether an order to find caution or to consign money with the court covering a party's expenses, as a condition precedent to proceeding with or defending a claim, is covered by r.46(1)(g). Equally, it is unclear whether an order on a party resident outwith Scotland to sist (in the sense of "add") a mandatary is covered by r.46(1)(g).

Sisting a mandatary involves the court ordering a party to add a person resident in Scotland into the action as his "mandatary" and thus potentially liable for all of the expenses of the litigation, including those before his addition. The mandatary is responsible to the court for the direction of the action, although he cannot settle his principal's claim. An order to sist a mandatary can be made in a Scottish litigation where the pursuer (claimant) is resident abroad in a country that is not within the European Union or party to the Brussels or Lugano Conventions on jurisdiction and enforcement of judgments. In deciding whether to grant the order, the court exercises its discretion in the interests of justice. Unless there is some difficulty with the directing of the action from abroad, the court may be slow to order the sisting of a mandatary if it can use its powers to make an order for caution or consignation of money instead. **R46–58**

Both of these court powers are concerned with a party being able to recover arbitration expenses from the other party in the event of success. In addition, the sisting of a mandatary is concerned with a party resident abroad being able to manage the Scottish proceedings properly. Leading commentators have discovered no case under common law in which the court has used these powers in relation to an arbitration and no case in which an arbitral tribunal purported to exercise such powers. It is unclear whether they would have been implied into an arbitration agreement at common law in a manner similar to the power to award expenses. **R46–59**

The question is whether such court orders in relation to caution and sist of a mandatary fall within the catch-all phrase "any other interim or permanent order". Rule 46(1) expressly provides that the court is able to make such orders in relation to an arbitration as it would in relation to a litigation, so that the tribunal, in deciding whether to grant consent to an application, should apply the test which the court would apply. **R46–60**

However, the Act also provides in r.64 (a default rule) that the tribunal has the power to order "security" for the arbitration expenses with a test that is more stringent than the court test in relation to a litigation. If a tribunal should be faced with an application for consent for the making of an application to the court for an order for caution, which criteria is it to apply? Should it be the r.64 criteria, with the restriction in r.64(2) in relation to foreign parties, or should it be the criteria applicable by a court in a litigation, without such a restriction (at least in relation to non-EU or non-Brussels or Lugano Convention countries)? It would seem odd that a party could bypass the provisions of r.64 by seeking to invoke r.46(1)(g). **R46–61**

The authors suggest that, despite the orders in question apparently falling within r.46(1)(g), the true legislative intent was that their subject matter be dealt with by the tribunal under r.64 and that, despite the catch-all wording of r.46(1)(g), orders in relation to security for expenses fall to the tribunal under r.64 and not to the tribunal and court under r.46(1)(g). Such a conclusion would also be beneficial from the point of view of attracting international arbitrations to a Scottish seat, which was one of the aims of the Act. **R46–62**

R46–63 The authors submit further that, as a general principle, where there is express statutory provision covering any matter, recourse to a catch-all provision must be considered inappropriate.

Rule 46(2)—Procedure

R46–64 An application may be made to either the Outer House or to a sheriff court of the sheriffdom where a respondent in the application is domiciled in terms of ss.41 or 42 of the 1982 Act.

R46–65 From a procedural point of view, it is important to bear in mind that the application is made under the appropriate part of r.46 which gives the court its jurisdiction in relation to the arbitration, rather than under the provision which would give the court its jurisdiction in relation to a litigation. That said, the petition or summary application will have to follow closely any substantive requirements for the equivalent application for a litigation so, for example, in relation to seeking diligence on the dependence, the petition or summary application should follow the requirements of s.15D of the Debtors (Scotland) Act 1987 (arrestment or inhibition) or s.9C of the Debt Arrangement and Attachment (Scotland) Act 2002 (attachment).

R46–66 If the application is made to the Outer House it is made by petition in the style contained in RCS Form 14.4 (RCS rr.100.5(1) and 14.4) or, if there are undisposed of Outer House proceedings, by note (RCS r.100.5). The requirements for the petition are set out in RCS r.14.4 and Ch.100 (r.15.2 for notes), together with the need to:

  (i) aver why the order is necessary;
  (ii) aver the circumstances in which the prerequisites for an application in terms of the relevant part of r.46 are satisfied;
  (iii) aver the consent of the tribunal (unless the arbitration has not begun or the case is one of urgency, in which case that should be averred);
  (iv) aver the reasons why the usual period of 21 days for answers should be dispensed with (if that is necessary); and
  (v) require service or intimation on the other parties to the arbitration, and, if appropriate, to the members of the tribunal, and the haver or witness in question.

If a shorter period of notice is required, then this should also be craved in the petition.

R46–67 Together with the petition, the applicant should lodge with the Court of Session:

  (i) as a production, any written arbitration agreement in which or other agreement or other document by virtue of which, the time limit is imposed;

(ii) any written statements of case and defence in the arbitration (the pleadings), if appropriate; and
(iii) the bundle of court documents known as the process (see RCS rr.4.3, 4.4).

Inventories of any productions should be intimated to the other parties and members of the tribunal.

If the petition is one where an urgent ex parte order is required, the court will immediately proceed to consider the petition. Regardless of whether such an order is sought or made, the applicant must move for a first order for service on the other party or parties to the arbitration or their representatives in the arbitration, and the members of the tribunal and anyone else who has an interest, to allow such persons to lodge answers opposing the petition if they wish within 21 days (RCS r.100.5). Therefore, it is advised that if a shorter period is required a motion for that shorter period should be sought. **R46–68**

After the end of the period for answers, whether answers have been lodged or not, the petitioner should enrol a motion to have the court determine the petition, with or without a hearing as may be appropriate in the circumstances. **R46–69**

If the application is made to the sheriff court, it is made by summary application in the style contained in SASAR Sch.1 Form 1 (SASAR r.2.4). The requirements for the summary application are broadly the same as for the petition described above. Detailed reference should be made to the SASAR. **R46–70**

Expenses of the application will not be included in the "arbitration expenses" (see the commentary to r.59 below), but will fall to be dealt with by the court rather than the tribunal, although, on an analogy with the preparation of the former stated case, the expenses of obtaining the consent of the tribunal fall to be dealt with by the tribunal in terms of r.60 (*Thomson v Earl of Galloway*, 1919 S.C. 611). **R46–71**

Rule 46(3)

The tribunal may continue with the arbitration whilst the court is determining the application. The preferred approach is to have the parties agree on the procedure whilst the application is ongoing. If the parties cannot agree, then while the tribunal has a duty to conduct the arbitration without unnecessary delay (r.24(1)(c)(i)) it also has a duty to treat the parties fairly (r.24(1)(b)). Everything will depend on the subject matter of the application to the court, the stage which the arbitration has reached and the nature of any prejudice that might be caused through the delay in not progressing with the arbitration balanced with any prejudice which might be caused through progressing with the arbitration. The authors submit that, given the provisional or interim nature of many of the court orders which would be made pursuant to applications under r.46, in most instances the tribunal **R46–72** should continue with the arbitration. Ultimately, the question of whether and, if so, how the arbitration should proceed will be a matter for the tribunal. In complying with its duties under r.24, the tribunal will seek to avoid any substantial injustice which could conceivably result in a challenge to the award for serious irregularity (see r.68).

Rule 46(4)

R46–73 Rule 46 does not affect other powers which a court may have, regardless of the rule, in relation to arbitrations or the powers of the tribunal. As noted above, the court's power to grant an order under s.1 of the 1972 Act in respect of an arbitration remains unaffected.

R46–74 In circumstances of a very exceptional kind, the Inner House may exercise its *nobile officium* to grant a commission to take evidence of a witness where there is not an action before it or an action immediately pending (*Galloway Water Power Co v Carmichael*, 1937 S.C. 135 at 140 where a witness was departing for Australia where he was likely to be for several years and for which evidence on commission or on interrogatories would be inappropriate; this might not now be followed with video conferencing). In such a case the petition would be to the Inner House of the Court of Session and not under r.46.

R46–75 Rule 1 addresses when an arbitration is said to have begun.

Part 6

Awards

Rule 47: Rules applicable to the substance of the dispute D

47.—(1) The tribunal must decide the dispute in accordance with—
    (a) the law chosen by the parties as applicable to the substance of the dispute, or
    (b) if no such choice is made (or where a purported choice is unlawful), the law determined by the conflict of law rules which the tribunal considers applicable.

(2) Accordingly, the tribunal must not decide the dispute on the basis of general considerations of justice, fairness or equity unless—
    (a) they form part of the law concerned, or
    (b) the parties otherwise agree.

(3) When deciding the dispute, the tribunal must have regard to—
    (a) the provisions of any contract relating to the substance of the dispute,
    (b) the normal commercial or trade usage of any undefined terms in the provisions of any such contract,
    (c) any established commercial or trade customs or practices relevant to the substance of the dispute, and
    (d) any other matter which the parties agree is relevant in the circumstances.

DEFINITIONS

"dispute": ss.2(1), 31(1)
"party": ss.2(1), 31(1), (2)
"tribunal": ss.2(1), 31(1)

STATUS

Rule 47 is a default rule so can be disapplied in whole or in part, or modified in any way, by the parties (s.9 refers). **R47–01**

If the parties have agreed to adopt institutional rules, those rules may have provisions relating to the rules under which the substance of the dispute must be decided. Examples include art.21(1) of the ICC Rules, art.22.3 LCIA Rules, and art.35 of the UNCITRAL Rules. These provisions will override r.47. A common feature of the ICC and UNCITRAL Rules is the greater discretion in choice which they give to the arbitral tribunal. In contrast, art.35(1) of the Swiss Rules requires the tribunal to apply the rules of law with which the dispute has the closest connection. **R47–02**

MODEL LAW

Article 28 of the Model Law is in substantially similar terms with differences in the detail (discussed below). **R47–03**

COMMENTARY

Introductory observations

In the overwhelming majority of "real" arbitrations, this rule (and its equivalent such as Model Law art.28 or s.46 of the 1996 Act) passes unnoticed. However, as was made comprehensively clear in the first edition of this book and is made no less clear below, there is scope for a great deal of theoretical discussion of the (very largely hypothetical) circumstances where r.47(1)(a) (or equivalents) does not apply. **R47–04**

That said, there are certain systems of arbitration where what is sought is something closer to equitable solutions but without expressly relying on r.47(2)(b). Such arbitrations may include some of those in the commodities trade association arbitrations, whether based in London or elsewhere, where, typically, a prerequisite to become registered as an arbitrator for commodity X is to have been a trader of that commodity; it follows that, in some such systems, barristers and solicitors are excluded from being registered even if they have been General Counsel of a large company trading in commodity X. That is what that commodity trade wants for itself so it is not for others to criticise or try to change it. In contrast, one well-known London-based arbitral institution is frequently criticised in its trade sector for being dominated by lawyers and for generating black-letter law awards divorced from the realities of what happens "on the ground" in that sector. **R47–05**

R47–06 This does not mean that tribunals in such arbitrations ignore the law—if they do, then e.g. a challenge under s.68 or an appeal (if not excluded in the relevant arbitration rules) under s.69 of the 1996 Act may follow. However, the English courts have shown themselves reluctant to disturb awards made by such tribunals except where (as happens rarely) there is a blatant error of law.

R47–07 In order to reinforce the desire (e.g. as was expressed during the Bill's consultation phase) of some industrial and commercial sectors for steering away from over black-lettering arbitration, r.47(3) was introduced reflecting Model Law art.28(4) and providing a flexibility absent from the 1996 Act.

General comments

R47–08 Although peremptory in form, r.47 is a default rule, i.e. the parties can ask the tribunal to decide the dispute in accordance with whatever norms they agree upon. For example, they could direct that the dispute be decided not according to strict law, but according to what might be just, fair or equitable. However, given the very wide flexibility created by r.47(2)(b), the authors cannot envisage any circumstances where the parties might agree to disapply r.47.

R47–09 Alternatively, the parties could invoke systems of law which do not form part of any national system of law, but which have been devised to facilitate international commerce, e.g. the Principles of European Contract Law or the UNIDROIT Principles of International Commercial Contracts.

R47–10 Similarly, the parties might invoke international conventions even if not yet part of the law of any state, or principles common to two or more legal systems. They might even refer to systems of law of questionable certainty such as *lex mercatoria*, general principles of law, international law, transnational commercial law and the like, or they might ask either that a particular national law be applied, but as it stood at a given point in time, or indeed agree that different national laws be applied to different aspects of the dispute, e.g. to the question of whether there has been a breach of contract, to issues such as frustration and to the question of remedies. It has even been known for parties to invoke the principles of law "created" by arbitral tribunals even though such have no formal status in any recognised system of law.

R47–11 Unless the parties have made one of the "exotic" choices set out above or, for example, a choice of rules of Shari'a or Jewish law (and see commentary on r.47(2) at R47–29 to R47–34 below), the provisions of r.47 apply.

Rule 47(1)(a)—Law chosen by the parties

R47–12 If the parties have chosen a specific system of law to apply to the substance of the dispute, the tribunal must apply that law regardless of the Scottish rules of private international law (conflict of law rules). The aim of r.47(1)(a) is to by-pass the need for a tribunal to have to consider rules of international private law. While the Model Law refers to "rules of law" chosen by the parties, r.47(1)(a) refers to "law" thus chosen. This appears to be intentional in seeking to restrict the choice to recognised legal systems and excluding international treaties and other legal instruments.

The tribunal will have to consider what the substance of the dispute is and whether the parties have chosen a system of law to apply to it. If the dispute concerns a contractual duty and (as is almost invariably the case in practice) the parties have nominated a particular law to govern their contract, that will amount to a choice of law under r.47(1)(a). Difficulties may arise if the nomination does not govern all matters in connection with or related to the contract and the tribunal will have to decide if the nomination does cover the substance of the dispute. There may also be different laws chosen for different aspects of a contract. **R47–13**

"Chosen" includes impliedly chosen. Given the modern recognition of the separability of an arbitration agreement from any contract within which it is included, the authors submit that the choice of seat in that arbitration agreement or choice of law in that agreement will not amount to an implied choice of law to govern the substantive dispute. **R47–14**

Whereas s.46(2) of the 1996 Act makes it clear that a choice of law refers to the substantive law of the state in question rather than its conflict of law rules, there is no such provision in r.47. Section 46(2) excludes *renvoi* whereby a national law is chosen but then its conflict of law rules direct that some other national law should govern the dispute (see DAC Report, para.224). The authors submit that the terms of r.47 are sufficiently clear to indicate that the choice of the parties relates to substantive law. **R47–15**

Should the tribunal require to apply conflict of law rules (under r.47(1)(b)), art.20 of the Rome I Regulation and art.15 of the Rome Convention (applicable by virtue of the Contracts (Applicable Law) Act 1990) exclude *renvoi*. **R47–16**

The case *B v A* [2010] EWHC 1626 (Comm) gave rise to an interesting example of an issue relating to choice of law. One arbitrator issued a dissenting opinion of some 19 pages, expressed in unusually trenchant, even intemperate, terms, in which she was highly critical of her colleagues. They had, she said, decided to ignore the parties' agreement to submit the contract to Spanish law and had in an arbitrary fashion proceeded to decide the dispute *ex aequo et bono*. They had, she said, done so for two reasons: (i) coming from a common law system, they did not feel comfortable with Spanish law and preferred "to grant an indemnity under Article 10.1 of the contract as if such clause would be self-governing, and not limited by Spanish law", and (ii) they had felt it necessary to punish reprehensible conduct, ignoring the question as to whether such conduct had caused any actual economic damage to A and imposing punitive and multiple damages in a manner which was not permitted under Spanish law and thus ignored the remedies available within the limits of the law of the contract. **R47–17**

Refusing the ss.67 and 68 challenges, Tomlinson J. said at [25]:

> "I should add for the avoidance of doubt that any suggestion of conscious disregard here is simply unsustainable. The arbitrators carefully considered the provisions of Spanish law. They concluded, at paragraphs G27 to G30, that Spanish law provides no impediment to the parties agreeing their own consensual remedy in lieu of applying provisions of the Spanish Civil Code. [B's expert on Spanish law] did not dispute this proposition. Nor as I understand him does [A's expert]."

R47–18 In the same case, Tomlinson J. also observed at [30]:

> "The essence ... of B's case is that the Tribunal erred in its construction of Article 10.1 [of the contract] under the relevant Spanish rules of contractual interpretation. That cannot possibly be a valid ground of challenge."

This highlights the important point that, while a tribunal's selection of a system of law or rules not in accordance with the provisions of r.47 will be an irregularity under r.68(2)(a), the tribunal's error in the application of those rules of law or other rules will not be an irregularity under r.68 and so not open to challenge. A tribunal's failure to abide by the choice of the parties renders its award open to challenge for serious irregularity (r.68(2)(a)(ii) refers).

The case *B v A* is discussed in Hew R. Dundas, "Alphabet Soup: Foreign Law and Dissenting Opinions in International Arbitration in London" (2010) 76 *Arbitration* 757–763.

Rule 47(1)(b)—Law determined by applicable conflict of law rules

R47–19 If the parties have not chosen such a legal system or their choice is unlawful, the law to be applied must be that determined by the conflict of law rules which the tribunal considers applicable. "Have not chosen" is self-explanatory.

Unlawful choice of law

R47–20 Neither the Model Law nor the 1996 Act mention an unlawful choice of law. By an "unlawful" choice is meant a choice contrary to the general public policy of Scots law or contrary to mandatory rules of Scots law that override any foreign law that would otherwise be applied by a Scottish forum. For example, if a dispute arose out of a contract between two parties incorporated in State X concerning a project within that state but the parties had agreed on the law of State Y to govern their dispute because the contract would be illegal under the law of State X, a tribunal would have to ignore that choice of law.

R47–21 Another example of an unlawful choice of law arises from s.27(2) and (3) of the Unfair Contract Terms Act 1977 which indicates that where a contract is made in the UK, and one party is a consumer who is habitually resident there, the terms of the Act cannot be excluded by a choice of law other than that of the UK.

Tribunal applies conflict of law rules

R47–22 The default position, absent choice by the parties, is that the governing law is to be determined by the conflict of law rules which the tribunal considers applicable. This derives from Model Law art.28(2) and mirrors s.46(3) of the 1996 Act.

R47–23 The tribunal is not required to apply the law determined by the applicable conflict of law rules but the law determined by the conflict of law rules which the tribunal *considers* applicable and this opens up a difficult question as to how wide a discretion is conferred thereby (authors' emphasis).

R47–24 The drafters of the Model Law thought that the discretion was considerable, acknowledging that a tribunal might first decide which substantive law it wishes to apply to the dispute, only thereafter looking for a set of conflict of law rules which would allow that choice (see *Report of the UNCITRAL on the work of its eighteenth session*, UN A/40/17, para.237). This is also reflected in art.35 of the UNCITRAL Rules.

R47–25 If, therefore, the tribunal wished to apply the law of State X, it would only be where no conflict of law rule could be found which would allow that choice that the tribunal would be prevented from doing so.

R47–26 The authors submit that, if a tribunal applied a law which was not authorised by any conflict of law rule, or if it ignored the law chosen by the parties, that would be a perverse (wholly unreasonable) exercise of discretion, therefore not only a failure to conduct the arbitration in accordance with r.47(1)(b) but also an irregularity in terms of r.68(2)(a)(ii), allowing the award to be challenged. If, for example, in a Franco-Brazilian dispute with no connection with Kazakhstan, the tribunal considered that determination by Kazakh conflict of law rules was applicable, the authors submit that would not amount to compliance with r.47(1)(b).

R47–27 In *Peterson Farms Inc v C&M Farming Ltd* [2004] EWHC 121 (Comm), a tribunal which was required to apply the law of Arkansas held, applying the "group of companies" doctrine which does not form part of the law of Arkansas, that the respondent was obliged to pay damages to the claimant for losses sustained by other entities in the claimant's group of companies. The award was set aside on the basis that the tribunal had decided to make the award not under the law of Arkansas but the "group of countries doctrine" itself. While a s.67 challenge was allowed in that particular case, the authors submit that a r.68/s.68 challenge will generally be appropriate.

R47–28 Whether a r.68 challenge would succeed for non-compliance with r.47(1)(b) would depend on whether the non-compliance caused substantial injustice.

Rule 47(2)—Decision according to fairness, etc.

R47–29 If the parties authorise the tribunal to decide the dispute according to equity rather than strict law then r.47(1) is disapplied as is r.69 since no point of Scots law can arise if Scots law is disapplied. The reference to considerations such as justice forming part of the law will be unfamiliar to many common law systems where such considerations tend to be reflected in particular rules and principles and where equitable exceptions tend to be part of the fabric of such rules. However, in some systems, e.g. those systems of law derived from a religion, it is common for arbitrators to depart from formal rules of law and decide according to equity. Rule 47(2) preserves that possibility.

R47–30 The concept of *amiable compositeur*, provided in Model Law art.28(3), permits the tribunal a wide range of solutions including readjusting the contract between the parties. This concept is well known in civil law systems and was well known under Scots common law up to the 18th century (see R.L.C. Hunter, *The Law of Arbitration in Scotland*, 2nd edn (Edinburgh: Butterworths Lexis Nexis, 2002), pp.31–38, 43). Section 46(1)(b) of the 1996 Act expressly permits decisions to be made according to a system other than national law or according to non-legal criteria (see also DAC Report, para.224).

R47–31 The Act also permits the parties to give the tribunal discretion to select such criteria, i.e. the parties can agree to any arrangement they wish, including empowering tribunals to make their own decisions as to the criteria they will employ.

R47–32 Model Law art.2(d) entitles the parties to empower a third party, such as an arbitral institution, to determine any matter which the Model Law empowers the parties to agree but that excludes art.28, because this would otherwise offend a key principle of private international law (see *Summary Record of the 327th meeting on the preparation of the UNCITRAL Model Law on International Commercial Arbitration*, UN A/CN.9/SR.327, paras 320–327). The question then arises as to the position under the Act if the parties agreed that a third party should decide what system of law or other criteria the tribunal must apply, an option which does not appear to be available under the 1996 Act. The authors submit that the answer, prima facie an unlikely one, is given by s.9(4)(a)(iii) whereby the parties may modify a default rule by agreement. To achieve this conclusion, however, necessitates taking the view that r.47's default status gives the parties complete freedom, and this is consistent with the explanatory notes at paras 153–154.

R47–33 It has been argued that by not expressly providing that the parties can invoke considerations such as those mentioned above, the Act has left the matter to be governed by the common law. The authors submit that it must be assumed that it could never have formed any part of the draftsman's or the legislators' intention to pass a piece of apparently comprehensive legislation with gaps deliberately left in it requiring the common law to fill.

Furthermore, given that r.47(2)(b) expressly provides that the tribunal can be authorised to decide the dispute on the basis of justice etc. rather than law, the authors submit that it must follow that any reference to quasi-legal principles is permissible and that the common law, even if it does contradict such a choice, is overridden by statute. **R47–34**

Rule 47(3)—Considerations to which tribunal should have regard

Rule 47(3) echoes Model Law art.28(4) which itself derives from art.33(3) of the UNCITRAL Arbitration Rules (1976) (now art.35(3) (2010 Rules)); see also art.21(2) of the ICC Rules and it is quite similar to art.7(1) of the European Arbitration Convention 1961 (which has never been adopted by the UK). Article 28(4) provides that the tribunal **R47–35**

> "shall decide in accordance with the terms of the contract and shall take into account the usages of trade applicable to the transaction".

The 1996 Act refers to no such factors, and the view of the DAC Report, at para.222, was that **R47–36**

> "if the applicable law allows this to be done, then the provision is not necessary; while if it does not, then it could be said that such a direction overrides that law, which to our minds would be incorrect."

The authors question whether English law does in fact incorporate these factors.

As stated above (paras R47–05 to R47–07), there are sectors of industry and commerce where the factors set out in r.47(3) are highly-valued and considered essential to give outcomes in line with the practical realities of that sector, rather than to arrive at black-letter law outcomes divorced from commercial realities. **R47–37**

The drafters of the Model Law themselves were not uniformly convinced of the value of art.28(4) and it was, at one point, discarded because of **R47–38**

> "the many questions and concerns it raised. For example, the reference to the terms of the contract could be misleading where such terms were in conflict with mandatory provisions of law or did not express the true intent of the parties. Also, this reference did not belong in an Article - dealing with the law applicable to the substance of the dispute, although appropriate in arbitration rules. As regards the reference to trade usages, the concerns related to the fact that their legal effect and qualification was not uniform in all legal systems" (UN A/CN.9/245, para.99).

However, art.28(4) was ultimately restored because (refer *Analytical Compilation of Comments on Article 28*, UN A/CN.9/263, para.12) "the parties, not without good reasons, expect from the arbitrators that they will, above all, base their decisions on the wording and history of the contract and usages of trade."

R47–39 The authors submit that the purpose of r.47(3)(b) and (c) is to allow the tribunal to have regard to usages, customs and practices in deciding the meaning of the contract or any provision within it and thereby to ensure that practical realistic outcomes are reached. Rule 47(3)(b) and (c) enable a tribunal to have regard to these matters and to raise them, even if they are not raised by the parties (subject always to the duty of fairness in r.24).

R47–40 It has been argued that, given that the tribunal must decide as directed by the parties in any event, r.47(3)(a) and (d) are redundant. The authors submit that, first, r.47(3)(a) is essential as a reminder that r.47(3) is not a licence for the tribunal to "frolic on its own" but that its decision must be rooted in the parties' contract and, secondly, that r.47(3)(d) is a valuable inclusion as a reminder that the parties can agree something at any time.

R47–41 It has also been suggested that the meaning of r.47(3)(c) is obscure but, for example, one of the authors has considerable experience of such trade customs and practices in the oil and gas industry.

R47–42 A question can arise in theory to what the tribunal should do when the law determined under r.47(1) (as modified by any institutional rule) prohibits reference to trade usages. In such an unlikely event, the authors submit that, very simply, a law determined under r.47(1) overrides r.47(3) to the extent that it is inconsistent with that law.

R47–43 While a failure to have regard to any of the r.47(3) factors may amount to a serious irregularity (r.68(2)(a)(ii) refers), it might, in certain circumstances, be difficult to establish that the tribunal has indeed contravened r.47(3)(b) or (c).

R47–44 Where the governing law of the contract is Scots law, if such a failure led to an erroneous interpretation of the contract, the award is open to challenge under r.69 (if not excluded and permitted under r.70) as an error of law.

Rule 48: Power to award payment and damages M

48.—(1) The tribunal's award may order the payment of a sum of money (including a sum in respect of damages).

(2) Such a sum must be specified—
   (a) in any currency agreed by the parties, or
   (b) the absence of such agreement, in such currency as the tribunal considers appropriate.

DEFINITION

"tribunal": ss.2(1), 31(1)

STATUS

Rule 48 is mandatory so cannot be disapplied, or modified in any way, by the parties. **R48–01**

MODEL LAW

There is no equivalent in the Model Law. **R48–02**

COMMENTARY

Introductory

Rule 48 was originally part of what is now r.49 (dealing with remedies) in general (just as in s.48 of the 1996 Act), but r.49 was then and remains a default rule and it was argued that the power to award damages was so fundamental that the parties should not be able to exclude them. One professional institution, in particular, argued that, if the rule was a default one, stronger parties such as main contractors and large retailers would abuse their position in respect of sub-contractors and suppliers in order to insist that the power was routinely excluded, hence the rule is mandatory. There is no corresponding provision of the Model Law. **R48–03**

Rule 48(1)

In the great majority of arbitrations (save where a claim is dismissed in its entirety), the principal remedy sought will be the payment of money by one party to the other. This might be payment of a sum owed under the contract or the payment of monetary compensation (damages) for breach of contract or the payment of expenses recoverable in the arbitration. **R48–04**

It is vitally necessary that r.48 has unequivocally established the principle that a Scots-seated tribunal has the implied power to award damages since one of the several notorious deficiencies of pre-2010 Scots arbitration law was that a tribunal had no implied power to award damages, instead of which such power had to be expressly conferred by the parties on the tribunal. This was established by the House of Lords in *Aberdeen Railway Co v Blaikie Brothers* (1853) 15 D. (HL) 20 and the rule had been followed ever since (see, e.g. *Whatlings (Foundations) Ltd v Shanks & McEwan (Contractors) Ltd*, 1989 S.C. 253). **R48–05**

A question arises as to whether the tribunal may award penal or exemplary damages despite such remedies being unavailable under Scots law. Rule 48 provides no express answer but, the authors submit, the answer must be "no". **R48–06**

A follow-up question then arises, given that r.48 is mandatory, whether the parties could confer a power to award penal damages by choosing a foreign law such as the many US state laws which permit such awards. While the principle of party autonomy is a founding principle of the Act **R48–07**

Arbitration (Scotland) Act 2010

(s.1(b) refers) it is "subject only to such safeguards as are necessary in the public interest" and, the authors submit, this is sufficient to prevent "damages" being interpreted as including penal damages which are clearly established as contrary to public policy (see ICC case 5946 (1991) XVI YCA 97).

R48–08 Even where it might be possible to award such remedies, there may be difficulties at the enforcement stage if the enforcing state does not countenance remedies of that kind, e.g. the BGH declined to enforce that part of a US award which awarded punitive damages (decision of June 4, 1992 BGHZ 118 at 312).

R48–09 If money is ordered to be paid, the award must specify the currency which will normally be the currency agreed by the parties in their contract but might also be some other currency claimed in the arbitration; in the absence of party agreement it will be in such currency as the tribunal considers appropriate and that might be a variety of currencies where that would be apt. This would mirror the position at common law (*Commerzbank AG v Large*, 1977 S.L.T. 219).

R48–10 Although the tribunal appears, subject to the agreement of the parties, to be given complete discretion here, the House of Lords held, in *Lesotho Highlands Development Authority v Impregilo SpA* [2005] UKHL 43 (a decision under the 1996 Act), that it cannot make a choice of currency which would not be open to the court in a similar situation.

R48–11 Their Lordships further held that a failure by the tribunal to render the award in the currency impliedly selected by the parties was challengeable only as an error of law. Applying that approach in a Scottish context, that would mean that the error could not be challenged under r.69 where the law governing the substance was not Scots Law, nor where the parties had disapplied r.69.

R48–12 The question of choice of currency arose in *Milan Nigeria Ltd v Angeliki B Maritime Co* [2011] EWHC 892 (Comm), where Gloster J. said:,

> "62. As [Counsel for Milan] submitted, the legal principles to be applied to the issue of the currency in which an award is to be made are well-established and clearly identifiable: cf *The Texaco Melbourne* [[1994] 1 Lloyd's Rep. 473 (HL)]; *The "Mosconici"* [[2001] 2 Lloyd's Rep. 313 at 315 LHC]. Pursuant to s.48(4) of the [1996] Act, a tribunal may order the payment of a sum of money in any currency. However, this does not give a tribunal an unfettered discretion as regards the currency of an award. It must act in accordance with the principles identified by Lord Wilberforce in *The Folias* [[1979] A.C. 685] and restated by Lord Goff in *The Texaco Melbourne* at 477–478:
>
> > 'First, it is necessary to ascertain whether there is an intention, to be derived from the terms of the contract, that damages for breach of contract should be awarded in any particular currency or

currencies. In the absence of any such intention, "the damage should be calculated in the currency in which the loss was felt by the plaintiff or 'which most truly expresses his loss'".'

63. The currency in which a claimant feels its loss is a question of fact to be determined by the tribunal having regard to all the circumstances of the case before it: see *The Texaco Melbourne*, (*supra*) at pages 478-480. The decision-maker's function is to identify 'the currency which most justly expresses the loss that has been suffered by the claimants': *The "Mosconici"*, at page 316. Thus, factors which are important in one case may or may not be important in another, and caution must be taken not to elevate factual observations made in one case into statements of principle to be applied generally in other cases. In the passage relied upon by Mr Karia in *The Texaco Melbourne,* Lord Goff was discussing the particular facts of the case before him. He was not attempting to lay down a principle of law applicable to all factual situations. The facts in that case were particular and readily distinguishable from those in the present case. In *The Texaco Melbourne* the operation of very strict exchange controls meant that, although the claimant could enter into transactions to buy or sell goods in foreign currency, all payments of foreign currency were to be made to or by the Ghanaian Central Bank who would then credit or debit the claimant's local currency accounts. The claimant itself never dealt with or handled foreign currency. In the circumstances, it was not surprising that the courts at all levels held that the currency in which the claimant suffered its loss was the local one.

64. Again, as [Counsel for Milan] submitted, the fact that replacement goods may have been purchased in a particular currency (see *The "Mosconici"*) or that the available market by reference to which the quantum of damages falls to be determined operates in a particular currency (see *The Texaco Melbourne*) are no more than factors to be taken into account and, even then, may well be of relatively limited importance. Matters that are likely to be more important are the claimant's currency of account and the nature of its business and also the nature of the particular transaction in question."

Rule 49: Other remedies available to tribunal D
49. The tribunal's award may—
   (a) be of a declaratory nature,
   (b) order a party to do or refrain from doing something (including ordering the performance of a contractual obligation), or
   (c) order the rectification or reduction of any deed or other document (other than a decree of court) to the extent permitted by the law governing the deed or document.

DEFINITIONS

"party": ss.2(1), 31(1), (2)
"tribunal": ss.2(1), 31(1)

STATUS

R49–01 Rule 49 is a default rule so can be disapplied in whole or in part, or modified in any way, by the parties (s.9 refers).

MODEL LAW

R49–02 There is no equivalent in the Model Law.

COMMENTARY

R49–03 Given the default status of r.49, the parties may restrict or remove the power of the tribunal to grant certain, or all, of these remedies or they might look to extend the available remedies (see DAC Report, para.234), and they may do so by invoking a set of arbitral rules or a foreign procedural law which contemplates such remedies (see *Kastner v Jason* [2004] EWHC 592) or by any other means (s.9(4)(a)(iii) refers).

R49–04 Pre-1996, it had been established in England that a tribunal had the implied authority to grant any remedy available to a court, save those which self-evidently lay only in the competence of the court (*President of India v La Pintada Compania Navigacion SA (La Pintada)* [1985] A.C. 104). The question then arose whether, post-1996, tribunals were confined to granting the remedies specified in s.48 of the 1996 Act other than where the parties extended their competence.

R49–05 In *Wealans v CLC Contractors Ltd* [1999] 2 Lloyd's Rep. 739, the court decided that s.48 of the 1996 Act had not been intended to restrict the range of remedies available to a tribunal, so that it might, for example, grant special remedies created by statutory provisions in situations where this would be available to a court.

R49–06 Under the pre-2010 Act law, the tribunal had the power to grant any remedy necessary to exhaust the reference (with the exception of damages): see *Irons and Melville on Arbitration*, pp.216–225. This accords with Lord Hoffmann's analysis in *Fiona Trust v Privalov* [2007] UKHL 40 under which it must be assumed that parties to an arbitration agreement intended that the tribunal would possess all remedies not excluded by law, in order to eliminate the need to engage in two separate sets of proceedings in respect of the same dispute. It follows, the authors submit, that the Scottish courts should take the Hoffmannesque view that r.49 is to be read widely and is not intended to restrict the tribunal's remedies.

Rule 49(a)—Declarator

A party may not be seeking compensation for an alleged wrong, but the **R49–07** determination of a contested issue such as the true meaning of a particular term of the contract, the level of rent, or which of the parties is the true owner of a copyright or patent. Further, in a case (possibly unique) of which one of the authors is aware, the supplier of a service, despite having been paid in full, went to arbitration solely to establish that the work had been done to the highest professional standard (the parties settled so no conclusion was needed). In such situations, the tribunal will issue a declarator as to the rights of the parties or as to the quality of the work.

Rule 49(b)—Interdict and specific implement

A tribunal may, by award, order a party to refrain from doing something **R49–08** (interdict in Scots law) and such power had already existed in Scots common law for many years (*Gray v Brown* (1833) 11 S. 353).

One example of a remedy excluded by law is that the Crown cannot be **R49–09** interdicted; Crown Proceedings Act 1947 ss.21 and 43 refer.

The authors submit that a tribunal has the power to issue an interim **R49–10** interdict (equivalent to an interlocutory injunction) since it may make a provisional award under r.53 unless the parties have agreed otherwise. In *Welex AG v Rosa Maritime Ltd (The Epsilon Rosa)* [2003] 2 Lloyd's Rep. 509, the court held that the similar power under the 1996 Act entitled a tribunal to issue an anti-suit injunction, i.e. to order a party to an arbitration agreement not to seek to litigate in breach of that agreement.

The tribunal can also order a party to do something, including ordering **R49–11** the performance of a contractual obligation. Such an order is commonly referred to as an order for "specific implement" (specific performance in England) or an order *ad factum praestandum*.

However, an order against the Crown for specific implement is not **R49–12** competent except where the Crown is in breach of EU law: Crown Proceedings Act 1947 s.21, and *R v Secretary of State for Transport ex parte Factortame Ltd* [1990] 2 A.C. 85 and [1991] 1 A.C. 603.

Interestingly, whereas under s.48(5)(b) of the 1996 Act (following s.15 of **R49–13** the 1950 Act) a court cannot order specific performance of a contract related to land, there is no such restriction under r.49 since arbitrators have always had this power in Scotland.

Specific implement might be ordered in situations where monetary compensation would not be an adequate remedy for breach of contract, or where, **R49–14** for example, a party is refusing to deliver a commodity or good as required by the contract, which commodity cannot reasonably be sourced elsewhere.

It is usually inappropriate to order the enforcement of the performance of **R49–15** obligations of some complexity, since such an order would require to have a high degree of specificity and there may be difficulties with the practicalities of enforcement. However, CIMAR r.12.7 empowers the arbitrator either to supervise performance or (the far more likely option) to appoint a third party to do so.

R49–16 In addition, in international arbitrations it will generally be wrong to assume that a court in another jurisdiction will be prepared to enforce an award which does anything other than order the payment of money and courts may be particularly reluctant to enforce awards which call on them to supervise the behaviour of a party (see Troy E. Elder, "The Case Against Arbitral Awards of Specific Performance in Transnational Commercial Disputes" (1997) 13 Arbitration Int. 1). Many would also see this as an argument for not empowering tribunals to award such remedies in domestic arbitrations.

Rule 49(c)—Rectification/reduction

R49–17 Reduction of a deed or document occurs where it is annulled (set aside). Typical grounds for reduction in Scots law include ultra vires (outwith the powers of a granter), forgery, fraud, coercion (duress), incapacity, facility and circumvention and undue influence. Reduction serves to deprive the deed or document of legal effect. There can be partial reduction if the document can be divided into lawful and unlawful parts.

R49–18 Rectification of a deed or document occurs where part of it is corrected in order to give effect to the intention of a sole granter or the common intention of both parties. Rectification of documents under Scots law is governed by ss.8 and 9 of the Law Reform (Miscellaneous Provisions) (Scotland) Act 1985 and see *Greens Annotated Rules of the Court of Session* (Edinburgh: W. Green), para.73.1.2. Whereas art.22.1(g) LCIA Rules (1998) provided for rectification, the 2014 Rules do not.

R49–19 Not every system of law permits arbitrators to reduce or to rectify a formal deed or document, so in the unlikely event that the parties choose a Scottish seat governed by a foreign procedural law (s.9(4)(b) refers) these remedies might be excluded.

R49–20 The authors further submit that r.49(c) authorises reduction or rectification unless the governing law actually forbids it.

R49–21 It is, however, axiomatic that a decree (judgment/order) of court cannot be rectified and the authors would be somewhat surprised if there was any legal system where such rectification can be countenanced. In addition, the authors submit that the fact that r.49(c) is a default provision does not allow the parties to confer that power via s.9(4)(a)(iii). In effect, decrees of court are not arbitrable on the grounds of public policy (s.30 refers).

R49–22 In any case, r.49(c) must be read in the context of s.11(2) which indicates that an award which purports to rectify or reduce a deed or document is of no effect in so far as it would adversely affect the interests of any third party acting in good faith—see the commentary on that provision.

Rule 50: Interest M

50.—(1) The tribunal's award may order that interest is to be paid on—
  (a) the whole or part of any amount which the award orders to be paid (or which is payable in consequence of a declaratory award), in respect of any period up to the date of the award,
  (b) the whole or part of any amount which is—
    (i) claimed in the arbitration and outstanding when the arbitration began, but
    (ii) paid before the tribunal made its award,
  in respect of any period up to the date of payment,
  (c) the outstanding amount of any amounts awarded (including any award of arbitration expenses or pre-award interest under paragraph (a) or (b)) in respect of any period from the date of the award up to the date of payment.
(2) An award ordering payment of interest may, in particular, specify—
  (a) the interest rate,
  (b) the period for which interest is payable (including any rests which the tribunal considers appropriate).
(3) An award may make different interest provision in respect of different amounts.
(4) Interest is to be calculated—
  (a) in the manner agreed by the parties, or
  (b) failing such agreement, in such manner as the tribunal determines.
(5) This rule does not affect any other power of the tribunal to award interest.

DEFINITIONS

"arbitration": ss.2(1), (2), 31(1)
"tribunal": ss.2(1), 31(1)

STATUS

Rule 50 is mandatory so cannot be disapplied, or modified in any way, by the parties R50–01

MODEL LAW

The Model Law makes no provision regarding interest. R50–02

COMMENTARY

Preliminary observations

While, as will be set out below, this rule (on its face) represents a major improvement on the common law, it introduces an issue of considerable controversy. In the original Bill, this rule was a default one, mirroring s.49 R50–03 of the 1996 Act but, in a late change (for the same reasons as set out in para.R48–03), it was changed to mandatory despite there being no visible evidence whatsoever that the default nature of s.49 of the 1996 Act had ever caused any difficulty of the nature being argued.

R50–04 In itself, that change causes no difficulty in the circumstances contemplated by para.R48–03 but it appears clear to the authors that the mandatory nature of r.50 prima facie excludes certain sectors of society from ever arbitrating under the Act since any connection with, or reference to, "interest" is wholly prohibited in those sectors. It has been suggested that either r.50(1)'s reference to "may" or r.50(4) give a "let-out" (e.g. that r.50(4)(a) permits the parties to agree something which is not called "interest") but that goes nowhere in dealing with an absolute prohibition since r.50 is headed "Interest" and r.50(4) begins with the language "Interest is to be calculated …".

R50–05 Further, the authors question but express no view on whether such an exclusion is in fact lawful under the Equality Act 2010.

Introductory comments

R50–06 Rule 50 is self-evidently modelled on s.49 of the 1996 Act, widely regarded around the world as outstanding draftsmanship and widely copied. Of course, r.50 has no counterpart in the Model Law since there was never any prospect of the participants in UNCITRAL agreeing anything of this nature.

R50–07 More importantly, r.50 is a considerable advance on the common law since, thereunder, an arbitrator had no implied power to award interest on sums due prior to the date of the award (see Lord Dunpark in *John G McGregor (Contractors) Ltd v Grampian Regional Council*, 1991 S.L.T. 136 at 137L).

> "Interest is the recompence [sic] due by the debtor, of a sum of money to the creditor for the use of it" (Erskine, 3.3.75).

R50–08 Broadly speaking, the payment of interest can (a) be agreed by the debtor and creditor, or (b) arise where a principal sum of money has been wrongly withheld by a debtor from a creditor (*Carmichael v Caledonian Railway Co* (1870) 8 M. (HL) 119 at 131 per Lord Westbury).

R50–09 The authors approach the whole matter of interest from the basic principle that it is compensatory, i.e. (subject to the agreement of the parties) the aggrieved party should be restored to the position it would have been in had the dispute never arisen; this "compensatory principle" will recur below since it is both fundamental and integral to r.50.

Rule 50(1)(a)—Interest to date of award

The tribunal may award interest on the whole or part of the amount **R50–10** awarded for any period up to the date of the award, e.g. from the date of breach (as under s.49(3)(a) of the 1996 Act). Applying this compensatory principle, interest could not be awarded from a date earlier than when the principal amount awarded became due (see *BP Chemicals Ltd v Kingdom Engineering (Fife) Ltd* [1994] 2 Lloyd's Rep. 373; *Durham CC v Darlington Borough Council* [2003] EWHC 2598 (Admin)). As under s.49(5) of the 1996 Act, it is also made clear that such interest may also be ordered to be paid on a sum which is not actually awarded but is nonetheless payable because the tribunal has issued a declarator to that effect (see *Durham CC v Darlington Borough Council* [2003] EWHC 2598 (Admin)).

It has been held in England that, if a sum has been found to be payable, it **R50–11** is not necessary for the tribunal to believe that the respondent acted wrongfully for it to be able to award interest (*Amec Building Ltd v Cadmus Investment Co Ltd* [1997] C.L.Y. 262).

The first edition of this book asserted that there was a general discretion **R50–12** not to award interest but the authors consider that there is no basis in Scots law for any such assertion.

If the tribunal erroneously awards interest, whether because neither party **R50–13** asked for it or because the parties had agreed that no interest should be awarded, the remedy is a challenge under r.68(2)(b) or, depending on the circumstances, possibly also r.68(2)(a).

Rule 50(1)(b)

If a party claims a sum in the arbitration which is still outstanding when **R50–14** the arbitration begins but that sum or any part thereof is paid by the time the award is made, clearly that amount may no longer be awarded. However, the tribunal is, applying the compensatory principle, still entitled (and, arguably, obliged) to award interest on any such amount up to the date of payment.

Pursuant to r.50(b)(i), interest cannot be awarded on a *principal* amount **R50–15** which is claimed but which has already been paid when the arbitration begins *unless such interest is itself claimed as a principal amount*.

Rule 50(1)(c)

The tribunal may also award interest on any amount awarded (including **R50–16** pre-award interest) but not paid from the date of the award up to the date of payment, it being made clear that the amount awarded can include any expenses awarded or indeed any interest in respect of a period prior to the award.

Rule 50(2) and (3)

R50–17 The award may specify the rate(s) of interest, the period for which it is payable and whether any rests apply. It may treat different amounts quite differently here, for example applying different rates to pre and post award interest or to expenses or damages. Absent exceptional circumstances, the compensatory principle must drive what the tribunal does in this regard so the flexibility accorded to the tribunal is more apparent than real.

Rule 50(4)

R50–18 Interest is to be calculated as agreed by the parties or is, absent such agreement, at the discretion of the tribunal. The question then arises at to whether there is any restriction on the power of the parties in this regard; for example, they cannot exclude the power to award interest, but could, without conflicting with the mandatory nature of r.50, agree that interest should be levied at 0.00001 per cent. They can also agree that an exorbitantly high rate should apply but the authors cannot envisage this ever happening in practice.

Compound interest

R50–19 In some legal systems (and in many minds), the award of compound interest is unacceptable, often because courts cannot award it. The authors submit that there was no need to provide expressly for compound interest because of the compensatory principle: if the claimant had not been deprived of its money by the respondent's non-payment then either (i) it could have invested that money in a bank account earning compound interest, or (ii) it would not have had to borrow to cover the shortfall, such borrowing inevitably attracting compound interest.

R50–20 It follows that, except as agreed by the parties, there is in principle no place for simple interest in commercial arbitration and, the authors submit, any award of such is open to challenge under r.68(2)(a)(ii) or even r.69. The authors fully appreciate that this view is controversial and that many tribunals follow court rules in awarding simple interest only.

R50–21 The question as to whether or not the foregoing view is controversial is rendered largely irrelevant by the simple fact that parties may competently confer such a power on the tribunal at common law and it is inconceivable that the Act, absent very clear language to the contrary, intended to deprive the tribunal of such power.

R50–22 The Scots common law is that compound interest cannot be awarded unless the contract specifically authorises it (see Lord Gifford in *Baird's Trustees v Baird & Co* (1877) 4 R. 1005 at 1015) or in the case of a fixed usage in commercial dealings or where a trustee has violated his trust (*Douglas v Douglas' Trs* (1867) 5 M. 827, LJ-C Patton at 836). The DAC Report, paras 235–238 felt that the power to award compound interest should be made explicit, since the English courts similarly have no inherent power to award compound interest (*Westdeutsche Landesbank Girozentrale v Islington London Borough Council* [1996] A.C. 669). Entrusting such a power to tribunals was justified on the basis that most of its respondents favoured such a power, while the DAC felt that fears that it might be abused were groundless.

An award which saw the tribunal exceed its powers regarding the award of interest or ignore the agreement of the parties would presumably be challengeable in the usual way under rr.67–69 (and see *Lesotho Highlands Development Authority v Impregilo SpA* [2005] UKHL 43). If the award were simply silent on interest it would, assuming the parties claimed interest (it is inconceivable in practice that they would not), remain to be seen whether it might be challengeable under r.68(2)(c) on the basis that the tribunal had failed to deal with all the issues that were put to it. Such a challenge would surely only be possible if the claimant had raised the issue of interest (*Pirtek (UK) Ltd v Deanswood Ltd* [2005] 2 Lloyd's Rep. 728). **R50–23**

While there is English authority to the effect that the tribunal has no jurisdiction to award interest where it has not been invited to consider the issue (*Westland Helicopters Ltd v Al-Hejailan* [2004] 2 Lloyd's Rep. 523), this is rendered irrelevant in Scotland by the mandatory nature of r.50. **R50–24**

Rule 50(5)

It is not clear what purpose this provision serves, although it echoes s.49(6) of the 1996 Act. It may be that it is drafted with statutory arbitrations in mind. In *Lesotho Highlands Authority v Impregilo SpA* [2005] 2 Lloyd's Rep. 310 the House of Lords held that s.49(6) was merely a saving provision which did not oust any other power to award interest conferred by the parties or the Act. **R50–25**

Rule 51: Form of award D

51.—(1) The tribunal's award must be signed by all arbitrators or all those assenting to the award.

(2) The tribunal's award must state—
   (a) the seat of the arbitration,
   (b) when the award is made and when it takes effect,
   (c) the tribunal's reasons for the award, and
   (d) whether any previous provisional or part award has been made (and the extent to which any previous provisional award is superseded or confirmed).

(3) The tribunal's award is made by delivering it to each of the parties in accordance with rule 83.

DEFINITIONS

"party": ss.2(1), 31(1), (2)

Arbitration (Scotland) Act 2010

"rules": ss.7, 31(1)

STATUS

R51–01 Rule 51 is a default rule so can be disapplied in whole or in part, or modified in any way, by the parties (s.9 refers).

R51–02 The UNCITRAL Rules art.34(2), (3) and (4) make similar provisions to modify or (to the extent applicable) supersede r.51, as do arts 31(1) and 32(2), (3) and (4) of the Swiss Rules. Both art.31 ICC Rules and art.26 LCIA Rules will also modify r.51.

MODEL LAW

R51–03 Article 31 of the Model Law is in broadly similar terms with differences in the detail (discussed below).

COMMENTARY

R51–04 This rule echoes s.52 of the 1996 Act and art.31 of the Model Law, although it is closer in form to the former as, in the former, it is a default rule, whereas art.31 is mandatory (in part).

Rule 51(1)—Award must be signed

R51–05 It must be signed by all the arbitrators or at least all those assenting to the award. Were this not so, then a dissenting arbitrator could effectively undermine the proceedings by refusing to sign, leading to impossibility of enforcement in some jurisdictions. However, since this is a default rule, the parties might agree that all the arbitrators should sign, whether assenting or not, but there is no means of enforcing this in Scotland. Remarkably, art.15(3) of the Bolivian Law of Arbitration and Conciliation (Law No.1770 (March 10, 1997)) has an elegant solution: the dissenting arbitrator's fees cannot be paid until he has signed the award. Certain institutional rules, e.g. GAFTA Arbitration Rules art.9.1, achieve the same result.

R51–06 Furthermore, an arbitrator who refused to sign could be pursued for breach of contract, inter alia because the arbitrators' primary obligation is to render an enforceable award; in addition, if that refusal were in bad faith, he might forfeit his immunity under r.73 (see *Cargill International SA Antigue (Geneva Branch) v Sociedad Iberica de Molturacion SA* [1998] 1 Lloyd's Rep. 489).

R51–07 Article 31(1) Model Law provides that it is sufficient that the majority of the arbitrators sign, whether there is dissent or not, provided the reason for the missing signature is stated. Since the Model Law is mandatory on this point, it would override any agreement of the parties that all arbitrators must sign. The approach of the Model Law may seem preferable to r.51 in being mandatory.

R51–08 The question of how many arbitrators must sign the award differs from the question of how many need agree to it: although the assumption under r.30 is that majority rule prevails, the parties may agree otherwise. Thus if they have agreed that all decisions must be reached unanimously, but say nothing about the form of the award, if there is no unanimity the award will be invalid, even if it is signed by those who have assented to it.

Under the former English common law, now almost certainly no longer applicable (see *Bank Mellat v GAA Development Construction Co Ltd* [1988] 2 Lloyd's Rep. 44), the arbitrators had to sign the award at the same time and in the same place (see, e.g. *Peterson v Ayre* (1855) 15 C.B. 724) but this is not included in the 1996 Act. It must be presumed that the arbitrators who do sign may do so at different times and in different places and there has never been any suggestion that Scotland follows that former English common law. **R51–09**

If an arbitrator simply signed a blank signature page on the basis that they would be prepared to concur with whatever award were produced by their colleagues, such signature would, the authors submit, be invalid (see, e.g. *European Grain & Shipping Ltd v Johnston* [1982] 3 All E.R. 989). **R51–10**

The notion of signature by the majority presupposes that all the arbitrators were permitted to participate in the decision so that, if one of the arbitrators was excluded from the tribunal's deliberations by the others, the award might be challenged on the basis of serious procedural irregularity (see r.27(2) and the decision in *Czech Republic v CME* Unreported May 15, 2003 Swedish Court of Appeal; in fact, in that case the challenge was rejected). This would be the position at common law (*McCallum v Robertson* (1825) 4 S. 66) and under the Model Law (*Report of the Working Group on International Contract Practices on the work of its fourth session*, UN A/CN.9/232, para.18). **R51–11**

The parties could agree that only one of a number of arbitrators need sign, e.g. the presiding arbitrator where there is no majority as in art.31(1) of the Swiss and ICC Rules, but this leads to potentially serious consequences, particularly as regards enforcement in certain jurisdictions which require all three arbitrators to sign. **R51–12**

In contrast to both the Model Law and the 1996 Act, r.51 does not expressly require that the award should be in writing but that is provided by r.83(1) and (2). **R51–13**

Dissenting opinions

In those instances where majority rule does apply, a dissenting arbitrator may wish to issue a separate opinion. National laws and institutional rules are generally silent on whether this is permissible. Only the ICSID Arbitration Rules r.47.3 (which is, of course, part of a very particular form of a-national arbitration) expressly provide for such a practice. **R51–14**

A question arises concerning the status of a dissenting opinion, in particular whether it forms part of the award; clearly it does if it is integrated into **R51–15** the award but, if issued as a separate, stand-alone document, it does not. In *B v A* [2010] EWHC 1626 (Comm), Tomlinson J. said at [21]:

> "At this point I should say a word about the status of the Dissenting Opinion. It is not in my view formally part of the Award of the Tribunal. I was helpfully referred to the Final Report on Dissenting and Separate Opinions prepared by a Working Party of the ICC Commission on International Arbitration chaired by [Professor] Martin Hunter. The Report was adopted by the Commission on 21 April 1988. I am comforted to find that a large majority of the members of the Working Party reached that same conclusion. A dissenting opinion might be admissible as evidence in relation to procedural matters, as where for example it is alleged that some aspect of the procedures adopted in the arbitration worked unfairly to the disadvantage of one party—see per Coulson J in *F Limited v M Limited* ([2009] 1 Lloyd's Rep. 537 at 543). So too where the proper law of the dispute is English law and there is an appeal on point of law, I can see that the views of a dissenting arbitrator might well inform the decision of the court. In the present case however I find it difficult to ascribe any formal status to the Dissenting Opinion. In so far as it expresses conclusions of Spanish law which go beyond any evidence as to the content of that law given at the arbitration, I do not see how I can have regard to it."

See Hew R. Dundas, "Alphabet Soup: Foreign Law and Dissenting Opinions in International Arbitration in London" (2010) 76 *Arbitration* 757–763.

R51–16 Dissenting opinions are generally to be discouraged: see Professor Alan Redfern's Freshfields Lecture, "Dissenting Opinions in International Commercial Arbitration: The Good, the Bad and the Ugly" (2004) 20(3) Arbitration Int. 223 and his Worshipful Company of Arbitrators Master's Lecture, "Dissent is Dangerous" at (2005) 71 *Arbitration* 3 at 200. These lectures are supported by two further articles by Hew R. Dundas addressing different aspects of dissenting opinions: (i) "*F Ltd v M Ltd*: The Implications of Dissenting Opinions on Serious Irregularity in Arbitration" (2009) 75 *Arbitration* 3 at 454–461 and (ii) "Alphabet Soup"—see para.R51–15.

R51–17 It may be impossible to prevent a dissenting arbitrator from issuing such an opinion and, while it has been suggested (e.g. in the first edition of this book) that such an opinion might prove useful where a party is considering challenging the award for error of law, that notion was firmly rebutted in *F v M* (see previous paragraph).

R51–18 Such opinions, if issued separately (and there is no requirement so to do) do not form part of the award (see *Stinnes Interoil GmbH v A Halcoussis & Co (The Yanxilas)* [1982] 2 Lloyd's Rep. 445) but that is different from the dissenter signing the award while simply indicating that he dissents from it.

Rule 51(2)(a)—Award must state seat

Pursuant to s.7, r.51 applies (being a default rule, if not deleted or to the extent not amended) to all arbitrations seated in Scotland, so the award must state that Scotland is the seat, unless the parties agree that it should not. However, there is no conceivable reason to omit this. **R51–19**

Failure to state the seat in the award, or stating an erroneous one, will not mean that Scotland is no longer the seat of the arbitration where it clearly has been so designated in terms of s.3, although such a step may be of more significance where the issue of the seat is debatable. Prima facie such a failure or error is a serious irregularity challengeable under r.68, but the challenging party will have to demonstrate substantial injustice, perhaps where the failure or error prevents enforcement. This is because an award which is not "made" in a Convention state usually cannot be enforced under the New York Convention. **R51–20**

Equally, a number of the grounds for refusing enforcement under the New York Convention refer to the law of the seat, so that a statement of the wrong seat (or no seat at all) could unexpectedly jeopardise enforcement. A party should check that the seat is stated and, if it is not, apply to the tribunal for correction under r.58. **R51–21**

The terms of s.52(5) of the 1996 Act are quite similar, while art.31(3) of the Model Law demands that the award "shall state the [seat] of arbitration as determined in accordance with Article 20". It is clear that a failure to comply with this provision does not invalidate an award (see *Report of the Working Group on International Contract Practices on the work of its third session*, UN A/CN.9/216, para.79). **R51–22**

For how the seat should be determined, see commentary on s.3. The tribunal should have established the seat under s.3 at the outset of the arbitration. **R51–23**

Rule 51(2)(b)—Award must state when it is made and when it takes effect

Unless otherwise agreed by the parties, the award must state the date when it is made and the date when it takes effect; these may be the same (the usual circumstance) or different. In r.51(2)(b), "made" means the date that the award is completed such that it cannot be altered (other than through correction or on appeal). **R51–24**

Certain rules, e.g. rr.58(6)(a) and 71(4)(a), specify time limits by reference to the award being "made" and some, e.g. r.58(4), merely refer to an application having to be made within a certain period "of the award" and r.50 (interest) makes reference to the date of the award. Where time limits are specified, certainly for the parties, by reference to the award being "made" this must be a reference to the "making" of the award through its delivery to each of the parties in r.51(3). Otherwise, a time limit for an appeal could expire without the potential appellant having become aware of the terms of the award. **R51–25**

R51–26 Section 54(1) of the 1996 Act provides that, absent agreement to the contrary by the parties, the tribunal has discretion as to the date of the award. There is no such discretion in r.51(2)(b). Given that an award cannot be "made" before it has been signed in terms of r.51(1), the date that the award is made must be the date of signature of the last arbitrator to sign in terms of r.51(1). This should be stated in the award if there is more than one arbitrator.

R51–27 In international practice, it is common for tribunals to share the final form of the award by e-mail in conjunction with circulating signature pages only. Absent any express requirements to the contrary (whether party-agreed or institutional), best practice (reflected in s.54(2) of the 1996 Act) is that the award be dated with the date of the last signature, usually the chairman's.

R51–28 An issue arising under the Act is as to when the award is actually made, irrespective of the date which it bears. An award that bears no date, or bears an inappropriate date, must be challengeable under r.68, inter alia since there are key provisions which refer to the date of the award. Further, an award that fails to indicate when it takes effect will certainly be challengeable since that is a key date and the rules contain no provision deeming a particular date to be the point at which the award takes effect in the absence of a statement in the award. Of course, where an award does not state its date or fails to say when it takes effect either party may ask that this be rectified under r.58(1)(a), and it may be that all legal consequences flow from the point when this is done (see *Weldon Plant Ltd v Commission for the New Towns* [2000] B.L.R. 496).

R51–29 The mere making of an award by the tribunal does not make it take effect. The earliest that an award can take effect is when it is intimated to the parties either under r.51(3) or by means specified in an institutional rule or other agreement of the parties. However, the tribunal could potentially postpone the effectiveness of the award beyond the intimation and r.51(2)(b) allows for that to be done. In most cases, however, the tribunal will simply provide that the award will take effect when delivered to all of the parties in accordance with r.83.

R51–30 The concepts of the date of the award, the date when it is made and the date it takes effect have the potential to cause confusion but this can be eliminated by best practice in award-writing, such as is taught by the CIArb, otherwise (which should not be necessary) by the courts adopting a purposive approach to interpretation.

R51–31 The Model Law is unhelpful in this regard, with art.31(3) merely requiring that the award shall state its date but without indicating how that is to be determined. During the drafting phase, the Model Law indicated that an award was made when signed by the tribunal (see *Note by UNCITRAL Secretariat on draft articles 25–36*, UN A/CN.9/WG.II/WP.38, art.27(2)) and, later, that it was deemed to be made on the date that it bore (*Note by UNCITRAL Secretariat on draft articles 1–26*, UN A/CN.9/WG.II/WP.40, art.22(3)), but both those provisions were ultimately discarded.

Of course, r.51 applies only if the parties do not agree otherwise, so that a clear statement by the parties on how such matters should be resolved will remove any uncertainties, e.g. art.31.3 ICC Rules provides that "[t]he award shall be deemed to be made at the place of the arbitration and on the date stated therein". Any such provision displaces r.51(2)(b). **R51–32**

Rule 51(2)(c)—Award must contain reasons

Unless the parties agree otherwise, the award must contain reasons. This is not the position at common law, but most institutional rules demand reasons as do art.6(1) of the ECHR (*Ruiz Torija v Spain* (1995) 19 E.H.R.R. 553 at [29]), the Model Law and the 1996 Act. Prior to the 1996 Act, the position in English law was, similarly, that reasons did not have to be provided unless the parties had required them. However, the DAC Report, para.247 stated that **R51–33**

> "it is a basic rule of justice that those charged with making a binding decision affecting the rights and obligations of others should (unless those others agree) explain the reasons for making this decision".

The reasons for an award are, of course, the reasons of the majority of the tribunal in cases of dissent (see *Cargill International SA Antigua (Geneva Branch) v Sociedad Iberica de Molturacion SA* [1998] 1 Lloyd's Rep. 489). **R51–34**

Rule 57(4) provides that, where the award reflects the terms of a settlement between the parties, reasons are not required (in practice there may be, and will often be, none), while r.69(2) provides that an agreement by the parties to dispense with reasons will be taken as an agreement to exclude the right to challenge an award on the basis of an error of (Scots) law. **R51–35**

If the parties agreed to arbitrate under a set of rules which contemplated that reasons should not be given, then that must suffice to exclude the need for reasons. **R51–36**

The authors submit that rules which give the arbitrator discretion whether or not to provide reasons (see, e.g. Law Society of Scotland Arbitration Rules, para.25.6) would have a similar effect. **R51–37**

In terms of s.9(4)(b), so would an agreement to arbitrate in Scotland under a procedural law which did not demand a reasoned award, e.g. US law (see *United Steelworkers of America v Enterprise Wheel & Car Corp*, 363 U.S. 593 (1960)). **R51–38**

Institutional rules might also allow the provision of very limited reasons. In *Bay Hotel and Resort Ltd v Cavalier Construction Co Ltd* [2001] UKPC 34, an arbitration seated in the Turks and Caicos Islands was conducted in Miami under a set of rules of the American Arbitration Association applicable to US domestic construction arbitrations, requiring only a "written explanation" of the award. The tribunal ordered the payment of a sum of compensation with a breakdown of the sums involved but without **R51–39** any reasons why it had determined those sums to be due other than that it was "on the basis of the testimony and evidence of the parties". The Privy Council recognised that, while this would not meet the requirement of providing reasons under the test set out by Donaldson L.J. in *Bremer Handelgesellschaft mbH v Westzucker GmbH (No.2)* [1981] 2 Lloyd's Rep. 130 (see R51–47 below), it was within what was contemplated by the AAA rules agreed by the parties. It is clear from their Lordships' judgment that such skeletal "reasons" would not suffice under the 1996 Act. (See article by Hew R. Dundas, "Joinder, Reasons and Seat: the Privy Council Decides: *Bay Hotel and Resort Ltd v. Cavalier Construction Co. Ltd*" (2002) 68 Arbitration 184).

R51–40 Some forms of arbitration appear to be incompatible with the provision of reasons, e.g. commodity quality arbitrations of the "look-sniff" type (now very rare in practice) but, unless the parties might be said to have impliedly agreed to forego reasons by electing for such an arbitration, r.51(2)(c) would appear to demand that such awards should be reasoned. Nonetheless, it might be noted that the *travaux preparatoires* to the Model Law suggested that such an implied exclusion might arise in relation to arbitrations where customarily no reasons were given (see *Analytical Commentary on Article 31*, UN A/CN.9/264, para.3).

R51–41 The fact that an award is reasoned does not exclude the possibility that the reasoning may be erroneous. No challenge to an award is available solely on the basis that the tribunal has obviously misunderstood the facts or evidence. Furthermore, since only an error of Scots law can be challenged under r.69, if the reasons demonstrate misapplication of foreign law, no challenge is competent however gross the error is. The same is true even if Scots law applies should the parties have contracted out of the right to challenge under r.69.

R51–42 Given that r.68(2)(c) gives as a ground of challenge to an award a failure by the tribunal to deal with all the issues put to it, an important question arises as to what lengths a tribunal should go to in order to be seen to have dealt with all the issues. There is ample jurisprudence to show that tribunals do *not* have to deal with every last iota of the parties' submissions; see paras R68–34 to R68–44. Inter alia, it has been held that a failure to deal with an aspect of a party's argument is not necessarily a failure to deal with the applicable issue (*Margulead Ltd v Exide Technologies* [2004] EWHC 1019). Further, there is no duty on an arbitrator to deal with each and every point in dispute so long as the critical ones are identified and decided; see *Checkpoint Ltd v Strathclyde Pension Fund* [2003] EWCA Civ 84 at [48]–[49], per Ward L.J. and see *Arbitration Application No.1 of 2013* [2014] CSOH 83 at [23] per Lord Woolman. It is not a failure to give reasons if reasons are not given on peripheral matters (see *Benaim (UK) Ltd v Davies, Middleton & Davies Ltd (No.2)* [2005] EWHC 1370 (TCC) at [82]).

R51–43 Where a tribunal comprises non-lawyers, there will normally be no justification for appointing a solicitor or advocate to draft the award (per

Thomas J. in *Agrimex Ltd v Tradigrain SA* [2003] 2 Lloyds Rep. 537 at [32] and [39(iv)]–[39(v)]—see paras R32–08 to R32–10).

It should be noted that all FCIArbs have had to pass an award-writing **R51–44** examination, the seriousness of which is demonstrated by the interesting and surprising fact that a relatively high proportion of barristers (and, it is understood, one retired (foreign) judge) fail at the first attempt.

Historically, in Scotland in general, and in some classes of arbitration in **R51–45** London, it was common to issue reasons separately from the award proper on the agreed basis that the reasons would never be relied upon in any application to the court. In *Tame Shipping Ltd v Easy Navigation Ltd* [2004] 2 Lloyds Rep. 626, a s.68 application was made and Moore-Bick J., following careful review of the authorities, decided (at [28]) that the court had to open up the reasons since otherwise it could not determine the application. See also para.R51–41.

Under r.71(2) no appeal is competent unless a party has exhausted all **R51–46** available recourse under r.58 which allows a tribunal to correct or clarify an award. These provisions echo ss.70(2) and 57 of the 1996 Act and in that context, in *Al-Hadha Trading Co v Tradegrain SA* [2002] 2 Lloyd's Rep. 512, it was held that a party would first be expected to invite the tribunal to provide reasons where none had been given or clarify its reasoning where this was ambiguous or inadequate, before bringing an appeal. This has been followed in *Torch Offshore LLC v Cable Shipping Inc* [2004] EWHC 787 (Comm) and *Sinclair v Woods of Winchester Ltd* [2005] EWHC 1631 (QB) and approved, tacitly, in *Arbitration Application No.1 of 2013* [2014] CSOH 83 at [15] per Lord Woolman.

Form, quality and extent of reasons

English authority recognises that an award written by arbitrators who are **R51–47** not lawyers might differ in form from a judgment. Thus Donaldson L.J. in *Bremer Handelgesellschaft mbH v Westzucker GmbH (No.2)* [1981] 2 Lloyd's Rep. 130 at 132 (see also the Model Law case of *Navigation Somanar Inc v Algoma Steamships Ltd* (1994) XIX YCA 256 Quebec Supreme Court) suggests that:

"All that is necessary is that the arbitrators should set out what, on their view of the evidence, did or did not happen and should explain succinctly why, in the light of what happened, they have reached their decision and what that decision is. Where [an] award differs from a judgment is that the arbitrators will not be expected to analyse the law and the authorities. It will be quite sufficient that they should explain how they reached their conclusion."

In *Arbitration Application No.1 of 2013* (above), Lord Woolman observed at **R51–48** [23]:

"The nature and length of reasons to be given in an individual case will depend on the whole context within which the decision is given. An arbitrator is only required to deal with the essential issues, not every point that is raised: *Fidelity Management SA v. Myriad International Holdings BV* [2005] EWHC 1193 (Comm.) at para. 9."

R51–49 The reasons to be expected from a tribunal need not match "the accuracy of writing or the cogency of expression that is required of a judgment" (per Colman J. in *General Feeds Inc, Panama v Slobodna Plovidba Yugoslavia* [1999] 1 Lloyds Rep. 688 at 694). Further, in *Compton Beauchamp Estates Ltd v Spence* [2013] EWHC 1101 (Ch), Morgan J. said at [50]:

" ... I consider that the duty on an arbitrator to provide a reasoned award under s.52(4) of the 1996 Act [equivalent to r.51(2)(c)] is not less than the duty in the above cases [*Bremer Handelsgesellschaft mbH v Westzucker GmbH (No.2)* [1981] 2 Lloyd's Rep. 130, *Save Britain's Heritage v Number 1 Poultry Ltd* [1991] 1 W.L.R. 153, *Curtis v London Rent Assessment Committee* [1999] Q.B. 92 at 119] dealing, in broadly similar ways with arbitrators, tribunals and planning inspectors. The two cases I have cited dealing with reasons to be given for court decisions (*Flannery v. Halifax Estate Agencies Ltd* [2000] 1 W.L.R. 377 and *English v. Emery Reimbold & Strick Ltd* [2002] EWCA Civ 605; [2002] 1 W.L.R. 2409) involved the need to give reasons in relation to disputes as to expert evidence. In a case like the present [rent review], where the arbitrator is chosen for his experience in the relevant expert discipline, I do not see any particular reason why the duty on such an arbitrator to explain why he has preferred one expert to another should be fundamentally different from the duty on a court in such a case."

And in relation to the appeal based on breach of the equivalent of r.51(2)(c), (at [79]):

"[H]having considered individually the various criticisms of the reasoning in the award, I ought to stand back and consider the position overall. The arbitrator's reasoning as set out in the award is poor. This has placed a considerable burden on the court of informing itself by reference to the evidence and the parties' submissions of what the parties themselves are taken to know about the issues in the case. If one is informed in that way, then save in a minor respect the reasoning in the award, although unimpressive, is just about enough to explain the conclusions reached. The minor respect in which the reasons do not explain the conclusions reached does not give rise to substantial injustice to the Claimant."

Power to order reasons

In this context, the reader is also referred to the commentary to r.71(8)(a) (paras R71–24 to R71–37). This is very similar to s.70(4) of the 1996 Act and relates to awards which are being appealed. It allows the Outer House to order the tribunal to state its reasons for the award being appealed in sufficient detail to enable the Outer House to deal with the appeal properly. **R51–50**

Given that an appeal is competent only if an appellant has exhausted any available arbitral process of appeal or review, including correction of the award under r.58, and correction can include the giving of reasons or further reasons (*Al-Hadha Trading Co v Tradegrain SA* [2002] 2 Lloyd's Rep. 512 and *Torch Offshore LLC v Cable Shipping Inc* [2004] EWHC 787 (Comm)), it is suggested that the power of the court to order reasons exists only where these alternative remedies have been exhausted or have been excluded by the parties. These observations were cited with approval by Lord Woolman in *Arbitration Application No.1 of 2013* (see para.R51–48 above). **R51–51**

The most obvious situation in which the Outer House might exercise this power is where a party wishes to challenge the tribunal's decision on the basis of a suspected error of law, but the tribunal has provided inadequately explained reasons, or has perhaps failed to provide any reasons at all. **R51–52**

However, nowhere does the Act provide that the power of the Outer House is confined to r.69 issues and it may be appropriate to seek fuller reasons in respect of either r.67 (jurisdictional) or r.68 (irregularity) appeals. Thus, while one might ordinarily suppose that the power under r.71(8)(a) would not be exercised where the award was not based on Scots law, since then it would not be challengeable on the basis of error of law under r.69, that restriction may not apply. **R51–53**

Even where the parties have agreed that the award should not contain reasons, the Outer House may find it necessary to see those reasons in order to assess whether any ground of appeal exists on the basis of excess of jurisdiction or serious irregularity (see Webster J. in *Atlantic Lines & Navigation Co Inc v Italmare SpA (The Appollon)* [1985] 1 Lloyd's Rep. 597 at 601). **R51–54**

It has also been held that a clear failure to deal with an issue in an award (r.68(2)(c) refers) cannot be cured by requesting the tribunal to elaborate on its reasons (see *Hussmann (Europe) Ltd v Al Ameen Development Trade Co* [2000] 2 Lloyd's Rep. 83). **R51–55**

If the decision in an award was not based on Scots law and stated no reasons in circumstances where neither excess of jurisdiction nor other irregularity was suspected, given that there could be no appeal based on error of law, it would be difficult to argue that the absence of reasons had caused substantial injustice to the appellant and that the award should be set aside. **R51–56**

Rule 51(2)(d)—Award must state whether any previous award was made

R51–57 Unless the parties agree otherwise, the award must state whether any previous provisional or part award has been made and, in respect of provisional (but not part) awards, the extent to which such has been superseded or confirmed (NB—a part award is final as to the matters it decides (r.54(2)).

R51–58 While this provision has no parallel in either the Model Law or the 1996 Act, it is necessary since, e.g. if a provisional award is made in respect of claim X in the sum of £50,000 (i.e. equivalent to a payment on account) and if claim X is finally determined as £75,000, credit must self-evidently be given for the £50,000 already paid.

R51–59 Standard practice in awards is to recite the procedural chronology from appointment so r.51(2)(d) will automatically be satisfied through that process.

Rule 51(3)—Award made by delivery to parties

R51–60 Rule 51(3) is a default rule and so may be excluded or amended or replaced by the parties, for example, by art.31(3) of the ICC Rules. Rule 51(3) is important for rules which provide for time limits calculated from the "making" of the award. Rule 51(3) pre-supposes that the award is "made" when it is delivered to each of the parties. It follows from this that whilst it remains undelivered to any party, the award has not been "made" and the time limit has not been triggered. See commentary on r.83 for a full discussion of "delivery".

R51–61 While the terms of r.51(3) do not oblige the tribunal to deliver the award, this is clearly implicit (*St Andrews Bay Development Ltd v HBG Management Ltd*, 2003 S.L.T. 740 at [16]). The only exception to the duty is where the tribunal refuses to deliver the award pursuant to r.56 (retention for non-payment of fees and expenses).

R51–62 If the parties have agreed with the tribunal that the award requires to be issued by a certain time, then if the award is not issued by that time and the time is not extended (prorogated) by the parties, the jurisdiction of the tribunal to make the award will fall (*Cunninghame v Drummond* (1491) Mor. 635; *Earl of Linlithgow v Hamilton* (1610) Mor. 636). In case readers are concerned at reliance on such ancient authorities, it should be noted that in *Cubitt Building & Interiors Ltd v Fleetglade Ltd* [2006] EWHC 3413 (TCC), H.H. Judge Coulson QC reached the same conclusion (at [76(c)]), albeit in the context of an adjudication under HGCRA, inter alia citing, with respectful approval, *Ritchie Brothers (PWC) Ltd v David Philp (Commercials) Ltd* [2005] CSIH 32. See paras R9–02 and R9–03 for a discussion of the implications of these old authorities.

R51–63 The authors submit that (subject to greater specification in the agreement) the date of issue will be determined by delivery under rr.51(3) and 83 except where the tribunal intimates to the parties within any time limit for issue that they have made an award and are withholding delivery under r.56. The existence of the mandatory provisions of r.56 must be seen as a statutory prorogation of the jurisdiction of the tribunal (which has been limited by the parties), to allow an award which has been made (in the narrow sense) to be delivered to the parties.

Rule 52: Award treated as made in Scotland D

52. An award is to be treated as having been made in Scotland even if it is signed at, or delivered to or from, a place outwith Scotland.

STATUS

Rule 52 is a default rule so can be disapplied in whole or in part, or modified in any way, by the parties (s.9 refers) **R52–01**

Since r.52 is very important, it is odd that, as with s.53 of the 1996 Act, it is non-mandatory. The authors cannot envisage why, in any Scots-seated arbitration, the parties should agree to vary or disapply it except perhaps in far-remotely hypothetical circumstances such as where (i) hostilities had broken out between the UK and the expected enforcement state, or (ii) Scotland was to achieve independence but failed to become party to the New York Convention. However, the artificial choice of country X as the one where the award was made (i.e. if the choice of France in *Hiscox v Outhwaite* (1992) 41 I.C.L.Q. 637 had been deliberate) certainly could not bind any foreign court and, in addition, it is difficult to see any such artificial choice being accepted either. **R52–02**

MODEL LAW

The Model Law has art.31(3) which provides that the award is deemed to have been made at the place (seat) of the arbitration. **R52–03**

COMMENTARY

This is the equivalent of s.53 of the 1996 Act, which makes it clear that this result follows where *either* England and Wales or Northern Ireland is the seat of the arbitration. While r.52 does not mention the seat, it applies (s.7 refers) only when the arbitration is seated in Scotland. As regard arbitrations held outwith the UK, s.18(2) provides than an award seeking enforcement under the New York Convention is to be treated as made at the seat of the arbitration. **R52–04**

Rule 52 prevents any recurrence of the House of Lords' astonishing decision in *Hiscox v Outhwaite* [1992] 1 A.C. 562 (see Fraser P. Davidson, "Where is an Arbitral Award Made?—*Hiscox v Outhwaite*" (1992) 41 I.C.L.Q. 637) that an award in an arbitration between two English parties, conducted in London by an English arbitrator under English substantive law and under the 1950 and 1979 Acts, was to be treated as a French award merely because the arbitrator indicated that he had signed it while in Paris. **R52–05**

R52–06 The *ratio* of that decision was that the award was "made" wherever the arbitrator happened to be when he signed the award, or presumably where the final arbitrator happened to be when he signed the award if there were several arbitrators. Their Lordships were influenced in reaching their decision by ancient English authority on where an award might be made but no substantive reference was made to the New York Convention. While *Hiscox v Outhwaite* [1992] 1 A.C. 562 was effectively "reversed" by s.53 of the 1996 Act, it remained, by virtue of its high authority under the 1975 Act, persuasive in Scotland until r.52.

R52–07 Several grounds for refusing enforcement of an award under the Convention refer to the law of the country where the award was made and this is meaningful only if that place is taken to be the seat of the arbitration, since it cannot be imagined that the framers of the Convention would have put the enforceability of the award in jeopardy by making it depend on the law of a country which might have no connection with the arbitration at all, merely because of the accidental fact that the arbitrator signed it there.

R52–08 It remains common practice for arbitrators to indicate the place where the award is signed and, in some jurisdictions, this is a requirement. However, in such cases it is the fact that the seat of the arbitration is in Scotland (s.3 refers) which determines where the award is made. As suggested in the discussion of r.51(2)(a) (see paras R51–19 to R51–23), while the award should ordinarily state that Scotland is the seat of the arbitration, the fact that the award fails to do so, or erroneously states that another country is the seat of the arbitration, will not prevent the award from being regarded as made in Scotland if, in terms of s.3 of the 2010 Act, the seat is in Scotland.

Rule 53: Provisional awards D

53. The tribunal may make a provisional award granting any relief on a provisional basis which it has the power to grant permanently.

DEFINITIONS

"tribunal": ss.2(1), 31(1)

STATUS

R53–01 Rule 53 is a default rule so can be disapplied in whole or in part, or modified in any way, by the parties (s.9 refers).

R53–02 The commentary at para.R54–02 explains that, under the ICC, LCIA or Swiss Rules, arbitrators have the power to make "interim awards" but these are what the 2010 Act calls part awards, i.e. are final, not provisional, as to the matters decided therein.

R53–03 CIMAR r.10 effects a detailed modification of r.53.

MODEL LAW

The Model Law has no directly equivalent provision. R53–04

COMMENTARY

In the discussions leading up to the submission of the Bill to the Scottish R53–05
Parliament, it was clear that widespread confusion between "part", "partial", "interim" and "provisional" awards, which had existed for a very long time (see *Irons and Melville on Arbitration*, p.185), continued to exist; see commentary on r.54 below. The aim of r.53 is to put an end to this confusion and to create one unambiguous term to denote an award of a temporary character, namely "provisional award". A provisional award should be clearly designated as such.

Under the Scots common law what is now described in r.53 as a provi- R53–06
sional award was known as an "interim award" or "interim decree arbitral" (*Irons and Melville on Arbitration*, p.184). The root of the common law confusion lay in the use of the word "interim" in Scottish litigation, the forms of which common law arbitration tended to follow. Thus, in Scottish litigation, an "interim decree" for payment of money is not a provisional measure but final and conclusive on the restricted matters dealt by it, but an "interim interdict" (injunction) is only a provisional measure. Scottish litigators have no difficulty in understanding these terms but it is easy to understand why they should have caused confusion to non-legally qualified arbitrators. Rules 53 and 54 put an end to such confusion and the authors submit that the word "interim" should no longer be used to designate or describe any award.

The Model Law does not provide for the issue of any provisional award. R53–07
However, a proposal (see *Report of the Secretary General on the possible features of a Model Law on International Commercial Arbitration*, UN A/CN.9/207, para.82) to empower tribunals to make "interim, interlocutory and partial awards" (as under art.32.1 of the UNCITRAL Arbitration Rules) was rejected on the basis that there was no clear consensus on what those terms meant in international practice (see UN A/CN.9/207, para.73). Certain jurisdictions (e.g. British Columbia), in adopting the Model Law, explicitly conferred on tribunals the power to make such awards but, in contrast, Scotland did not follow this lead when it adopted the Model Law in 1990. An informal survey by one of the authors of colleagues in Model Law jurisdictions failed to reveal either (i) any example following British Columbia's lead, or (ii) any example in any civil law jurisdiction of the concept of the Scots "provisional award".

In the authors' experience and anecdotal knowledge, provisional awards R53–08
are extremely rare; see the extract from the DAC Report at R53–12 below.

While the parties could, at common law, certainly confer power on the R53–09
tribunal to make a provisional award, it was unclear whether a tribunal had any inherent power to make such awards absent express agreement. Lord

President Boyle, in *Lyle v Falconer* (1842) 5 D. 236 at 239, seemed to assume that there was such a power.

R53–10 Most recently, while Lord Malcolm held in *Apollo Engineering Ltd v James Scott Ltd*, 2008 S.L.T. 472 that there was such a power, the Inner House ([2009] CSIH 39) seemed more doubtful, but ultimately ruled that the matter did not arise for decision in that case.

R53–11 Rule 53 removes any doubt in the matter but with the caveat that it is a default rule.

R53–12 In the January 2009 Bill, r.53 was mandatory in order, so it was argued by one professional body, to protect the weaker party in cases where there was "inequality of arms", i.e. the rule would prevent stronger parties from routinely excluding the power to make provisional awards (see paras 127, 128 of the consultation paper). The authors (and others) considered this an unlikely scenario and the provision became a default one, effectively becoming comparable to s.39 of the 1996 Act, where s.39(4) states that a tribunal has the power to make such awards only if expressly conferred on it by the parties. The draft of s.39 of the 1996 Act was amended so that it would take this form (i.e. non-mandatory) because (see DAC Report, para.201):

> "enormous care has to be taken to avoid turning what can be a useful judicial tool into an instrument of injustice [and] we received responses from a number of practising arbitrators to the effect that they would be unhappy with such powers and saw no need for them."

R53–13 The authors stress that, while s.39 of the 1996 Act and r.53 both leave the matter of provisional awards at the option of the parties, the former does so on an opt-in basis, the latter on an opt-out one.

R53–14 The provision in the January 2009 Bill followed the example of s.39 of the 1996 Act and gave examples of what a provisional award might order, but r.53 omits any such examples because the power of the tribunal in this regard is limited by the range of remedies which the parties have empowered it to exercise. The range of remedies open to the tribunal could be wider than might be supposed because, although remedies are specified by r.49, that is a default rule and the parties might expand on those remedies either explicitly, or by invoking a particular set of rules or a particular foreign law to govern the matter.

R53–15 This power should be exercised with considerable care. To give one example, ordering the advance payment of monies by one party to the other in advance of the final determination of liability opens up a risk that the recipient becomes insolvent before that determination.

R53–16 The authors consider that the most likely form of provisional award is a monetary one, effectively making one party pay the other a payment on account, e.g. where (say) there appeared to be a strong case for 25 per cent of a claim, the claimant appeared to be in financial difficulties and the respondent was covered by insurance, the tribunal might then consider awarding that 25 per cent now rather than delay the claimant's receipt thereof until the end of the arbitration (see *BMBF (No.12) v Harland & Wolff Shipbuilding & Heavy Industries Ltd* [2001] 2 Lloyd's Rep. 227). Such situations are commonplace in the construction industry, and standard arbitration rules in that industry have long conferred power on tribunals to order provisional relief (see, e.g. ICE Arbitration Procedure r.19.3, CIMAR Rules r.10). The authors respectfully agree with the suggestion that it may be appropriate in rent review arbitrations where there is no dispute that the rent will be increased (B. Harris, R. Planterose and J. Tecks, *The Arbitration Act 1996—A Commentary*, 4th edn (Oxford: Blackwell Publishing, 2007), p.195), in which case the award would take the form of a provisional declarator.

R53–17 A provisional award under r.53 is, in its terms, intended to operate as an award so that it must comply with the requirements as to form (see commentary on r.51 above). Rule 71(3) provides that no appeal may be made against a provisional award and this must, on its terms, exclude a r.68 challenge for serious irregularity, even where the tribunal makes a provisional award in favour of the claimant without giving the respondent the opportunity to make representations. Such a provisional award by virtue of its nature must be subject to recall or modification by the tribunal following a relevant change of circumstances. A tribunal could make a provisional award of interdict which might be made ex parte due to urgency. However, if a tribunal failed to adhere to its r.24 duties in making a provisional award or at least in considering an application to it for recall or modification, it could open itself up for removal under r.12 given the potential prejudice.

R53–18 A tribunal that is minded to make a provisional award may, in advance of making it, wish to suggest to the parties that the award includes within it a condition that the claimant may be liable for any loss or expense caused to the respondent by the award should the tribunal determine in a partial or final award that the claimant was not entitled to anything granted to him in the provisional award and that the tribunal shall decide any difference or dispute between the parties arising therefrom.

R53–19 Given that the r.53 power to make a provisional award is prefaced "The tribunal *may* ..." (emphasis added) and given that there can be no challenge thereto of any nature when made, it follows that there can be no challenge to the tribunal's declining to make one. This is consistent with pre-1996 Act authority in England suggesting that the decision *not* to make a provisional order is not capable of challenge (*Japan Line Ltd v Aggeliki Charis Compania Maritima SA (The Angelic Grace)* [1980] 1 Lloyd's Rep. 288).

R53–20 The authors consider it highly unlikely that any provisional award would be recognised as "an award" in the context of the New York Convention, particularly in the many jurisdictions which have no concept of one.

Rule 54: Part awards M

54.—(1) The tribunal may make more than one award at different times on different aspects of the matters to be determined.

(2) A "part award" is an award which decides some (but not all) of the matters which the tribunal is to decide in the arbitration.

(3) A part award must specify the matters to which it relates.

DEFINITIONS

"arbitration": ss.2(1), (2), 31(1)
"tribunal": ss.2(1), 31(1)

STATUS

R54–01 Rule 54 is mandatory so cannot be disapplied, or modified in any way, by the parties.

R54–02 Under the ICC Rules, tribunals have power to make "interim" awards (art.2) in the same way as "final" awards but nowhere is "interim" defined. Article 32(1) of the Swiss Rules is entirely consistent with r.54 and empowers tribunals to make "interim" and "interlocutory" awards. However, the ICC, LCIA and Swiss references to "interim awards" equate to "part awards", not "provisional awards" as is demonstrated (e.g.) by LCIA art.26.1 which provides that the Arbitral Tribunal

> "may make separate awards on different issues at different times, including interim payments on account of any claim or cross-claim (including Legal and Arbitration Costs). Such awards shall have the same status as any other award made by the Arbitral Tribunal."

MODEL LAW

R54–03 The Model Law has no provision equivalent to a "part award" but it is clear from art.32(1) that there may be a series of awards of which the last is "final".

COMMENTARY

Rule 54(1) and (2)—Part awards

R54–04 A part award deals finally and conclusively with a particular issue or set of issues so that, in contrast to a provisional award, such matters not only need not but cannot, on the basis of res judicata, be revisited in any subsequent award (save only as to recitation) (see DAC Report, para.202). In any event, it is standard practice to summarise the chronology of all previous awards, of whatever type, in the final award. A part award is subject to the rights of correction under r.58 and appeal under rr.67, 68 and 69.

R54–05 See R53–05 to R53–11; some arbitrators and some institutions (see para.R54-02), refer to "interim" or "partial" awards but, in Scotland, it was decided to use only "part'" and eliminate "interim" and "partial", both in order to simplify the terminology and because it was felt that "part" clearly meant an award on part of the dispute while "interim" (e.g. as in "interim government") was too close to "provisional" and "partial", too close to "incomplete".

While r.51(1)(d) (a default rule) requires that a final award must note that **R54-06** a previous part award has been made, the tribunal has no power to reconsider any matter dealt with in that part award (*Charles M Willie & Co (Shipping) Ltd v Ocean Laser Shipping Ltd (The Smaro)* [1999] 1 Lloyd's Rep. 225). It is an award in all respects, including requirements of form and susceptibility to challenge.

Such an award might be made if there are a number of issues before the **R54-07** tribunal and some may be conveniently dealt with before others. A very common form of part award is one deciding liability with a subsequent one deciding quantum (see *Trans Trust SPRL v Danubian Trading Co Ltd* [1952] 2 Q.B. 297); another is where, after deciding liability and quantum, a separate part award is made addressing expenses (see *Exmar BV v National Iranian Tanker Co (The Trade Fortitude)* [1992] 1 Lloyd's Rep. 169). Further, it may be that several part awards made at different times decide a variety of claims before the tribunal (see DAC Report, para.227).

Exercising this power might indeed assist the tribunal in its duty under **R54-08** r.24(1)(c) to conduct the arbitration without unnecessary delay and avoiding unnecessary expense (see DAC Report, para.227). Subject to its general duties a tribunal would have discretion whether or not to make such an award (see *The Trade Fortitude* [1992] 1 Lloyd's Rep. 169). In England a tribunal has occasionally found it more convenient to make an award on a claim before considering a counterclaim (*SL Sethia Liners v Naviagro Maritime Corp (The Kostas Meals)* [1981] 1 Lloyd's Rep. 18, where the tribunal took the view that the counterclaim was not made in good faith); however, such circumstances will necessarily be rare.

In contrast to r.53, r.54 is a mandatory rule so the parties cannot amend **R54-09** or disapply it, either explicitly or by invoking arbitral rules or a foreign law (e.g. that of Gibraltar) which do not permit the making of part awards, although the authors are unaware of any institutional rules which have this effect.

Part awards are regarded as awards under the New York Convention, **R54-10** and thus could be expected to be enforced, assuming that there was anything to enforce (see Robert B. von Mehren, "The Enforcement of Arbitral Awards under Conventions and United States Law" (1985) 9 Yale J. World Pub. Ord. 343). Thus a part award which ordered the payment of money should be enforced, but an award which dealt with liability but not quantum or which was merely declaratory could not be (see *FCLG Enterprises v Golden Margarine Ltd* [2004] O.J. 3804).

Rule 54(3)

R54–11 Rule 54(3) might seem to state the obvious but is a necessary reminder that a part award must not only state that it is a part award but also state clearly what issues it is dealing with. Thus, for example, an award which stated that it was a part award but then simply awarded a money sum to one party without further explanation would fail the requirement of r.51(2)(c) (if applicable, it being a default rule) and be open to challenge. A party would thus be entitled to ask the tribunal for a clarification of the award under r.58(1)(b), and if such a step failed, to challenge the award on the basis of a serious irregularity in terms of r.68(2)(a)(ii) (see *Leach v Haringey London BC*, *The Times*, March 23, 1977).

Rule 55: Draft awards D

55. Before making an award, the tribunal—
   (a) may send a draft of its proposed award to the parties, and
   (b) if it does so, must consider any representations from the parties about the draft which the tribunal receives by such time as it specifies.

DEFINITIONS

"party": ss.2(1), 31(1), (2)
"tribunal": ss.2(1), 31(1)

STATUS

R55–01 Rule 55 is a default rule so can be disapplied in whole or in part, or modified in any way, by the parties (s.9 refers).

R55–02 Given what is said below, parties may agree that no draft award should be made; however, certain institutional rules do provide for one. For example, CIMAR r.12.10 gives the tribunal discretion to make a draft award and art.33 of the ICC Rules provides that the award must be scrutinised by the ICC Court (see also art.6 of Appendix II—Internal rules of the International Court of Arbitration) but the ICC does not issue draft awards to the parties.

MODEL LAW

R55–03 The Model Law has no equivalent provision.

COMMENTARY

Rule 55(a)—Draft awards

R55–04 Essentially, r.55 codifies Scots common law in relation to draft awards (see *Bell on Arbitration*, para.312). The purpose of draft awards was not only to allow parties to check for any errors, typographical, terminological or factual but also to ensure that if the tribunal had made use of any matter upon which the parties had not had an opportunity to comment, they could do so. The existence of powers of correction under r.58 take away the first rationale. The express provision of a duty to treat parties fairly in r.24(1)(b) should obviate the second rationale.

At common law, a tribunal had discretion to issue draft awards, but they were under no obligation to do so (see Lord Gifford in *McCallum v Robertson* (1826) 2 W. & S. 344 at 352), except where the parties had agreed that a draft award would be issued (e.g. the Law Society of Scotland Arbitration Rules r.25.5.). **R55–05**

Following s.3 of the 1972 Act, which allowed parties to obtain a binding opinion of the Inner House on any question of law arising in the arbitration before the making of a final award, parties tended to insist on the issue of draft awards to allow the opinion to be obtained by means of the stated case procedure. With the repeal of s.3, that rationale for draft awards has ceased also: see also rr.41 and 42 and the commentary thereon. **R55–06**

Given the flexibility of r.58, the authors submit that the issue of draft awards has, in most cases, no continuing useful purpose and, in particular, there is a real risk, borne out by much practical experience, that such issue becomes an invitation to the parties to debate the contents, leading to unnecessary, time-consuming and expensive complications and a breach of the tribunal's r.24(1)(c) duty. **R55–07**

Rule 55 restates the common law power in statutory form on a default basis, i.e. it may be amended or deleted by party agreement, whether explicit or via the adoption of arbitral rules, **R55–08**

Subject (as above) to contrary party agreement, the tribunal's discretion to issue a draft award must be exercised having regard to its duties under r.24 and in accordance with s.1(c) (general principle to resolve dispute without unnecessary delay or expense). **R55–09**

The general practice outside Scotland is *not* to issue draft awards except in one or more of three circumstances, usually in particularly complex cases especially in the construction sector: **R55–10**

(i) to secure the parties' joint agreement to the recitals of the procedural history of the arbitration;
(ii) to secure each party's agreement that the summary of its case and its arguments is fair and accurate (NB this would not include the tribunal's analysis thereof); and
(iii) ditto in respect to the facts of the case (but, of course, excluding the tribunal's findings of fact).

Rule 55(b)

R55–11 If it does issue a draft award, the tribunal must send a copy to both parties and consider any representations they wish to make about the draft award.

R55–12 A refusal to consider the parties' representations must be an irregularity which, if it gives rise to substantial injustice, will give rise to a serious irregularity appeal. It would similarly be an irregularity to send the draft only to one of the parties or to consider representations from only one of the parties.

R55–13 While the tribunal has discretion as to the period within which such representations might be made, if it were to specify an unreasonably short period, then it would not be treating the parties fairly in terms of r.24(1)(b), and that would also amount to a serious irregularity (r.68(2)(h) refers).

R55–14 If an "award" clearly indicates that it is a draft award (as a practical matter, it should be neither signed nor dated and should be printed on paper with the word "DRAFT" integral to the actual paper), then it is not an award at all, and has no legal status and need not comply with any requirements as to form. However, best practice is that it should be issued in a form that, assuming no comment by the parties, it can, without any addition, be signed, dated and issued as an award.

R55–15 If it is clear from a draft award that the tribunal has exceeded its jurisdiction and should a party fail to make any representations about this, it would lose its right to object by reason of r.76 and would therefore be precluded from challenging the award when finally issued.

R55–16 A draft award, properly prepared, is neither (i) open to challenge nor (ii) capable of being enforced.

Rule 56: Power to withhold award on non-payment of fees or expenses M

56.—(1) The tribunal may refuse to deliver or send its award to the parties if any fees and expenses for which they are liable under rule 60 have not been paid in full.

(2) Where the tribunal so refuses, the court may (on an application by any party) order—
- **(a) that the tribunal must deliver the award on the applicant paying into the court an amount equal to the fees and expenses demanded (or such lesser amount as may be specified in the order),**
- **(b) that the amount paid into the court is to be used to pay the fees and expenses which the court determines as being properly payable, and**
- **(c) that the balance (if any) of the amount paid into the court is to be repaid to the applicant.**

(3) The court may make such an order only if the applicant has exhausted any available arbitral process of appeal or review of the amount of the fees and expenses demanded.

(4) The court's decision on an application under this rule is final.

DEFINITIONS

"court": s.31(1)
"party": ss.2(1), 31(1), (2)
"tribunal": ss.2(1), 31(1)

STATUS

Rule 56 is a mandatory rule which cannot be disapplied or modified by the parties. **R56–01**

MODEL LAW

The Model Law has no equivalent provision. **R56–02**

COMMENTARY

Rule 56(1)—Withholding of award

This rule is based on s.56 of the 1996 Act which in turn was based on s.19 of the 1950 Act. **R56–03**

Rule 56 permits the tribunal to refuse to send or deliver the award to the parties if any fees or expenses for which they are liable under r.59 remain unpaid. The term "deliver" was added while the Bill was progressing through the Scottish Parliament, presumably because under r.51(3) an award is made through delivery to the parties in terms of r.83. The question of when an award is made and when it takes effect, and whether those two dates might be different is discussed in the context of r.51(2)(b) and r.51(3) (see paras R51–24 to R51–32 and R51–60 to R51–63) and is not repeated here. **R56–04**

The rules of the ICC, LCIA and other leading institutions require advance payment by the parties of deposits to cover the entire costs of the arbitration so that there will never be any need to resort to r.56. The risk to the arbitrators is in ad hoc (i.e. non-institutional) cases where some arbitrators are reluctant (some very) either to ask for deposits or to apply r.56. A well-known London arbitrator in a specialist sector told one of the authors (i) that he had just been paid his fees in a case seven years after rendering his award and (ii) that if he applied s.56 of the 1996 Act he would never be appointed again. **R56–05**

Given that r.71(4)(a) provides that an award is generally open to appeal (or application for leave to appeal) only within 28 days of it being "made" by means of delivery under rr.51(3) and 83, non-delivery by the tribunal of the award pursuant to r.56 will not prejudice the parties' rights of appeal. **R56–06**

The parties are jointly (indirectly) and severally (directly) liable for arbitrators' fees and expenses of the arbitration in terms of rr.60(1) and **R56–07**

62(3), including the fees of anyone engaged by the tribunal and any expert from whom it might seek an opinion. In terms of r.60(2), the parties are also jointly and severally liable for all the fees and expenses of any arbitral appointments referee and any other third party to whom the parties have given power in relation to the arbitration, e.g. a contractually stipulated appointing authority. This last category embraces, e.g. the ICC in an ICC-administered arbitration but, even if it did not, r.56 does not exclude the operation of art.34(1) ICC Rules pursuant to which the ICC Secretariat will issue the award to the parties only if they have paid all necessary expenses including those of the ICC itself.

R56–08 It follows that the tribunal may therefore decline to deliver the award even if all its own fees and expenses have been paid, but the fees and expenses of any arbitral appointments referee remain unpaid. Of course, it need not decline to deliver the award in those circumstances. If it does not, then the parties are still liable to the arbitral appointments referee, but the latter cannot rely on this lever to encourage payment. It is, indeed, entirely within the discretion of the tribunal whether it will decline to deliver the award even if its own fees and expenses have not been paid, and tribunals may choose to trust parties in this regard.

R56–09 It is clear that the fees and expenses of the arbitration include those of an umpire (see r.82) but there is nothing in r.56 equivalent to s.56(5) of the 1996 Act, which expressly provides that the reference to arbitrators includes any arbitrator who has ceased to act and an umpire who has not replaced the other arbitrators, both being very rare circumstances (and it is not obvious how that umpire could have earned any fees since he has not yet taken over the reference). Prima facie, the award cannot be withheld because the fees and expenses of a former member of the tribunal, or the umpire-in-waiting, have not been paid. In the authors' view the remedy of a former member of the tribunal is to apply to the court under r.16.

R56–10 Historically, arbitration was usually undertaken on a gratuitous basis and pre-19th century case law suggested that where an arbitrator had refused to release an award unless he was paid a fee, that rendered that award susceptible to being set aside under art.25 of the 1695 Articles on the basis that it was procured by "bribery" (see *Blair v Gibb* (1738) Mor. 664).

R56–11 More "recent" authority (*Fraser v Wright* (1838) 16 S. 1049) declined to follow this line, although falling short of unambiguously stating that the practice was entirely proper. The practice of withholding an award until fees and expenses were paid was, however, commonplace and sanctioned by various sets of arbitration rules.

R56–12 These considerations are now, of course, unnecessary, since the practice is now supported by a statutory rule. The rule is of course mandatory, since there would be no point in conferring such a power on the tribunal if the parties were allowed to withdraw it.

R56–13 Rule 56(1) allows the tribunal to "refuse" to deliver the award. The authors submit that, in order to take advantage of r.56, the tribunal must

Arbitration (Scotland) Act 2010 (r.56)

intimate the refusal to the parties. The intimation should state that the award has been made but that it will not be delivered until the outstanding fees and expenses have been paid. The intimation of the refusal may be important in relation to any time limit that the tribunal may be under to issue an award (see commentary on r.51(3) at paras R51–60 to R51–63). Any party aggrieved by the exercise of this power may ask the court to intervene under r.56(2).

Finally, although either party may pay the relevant fees and expenses in order to obtain the award, the award itself might (if it is a final award) or might not (e.g. a part award on liability or quantum) have determined the entitlement of a party to recover its payment of those fees and expenses from the other party. Rule 62 governs this matter. **R56–14**

Rule 56(2)—Payment into court

Where a tribunal refuses to release the award, any party to the arbitration may make an application to the court (the sheriff court or Outer House, but the Inner House when the arbitrator or one of the arbitrators is a judge). In contrast to the position under s.56(2) of the 1996 Act, that party need not give notice of that application to the tribunal and other parties, but such a requirement is given by r.100.5(3) of the RCS and rr.2.4(8) and 2.5 of the SASAR. **R56–15**

The court may then order, first, that the award should be delivered on the applicant paying into court the amount demanded or such lesser sum as the court may specify. While it is the applicant who has to pay this sum into court, he may in practice seek a contribution from the other party. A court may perhaps exercise its discretion to order delivery on payment of a lesser sum where the applicant is struggling to find the whole sum themselves, or where the amount demanded seems obviously excessive. In this context the DAC Report, para.259, said, in relation to the corresponding provision in the 1996 Act, that if the power to order payment into court of a lesser sum were not there, **R56–16**

> "an arbitrator could demand an extortionate amount, in effect preventing a party from taking advantage of the mechanism provided for here".

The court will then determine the amount which is properly payable and, if necessary, make a remit to the Auditor of the Court of Session under r.60(3) for that purpose. Having ascertained the amount properly payable, the court will order the equivalent amount from the money that has been lodged to be used to pay the fees and expenses, with any balance being repaid to the applicant. **R56–17**

For details of how payments are made (consigned) into court for the Court of Session see the commentary on RCS r.33.4 in *Greens' Annotated* **R56–18**

Rules of the Court of Session (Edinburgh: W. Green) also available in Vol.2 of *The Parliament House Book* (Edinburgh: W. Green) and for the sheriff court see *Sheriff Court Practice*, edited by Sheriff T. Welsh QC, 3rd edn (Edinburgh: Sweet & Maxwell, 2005), paras 11–48 to 11–49.

R56–19 Rule 56(2) provides recourse for a party who thinks that the amount demanded for the release of the award is or may be excessive. It does not assist a party who has already paid the fees and expenses demanded but considers them to be excessive (see in this context the decision of the Swedish Supreme Court in *Hobér, Kraus and Melis v Soyak International Construction & Investment Inc*, Case Ö 4227-06, reported in *Mealey's International Arbitration Report*, Vol.24 No.3 (March 2009)). Any recourse for such a party lies through applying to the Auditor under r.60(3) for a determination of the amount properly payable and an order for repayment, if appropriate, under r.60(5).

R56–20 However, under the 1996 Act, only those fees and expenses which have been fixed by the tribunal are capable of challenge (*Agrimex Ltd v Tradigrain SA* [2003] EWHC 1656 (Comm), see para.R60–15 below). Agreed fees cannot be challenged. While it is "theoretically" possible that a Scottish court might, under r.56(2)(b), decide that agreed fees are not properly payable, that would be an extraordinary position for any court to adopt.

R56–21 If the Auditor has already issued a determination under r.60(3) then, in practical terms, the court has no discretion to decide what fees and expenses are "properly payable" since that is, in effect, res judicata.

R56–22 There will be practical difficulties in enforcing an order under r.56 on an arbitrator who does not live in the UK.

Rule 56(3)

R56–23 As under s.56(4) of the 1996 Act, the court may not make such an order if there is available any arbitral process of review of the amount demanded. This is self-evident.

Rule 56(4)

R56–24 No appeal is possible under r.56, consistent with the policy throughout the 2010 Act that, other than in respect of rr.67/68/69, all first instance decisions are final. In contrast, although s.56(7) of the 1996 Act requires the applicant party to obtain the leave of the court to appeal its decision on such a matter, such an appellate process (as throughout the 1996 Act) can go as far as the UKSC.

Rule 57: Arbitration to end on last award or early settlement D

57.—(1) An arbitration ends when the last award to be made in the arbitration is made (and no claim, including any claim for expenses or interest, is outstanding).

(2) But this does not prevent the tribunal from ending the arbitration before then under rule 20(3) or 37(1).

(3) The parties may end the arbitration at any time by notifying the tribunal that they have settled the dispute.

(4) On the request of the parties, the tribunal may make an award reflecting the terms of the settlement and these rules (except for rule 51(2)(c) and Part 8) apply to such an award as they apply to any other award.

(5) The fact that the arbitration has ended does not affect the operation of these rules (in so far as they apply) in relation to matters connected with the arbitration.

DEFINITIONS

"arbitration": ss.2(1), (2), 31(1)
"party": ss.2(1), 31(1), (2)
"rules": ss.7, 31(1)
"tribunal": ss.2(1), 31(1)

STATUS

Rule 57 is a default rule so can be disapplied in whole or in part, or modified in any way, by the parties (s.9 refers). **R57–01**

If a tribunal decides not to seek the payment of a deposit to cover its fees and expenses, it may wish to ask parties as part of its terms and conditions to modify this r.57 to allow it, following notification of settlement, to make an award in respect of the parties' liability to it for fees and expenses. **R57–02**

MODEL LAW

Article 32 of the Model Law ("Termination of Proceedings") expressly addresses termination. **R57–03**

COMMENTARY

Rule 57(1)

Article 32 Model Law contrasts with the 1996 Act, since it was necessary, for three main reasons, to provide that the final award terminates proceedings: first, fix a date when the proceedings did indeed terminate; secondly, to make it clear that the tribunal became, on that date, *functus officio;* and thirdly, to provide a clear starting point for the running of time limits (see *Report of the Secretary General on the analytical commentary on the draft text of the Model Law on International Commercial Arbitration*, UN A/CN.9/264, paras 1, 2). Note that the 1996 Act does not deal explicitly with termination except in respect of settlement. **R57–04**

Rule 57 provides that no award can be a final award unless all claims have been disposed of, including any claim for interest or expenses. An expenses **R57–05** award may, under r.66, be made either together with or separately from an award on the substance, so it may be that an expenses award is the final award in an arbitration. An award of interest would, in practice, normally be made as part of an award on the merits, and the fact that the tribunal decides not to award interest would, given an express decision to that effect, not mean that the matter remained outstanding.

R57–06 No award can be a final award until exhaustion of the sequential processes (i) of correcting an award under r.58, and (ii) the court's possibly ordering, under r.71(8), the tribunal to state its reasons in more ("sufficient") detail; note that r.71(8) reflects art.34(4) of the Model Law. It may also be open to some other person or body to ask a tribunal to revise an award under institutional rules, e.g. under art.33 of the ICC Rules.

R57–07 The ICC example is one way the parties might vary the effect of r.57, otherwise the parties cannot disapply the logical conclusion that a tribunal which has dealt with all issues is functus officio. The Model Law is mandatory in this respect.

R57–08 The question of when a tribunal (other than as specified in r.9) becomes functus officio is a surprisingly difficult one as was demonstrated in *Martin Dawes v Treasure & Son Ltd* [2010] EWHC 3218 (TCC), where Akenhead J. opened by saying:

> "These claims raise interesting issues about the point or stage at which an arbitrator becomes *functus officio* or ceases to have jurisdiction and the extent, ambit or scope of a settlement of an arbitration."

He later said at [26]:

> "The efforts of experienced Counsel have failed to locate much of relevance by way of authority as to when and how an arbitrator becomes *functus officio*. This may not be altogether surprising because arbitrations and arbitration appointments vary and in almost every case, once the arbitration is over, the parties are usually delighted not to have to revert back to the arbitrator for any reason."

He also cited Merkin's *Arbitration Law* (2009), para.11.7 as providing some general light on the topic as well as *Russell on Arbitration*, 23rd edn, para.6–024.

R57–09 In that case, Akenhead J. drew the following conclusions at [29]:

> "(a) primarily, as arbitration is, usually, a consensual process, one must look to the contract between the parties pursuant to which the arbitrator has been appointed to determine what the parties have agreed, expressly or by implication, about when an arbitrator's jurisdiction becomes exhausted; (b) the settlement of a dispute after it has been referred to arbitration but before any final award does not generally,

and certainly does not necessarily, bring to an end to the jurisdiction. S.51 suggests that even if the dispute is settled there remains a jurisdiction to terminate the substantive proceedings and to resolve issues of costs or indeed any other matters remaining in dispute at that time. That jurisdiction is not expressed to be statutorily limited."

Rule 57(2)

Rule 57(1) is subject to the qualification that the tribunal may already have ended the arbitration, either under r.20(3) by having ruled that it does not have jurisdiction or under r.37 where it has decided that the claimant has delayed unnecessarily in pursuing or submitting a claim. In the former case, the arbitration would revive if a court ruled under r.21(1) that the tribunal did have jurisdiction. **R57–10**

Rule 57(3)

Rule 57(1) is also subject to the qualification that the parties can agree to end the arbitration by notifying the tribunal that they have settled the dispute. Notification requires a "notice" in terms of r.83, i.e. must be a formal communication in writing and delivered as contemplated by that rule. Article 30(1) of the Model Law places the obligation on the tribunal to terminate the proceedings when a settlement is reached. If it does not, the authors submit that proceedings terminate anyway since there is no dispute left to arbitrate so that the tribunal has no continuing jurisdiction. The authors submit that the approach of r.57(3) is preferable in this regard. **R57–11**

Rule 57(4)—Settlement in the form of an award

The parties may wish their settlement to be recorded in the form of an award (a "consent award") both because the matter then becomes res judicata and because such an award is immediately enforceable, e.g. via the New York Convention. Article 30(1) of the Model Law has the same effect, as does s.51 of the 1996 Act. **R57–12**

It had originally been suggested that the Model Law should empower the tribunal to record a settlement in the form of an award unless the parties had provided otherwise (see *Report of the Working Group on International Contract Practices on the work of its third session*, UN A/CN.9/216, para.96), but since the parties may not always wish this to happen, the more sensible view prevailed that the parties should have to request this step. **R57–13**

It had also been suggested that it should be enough that one party should request that their settlement be recorded in the form of an award, given that only the party seeking enforcement had an incentive to take this step (*Report of the Working Group on International Contract Practices on the work of its fourth session*, UN A/CN.9/232, para.174). Once again, however, this view did not prevail, since "a settlement may be ambiguous or subject to **R57–14** conditions that may not be apparent to the arbitral tribunal", so that there were, "fewer dangers of injustice by requiring both parties to request [such] an award" (*Report of the Working Group on International Contract Practices on the work of its fourth session*, UN A/CN.9/232, para.174). The *travaux preparatoires* record, however, that the formal request for a settlement to be rendered as an award need only be made by one party, provided it is clear that the request expresses the will of both parties (*Report of the UNCITRAL on the work of its eighteenth session*, UN A/40/17, para.250). It remains to be seen whether a similar approach will be adopted under r.57(4).

Tribunal discretion

R57–15 The tribunal "may" make such an award, i.e. it has discretion in this matter. There may be good reasons why it may wish to decline to do so, e.g. where the settlement seems to be in restraint of trade or otherwise illegal or contrary to public policy. For example, there is evidence in the USA of wholly artificial arbitrations being constructed with fake parties, fictitious facts, fake documents etc. with a view to the tribunal ordering A to pay money to B in an award which A then enforces through the courts. Once the award is stamped by the court, A proceeds to B's bank and collects under what has become a court order so appears wholly legitimate but where the underlying objective is money-laundering and A and B are controlled by the same persons.

R57–16 One of the authors has been told by certain US arbitrators that they never issue consent awards for this reason; in the UK, an arbitrator who, however unwittingly or innocently, issues a consent award which is in fact a money-laundering scheme may have serious difficulties to face under the Proceeds of Crime Act 2002 and/or the Money-Laundering Regulations 2007 (SI 2007/2157). For further information and advice, readers are referred to the CIArb's Practice Guideline 12, "The Proceeds of Crime Act 2002: Guidance for arbitrators and mediators"; see *http://www.ciarb.org/resources/practice-guidelines-and-protocols/list-of-guidelines-and-protocols/* [Accessed June 19, 2014].

R57–17 Early in the drafting of the Model Law, the tribunal was to be permitted to decline to make such an award only if it had good reasons for doing so (*Note by UNCITRAL Secretariat on draft articles 25–36*, UN A/CN.9/WG.II/WP.38, art.33, alternative B), but it was recognised that such a qualification would be difficult to interpret and even more difficult to make effective (*Report of the UNCITRAL on the work of its eighteenth session*, UN A/40/17, para.249), so that the tribunal was, ultimately, left with complete discretion.

R57–18 The same position prevails under r.57(4) (and under s.51(2) of the 1996 Act); the tribunal may refuse to make such an award for any reason or for none.

R57–19 Since r.57 is a default rule, the parties could agree that, should they reach a settlement, the tribunal is to be bound to issue an award on those terms.

While such an agreement post-appointment could, prima facie, not bind the tribunal, if the tribunal clearly entered the arbitration on that basis, there is no obvious reason why they could not be bound thereto as a matter of contract at appointment. In practice, while the tribunal might still decline to make a consent award, it would then be in breach of contract. The parties could then remove the tribunal under r.12(1)(a) and appoint another who would be willing to render an award on agreed terms.

In the "theoretical" circumstance of a tribunal being trapped in the foregoing dilemma, it has a possible exit route by resigning pursuant to r.15(1)(e) and 15(2). **R57–20**

Tribunal promoting settlement

One situation where a tribunal might consider recording a settlement in the form of an award is where it has actively promoted that settlement (see Christopher Newmark and Richard Hill, "Can a Mediated Settlement Become an Enforceable Arbitral Award?" (2000) 16 Arbitration Int. 81 and the Centre for Effective Dispute Resolution's ("CEDR"), *Rules for the Facilitation of Settlement in International Arbitration*, found at http://www.cedr.com/about_us/arbitration_commission/Rules.pdf [Accessed June 19, 2014]). The latter are based largely on German and Swiss practice in both litigation and (derived therefrom) in arbitration whereby judges (see §278 ZpO) and arbitrators play an active role in assisting the parties to settle. Note that this practice is wholly distinct from, and does *not* constitute, "mediation" as generally understood and practiced in the UK. **R57–21**

This book is not the place to enter into a discussion of the several difficult questions arising from a tribunal's adoption of a role as any one or more of settlement facilitator, conciliator or mediator. However, we note in passing that the decision in the English case of *Glencot Development and Design Co Ltd v Ben Barrett & Son (Contractors) Ltd* [2001] B.L.R. 207 places a serious difficulty (in that case, the adjudicator's decision was set aside because he had acted as mediator during the process before reverting to acting as adjudicator) on any arbitrator wishing to probe the boundary between arbitration and mediation. **R57–22**

In stark contrast, *Gao v Keeneye Holdings Ltd* [2011] HKCA 459 arose from the attempted enforcement in Hong Kong of an award issued under the auspices of the Xian Arbitration Commission (in the PRC), the rules of which, as is the norm in the PRC, expressly provide for the tribunal (often in the person of the chairman) to act as mediator and, following common PRC practice, that does not exclude the tribunal meeting one of the parties alone. **R57–23**

At first instance in Hong Kong, enforcement of the award was refused because the chairman's meeting one party in the absence of the other was held contrary to public policy. The judge said (at [99]):

"Second, it would, however, be wrong to uphold an award tainted by an appearance of bias. Upholding such an award will have the consequence that justice would not be seen to be done. Enforcement of such award would be an affront to this Court's sense of justice ... "

The Court of Appeal, with a very detailed survey of the authorities, reversed the first instance refusal, with Tang VP saying (at [106]):

"In the circumstance of this case, I am not satisfied that a sufficient case of apparent bias, contrary to the fundamental conceptions of moral and justice in Hong Kong, has been established such that it would be right for our court to refuse to enforce the Award."

This decision caused a significant shockwave through the Anglo-American arbitral community.

R57–24 A consent award is like any other award in terms of form and effect, save that the parties might not require reasons as would otherwise be required by r.51(2)(c). However, omission of reasoning could cause enforcement difficulties.

R57–25 There is no requirement in r.56 for a consent award to state that it is one but such would be normal practice, e.g. as required by art.26.9 of the LCIA Rules, whereas the DAC Report, para.244, explains why no such requirement was included in the 1996 Act. However, in England the Civil Procedure Rules (at CPR r.62.18.5) direct that where enforcement of a consent award is sought, the enforcement form must state that it is one. This might be of significance to third parties, such as insurers, who may be bound to compensate a party if he is found liable in litigation or arbitration but not if his liability is effectively self-admitted.

R57–26 Importantly, a consent award is not open to challenge under Part 8 of the Act. Despite the matter having been raised during the drafting of the Model Law (see *Report of the Working Group on International Contract Practices on the work of its sixth session*, UN A/CN.9/245, para.107), ultimately the Model Law made no provision for challenges of such awards, leaving the issue hanging in the air. Although the position under r.57(4) has the merit of certainty, it means of course that such an award is unchallengeable even if it deals with matters which are not arbitrable under Scots law, or if it is illegal or contrary to public policy. This means that the focus then shifts to whether such an award is enforceable (see DAC Report, paras 373–374).

R57–27 As in the Model Law and the 1996 Act, r.57 appears to contemplate only a final settlement of the dispute, and does not provide for a part settlement to be expressed as an award. Since r.57 is a default rule, it is open to the parties to agree that the rule be extended to cover consent part awards.

Rule 57(5)

Although the arbitration has ended, some of the SAR (but nowhere is it stated which ones) must remain in force to govern such issues as recourse against the award, liability for fees and expenses, and other relevant matters. Section 51(5) of the 1996 Act provides merely that the provisions as to costs remain in force in so far as costs have not been dealt with by the settlement. While the simpler approach of the 1996 Act may appeal, the advantage of r.57 is that, being completely flexible, it covers the possibility of an unexpected requirement to resuscitate one or more SAR.

R57–28

Rule 58: Correcting an award D

58.—(1) The tribunal may correct an award so as to—
  (a) correct a clerical, typographical or other error in the award arising by virtue of accident or omission, or
  (b) clarify or remove any ambiguity in the award.

(2) The tribunal may make such a correction—
  (a) on its own initiative, or
  (b) on an application by any party.

(3) A party making an application under this rule must send a copy of the application to the other party at the same time as the application is made.

(4) Such an application is valid only if made—
  (a) within 28 days of the award concerned, or
  (b) by such later date as the Outer House or the sheriff may, on an application by the party, specify (with any determination by the Outer House or the sheriff being final).

(5) The tribunal must, before deciding whether to correct an award, give—
  (a) where the tribunal proposed the correction, each of the parties,
  (b) where a party application is made, the other party,
a reasonable opportunity to make representations about the proposed correction.

(6) A correction may be made under this rule only—
  (a) where the tribunal proposed the correction, within 28 days of the award concerned being made, or
  (b) where a party application is made, within 28 days of the application being made.

(7) Where a correction affects—
  (a) another part of the corrected award, or
  (b) any other award made by the tribunal (relating to the substance of the dispute, expenses, interest or any other matter),
the tribunal may make such consequential correction of that other part or award as it considers appropriate.

(8) A corrected award is to be treated as if it was made in its corrected form on the day the award was made.

DEFINITIONS

"Outer House": s.31(1)
"party": ss.2(1), 31(1), (2)
"tribunal": ss.2(1), 31(1)

STATUS

R58–01 Rule 58 is a default rule so can be disapplied in whole or in part, or modified in any way, by the parties (s.9 refers). If the parties have agreed to adopt well known arbitral rules, they will usually have provisions relating to the correction and interpretation of awards (e.g. art.19 SAC07, arts 37 and 38 of the UNCITRAL Rules, art.35 of the ICC Rules, and arts 35 and 36 of the Swiss Rules). Article 27 LCIA Rules does not provide for the "interpretation" of an award but instead allows for the correction of "any ambiguity" in the award.

R58–02 A common feature of all of these rules is that they empower correction of "errors in computation, any clerical or other typographical errors or any errors of similar nature" in line with art.33(1)(a) of the Model Law. Such rules may be seen as modifying and restricting the scope of r.58(1)(a), given its wide scope. The origin of the provisions on the "interpretation" of awards also lies in the Model Law and, if adopted, such provisions will also modify the scope of r.58(1)(b).

MODEL LAW

R58–03 Article 33 of the Model Law allows a party to request the arbitral tribunal:

- to "correct in the award any errors in computation, any clerical or other typographical errors or any errors of similar nature";
- provided that the parties agree, to give "an interpretation of a specific point or part of" an award;
- to make an additional award to cover claims omitted from the award (as in s.57(3)(b) of the 1996 Act).

Rule 58 appears to give greater powers of correction and clarification to the tribunal than the Model Law.

COMMENTARY

R58–04 At common law the authorities were divided as to whether a tribunal did or did not have power to correct clerical errors and errors of calculation in its award (compare *Simpson v Strachan* (1736) Mor. 17007; *MacBryde v Macrae's Executors* (1748) Mor. 657; *Nasmyth v Magistrates of Glasgow* (1777) 5 Br. Supp. 427); importantly, there was no clear authority to support such a power. The creation of an express, detailed statutory power is an important step forward.

Equally important is the new r.58 power, certainly absent from the common law, to clarify an award so that if an award could not be saved by a court imposing a commonsense construction (see Lord Cowan in *Patrick v McCall* (1867) 4 S.L.R. 12 at 13), it would have to be held to be void from uncertainty (*McKenzie v Aberdeen and Inverness Junction Railway Co* (1866) 4 M. 810). **R58–05**

The r.58 powers extend also to part and provisional awards. Where a party has recourse in respect of an award under r.58 but does not exercise that recourse, any subsequent appeal against the award in respect of the matter that could have been cured by r.58 is incompetent (see r.71(2)). **R58–06**

While s.57 of the 1996 Act is very similar to r.58, it is not as broad in its scope. **R58–07**

Both art.33 and s.57 also empower the tribunal to make an additional award to cover any matter submitted to the tribunal but omitted from the award, but r.58 includes no such power. Instead, under r.58 the tribunal can simply correct the award by adding the matter omitted from it, if appropriate. **R58–08**

The question of whether the tribunal is entitled to charge further fees for the making of such corrections or clarifications has different answers. While fees in certain types of arbitration are paid on an ad valorem basis (e.g. ICC and SIAC), most are paid on hourly rates (LCIA, HKIAC, CIETAC, CEAC) but, with one exception, the authors are unaware of any provision in any such set of rules, or in any arbitral statute, preventing the earning of additional fees. The exception is UNCITRAL Arbitration Rules (1976) art.40(4) and (2010) art.40(3). **R58–09**

The award does not cease to be binding merely because a party has sought a correction or clarification, and the other party is not prevented from seeking to enforce the award. However, the fact that such a request is under consideration obliges the court to defer any decision on enforcement until the issue is disposed of: see s.12(2)(c). **R58–10**

Rule 58(1)(a)—Correcting errors

A tribunal may correct a clerical or typographical error arising from accident or omission. Article 33(1)(a) of the Model Law refers to "errors in computation, any clerical or typographical errors or any errors of a similar nature", whereas s.57(3) of the 1996 Act refers only to a clerical error, while it is clear, however, that s.57(3) would embrace any computational or typographical error (see *Omnibridge Consulting Ltd v Clearsprings (Management) Ltd* [2004] EWHC 2276 (Comm)). **R58–11**

Rule 58(1)(a)'s reference to "other error" clearly extends to a computational one but a question arises as to how widely "other error" can be **R58–12** interpreted, particularly given that there is no suggestion that this error should be of the same kind as a clerical or typographical error.

R58–13 Rule 58(1)(a) does not allow an arbitrator to rewrite a determination but it does provide significant corrective powers beyond minor matters such as typographical errors (*Arbitration Application No.1 of 2013* [2014] CSOH 83 at [15] per Lord Woolman). In that case, the question was whether it had been open to the appellant to have applied under r.58 seeking clarification of arguably incomplete or absent reasons for the award. That question did not require to be decided but Lord Woolman expressed the view that the provision, by the rule, of "significant corrective powers" implemented the philosophy that arbitration is intended to be a stand-alone process with its own remedial mechanisms (*Arbitration Application No.1 of 2013* (above) at [15]). This supports a wide interpretation of "other error" arising by virtue of "accident or omission" provided that it does not involve a re-writing of the award. Given that, if the error does not involve an omission, it must arise through "accident", the authors submit that the effect of r.58 is adequately controlled.

R58–14 For example, there is no r.58 correction available if the passage did express what the tribunal intended to say but it had reached those views on the basis of flawed reasoning or a mistaken understanding of the facts or the evidence (see *Fuga AG v Bunge AG* [1975] 2 Lloyd's Rep. 192; *Al Hadha Trading Co v Tradigrain SA* [2002] 2 Lloyd's Rep. 512). Lloyd L.J. suggested in *The Trade Fortitude* [1987] 1 W.L.R. 134 at 147 that, to be correctable, "it must be an error affecting the expression of the tribunal's thought, not an error in the thought process itself".

R58–15 The authors are aware of an arbitration where an item had to be computed for years 1 to 5 of a 5-year contract but the award stopped (by simple oversight) at year 2; the parties separately applied for a correction under s.57(3)(a) of the 1996 Act and this must be the correct answer,

R58–16 Further, even if the error is not one capable of correction by the tribunal even on a wide interpretation of "other error", then a solution is for the tribunal to admit the error so that the award may be challenged under r.68(2)(j)(i) on the basis that there has been an irregularity in the award that is admitted by the tribunal, and the tribunal may be ordered to reconsider the award under r.68(3)(b).

R58–17 However, it cannot be in the interests of ether party to go down the r.68(2)(a)(ii)/r.68(2)(e)/r.68(3)(b) road at no little cost and expense; common sense and commercial realities suggest that it is much better if the parties agree to allow the tribunal to make the correction under r.58

Rule 58(1)(b)—Clarifying award

R58–18 A tribunal may also clarify or remove any ambiguity in the award. The terms of s.57(3)(a) of the 1996 Act are identical and this approach is, the authors submit, preferable to art.33(1)(b) of the Model Law under which a party may request the tribunal to interpret a specific point of the award, but only if the parties agreed to the tribunal having this power.

Under the 1996 Act, it has been held appropriate for parties to seek clarification of the reasons for the award (*Torch Offshore LLC v Cable Shipping Inc* [2004] 2 All E.R. (Comm) 365) and indeed even to seek reasons where none have been provided (*Groundshire v VHE Construction* [2001] B.L.R. 395), but not to challenge the reasons provided where these were quite clear (see *World Trade Corp Ltd v Czarnikow Sugar Ltd* [2005] 1 Lloyd's Rep. 422). In the language of the rule, there must be an *ambiguity* which can be *clarified* or *removed*, hence the authors are unpersuaded by *Groundshire* but are ad idem with *World Trade*. **R58–19**

Equally where it was unclear whether a tribunal had dealt with an issue concerning interest, it was held that this was an ambiguity which could be resolved by an application under s.57(3)(a) (*Bulk Ship Union SA v Clipper Bulk Shipping Ltd* [2012] EWHC 2595 (Comm) at [31] per Popplewell J. Under r.58 the situations in *Groundshire* and *Bulk Union* could potentially be covered by r.58(1)(a) if not under r.58(1)(b) (see *Arbitration Application No.1 of 2013* (above)). **R58–20**

Rule 58(2)

The tribunal may make such a correction or clarification on its own initiative, or on the application by any party, mirroring the position under s.57(3)(a) of the 1996 Act, but in each case further conditions require to be met. A tribunal may make a correction on its own initiative where, for example, it realises that an error has been made, or where a party informally queries an award and it becomes evident that there has been an error. If both parties agree that there has been an error and insist that it should be corrected, the tribunal may do so on its own initiative, but the rule contains no provision compelling it to do so; see the commentary to r.58(4) at para.R58–23 below. **R58–21**

Rule 58(3)

A party making an application must, simultaneously with making the r.58 application, send a copy thereof to the other party or parties. The rule contains no provision for sanction for failure in this obligation but there might conceivably be adverse consequences if the disadvantaged party is thereby deprived of a reasonable opportunity to make representations regarding the proposed correction (see the discussion of a similar requirement under the Model Law at *Report of the Working Group on International Contract Practices on the work of its seventh session*, UN A/CN.9/246, para.124). In any event, as a practical matter, the chairman of the tribunal will automatically acknowledge receipt of the application and will copy that acknowledgement to the other party. It follows that the "conceivable adverse consequences" *should* never arise in practice. **R58–22**

Rule 58(4)

R58–23 An application must be made within 28 days of the award. This must mean within 28 days of the "making" of the award under r.51(3), assuming that that rule has not been modified, but the sheriff or Outer House may extend that period on application by a party. Since this is a default rule, the parties may agree upon a longer or shorter period, and/or exclude the power of the court. If they arbitrate under certain institutional rules, they will impliedly agree on a longer period (see, e.g. Arbitration Rules of the Stockholm Chamber of Commerce r.20).

R58–24 If the 28 day period is to be extended, an application should be made to the court within the 28 days. This is consistent with the principle in s.1(a) and is not a difficult requirement. For the procedure in applying to the court, see the commentary on r.44 which applies equally to r.58(4)(b).

R58–25 The reference to 28 days "of" the award can mean only from the date when it is "made" since all other dates are irrelevant. In the context of the 1996 Act, it has been held (but, perhaps, questionably in black-letter law terms) that if the application has been made timeously, the tribunal should consider all potential errors or ambiguities drawn to its attention even if some are not raised until after the expiry of this period (*RC Pillar & Sons v Edwards* [2002] C.I.L.L. 1799). Obviously, in such a case the tribunal should give the other party a proper opportunity to make representations regarding such matters, including the matter of whether apparently out-of-time submissions should be allowed

Rule 58(5)

R58–26 A tribunal may decide that a correction is appropriate or that no correction is necessary at all, but before reaching such a decision it must give the parties, or the other party when one has applied for a correction, a reasonable opportunity to make representations about the proposed correction. Obviously, for this to happen the parties must be made aware of the proposed correction, and the parties will not be treated fairly in terms of r.24(1)(b) if this was not properly done, or the parties were given insufficient time in which to make representations.

R58–27 The same would, of course, apply if this was the effect of a party failing to copy the application for a correction to the other but (per para.R58–21) this is, in practice, a non-issue.

R58–28 There is a question as to whether if, after considering an application for a correction, the tribunal still left a glaring error in place, the award could be appealed successfully. In *Danae Air Transport SA v Air Canada* [2000] 1 W.L.R. 395 the tribunal had issued a draft award in which it made a glaring arithmetical error in finding that the claimants had not bettered the respondents' Calderbank offer (akin to a tender), and awarding significant costs to the respondents. Despite submissions pointing out the mistake it was not corrected. The Court of Appeal, under the pre-1996 Act legislation not repeated in the 1996 Act, found the error to be a "procedural mishap" and remitted the costs issue to the tribunal. It is difficult to see how such an outcome could occur under the 2010 Act given that tribunals are masters of the facts and are entitled to err in deciding them.

The tribunal would have a similar discretion as to whether to make a clarification and, if it declines to do so, a party's only recourse is to challenge the award under r.68(2)(e) (on the basis that it is uncertain or ambiguous in its effect) or r.68(2)(h). It has been held in England that a party should not challenge the award under the 1996 Act equivalent of r.68(2)(e) without first seeking a clarification from the tribunal (*Gbangola v Smith and Sheriff Ltd* [1998] 3 All E.R. 730), unless the award is plainly "unsalvageable" (*Sinclair v Woods of Winchester Ltd* [2005] EWHC 1631 (QB) at [38])) and indeed r.71, in indicating that an appeal under rr.67–69 is only competent where an appellant has exhausted any available arbitral process of appeal or review, expressly requires exhaustion of any recourse available under r.58. **R58–29**

While in terms of r.71(4)(a) an appeal must be made no later than 28 days after the award takes effect, under r.71(4)(b) if there has been an arbitral process of appeal or review, the 28 day period runs from the date when the appellant is notified of the result of that process. Thus, should the correction of the award itself create a ground of appeal, a party's position is protected. **R58–30**

Rule 58(6)

The time limit for making such a correction is fairly tight, given the need to allow representations to be made: 28 days of the award, if the correction is made on the tribunal's own initiative, otherwise 28 days of the application being made. The parties may agree on a different period (see *Home of Homes Ltd v Hammersmith and Fulham London Borough Council*, 92 Con. L.R 48), and will do if they arbitrate under certain arbitration rules (e.g. UNCITRAL Arbitration Rules (1976) art.36; (2010) art.37(2)), while other rules see the tribunal being accorded discretion to extend the period (e.g. LMAA Terms, para.25). **R58–31**

Nowhere does the Act provide that the Sheriff Court or Outer House may extend this period, by contrast with s.79 of the 1996 Act which confers a general power on the court to extend time limits imposed by the Act or the parties, while art.33(4) of the Model Law gives the tribunal itself power to extend the time limit for making a correction "if necessary". The framers of the Model Law thought that it was particularly important for this power to exist in the context of international arbitration since it might occasionally be difficult to comply with the 30 day time limit which the Model Law would otherwise impose (see *Analytical Commentary on Article 33*, UN A/CN.9/264, para.4). It is clear from the general context of the Act that this inability of any court to modify the time limit is deliberate in order to expedite the process. **R58–32**

Rule 58(6) is very similar to s.57(5) of the 1996 Act, and was practically **R58–33** identical until, midway through the parliamentary process, the 28 day time limit under r.58(6)(b) was altered from running from the date when the tribunal received the application to running from the date when the application was made. The authors submit that this fits rather better with the overall scheme of the Act, especially r.83, dealing with formal communications, including applications. In particular, r.83(5)(b) indicates that where a formal communication is posted it is treated as having been served on the day on which it would be delivered in the ordinary course of post and says nothing about when such a communication is treated as having been "received", an issue which has caused difficulty in England (see *RC Pillar & Sons v Edwards* [2002] C.I.L.L. 1799). The current approach allows the 28 day period to be measured with a degree of certainty, albeit that it might make the 28 day period rather tight, especially where, as in the *Pillar* case, the arbitrator is out of the office for a significant period.

R58–34 Correction is achieved through the delivery of the corrected award (rr.51(3) and 83 refer). That will then trigger the time limits for appeal under r.71(4) (see commentary thereon). If the tribunal is concerned that it might not be able to comply with the time limit for correction it should inform the parties and seek their agreement to an extension. Equally, the parties should be pro-active and try to find out any reason for non-compliance and, if it is appropriate, agree an extension.

R58–35 If there is non-compliance with the time limit, no extension agreed, and continuing delay by the tribunal in making a decision the parties may be placed in a difficult position where the only remedy would be the "nuclear" one of removal of the tribunal.

Rule 58(7)

R58–36 This is a provision with no counterpart in either the 1996 Act or the Model Law but is a necessary addition to cover the lacuna revealed in *Gannet Shipping Ltd v Eastrade Commodities Inc* [2002] 1 Lloyd's Rep. 713. In that case, the arbitrator corrected (under s.57) a simple error in his award but that led him to revise, in consequence, the principle of his costs award. The 1996 Act makes no provision for such a consequential amendment.

R58–37 Rule 58(7) therefore recognises that a correction may entail consequential corrections elsewhere in the award or in an earlier award and empowers the tribunal to make such corrections. Applying r.58(5), the parties are entitled to be made aware of these proposed consequential corrections and to have a reasonable opportunity to make representations about the proposed corrections.

Rule 58(8)

Any correction is to have retrospective effect and to be treated as part of the award from the day the award was made, in the sense of signed by the parties (r.51 refers). To suggest otherwise, the authors submit, would be nonsensical. **R58–38**

Part 7
Arbitration Expenses

Rule 59: Arbitration expenses D

59. "Arbitration expenses" means—
   (a) the arbitrators' fees and expenses for which the parties are liable under rule 60,
   (b) any expenses incurred by the tribunal when conducting the arbitration for which the parties are liable under rule 60,
   (c) the parties' legal and other expenses, and
   (d) the fees and expenses of—
       (i) any arbitral appointments referee, and
       (ii) any other third party to whom the parties give powers in relation to the arbitration,

for which the parties are liable under rule 60.

DEFINITIONS

"arbitral appointments referee": ss.22, 31(1), r.7
"arbitrator": ss.2(1), 31(1)
"party": ss.2(1), 31(1), (2)
"tribunal": ss.2(1), 31

STATUS

This is a default rule so it is open to the parties to modify it, agree something different or disapply it completely (see s.9). The default status is necessary because the term "arbitration expenses" is used in rr.61, 62 and 64–66, which are themselves all default rules. **R59–01**

The parties can agree some different definition of "arbitration expenses", e.g. if they had adopted the UNCITRAL Rules art.40 provides a definition of "costs", and arts 41–43 provide specific rules in relation to expenses. **R59–02**

MODEL LAW

There is no provision in the Model Law dealing with expenses (costs), principally because no consensus could be reached in 1985 on how to handle expenses, the "winner takes all" approach common (but not universal) in common law jurisdictions while being rejected by most (but not all) civil law jurisdictions. In most states of the USA, the parties' costs in arbitration fall **R59–03** where they lie since US litigation does not normally award costs in either direction. The authors understand that, in the Philippines, anything other than a 50:50 split is unlawful being in contravention of the Civil Code.

COMMENTARY

R59–04   Rule 59 defines the critical concept of "arbitration expenses", in brief the whole costs of the persons and entities, other than the courts, carrying out functions in connection with the arbitration, i.e. the parties, the tribunal, any AAR, any appointing body or administering institution and any other third party empowered by the parties in relation to the arbitration.

R59–05   Although not treated differently in r.59, it will be helpful in practice to distinguish between: (i) arbitration expenses excluding the parties' legal and other costs and (ii) such excluded costs; this is because, in practice different considerations will apply to these two categories

R59–06   A question may arise as to the scope of the phrase "parties' legal and other expenses", in particular whether these include the expenses of any court proceedings ancillary to the arbitration. In *McQuater v Fergusson*, 1911 S.C. 640 it was held that the phrase, "the expenses of and incidental to the arbitration" did not include the expenses of a stated case to the court under an equivalent of r.41 on the basis that Parliament did not indicate that the usual rule that the expenses of a court process should be determined by the court should be departed from.

R59–07   The authors submit that the words "incidental to the arbitration" fall to be implied in the phrase, "parties' legal and other expenses" and that the rationale of *McQuater* applies to exclude the expenses of court proceedings from the concept of "parties' legal and other expenses" and, therefore, from the concept of "arbitration expenses" as a whole, at least unless the parties agree to modify r.59(c) to include court expenses which are incidental to the arbitration.

R59–08   English authority supports the authors' approach in para.R59–07; see *Marc Rich & Co AG v Beogradska Plovidba (The Avala)* (1994) 1 Lloyds Rep. 363.

R59–09   Parties' "other expenses" may include witness costs, fees of professional witnesses, travelling and accommodation costs of parties, witnesses, lawyers and administrative costs such as copying charges, telephone and other communication media charges, recording of evidence charges and so forth. They may be substantial. For an early example of a claim for the time of non-professional witnesses in an arbitration being disallowed see *Younger v Caledonian Railway Co* (1847) 10 D. 133.

R59–10   There is continuing English and international debate on whether contingency/conditional fee arrangements ("CFAs"), success fees and the like fall within "arbitration expenses" and no firm consensus has been reached. In simplified terms, one approach is that if a party pays £X to its solicitors by way of fees, that is a valid arbitration expense irrespective of how X is arrived at whereas the main opposing argument is that "costs" can be measured only in terms of hours worked and that percentage uplifts, etc. are not "expenses".

In England and Wales, s.58 of the Courts and Legal Services Act 1990 **R59–11** recognised CFAs in litigation and s.58A (inserted by s.27 of the Access to Justice Act 1999) gave statutory effect to the Court of Appeal's decision in *Bevan Ashford v Geoff Yeandle (Contractors) Ltd* (1998) 3 All E.R. 238 that s.58 extended to arbitration despite not expressly referring thereto. No equivalent extension has been made to the uplift for speculative fees enabled by s.36 of the Law Reform (Miscellaneous Provisions) (Scotland) Act 1990.

In *Protech Projects Construction (Pty) Ltd v Al-Kharafi & Sons* [2005] **R59–12** EWHC 2165 (Comm), the arbitrator had considered claims for CFAs and had concluded that: (i) costs arising from CFAs should not be disallowed as a matter of principle (see above); and (ii) whether uplifts above normal rates should be allowable was subject to the "reasonable" cost test in s.63(5) of the 1996 Act.

In considering "reasonableness", the arbitrator said:

> " ... do [the CFAs] meet the test of 'reasonable' costs as set out in Article 31.1 of ICC Rules? In my view they do not. These are not CFAs where work is undertaken below normal rates but uplifted on success. These are CFAs which effectively double normal fee rates. The justification given [by Al-Kharafi ... referred to the] risks involved in international arbitration, risks in enforcement of awards overseas [and] postponement of fee recovery. I am not persuaded that the risks in international arbitration justify, and/or make reasonable, fee uplifts of the amounts claimed in this arbitration. Nor am I persuaded that enforcement risks justify, and/or make reasonable, such uplifts. As to postponement of fee recovery I am not persuaded that the costs of such an arrangement are costs within the ambit of Article 31 of ICC Rules whether they be included within a CFA or otherwise."

On a s.68 challenge, Langley J. agreed with Counsel for Al-Kharafi that "incurred" meant incurred by the party (or client) and carried the connotation of actual payment or an obligation to make payment, analogous to English law's indemnity principle. It followed that it was strongly arguable that costs that cannot be enforced against a client are not "incurred" by the client. Further, the judge saw no substantial injustice to Al-Kharafi in having to meet the award of costs which the arbitrator had in fact made which had excluded any mark-up or success fee, those costs being reasonably charged. Al-Kharafi's being deprived of an unexpected and unearned bonus did not readily constitute substantial injustice.

The judge considered the authorities, including *Sharrat v London Bus Co Ltd* [2003] EWCA Civ 718; *Spencer v Wood* [2004] EWCA Civ 352, but, obiter, he said that these were personal injury actions whereas, in a commercial arbitration, different considerations might, at least arguably, apply. More importantly, consideration of the very different facts of the present case was, the Judge thought, of some relevance to the overall consideration of "substantial injustice" with which the court was ultimately concerned on hearing a s.68 challenge.

R59–13 The CIArb's Practice Guideline 9, although focused on ss.59–65 of the 1996 Act, offers helpful advice and guidance; see *http://www.ciarb.org/ information-and-resources/PracticeGuideline9.pdf* [Accessed June 20, 2014]. There is an important caveat in that some parts of that Practice Guideline, e.g. paras 4.8, 5.7.1.3, are inapplicable to Scotland.

Rule 60: Arbitrators' fees and expenses M

60.—(1) The parties are severally liable to pay to the arbitrators—
  (a) the arbitrators' fees and expenses, including—
    (i) the arbitrators' fees for conducting the arbitration,
    (ii) expenses incurred personally by the arbitrators when conducting the arbitration, and
  (b) expenses incurred by the tribunal when conducting the arbitration, including—
    (i) the fees and expenses of any clerk, agent, employee or other person appointed by the tribunal to assist it in conducting the arbitration,
    (ii) the fees and expenses of any expert from whom the tribunal obtains an opinion,
    (iii) any expenses in respect of meeting and hearing facilities, and
    (iv) any expenses incurred in determining recoverable arbitration expenses.

(2) The parties are also severally liable to pay the fees and expenses of—
  (a) any arbitral appointments referee, and
  (b) any other third party to whom the parties give powers in relation to the arbitration.

(3) The amount of fees and expenses payable under this rule and the payment terms are—
  (a) to be agreed by the parties and the arbitrators or, as the case may be, the arbitral appointments referee or other third party, or
  (b) failing such agreement, to be determined by the Auditor of the Court of Session.

(4) Unless the Auditor of the Court of Session decides otherwise—
  (a) the amount of any fee is to be determined by the Auditor on the basis of a reasonable commercial rate of charge, and
  (b) the amount of any expenses is to be determined by the Auditor on the basis that a reasonable amount is to be allowed in respect of all reasonably incurred expenses.

(5) The Auditor of the Court of Session may, when determining the amount of fees and expenses, order the repayment of any fees or expenses already paid

which the Auditor considers excessive (and such an order has effect as if it was made by the court).
(6) This rule does not affect—
(a) the parties' liability as between themselves for fees and expenses covered by this rule (see rules 62 and 65), or
(b) the Outer House's power to make an order under rule 16 (order relating to expenses in cases of arbitrator's resignation or removal).

DEFINITIONS

"arbitral appointments referee": ss.22, 31(1), r.7
"arbitrator": ss.2(1), 31(1)
"Outer House": s.31(1)
"party": ss.2(1), 31(1), (2)
"tribunal": ss.2(1), 31(1)

STATUS

This is a mandatory rule (see s.8) so the parties cannot disapply or modify it. Furthermore, s.8 prohibits disapplication or modification of any mandatory rule "by any other means", i.e. including waiver. **R60–01**

The authors submit, however, that s.8 does not prevent arbitrators and parties from agreeing to augment (but not to detract from or alter the substance of) r.60 by adding terms and conditions which legally bind both arbitrators and parties. The reason for r.60 being mandatory is to protect the interests of arbitrators, and any agreed addition to r.60 that does not detract from the protection given by the rule is entirely in accordance with the spirit of the rule. **R60–02**

Practice Guideline 3 issued by the CIArb (available at *http://www.ciarb.org/information-and-resources* [Accessed June 20, 2014]) assists arbitrators in formulating their terms and conditions and indicates what should be covered in an agreement between the parties and the tribunal. **R60–03**

It is recognised practice for arbitrators to require security for their fees and expenses, often by means of a cash sum to be lodged in the hands of an interest bearing account in trust for the parties; see, e.g. UNCITRAL Rules art.43. Both the ICC Rules at art.36 and the LCIA Rules at art.24 provide for the parties to make deposits against fees and expenses. Under the latter's art.24(3), the tribunal shall not proceed with the arbitration without ascertaining from the LCIA that it is in requisite funds. Analogously, the ICC Secretariat will not "transmit the file" to the tribunal (i.e. to commence the arbitration) until the requisite deposits have been made (art.16 refers). For ad hoc arbitrations, the CIArb provides a service as neutral depositholder. Further it was formerly common practice for arbitrators to hold parties' deposits in individual quasi client accounts (with one for each arbitration) where the monies were deemed held in trust for the parties. **R60–04**

However, modern money-laundering and related regulations now make this all but impracticable.

MODEL LAW

R60–05 There is no provision in the Model Law dealing with expenses, principally because no consensus could be reached in 1985 on how to handle expenses, the "winner takes all" approach common (but not universal) in common law jurisdictions while being rejected by most (but not all) civil law jurisdictions.

COMMENTARY

Introductory

R60–06 Rule 60 addresses the liability of the parties to the arbitration to pay for the fees and expenses of all those, i.e. the tribunal, any arbitral appointments referee and any other third party to whom the parties gave powers in relation to the arbitration, with a role in the arbitration. Rule 60 is not concerned with the parties' own legal and other costs.

R60–07 Rule 60 also addresses the rights of the arbitrators etc. to remuneration and reimbursement. Historically, under the common law, an arbitral tribunal had no implied right to remuneration, the presumption being that the work was to be done gratuitously. However, by the time of *Macintyre Brothers v Smith*, 1913 S.C. 129, that had been modified and the common law rule came to be that there was an implied term in the contract between the arbitrators and the parties that, where the arbitrator was a professional man, he was entitled to remuneration from the parties on a joint and several basis.

R60–08 Liability under r.60 will arise in every arbitration seated in Scotland although arbitrators can agree to reduce or even waive the parties' liability to them (i.e. agree that their fees will be £0), under r.60(3). Per para.R60–02, r.60 will normally be augmented by the parties' agreement to the arbitrator's terms and conditions. Similarly an AAR may charge a fee for the appointment service provided with terms and conditions attached.

Rule 60(1) and (2)

R60–09 The liability of the parties to an arbitrator is "several" rather than "joint and several" and it is unclear why r.60 does not simply—as the CIArb argued in the Bill's drafting phase—provide for the liability to be joint and several as was the case under the common law (*Macintyre Brothers v Smith*, 1913 S.C. 129). However, r.62(3) provides that until or unless an award is made under r.62(1) the parties are, *inter se*, liable for an equal share of any fees or expenses for which they are liable under r.60 (see para.R62–26). This somewhat circuitous drafting has the effect of making the liability under r.60 joint and several.

"Several" liability means that the arbitrator can claim the whole of his fees and expenses from any one of the parties (*Fleming v Gemmill*, 1908 S.C. 340 at 345) and the paying party must pay the whole amount without a right of relief against any other party unless or until the arbitrator makes an award under r.62(1) (or the equivalent institutional rule) making the other party partly liable for his fee.

Rule 60(3)

Rule 60(3) expresses the important principle that the quantum of fees and expenses and the payment terms payable to the arbitrators etc. shall be as agreed contractually by the parties and the arbitrators etc. before they are incurred, failing which not only the quantum but also the payment terms will be determined by the auditor of the Court of Session. From the point of view of all concerned, especially the arbitrators, it is highly desirable to agree the quantum of fees and terms of payment and all other matters between the parties and the arbitrators beforehand, a matter emphasised by the CIArb Practice Guideline (see para.R60–03).

Per r.60(3)(b), the auditor has jurisdiction only if the fees and expenses have not been contractually agreed. In *Hussman (Europe) Ltd v Al Ameen Development and Trade Co* [2000] 2 Lloyd's Rep. 83 at 99 (in relation to s.28(5) of the 1996 Act), it was held that the mere fact that the fees were paid through the medium of an arbitral institution did not mean that they had been contractually agreed with the arbitrators and therefore the court had the jurisdiction given to it under the equivalent provision of the 1996 Act to adjust the fees.

Rule 60(4) and (5)

Rule 60(4) and (5) provide for the situation where the fees and expenses or payment terms have not been agreed between the parties and the arbitrators. Rule 60(5) is one for arbitrators to watch since, on the face of it, it would appear to allow the auditor to reopen a payment of expenses that has been made with the agreement of both the parties and the arbitrator. It is suggested that if both parties and the arbitrator have agreed a payment of fees and expenses and it has been made, the auditor should be slow to order the arbitrator to repay that amount unless the payment was made by the parties under such error as to make it clearly equitable for such an amount to be repaid.

The Act does not provides for any appeal against the auditor's decision under r.60(4) and (5) and, while the auditor is not a "court" in the context of s.1(c), the authors submit that the auditor's decision is final and not open to any appeal, this view being wholly consistent with the overall policy of finality universally (save only rr.67/68/69) inherent to the Act. The authors can envisage, but do not accept, an alternative view that there is a possible remedy for either a party or an arbitrator to petition the Outer House for judicial review of the decision.

R60–15 In *Agrimex Ltd v Tradigrain SA* [2003] EWHC 1656 (Comm), Thomas J. reduced the expenses charged by the tribunal because they included an amount charged by an external solicitor employed by the tribunal to draft the award in legally appropriate form, which charge Thomas J. considered to be excessive. At [30]–[36] he also expressed a strongly negative view about tribunals employing external solicitors in such circumstances. He observed that he had no power under the 1996 Act to determine issues of liability as between the arbitrators and draftsman. See R32–08 to R32–10 for additional commentary on this case.

Rule 61: Recoverable arbitration expenses D

61.—(1) The following arbitration expenses are recoverable—
   (a) the arbitrators' fees and expenses for which the parties are liable under rule 60,
   (b) any expenses incurred by the tribunal when conducting the arbitration for which the parties are liable under rule 60, and
   (c) the fees and expenses of any arbitral appointments referee (or any other third party to whom the parties give powers in relation to the arbitration) for which the parties are liable under rule 60.

(2) It is for the tribunal to—
   (a) determine the amount of the other arbitration expenses which are recoverable, or
   (b) arrange for the auditor of the Court of Session to determine that amount.

(3) Unless the tribunal or, as the case may be, the auditor decides otherwise—
   (a) the amount of the other arbitration expenses which are recoverable must be determined on the basis that a reasonable amount is to be allowed in respect of all reasonably incurred expenses, and
   (b) any doubt as to whether expenses were reasonably incurred or are reasonable in amount is to be resolved in favour of the person liable to pay the expenses.

DEFINITIONS

"arbitration expenses": r.59
"Outer House": s.31(1)
"party": ss.2(1), 31(1), (2)
"tribunal": ss.2(1), 31(1)

STATUS

R61–01 This is a default rule so it is open to the parties to modify it, agree something different or disapply it completely (see s.9).

Many institutional rules contain detailed provisions on expenses. These include SAC 2007 art.20, the ICC Rules art.37, LCIA Rules art.28, and UNCITRAL Rules arts 41–43. In assessing the effect of these rules on r.61, the starting point is, as with all default rules, to begin with r.61 and then to assess the extent to which the parties' agreement of institutional rules has disapplied or modified r.61. **R61–02**

MODEL LAW

There is no provision in the Model Law dealing with expenses; see para.R59–03 above. **R61–03**

COMMENTARY

Rule 61 is important because it defines the quantum of expenses one party to the arbitration might recover from the other in terms of an award by the tribunal under r.62. The phraseology of r.61 is a little confusing in that not only is there no express reference to the parties' legal and other expenses but also r.61(1) may be perceived as excluding them. However r.61(2) refers to "other arbitration expenses" meaning anything in r.59 save what has already been dealt with in r.61(1) and r.59(c) covers the parties' legal and other expenses. **R61–04**

It is important to appreciate that neither the Act's provisions on recoverability nor those on cost-capping (see r.65) affect what a party can actually spend by way of its own legal and other expenses; this will be addressed in detail in the commentary on r.65. **R61–05**

Rule 61(1) and (2)

While r.61(1) and (2) together provide that all of the categories of arbitration expenses defined in r.59 are recoverable, the quantum of legal and other expenses of the parties recoverable is either to be determined by the tribunal under r.61(2)(a) (excluding the tribunal's own fees and expenses) or is to be referred by the tribunal to the auditor under r.61(2)(b). It is all but unknown for a tribunal in England and Wales to make a reference to the court under the equivalent s.63(4) of the 1996 Act and, the authors submit, having regard to its duty under r.24, a tribunal should not normally have recourse to r.61(2)(b) unless it could clearly be justified under r.24. Reference to the auditor should be the (rare) exception and certainly not routine. **R61–06**

One example possibly (but only possibly) justifying a r.61(2)(b) reference is an English-seated case where A claimed, in a single arbitration, many millions of dollars separately against each of B (25 per cent of $X) and C (10 per cent of the same $X) but C settled with A soon after lodging of claim and defences and the latter subsequently won a substantial award against B. There were, therefore, significant complications in allocating A's costs as **R61–07** between B and C, a matter wholly familiar to the taxing masters of the court but wholly novel to the majority of the tribunal.

R61–08 Rule 61(2) represents a welcome reform of the common law under which, if the tribunal made an award of expenses, it had to quantify those expenses in the award (*Younger v Caledonian Railway Co* (1847) 10 D. 133) or at least fix a means of those determining those expenses (*Paterson v Sanderson* (1829) 7 S. 616; *Deko Scotland Ltd v Edinburgh Royal Joint Venture*, 2003 S.L.T. 727 at 730). If the tribunal did not quantify the expenses or fix a means for their ascertainment, they were not recoverable unless, in the proceedings for recovery, the unsuccessful party waived its right to plead incompetency of recovery, in which event the court would remit the account of expenses sought to be recovered to its auditor of court for taxation (assessment). That is what occurred in the *Younger* case.

R61–09 Under the common law, it was open for the parties to agree to remit an account of expenses to taxation by an auditor of court. However, subject to compliance with its duties under r.24, r.61(2) specifically empowers only the tribunal, not the parties, to make the reference to the auditor in relation to the taxation of the "legal and other expenses" of a party.

R61–10 The expense incurred by the tribunal in the making of the reference is itself a recoverable arbitration expense under r.61(1)(b) combined with r.60(1)(b)(iv).

R61–11 If the tribunal arranges for the auditor to quantify the quantum of the recoverable legal and other expenses, that quantification is not open to appeal unless it was incorporated into the tribunal's award. As at para.R60–14 above, this is wholly consistent with the Act's ethos of allowing no appeals (save rr.67, 68, 69) from court decisions.

Rule 61(3)

R61–12 Both the tribunal and the auditor are given discretion as to how to assess and quantify the legal and other expenses of a party. They can either follow the default provisions of r.61(3)(a) and (b) or they can choose some other method of assessment or quantification. Fairness and good practice suggests that, if either the tribunal or the auditor are minded to choose another method of assessment or quantification, for example by reference to a "party-party" litigation basis, they should invite the parties to make representations as to the appropriateness of that basis and a failure to do so might render the subsequent award appealable under r.68 on the grounds of serious irregularity.

R61–13 Equally, if a party wishes assessment or quantification on a basis other than the default basis, they should apply to the tribunal (or auditor) for assessment or quantification on its proposed basis. A decision on the basis of assessment and quantification will also allow the parties to be able to estimate the quantum of expenses and assist them in reaching agreement as to quantification which in itself may save the expense of the tribunal or the auditor carrying out the task themselves.

Under the Scots common law there was little authority on how legal and **R61–14** other expenses of a party should be quantified. *Irons and Melville on Arbitration* took the view (at p.228) that assessment and quantification should be carried out on the same principles as litigation, that is to say that it should be carried out on the basis of restricted recovery by reference to a party-party scale rather than on an indemnity (agent-client) basis. That view was followed by Lord Drummond Young in *Deko Scotland Ltd v Edinburgh Royal Joint Venture*, 2003 S.L.T. 727.

However neither Irons and Melville nor the court in *Deko* had noticed **R61–15** that, in *Younger v Caledonian Railway Co* (1847) 10 D. 133, the Inner House had observed, in relation to an arbitration on the extent of compensation payable for compulsory purchase, that the phrase, "all the expenses of the arbitration and incident thereto" could cover a good deal of expense preparatory to the arbitration which would not be recoverable in an ordinary (party-party) account of expenses in a litigation (*Younger v Caledonian Railway Co* (1847) 10 D. 133 per Lord Justice-Clerk Hope at 137). This suggests that, at common law, the quantification of expenses in arbitration was not restricted by the rules relating to litigation, although it was clearly influenced by them.

With regard to the basis of assessment in r.61(3)(a) and (b) neither the **R61–16** tribunal nor the auditor are given any guidance on how reasonableness is to be assessed: everything will depend upon circumstances. However the reasonableness of any claim for an item of expense or for the quantum of that item must exist beyond any doubt, that being the effect of r.61(3)(b). That is not a test applied to the taxation of accounts of expenses in Scottish litigations. It appears to originate from s.63(5)(b) of the 1996 Act which in turn originates from r.44.4(2) and (3) of the CPR.

The authors submit that, in these circumstances, the presence of the test of **R61–17** "reasonableness" removes any need to imply an agreement for taxation on a litigation basis as occurred in *Cole v Silvermills Estates and Land Ltd* [2011] CSIH 37. In particular, the exercise of the power in r.61(2)(b) to remit to the auditor does not entail his being required to assess the expenses on a Court of Session litigation scale; the same applies if, by party agreement, the taxation is remitted to any third party such as counsel or a law accountant.

Importantly, the test of "reasonableness" also features in ICC Rules **R61–18** art.37.1 and UNCITRAL Rules art.41(1) and is very widely recognised in international arbitration. In a case before the Iran-US Claims Tribunal governed by the 1976 UNCITRAL Rules (art.38(c)) (separate opinion of Judge Holtzmann, reported in *Iranian Assets Litigation Reporter* 10860 at 10863; 8 Iran-US C.T.R. 329 at 332–333):

> "A test of reasonableness is not, however an invitation to mere subjectivity. Objective tests of reasonableness of lawyers' fees are well known. Such tests typically assign weight primarily to the time spent and complexity of the case. In modern practice the amount of time required

Arbitration (Scotland) Act 2010

to be spent is often a gauge of the extent of the complexities involved. When the Tribunal is presented with copies of bills for services, or other appropriate evidence, indicating the time spent, the hourly billing rate, and a general description of the professional services rendered, its task need be neither onerous nor mysterious. The range of typical hourly billing rates is generally known and, as evidence before the Tribunal in various cases including this one indicates, it does not greatly differ between the US and countries of Western Europe, where both claimants and respondents before the Tribunal typically hire their outside counsel. Just how much time any lawyer reasonably needs to accomplish a task can be measured by the number of issues involved in a case and the amount of evidence requiring analysis and presentation. While legal fees are not to be calculated on the basis of the pounds of paper involved, the Tribunal by the end of a case is able to have a fair idea, on the basis of submissions made by both sides, of the approximate extent of the effort that was reasonably required. Nor should the Tribunal neglect to consider the reality that legal bills are usually first submitted to businessmen. The pragmatic fact that a businessman has agreed to pay a bill, not knowing whether or not the Tribunal would reimburse the expenses, is a strong indication that the amount billed was considered reasonable by a reasonable man spending his own money or the money of the corporation he serves. That is a classic test of reasonableness."

R61–19 The basis of "reasonableness beyond doubt" should not be used to bring in a party-party litigation basis via the back door and, in principle there is no reason why a winning party cannot recover 100 per cent of his legal and other expenses.

R61–20 Frequently-occurring examples of questions that may arise in practice concerning what is/is not reasonable include: (i) in many domestic cases, was it necessary (i.e. was the cost reasonable?) for the party to be represented by an advocate *and* a solicitor?; (ii) was it reasonable to have commissioned a second expert opinion from (e.g.) two architects?; and (iii) was it reasonable to have stayed at a 5-star hotel and/or eaten at a Michelin-starred restaurant?

R61–21 It may be difficult to challenge the tribunal's award on assessment and quantification of recoverable expenses. The two possible routes are a serious irregularity appeal under r.68(2) perhaps under heads (a) (failure to follow r.61 or the arbitration agreement), (h) (failure to treat the parties fairly) or a legal error appeal under r.69. Since these heads refer to irregularities by the tribunal, they do not apply to the conduct of the auditor, an officer of the court. A r.68 appeal is the correct route: see para.R62–08.

Rule 62: Liability for recoverable arbitration expenses D

62.—(1) The tribunal may make an award allocating the parties' liability between themselves for the recoverable arbitration expenses (or any part of those expenses).

(2) When making an award under this rule, the tribunal must have regard to the principle that expenses should follow a decision made in favour of a party except where this would be inappropriate in the circumstances.

(3) Until such an award is made (or where the tribunal chooses not to make such an award) in respect of recoverable arbitration expenses (or any part of them), the parties are, as between themselves, each liable—
  (a) for an equal share of any such expenses for which the parties are liable under rule 60, and
  (b) for their own legal and other expenses.

(4) This rule does not affect—
  (a) the parties' several liability for fees and expenses under rule 60, or
  (b) the liability of any party to any other third party.

DEFINITIONS

"arbitration expenses": r.59
"party": ss.2(1), 31(1), (2)
"tribunal": ss.2(1), 31(1)

STATUS

This is a default rule so it is open to the parties to modify it, agree something different or disapply it completely (see s.9). **R62–01**

Many institutional rules contain detailed provisions on expenses. These include the SAC 2007 art.20, the ICC Rules art.37, the LCIA Rules art.28 and the UNCITRAL Rules arts 40–43. In assessing the effect of these rules on r.62 the starting point is, as with all default rules, to begin with r.62 and then to assess the extent to which the parties' agreement of institutional rules has disapplied or modified r.62. **R62–02**

MODEL LAW

This is no equivalent to this rule in the Model Law. See para.R59–03 above. **R62–03**

COMMENTARY

Introductory

Different countries have different provisions in relation to who is to bear the expenses of an arbitration. Under Scots common law a tribunal had an inherent power to award the expenses of the arbitration (*Pollich v Heatley*, **R62–04**

1910 S.C. 469 at 482) except as modified by agreement of the parties in their joint submission or reference to the tribunal.

R62–05 The award of the tribunal allocating liability for expenses may take place at the same time or before the award quantifying the expenses under r.61.

R62–06 Rule 62 does not contain any provisions in relation to appeals. An award of expenses under r.62, whether it be a part award or an award dealing with the whole of the recoverable arbitration expenses, is appealable under r.68. At common law the setting aside of an award in relation to expenses was not possible at all in relation to errors of law and there had to be some procedural irregularity or lack of jurisdiction or fundamental unreasonableness that rendered the award ultra vires.

R62–07 In England, in a controversial judgment in *Fence Gate Ltd v NEL Construction Ltd* (2001) 82 Con. L.R. 41, a TCC judge identified questions of law arising out of a costs award and said (at [30]):

> "An appeal arising out of a costs award may be brought: 'on a question of law arising out of an award' (section 69(1) of the Act) ... Further, a costs award may be made the subject of a challenge under section 68 of the Act on the ground of serious irregularity of a kind defined in section 68(2). As I have already stated, that section includes, as one of the defined specific grounds for challenge, a complaint that the arbitrator exceeded his powers."

Unfortunately, although the judge gave leave to appeal against his decision, the parties settled before the issue could be heard by the Court of Appeal so the decision was not reconsidered.

R62–08 The authors respectfully disagree with the learned judge. The structure of both ss.68 and 69 of the 1996 Act and rr.68 and 69, 70 make it plain that "errors of law" which fall within s.68 and r.68 (e.g. breach of natural justice (unfairness), or dealing with a matter not referred for decision) are to be dealt with by means of a serious irregularity appeal under s.68 or r.68 but errors in application of the substantive law to the merits are covered by the restricted legal error appeal provisions of s.69 and rr.60, 70. Errors in applying the SAR, e.g. rr.60, 61 and 62, in expenses awards fall clearly within r.68(2)(a)(ii).

R62–09 Where there was a statutory right to state a case to a court in relation to awards of expenses in workmen's compensation arbitrations, the Inner House held that an arbitrator had a right to be wrong and that the court would interfere only where it was plain that the tribunal had failed to apply the judicial principle in the award of expenses (see below at para.R62–15) (*McArdle v J&R Howie Ltd*, 1927 S.C. 779—appeal unsuccessful; contrasted with *O'Neill v Giffnock Collieries Ltd*, 1924 S.C. 376—appeal successful).

Arbitration (Scotland) Act 2010 (r.62)

Rule 62(1)—Allocation of liability between the parties

Rule 62(1) enables a tribunal to make an award allocating the parties' liability for the whole or part of the recoverable arbitration expenses, as specified in r.61. While r.62 is worded in the singular, it must be read with r.54 which allows the making of a part award on some of the matters to be decided in the arbitration and such "matters" include liability for expenses. **R62–10**

There would appear to be nothing to stop a tribunal from making a part award in relation to some specific aspect of the recoverable arbitration expenses. That was the case under the old Scots common law (*Apollo Engineering Ltd v James Scott Ltd*, 2008 S.L.T. 472). That part award would be subject to quantification and enforcement or appeal in the same way as an award dealing with all of the recoverable arbitration expenses in the arbitration. See para.R66–04 for an example of this. **R62–11**

An award of expenses may be made together with or separate from an award on the merits of the dispute (r.66). **R62–12**

The question arises whether, in the light of r.62(1), the tribunal must deal with expenses in order to exhaust the reference. At common law, in *Pollich v Heatley*, 1910 S.C. 469, an award was sought to be set aside on the ground that it did not deal with expenses but the Inner House rejected the application on the grounds that, while the tribunal had an inherent power to deal with expenses, since expenses were not sought in the parties' submission to the tribunal, the tribunal did not have to deal with them in order to exhaust the reference. **R62–13**

In *Grampian Regional Council v John G McGregor (Contractors) Ltd*, 1994 S.L.T. 133 at 138, Lord President Hope noted that whether the tribunal was obliged to deal with expenses depended on a construction of the submission being made to the tribunal. **R62–14**

These decisions are no longer good law since r.62(1) has to be read with r.57(1) which provides that "an arbitration ends when the last award to be made in the arbitration is made (and no claim, including any claim for expenses or interest, is outstanding)". Further, r.57(1) and r.62(1) are subject to r.68(2)(c) which provides that the tribunal's failure to deal with all the issues that were put to it constitutes a serious irregularity which, if causing substantial injustice, could give rise to an appeal. The tribunal is therefore obliged to award expenses if that matter is put to it, whether in the original submission or reference or pleadings or in a request during the course of the arbitral proceedings. Only if there is no mention of expenses at all (highly unlikely in practice) could a tribunal be justified in not dealing with expenses without the risk of an appeal under r.68(2)(c). **R62–15**

It follows that, if the parties settle the dispute, they should take care to deal with issues of expenses since if expenses have not been sought up to that point, a consent award could be made without any reference to expenses. **R62–16**

Rule 62(2)—The test for awards of expenses

R62–17 Rule 62(2) reflects the principle for the award of expenses in a Scots litigation, a principle stated as follows:

> "The principle upon which the Court proceeds in awarding expenses is that the cost of litigation should fall on him who has caused it. The general rule for applying this principle is that costs follow the event, the ratio being that the rights of parties are to be taken to have been all along such as the ultimate decree declares them to be, and that whosoever has resisted the vindication of those rights, whether by action or by defence is prima facie to blame. In some cases, however, the application of the general rule would not carry out the principle and the Court has always, on cause shewn, considered whether the conduct of the successful party, either during the litigation or in the matters giving rise to the litigation, has not either caused or contributed to bring about the law suit." (*Shepherd v Elliot* (1896) 23 R. 695 per Lord President Robertson at 696).

R62–18 That principle, focusing on who caused the litigation or procedural steps within it, was also reflected in the Scots common law approach to expenses in arbitration. Thus it was held that, where one party was entirely successful in the arbitral proceedings, the tribunal ought to award him the expenses unless there was something in his conduct to disentitle him to expenses or unless there was some other statable ground which rendered a departure from the ordinary rule desirable (*Feeney v Fife Coal Co*, 1918 S.C. 197 at 201).

R62–19 Rule 62(2) sets out the general rule which is that expenses should follow a decision made in favour of a party except where it would be inappropriate in the circumstances. The question is, in what circumstances would it be "inappropriate" that expenses should follow success? Applying the general principle relating to expenses, the circumstances will be ones where the unsuccessful party has not wholly caused the arbitration or certain steps of it, or in certain circumstances, where the successful party has caused the arbitration. This has been illustrated in cases where the unsuccessful party has made an offer to the successful party which has not been bettered by the award made to the latter.

R62–20 One way in which a respondent can protect itself against an award of expenses is to make a protective offer to the claimant (when made sealed and expressed to be "without prejudice save as to costs", known in England and elsewhere as a Calderbank offer—see *Calderbank v Calderbank* [1976] Fam. 93) in the hope that any ultimate award to the claimant will not exceed it and the claimant can therefore be held to have caused the arbitral procedure after the date of the offer. Calderbank offers can be made both before or after the commencement of proceedings.

The protective offer made after the commencement of Scots litigation is known as a "judicial tender" or "tender" where a defender offers to a pursuer a sum (inclusive of interest) plus expenses to date. The offer is lodged with the court in a sealed envelope. If, at the end of the litigation, the ultimate judgment is equal to or less than the amount offered (making due allowance for interest between the date of the offer and the date of the judgment), the defender is entitled to expenses from the date of the offer. **R62–21**

While it has been observed that there is no normal or general rule of practice in arbitrations relating to tenders (*Carnegie v Nature Conservancy Council*, 1992 S.L.T. 342), there is no reason in principle why tenders cannot be made in arbitrations with results similar to those in litigation. Indeed, Calderbank offers are understood to be very much the norm in English construction cases. **R62–22**

In contrast to Scots litigation, even once the arbitration has commenced it may not be necessary in all circumstances for the respondent to offer expenses to date. A Calderbank offer may be effective when made during, as well as before, the arbitration. In *Mikuta v William Baird & Co*, 1916 S.C. 194, the respondent offered, during the arbitration, a sum to the claimant but without an offer to pay expenses to date. If accepted the offer would have left the tribunal to decide the question of expenses. The claimant did not accept the offer and after obtaining from the tribunal a sum less than the sum offered, the tribunal awarded expenses to the claimant up to the date of the offer and to the respondent from the date of the offer. The basis of the award to the respondent was that it was likely that had the offer been accepted the tribunal would have awarded the claimant the expenses and that being the case it could be said, fairly, that the claimant had caused the procedure in the arbitration after that date. **R62–23**

Circumstances where it would be inappropriate for the general rule to apply have included, where before the arbitration the respondent offered to the claimant more than the claimant ultimately obtained and the unsuccessful respondent was awarded the expenses (*Murphy v Farme Coal Co Ltd*, 1918 S.C. 659). They might also include hearings that have been caused or in which time has been taken up by arguments in which both sides have enjoyed significant success where an award of no expenses might be appropriate. **R62–24**

It is important to remember that, if a party wishes to found on "inappropriate circumstances" or to rely on an offer in connection with a request for an award of expenses, it should bring the offer and the circumstances to the attention of the tribunal. In *Carnegie v Nature Conservancy Council*, 1992 S.L.T. 342 the petitioner failed to draw the tribunal's attention to the terms of the tender that was below the award and ended up with an award of no expenses due in respect of his legal costs. **R62–25**

Rule 62(3) and (4)

R62–26 Rule 62(3)(a) is necessary to allow for the parties' liabilities for the tribunal's fees and expenses to be joint and several. It is therefore a consequence of the curious omission of "joint liability" in r.60(1) (see para.R60–09). Rule 62(4)(a) does not be read as taking away the effect of r.62(3)(a). The reader is referred to the commentary to r.60 above.

R62–27 It is self-evident that parties must bear their own legal and other expenses until such time as an award is made transferring that liability or part of it to another party; as with several other "for the avoidance of doubt" provisions in the Act, this is helpfully restated in r.62(3)(b).

Rule 63: Ban on pre-dispute agreements about liability for arbitration expenses M

63. Any agreement allocating the parties' liability between themselves for any or all of the arbitration expenses has no effect if entered into before the dispute being arbitrated has arisen.

DEFINITIONS

"arbitration expenses": r.59
"dispute": s.2(1)
"party": ss.2(1), 31(1), (2)
"tribunal": ss.2(1), 31(1)

STATUS

R63–01 This is a mandatory rule which cannot be modified or disapplied by the parties.

MODEL LAW

R63–02 There is no equivalent to this rule in the Model Law.

COMMENTARY

R63–03 Rule 63 appears to be a straightforward import from English law in the shape of s.60 of the 1996 Act; there was no such rule under the Scots common law.

R63–04 The rationale behind the "English rule" is that there used to exist standard-form contracts which provided, in one way or another, that a precondition of a claimant was that it (e.g. a sub-contractor or supplier, i.e. generally the weaker party resorting to arbitration) had to bear not only the tribunal etc's fees and expenses but also all of its own costs irrespective of the outcome; this was perceived to be unfair. Rule 63 (and s.60) renders any such pre-dispute agreement void and that will leave the other provisions of the Act to apply in full.

When the Act reached the statute book, the rent review fraternity became **R63–05**
very unhappy with r.63 since it was reportedly common in commercial leases
for the parties to agree to bear their own legal and other costs in any
arbitration and share the arbitrators' costs 50:50. There are three responses
to this: first, such an arrangement is inconsistent with the general principle
of Scots law outlined at paras R62–10 to R62–16 above; second, it is open to
the parties in a rent review (or any other such) case to agree, after the
dispute has arisen, that that "norm" apply; third, r.62(2) empowers the
arbitrator to award expenses on some basis other than "expenses follow the
event" so it is open to any party to submit that "trade practices" should be
followed in which event r.47(3)(c) might be cited.

Rule 64: Security for expenses D

64.—(1) The tribunal may—
  (a) order a party making a claim to provide security for the recoverable arbitration expenses or any part of them, and
  (b) if that order is not complied with, make an award dismissing any claim made by that party.
(2) But such an order may not be made only on the ground that the party—
  (a) is an individual who ordinarily resides outwith the United Kingdom, or
  (b) is a body which is—
     (i) incorporated or formed under the law of a country outwith the United Kingdom, or
     (ii) managed or controlled from outwith the United Kingdom.

DEFINITIONS

"party": ss.2(1), 31(1), (2)
"tribunal": ss.2(1), 31(1)
"United Kingdom": s.5 and Interpretation Act 1978 Sch.1

STATUS

This is a default rule so it is open to the parties to modify it, agree **R64–01**
something different or disapply it completely (see s.9).

Some institutional rules, mainly those with a common law basis, provide **R64–02**
for security for expenses but it is not a universal clause. Whereas the LCIA
Rules art.25.2 provide for such security, the ICC Rules do not. In assessing
the effect of such rules on r.64, the starting point is, as with all default rules,
to begin with r.64 and then to assess the extent to which the parties'
agreement of institutional rules has (if at all) disapplied or modified r.64.

Since (e.g.) the ICC Rules do not address security for expenses, r.64 **R64–03**
applies unless disapplied (per s.9(2)) so, in any ICC arbitration in Scotland,
an express disapplication will be necessary.

MODEL LAW

R64–04 The Model Law provides for "interim measures" which are defined in art.17(2) as,

> "any temporary measure, whether in the form of an award or in another form, by which at any time prior to the issuance of the award by which the dispute is finally decided, the arbitral tribunal orders a party to ... (c) provide a means of preserving assets out of which a subsequent award may be satisfied".

R64–05 Under art.17(1), unless the parties otherwise agree, the tribunal is given power, at the request of a party, to grant such interim measures. Article 17E(1) provides that the tribunal may require that the applicant for an interim measure shall provide appropriate security in connection with that measure. Article 17F(2) empowers the tribunal to require any party to disclose promptly any material change in the circumstances on the basis of which the measure was requested or granted.

R64–06 The Model Law's provisions are limited to the provision of security by the applicant in connection with an application for an interim measure, e.g. where the applicant seeks the production of relevant evidence the production of which might entail some prejudice to the producing party, or where the applicant seeks an interim interdict which may turn out to be wrongful having regard to the final outcome. Rule 64 has a different focus being concerned with providing a remedy to respondents in relation to impecunious claimants. In the language of Scottish litigation, it is the equivalent of an order for caution for expenses as a condition precedent to further procedure.

COMMENTARY

Introductory

R64–07 Rule 64 represents an increase in the powers of the tribunal in comparison with the previous common law. In effect the tribunal is given a power similar to that of the court to order a party (usually a pursuer/claimant) to find caution for expenses. Unlike the court order, the tribunal's order, being for the "recoverable arbitration expenses" can include, for example, the fees and expenses of the tribunal itself and the other elements set out in r.59.

R64–08 The tribunal may not make the order on the sole ("only") ground that the party from whom security is sought is an individual who ordinarily resides outwith the UK or is a body which is formed under the law of a country outwith the UK or is managed or controlled from outwith the UK. The 1996 Act omitted the word "sole" for reasons explained in the DAC Supplementary Report at para.28 but that rationale was contradicted by the Court of Appeal in *Nasser v United Bank of Kuwait* [2001] EWCA Civ 556.

The tribunal's power is, therefore, more restricted than that of a court in a Scottish litigation where the party in question is resident outwith the EU or a country which is party to the Brussels or Lugano Conventions on jurisdiction and the enforcement of judgments. The court may require security (in the form of the sisting of a mandatary or the obtaining of caution for expenses) on that sole ground whereas the tribunal may not. **R64–09**

On one view the court, with the consent of the tribunal, has that power under r.46(1)(g) in relation to an arbitration but it is suggested that the better view is that the powers of the tribunal are as set out in r.64 and that the tribunal has no power under r.46(2) to consent to the court granting an order for caution for expenses or to sist a mandatary as it would in ordinary court litigation. See also the commentary to r.46(1)(g) above (paras R46–57 to R46–63). **R64–10**

Rule 64 does not set out the test which has to be met by a party, typically a respondent, seeking security for recoverable arbitration expenses. In Scots litigation the court applies a number of factors and weighs them against each other to assess the requirements of justice in the matter. In deciding where the interests of justice lie, a court will weigh up: **R64–11**

- the impecuniosity of the pursuer (impecuniosity alone may not be sufficient);
- the nature of the case being made by pursuer and whether it has prima facie merit;
- the conduct of the litigation by the pursuer; and
- other factors that are not exhaustive but which bear upon whether it is unfair in the circumstances for the defender to have to take the risk of not recovering his expenses if he is successful.

Each case will turn on its own facts but there are, however, some well established situations where courts have ordered the lodging of caution (security). Where the pursuer is insolvent in the sense that liabilities exceed assets (though not necessarily sequestrated by formal order) the court will order the lodging of caution. Where the pursuer is resident abroad in a country not in the EU or party to the Brussels or Lugano Conventions the court will order the lodging of caution in place of a mandatary (a Scottish agent who is liable for expenses) being required. Subject to the proviso in r.64(2), the approach of a court in a Scottish litigation may offer some guidance to parties and tribunals. For further information the reader is referred to the commentary in Ch.33 of *Greens' Annotated Rules of the Court of Session* (Edinburgh: W. Green). **R64–12**

The tribunal will necessarily be careful to specify in its order the form of the security and how it is to be provided. **R64–13**

Rule 65: *Limitation of recoverable arbitration expenses* D

65.—(1) A provisional or part award may cap a party's liability for the recoverable arbitration expenses at an amount specified in the award.

(2) But an award imposing such a cap must be made sufficiently in advance of the expenses to which the cap relates being incurred, or the taking of any steps in the arbitration which may be affected by the cap, for the parties to take account of it.

DEFINITIONS

"arbitration expenses": r.59
"party": ss.2(1), 31(1), (2)
"tribunal": ss.2(1), 31(1)

STATUS

R65–01 This is a default rule so it is open to the parties to modify it, agree something different or disapply it completely (see s.9).

R65–02 Institutional rules such as the LMAA's Small Claims Procedure (but neither the ICC Rules nor the LCIA Rules) include a cost cap; while it was originally proposed that the CIArb SSFARs should do so, the as-issued rules (2012) do not. In such situations, the starting point will be to consider the extent to which r.65 is inconsistent with or disapplied by any institutional rule.

MODEL LAW

R65–03 There is no equivalent provision in the Model Law; see the commentary to r.59 above (para.R59–03).

COMMENTARY

R65–04 This rule had no equivalent in Scots common law and is a straightforward import from of s.65 of the 1996 Act. Section 65 had its origin in the DAC Report, para.272, which stated:

> "We consider that such a power [in cl.65, equivalent to that contained in r.65], properly used, could prove to be extremely valuable as an aid to reducing unnecessary expenditure. It also represents a facet of the duty of the tribunal as set out in Clause 33 [equivalent to that contained in r.24]. The Clause enables the tribunal to put a ceiling on the costs so that while a party can continue to spend as much as it likes on an arbitration it will not be able to recover more than the ceiling amount from the other party. This will have the added virtue of discouraging those who wish to use their financial muscle to intimidate their opponents into giving up through fear that by going on they might be subject to a costs order which they could not sustain."

The purpose is to offer some protection to a financially weak party facing financially stronger opponents. The duty referred to in r.24 is that of conducting the arbitration without incurring unnecessary expense. **R65–05**

Section 65 of the 1996 Act has (as best the authors can ascertain) hardly been used at all (except via rules such as the LMAA SCP), although this may be due to some doubt as to how it is to be applied. Other ways of achieving (at least in part) the same outcome include: (i) limiting each party to a single expert; and (ii) disallowing recovery of unreasonably expensive legal representation in the assessment and quantification of expenses. **R65–06**

Indicative of the invisibility of s.65 of the 1996 Act in practice is the fact that the massive (2,800 responses) 10-Year Survey of the workings of that Act in 2006 did not even mention it. Further, one of the authors attended (in 2001) the annual seminar of the arbitration scheme of a well-known trade association where the distinguished panel, in response to a question from the floor, refused to accept that they even had the s.65 power until a copy of the 1996 Act was shown to them. **R65–07**

Rule 65 and s.65 of the 1996 Act differ in one significant respect in that the former requires an award, the latter merely a direction. With respect to the drafters of the Act, the latter is clearly the better approach. **R65–08**

Irrespective of the authors' views, r.65 (unless disapplied) does indeed require a part award to be made, we assume for "instant appeal" purposes under r.68. Such a part award would fix a figure for expenses that would then have to be applied (unless successfully challenged) in the final award on expenses. **R65–09**

It should be stressed that r.65 places no limit on what a party can actually spend on an arbitration, merely caps the liability of the other party to be liable for such expenses **R65–10**

That said, clearly a party may request the tribunal to make an expenses-capping award. Further, as part of the tribunal's duties under r.24, in appropriate cases it should raise the issue with the parties and ask to be addressed on it. The issue of the likely cost of the arbitration should be addressed by the tribunal at the preliminary hearing with parties being directed under r.28 to give and exchange estimates as to their likely expenses; this is how post-Jackson litigation operates in England (see *Andrew Mitchell MP v News Group Newspapers Ltd* [2013] EWCA Civ 1537). This may itself trigger an application under r.65 if there is a material disparity in the estimates. It may also stir the tribunal into raising the issue of expense and a possible r.65 "award" if the tribunal takes the view that the expenses are wholly excessive or disproportionate to what is at stake in the arbitration. **R65–11**

In relation to the making of a r.65 award the main questions for parties and tribunals, are: **R65–12**

- What test requires to be satisfied for the making of an award capping liability for recoverable expenses?

- What form would the r.65 award take?

R65–13 No guidance as to the test is given either by the DAC or by r.65 itself. An order must be made sufficiently in advance of the taking of steps in the arbitration which may be affected by the order. The authors submit that it must be shown that there is a risk that one party may incur unreasonable expense in relation to its conduct of the arbitration. This may be difficult to show, but circumstances do occur in practice where senior lawyers are being retained for a simple claim, large numbers of experts are being instructed, unascertained or unjustifiable expense relative to the issues at stake is being incurred or where it can be shown that unnecessary work has been or is being carried out which gives rise to an inference that this may continue into or take place in the future.

R65–14 The tribunal will have to decide whether the items of expense are reasonable and if so whether the quantum of that expense is reasonable, and if not what would be a reasonable cap. Essentially the tribunal will have to carry out an exercise in determining the recoverable expenses under r.61 in advance of them being incurred. The tribunal will have to be supplied with figures with which it can justify the cap sought. Clearly a tribunal will have to act carefully having regard to its various duties under r.24.

R65–15 A r.65 award may be a part award or a provisional award. A provisional award can be varied later on a change of circumstances but is not subject to appeal during the course of the arbitration (see r.71(3)) until it is incorporated into or confirmed in a permanent part or final award. For part awards see paras R54–01 to R54–11.

R65–16 The r.65 award will have to be clear and precise in its specification of the recoverable arbitration expenses in particular and the monetary caps which it imposes, so that there is no room for argument as to what it means.

R65–17 Paragraph 6 of the CIArb's Practice Guideline 9, although focused on s.65 of the 1996 Act, offers helpful advice and guidance; see *http://www.ciarb.org/ informationandresources/PracticeGuideline9.pdf* [Accessed June 20, 2014].

Rule 66: Awards on recoverable arbitration expenses D

66. An expenses award (under rule 62 or 65) may be made together with or separately from an award on the substance of the dispute (and these rules apply in relation to an expenses award as they apply to an award on the substance of the dispute).

DEFINITIONS

"rules": s.31(1)

STATUS

R66–01 This is a default rule so it is open to the parties to modify it, agree something different or disapply it completely (see s.9).

MODEL LAW

There is no equivalent provision in the Model Law. See the commentary **R66–02**
on r.59 above (para.R59–03).

COMMENTARY

The purpose of r.66 is to emphasise that part awards of expenses can be **R66–03**
made and that both part awards and final awards of expenses can be
appealed in the same way as an appeal against an award on the merits. In
practice, it may however be more difficult to appeal an award in relation to
expenses.

A very common form of part award on expenses is where both claimant **R66–04**
and respondent are obliged to lodge an advance deposit of 50 per cent of the
estimated tribunal and institutional costs of the arbitration but respondent
fails to do so, thereby forcing claimant to pay both tranches of 50 per cent.
Formerly, claimants waited until the final award to collect but now they
apply immediately for an award (enforceable in 150 states) of the 50 per cent
which respondent failed to pay. London tribunals issue such awards as a
matter of course.

An expenses award may be a part award made during the course of the **R66–05**
arbitration dealing with a specific element of arbitral procedure. Rule 66
supersedes the pre-2010 Act law as to part awards of expenses set out in
Apollo Engineering Ltd v James Scott Ltd, 2009 S.C. 525. The provisions of
all of the SAR, including in particular rr.59–66 and r.68 (appeals) apply to
part awards of expenses as they do to final expenses awards.

PART 8

CHALLENGING AWARDS

Rule 67: Challenging an award: substantive jurisdiction M

67.—(1) A party may appeal to the Outer House against the tribunal's award on the ground that the tribunal did not have jurisdiction to make the award (a "jurisdictional appeal").

(2) The Outer House may decide a jurisdictional appeal by—
  (a) confirming the award,
  (b) varying the award (or part of it), or
  (c) setting aside the award (or part of it).

(3) Any variation by the Outer House has effect as part of the tribunal's award.

(4) An appeal may be made to the Inner House against the Outer House's decision on a jurisdictional appeal (but only with the leave of the Outer House).

(5) Leave may be given by the Outer House only where it considers—
  (a) that the proposed appeal would raise an important point of principle or practice, or

(b) that there is another compelling reason for the Inner House to consider the appeal.

(6) The Outer House's decision on whether to grant such leave is final.

(7) The Inner House's decision on such an appeal is final.

DEFINITIONS

"Outer House": s.31(1)
"party": ss.2(1), 31(1), (2)
"tribunal": ss.2(1), 31(1)

STATUS

R67–01 Rule 67 is mandatory so cannot be disapplied, or modified in any way, by the parties.

MODEL LAW

R67–02 Article 34 provides that an arbitral award may be set aside if the party applying for the setting aside furnishes proof inter alia that:

(a) a party to the arbitration agreement was under some incapacity; or the said agreement is not valid under the law to which the parties have subjected it or, failing any indication thereon, under the law of the state whose court is to decide the application; or

(b) the award deals with a dispute not contemplated by or not falling within the terms of the submission to arbitration, or contains decisions on matters beyond the scope of the submission to arbitration, provided that, if the decisions on matters submitted to arbitration can be separated from those not so submitted, only that part of the award which contains decisions on matters not submitted to arbitration may be set aside; or

(c) the composition of the arbitral tribunal was not in accordance with the agreement of the parties, unless such agreement was in conflict with a provision of the law of the state whose court is to decide the application from which the parties cannot derogate, or, failing such agreement, was not in accordance with such a law.

R67–03 Rule 67 is partly based on art.34 of the Model Law but the latter contains other grounds for setting aside, some of which are contained in r.68.

COMMENTARY

Introductory

A r.67 appeal on jurisdiction provides the first of the three means of appealing an arbitral award. The second is an appeal under r.68 to the manner in which, or process by which, the tribunal reached its award. The third is an appeal under rr.69 and 70 to the merits of the award on the basis of an obviously wrong or seriously doubtful application of Scots law. **R67–04**

The Act does not define what is meant by the tribunal "not having jurisdiction". However, r.19 sets out the matters on which a tribunal may rule as to its own jurisdiction and, on that basis, a tribunal lacks jurisdiction where: **R67–05**

- there is no valid arbitration agreement providing for the resolution of the dispute (or in the case of a statutory arbitration, the dispute is not covered by the enactment providing for arbitration);
- the tribunal has not been properly constituted; or
- the tribunal deals with or decides matters which have not been submitted to arbitration in accordance with the arbitration agreement.

The reader is referred to the commentary on r.19 in relation to these grounds of lack of jurisdiction. More detailed commentary is also contained in the commentaries to ss.4 and 5 (in relation to valid arbitration agreements) and rr.2–7 (in relation to the proper constitution of the tribunal). **R67–06**

Since r.67 is not tied to r.19, it is possible that an appellant might find some other basis for a challenge but, the authors submit, reading the Act as a whole points clearly to "jurisdiction" comprising the matters stated above. **R67–07**

The general rule is that an appeal has to be made within 28 days of the date when the award is "made". There are exceptions to this and the reader is referred to the commentary to r.71(4) at paras R71–09 to R71–22 below, for more detail in relation to time limits. **R67–08**

Before making an appeal, the appellant must (per r.71(2)) exhaust any available arbitral process of appeal or review, including any recourse under r.58. **R67–09**

An appeal is made by a petition in the style contained in RCS Form 14.4 (RCS rr.100.5, 14.4) or, if there is an undisposed of Outer House petition, by note (RCS rr.100.5, 15.2). The petition or note must set out the grounds of appeal and any other relevant matters required by r.100.7 of the RCS. The petition or note must be lodged with the relevant productions referred to in the commentary on r.42(2) at paras R42–06 to R42–18 above. **R67–10**

Whether an appeal under r.67 will involve the leading of evidence will depend on the grounds of lack of jurisdiction being put forward. If evidence is required, this should be indicated to the court at the time of the motion for additional procedure at which point a warrant to cite the witnesses in **R67–11** question to the hearing should be sought from the court (RCS r.100.5). In most appeals under r.67 the authors do not envisage the leading of evidence.

R67–12 The Act does not state whether an appeal against jurisdiction should entail a de novo hearing where the court reconsiders the whole issue afresh, including the possible leading of evidence to re-determine facts relevant to jurisdiction found by the arbitrator.

R67–13 Extensive English jurisprudence, including UKSC, has made it clear that the court will consider the whole jurisdictional issue de novo; see, e.g. *Dallah Real Estate and Tourism Holding Co v The Ministry of Religious Affairs, Government of Pakistan* [2011] 1 A.C. 763 (with Lord Hope presiding), per Lord Mance at [26] and with Lord Collins saying this at [96]:

> "The consistent practice of the courts in England has been that they will examine or re-examine for themselves the jurisdiction of arbitrators. This can arise in a variety of contexts, including a challenge to the tribunal's jurisdiction under [s.67] .... Thus in *Azov Shipping Co v Baltic Shipping Co* [1999] 1 Lloyd's Rep 68 Rix J decided that where there was a substantial issue of fact as to whether a party had entered into an arbitration agreement, then even if there had already been a full hearing before the arbitrator the court, on a challenge under [s.67], should not be in a worse position than the arbitrator for the purpose of determining the challenge. This decision has been consistently applied at first instance (see, eg. *Peterson Farms Inc v C&M Farming Ltd* [2004] EWHC 121 (Comm), [2004] 1 Lloyd's Rep 603) and is plainly right."

R67–14 Given the close similarity of r.67 with s.67 of the 1996 Act, and given that in *Arbitration Application No.3 of 2011* [2011] CSOH 164, Lord Glennie said (at [8]):

> "Since the Act was closely and unashamedly modelled on the [1996] Act, and reflects the same underlying philosophy, authorities on the Act (and its predecessor, the Arbitration Act 1979) in relation to questions of interpretation and approach will obviously be of relevance. There is no point in re-inventing the (arbitration) wheel",

it can be expected that the Outer House will very likely choose to hear r.67 applications on a de novo basis. However, the authors are aware that there are jurisdictions where the court does not engage in such a de novo hearing.

R67–15 An issue as to jurisdiction will arise where the principal question is whether a condition precedent to arbitration had been satisfied; see *Tang Chung Wah vs Grant Thornton International Ltd* [2012] EWHC 3198 (Ch) which was discussed in Hew R. Dundas, "ADR-Related Conditions Precedent to Arbitration: When Are They Effective and When Not?" (2013) 79 *Arbitration* 221–227.

Matters affecting each of rr.67, 68 and 69

The question arises whether the parties can, by agreement, widen the scope of judicial review as established by rr.67, 68 and 69. The authors submit (i) that s.1(c) of the Act excludes any such widening, and (ii) in any event, that s.9 of the Act is clear in that rr.67, 68 and 70 cannot be modified. The question surrounding r.69 has been considered by the court in England and in the USA; see commentary on r.69 at paras R69–02 and R69–03. **R67–16**

A practical question arises as to what should be submitted to the court in lodging an appeal under any of rr.67, 68 or 69. In this regard, the English High Court and Court of Appeal have become increasingly critical of the excessive volume of some submissions, see *MidGulf International Ltd v Groupe Chimique Tunisien* [2010] EWCA Civ 66 at [71]–[72], where Toulson L.J. expressed strong disapproval of the lodging of 5 lever arch volumes of over 100 authorities and a 132 page "skeletal" argument. The authors respectfully suggest that equally forceful disapproval would be wholly appropriate for appeals under the 2010 Act. **R67–17**

It should be noted that a r.67 appeal relates to an award covering both jurisdiction and merits (or an award where the tribunal has found jurisdiction to be absent on its own initiative); in contrast to a r.21 appeal which relates only to a tribunal decision made under r.20(4)(a) (see also para.R21–14). However, only the jurisdictional issue(s) can be appealed under r.67 and any appeal on other issues will have to be made under rr.68 or 69. **R67–18**

Rule 67(1)

As with rr.68 and 69, an r.67 appeal is to the Outer House only. **R67–19**

A party's entitlement to make a r.67 appeal must be viewed in the context of other rules relating to the jurisdiction of the tribunal. Whereas r.19 empowers the tribunal to rule on its own jurisdiction, r.76 provides that a party who participates in an arbitration without making a timeous objection (as defined in r.76(2)) on the ground that the tribunal lacks jurisdiction may not raise the objection later before the tribunal or the court. **R67–20**

Rules 20–22 cover the contesting of jurisdiction prior to the tribunal's issue of an award. Under r.21(1), a party may appeal directly to the Outer House for an order that the tribunal lacks jurisdiction; the decision of the Outer House is final (r.23(4)) and, the authors submit, no appeal on the same basis can be made under r.67 at any later date. **R67–21**

Circumstances might arise where a party makes an objection to the tribunal under r.20 but the other party does not insist that the tribunal decide the matter immediately. In such event, the tribunal has the discretion to decide whether it should decide the objection immediately or delay a decision until its final award (r.20(4)). Rule 67 does not permit an appeal against that decision (*AOOT Kalmneft v Glencore International AG* [2002] 1 Lloyd's Rep. 128 at 139). **R67–22**

If an objection to jurisdiction is made to a tribunal and it has to be **R67–23** decided by the parties, failing whom the tribunal, whether the objection should be dealt with immediately or left to the end of the arbitration, the parties and the tribunal should be aware of the different routes of appeal from a part award under r.20 and an award at the end of the arbitration. The first is to appeal the part award to the Outer House within 14 days under r.21 while the arbitration is ongoing (assuming there is a part award upholding jurisdiction). If that route is followed then the decision of the Outer House is final (r.21(3)) and, the authors submit, no further appeal on the same basis can be made under r.67 at any later date. The second option is to wait until the tribunal makes its final award and then to appeal the final award under r.67.

R67–24 Both options bring advantages and disadvantages. In the first, there is the advantage of the early disposal of the arbitration proceedings if the appeal is successful and the arbitration proceedings have not yet concluded at the time that the court allows the appeal. In the second option, there is the possibility of a further appeal to the Inner House (see r.67(5)) but in the meantime the tribunal will have been obliged to have decided the merits of the claim. Another risk with the second option is that, while a r.67 appeal is ongoing, the award might be enforced in a foreign jurisdiction or the sum awarded might be required to be paid into court or otherwise secured under r.71(12).

R67–25 Except where an appeal is made by a party who claims to have had no notice of the arbitration (as in *Bernuth Lines Ltd v High Seas Shipping Ltd* [2006] 1 Lloyd's Rep. 537) the award being appealed under r.67 must deal in some way, at least in substance if not in form, with an objection on the ground of lack of jurisdiction (*Vee Networks Ltd v Econet Wireless International Ltd* [2005] 1 Lloyd's Rep. 192 at 198).

R67–26 That latter case also appears to suggest that parties may contract out of the possibility of an appeal from a tribunal's decision on jurisdiction (para.26) but the authors respectfully submit that this cannot be possible since it would circumvent the mandatory nature of s.67 of the 1996 Act.

R67–27 There is English authority, relating to the equivalent to r.76, that an appeal on the ground of lack of jurisdiction may not be based on any argument not made before the tribunal unless the appellant shows that it did not know of the argument and could not with reasonable diligence have discovered that ground (*JSC Zestafoni G. Nikoladze Ferroalloy Plant v Ronly Holdings Ltd* [2004] 2 Lloyd's Rep. 335 at 345). For further discussion, see the commentary on r.76.

R67–28 Whether an argument made on appeal was within the ground of objection made to the tribunal is a matter of degree (see *Primetrade AG v Ythan Ltd* [2006] 1 Lloyd's Rep. 457 at 474). This suggests that a party making an objection to jurisdiction that could give rise to an appeal should frame their grounds of objection to a tribunal broadly so as to allow some flexibility at an appeal, but not so broad as not to give fair notice of the ground to the respondent.

An example of a lack of jurisdiction is where the tribunal makes an award **R67–29** in favour of a person who was not a party to the arbitration agreement, e.g. *Hussman (Europe) Ltd v Al Ameen Development and Trade Co* [2000] 2 Lloyd's Rep. 83.

In deciding a jurisdictional appeal, if the "English approach" is to be **R67–30** followed (see para.R67–13), the Outer House will hear the case de novo (see citations in para.R67–13).

A r.67 hearing by the Outer House may therefore necessitate hearing oral **R67–31** evidence, if this cannot be agreed. If this is the intention, parties should be clear on whether oral evidence will be necessary by the time that the appellant applies under RCS r.100.5 for an order as to further procedure or an order for a hearing. If oral evidence will be necessary, the order should include a warrant to the parties to cite witnesses and havers of documents.

Rule 67(2) and (3)

The remedies for an appellant under r.67 are variation or setting aside of **R67–32** the award or part of it. The setting aside of the award corresponds to the former remedy at common law which was to have the award "reduced". In both instances the effect is that the part or whole of the award which is set aside is rendered null and void. The provision for part of the award to be set aside is to allow for an award which contains a part which the tribunal had jurisdiction to make and a part where it lacked jurisdiction. In such a situation the court would set aside only the part where the tribunal lacked jurisdiction.

Rule 67(2) also allows the court to vary the award or part of it. It is **R67–33** suggested that the purpose of this power is to allow the court some flexibility in setting aside part of an award, so that if in substance the award is separable into parts where the tribunal had and where it lacked jurisdiction, the court can vary it (by implication only slightly) in order to avoid setting aside part of an award. However, it cannot have been intended to allow the court to vary the substantive terms of the award as that would be to usurp the jurisdiction of the tribunal given to it by the parties. Variation is rare but one example is *Lobb Partnership Ltd v Aintree Racecourse Co Ltd* [2002] EWHC (TCC) 3094 where H.H. Judge Thornton QC varied the arbitrator's award (at [90]).

Rule 67(3) is a necessary provision deeming the variations consequential **R67–34** on a separation of the award to have been part of the tribunal's award.

Rule 67(4)–(6)—Further appeals

These provisions provide limits to the right of appeal in order that the **R67–35** finality of the arbitration process be compromised as little as possible, compatible with avoiding substantial injustice to a party. Thus, appeals from the Outer House to the Inner House can occur only with leave of the former and such leave may be granted only in circumstances (see r.67(5)) intended by the drafters of the Act to be exceptional. The criteria in r.67(5) will be considered in more detail at paras R70–11 to R70–28.

R67–36 Appeal to the UKSC under s.40 of the Court of Session Act 1988 is excluded by r.67(7).

R67–37 For the time limit for seeking leave see r.71(5), below, and the commentary to that rule. See also RCS r.38.5 in relation to applications for leave to appeal (reclaim).

R67–38 A requirement that leave be obtained for a further appeal is not incompatible with the right to a fair trial under art.6 ECHR (*Kazakhstan v Istil Group Ltd* [2007] 2 Lloyd's Rep. 548).

R67–39 The question of whether the Outer House's refusal to grant leave can itself be appealed to the Inner House on the ground that the refusal followed Outer House action which was incompatible with the appellant's right under art.6 of the ECHR is addressed in the commentary to r.70(9), (10) and (11) at paras R70–43 to R70–51 below.

Rule 68: Challenging an award: serious irregularity M

68.—(1) A party may appeal to the Outer House against the tribunal's award on the ground of serious irregularity (a "serious irregularity appeal").

(2) "Serious irregularity" means an irregularity of any of the following kinds which has caused, or will cause, substantial injustice to the appellant—

    (a) the tribunal failing to conduct the arbitration in accordance with—
        (i) the arbitration agreement,
        (ii) these rules (in so far as they apply), or
        (iii) any other agreement by the parties relating to conduct of the arbitration,
    (b) the tribunal acting outwith its powers (other than by exceeding its jurisdiction),
    (c) the tribunal failing to deal with all the issues that were put to it,
    (d) any arbitral appointments referee or other third party to whom the parties give powers in relation to the arbitration acting outwith powers,
    (e) uncertainty or ambiguity as to the award's effect,
    (f) the award being—
        (i) contrary to public policy, or
        (ii) obtained by fraud or in a way which is contrary to public policy,
    (g) an arbitrator having not been impartial and independent,
    (h) an arbitrator having not treated the parties fairly,
    (i) an arbitrator having been incapable of acting as an arbitrator in the arbitration (or there being justifiable doubts about an arbitrator's ability to so act),
    (j) an arbitrator not having a qualification which the parties agreed (before the arbitrator's appointment) that the arbitrator must have, or
    (k) any other irregularity in the conduct of the arbitration or in the award which is admitted by—

(i) the tribunal, or
(ii) any arbitral appointments referee or other third party to whom the parties give powers in relation to the arbitration.

(3) The Outer House may decide a serious irregularity appeal by—
 (a) confirming the award,
 (b) ordering the tribunal to reconsider the award (or part of it), or
 (c) if it considers reconsideration inappropriate, setting aside the award (or part of it).

(4) Where the Outer House decides a serious irregularity appeal (otherwise than by confirming the award) on the ground—
 (a) that the tribunal failed to conduct the arbitration in accordance with—
  (i) the arbitration agreement,
  (ii) these rules (in so far as they apply), or
  (iii) any other agreement by the parties relating to conduct of the arbitration,
 (b) that an arbitrator has not been impartial and independent, or
 (c) that an arbitrator has not treated the parties fairly,
it may also make such order as it thinks fit about any arbitrator's entitlement (if any) to fees and expenses (and such an order may provide for the repayment of fees or expenses already paid to the arbitrator).

(5) An appeal may be made to the Inner House against the Outer House's decision on a serious irregularity appeal (but only with the leave of the Outer House).

(6) Leave may be given by the Outer House only where it considers—
 (a) that the proposed appeal would raise an important point of principle or practice, or
 (b) that there is another compelling reason for the Inner House to consider the appeal.

(7) The Outer House's decision on whether to grant such leave is final.

(8) The Inner House's decision on such an appeal is final.

DEFINITIONS

"arbitration agreement": ss.4, 31(1)
"Outer House": s.31(1)
"party": ss.2(1), 31(1), (2)
"rule": s.31(1)
"tribunal": ss.2(1), 31(1)

STATUS

Rule 68 is mandatory so cannot be disapplied, or modified in any way, by the parties. **R68–01**

MODEL LAW

R68–02 Article 34 provides that an arbitral award may be set aside if the party applying for set-aside furnishes proof inter alia that:

   (a) the party making the application was not given proper notice of the appointment of an arbitrator or of the arbitral proceedings or was otherwise unable to present his case; or
   (b) the arbitral procedure was not in accordance with the agreement of the parties, unless such agreement was in conflict with a provision of the law of the state whose court is to decide the application from which the parties cannot derogate, or, failing such agreement, was not in accordance with such a law; or
   (c) (i) the subject matter of the dispute is not capable of settlement by arbitration under the law of that state; or
       (ii) the award is in conflict with the public policy of that state.

R68–03 Rule 68 reflects the grounds for setting aside contained in the Model Law but contains additional grounds therefor which relate to the manner in which, or process by which, the tribunal reached its award.

COMMENTARY

Introductory

R68–04 A r.68 serious irregularity challenge is the second of the three available means of appealing an arbitral award. The first (r.67) is a jurisdictional appeal and the third is a r.69 legal error appeal.

R68–05 Matters affecting each of rr.67, 68 and 69 are set out in paras R67–16 to R67–18.

R68–06 Arbitration constitutes a derogation from state courts hence, as a matter of public policy, certain safeguards are required to underpin the arbitral process to ensure that essential minimum standards in a private system of justice are met; r.68 and the closely related r.24 are central to this and are necessarily mandatory.

R68–07 The list of grounds of challenge seeks to strike a balance between the objectives of achieving finality of an arbitral award and of ensuring that tribunals meet the necessary standards. The emphasis in most of the grounds is on defects in the process rather than in the result. Some of these grounds were in existence as grounds of reduction at common law but others are new. So far as a complaint about the result is concerned, the remedy, if any exists, lies in r.69.

R68–08 The general rule is that an appeal has to be made within 28 days of the date when the award is "made". There are exceptions to this and the reader is referred to the commentary to r.71(4) below for more detail in relation to time limits.

Before making an appeal the appellant must (per r.71(2)) exhaust any available arbitral process of appeal or review including any recourse under r.58. **R68–09**

An appeal is made by a petition in the style contained in RCS Form 14.4 (RCS rr.100.5, 14.4) or, if there is an undisposed of Outer House petition, by note (RCS rr.100.5, 15.2). The petition or note must set out the grounds of appeal and any other relevant matters required by r.100.7 of the RCS. The petition or note must be lodged with the relevant documents referred to in the commentary to r.42(2). **R68–10**

Rule 68 discards the previous common law remedy of the setting aside of an award through either a defence of setting aside in court proceedings for implement of an award (reduction of the award *ope exceptionis*) or court proceedings, typically judicial review, for setting aside of an award (reduction of the award). Section 13 provides that legal proceedings are competent in respect of a tribunal's award or any other act or omission by a tribunal when conducting an arbitration only as provided for in the SAR and that, in particular, a tribunal's award is not subject to review in any legal proceedings except as provided for in Part 8 of the rules (i.e. rr.67–72), consistent with the founding principle of s.1(c). **R68–11**

Given the close similarity to r.68 with s.68 of the 1996 Act and given that, in the inaugural 2010 Act case *Arbitration Application No.3 of 2011*, 2012 S.L.T. 150, Lord Glennie said: **R68–12**

> "Since the Act was closely and unashamedly modelled on the [1996] Act, and reflects the same underlying philosophy, authorities on the Act (and its predecessor, the Arbitration Act 1979) in relation to questions of interpretation and approach will obviously be of relevance. There is no point in re-inventing the (arbitration) wheel",

the extensive English s.68 jurisprudence will be very persuasive in applications under the 2010 Act.

Rule 68(1)

Rule 68's heading includes the key phrase "serious irregularity", defined in r.68(2), emphasising that, for the appeal to succeed, the irregularity in question must be serious. **R68–13**

As with rr.67 and 69, any appeal is to the Outer House only. **R68–14**

Rule 68(2)—Qualifying irregularity and "substantial injustice"

A "serious irregularity" requires two elements: first, there must be one of the qualifying irregularities exhaustively listed in r.68(2) and, secondly, that irregularity must have caused or will cause "substantial injustice" to the appellant (*Lesotho Highlands Development Authority v Impreglio SpA* [2006] 1 A.C. 221 at [28] per Lord Steyn). There have been many examples in **R68–15** practice where an appellant has shown irregularity but has failed to demonstrate substantial injustice.

R68–16 The authors stress that r.68(2) constitutes an exhaustive list (see Lord Steyn in *Lesotho* [2006] 1 A.C. 221 at [28]); there have been many examples in practice where an appellant has failed to bring its complaint within the list.

R68–17 Where a qualifying irregularity has been established, the appeal fails unless the Outer House is also satisfied that the irregularity in question has caused or will cause "substantial injustice" to the appealing party. "Substantial injustice" has not been defined further, leaving the Outer House to assess the issue on a case by case basis. The word "substantial" has often been seen as having two different meanings, namely (1) large or big; or (2) anything having content which is more than de minimis and the word must be read in the context of the need for a "serious" irregularity. It must also be viewed against the background of being one of the three exceptions to the finality of an arbitral award, finality being one of the cornerstones of arbitration. If r.68 was applicable to any injustice, then finality would be seriously compromised and the proceedings prolonged, contrary to the founding principle of s.1(a).

R68–18 The DAC Report stated (at para.280):

> "We have listed the specific cases where a challenge can be made under this Clause. The test of "substantial injustice" is intended to be applied by way of support for the arbitral process, not by way of interference with that process. Thus it is only in those cases where it can be said that what has happened is *so far removed from what could reasonably be expected of the arbitral process* that we would expect the Court to take action. In short, Clause 68 is really designed as a long stop, only available in extreme cases where the tribunal has gone so wrong in the conduct of the arbitration that justice calls out for it to be corrected" (authors' emphasis added).

R68–19 This passage was approved by Lord Woolman in *Arbitration Application No.1 of 2013* [2014] CSOH 83 at [18]. However, Lord Woolman does not mention Christopher Clarke J.'s observation in *Bandwidth Shipping Corp v Intaari (the Magdalena Oldendorff)* [2006] EWHC 2532 (Comm) (undisturbed on appeal [2008] 1 Lloyd's Rep. 7; [2007] EWCA Civ 998) at [61] that the passage was not intended to add gloss to, or to displace the language of, s.68 of the 1996 Act.

R68–20 That passage has been applied in numerous English cases such as in *ABB AG v Hochtief Airport GmbH* [2006] 1 All E.R. (Comm) 529 per Tomlinson J. at [63]. However, it is not intended to add any gloss to, or to displace the language of, s.68 of the 1996 Act (*Bandwidth Shipping Corporation v Intaari (the Magdalena Oldendorff)* [2006] EWHC 2532 (Comm) at [61] per Christopher Clarke J., undisturbed on appeal [2008] 1 Lloyd's Rep. 7). The same applies to r.68.

Where, but for the irregularity, the appellant would still have failed will **R68–21** make it very difficult for it to demonstrate that it suffered substantial prejudice as a result of the irregularity (*Margulead Ltd v Exide Technologies* [2005] 1 Lloyd's Rep. 324 at 330, [36]).

While each r.68 application must be looked at on its own merit, the **R68–22** extensive English jurisprudence provides valuable guidance (see R68–18 above) on "substantial injustice". Examples include:

- Where, had the irregularity not occurred, it is clear that the decision of the tribunal would have been the reverse of the decision actually made, there will be substantial injustice (*Newfield Construction Ltd v Tomlinson* 97 Con. L.R. 148, per H.H. Judge Coulson QC at [44]).
- Similarly, it has been suggested, in passing, that if the duty to give reasons has not been excluded and no or insufficient reasons were given then the substantial injustice would be automatic. In *Benaim (UK) Ltd v Davies Middleton & Davies Ltd (No.2)* 102 Con. L.R. 1, H.H. Judge Coulson QC said at [95]:

    "At para.21.16 of Arbitration Law, by Professor Robert Merkin (December 2004 update) the learned editors say that, 'It is strongly arguable that unless a party knows the reasons for an award there is automatically substantial injustice to him', and the relevant footnote suggests that, 'This is indeed the very rationale of the requirement that arbitrators are to give reasons'. I respectfully agree with those comments."

- Where a tribunal awarded interest at a rate which neither party had asked for, and on which neither had been invited to make submissions, and which resulted in an extra payment of nearly €1 million, it was held that the tribunal's irregularity had caused substantial injustice (*Van der Giessen-de Noord Shipbuilding Division BV v Imtech Marine & Offshore BV* [2009] 1 Lloyd's Rep. 273 at 280).
- Where, in an arbitration conducted by trade arbitrators on documents and notwithstanding the respondents' admission of default and the refinement of the dispute in the pleadings to one of quantum, the arbitrators dismissed the claim in its entirety, their failure to treat the parties fairly gave rise to substantial injustice (*Pacol Ltd v Joint Stock Co Rossakhar* [2000] 1 Lloyd's Rep 108).

Examples of what did not cause substantial injustice include: **R68–23**

- The tribunal met an expert without informing the parties and thereby breached the equivalent of r.24 but that meeting did not prejudice either party and the irregularity did not cause any injustice, let alone substantial, to the appellant (*Hussman (Europe) Ltd*

v Al Ameen Development & Trade Co [2000] 2 Lloyd's Rep. 83 per Thomas J. at 95).
- The tribunal failed to give a party an opportunity to cross-examine but this did not give rise to substantial injustice; *Compania Sud-Americana De Vapores SA v Nippon Yusen Kaisha* [2009] EWHC 1606 (Comm).

Rule 68(2)(a)—Tribunal failure to conduct in accordance with the agreed procedures

R68–24 This irregularity is defined as having three branches: failure to conduct the arbitration in accordance with (a) the arbitration agreement; (b) the SAR; or (c) other agreement between the parties relating to the conduct of the arbitration.

R68–25 It is particularly important to note that r.68(2)(a) is, in conjunction with r.68(2)(g) and (h), elevated to a higher level of seriousness by application of r.68(4).

R68–26 A r.68(2)(a)(i) challenge will concern a failure by the tribunal to follow a procedure set out in the arbitration agreement but this is a separate matter from a challenge to the jurisdiction of the tribunal which would be made under rr.20, 22 or 67. While relatively few arbitration agreements provide much procedural detail, one common example is the requirement that the arbitration be conducted in the English language so that failure to do so could trigger a s.68(2)(a)(i) challenge. That said, in such a circumstance the loss of the right to object (r.76(1)(e)) would very likely be relevant.

R68–27 A failure by the tribunal to follow the SAR (to the extent applicable since some of the default rules might have been displaced or modified) is itself an irregularity. This includes, in particular, a failure to comply with rr.24 and 26. In England, a high hurdle has been placed for appellants seeking to rely on a breach of the equivalent of r.24 as an irregularity giving rise to substantial injustice (*Bandwidth Shipping Corp v Intaari (A Firm) (The Magdalena Oldendorff)* [2008] 1 Lloyd's Rep. 7 per Waller L.J. at [38]).

R68–28 Only clear breaches by the tribunal of its statutory duties have resulted in successful appeals under s.68 of the 1996 Act. Examples include:

- giving a higher award of costs due than would otherwise have been due because of an arithmetical error in the main claim (*Gannet Shipping Ltd v Eastrade Commodities Inc* [2002] 1 Lloyd's Rep. 713);
- making an award on a basis contrary to the common position of the parties without giving them an opportunity to make submissions on it (*Omnibridge Consulting Ltd v Clearsprings (Management) Ltd* [2004] EWHC 2276 (Comm)); and
- the tribunal's contact of potential witnesses outwith the presence of the parties' representatives and a failure to note what they said to it

and to disclose the contact (see *Norbrook Laboratories Ltd v Tank* [2006] 2 Lloyd's Rep. 485 per Colman J. at [142] to [147]).

R68–29 In contrast, the tribunal's appointing its own expert without reference to the parties was, in the circumstances, not a breach of the equivalent of r.24; see *Hussman (Europe) Ltd v Al Ameen Development & Trade Co* [2000] 2 Lloyd's Rep. 83.

R68–30 Rule 68(2)(a)(iii) envisages the parties agreeing aspects of conducting the arbitration but in an agreement quite separate from the original arbitration agreement. Examples include:

- agreement on procedure, whether ad hoc or through the adoption of institutional rules (but it is very rare to find such adoption not already incorporated in the arbitration agreement);
- an agreement contained in the pleadings as to the arguments to be submitted to the tribunal, e.g. *Newfield Construction Ltd v Tomlinson*, 97 Con. L.R. 148 at [43] where an arbitrator did not base his decision on expenses on success in terms of the pleadings of the parties and was held to have failed to conduct the arbitration in accordance with the agreement of the parties, that agreement being contained in the procedure agreed by the parties requesting a decision on the cases presented in the written pleadings and not other matters.

Rule 68(2)(b)—Tribunal acting outwith its powers (other than exceeding its jurisdiction)

R68–31 Jurisdiction is dealt with by rr.20, 22 or 67. An example of a r.68(2)(b) failure is where the tribunal appoints an expert under r.34 but the parties had excluded that default power. This might also be challengeable under r.68(2)(a)(i), (ii) or (iii).

R68–32 However, in a case where a tribunal erroneously exercised a power that it did have, this was held not to constitute "acting outwith" powers under s.68(2)(b) of the 1996 Act (*Lesotho Highlands Development Authority v Impregilo SpA* [2006] 1 A.C. 221 per Lord Steyn at 233, [24]).

R68–33 Rule 68(2)(b) cannot be used to complain that an award is wrong as a matter of fact and law (*Lesotho Highlands Development Authority* [2006] 1 A.C. 221 per Lord Steyn at 231, [31]).

Rule 68(2)(c)—Not dealing with all the issues

R68–34 "Issues" in r.68(2)(c) mean issues the determination of which is essential to a decision on the claim or defence raised in the course of the reference (*World Trade Corp Ltd v C Czarnikow Sugar Ltd* [2005] 1 Lloyd's Rep. 422 per Coleman J.). It follows that not every matter raised during the course of the arbitration proceedings is therefore an "issue".

R68–35 In *Schwebel v Schwebel* [2010] EWHC 3280 (TCC), Akenhead J. gave a helpful summary:

> "23. I draw from these cases and from s.68 itself the following general conclusions:
>
> (a) Arbitrators and awards cannot be criticised simply because they do not address each and every item of contentious or even non-contentious evidence. Omission to address particular items of evidence is not necessarily in itself a serious irregularity, let alone one which will give rise to serious injustice.
>
> (b) Arbitrators who are required to give reasons in their awards do not have to list all the arguments or items of evidence as advanced which they accept and which they reject. They should identify usually the primary evidence which they do find compelling where the case depends upon factual findings because that will be part of the reasoning.
>
> (c) Great care and circumspection should be exercised by the Court to identify cases which genuinely give rise to a serious irregularity and those which essentially reflect a losing party's upset that its evidence was not accepted or that inferences were made against it or for the other party. There will be no serious irregularity simply because the Claimant in the Court proceedings considers that the tribunal failed to arrive at the right decision, factual or legal.
>
> (d) It is wrong for the Court to allow a party to use s.68 to challenge the decision on a question of fact.
>
> (e) It will be a very rare and exceptional case for the Court to interfere pursuant to s.68 on the grounds that the arbitrator reached the wrong findings of fact, should have reached different factual conclusions, given greater weight to some evidence or failed to explain why weight or importance was not given to some evidence. It will be an even rarer case for the Court to find that even if there was some serious irregularity with regard to a failure to take into account evidence that there was substantial injustice, which is of course a precondition to the involvement of the court under s.68, along with the need for there to be a serious irregularity."

R68–36 The "issue" must therefore be a fundamental issue which had been put to the tribunal for it to decide since only such an issue could be capable of causing substantial injustice to the party putting it to the tribunal (*Fidelity Management SA v Myriad International Holdings Ltd BV* [2005] 2 Lloyd's Rep. 508 at 510).

R68–37 The distinction between a primary issue which must be dealt with and a subsidiary issue can be difficult to draw (*Van der Giessen-de Noord Shipbuilding Division BV v Imtech Marine & Offshore BV* [2009] 1 Lloyd's Rep. 273 at 282, [43]).

Subsidiary issues which are not critical to the primary issues are not "issues" for the purpose of r.66(2)(c) (*Benaim (UK) Ltd v Davies Middleton & Davies (No.2)*, 102 Con. L.R. 1 at [51]–[53]). **R68–38**

In *Van der Giessen-de Noord Shipbuilding Division BV v Imtech Marine & Offshore BV* [2009] 1 Lloyd's Rep. 273, Christopher Clarke J. said (at [8]), on the basis of *Petroships Pte Ltd of Singapore v Petec Trading & Investment Corp of Vietnam (The Petro Ranger)* [2001] 2 Lloyd's Rep. 348, that the power to set aside an award was **R68–39**

> "not available simply because the Tribunal has made a mistake, whether of fact or law; or because the arbitrators did not deal with all the points made or arguments advanced or did not set out each step by which they reached their conclusion."

In this context "failure to deal with all the issues" is a different matter from giving clear or adequate reasons for the decisions on the issues (*Ispat Industries Ltd v Western Bulk Pte. Ltd* [2011] EWHC 93 (Comm) at [14] per Teare J.). If parties have agreed that no reasons should be given then there is no duty to give reasons and no irregularity if they are not given. If the court cannot deal with the appeal properly without the tribunal giving reasons or further detailed reasons, then it has the power to order the tribunal to give such reasons (see the commentary to r.71(7) below). **R68–40**

A failure to set out each step by which a conclusion was reached or a failure to deal with each point raised by a party under an issue will not amount to a failure to "deal with all the issues" put to the tribunal (*Hussman (Europe) Ltd v Al Ameen Development & Trade Co* [2000] 2 Lloyd's Rep. 83 per Thomas J. at 97). **R68–41**

If the tribunal fails to give clear reasons then this may amount to an irregularity under r.68(2)(a)(ii) being a failure to conduct the arbitration in accordance with r.48(2)(c) which requires a tribunal to give reasons. **R68–42**

If a tribunal has, in some way, been expressly asked to deal with the expenses of an arbitration, its failure to do so would amount to a qualifying irregularity (see also the commentary to r.62) and could be a serious irregularity; see *Gannet Shipping Ltd v Eastrade Commodities Inc* [2002] 1 Lloyd's Rep. 713 at para.R68–28 above. **R68–43**

In *Soeximex SAS v Agrocorp International Pte Ltd* [2011] EWHC 2743 (Comm), Gloster J. said this: **R68–44**

> "25. The Commercial Court is very sensitive to the fact that parties have chosen to have their disputes resolved by an industry or trade arbitral tribunal, rather than by the Courts. As a matter of general approach, it tries to uphold arbitration awards and to read them in a

sensible and commercial way. It is very mindful that the Court's role on a s.68 application is not to pick holes in an award, or to indulge in an over-nice analysis of what may be understandably brief reasons given by commercial men in areas with which they are far more familiar than the Court. However, in this case, there were clearly legal issues which had to be addressed and were not; the Award took some time to be produced, which may explain why some issues were overlooked. In all the circumstances, I conclude that there was indeed a failure by the Board to deal with all the issues that were put to it, and that, given the arguments which were available to the Buyers, this failure amounted to a serious irregularity which has caused the Buyers substantial injustice, since (absent a remission to the Board) they have been deprived of the opportunity of having their arguments on these important points resolved, whether by the Board, or on an appeal under s.69."

Rule 68(2)(d)—AAR or third party acting outwith powers

R68–45 This type of irregularity is closely related to a r.68(2)(b) one by the tribunal itself (*Lesotho Highlands Development Authority v Impregilo SpA* [2006] 1 A.C. 221 at 236, [29]); however, the range of powers given to an AAR is very narrow compared to those given to the tribunal. An example would be where an AAR appointed a 3-person tribunal where the arbitration agreement specified a sole arbitrator.

Rule 68(2)(e)—Uncertainty or ambiguity as to award's effect

R68–46 If a party considers that the effect of an award is uncertain or ambiguous, it must apply to the tribunal under r.58(2)(b) and (1)(b) for the correction of the award so as to clarify or remove any ambiguity; see the commentary at r.58 above.

R68–47 Only if the tribunal's decision on the application is unsatisfactory is there a right of appeal under r.68 in respect of the uncertainty or ambiguity of effect of the award (r.71(2)).

R68–48 For the r.68 appeal to be successful, there must not merely be uncertainty or ambiguity as to the effect of the award but such uncertainty or ambiguity must cause substantial injustice to the appellant, something which is not required under r.58.

R68–49 In *Tongyuan (USA) International Trading Group v Uni-Clan Ltd* Unreported January 19, 2001 QB, in connection with opposition to the enforcement of a foreign award on the grounds of uncertainty or ambiguity, Moore-Bick J. said:

"The court should not, in my view, be astute to find difficulties of construction of awards or, for that matter, judgments, where none really exist."

As a matter of Scots common law, if an award directs a party to pay a sum **R68–50** of money or perform some act, while it is advisable that the award give a time limit for the implementation of the payment or the act, the absence of a time limit will leave an implied term that the payment or performance be within a reasonable time (*Irons and Melville on Arbitration*, p.201).

The effect of a successful appeal on this ground may result in an order to **R68–51** the tribunal to reconsider the award or part of it. See the commentary to rr.68(3) and 69 below.

Rule 68(2)(f)—Contrary to public policy, obtained by fraud

This paragraph contains three possible irregularities, i.e. the award being **R68–52** (a) contrary to public policy, (b) obtained by fraud, and (c) obtained in a way contrary to public policy.

The fact that an award in itself, as opposed to the means by which it was **R68–53** obtained from a tribunal, was contrary to public policy has never been invoked as a discrete ground for setting aside an award either under the common law or under the 25th Act of the 1695 Articles (now disapplied by s.26).

If the court had been faced with, for example, enforcement proceedings in **R68–54** respect of a Scottish award relating to a contract involving smuggling or illegal or immoral activity, the court would have set aside the award on the grounds of the tribunal having acted outwith its powers in having made an award on an illegal and therefore unarbitrable contract. This common law approach remains open to the court under r.67 where a tribunal lacked jurisdiction because of an invalid arbitration agreement.

The concept of "public policy" as a ground for setting aside a Scottish **R68–55** award is something new, introduced by the Act, whose ultimate origins lie in art.V(2)(b) of the New York Convention. Interestingly, "public policy" did feature as a ground in Scots common law for the refusal of recognition of foreign arbitral awards (see *Hamlyn v Talisker Distillery Co* (1894) 21 R. (HL) 21).

Whilst the rule does not state that it is the public policy of Scots law, given **R68–56** that the rule (unlike its Convention equivalent: see s.20(4)(b) above) is being applied in an arbitration with a Scots seat, it is difficult to see what other public policy could be covered. Such an interpretation would be consistent with the Model Law. This can include EU law as part of Scots law: see para.S20–128.

The authors submit that "public policy" in terms of r.68 is different to **R68–57** "public policy" in terms of the Model Law or the Convention (see s.20(4)(b)) because "public policy" under the Convention was intended to be international in concept . In the final report leading up to the enactment of the Model Law, the UN Commission observed that, in the Model Law as well as in the Convention, the term "public policy" ("ordre publique" in the French sense) was not the equivalent to the political stance or international policies of a state but comprised the fundamental notions and principles of justice, which in France and some civil law jurisdictions included fundamental procedural justice (*Report of the UN Commission on International Trade Law on its work in its 18th Session* (A/40/17), paras 296, 297).

R68–58 Instances such as corruption, bribery or fraud and similar serious cases could, in the French sense, be covered by the concept and in that connection, that the wording "the award is in conflict with the public policy of this State" in art.V(2)(b) was not to be interpreted as excluding instances or events relating to the manner in which an award was arrived at. Given that procedural injustice is covered by r.68(2)(a), (g) and (h) (at least), "public policy" in terms of this rule is, the authors submit, intended to have a narrower meaning than its use in the New York Convention and the Model Law.

R68–59 Under the pre-2010 Act common law, "public policy" was held to be "a deeply rooted and important consideration of local policy" (*Hamlyn v Talisker Distillery Co* (1894) 21 R. (HL) 21 per Lord Watson at 27) or "a fundamental principle of the law of Scotland founded on considerations of public policy" (*Hamlyn* (1894) 21 R. (HL) 21 per Lord Herschell at 23).

R68–60 Contracts *contra bonos mores* have always been regarded as void or unenforceable and therefore not giving rise to arbitrable disputes. In England, it has been held that an award in an English arbitration following a dispute under a contract which would be illegal under English law was itself contrary to public policy and an appeal against it was allowed (*Soleimany v Soleimany* [1999] Q.B. 785, per Court of Appeal at 799).

R68–61 By contrast, in *R v V* [2009] 1 Lloyd's Rep. 97 the court found that an award based on a contract alleged to be illegal under Libyan law on grounds of "purchase of influence" was not contrary to the principles of English public policy as set out in *Lemenda Trading Co Ltd v African Middle East Petroleum Co Ltd* [1988] Q.B. 448 so the appeal against the arbitrator's award was dismissed.

R68–62 The authors submit that such an approach should be followed in Scotland.

R68–63 The second and third irregularities concern the means by which the award was obtained, i.e. a very different set of considerations to those concerning the award itself

R68–64 The obtaining of an award through a party's fraud has, for very many years, been a ground under the Scots common law for the setting aside of an award (see, e.g. the case law cited in *Irons and Melville on Arbitration*, pp.407–408).

R68–65 In *Boyd & Forrest v Glasgow & South Western Railway Co (No.1)*, 1912 S.C. (HL) 93 at 99, Lord Atkinson quoted with approval Lord Herschel's classic definition of fraud in *Derry v Peek* (1889) 14 App. Cas. 337 as follows:

"fraud is proved where it is shown that a false representation has been made (1) knowingly, or (2) without belief in its truth, or (3) recklessly, careless whether it be true or false. Although I have treated the second and third as distinct cases, I think the third is but an instance of the second, for one who makes a statement under such circumstances can have no real belief in the truth of what he states. To prevent a false statement being fraudulent, there must, I think, always be an honest belief in its truth. And this probably covers the whole ground for one who knowingly alleges that which is false has obviously no such honest belief if fraud be proved, the motive of the person guilty of it is immaterial. It matters not that there was no intention to cheat or injure the person to whom the statement was made."

In the context of obtaining an award by fraud, the onus on the person alleging it is to make good the allegation by exhibiting cogent evidence (*Double K Oil Products 1996 Ltd v Neste Oil OYJ* [2009] EWHC 3380 (Comm) per Blair J. at [33]). **R68–66**

Mere inadvertent misleading of a party, or an innocent production of false evidence, will not suffice. In addition to the making of the false representation it must be shown that it had a causal effect on the terms of the award. **R68–67**

The following applies in these r.68(2)(f) circumstances: **R68–68**

"... it is difficult to think that if under section 68(2)(g) [the 1996 Act equivalent] it were suggested an award had been obtained by fraud and that relief under section 68(3) should be granted, the court would not insist on the same condition, i.e., unavailability of the evidence produced as at the time of the arbitration, and that such evidence would have had an important influence on the result" (*Westacre Investments Inc v Jugoimport SDPR Holding Co Ltd* [1999] 2 Lloyd's Rep. 65 per Waller L.J. at 77).

Finally, although r.68(2)(f) merely states "obtained by fraud", thereby leaving it open by whose fraud the award might have been obtained, it has been observed that it should be read as referring to the fraud of a party to the arbitration or the fraud of some other person to which a party was privy (see *Double K Oil Products* [2009] EWHC 3380 (Comm) at [35], following Aikens J. in *Elektrim SA v Vivendi Universal SA* [2007] 1 Lloyd's Rep. 693 at [79]). **R68–69**

Where the allegation is that the award was obtained by perjury, the appellant must produce evidence which, with reasonable diligence, could not have been produced at the evidential hearing and would have probably affected the result and it must be sufficiently strong that it could be expected to be decisive at the rehearing (*DDT Trucks of North America Ltd v DDT Holdings Ltd* [2007] 2 Lloyd's Rep. 213 per Cooke J. at [22]). **R68–70**

Prior to the Act, the obtaining of an award from arbitrators who were guilty of "corruption, bribery, or falsehood" was a ground for the setting **R68–71** aside of an award under the now disapplied (see s.28) 25th Act of the 1695 Articles. In place of the disapplied 25th Act we now have a broader new concept of the obtaining of an award in a way contrary to public policy. This concept has been held to require normally the demonstration of some form of reprehensible or unconscionable conduct which has contributed in a substantial way to the obtaining of the award (see *Double K Oil Products* [2009] EWHC 3380 (Comm); *Protech Projects Construction (Pty) Ltd v Al-Kharafi & Sons* [2005] 2 Lloyd's Rep. 779; and the commentary to s.20 above).

R68–72 The cases under the equivalent provision in the 1996 Act indicate that the court should be slow to find reprehensible or unconscionable conduct.

Rule 68(2)(g), (h), (i), and (j)

R68–73 Rule 68(2)(g), (h), (i) and (j) relate directly to other rules as set out below:

- r.68(2)(g) (arbitrator not having been impartial and independent): see the commentary on r.24(1)(a) at paras R24–04 to R24–21;
- r.68(2)(h) (arbitrator not having treated the parties fairly): see the commentary on r.24(1)(b) at paras R24–22 to R24–41;
- r.68(2)(i) (arbitrator incapable or justifiable doubts about capability): see the commentary on r.12(c) at para.R12–18; and
- r.68(2)(j) (arbitrator lacking agreed qualification): see the commentary to rr.10(2)(a)(iii) and 12(d) both at paras R10–12 to R10–13.

R68–74 It is particularly important to note that r.68(2)(g) and (h) are, in conjunction with r.68(2)(a), elevated to a higher level of seriousness by application of r.68(4).

Rule 68(2)(k)—Admitted irregularity

R68–75 This provision is self-explanatory and needs no commentary.

Rule 68(3)—Remedies

R68–76 Rule 68(3) sets out the possible outcomes of a serious irregularity appeal: (a) confirmation of the award (i.e. dismissal of the appeal), (b) the Outer House's ordering the tribunal to reconsider the award (or part of it), or (c) if the Outer House considers reconsideration inappropriate, setting aside the award (or part of it).

R68–77 Note that while r.67(2) of the Act (but not r.70(8)) and s.67(3) and s.69(7) of the 1996 Act provide for the court to vary the award, there is no power of variation under r.68 or s.68; this is because few of the listed types of serious irregularity can ever be cured by any amount of judicial tinkering with the award.

R68–78 The first issue for the court to consider is whether an order requiring the arbitrator to reconsider the award, or any part of it, is appropriate. While that is likely to be appropriate in respect of rr.68(2)(c) (failing to deal with all the issues) or (e) (uncertainty or ambiguity), it will be only in exceptional circumstances that remission is appropriate where serious irregularities arise under r.68(2)(a) (failure to conduct that arbitration as agreed by the parties, particularly r.68(2)(a)(ii), i.e. breach of the SAR including the tribunal's r.24 duties), r.68(2)(g) (arbitrator not impartial and independent), or r.68(2)(h) (treating the parties unfairly). It is impossible to envisage reconsideration where r.68(2)(i) (arbitrator incapable), r.68(2)(j) (arbitrator not qualified) have been satisfied. A useful test here is whether or not the award can be corrected in a manner similar to that under r.58.

R68–79 A rare example, believed to be the first such case in England, of a breach of s.33 of the 1996 Act leading to a successful s.68(2)(a) challenge (i.e. equivalent to r.68(2)(a)(ii) and r.68(2)(h)) but where the court remitted the award to the tribunal for reconsideration occurred in *Brockton Capital LLP v Atlantic-Pacific Capital Inc* [2014] EWHC 1459 (Comm). There, in post-hearing written submissions, one party had submitted, for the first time, that only one of two sub-clauses in the contract was void as a penalty provision. In its award the tribunal had found that the clause containing both sub-clauses was void as a penalty provision. The court found that the tribunal had failed to give the parties an opportunity to address the potential invalidity of the second sub-clause, which submission could have persuaded the tribunal not to have held it void. However, the court rejected a motion to set aside the award entirely, noting that the members of the tribunal were distinguished lawyers and arbitrators of high reputation and finding that there were no grounds for an objective conclusion that confidence could not be placed in the tribunal to reach a fair conclusion on the matter to be reconsidered. The authors submit that the circumstances in which the error was made, where a submission based on a sub-clause was in effect treated as one bearing on the entire clause, were clearly also of relevance.

R68–80 In *Ascot Commodities NV v Olam International Ltd* [2002] C.L.C. 277, Toulson J. indicated (at 286), obiter in post-judgment discussions with Counsel, that "reconsideration" meant the same arbitrator using the existing material which has been presented to him for the purposes of the award plus any supplementary submissions which are consequential upon the successful appeal. The authors' view of *Ascot v Olam* was confirmed in *Cottonex Anstalt v Patriot Spinning Mills Ltd* [2013] EWHC 236 (Comm) where Hamblen J. said at [88]:

> "As matters stand the [tribunal] is *functus officio. It retains jurisdiction only to the extent covered by any remission.* If there is to be a new claim it would therefore need to be in a further arbitration. It should only determine Patriot's alleged damages claim if satisfied that such a claim is within the existing arbitration reference/appeal" (authors' emphasis added).

R68–81 In relation to a similar provision in the Jamaican Arbitration Act, the Privy Council observed in *Sans Souci Ltd v VRL Services Ltd* [2012] UKPC 6 at [10]:

> "It [the power to order reconsideration] exists in order to enable the tribunal, which would otherwise have been *functus officio* from the publication of its award, to address issues which were part of the submission to arbitration but were not resolved, or not properly resolved, in the award. Leaving aside the perhaps anomalous category of cases in which an award has been remitted on the ground that fresh evidence has become available since it was made, the essential condition for the exercise of the power is that something has gone wrong with the proceedings before the arbitrators. Some error, oversight, misunderstanding or misconduct must have occurred which resulted in the tribunal failing to complete its task and justifies reopening what would otherwise be a conclusive resolution of the dispute."

R68–82 With the greatest of respect, the authors take the view that, given the very close relationship between the 1996 and 2010 Acts, a judicial decision in respect of the former is to be considered more persuasive than a decision on a foreign law whose relationship to the 2010 Act is highly uncertain. It follows that, on rendering the final award (and subject to r.58), the arbitrator becomes *functus officio* and cannot reopen the arbitral proceedings; note that r.57(5) keeps r.70(8) alive so that the arbitrator can reconsider the award but it does not reopen the entire SAR so no form of arbitral proceedings is competent.

R68–83 One of the authors is aware, privately, of an unreported English case where the award was sent back to the arbitrator for reconsideration and his response was a 1-line letter to the court "I hereby confirm my award" which, in the particular circumstances, was accepted. See below under r.70(8)(b) and, for the consequences of remission for reconsideration, see the commentary to r.72 below.

R68–84 With regard to the scope of a remission for reconsideration, in *Sans Souci* (see para.R68–81 above), the Privy Council approved Rix J. (as he then was) in *Glencore International AG v Beogradska Plovidba (The Avala)* [1996] 2 Lloyd's Rep. 311 at 316 where he said:

> "When ... a court remits an award to an arbitrator, it is not remitting a whole dispute, unless upon the terms of the order it expressly does so. It generally remits something narrower, and where it does so against the background of an arbitration which has already been defined by the pleadings and argument before an arbitrator, it is some one or more of the issues as so defined within the scope of the reference that in general must be considered to be subject matter of the remission."

R68–85 The time gap between the court's decision and the original award may cause difficulties for the tribunal and this may point towards set-aside being appropriate (see *Ascot Commodities NV v Olam International Ltd* [2002] C.L.C. 277).

However, if an appeal is successful under (say) r.68(2)(g), (h) or (i) remission for reconsideration may be inappropriate and set-aside will be the proper course to follow. Appeals under r.68(2)(a) will almost always (see para.R68–78) fall into this category also. This may have an impact on the arbitrator's entitlement to his fees. **R68–86**

If the court orders the tribunal to reconsider the award or any part of it, the reconsidered award must be made by no later than three months after the date of the court's order unless the court specifies a different deadline (r.72(1)). For the effects of remission see the commentary to r.72 below. **R68–87**

Rule 68(4)—Arbitrator's fees and expenses

Rule 68(4) deals with successful appeals under r.68(2)(a), (g) and (h) and, inter alia, elevates those three sub-rules to a higher level of seriousness. **R68–88**

Such appeals are caused by defective personal conduct of the arbitrator, not that of the parties, and indeed will probably, certainly in the event of set-aside, have caused substantial wasted arbitral expenses. However, the arbitrator will not be party to the appeal and so the court will have no power to find him liable for any expenses arising as a result thereof. This rule therefore gives the court power to adjust (assumed downwards) the fees charged or chargeable by the arbitrator. **R68–89**

The quantum of the parties' wasted expenses will very likely far exceed the quantum of the tribunal's fees (an ICC study showed that 12 per cent of the costs of arbitrations were the tribunal's fees and expenses, 80 per cent the parties') so r.68(4) appears to fall short of providing full recompense. However, disgruntled parties may be able to apply r.73(2)(a) to negate the tribunal's immunity from civil proceedings for recovery of the wasted expenses. **R68–90**

The power is stated to be as the court "thinks fit" but this does not mean that the court has an unfettered discretion in the exercise of its power, instead that it should be exercised to give effect to the principle that the tribunal should not be entitled to fees and expenses for time expended on part of the proceedings rendered abortive through its failure under r.68(2)(a), (g) or (h). Per the mandatory r.60(1), the tribunal is entitled to fees and expenses relating to other, non-aborted, parts of the proceedings but, in the context of r.68(2)(a), (g) and (h), it may be relatively rare that part of the proceedings are contaminated and part not. Where r.68(2)(g) applies, the court must apply r.78. **R68–91**

As a matter of natural justice and the right to a fair trial (ECHR art.6 refers), the arbitrator, or his representative, should be given a full opportunity to address the court on any proposal to exercise the r.68(4) power. Failure to notify such a proposal fairly in advance can result in a blatant miscarriage of justice as in an unreported English case (*WS v BB* **R68–92**

Unreported June 8, 2001 TCC) concerning an application under s.24 of the 1996 Act to remove the arbitrator, where in his presence, unrepresented and under the impression that he was present merely to assist the court, and with the judge refusing to consider application of s.29 of the 1996 Act (immunity of the arbitrator), the arbitrator's fees were approximately halved. The arbitrator was also made liable for the costs of this (and one other) court hearing and these exceeded his (now-reduced) fees. The authors respectfully submit that the Court of Session would not tolerate any such miscarriage of justice.

Rule 68(5), (6), (7) and (8)—Further appeals

R68–93 These provisions provide a strict limit to the right of appeal in order that the finality of the arbitration process be reinforced while remaining compatible with avoiding substantial injustice to a party. Thus, appeals from the Outer House to the Inner House can be made only with leave of the former and there is no appeal to the UKSC; s.40 of the Court of Session Act 1988 is excluded.

R68–94 These provisions (and others described below) are much stricter than the equivalent ones in England.

R68–95 For the time limit for seeking leave see r.71(5) below, and the commentary to that rule. See also RCS r.38.4 in relation to applications for leave to appeal (reclaim).

R68–96 The requirement that leave be obtained for a further appeal is not incompatible with the right to a fair trial under ECHR art.6 (*Kazakhstan v Istil Group Ltd* [2007] 2 Lloyd's Rep. 548).

R68–97 See the commentary to r.70(9), (10) and (11) at paras R70–43 to R70–51 below in respect of the question of whether, if leave is refused, the refusal to grant it can be appealed to the Inner House on the ground that the refusal followed action of the Outer House which was incompatible with the appellant's rights under art.6 of the ECHR .

Rule 69: Challenging an award: legal error D

69.—(1) A party may appeal to the Outer House against the tribunal's award on the ground that the tribunal erred on a point of Scots law (a "legal error appeal").

(2) An agreement between the parties to disapply rule 51(2)(c) by dispensing with the tribunal's duty to state its reasons for its award is to be treated as an agreement to exclude the court's jurisdiction to consider a legal error appeal.

DEFINITIONS

"Outer House": s.31(1)
"legal error appeal": r.69(1)
"party": ss.2(1), 31(1), (2)
"rule": s.31(1)

"tribunal": ss.2(1), 31(1)Arbitration (Scotland) Act 2010 (r.69)

STATUS

R69–01 This is a default rule so it is open to the parties to modify it, agree something different or disapply it completely (see s.9). The adoption by parties of various institutional rules will exclude r.69, as is discussed below (see paras R69–08 to R69–10).

R69–02 A question has arisen in English and US courts as to whether parties can agree to confer rights on courts to consider challenges to tribunal awards on findings of fact. In *Guangzhou Dockyards Co Ltd v E.N.E. Aegiali I* [2010] EWHC 2826 (Comm), the issue between the parties was essentially that GDC argued that it was open to the parties to an arbitration agreement to agree that questions of fact (as well as questions of law) arising out of an arbitration award can be the subject of an appeal to the English court, and that they had so agreed in that case. This was argued to follow from the principle of party autonomy enshrined in the 1996 Act. Blair J. decided that there had been no such agreement and, disappointingly, declined to express a definitive view on the main principle at stake, commenting at [29] that it was "very doubtful" that the court could have jurisdiction to hear an appeal from arbitrators on questions of fact, even if the parties were to agree to such an appeal. However, he did (helpfully) add:

> "29. In the light of [the absence of such an agreement], I do not need to express a view on the additional case law from outside the arbitration field cited by the Owners in support of a more general principle that parties cannot by agreement confer jurisdiction on a court which the court does not otherwise possess. It is worth however noting that in the United States, albeit on different statutory wording, it has been held that private parties have no power to alter or expand the grounds identified in the Federal Arbitration Act on which a federal court might review an arbitral decision, and that a contractual provision purporting to do so is legally unenforceable: see *Kyocera Corp vs Prudential-Bache Trade Services Inc* 341 F 3d 987 (9th Cir 2003), and *Hall Street Associates LLC vs Mattel Inc* (2008) 552 US 576 (Sup Ct), discussed in *Redfern & Hunter on International Arbitration*, 5th edn, (OUP, 2009), at p.612 et seq."

R69–03 The authors submit that having regard to the founding principle in s.1(c), and the existence of the mandatory r.70, the power in s.9 should, in relation to r.69, be interpreted restrictively as not enabling parties to confer on the court jurisdiction to intervene in a tribunal's award except as set out in r.70. See also s.13(2). Intervention under r.70 does not, of course, relate to findings of fact of the tribunal (see below).

R69–04 It follows that r.69 is not excluded in agricultural arbitration agreements

Arbitration (Scotland) Act 2010

entered into in pursuance of the Agricultural Holdings (Scotland) Acts 1991 and 2003: see commentary on s.16(1) at paras S16–06 to S16–10.

MODEL LAW

R69–05 There is no equivalent provision in the Model Law but this does not mean, as has been suggested, that the principle of r.69 is wholly alien thereto. Model Law art.5 states "In matters governed by this Law, no court shall intervene except where so provided in this Law" and ss.1(c) and 13, the latter emphatically, reflect that principle (in particular, excluding rights of appeal given by the Court of Session Act 1988) and the inclusion of rr.69/70 in the SAR does not, per se, conflict with art.5.

COMMENTARY

Introductory

R69–06 A r.69 legal error appeal is, notwithstanding being on an opt-out basis, the third of the three available means of appealing an arbitral award. The first (r.67) is a jurisdictional appeal and the second (r.68) is a serious irregularity appeal.

R69–07 Matters affecting each of rr.67, 68 and 69 are set out in paras R67–16 to R67–18.

R69–08 Most sets of institutional rules contain a mandatory provision which disapplies r.69, e.g. ICC Rules art.34(6) states:

> "Every award shall be binding on the parties. By submitting the dispute to arbitration under the Rules, the parties undertake to carry out any award without delay *and shall be deemed to have waived their right to any form of recourse insofar as such waiver can validly be made*" (authors' emphasis added).

Similarly, LCIA Rules art.26.8 states that:

> "Every award (including reasons for such award) shall be final and binding on the parties. The parties undertake to carry out any award immediately and without any delay (subject only to Article 27); *and the parties also waive irrevocably their right to any form of appeal, review or recourse to any state court or other legal authority, insofar as such waiver shall not be prohibited under any applicable law*" (authors' emphasis added).

R69–09 Note that both the ICC and LCIA Rules contain an express waiver of certain rights of appeal covering r.69: the mere provision in an institutional rule, or an arbitration agreement (whether it is part of a larger contract or is a joint submission or reference independent of or consequential to the larger contract) that the arbitrator's decision is to be "final and binding" is likely to be insufficient to exclude a legal error appeal (for a review of English, Canadian and Australian case law see *Essex CC v Premier Recycling Ltd* [2006] EWHC 3594 (TCC)). This is because it is not inconsistent with r.69 nor does it amount to an express agreement to modify or disapply r.69.

The same can be said for a rule that an award is to be "final conclusive **R69–10** and binding on the parties". The use of the word "conclusive" in that phrase has been held to be insufficient to amount to an agreement to disapply the similar s.69 of the 1996 Act, it being a mere emphasis of the position that an arbitral award is res judicata (*Shell Egypt West Manzala GmbH v Dana Gas Egypt Ltd* [2009] EWHC 2097 (Comm)).

If r.69 has been disapplied then the issue of disapplication is likely to be **R69–11** raised at the stage of the application for leave to appeal.

An arbitration agreement made before June 7, 2010 (i.e. the commence- **R69–12** ment of the Act) which disapplied the now-repealed default provision in s.3 of the 1972 Act is, per s.36(8), deemed to be an agreement to disapply r.69 unless the parties otherwise agree. Given that many arbitration clauses excluded the unpopular s.3 it is important to note that these clauses will still be effective to exclude r.69, unless the parties agree that r.69 should apply.

An agreement between the parties to disapply r.51(2)(c) (requiring the **R69–13** arbitrator to give reasons for his award) operates to exclude legal error r.69 appeals.

Rule 69 is applicable only to arbitrations (i) seated in Scotland where (ii) the **R69–14** tribunal has decided the dispute by applying Scots law to the facts (see the commentary to r.47 above). If, under r.47, the tribunal requires to decide the dispute in accordance with a non-Scots law, but is not provided with satisfactory evidence of the relevant rules of that non-Scots law, it must apply rules of Scots law on the basis that the rules of the non-Scots law are presumed to be the same as Scots law (*Bonnor v Balfour Kilpatrick Ltd*, 1974 S.C. 223).

If the parties have chosen a law other than Scots law as the applicable law **R69–15** to decide their dispute, or have required the arbitrator to take non-legal matters of equity into account and to act as an "*amicable compositeur*", the parties have not so much disapplied r.69 as taken the arbitration beyond the scope of r.69 in that the tribunal will not be making its award through the application of Scots law, an error of which could give rise to an appeal. See also the commentary below.

Since foreign law is a question of fact to be proved by expert evidence, it **R69–16** follows that if the tribunal errs on a point of non-Scots law, r.69 does not extend to appeals on such points. An analogous example in England was *Schwebel v Schwebel* [2010] EWHC 3280 (TCC) which arose from a Beth Din arbitration under the 1996 Act but applying Jewish substantive law, where Akenhead J. said at [29]:

> "No appeal can be made pursuant to s.69 as there is no question of English law which arises in connection with the award."

R69–17 In enacting rr.69 and 70, the 2010 Act has departed from the common law position which did not allow any appeal against an arbitral award on the merits of the award, even if the arbitrator had erred in law. The common law position had been the subject of criticism in the early 1970s which had resulted in the enactment of a default rule (in s.3 of the 1972 Act) whereby a party could apply to the Court of Session, at any stage of the arbitration up to the time of the making of the award, for a binding opinion of the court on any question of law whatsoever. This had the effect of significantly slowing down the arbitral process.

R69–18 Rules 69 and 41 can be seen as providing a compromise between the common law position and that under the former s.3. Fundamentally, r.69 seeks to reflect the presumed wishes of the parties that they wish to have the merits of the dispute decided by Scots law and that, where the arbitrator has failed to understand or apply that law, they should not be bound by such a failure; note, however, that the main application of s.69 in England has not been in respect of any arbitrator failure—see para.R69–22.

R69–19 A legal error appeal against an award is, however, significantly more restricted than such an appeal from any other statutory tribunal or from a court decision in a litigation at first instance. If something is an error of law it cannot also be a qualifying irregularity under r.68(2) (*Arbitration Application No.1 of 2013* [2014] CSOH 83 at [28]—a case where the appellant sought to rely on the same grounds for both a r.68 appeal and a r.70 application for leave to appeal under r.69 which grounds were found to be alleged irregularities under r.68 and not alleged errors of law within the meaning of r.69 at all).

R69–20 In particular, as under the pre-Act position, the facts found by the tribunal cannot be questioned (see the commentary to r.70(3)(c) at paras R70–17 to R70–28 below). This is in line with the advantage of finality given to parties choosing to resolve their dispute by arbitration. For example, a decision as to whether a loss was sustained in a foreign currency is a question of fact (*Milan Nigeria Ltd v Angeliki B Maritime Co* [2011] EWHC 892 (Comm) at [67]). In contrast, whether under the law of damages such a loss should be reflected in an award in domestic or foreign currency is a question of law.

R69–21 Respondents should be aware of the possibilities of seeking caution for expenses and also seeking payment of the sum awarded into the court as a condition precedent to an appeal or application proceeding (see r.71(10)–(12) below).

R69–22 In the development and parliamentary phases of the Bill, some parties appeared to perceive r.69 as being to rectify blunders made by non-lawyer arbitrators. However, a survey of the extensive jurisprudence under the equivalent s.69 of the 1996 Act shows that, with rare exceptions (e.g. occasional errors of law made by commodity trade association arbitrators who are, by definition, non-lawyer commodity traders), s.69 has operated completely differently. Three examples demonstrate what s.69 actually achieves and why it is necessary:

- In *Golden Strait Corp v Nippon Yusen Kubishika Kaisha (The Golden Victory)* [2007] 2 A.C. 353 the sole arbitrator decided a dispute by applying the law (a Court of Appeal decision by which he was, of course, bound) although he said that it led to the "wrong answer"; on appeal, the judge said much the same and on further appeal the Court of Appeal echoed that, being bound by its own previous decision. The House of Lords, in a 3–2 decision (with Lord Bingham, in the minority, delivering a notable and very powerful speech) reversed the Court of Appeal decision and therefore, in effect, changed the law. In the absence of s.69, this could not have happened and the parties would have been left with a decision causing substantial injustice.
- In *CMA CGM SA v Beteiligungs KG MS Northern Pioneer Schiffahrtsgesellschaft mbH & Co* [2003] 1 Lloyd's Rep. 204 a tribunal comprising a former Court of Appeal judge and two very senior QCs disagreed on the interpretation of a clause in a standard-form contract, such contract being in worldwide use with, probably, many thousands in use at any one time. Section 69 enabled such an important matter to be determined in an open court, instead of in private, in a precedential manner giving the necessary certainty.
- An LMAA tribunal was faced with a point of law upon which there was no authority and duly decided it; left there, the decision would have remained private to the parties and, even if published in anonymised form (as some LMAA awards are), would neither carry any precedential weight nor constitute part of the law of England. Section 69 solved both problems since, on appeal (*Mediterranean Salvage & Towage Ltd v Seamar Trading & Commerce Inc* [2008] EWHC 1875 (Comm)), Aikens J. agreed with the tribunal. His decision was subsequently upheld in the Court of Appeal ([2009] EWCA Civ 531).

Furthermore, giving the lie to the idea of the blundering non-lawyer, in *Lobb Partnership Ltd v Aintree Racecourse Co Ltd* [2002] EWHC (TCC) 3094, a non-lawyer arbitrator was, in effect, sandwiched between two apparently conflicting House of Lords decisions, the later of which post-dated the date of his award. On a s.69 appeal, the judge varied the award to take account of the later decision (and reconciled the apparent conflict) and remitted the award for reconsideration. **R69–23**

During the pre-Act phase, the view was also expressed that rr.41 and 69 would "open the floodgates"; first, the evidence in Scotland since 2010 has shown that that has not been the case and, secondly, there are approximately only 40 or so s.69 applications per year in England and, thirdly, it is understood that only 10–20 per cent of these are given leave to appeal and, of those that are, approximately 10–15 per cent are successful. Combining, we see that the overall success rate is between 1 and 3 per cent. **R69–24**

Rule 69(1)

R69–25 The right to appeal depends on the granting of an application for leave to allow the appeal to proceed (see r.70(2) and (3) below) so there is a 2-stage process.

R69–26 Both the application for leave and the appeal itself must be made within short time limits (see r.71(4) and (5) below).

R69–27 Before making an application a party must exhaust any available arbitral process of appeal or review (r.71(2)). For further detail on the procedure for applications for leave to appeal and appeals themselves, see commentary on r.70 below.

R69–28 In the TCC, it is normal for the judge to hear the application for leave to appeal and the appeal itself together since, in most cases, the facts and the arguments overlap significantly and it is cost-effective to hear them sequentially; of course, if leave is not granted, the hearing of the appeal becomes otiose but TCC judges normally express an obiter view on the merits of the appeal, almost invariably negative where leave to appeal has been refused.

R69–29 In contrast, in the English Commercial Court it is normal for the leave application to be dealt with on paper then, if leave is granted, for the hearing of the appeal itself to take place at a later date in front of a different judge.

Rule 69(2)

R69–30 If the parties have chosen to disapply r.51(2)(c) requiring the arbitrator to give reasons for his award, they will be treated as having excluded the right to make legal error appeals.

Rule 70: Legal error appeals: procedure etc. **M**

70.—(1) This rule applies only where rule 69 applies.

(2) A legal error appeal may be made only—
    (a) with the agreement of the parties, or
    (b) with the leave of the Outer House.

(3) Leave to make a legal error appeal may be given only if the Outer House is satisfied—
    (a) that deciding the point will substantially affect a party's rights,
    (b) that the tribunal was asked to decide the point, and
    (c) that, on the basis of the findings of fact in the award (including any facts which the tribunal treated as established for the purpose of deciding the point), the tribunal's decision on the point—
        (i) was obviously wrong, or Arbitration (Scotland) Act 2010 (r.70)
        (ii) where the court considers the point to be of general importance, is open to serious doubt.

(4) An application for leave is valid only if it—
    (a) identifies the point of law concerned, and
    (b) states why the applicant considers that leave should be granted.

(5) The Outer House must determine an application for leave without a hearing (unless satisfied that a hearing is required).

(6) The Outer House's determination of an application for leave is final.

(7) Any leave to appeal expires 7 days after it is granted (and so any legal error appeal made after then is accordingly invalid unless made with the agreement of the parties).

(8) The Outer House may decide a legal error appeal by—
- (a) confirming the award,
- (b) ordering the tribunal to reconsider the award (or part of it), or
- (c) if it considers reconsideration inappropriate, setting aside the award (or part of it).

(9) An appeal may be made to the Inner House against the Outer House's decision on a legal error appeal (but only with the leave of the Outer House).

(10) Leave may be given by the Outer House only where it considers—
- (a) that the proposed appeal would raise an important point of principle or practice, or
- (b) that there is another compelling reason for the Inner House to consider the appeal.

(11) The Outer House's decision on whether to grant such leave is final.

(12) The Inner House's decision on such an appeal is final.

DEFINITIONS

"Outer House": s.31(1)
"legal error appeal": r.69(1)
"party": ss.2(1), 31(1), (2)
"rule": s.31(1)
"tribunal": ss.2(1), 31(1)

STATUS

Rule 70 is mandatory so cannot be disapplied, or modified in any way, by the parties. This is to ensure that, if the default r.69 applies, the parties cannot alter the binding conditions upon which the Scottish Parliament has agreed to allow legal error appeals. It is not for the parties to an arbitration to try, by contractual agreement, to modify or disapply any part of a rule dealing with the functioning of the court. R70–01

MODEL LAW

There is no equivalent provision in the Model Law. R70–02

Arbitration (Scotland) Act 2010

COMMENTARY

Rule 70(2) and (4)—Application to allow legal error appeal to proceed

R70–03 A legal error appeal may proceed only with the leave of the Outer House, or with the agreement of the parties.

R70–04 The result of the somewhat circuitous drafting in r.70 and r.71(4) means that the general rule is that an application for leave has to be made within 28 days of the date when the award is "made". There are exceptions to this and the reader is referred to the commentary to r.71(4), below, for more detail in relation to time limits. In the unusual circumstances of an appeal by agreement, no leave is necessary and the appeal itself has to be made within 28 days of the date when the award is "made". See again the commentary to r.71(4) at paras R71–09 to R71–22 below.

R70–05 An application for leave is made by petition (in the style contained in RCS Form 14.4 (RCS rr.100.5, 14.4) or, if there is an undisposed of Outer House petition, by note (RCS rr.100.5, 15.2). The content of such a petition is discussed in the commentary on r.42(1) and (2) at para.R42–13 above.

R70–06 In *Arbitration Application No.1 of 2013* [2014] CSOH 83, the application did not identify any point of law at all in terms of r.69 and was therefore refused (at [28]).

R70–07 In *Arbitration Application No. 2 of 2011* [2011] CSOH 186, Lord Glennie commented at [3] that, given that the tribunal's findings of fact could not be disputed, detailed pleading of fact was to be avoided unless a party wished to put down a factual basis for seeking ancillary orders such as that for further reasons under r.71(8). He observed that adjustment to the petition and answers would seldom, if ever, be required and the hearing of the appeal itself would usually proceed on a basis of written notes of argument lodged in advance of the hearing, rather than on the basis of the formal pleadings.

R70–08 The RCS, at the time of writing, are unusual in that they appear to require the petition for leave also to contain the appeal itself on the assumption that leave is granted (RCS r.100.8). Upon lodging of the petition, the petitioner must enrol a motion for intimation and service of the petition (RCS r.100.5(3)). Rather oddly, at the same time the petitioner must also enrol another motion (which does not need to be intimated to the respondent and tribunal) seeking leave to appeal (RCS r.100.8(1)(a)). With this second motion any documents intended to be relied upon in the application, and if successful, the appeal, must be lodged.

R70–09 Given that RCS r.100.5 provides that any application under the Act is to be made by petition, and RCS r.100.8(3) provides a time limit for the respondent to lodge grounds of opposition within 14 days of service of the petition or note, the purpose of the petitioner having to make an unintimated motion under r.100.8(1)(a) is unclear and its role productive of unnecessary confusion to practitioners. The authors trust that the matter will soon be addressed by the new Scottish Civil Justice Council. The reader is referred to the most up to date version of the *Greens Annotated Rules of* *the Court of Session* (Edinburgh: W. Green) which are also contained in Vol.2 of *The Parliament House Book* (Edinburgh: W. Green).

If leave is granted, the appeal must be made within seven days of the date **R70–10** of grant. See the commentary on r.70(7) below. With the current requirement to lodge the appeal at the same time as the application for leave, perhaps a grant of leave automatically "makes" the appeal in the remainder of the petition, although there is a (technical) argument that this is not compliant with r.70(7) and some step by the appellant to "make" the appeal is required.

Rule 70(3)—Preconditions for legal error appeal

This subpara. sets out the three preconditions which must be satisfied **R70–11** before the Outer House will allow the appeal to proceed. These conditions are essentially very similar to those in the equivalent s.69 of the 1996 Act.

Given the close similarity of rr.69/70 with s.69 of the 1996 Act and given **R70–12** that in *Arbitration Application No.3 of 2011*, 2012 S.L.T. 150 Lord Glennie said at [8]:

"Since the Act was closely and unashamedly modelled on the [1996] Act, and reflects the same underlying philosophy, authorities on the Act (and its predecessor, the Arbitration Act 1979) in relation to questions of interpretation and approach will obviously be of relevance. There is no point in re-inventing the (arbitration) wheel",

it can be expected that the Outer House will play close attention to the extensive English jurisprudence covering s.69 in general and s.69(3) in particular.

Rule 70(3)(a)—"Substantially affect" parties' rights

The first precondition is that a decision on the point of Scots law in **R70–13** question will "substantially affect" a party's rights. The "rights" in question must be the rights or liabilities under the award itself since it is the award which gives rise to the wish to appeal. In this context, given the founding principles in s.1(a) of the resolution of disputes without unnecessary delay or expense and (per s.1(c)) that the court should not intervene except as provided for, the authors submit that "substantially" should be interpreted as meaning "greatly" or "essentially".

This has been the approach adopted in England, e.g. where the tribunal **R70–14** may have erred on two grounds of its decision but on the third ground had not been asked to make a decision on the point of law being applied, a decision by the court on the points of law in the two grounds relied upon could not substantially affect the appellant's rights, and on that basis permission to appeal was properly refused (*CMA CGM SA v Beteiligungs KG*

MS Northern Pioneer Schiffahrtsgesellschaft mbH & Co [2003] 1 W.L.R. 1015 at 1023, [25]–[27].

R70–15 Rule 70(3)(a) ultimately derives from s.1(4) of the now-repealed 1979 Act. There is much case law concerning whether an appellant's rights would be "substantially affected" by the point of law in question, e.g. in *Coal Authority v Trustees of the Nostell Trust* [2005] EWHC 154 (TCC) an appeal was sought by a public authority in respect of an award against it of (1) £191,000, and (2) £12,500. It was held that in the context of the award as a whole, the £12,500 element was not something which substantially affected the rights of the parties.

Rule 70(3)(b)—Tribunal was "asked to decide" the point of law

R70–16 The second precondition is that the tribunal had been "asked to decide" the point of Scots law on which the tribunal had allegedly erred. In England, this has been held to include the raising of the point before the tribunal without conceding that it should be decided a certain way (*CMA CGM SA* [2003] 1 W.L.R. 1015 per Court of Appeal at 1030–1032, [32]–[36]) and to require that the point has been fairly and squarely put to the tribunal for its decision (*House of Fraser Ltd v Scottish Widows Plc* [2011] EWHC 2800 (Ch) at [26] following *Safeway Stores v Legal and General Assurance Society Ltd* [2005] 1 P. & C.R. 9 at [8]; this was followed in *Arbitration Application No.1 of 2013* [2014] CSOH 83 at [30]). If the point has not been expressly raised with the tribunal it is difficult to see how it can have been asked to decide it.

Rule 70(3)(c)—Findings in fact (actual or deemed) unalterable

R70–17 The third precondition has two possible limbs with both proceeding on the basis that the findings of fact are not open to challenge. This indicates the intention of the Scottish Parliament to exclude any challenge to the findings in fact whether or not they proceeded on the basis of an error of law by the tribunal, e.g. lack of evidence or perverse interpretation of the evidence. This accords with the approach under s.69 of the 1996 Act (*Demco Investments & Commercial SA v SE Banken Forsakring Holding AB* [2005] 2 Lloyd's Rep. 650 per Cooke J. at [35] to [45], followed in *House of Fraser Ltd v Scottish Widows Plc* [2011] EWHC 2800 (Ch)). This reinforces the limited nature of the court's role in relation to review the merits of the tribunal's decision. Even if a r.69 legal error appeal is permitted, such is therefore more restricted than appeal in litigation from the decision of a court at first instance. Factual and evidential matters decided by the tribunal, including relevancy, admissibility, materiality and weight of any evidence, will not involve "points of law" which can be appealed under r.69. See also para.R69–17.

R70–18 The tribunal may make an award on the basis that even if the claimant's factual allegations are treated as established, i.e. taken *pro veritate*, the law does not entitle him to the remedy which he seeks. If such an award is made then the deemed facts are treated as established in relation to any legal error appeal.

Rule 70(3)(c)(i)—Decision on point of law was "obviously wrong"

R70–19 The first possible limb is that, based on the findings in fact, the tribunal's decision on the point of law which it had been asked to decide was "obviously wrong". If the decision on the point of law, following complex legal analysis and opposing legal argument, was wrong, then it will not be "obviously wrong" and so will not be reviewable on this basis. The mere fact that the decision was wrong or that another tribunal, or the court, might have reached a different decision will not make the decision "obviously wrong", nor is there any threshold of the length of time taken by the judge to understand the alleged wrongfulness (*Braes of Doune Wind Farm (Scotland) Ltd v Alfred McAlpine Business Services Ltd* [2008] 1 Lloyd's Rep. 608 per Akenhead J. at 615, [28]).

R70–20 It has recently been said that:

> "For a decision to be obviously wrong, it must involve something in the nature of a major intellectual aberration or 'making a false leap in logic or reaching a result for which there was no reasonable explanation': *HMV UK Ltd v Propinvest Friar Ltd Partnership* [2012] 1 Lloyd's Rep 416" (*Arbitration Application No.1 of 2013* [2014] CSOH 83 at [32] per Lord Woolman).

It has been observed that the "obviously wrong" test is a stringent one which will seldom be satisfied (*National Trust for Places of Historic Interest or Natural Beauty v Fleming* [2009] EWHC 1789 (Ch) per Henderson J. at [12]).

R70–21 The distinction between r.70(3)(c)(i) and (ii) can be viewed this way: the former (broadly applicable to bespoke contracts) sets, as given by *National Trust* and *HMV*, a very high threshold while the latter (broadly applicable to standard-form contracts in widespread usage) sets a slightly lower one.

Rule 70(3)(c)(ii)—Decision of "general importance" and "open to serious doubt"

R70–22 If the court takes the view that the tribunal's decision was not obviously wrong, the next issue is whether the point of law is "of general importance". In s.69 of the 1996 Act there is a similar provision, albeit that it requires the point of law to be of "general public importance". The reason for the difference appears to flow from the purpose of the provision not requiring the public as a whole to have an interest but merely a section of the public.

R70–23 An example clearly being of general importance is *Northern Pioneer* [2002] EWCA Civ 1878 (see para.R69–22 above).

R70-24 In contrast to *Northern Pioneer*, the interpretation of a clause in a charterparty that was said to be "common" without any indication that the market needed a resolution of the interpretation issue, or the extent of its use or the existence of other cases where the interpretation issue had arisen, has been held not to be a point of law of "general public importance" (*Bottiglieri di Navigazione SpA v Cosco Qingdao Ocean Shipping Co (The Bunga Saga Lima)* [2005] 2 Lloyd's Rep. 1 per Gloster J. at 8, [18]. A similar outcome occurred in relation to a rent review clause in a bespoke 125-year lease (*Arbitration Application No.1 of 2013* [2014] CSOH 83).

R70-25 The question of what constitutes "general public importance" has arisen in many different guises but the judgment in the case *Martrade Shipping and Transport Gmbh v United Enterprises Corporation* [2014] EWHC 1884 (Comm), while strictly an appeal by Martrade under s.69 of the 1996 Act, reads more as a combined claimant/respondent/tribunal application to the court for a ruling; Popplewell J. said at [1]:

> "This is an appeal pursuant to [s.69] from [an award]. It raises a short point in relation to the applicability of the Late Payment of Commercial Debts (Interest) Act 1998 to charterparties providing for English law and London arbitration. It is a point which the tribunal described as arising in an increasing number of cases and upon which the Court's guidance would be welcomed."

R70-26 Similarly, in *Mediterranean Salvage & Towage Ltd v Seamar Trading & Commerce Inc* [2008] 2 Lloyd's Rep. 628; [2008] EWHC 1875 (Comm), Aikens J. said at [9]:

> "In their award the arbitrators correctly noted that there is no direct authority on this particular issue. The question [at issue] has been the subject of debate in the textbooks and amongst shipping lawyers for many years. The present question is therefore of interest and perhaps importance to the shipping industry ... In view of the fact that this is a point on which there is no direct authority and its possible general interest to the industry, I decided to reserve judgment."

After full consideration of the authorities Aikens J. effectively confirmed the tribunal's award; in turn, he was unanimously upheld by a strong Court of Appeal (*Mediterranean Salvage & Towage Ltd v Seamar Trading & Commerce Inc* [2009] 2 Lloyd's Rep 639; [2009] EWCA Civ 531). A further example clearly being of general importance is *Northern Pioneer* [2003] 1 W.L.R. 1015.

R70-27 If, and only if, the court takes the view that the point of law is of general importance does it have to ask itself whether the tribunal's decision on it was "open to serious doubt"; see *Northern Pioneer* [2002] EWCA Civ 1878 at para.R69-22 above.

In *Coal Authority v Trustees of the Nostell Trust* (see para.R70–14 above), **R70–28** the proper interpretation of s.19 of the Coal Mining Subsidence Act 1991 relating to the assessment and quantification of remedial work caused by subsidence to listed buildings was said to have been in issue in some 36 claims in the period before the appeal and occurred with reasonable regularity such that it was of "general public importance" (*Coal Authority v Trustees of the Nostell Trust* [2005] EWHC 154 (TCC) per H.H. Judge Coulson QC at [13]).

Rule 70(5)—Decision on application without a hearing

See paras R69–28 and R69–29 above. The purpose of this rule is to **R70–29** expedite the process relating to appeals.

The parties should be informed as soon as possible whether leave has been **R70–30** granted. The question may arise as to whether this is compatible with art.6 of the ECHR but, given that the parties have chosen to have their dispute dealt with by arbitration rather than in a court, they have implicitly accepted that their appeal rights, including the right to have a hearing on the application for leave to make a legal error appeal, might be curtailed in the interests of the advantages of the arbitral process (para.S1–21 refers).

There is another strong answer to the question as to whether r.70(3)'s very **R70–31** tight restrictions on leave to appeal are at risk under art.6 ECHR. Other than in England and Wales, there is no right in any ECHR jurisdiction to make any legal error appeal whatsoever so the fact that Scotland and the rest of the UK offers such a right cannot, by virtue of the restrictions, be seen as being a disproportionate means of fulfilling a legitimate aim (reconciliation of finality, fairness, expedition and cost in arbitration) where state authorities have considerable discretion in regulating the setting aside of arbitral awards (see commentary on s.1).

Rule 70(6)—Finality of decision on allowance of making of legal appeal

The Outer House's decision on whether a legal error appeal may proceed **R70–32** is final and the right of appeal to the Inner House, given by s.18 of the Court of Session Act 1988, is excluded.

In *BLCT (13096) Ltd v J Sainsbury Plc* [2004] 2 P. & C.R. 3, the Court of **R70–33** Appeal held (at [33]) that statutory provisions limiting the right of appeal from an arbitral award do not offend art.6 ECHR. This was because the parties had chosen that course and, by implication, it was open to parties to agree to waive the protection of a public hearing to which they would otherwise be entitled under art.6. See also para.R70–29 above.

There is nothing in the RCS equivalent to either CPR 3.1(7) ("A power of **R70–34** the court under these Rules to make an order includes a power to vary or revoke the order") or CPR 52.9(1)(b) (which confers a power on the Court of Appeal to set aside permission to appeal in whole or part where there is a compelling reason to do so). Rule 70(6) makes it clear that the decision of the Outer House is final, consistent with s.1(c).

Rule 70(7)—Legal error appeal—Time limit

R70–35   The leave to appeal has a time limit attached to it of seven days after its grant, with the obvious intention of expediting procedure. An appeal outside the seven days is invalid but it is open to the parties to agree to extend that. For the method of appeal the reader is referred to Ch.100 of the RCS.

Rule 70(8)—Remedies

R70–36   There are a number of possible outcomes for a legal error appeal. The first, confirmation of the award, is another way of saying that the appeal is dismissed. If the appeal is to any extent successful, the question for the court will lie between the second (tribunal reconsideration) and third (set-aside) options.

R70–37   The first issue for the court is whether an order requiring the arbitrator to reconsider the award or any part of it is appropriate. Only if that is inappropriate is it open to the court to set aside the award or part of it.

R70–38   See paras R68–79 to R68–82 concerning reconsideration and see para.R71–07 for an interesting example of remission.

R70–39   The question of whether or not to remit for reconsideration arose in *E D and F Man Sugar Ltd v Unicargo Transportgesellschaft GmbH* [2013] EWCA Civ 1449 where Tomlinson L.J. (with whom Christopher Clarke and Patten L.JJ. agreed) said at [20]:

> "In my judgment it would be highly inappropriate to remit the matter to the arbitrators. The original arbitration Claim Form sought only remission of the Award for reconsideration in the light of the judgment of the court, which judgment in turn could be expected only to deal with the question of law identified in the application made pursuant to s.69 of the Arbitration Act 1996 ... It would not be appropriate to permit [Charterers] now to re-open the arbitration and to seek from the arbitrators findings which they had contended at the arbitration were irrelevant and unnecessary. That is sufficient to dispose of [their] application. However, I would go further, as I suspect that a remission would in any event be to no purpose. Whilst mindful that we do not know precisely what evidence the arbitrators had before them, I infer that [Charterers] in fact adduced no evidence on the basis of which the arbitrators could have made a finding as to the cause of the fire. [Counsel for Owners] described the evidence on this point as 'not extensive' and that may be a euphemism. It would be doubly inappropriate for [Charterers] now to be permitted to introduce fresh evidence which, had they thought it relevant, they could have obtained for use at the arbitration."

Arbitration (Scotland) Act 2010 (r.70)

See paras R71–30 to R71–32, concerning whether or not the court can order the arbitrator to appear to be cross-examined, which also applies to r.70(8)(b). **R70–40**

The time gap between the court's decision and the original award may cause difficulties for the tribunal and this may point towards set-aside being appropriate (see *Ascot Commodities NV v Olam International Ltd* [2002] C.L.C. 277). **R70–41**

If the court orders the tribunal to reconsider the award or any part of it, the reconsidered award must be made by no later than three months after the date of the court's order, unless the court specifies a different deadline (r.72(1)). For the effects of remission see the commentary to r.72 below. **R70–42**

Rule 70(9), (10), (11) and (12)—Further appeals

These four paragraphs must be read together. They apply to the decision of the Outer House on the appeal itself rather than the preceding decision of the Outer House on whether it should grant leave to appeal, such latter decision being final (per r.70(6)). **R70–43**

The Outer House's decision on a legal error appeal can be appealed only with its leave, i.e. there is no "leapfrog" appeal direct to the Inner House as there is to the UKSC in England. **R70–44**

Leave must be sought within 28 days (r.71(5)). **R70–45**

The appeal must be made by reclaiming motion within seven days of leave being granted (r.71(5)). **R70–46**

If leave is refused, the question arises as to whether the refusal to grant leave can be appealed to the Inner House on the ground that the refusal followed action of the Outer House which was incompatible with the appellant's right under art.6 of the ECHR. **R70–47**

It has been held in England that, under the 1996 Act, there is a possible appeal against a refusal to grant leave to appeal to the Court of Appeal on the ground that the refusal followed action by the first instance court which was incompatible with the appellant's art.6 rights (*CGU International Insurance Plc v AstraZeneca Insurance Co Ltd* [2007] 1 Lloyd's Rep. 142 per Rix L.J. at 155, 156, [73], following *North Range Shipping Ltd v Seatrans Shipping Corp (The Western Triumph)* [2002] 2 Lloyd's Rep. 1). This rests on the residual jurisdiction of the Court of Appeal to hear appeals from any court or judgment of the High Court (Senior Courts Act 1981 s.16) combined with the existence of a remedy under s.9(1) of the Human Rights Act 1998 against an act of a court which is incompatible with Convention rights. **R70–48**

In Scotland, the Outer House and the Inner House are part of the same court, the Court of Session. Every order of the single judge in the Outer House is subject to review of the Inner House in accordance with the Court of Session Act 1988 s.18. Review is by means of a "reclaiming" motion against the interlocutor (order) of the Outer House (RCS r.38.2). If the interlocutor refuses leave (as in *CGU International Insurance Plc* [2007] 1 **R70–49**

Arbitration (Scotland) Act 2010

Lloyd's Rep. 142), then such an interlocutor cannot be appealed (RCS r.38.4(6)). In relation to the seeking of leave, it appears that the Inner House's residual jurisdiction under the 1988 Act has been excluded by RCS r.38.4(6).

R70–50 The authors submit that RCS r.38.4(6) is not incompatible with art.6(1) of the ECHR. A requirement that leave be obtained for a further appeal is not incompatible with the art.6(1) right (*Kazakhstan v Istil Group Ltd* [2007] 2 Lloyd's Rep. 548).

R70–51 There is no right of appeal to the UKSC and the right otherwise given by s.40 of the Court of Session Act 1988 is excluded.

Rule 71: Challenging an award: supplementary M

71.—(1) This rule applies to—
    (a) jurisdictional appeals,
    (b) serious irregularity appeals, and
    (c) where rule 69 applies to the arbitration, legal error appeals,
and references to "appeal" are to be construed accordingly.

(2) An appeal is competent only if the appellant has exhausted any available arbitral process of appeal or review (including any recourse available under rule 58).

(3) No appeal may be made against a provisional award.

(4) An appeal must be made no later than 28 days after the later of the following dates—
    (a) the date on which the award being appealed against is made,
    (b) if the award is subject to a process of correction under rule 58, the date on which the tribunal decides whether to correct the award, or
    (c) if there has been an arbitral process of appeal or review, the date on which the appellant was notified of the result of that process.
A legal error appeal is to be treated as having being made for the purposes of this rule if an application for leave is made.

(5) An application for leave to appeal against the Outer House's decision on an appeal must be made no later than 28 days after the date on which the decision is made (and any such leave expires 7 days after it is granted).

(6) An appellant must give notice of an appeal to the other party and the tribunal.

(7) The tribunal may continue with the arbitration pending determination of an appeal against a part award.

(8) The Outer House (or the Inner House in the case of an appeal against the Outer House's decision) may—
    (a) order the tribunal to state its reasons for the award being appealed in sufficient detail to enable the Outer House (or Inner House) to deal with the appeal properly, and
    (b) make any other order it thinks fit with respect to any additional expenses arising from that order.

(9) Where the Outer House (or the Inner House in the case of an appeal

against the Outer House's decision) decides an appeal by setting aside the award (or any part of it), it may also order that any provision in an arbitration agreement which prevents the bringing of legal proceedings in relation to the subject-matter of the award (or that part of it) is void.

(10) The Outer House (or the Inner House in the case of an appeal against the Outer House's decision) may—
    (a) order an appellant (or an applicant for leave to appeal) to provide security for the expenses of the appeal (or application), and
    (b) dismiss the appeal (or application) if the order is not complied with.

(11) But such an order may not be made only on the ground that the appellant (or applicant)—
    (a) is an individual who ordinarily resides outwith the United Kingdom, or
    (b) is a body which is—
        (i) incorporated or formed under the law of a country outwith the United Kingdom, or
        (ii) managed or controlled from outwith the United Kingdom.

(12) The Outer House (or the Inner House in the case of an appeal against the Outer House's decision) may—
    (a) order that any amount due under an award being appealed (or any associated provisional award) must be paid into court or otherwise secured pending its decision on the appeal (or the application for leave to appeal), and
    (b) dismiss the appeal (or application) if the order is not complied with.

(13) An appeal to the Inner House against any decision of the Outer House under this rule may be made only with the leave of the Outer House.

(14) An application for leave to appeal against such a decision must be made no later than 28 days after the date on which the decision is made (and any such leave expires 7 days after it is granted).

(15) Leave may be given by the Outer House only where it considers—
    (a) that the proposed appeal would raise an important point of principle or practice, or
    (b) that there is another compelling reason for the Inner House to consider the appeal.

(16) The Outer House's decision on whether to grant such leave is final.

(17) A decision of the Inner House under this rule (including any decision on an appeal against a decision by the Outer House) is final.

DEFINITIONS

    "appeal": r.71(1)
    "arbitration agreement: ss.4, 31(1)
    "jurisdictional appeal": r.67(1)
    "legal error appeal": r.69(1)
    "notice": r.83

"Outer House": s.31(1)
"party": ss.2(1), 31(1), (2)
"provisional award": r.53
"serious irregularity appeal": r.68(1)
"tribunal": ss.2(1), 31(1)

STATUS

R71-01 Rule 71 is mandatory so cannot be disapplied, or modified in any way, by the parties. This is necessary because it relates to the court procedures for appeals under rr.67, 68 and 69 and it is not for the parties to an arbitration to modify or disapply any part of a rule dealing with the functioning of the court. Further, since the rights of appeal to the Outer House in rr.67 and 68 are mandatory and, while r.69 (legal error appeals) is a default rule, r.70 is mandatory, it is logical for the procedures to be mandatory also.

MODEL LAW

R71-02 This rule has no equivalent in the Model Law. Article 34(4) does however provide that in an application to set aside (appeal) a party may ask the court to suspend the setting aside proceedings for a period of time fixed by the court to enable the tribunal to resume the arbitral proceedings or to take such action as would, in the tribunal's opinion, eliminate the grounds for setting aside. This has some resonance in r.71(8) allowing the court to order the tribunal to provide reasons.

COMMENTARY

Rule 71(1)

R71-03 Rule 71 applies equally to all three means of challenge to an arbitral award, except only if r.69 is disapplied.

Rule 71(2)—Requirement to exhaust other remedies

R71-04 Given that parties have chosen arbitration in preference to litigation to resolve the dispute, one of the founding principles of the Act (s.1(c)) is that the court should not intervene in an arbitration except as provided in the Act. The requirement on parties to exhaust arbitral remedies before applying to the Outer House is a consequence of that policy.

R71-05 Arbitral remedies may include (i) any arbitral process of appeal or review contained in the arbitration agreement or institutional rules incorporated therein, or (ii) the correction and clarification process provided under r.58 (unless excluded by the parties).

R71-06 In connection with the latter process, a party discontent with an award that might be appealed must first seek a remedy under r.58. The consequence of failing to consider such a remedy is that the appeal or application could be held to be incompetent for failure to exhaust the r.58 remedy but the r.58 remedy itself may by then be time-barred, subject to an application for relief under r.58(4). Examples under the 1996 Act where a party's appeal was held to be incompetent for such a reason was *Torch Offshore LLC v Cable Shipping Inc* [2004] 2 Lloyd's Rep 446 at [28] and *Sinclair v Woods of Winchester* [2005] EWHC 1631.

Rule 71(2) requires the appellant, prior to making any appeal under rr.67, 68 or 69, to exhaust any available arbitral process of appeal or review including any recourse available under r.58. The latter is both straightforward (see the commentary on r.58) and relatively common but examples of arbitral appeal processes are not common, typically occurring in the narrowly focused London-based commodity trade association arbitral systems (e.g. GAFTA and FOSFA) where arbitrations take place, under restricted procedures, before a tribunal of three trade arbitrators with a right of appeal to a Board of Appeal, a tribunal of five (also normally trade arbitrators). **R71–07**

A review of those cases that have come before the court shows that, as often happens in practice, where the second tier decision confirms the first, the court will be highly reluctant to overturn an 8–0 decision by trade arbitrators. In *Bunge SA v Nibulon Trading BV* [2013] EWHC 3936 (Comm) there was a very rare occurrence of the second tier tribunal overturning the first but then itself being overturned by the court. The award was remitted to the Board for reconsideration; see para.R70–39.

Rule 71(3)—No appeal against provisional award

There is no right of appeal against a provisional award, on any ground; see commentary on r.53. **R71–08**

Rule 71(4), (5) and (6)—Time limits

A jurisdictional or serious irregularity appeal or an application for leave to make a legal error appeal must be made within the short time limit of 28 days, the trigger point for which depends on whether there has been an arbitral process of appeal or review or a r.58 process for correction (including clarification—see r.58(1)(b)). **R71–09**

The basic position is that, where there has been no arbitral appeal or review and no r.58 process, the trigger point is the date on which the award is made, which is the date the award is delivered to each of the parties in accordance with r.83 (see r.51(3)). Where the award is delivered on different dates, the "making" of the award will be the last of those dates otherwise there could be appeals occurring at different times. The first of the 28 days is then the day after the trigger point date. **R71–10**

The parties' arbitration agreement may expressly, or by incorporation of separate rules, contain its own arbitral appeal or review process. For the trigger point for the 28 days to be delayed, an arbitral process of appeal or **R71–11**

Arbitration (Scotland) Act 2010

R71–12 If there has been an arbitral process of appeal or review, the trigger point is the date of notification of the result of that process. The first of the 28 days begins with the day after the date on which the appellant was notified of the result of that process. For what amounts to "notification" see r.83 below.

R71–13 If there has been a r.58 process for correction, r.71(4)(b) provides that the trigger point is the date on which the tribunal "decides" whether to correct the award. Given the emphasis in s.1(a) on fairness in arbitration, with the House of Lords having ruled that a decision is ineffective until it has been notified to a party (see *R (on the application of Anufrijeva) v Secretary of State for the Home Department* [2004] 1 A.C. 604) and with the existence of the duty of the tribunal to notify the parties of the decision under r.24(1)(b) and (c)(i), the authors submit that, on a proper construction of r.71(4)(b), the trigger point is the date of notification or service of the tribunal decision to the parties. The date of notification or service of the document would then be ascertained under r.83.

R71–14 While a r.58 correction process can be initiated by the tribunal itself, prudence suggests that the possibility of the tribunal initiating the process should not be relied on by parties in deciding whether to appeal.

R71–15 If both an internal arbitral appeal or review process or a r.58 correction process are competent then the trigger point for the 28 days is the trigger point latest in time under those processes.

R71–16 If an appeal or application is not lodged within the 28-day period prescribed by r.71(4), an appellant or applicant will also have to lodge a motion with the Outer House to obtain relief under RCS r.2.1 (*Hume v Nursing and Midwifery Council*, 2010 S.C. 246), albeit the ability to seek relief under the RCS has been questioned in *Holmes v Nursing and Midwifery Council* [2009] CSIH 82. Under RCS r.2.1, the court has a discretion to grant relief if the failure has been due to "mistake, oversight or other excusable cause" on such conditions, if any, as the court thinks fit. In other words, first the failure must be due to the specified cause. Then, even if the failure is of that type, the court has an overriding discretion in the matter.

R71–17 In relation to extension of time for lodging arbitration appeals in England (refer s.79 of the 1996 Act), in *AOOT Kalmneft v Glencore International AG* [2002] 1 Lloyd's Rep. 128 at 137, Colman J. set out the following material factors to be taken into account:

    (i) the length of the delay;
    (ii) whether, in permitting the time limit to expire and the subsequent delay to occur, the appellant was acting reasonably in all the circumstances;
    (iii) whether the respondent to the appeal or the arbitrator caused or contributed to the delay;

(iv) whether the respondent to the appeal would by reason of the delay suffer irremediable prejudice in addition to the mere loss of time if the appeal were permitted to proceed;
(v) whether the arbitration has continued during the period of delay (i.e. where the appeal is against a part award) and, if so, what impact on the progress of the arbitration or the costs incurred in respect of it the determination of the appeal by the court might now have;
(vi) the strength of the appeal;
(vii) whether in the broadest sense it would be unfair to the appellant for him to be denied the opportunity of having the appeal determined.

While Colman J.'s criteria have been cited often in subsequent judgments, it should be noted that, in *Nagusina Naviera v Allied Maritime Inc* [2003] 2 C.L.C. 1 at [39]–[42], Mance L.J. considered that criteria (i), (ii) and (iii) were the primary ones, whereas (iv) was not essential, (v) was minor, (vi) was where the appellant's case was so strong that it would be an obvious hardship not to grant relief; and (vii) had to be considered in the context of the importance of finality and restriction of court intervention by means of time limits. **R71–18**

AOOT Kalmneft v Glencore International AG [2002] 1 Lloyd's Rep. 128 was a case involving international parties and the authors submit that the court is likely to be less sympathetic to appeals by Scottish parties and the factors may be more relevant to the discretion to be exercised by the court. The weight to be given to each of the factors will vary in each case (see, e.g. *Thyssen Canada Ltd v Mariana Maritime SA* [2005] 1 Lloyd's Rep. 640; and *Sinclair v Woods of Winchester Ltd*, 102 Con. L.R. 127 where a delay of one day was fatal). **R71–19**

Rule 71(5) provides for a relatively lengthy period of 28 days for a party to seek leave to appeal to the Inner House against the decision of the Outer House on an appeal. **R71–20**

If such leave is granted, the appeal (by reclaiming motion under Ch.38 of the RCS) must be enrolled within seven days of such granting. This overrides the default provisions of RCS Ch.38 which provide that a reclaiming motion must be enrolled within 14 days and that leave must be obtained within that time limit (albeit for the possibility of the suspension of that time limit if the judge who made the decision cannot be obtained to consider leave within the 14 days). See also RCS r.38.4 in relation to applications for leave to appeal (reclaim). **R71–21**

Rule 71(6) provides that an appellant must give notice of an appeal to the other party or parties and to the tribunal. This would normally be given after the Outer House makes its order under RCS 100.5(3) for service of the appeal. **R71–22**

Rule 71(7)—Continuation of the arbitration

R71–23 Notwithstanding the making of an appeal against a part award, the tribunal has a power to continue with the arbitration and this must be exercised in the light of the tribunal's duties under r.24. Where there is a part award there may be another aspect of the case which can be dealt with without the need for the court's decision on the part award and, if that is the case, the tribunal should not normally suspend proceedings, thereby causing delay in the resolution of such other aspect, merely because its part award is being appealed.

Rule 71(8)—Order for reasons

R71–24 The award must contain reasons unless the parties have contracted out of this requirement or the award reflects the terms of a settlement (see the commentary to rr.51(2)(c) (paras R51–33 to R51–56) and 57(4).

R71–25 If the parties have not contracted out of the r.51(2)(c) requirement, the award will contain reasons but these may be insufficient, either through brevity, incompleteness or their confused and/or illogical nature, for the court to decide the appeal. In such event, the first remedy is an application to the tribunal under r.58(1)(a) or (b) for a correction of the award (see commentary on r.71(2) and r.58). If the tribunal does not provide the correction or clarification sought, the court can be expected to exercise its power under r.71(8) to order the tribunal to state its reasons. This is consistent with the founding principle in s.1(c) under which court intervention is to be reduced to the minimum.

R71–26 Such a failure to provide adequate reasons could, if it caused substantial injustice to a party e.g. by leaving it in the dark as to a material part of its case, amount to a serious irregularity giving rise to an appeal under r.68 and to an order from the court requiring the tribunal to reconsider the award.

R71–27 Rule 71(8), in terms, applies only where an appeal has been made and not where a mere application to the Outer House for leave to appeal has been made; r.71(8) is not triggered by an application for leave to make a legal error appeal. The equivalent s.70(4) of the 1996 Act applies both to an application and an appeal and, in relation to an application, provides that the power is to enable the court properly to consider the application or appeal. While r.71(8) makes no reference to an application, r.71(4) provides that a legal error appeal is to be treated as having been made for the purposes of r.71 if an application is made. It follows that "appeal" in r.71 is to be read as "appeal or application" where appropriate.

R71–28 If the reasons have been given in a document separate from the award and which, by agreement of the parties, is confidential and privileged, the court is nevertheless entitled to look at it to see the reasons of the tribunal if this is necessary to enable it to deal with the appeal properly (*Tame Shipping Ltd v Easy Navigation Ltd* (*The Easy Rider*) [2004] 2 Lloyd's Rep. 626 per Moore-Bick J. at 634, [28]).

The court can be assumed to be alert to the possible misuse of r.71(8). In **R71–29** *Eitzen Bulk A/S v TTMI SARL* [2012] EWHC 202 Comm, Eder J. said this:

> "34. Notwithstanding, Mr Passmore submitted that I should make an order requiring the Tribunal to state further reasons because even if such further reasons would not assist in establishing an estoppel, nevertheless it would assist his first main argument in relation to "unworkability"..... However, it seems to me that this attempted use of the power to order further reasons is misconceived. As I have said, my view is that the application for further reasons was out of time. In any event, it seems to me that in truth Mr Passmore is seeking in this context to rely upon the post-contractual conduct of the parties as an aid to construction. On well-established principles, that is impermissible. For all these reasons I reject the application by Eitzen for further reasons."

The English case *Sumner v Costa Ltd and D* [2013] EWHC 4116 (Ch) saw an **R71–30** attempt by the appellants, believed to be the first such in a reported case under the 1996 Act, in an "inadequate reasons appeal" to have the court order D, the arbitrator, to appear in court to be cross-examined to discover his true reasons for the award. The judge, having noted that he had the power ("jurisdiction") to make such an order, refused to exercise it, concluding:

> "43. For my own part, I view the application [for] the cross-examination as unnecessary and inappropriate in this case. If the reasons given in the award can be shown on the face of what the second defendant has written to be not good enough or worse then the claimants will succeed.
> 44. Further, interrogation of the arbitrator would be contrary to the principles which underpin the process of arbitration, both generally and as deliberately selected by the parties in this case, namely a relatively inexpensive and swift mechanism for obtaining an expert final decision to resolve the commercial dispute."

For a discussion of *Sumner*, see Hew R. Dundas, "Two Rarities: Subpoenaing an Arbitrator for Cross-Examination and Court Enforcement of a Peremptory Order" [2014] 80 *Arbitration* 2, 196–203.

The authors submit not only that the decision in *Sumner* is correct but **R71–31** that the 2010 Act must be applied in like manner: r.71(8)(a) does not give the court any power other than to order the arbitrator to be cross-examined to give reasons, and the ability to hear the evidence of an arbitrator in a r.68 appeal (in *Sumner* under the equivalent of rr.68(2)(a)(ii) and r.51(2)(c)) does not allow him to expand on his reasoning orally.

A similar question had arisen in the case *Glasgow City and District* **R71–32**

Railway Company v MacGeorge, Cowan and Galloway (1886) 13 R. 609 where a common law challenge was made to an award on the grounds of it being *ultra fines compromissi* (ultra vires) in covering matters not authorised by the statutory arbitration provision (now r.68(2)(a)(i) or (b)). There, the arbitrator (umpire) was cross-examined. The court rejected the challenge, finding that the award did not contain any ultra vires elements and that the arbitrator was entitled to decide the method to be applied to calculate compensation.

R71–33 An application for the exercise of the r.71(8) power should be made by motion (RCS r.23.11), notwithstanding Ch.100 of the RCS. For guidance on when the application should be made and factors to be taken into account in its granting see *Navios International Inc v Sangamon Transportation Group* [2012] EWHC 166 (Comm).

R71–34 If the Outer House makes an order under r.71(8), it may make such ancillary order as it thinks fit with respect to additional expenses *arising from its order* (authors' emphasis added). The authors submit that such an order will not cover expenses arising from an unsuccessful resistance to the making of the order but will deal with additional expenses which arise from the need for compliance with it.

R71–35 The intention behind r.71(8)(b) appears to be that the party (or the tribunal) who has caused the need for reasons, or further and better reasons, to be obtained should bear the expense of the obtaining of that statement.

R71–36 Where the tribunal is potentially liable under r.71(8)(b), the Outer House must bear in mind both the need for the tribunal to be given an opportunity to make representations (see para.R68–92 above) and also the tribunal's immunity under r.73 (subject to the exceptions in r.73(2)), for anything omitted in the performance or purported performance of its functions.

R71–37 To a layman, if the tribunal's reasons are sufficiently defective (let alone non-existent) that it has to rewrite them, it should not expect to be paid for failure, i.e. it should rectify its defective work at no cost to the parties.

Rule 71(9)

R71–38 This prima facie odd-looking rule covers the (probably rare) situation where a provision in an arbitration agreement prevents the bringing of legal proceedings in relation to the subject-matter of the award. Such a provision can include a "*Scott v. Avery*" clause: see para.S10–69. If that award, or part of it, has been set aside, that provision may be declared void by court order. This is wholly logical: where the award (or any part of it) has been set aside, then the bar on the bringing of legal proceedings cannot survive.

Rule 71(10) and (11)—Security for expenses of appeal

R71–39 These sub-rules give the court power to order an appellant, or an applicant for leave to appeal from a decision of the Outer House, to provide security for the expenses of the appeal, or the application for leave to appeal. These provisions are a mirror image of the provisions of r.64 enabling an arbitrator to order a party to provide security for the arbitration expenses; see the commentary to r.64, above.

An application for the exercise of this power is made by motion setting out the grounds (RCS r.33.2) notwithstanding Ch.100 of the RCS. **R71–40**

Where the order is made, it will specify the time within which the security is to be provided (RCS r.33.3). **R71–41**

The security can be of different forms. Traditionally, it was in the form of a "bond of caution" (pronounced "kayshun"), being a guarantee from certain guarantee-providing or insurance companies (RCS rr.33.4, 33.5). Another more flexible form is "consignation", being the payment (consignation) of a sum of money into a bank account in the name of the Accountant of Court (RCS r.33.4). Once consigned the money is held under the Court of Session Consignations (Scotland) Act 1895. **R71–42**

However, the security can be provided by other means if these are approved by the Outer House, e.g. a deposit of a sum of money in the joint names of the parties' respective solicitors (see RCS r.33.4). **R71–43**

For further details of the way in which security is provided and also the common law test for the ordering of security, see the commentary in Ch.33 of *Greens' Annotated Rules of the Court of Session* (Edinburgh: W. Green) also available in Vol.2 of *The Parliament House Book* (Edinburgh: W. Green). **R71–44**

There is no formal fetter on the court's discretion except that the order cannot be made on the *sole* ground that the appellant or applicant resides, is formed, or is managed or controlled from outwith the UK. The DAC Supplementary Report (at para.28) explains why "only" was dropped from the 1996 Act (i.e. the criterion can never be taken into account at all) and this is expanded by the learned authors Harris, Planterose and Tecks in *The Arbitration Act 1996: A Commentary*, 5th edn (2014), p.199. While EU law prohibits the residence criterion from being applied against EU-resident parties, the Court of Appeal held in *Nasser v United Bank of Kuwait* [2001] EWCA Civ 556 that it could legitimately be applied to non-EU parties. **R71–45**

In the exercise of its discretion in an ordinary litigation, the court has to weigh up a number of factors (see the commentary to r.64 above). In relation to an appeal or application, the critical factor will be whether the appellant or applicant has sufficient assets readily available to satisfy any award of expenses against him if his appeal or application is unsuccessful (see *Azov Shipping Co v Baltic Shipping Co (No.2)* [1999] 2 Lloyd's Rep. 39 per Longmore J. at 41). **R71–46**

In *Azov Shipping Co* [1999] 2 Lloyd's Rep. 39, it was commented that the existence of the existing award against the appellant would be a factor only if the evidence as to readily available assets was uncertain. If the motion for the order arises after the court has already upheld an arbitrator's decision, and there is an application for leave to appeal to the Inner House, then it is suggested that the existence of two awards against the applicant may be of greater weight. **R71–47**

R71–48 Where a party who has been ordered to provide security for expenses has not done so, the court has power to dismiss the appeal or application.

Rule 71(12)—Payment into court of sums awarded

R71–49 The Outer House also has power to order that the appellant pay the actual sum awarded against him by the award being appealed into the court. No test is given to guide the court in its decision on whether to exercise the power. Two of the founding principles in s.1 of the Act are relevant, namely (a) that the object of arbitration is to resolve disputes fairly, impartially and without unnecessary delay or expense, and (c) that the court should not intervene in an arbitration except as provided by the Act. The purpose of the provision is to support the arbitration process which has found for the claimant and who should not on the face of it be prejudiced in recovering the sum awarded to him by any delay caused in the appeal process. It therefore encourages the attractiveness of arbitration as an expedited method of dispute resolution, in contrast to the ordinary court process where nothing is payable until the appeal process is exhausted. It should therefore be applied in that light rather than in the light of the ordinary court process of appeal.

R71–50 The power under r.71(12) is similar to that under s.20(6)(b) (see paras S20–144 to S20–147 and S20–138) in relation to applications in foreign jurisdictions to set aside arbitral awards made in those jurisdictions. That latter power derives from art.VI New York Convention (and is restated in art.36(2) of the Model Law), which provides that if an application for setting aside, e.g. an appeal, has been made to a competent authority of the law of the seat, the authority where enforcement is sought may, if it considers proper, adjourn the decision on enforcement and may, on the application of the party claiming enforcement of the award, order the other party (the appellant) to give suitable security.

R71–51 In relation to what is now s.20(6)(b), it was said that there were two important factors to be considered in deciding whether to require the respondent to pay the sum awarded against him into the court as security pending the disposal of the appeal, namely (a) the strength of the argument against the award; and (b) the ease or difficulty of enforcement of the award and whether it would be rendered more difficult, for example, through the movement of assets or improvident trading if enforcement was delayed (*Soleh Boneh International Ltd v Government of Uganda* [1993] 2 Lloyd's Rep. 208 per Staughton L.J. at 212). These seem to be relevant factors in relation to r.71(12).

R71–52 The court is not restricted to ordering the payment of the whole amount or nil. Thus in *Soleh Boneh* [1993] 2 Lloyd's Rep. 208 the court weighed up the factors and required the respondent to pay into court part of the amount awarded against him.

Arbitration (Scotland) Act 2010 (r.71)

There seems to be no reason why a similar approach should not be followed for a court in deciding whether to make an order under r.71(12). **R71–53**

English case law is undeveloped on the equivalent s.70(7) of the 1996 Act. The purpose of introducing s.70(7) was to avoid the risk that, while an appeal was pending, the ability of the losing party to honour the award might be diminished (DAC Report, para.380, where the proposal was described as a "tool of great value"). **R71–54**

In *Peterson Farms Inc v C&M Farming Ltd* [2004] 1 Lloyd's Rep. 614 (not to be confused with the judgment on the merits at [2004] 1 Lloyd's Rep. 603), Tomlinson J. suggested that there should be a difference in the approach to the decision on whether to require payment depending on whether the appeal was to be on jurisdiction, on serious irregularity or on an error of law. The authors respectfully submit that that approach appears misconceived given that an appeal on any of these is capable of otherwise delaying the making of payment as required by the award. In addition, Tomlinson J. took account of the fact that the appellant was not likely to be in funds and that he might require to obtain financial support from a third party in order to make the payment as a factor against ordering payment. It is suggested that such a factor is one for the ordering of payment since it tends to suggest that the appellant will indeed be unable to make payment of the award if he is unsuccessful in the appeal. **R71–55**

An application for the exercise of this power is made by motion setting out the grounds (RCS r.33.2). **R71–56**

Where the order is made it will specify the time within which the security is to be provided (RCS r.33.3). **R71–57**

The presumption is that security must be provided by the payment (consignation) of a sum of money into the court in the name of the Accountant of Court (RCS r.33.4). Once consigned, the money is held under the Court of Session Consignations (Scotland) Act 1895. However, the security can be provided by other means if these are approved by the Outer House. These can include a deposit of a sum of money in the joint names of the solicitors of the parties (see RCS r.33.4). **R71–58**

Where a party who has been ordered to pay in the whole or part of the payment awarded against him has not done so, the court has power to dismiss the appeal or application. **R71–59**

Rule 72: Reconsideration by tribunal M

72.—(1) Where the Outer House or, as the case may be, the Inner House decides a serious irregularity appeal or a legal error appeal by ordering the tribunal to reconsider its award (or any part of it), the tribunal must make a new award in respect of the matter concerned (or confirm its original award) by no later than—

    (a) in the case of a decision by the Outer House—

        (i) where the decision is appealed, the day falling 3 months after the

Arbitration (Scotland) Act 2010

          appeal (or, as the case may be, the application for leave to appeal) is dismissed or abandoned,
        (ii) where the decision is not appealed, the day falling 3 months after the decision is made, or
        (iii) such other day as the Outer House may specify,
    (b) in the case of a decision by the Inner House—
        (i) the day falling 3 months after the decision is made, or
        (ii) such other day as the Inner House may specify.

(2) These rules apply in relation to the new award as they apply in relation to the appealed award.

DEFINITIONS

"legal error appeal": r.69(1)
"Outer House": s.31(1)
"serious irregularity appeal": r.68(1)
"tribunal": ss.2(1), 31(1)

STATUS

R72–01 Rule 72 is mandatory so cannot be disapplied, or modified in any way, by the parties. This is consistent with rr.68 and 70 to which it is closely related.

MODEL LAW

R72–02 There is no equivalent provision in the Model Law.

COMMENTARY

R72–03 Following remission by the court, the part of the award which is to be reconsidered is suspended and no longer binding in respect of any of the matters to be reconsidered unless it is reaffirmed (confirmed) by the tribunal in its reconsidered award (*Huyton SA v Jakil SpA* [1999] 2 Lloyd's Rep. 83 per Brooke L.J. at 87).

R72–04 Once the tribunal has delivered its reconsidered award, that part of the award which had previously been remitted falls away and becomes null and void (*Huyton SA v Jakil SpA* [1999] 2 Lloyd's Rep. 83).

R72–05 Any part of the award which is not to be reconsidered remains in full force and effect.

R72–06 If the remission has been made in order to remove any uncertainty or ambiguity as to the award's effect, this does not affect the substance of the award and the tribunal has no power to alter or revisit any aspect of the substance of the award (*Carter (t/a Michael Carter Partnership) v Harold Simpson Associates (Architects) Ltd* [2004] 2 Lloyd's Rep. 512).

R72–07 The tribunal must make either a new award in respect of the matter remitted to it or confirm the original award having regard to the findings of the court. It has three months in which to make the fresh award, although if the remit is made by the Outer House and is appealed unsuccessfully to the Inner House the three months runs from the dismissal or abandonment of the appeal.

Part 9

Miscellaneous

Rule 73: Immunity of tribunal etc. M

73.—(1) Neither the tribunal nor any arbitrator is liable for anything done or omitted in the performance, or purported performance, of the tribunal's functions.

(2) This rule does not apply—
  (a) if the act or omission is shown to have been in bad faith, or
  (b) to any liability arising from an arbitrator's resignation (but see rule 16(1)(c)).

(3) This rule applies to any clerk, agent, employee or other person assisting the tribunal to perform its functions as it applies to the tribunal.

DEFINITIONS

"arbitrator": ss.2(1), 31(1)
"tribunal": ss.2(1), 31(1)

STATUS

Rule 73 is mandatory so cannot be disapplied, or modified in any way, by the parties, or by any other means (s.8 refers). **R73–01**

MODEL LAW

There is no provision in the Model Law on the immunity of arbitrators for the simple reason that while in some jurisdictions it is provided by statute, in others it is restricted by statute (e.g. ÖZpO art.594(4)), or even unconstitutional, so the parties to UNCITRAL could never have agreed any compromise. **R73–02**

COMMENTARY

Introductory

Rule 73 enacts in statute Scotland's traditional common law favouring of immunity. The rationale for this was stated obiter in *McMillan v Free Church of Scotland* (1862) 24 D. 1282 at 1295 where, in relation to a claim for damages against members of the General Assembly of the Church of Scotland who had exercised a jurisdiction to make a decision against the claimant, Lord Curriehill said: **R73–03**

"[P]arties upon whom judicial functions are lawfully conferred, and who in the bona fide exercise of these functions over parties subject to their authority, fall into errors of judgment, are not liable in damages to their parties in consequence of such errors. *Humanum est errare.* Infallibility of judgment is attainable by no man, however laboriously or conscientiously he may exert his powers to do what is right, and if notwithstanding a judge's best and bona fide endeavours to do so, he should be liable in damages for errors into which he might fall, such offices would be shunned by those best qualified for performing their functions. But such functionaries have an immunity from liability for errors in judgment, unless their errors arise from corruption or malice. The law unquestionably confers such an immunity upon judges officiating in the public judicial institutions of the country. It also extends such immunity to private persons, upon whom parties, by voluntary agreement, confer authority to adjudicate certain matters among themselves; it being the policy of our law to encourage and support the settlement of disputes by such private arrangements. Such arbitrators are not liable in damages to the contracting parties for errors of judgment into which they happen to fall in the bona fide exercise of the functions so conferred upon them."

R73–04 Some institutional rules provide for immunity, e.g. art.31(1) LCIA Rules (qualified by the language "save (i) where the act or omission is shown by that party to constitute conscious and deliberate wrongdoing committed by the body or person alleged to be liable to that party and (ii) the extent to which any part of this provision is prohibited by any applicable law") and art.40 ICC Rules ("except to the extent such limitation of liability is prohibited by applicable law") and SAC 07 art.8 (qualified by "except that that individual may be liable for the consequences of conscious and deliberate wrongdoing").

R73–05 Since r.73 is mandatory, its terms prevail over the provisions of any such set of rules, whether such rules are or are not inconsistent with r.73.

Rule 73(1)

R73–06 The immunity applies to liability for breach of the express or implied terms of the arbitration agreement or for delictual (tortious or quasi-delictual) wrong during the performance or purported performance of the tribunal's functions.

R73–07 The immunity does not apply to other forms of liability that the arbitrator may incur.

R73–08 A disturbing example was an unreported English case (*WS v BB*) concerning an application under s.24 of the 1996 Act to remove the arbitrator. He was in court, unrepresented and under the impression that he was present merely to assist the court but the judge refused to consider application of s.29 of the 1996 Act (immunity of the arbitrator); not only were the arbitrator's fees approximately halved but he was also made liable for the costs of this court hearing (and a previous one) and these exceeded his (now-reduced) fees. See also paras R14–04 to R14–08 and R16–14.

Before the immunity applies, there has to be breach of the arbitration agreement or a delictual wrong by the arbitrator in the fulfilment of his functions as an arbitrator. Whether there has been a breach of the arbitration agreement or there has been a delictual wrong in the performance or purported performance of the tribunal's functions are separate issues of fact and/or law. If there has been such a breach or delictual wrong, the immunity will apply unless r.73(2) applies. **R73–09**

The immunity exists only in relation to liability for anything done or omitted to be done in the performance or purported performance of functions by the tribunal. If an arbitrator incurs liability when he is not performing or purportedly performing the functions of the tribunal, then the immunity will not cover that liability. **R73–10**

Rule 73(2)

The immunity is based on the understanding that to err is human (per Lord Curriehill at para.R73–03 above) and that without such immunity capable persons would be discouraged from accepting arbitral appointments. **R73–11**

However, where the conduct goes beyond mere error but involves bad faith by the arbitrator, the understanding upon which the immunity is conceived no longer applies. There is no conceivable reason why the arbitrator should enjoy immunity if his breach of contract or delictual wrong was in bad faith. Rule 73(2) reflects this. **R73–12**

The act of resignation is a conscious and deliberate refusal to carry out the duty to resolve the dispute that the arbitrator has agreed, in contract, to resolve. Therefore, on the face of it, it involves something which is akin to a breach of the arbitration agreement in bad faith. Resignation is no part of "the performance or purported performance of an arbitrator's functions". **R73–13**

If an arbitrator wishes to resign without incurring the real risk of loss of immunity, he must comply with rr.15 and 16. **R73–14**

Rule 73(3)

The immunity also applies to any clerk to the arbitration or any agent, employee or other person assisting the tribunal to perform its functions; this is self-evidently logical as is r.74 (below). **R73–15**

Rule 74: Immunity of appointing arbitral institution etc. M

74.—(1) An arbitral appointments referee, or other third party who the parties ask to appoint or nominate an arbitrator, is not liable—

(a) **for anything done or omitted in the performance, or purported performance, of that function (unless the act or omission is shown to have been in bad faith), or**
(b) **for the acts or omissions of—**
   (i) **any arbitrator whom it nominates or appoints, or**
   (ii) **the tribunal of which such an arbitrator forms part (or any clerk, agent or employee of that tribunal).**

(2) **This rule applies to an arbitral appointments referee's, or other third party's, agents and employees as it applies to the referee or other third party.**

DEFINITIONS

"arbitral appointments referee": ss.22, 31(1)
"arbitrator": ss.2(1), 31(1)
"tribunal": ss.2(1), 31(1)

STATUS

R74–01 Rule 74 is mandatory so cannot be disapplied, or modified in any way, by the parties.

MODEL LAW

R74–02 There is no provision in the Model Law for the immunity of appointing arbitral institutions; see R73–02 above.

COMMENTARY

Introductory

R74–03 Section 22 and r.7 provide for the appointment of an arbitrator by an AAR, failing which by the court.

R74–04 In addition other persons (e.g. the Chairman of the CIArb Scottish Branch, the President of the Law Society of Scotland or the Dean of the Faculty of Advocates or other heads of professional bodies or sheriffs principal or sheriffs) may have been agreed upon as a person who may nominate an arbitrator (arbiter).

R74–05 Extending the logic of r.73, r.74 is necessary to prevent individuals or institutions from being discouraged, by fear of contractual or delictual liability, from seeking appointment as and acting appointors, whether as AAR or otherwise.

R74–06 Pre-2010 Act, if the parties had agreed on a private arbitral appointor (e.g. the Chairman, CIArb Scottish Branch) who omitted to make immunity part of his contractual terms of reference, it was uncertain whether he could be liable to the parties for making an unreasonable appointment.

R74–07 As standard practice (see para.R73–04 above), international and other arbitral institutions exclude their liability in respect of the arbitral appointments which they make. Where the court made the appointment, it was protected by its immunity. It was, therefore, wholly appropriate that the SAR provide for the immunity of both arbitral appointment referees as designated under the Act and also "other third parties", that is to say private appointors designated in the parties' own agreement or otherwise, e.g. by the PCA.

It is also wholly appropriate that r.74 exclude any possibility of vicarious liability of the appointers of arbitrators (and their employees and agents) for any liability of the arbitrator. **R74–08**

There is nothing to prevent (and it would be highly recommended that) an appointor of arbitrators agreeing with the parties appropriate immunity before exercising his power. **R74–09**

Rule 74(1) and (2)

In this paragraph, "other third party" includes persons such as listed (non-exhaustively) in para.R74–04 or any other person whom the parties have nominated in their arbitration agreement to appoint the arbitrator. It would also include the court, if there was any doubt over whether the court was entitled to its judicial immunity in exercising its function of appointment. **R74–10**

Rule 75: Immunity of experts, witnesses and legal representatives M

75. Every person who participates in an arbitration as an expert, witness or legal representative has the same immunity in respect of acts or omissions as the person would have if the arbitration were civil proceedings.

DEFINITIONS

"legal error appeal": r.69(1)
"Outer House": s.31(1)
"serious irregularity appeal": r.68(1)
"tribunal": ss.2(1), 31(1)

STATUS

Rule 75 is mandatory so cannot be disapplied, or modified in any way, by the parties. **R75–01**

MODEL LAW

There is no provision in the Model Law on the immunity of experts, witnesses and legal representatives; see para.R73–02. **R75–02**

COMMENTARY

R75–03　Rule 75 places arbitral proceedings on a par with civil court proceedings in Scotland for the purpose of any question of the liability of experts, witnesses and legal representatives.

R75–04　Whether liability actually arises against any of these persons will depend on various criteria depending on the ground of liability in question. For the position in Scotland see *Karling v Purdue*, 2004 S.L.T. 1067 where Temporary Judge J.G. Reid QC FCIArb followed the Scottish House of Lords case *Watson v McEwan* (1905) 7 F. (HL) 109. The authors submit that at the time of writing these cases—under which expert witnesses have immunity in respect of their evidence whether in court or any other proceedings, including arbitral and tribunal proceedings, and their statements made in preparation for that evidence—continue to represent the law of Scotland.

R75–05　It remains to be seen whether the position in *Karling* will continue in Scotland following the UKSC decision in an English case *Jones v Kaney* [2011] 2 A.C. 398. The authors, noting in passing that Lord Hope dissented in *Jones*, express no view on this question.

Rule 76: Loss of right to object M

76.—(1) A party who participates in an arbitration without making a timeous objection on the ground—
- (a) that an arbitrator is ineligible to act as an arbitrator,
- (b) that an arbitrator is not impartial and independent,
- (c) that an arbitrator has not treated the parties fairly,
- (d) that the tribunal does not have jurisdiction,
- (e) that the arbitration has not been conducted in accordance with—
    - (i) the arbitration agreement,
    - (ii) these rules (in so far as they apply), or
    - (iii) any other agreement by the parties relating to conduct of the arbitration,
- (f) that the arbitration has been affected by any other serious irregularity,

may not raise the objection later before the tribunal or the court.

(2) An objection is timeous if it is made—
- (a) as soon as reasonably practicable after the circumstances giving rise to the ground for objection first arose,
- (b) by such later date as may be allowed by—
    - (i) the arbitration agreement,
    - (ii) these rules (in so far as they apply),
    - (iii) the other party, or
- (c) where the tribunal considers that circumstances justify a later objection, by such later date as it may allow.

(3) This rule does not apply where the party shows that it did not object timeously because it—
  (a) did not know of the ground for objection, and
  (b) could not with reasonable diligence have discovered that ground.
(4) This rule does not allow a party to raise an objection which it is barred from raising for any reason other than failure to object timeously.

DEFINITIONS

"arbitration agreement": ss.4, 31(1)
"court": s.31(1)
"party": ss.2, 31(1), (2)
"rules": s.31(1)
"timeous objection": r.76(2)
"tribunal": ss.2(1), 31(1)

STATUS

Rule 76 is mandatory so cannot be disapplied, or modified in any way, by the parties. **R76–01**

MODEL LAW

Article 4 of the Model Law is broadly the same. **R76–02**

COMMENTARY

The purpose of r.76 is to preserve the speed and openness of arbitration as a form of dispute resolution by restricting the ability of a party to make challenges which, whether meritorious or not, could cause delay and additional expense. If, during the proceedings, one of the qualifying objections set out in the rule arises and a party is either aware of it or could with reasonable diligence have discovered it, then it must make the objection at that time and not keep it to itself to be used at a later date as a secret insurance should the decision on the merits appear to be going against it. Early intervention should also maximise the tribunal's ability to find an early cure. **R76–03**

Paragraph R8–18 above gives a US example of the sort of mischief r.76 is intended to prevent; in the US case, the complaining party could and should have hired private detectives before the arbitration commenced (e.g. pre-appointment), not after the award was issued. A similar conclusion was reached in the celebrated English case (on bias) *Locabail Ltd v Bayfield Properties Ltd* [2000] Q.B. 451.

Rule 76(1)—The need for timeous objection

R76–04 This sets out the types of objection which must be made timeously if they are not to be waived. The common feature of all of these is that they are the type of objection which relates to either the jurisdiction of the tribunal or a qualifying procedural irregularity both of which could give rise to a challenge to an arbitral award under rr.67 and 68.

R76–05 An "objection" in terms of the rule means a ground of objection in the sense that, for example, an objection to jurisdiction on one ground need not cover an objection to jurisdiction on an entirely different ground (*Primetrade AG v Ythan Ltd* [2006] 1 Lloyd's Rep. 457 at 474, and the cases cited therein). This stems from the purpose of the provision being to encourage open dealing and to ensure that all arguments are raised at the earliest opportunity.

R76–06 Whether a later argument, e.g. at appeal, was within an earlier ground of objection made to the tribunal is a matter of degree. This suggests that a party making an objection that could give rise to an appeal should frame their grounds of objection to a tribunal broadly so as to allow some flexibility at an appeal, but not so broad as not to give fair notice of the ground to the respondent.

R76–07 In *Athletic Union of Constantinople (AEK) v National Basketball Association* [2002] 1 Lloyd's Rep. 305 at 311, the appellant's ground of appeal on lack of jurisdiction was not within an earlier ground on lack of jurisdiction and the appellant was barred from raising this new ground in an appeal.

R76–08 The following have been dealt with above:

- r.76(1)(a) (ineligibility to act as an arbitrator): see commentary on r.4;
- r.76(1)(b) (impartiality and independence): see commentary on r.24(1)(a) at paras R24–04 to R24–22;
- r.76(1)(c) (fair treatment of the parties): see commentary on r.24(1)(b) at paras R24–23 to R24–42;
- r.76(1)(d) (lack of jurisdiction): see commentary on r.20(2)(a) at paras R20–04 to R20–20;
- r.76(1)(e) (the arbitration has not been conducted in accordance with the arbitration agreement, the rules, or any other agreement of the parties relating to its conduct): see commentary on r.68(2)(a) at paras R68–23 to R68–29; and
- r.76(1)(f) (any other serious irregularity): see commentary on r.68(2)(b), (c), (d) and (k) at paras R68–30 to R68–44.

Rule 76(2)(a)—"timeous"

Any objection must be made no later than the date at which it became **R76–09** reasonably practicable to have made it, clearly after the circumstances giving rise to the ground for objection first arose; see para.R76–03 for two examples.

The "reasonably practicable" test sets an objective standard applicable to **R76–10** a reasonable party in the position of the objecting party. The tribunal or court must assess when it would have become not merely practicable but reasonably practicable for that reasonable party to make that objection. It is a test that has been used in other contexts to impose time-bars on personal injury claims (*Agnew v Scott Lithgow Ltd (No.2)*, 2003 S.C. 448) and employment tribunal claims (*Royal Bank of Scotland Plc v Theobald* Unreported January 10, 2007 EAT Scotland). The date at which it first became "reasonably practicable" for a party to make an objection will be a question of fact which will vary from case to case.

In *ASM Shipping Ltd of India v TTMI Ltd of England* [2006] 1 Lloyd's **R76–11** Rep. 375, the issue of timeous objection was raised in relation to s.73 of the 1996 Act which, in contrast to r.76, requires objection to be made "forthwith".

ASM and TTMI were engaged in a London arbitration arising out of a charterparty where Mr X QC was appointed chairman of the tribunal. ASM's principal witness was Mr M, a shipbroker. In a wholly separate (but relatively recent) arbitration (the "other arbitration") between entirely unrelated parties, M had been a key witness for one of the parties and TTMI's solicitors in the present case, WH, had represented the other side and, for a short time and in respect of one preliminary issue only (which was settled), Mr X QC had been instructed by WH and had drafted certain disclosure applications. M had been the target, so he alleged, of an attack by WH in the other arbitration.

On the morning before M gave evidence, ASM were made aware of M's allegation. M's evidence started after lunch. Mr X QC had no recollection of meeting M and had not conducted any part of any hearing or other proceeding involving him. M's evidence was not completed that day and ASM's legal team considered the matter overnight. On the following day, at the end of M's evidence, they objected to Mr X QC's participation in the tribunal under reservation of taking instructions in the course of M's evidence. Having obtained instructions to object, ASM's legal team maintained the objection.

ASM took up the subsequent award and, it was held, thereby waived its right to object to the chairman of the tribunal so he was not removed but, in a strongly-criticised judgment (e.g. see H.R. Dundas, "Arbitration Case in English High Court—Bias/Removal Of Arbitrator", Arbitration Newsletter 12 (December 2005) at *http://www.dundasarbitrator.com* [Accessed February 5, 2014]) the judge made it clear that (in his opinion) the arbitrator should have been. The judge rejected a submission that the objection should have been made before M began to give evidence. Applying the reasonable practicability test in r.76, the authors submit that it was *reasonably* practicable for ASM to have objected before M began to give evidence.

Rule 76(2)(b) and (c)—Timeous objection: later dates

R76–12   If it is found that the objection was not made by the "reasonable practicability" date, the tribunal or court must consider whether it was made within any later date that:

- the arbitration agreement allows;
- the rules allow;
- the other party has allowed, other than in the arbitration agreement, for example by waiver of the point; or
- is justified by circumstances.

R76–13   "Justified by circumstances" is a sensible escape route, giving the tribunal or the court the ultimate discretion.

Rule 77: Independence of arbitrator M

77. For the purposes of these rules, an arbitrator is not independent in relation to an arbitration if—
   (a) the arbitrator's relationship with any party,
   (b) the arbitrator's financial or other commercial interests, or
   (c) anything else,
gives rise to justifiable doubts as to the arbitrator's impartiality.

DEFINITIONS

"arbitration": ss.2(1), 31(1)
"arbitrator": ss.2(1), 31(1)
"party": ss.2, 31(1), (2)

STATUS

R77–01   Rule 77 is mandatory so cannot be disapplied, or modified in any way, by the parties. This is because it effectively extends r.24(1)(a), i.e. self-evidently critically important.

MODEL LAW

R77–02   Article 12 Model Law allows for challenge to an arbitrator if, "circumstances exist that give rise to justifiable doubts as to his impartiality or independence", thereby distinguishing between "impartiality" and "independence".

COMMENTARY

The SAR use different terminology from the Model Law in the sense that **R77–03**
lack of independence is defined by various features which give rise to justifiable doubts as to the arbitrator's impartiality. For the purposes of the SAR, partiality is linked to actual bias whereas non-independence is linked to justifiably feared bias. The rules do not subdivide lack of independence, or justifiably feared bias further, but simply give examples of where such justifiable fear could emerge from and then finish with a catch all provision of "anything else" which could give rise to the justifiable doubts.

Rule 77 provides a definition of lack of independence for the purposes of **R77–04**
rr.8(2), 10(2)(a), 12(a) and 24(1)(a). The reader is referred to the commentary to those rules above.

See commentary on r.24(1)(a) at paras R24–15 to R24–17 for commen- **R77–05**
tary on two key cases concerning independence: (i) the English case *AT&T Corporation v Saudi Cable Co* [2000] 2 Lloyd's 127; and (ii) the Australian case *Smits v Roach* [2006] HCA 36.

Rule 78: Consideration where arbitrator judged not to be impartial and independent D

78.—(1) This rule applies where—
  (a) an arbitrator is removed by the Outer House under rule 12 on the ground that the arbitrator is not impartial and independent,
  (b) the tribunal is dismissed by the Outer House under rule 13 on the ground that it has failed to comply with its duty to be impartial and independent, or
  (c) the tribunal's award (or any part of it) is returned to the tribunal for reconsideration, or is set aside, on either of those grounds (see rule 68).

(2) Where this rule applies, the Outer House must have particular regard to whether an arbitrator has complied with rule 8 when it is considering whether to make an order under rule 16(1) or 68(4) about—
  (a) the arbitrator's entitlement (if any) to fees or expenses,
  (b) repaying fees or expenses already paid to the arbitrator.

DEFINITIONS

"arbitrator": ss.2(1), 31(1)
"Outer House": s.31(1)
"party": ss.2, 31(1), (2)
"tribunal": ss.2(1), 31(1)

STATUS

Rule 78 is a default rule so can be disapplied in whole or in part, or **R78–01**
modified in any way, by the parties (s.9 refers).

MODEL LAW

R78–02 There is no equivalent provision in the Model Law.

COMMENTARY

R78–03 The requirement that an arbitrator be both independent (see r.77) and impartial is a fundamental one for any person undertaking that role, so fundamental that breach thereof may engage the Outer House's power under rr.16(1) and 68(4) to restrict or exclude the arbitrator's entitlement to his fees and expenses.

R78–04 Rule 78 provides that, in considering whether and if so how to exercise that power, the court must have particular regard to whether the arbitrator has complied with his duty under r.8 to disclose without delay to parties any circumstance known to him, or which becomes known to him during the arbitration, which might be considered relevant to the question of whether he was independent and impartial. See further the commentary to r.8 above at para.R08–01ff.

R78–05 There is no direct equivalent in the 1996 Act but ss.24(4) and 25 achieve essentially the same result with the key difference that r.8 (continuing disclosure obligation) has no equivalent in the 1996 Act so aggrieved parties will need to find another, less direct, route for any challenge. See the commentary at paras R24–15 to R24–17 above.

R78–06 Institutional rules differ in this context, e.g. art.10.1 LCIA Rules gives the LCIA Court similar powers but, whereas arts 11(2) and (3) ICC Rules place arbitrators under disclosure obligations consistent with r.8, the Rules do not expressly empower the ICC Court to adjust the arbitrator's fees and expenses.

R78–07 Rule 78 can be seen as part of one of the Act's less visible themes, that of ramping up the pressure on arbitrators to conduct themselves to the highest professional standards, failing which the consequences could be painful. See also r.16 and r.73(2)(b) (see paras R73–11 to R73–14).

Rule 79: Death of arbitrator **M**
79. An arbitrator's authority is personal and ceases on death.

DEFINITIONS

"arbitrator": ss.2(1), 31(1)

STATUS

R79–01 Rule 79 is mandatory so cannot be disapplied, or modified in any way, by the parties. This is so because: (a) no arbitrator can fulfil any of his functions after he dies; and (b) an arbitrator's duties are non-delegable so neither his executors nor his partners (if applicable) nor employees can take over the arbitration.

MODEL LAW

There is no equivalent provision in the Model Law. R79–02

COMMENTARY

The purpose of this rule is to make it clear beyond doubt that an arbitrator's appointment has *delectus personae* and falls with his death and does not transmit to his executor. For the continuing liability to pay the deceased arbitrator's outstanding fees and expenses see the commentary on r.16 and paras R16–05 to R16–07 above. R79–03

Section 26 of the 1996 Act adds an otiose clarification (derived from s.2(2) of the 1950 Act) that the death of the arbitrator's appointor (necessarily only when that is an individual) has no effect on the arbitrator's authority. R79–04

Article 10.1 LCIA Rules (1998) provided, anomalously, only that the LCIA Court *may* revoke the arbitrator's appointment on his death. The 2014 Rules make no reference to the death of an arbitrator but art.10.1 provides at (ii) "[the] arbitrator … becomes unable … to act"; for an English-seated arbitration, the mandatory s.26(1) overrides that, leaving open the question as to what the position might be in an LCIA arbitration seated outside the UK. R79–05

Article 15(1) of the ICC Rules provides mandatorily for the replacement of a deceased arbitrator. R79–06

Rule 80: Death of party D

80.—(1) **An arbitration agreement is not discharged by the death of a party and may be enforced by or against the executor or other representative of that party.**

(2) This rule does not affect the operation of any law by virtue of which a substantive right or obligation is extinguished by death.

DEFINITIONS

"arbitration agreement": ss.4, 31(1)
"party": ss.2, 31(1), (2)

STATUS

Rule 80 is a default rule so can be disapplied in whole or in part, or modified in any way, by the parties (s.9 refers). Where the arbitration agreement is governed by Scots law (s.6 refers), the authors cannot conceive of any practical circumstance where the parties might agree something different. R80–01

MODEL LAW

There is no equivalent provision in the Model Law. R80–02

COMMENTARY

R80–03　Upon the death of a party a tribunal will wish to seek to trace the executor or deceased representative of the deceased party and invite them to participate in the arbitration. The tribunal may exercise its powers under r.28 in that connection, bearing in mind its duties under r.24. From the point of view of the executor or representative it should be borne in mind that, should he participate in the arbitration, then from the date the participation begins he will be personally liable for the expenses both as found liable to the other party and as liable to the arbitrator. It is therefore strongly recommended that an executor does not participate in an arbitration without having obtained security for such liabilities from those succeeding to the deceased's estate.

R80–04　Rule 80 clarifies the position regarding rights and obligations under an arbitration agreement following the death of a party to it; this, of course, assumes that the deceased party was an individual such as might happen, e.g. in a house-building or other consumer-type case.

R80–05　Rule 80 does not apply to parties who are legal persons rather than individuals (typically companies, but also including Scottish but not English and Welsh partnerships), given that: (i) legal persons do not "die" but are "dissolved"; and (ii) r.80 contemplates an executor or other representative continuing with the arbitration which is not possible after the dissolution of a legal person. For legal persons insolvency is a separate matter from dissolution and a legal person who is insolvent is not necessarily dissolved and, during administration or liquidation, the legal person will remain in existence.

R80–06　The common law position is that prima facie all contractual rights and obligations pass on to the executors of the deceased party, whose duty it is to ingather the estate, settle the deceased's debts and obligations and distribute the residue to beneficiaries either under a will or under the law of intestacy. The matter is now put beyond any doubt in relation to arbitration agreements.

R80–07　Rule 80(2) makes it clear that the continuation of an arbitration agreement does not otherwise alter the effect that death might have on other rights and obligations of the parties. These could include those under the contract giving rise to the dispute, if for example it was governed by Scots law and any duty of a respondent was *delectus personae*.

Rule 81: Unfair treatment　D

81. A tribunal (or arbitrator) who treats any party unfairly is, for the purposes of these rules, to be deemed not to have treated the parties fairly.

DEFINITIONS

"arbitrator": ss.4, 31(1)
"party": ss.2, 31(1), (2)
"tribunal": ss.2(1), 31(1)

STATUS

Rule 81 is a default rule so can be disapplied in whole or in part, or modified in any way, by the parties (s.9 refers). R81–01

MODEL LAW

There is no equivalent provision in the Model Law. R81–02

COMMENTARY

The purpose of r.81 might appear unclear at first sight but, given, e.g. the language of r.10(2)(a)(ii) " ... [the arbitrator] has not treated the parties fairly", what it does is put it beyond doubt that the positive language "treats any party unfairly" equates to the negative "not to have treated the parties fairly". Five years on, the authors can no longer recall why the draftsman thought this was necessary. R81–03

Rule 82: Rules applicable to umpires M

82.—(1) The following rules apply in relation to an umpire appointed under rule 30 (or otherwise with the agreement of the parties) as they apply in relation to an arbitrator or, as the case may be, the tribunal—
>rule 4
>rule 8
>rules 10 to 14
>rule 24
>rule 26
>rules 59, 60 and 61(1)
>rule 68
>rule 73
>rules 76 to 79

(2) But the parties are, in so far as those rules are not mandatory rules, free to modify or disapply the way in which those rules would otherwise apply to an umpire.

DEFINITIONS

"arbitrator: ss.4, 31(1)
"court": s.31(1)
"party": ss.2, 31(1), (2)
"tribunal": ss.2(1), 31(1)

STATUS

Rule 82 is mandatory so cannot be disapplied, or modified in any way, by the parties. R82–01

MODEL LAW

R82–02 There is no equivalent provision in the Model Law, no doubt because the concept of an "umpire", i.e. a third arbitrator who takes on the reference alone after the two appointed arbitrators disagree, appears to be unknown in most civil law jurisdictions.

COMMENTARY

R82–03 See the commentary to r.30 above in relation to umpires (formerly known under Scots common law as "oversmen"). Essentially the same key rules apply to umpires as they do to arbitrators.

R82–04 For ease of reference we append a brief description of the rules listed in r.82(1), noting that r.82(2) permits modification or disapplication of any default rules so listed:

- r.4 D excludes children and incapax adults from acting as arbitrator;
- r.8 M disclosure of conflicts of interest;
- rr.10–11 D Challenge to and removal of arbitrators/tribunals by the parties;
- rr.12–14 M Removal or dismissal of arbitrators/tribunals by the court;
- r.24 M general duties of the tribunal;
- r.26 D confidentiality;
- rr.59/61(1) D arbitration expenses;
- r.60 M arbitrators' fees and expenses;
- r.68 M serious irregularity appeal;
- r.73 M immunity of arbitrator;
- r.76 M loss of right to object;
- r.77 M arbitrator independence;
- r.78 D considerations affecting r.77; and
- r.79 M death of the arbitrator.

R82–05 It should be noted that, per s.8, all mandatory rules apply to an umpire conducting an arbitration seated in Scotland irrespective of the list given by r.82(1).

Rule 83: Formal communications **D**

83.—(1) A "formal communication" means any application, award, consent, direction, notice, objection, order, reference, request, requirement or waiver made or given or any document served—
    (a) in pursuance of an arbitration agreement,
    (b) for the purposes of these rules (in so far as they apply), or
    (c) otherwise in relation to an arbitration.
(2) A formal communication must be in writing.
(3) A formal communication is made, given or served if it is—

(a) hand delivered to the person concerned,
(b) sent to the person concerned by first class post in a properly addressed envelope or package—
   (i) in the case of an individual, to the individual's principal place of business or usual or last known abode,
   (ii) in the case of a body corporate, to the body's registered or principal office, or
   (iii) in either case, to any postal address designated for the purpose by the intended recipient (such designation to be made by giving notice to the person giving or serving the formal communication), or
(c) sent to the person concerned in some other way (including by email, fax or other electronic means) which the sender reasonably considers likely to cause it to be delivered on the same or next day.

(4) A formal communication which is sent by email, fax or other electronic means is to be treated as being in writing only if it is legible and capable of being used for subsequent reference.

(5) A formal communication is, unless the contrary is proved, to be treated as having been made, given or served—
(a) where hand delivered, on the day of delivery,
(b) where posted, on the day on which it would be delivered in the ordinary course of post, or
(c) where sent in any other way described above, on the day after it is sent.

(6) The tribunal may determine that a formal communication—
(a) is to be delivered in such other manner as it may direct, or
(b) need not be delivered,

but it may do so only if satisfied that it is not reasonably practicable for the formal communication to be made, given or served in accordance with this rule (or, as the case may be, with any contrary agreement between the parties).

(7) This rule does not apply in relation to any application, order, notice, document or other thing which is made, given or served in or for the purposes of legal proceedings.

DEFINITIONS

"arbitration": ss.2(1), 31(1)
"arbitration agreement": ss.4, 31(1)
"party": ss.2, 31(1), (2)
"rules": s.31(1)
"tribunal": ss.2(1), 31(1)

STATUS

Rule 83 is a default rule so can be disapplied in whole or in part, or modified in any way, by the parties (s.9 refers). **R83–01**

R83–02 If the parties have agreed to adopt institutional rules, those rules will usually have provisions relating to communications between parties. Examples include art.2 SAC 07, art.3 of the ICC Rules, art.13 LCIA Rules, and art.2 of the UNCITRAL Rules. In such situations, the starting point will be to consider what is the position under r.83 and then to see the extent to which r.83 is inconsistent with or disapplied by the institutional rule.

R83–03 In addition, parties can agree to disapply r.83 ad hoc in relation to particular communications (see s.9(3)(b)). For example where a party makes an oral request at a hearing and there is no objection from the other parties to the arbitration, the parties will have agreed to disapply r.83(2) requiring the request to be in writing, and with it any other rules consequential upon the need for a request to be in writing.

MODEL LAW

R83–04 Rule 83 is broadly consistent with art.3(1) of the Model Law but is in more detail.

COMMENTARY

R83–05 Essentially r.83 provides a comprehensive code for communications between the parties and the tribunal and between the parties themselves in relation to the arbitration.

R83–06 While the term "formal communication" is used both in the rule's heading and in the definition of its subject matter, it is given a wide definition including, in particular, any "notice", "objection", "request" or "requirement" made or given in pursuance of the arbitration agreement, for the purposes of the rules or otherwise in relation to an arbitration.

R83–07 Rule 83(7) provides (as does art.3(2) of the Model Law) that r.83 does not apply to communications made in or for the purposes of "legal proceedings", i.e. proceedings before any court.

Rule 83(1), (2), and (4)—Requirement of writing

R83–08 The general rule is that the communication in question must be in writing. With communications such as awards, directions, notices, orders and references this is what one would expect. However r.83 goes further and requires all of the communications covered by the rule to be in writing. Thus any application, notice, objection, request, requirement, or perhaps more controversially, any waiver, must be in writing.

R83–09 Per r.83(4), for any communication sent by email, fax or other electronic means to be treated as being in writing, it must be legible and capable of being used for subsequent reference. However, the rule does not state whether those tests apply to the sender or recipient, thereby leaving open the possibility that something sent was never actually received; of course, this also applies to hard copy communications. It has been standard practice for decades to rely on telex answerback and fax journals and email read receipts are no different in principle. Text messages might perhaps appear more problematic but, for example, a BlackBerry can be set up to record "proof" both of sending and (separately) of delivery of a text message.

There is no requirement for the written communication to be signed but it is good practice to do so in order that any confusion between drafts and final versions and copies and originals is avoided. In *Lafarge (Aggregates) Ltd v London Borough of Newham* [2005] 2 Lloyds Rep. 577, an adjudicator's decision had been sent, unsigned, by email, with the signed version sent by mail the same day and the court accepted the email as constituting sending the decision to the parties. **R83–10**

Rule 83(3)(a) and (5)(a)—Hand delivery

A formal communication is made if it has been hand-delivered to the person concerned. While that appears straightforward, there might be an issue as to whether the test has been satisfied. Clearly, if the sender merely goes to an individual recipient's address and puts the document through his letterbox, that cannot amount to hand delivery, e.g. if the recipient is not present. **R83–11**

Whereas r.83(3)(b), dealing with delivery by post, distinguishes between those "persons concerned" who are individuals and those who are bodies corporate, r.83(3)(a) does not; it follows that there can be hand delivery to a corporate body or other legal person. This would also accord with a practical approach, e.g. there is no good reason why delivery to a sole director of a small company, or a partner of a partnership, should not count as hand delivery to the company or partnership. One of the authors had an instance where a third party sought to serve a notice on his employer but the latter was operating temporarily from the third floor of a management contractor's office; the question arose whether delivery to the management contractor's (not employer's) reception staff at ground floor level was sufficient and the answer was clearly "no". **R83–12**

Corporate bodies or other legal persons, in particular large organisations, lead to the question of whether delivery to an individual within the body who is not authorised to receive it amounts to delivery to the corporate body. It has been held that an email sent to an "info@" email address which was received by a company's customer service representative, but then not forwarded to the relevant individual within the body, was in fact served on the body in question (*Bernuth Lines Ltd v High Seas Shipping Ltd "The Eastern Navigator"* [2006] 1 Lloyd's Rep. 537). **R83–13**

On the same principle a delivery to an individual employee of a body might amount to delivery to that body. Clearly, if the individual in question is authorised to receive post, that would be sufficient for hand delivery (*Burt v Kirkcaldy* [1965] 1 W.L.R. 474 applied in *Duffy v Normand*, 1995 S.L.T. 1264). Whether, on an analogy with *The Eastern Navigator*, delivery **R83–14** to any employee or agent of the body would be sufficient, however unconnected they were from the function of receiving post, is open to question.

R83–15 Rule 83(5)(a) provides that a formal communication is, unless the contrary is proved, to be treated as having been made given or served where hand delivered on the day of delivery. From a practical point of view, given both that there is no presumption of the making of hand delivery and the necessity of proof of hand delivery, r.83(5)(a) does not alter the need for the party making the hand delivery to provide evidence that the delivery was made. If that evidence exists, then the presumption in r.83(5)(a) comes into play and it is for the recipient to disprove it.

Rule 83(3)(b) and (5)(b)—First class post

R83–16 Another form of communication is the sending of the written communication to the person concerned by first class post. For this form of communication to be effective, sending is sufficient and there is no requirement that it be received. Rules 83(3)(b) and (5)(b) thereby supersedes most of s.7 of the Interpretation Act 1978 in effect for most purposes. Apart from its possible applicability in relation to service on Scottish partnerships by post, the only requirement of s.7 which is not reflected in r.83 but which must be read with it is that the postage must be pre-paid.

R83–17 It is unfortunate that the phrase "body corporate" is used given that a Scottish partnership without limited liability is a legal person in its own right, separate from the individuals who may be partners therein, but is, self-evidently, not a body corporate. There may be other legal persons who are not "bodies corporate". Unless the phrase "body corporate" can be construed as including a Scottish partnership, the making, giving or serving of a formal communication by post on such a partnership is to be done either under the "other means" head of r.83(3)(c) (see below).

Rule 83(3)(c) and (5)(c)—Other means

R83–18 The only restriction on other methods of transmission of formal communications, not being covered by the earlier parts of r.83(3), is that the sender must reasonably consider the method to be likely to cause the communication to be delivered on the same day as or the next day after sending. Thus the methods can include email, fax, or other electronic means, or by other postal means not involving r.83(3)(b). Thus a private postal service such as document exchange or, in Scotland, Legal Post, would be covered. First class post to legal persons who are not corporate bodies, e.g. a Scottish unlimited liability partnership, would be covered. For both private post and first class post in this limited sense, s.7 of the Interpretation Act 1978 would appear to apply where there is a gap in r.83. The provisions of s.7 are as follows:

"Where an Act authorises or requires any document to be served by post (whether the expression 'serve' or the expression 'give' or 'send' or any other expression is used) then, unless the contrary intention appears, the service is deemed to be effected by properly addressing, pre-paying and posting a letter containing the document and, unless the contrary is proved, to have been effected at the time at which the letter would be delivered in the ordinary course of post."

Rule 83(6)—Communication not reasonably practicable

Rule 83(6) provides for the situation where the tribunal is satisfied that it is not reasonably practicable for r.83 to be complied with so the tribunal is given wide powers to provide for the delivery of formal communications in such other manner as it may direct or to dispense with delivery entirely. The purpose of the powers in r.83(6) is to deal with the situation where the location of a party is unknown or a party is evading service such that it is not practicable for that party to be communicated with using the methods of r.83 or other methods agreed by the parties. Given the wide variety of methods in r.83 (as included in institutional rules) it is unlikely that these powers will often be used. **R83–19**

A common feature of the standard r.83 methods is that the communication must be delivered to the person concerned. If that is not practicable by those methods it is conceivable that the tribunal could determine that the communication should be delivered to some other person where there is reason to believe that in this way the person concerned could become aware of the communication, e.g. a relative of or solicitor or other agent who had recently acted for the person concerned. Another method may be by an advertisement in a newspaper circulating in the area of the last known residence or whereabouts of the person concerned. **R83–20**

In any determination by the tribunal under r.83(6), it is important that it bears in mind its overriding duty under r.24 to be impartial and independent, treat the parties fairly and conduct the arbitration without unnecessary delay or expense. **R83–21**

Rule 83(6) cannot be applied in the giving of a notice of arbitration under r.1 given that no tribunal will have been appointed at that time. **R83–22**

A determination by the tribunal that a formal communication need not be delivered is one which the tribunal is likely to reach only in extreme circumstances. It will require to be convinced that, if it made such a determination, its award would still withstand an appeal on the grounds of serious irregularity or lack of jurisdiction. **R83–23**

Rule 84: Periods of time D

84. Periods of time are to be calculated for the purposes of an arbitration as follows—

(a) where any act requires to be done within a specified period after or

from a specified date or event, the period begins immediately after that date or, as the case may be, the date of that event, and

(b) where the period is a period of 7 days or less, the following days are to be ignored—
  (i) Saturdays and Sundays, and
  (ii) any public holidays in the place where the act concerned is to be done.

DEFINITIONS

"arbitration": ss.2(1), 31(1)

STATUS

R84–01   Rule 84 is a default rule so can be disapplied in whole or in part, or modified in any way, by the parties (s.9 refers).

R84–02   If the parties have agreed to adopt institutional rules, those rules will usually have provisions relating to periods of time. Examples include art.3(4) of the ICC Rules, art.4 LCIA Rules, and art.2 of the UNCITRAL Rules. In such situations, the starting point will be to consider what is the position under r.84 and then to see the extent to which r.84 is inconsistent with or disapplied by the institutional rule.

MODEL LAW

R84–03   The Model Law does not cover the matters addressed by r.84(b).

COMMENTARY

R84–04   The purpose of this rule is to set out how time is to be calculated for the purposes of an arbitration. The rule applies not merely to time limits set out in the rules but also to time limits fixed by a tribunal in its directions.

R84–05   Rule 84 does not apply where time is calculated by the rules of court (RCS or SASAR). In those situations calculation of time is determined by the application of the relevant rule.

R84–06   The basic rule is that where something has to be done "within" a specified period then the period begins to run immediately after the date of commencement. So, for example, where on March 1 it was ordered that a document had to be lodged within 14 days, then the period begins to run with March 2 and the last day of the period will be March 15.

R84–07   The time of an act is always linked to the place where the act in question has to be done. The location of such an act depends on what it is. The place of the making of a formal communication, for example, under r.83 will be where the relevant part of r.83 (or the rule displacing it) was satisfied. That place may differ, for example on whether there is hand delivery or posting. This is important where parties and their advisers are located in different time zones. It is standard practice for a tribunal to specify time limits with reference to a particular recognised time zone, e.g. 18:00 GMT for a London-seated arbitration.

Tribunals, the parties, and their advisers must be careful concerning the effect of public holidays and weekends. Rule 84, indicates, by implication, that a period of time is not suspended merely because the last day falls within a public holiday unless the period in question was seven days or less. If a period of time happens to end on a UK Bank Holiday Monday, it may in practice, at least in certain types of organisation (e.g. the civil service, government agencies or local authorities), be necessary to comply with it by the previous Friday. However, in the commercial sphere, with the universal use of laptops and smartphones, compliance with a deadline falling on a weekend or a public holiday is no burden. R84–08

A "public holiday" is determined by reference to the place where the act for which the period of time exists is to be done (r.84(b)). R84–09

Public holidays in Scotland are either bank holidays or local holidays. R84–10

Bank holidays are set out in Sch.1 to the Banking and Financial Dealings Act 1971. In Scotland these are, at present, January 1, January 2 (or if it is a Saturday or a Sunday, Monday January 3 or 4 as appropriate), Good Friday, Easter Monday, the first Monday in May, the first Monday in August, November 30 (or if it is a Saturday or Sunday, Monday December 1 or December 2 as appropriate), Christmas Day (or if it is a Sunday, December 26), and any other day that Her Majesty may from time to time appoint by royal proclamation. The other days that have in the past been made bank holidays by royal proclamation are the English ones of the last Monday in May (the Whitsun holiday) and December 26 (if it is not a Monday). R84–11

The Scottish Government website lists Scottish bank holidays—see *http://www.scotland.gov.uk/Topics/People/bank-holidays* [Accessed June 21, 2014]. R84–12

Local public holidays are common in Scotland and vary between different localities. Local councils or chambers of commerce will be able to advise on whether any given day is a local holiday. Popular local holidays can include Easter Monday, Edinburgh Victoria Day being the third Monday in May, Glasgow Fair, or various "trades" holidays in July or August, and a Monday in September which varies from locality to locality. R84–13

INDEX

The words and other expressions listed in the following index are defined or otherwise explained for the purposes of these rules by the provisions indicated in the index.

Expression	Interpretation provision
arbitral appointments referee	section 24
arbitration	section 2
arbitration agreement	section 4

arbitration expenses	rule 59
arbitrator	section 2
claim	section 31(1)
court	section 31(1)
default rule	section 9(1)
dispute	section 2
independent	rule 77
Inner House	section 31(1)
mandatory rule	section 8
Outer House	section 31(1)
part award	rule 54
party	sections 2 and 31(2)
provisional award	rule 53
recoverable arbitration expenses	rule 61
rule	section 2
statutory arbitration	section 16(1)
tribunal	section 2

SCHEDULE 2

REPEALS

(introduced by section 29)

Enactment	Extent of repeal
Arbitration (Scotland) Act 1894 (c.13)	The whole Act
Arbitration Act 1950 (c.27)	The whole Act
Administration of Justice (Scotland) Act 1972 (c.59)	Section 3
Arbitration Act 1975 (c.3)	The whole Act
Law Reform (Miscellaneous Provisions) (Scotland) Act 1980 (c.55)	Section 17
Law Reform (Miscellaneous Provisions) (Scotland) Act 1990 (c.40)	Section 66 Schedule 7

APPENDIX 1

ARBITRATION INVOLVING CONSUMERS

Sections 89–91 of the 1996 Act are the only sections of that Act which ever applied in Scotland and they continue to be in force.

This might appear anomalous but regulation of the sale and supply of goods and services to consumers, almost wholly EU-driven, is a matter reserved to the Westminster Parliament under the Scotland Act 1998 and the Scottish Government is not competent to legislate in this area.

Sections 89–91 subject consumer arbitration agreements to the Unfair Terms Regulations (the "Regulations") despite the Regulations (and their 1994 predecessors) already applying to such agreements.

More importantly, ss.89–91 also provide that an arbitration agreement will be automatically unfair and thus not bind the consumer where the amount sought to be recovered does not exceed £5,000 (Unfair Arbitration Agreements (Specified Amounts) Order 1999 (SI 1999/2167)).

Even if such an agreement is not automatically unfair because the sum sought exceeds those limits, it may be found to be unfair as a result of the application of the fairness test under the Regulations.

This was indeed the outcome in *Zealander v Laing Homes Ltd* (2000) 2 T.C.L.R. 724 and in *Mylcrist Builders Ltd v Buck* [2009] 2 All E.R. (Comm) 259; for a discussion of the latter case, see Hew R. Dundas, "Recent Developments in English Arbitration Law: Arbitrations Involving Consumers, Whether to Hold a Hearing, Enforcement of Foreign Awards and a Postscript" (2009) 75 *Arbitration* 1 at 115–125.

In *Mylcrist*, the court considered that the arbitration clause was financially disadvantageous to the consumer and that its impact would not have been apparent to a layperson.

While, under the Regulations, a consumer ordinarily requires to be a natural person acting for non-business purposes, s.90 of the 1996 Act makes it clear that a consumer may be a legal person.

Regulation 3(1) defines consumer as

"any natural person [or company] who in contracts covered by these Regulations is acting for purposes which are outside his trade, business or profession",

i.e. a company which contracts for non-business purposes can challenge the fairness of an arbitration clause in that contract. Such was the case in *Heifer International Inc v Christiansen* [2008] 2 All E.R. (Comm) 831 where the company bought a residential property for an individual employee; however, the clause was held not to be unfair in that instance.

A1–10 The Scottish Government had (in 2009/10) intended to make an order under s.104 of the Scotland Act 1998 in order to disapply ss.89–91 in Scotland and to recast those provisions, suitably amended, as sections of the 2010 Act (*SP Official Report*, col.216267 (November 18, 2009)) but this intention appears to have been shelved. It would have been, of course, both unnecessary and, in the authors' view, wholly unhelpful—see para.A1–02, above.

A1–11 The CIArb Scottish Branch's SSFARs (modelled (in part) on the LMAA SCP and on IDRS Ltd's Arbitration Scheme for the Travel Industry) provide, should the parties agree to adopt them, a simplified set of rules intended for application to "small" disputes, be they consumer or small business ones. The SSFARs give a guideline range of "up to £25,000" (excluding VAT) but they can be adopted by agreement for larger disputes. The intention is that this becomes the dispute resolution process of choice over litigation in court.

Appendix 2

ANNOTATED RULES OF THE COURT OF SESSION

CHAPTER 62

Recognition, Registration and Enforcement of Foreign Judgments, etc.

. . . . .

[1]Part IX—Enforcement of Arbitral Awards under the New York Convention on the Recognition and Enforcement of Foreign Arbitral Awards

Note

1. Substituted by the Act of Sederunt (Rules of the Court of Session Amendment No.4) (Miscellaneous) (SSI 2010/205) r.10 (effective June 7, 2010).

Interpretation and application of this Part

62.56.—(1) In this Part—

"the 2010 Act" means the Arbitration (Scotland) Act 2010;

"the Convention" means the New York Convention on the Recognition and Enforcement of Foreign Arbitral Awards;

"Convention award" means an award made in pursuance of a written arbitration agreement in a territory of a state (other than the United Kingdom) which is a party to the Convention.

(2) This Part applies to an application under section 19 of the 2010 Act (recognition and enforcement of New York Convention awards).

General Note

Part IX of this Chapter provides for recognition and enforcement of non-UK awards under the 1958 New York Convention for the Recognition and Enforcement of Foreign Arbitral Awards by means of the flexible petition procedure in place of the former procedure by ordinary action. The 1958 Convention is an international treaty under which the State parties to the Convention agreed under certain conditions to recognise and allow the enforcement of arbitral awards seated in other State parties. Since 1975 the

A2–01

United Kingdom has been party to the Convention, to which there are now 150 States party. A copy of the Convention and further details on states that are party to it can be obtained via the UNCITRAL website at *http://www.uncitral.org* [Accessed June 21, 2014]. An arbitral award made in the territory of a State other than the United Kingdom which is party to the Convention and which was made pursuant to a written agreement or clause submitting the dispute to arbitration is known in Ch.100 of the RCS 1994 as a "Convention award". See in general the commentary at paras S18–01 to S18–15.

Unfortunately the rules on enforcement of Convention awards were not put into one place and the petitions under Part IX of Ch.62 are also covered by Ch.100, apart from rr.100.5 and 100.7, as well as by the general rules on petitions which have not been excluded by r.104.

Applications for enforcement of a Convention award

62.57.—(1) An application for enforcement of a Convention award under section 19(2) of the 2010 Act shall be made by petition or, where there are proceedings depending before the court under the 2010 Act in relation to the same arbitration process, by note in the process of the petition.

(2) There shall be produced with such a petition or note—

(a) the duly authenticated original award or a certified copy of it;
(b) the original agreement referred to in article II of the Convention or a certified copy of it;
(c) a translation of any award or agreement which is in a language other than English, certified by an official or sworn translator or by a diplomatic or consular agent;
(d) an affidavit stating—

   (i) the full name, title, trade or business and the usual or last known place of residence or, where appropriate, of the business of the petitioner or noter and the party against whom the Convention award was made;
   (ii) the amount of the Convention award which is unsatisfied; and
   (iii) that the Convention award has become binding on the parties and has not been set aside or suspended by a court of the country which, or under the law of which, the award was made.

"PETITION"

A2–02 A petition must be presented in the Outer House (RCS r.14.2(h)) and must be in Form 14.4 in the official printed form (RCS rr.4.1 and 14.4). The petition may be signed by the petitioner, counsel or other person having a right of audience or an agent (RCS r.4.2); and see r.1.3(1) (definition of "counsel", "other person having a right of audience" and "agent").

The petitioner must lodge the petition with the required steps of process (RCS r. 4.4) and any documents founded on or adopted (RCS r.27.1(1)). A fee is payable on lodging the petition.

On petitions generally, see RCS Ch.14.

PRODUCTIONS

The petitioner must produce with the petition (1) the items listed in RCS r.68.57(2), those listed in subparas (a) and (b) of RCS r.68.57(2) being also required by the Model Law; and (2) if necessary, a translation of any document lodged appropriately certified: see paras S21–14 to S21–16. While RCS r.62.3 imposes a more stringent requirement in that the translation must be certified as correct by the translator with the certificate including his full name, address and qualification that rule was intended to apply to the recognition and enforcement of all types of judgment or award. The authors submit that the particular provisions of RCS r.62.57 which are intended to cater for Convention enforcement in particular take precedence over RCS r.62.3. Such an interpretation would accord with the UK's obligations under the New York Convention and the pro-enforcement bias of the Convention. **A2–03**

AFFIDAVIT

The affidavit should be in the form of a statement of evidence written in the first person and should contain the evidence of the deponent in support of the averments in the petition. In particular it should deal with the matters listed in RCS r.62.57(2)(c). **A2–04**

An affidavit should be sworn and signed by the deponent before any person who may competently take an oath, whether in Scotland or in any other country. In Scotland such a person may include a notary public, justice of the peace, sheriff or any judge. The person taking the oath should also sign the affidavit. Where it is not in English a duly certified translation should also be lodged.

See also definition of affidavit in RCS r.1.3(1).

Registration of Convention award

62.58.—(1) The court, on being satisfied that the Convention award may be registered, shall grant warrant for registration.

(2) Where the court pronounces an interlocutor under paragraph (1), the Deputy Principal Clerk shall enter the Convention award in a register of Convention awards.

(3) Where the Keeper of the Registers receives from the petitioner or noter the documents referred to in paragraph (4), he or she shall register them in the register of judgments of the Books of Council and Session.

(4) The documents are—

(a) a certified copy of the interlocutor of the warrant of registration,
(b) a certified copy of the Convention award to be registered, and any translation of it, and
(c) any certificate of currency conversion under rule 62.2(1)(b).

(5) An extract of a registered Convention award with warrant for execution shall not be issued by the Keeper of the Registers until a certificate of service under rule 62.59 (service on party against whom Convention award made) is produced to him or her.
Other proceedings in relation to statutory applications

"Keeper of the Registers"

A2–05   This is the Keeper of the Registers of Scotland (RCS r.1.3(1)). The Register of Judgments is at Meadowbank House, 153 London Road, Edinburgh EH8 7AU; tel. 0131-659 6111; fax 0131-459 1221; DX ED300; e-mail: customer.services@ros.gov.uk

"Certified copy of the interlocutor"

A2–06   A copy of the interlocutor must be typed by the agent and presented to the Clerk of Session in the Petition Department. The clerk checks it, certifies it as a true copy and stamps it with the court stamp. A fee is payable.

"Certified copy of the award"

A2–07   It is not clear how the award should be certified; but presumably this may be done by the arbitrator or by any solicitor or his clerk; see paras S21–09 to S21–10.

"Translation"

A2–08   See RCS r.62.3.

"Certificate of currency conversion"

A2–09   The certificate should be obtained from the clerk of session in the Petition Department and should be signed by him (RCS r.62.2(3)).

Registration fee

A2–10   A fee will be payable to the Keeper of the Registers for registration and any extract: see the Fees in the Registers of Scotland Order 1991 (SI 1991/2093).

Service on party against whom Convention award made
62.59. On registration under rule 62.58, the petitioner or noter shall forthwith serve a notice of registration on the party against whom the Convention award was made in Form 62.59.

Rules of the Court of Session

"SERVE"
For methods of service, see RCS Ch.16 Pt I.

Application for refusal of recognition or enforcement of a Convention award

62.60.—(1) An application under article V of the Convention (request by party against whom Convention award made for refusal of recognition or enforcement) shall be made by note.

(2) A note referred to in paragraph (1) may crave—

(a) suspension or interdict of any past or future steps in the execution of the Convention award, including registration or enforcement of the award; and
(b) recall of the interlocutor pronounced under rule 62.58(1) (registration under the Convention).

(3) The note shall be supported by affidavit and any relevant documentary evidence.

[1](4) Where any interlocutor pronounced under rule 62.58(1) is recalled, a certificate to that effect issued by the Deputy Principal Clerk shall be sufficient warrant to the Keeper of the Registers to cancel the registration and return the documents registered to the petitioner or noter on whose application the interlocutor under that rule was pronounced.

NOTE
1. As amended by the Act of Sederunt (Rules of the Court of Session Amendment No. 4) (Miscellaneous) (SSI 2011/288) (effective July 21, 2011).

GENERAL NOTE
For the grounds on which an application may be made for refusal of recognition or enforcement of an arbitral award under the New York Convention see s.20(2) to (4) and the commentary thereon.

"NOTE"
For applications by note, see RCS r.15.2.

"AFFIDAVIT"
See the commentary on RCS r.62.57.

Arbitration (Scotland) Act 2010

CHAPTER 100[1]

Arbitration

Note

1. Chapter 100 inserted by the Act of Sederunt (Rules of the Court of Session Amendment No.4) (Miscellaneous) (SSI 2010/205) r.10 (effective June 7, 2010).

Interpretation and application

100.1.—(1) In this Chapter—

"the 2010 Act" means the Arbitration (Scotland) Act 2010;

"Convention award" means an award made in pursuance of a written arbitration agreement in a territory of a state (other than the United Kingdom) which is a party to the New York Convention on the Recognition and Enforcement of Foreign Arbitral Awards;

"Scottish Arbitration Rules" means the Scottish Arbitration Rules set out in schedule 1 to the 2010 Act;

"tribunal" means a sole arbitrator or panel of arbitrators.

(2) Subject to paragraph (3), this Chapter applies to applications and appeals made under the 2010 Act (including applications and appeals made under the Scottish Arbitration Rules).

(3) Rules 100.5 and 100.7 do not apply to an application under section 19(2) of the 2010 for enforcement of a Convention award.

General Note

A2–15 This Chapter provides rules for the making of applications under the Arbitration (Scotland) Act 2010 which came into force on 7th June 2010 in relation to all arbitrations begun on or after that date except for referrals to arbitration under statute (Arbitration (Scotland) Act 2010 (Commencement No. 1 and Transitional Provisions) Order 2010 (SSI 2010/195) arts 2(2) and 3(1)(b). The 2010 Act, and this Chapter, do not apply to causes relating to arbitrations begun before June 7, 2010 nor to causes relating to arbitration (whether or not begun before that date) raised or depending before the court before June 7, 2010 (2010 Order art.3(1)(b)). Such causes are governed by other provisions of the RCS 1994 (e.g. Ch.58 relating to judicial review) or other enactments or by the common law applicable to procedure or by a mixture of these.

Given that Ch.100 was not enacted by application of any power given by the 2010 Act, it follows that the definitions in the Act do not necessarily apply to the words used in the Chapter.

Applications ancillary to ongoing arbitration

A2–16 One of the principal aims of arbitration is to allow a dispute to be resolved by an arbitrator or arbitrators in a prompt and cost-effective manner which allows for a flexibility of procedure not allowed for by the normal process of litigation in a court.

The SAR give arbitrators extensive powers of case management to allow the dispute to be resolved in a prompt, cost-effective and fair manner. It is a founding principle of the 2010 Act that the court should not intervene in an arbitration except as provided by the Act itself: 2010 Act s.1(c). However, notwithstanding the powers given to the arbitrator by the parties and the SAR, no arbitrator has power over third parties such as witnesses who are not parties or havers of documents. Nor can an arbitrator enforce a provisional award of interdict or enforce an interim measure such as inhibition, arrestment or attachment to secure assets from which an award may be satisfied.

For all of these reasons it is necessary for the parties to be able to apply to the court that it exercise its powers to assist the arbitration. In response to this need, the 2010 Act provides for parties to an arbitration to make a number of applications to the court in connection with the ongoing arbitration or issues relating to expenses arising out of it. Thus a party can apply to the court under the following provisions of the SAR:

Rule 7(6) (appointment of arbitrator)

Rule 12 (removal of arbitrator)

Rule 13 (dismissal of arbitrator)

Rule 15(2) (authorisation of resignation of arbitrator)

Rule 16(1) (orders as to fees, expenses and liability consequent on cessation of arbitrator's tenure)

Rule 43 (variation of time limits set by parties)

Rule 45 (attendance of witnesses and disclosure of documentary and other material evidence)

Rule 46 (orders as to appointment of safeguarder, securing amounts in dispute, diligence on the dependence, or interim diligence, interdict or interim interdict, or recovery of evidence under s.1 of the 1972 Act)

Rule 56(2) (issue of award pending resolution of dispute over arbitrator's fees etc.)

Rule 58(3) (extension of time to seek correction of award)

APPEALS AND THE SUPERVISORY ROLE OF THE COURT

In addition to the court having a role supporting the arbitration, it also has a supervisory role. This is to ensure the quality of the decision-making procedure used by an arbitrator and, to a limited extent, the quality of any award (formerly known as a decree arbitral) made by the arbitrator. Again, this has been recognised internationally and in Scotland over many years. Until the 2010 Act, the supervisory role was exercised by the court by means of its common law supervisory jurisdiction over inferior tribunals. Until the 2010 Act, the supervisory jurisdiction could be exercised as part of a number of different procedures.

A party to an arbitration could raise an ordinary action of reduction of

A2–17

the award or interdict of an apprehended or ongoing step of procedure or specific implement of a failure to act. From 1985 the ordinary action seeking these remedies was replaced by a petition for judicial review under what is now Ch.58 of the RCS 1994. Alternatively, a party could, at any time until the issue of the final award, ask the arbitrator under s.3 of the 1972 Act to state a case to the Inner House asking it to give a binding opinion on any question of law which had arisen.

Finally, if an award was issued and the successful party raised an action seeking implement thereof, for example through seeking an order for payment, the unsuccessful party could seek to invoke the court's supervisory jurisdiction with the result that the award would be reduced by way of exception (*ope exceptionis*).

Under the 2010 Act, these common law methods of challenge to the arbitral procedure and any award following thereon are no longer competent (2010 Act s.13) nor is the stated case procedure competent (2010 Act Sch.2). In their place the 2010 Act has provided a comprehensive code in the SAR for the making of challenges to arbitral procedure and awards. It has also provided more limited powers to allow parties to obtain a binding decision of the court on certain issues. This code allows for the challenging of awards by means of appeals and the obtaining of binding opinions by means of references.

ENFORCEMENT OF CONVENTION AWARDS

A2–18 Since 1975 the UK has been party to the New York Convention. This is an international treaty under which the state parties to the Convention agreed under certain conditions to recognise and allow the enforcement of arbitral awards seated in other state parties. There are now 150 states which are parties to the New York Convention and a copy thereof and further details on states that are party to the Convention can be obtained via the UNCITRAL website at *www.uncitral.org*. An arbitral award made in the territory of a state other than the UK which is party to the Convention and which was made pursuant to a written agreement or clause submitting the dispute to arbitration is known in Ch.100 as a "Convention award".

The New York Convention was originally implemented by the 1975 Act under which a party seeking recognition or enforcement of Convention award required to raise an ordinary action seeking payment under or other implement of the award. The 1975 Act, in so far as it applied to Scotland, was repealed by the 2010 Act and the opportunity was taken to reform the method of enforcement of a Convention award. Unfortunately the rules on enforcement of Convention awards were not put into one place and the rules are to be found in rr.100.2, 100.3, 100.4 and 100.9 and also in rr.62.56 to 62.60.

Rules 100.5 and 100.7 do not apply to an application to enforce a Convention award.

Proceedings before a nominated judge

100.2. All proceedings in the Outer House in a cause to which this Chapter applies shall be brought before a judge of the court nominated by the Lord President as an arbitration judge or, where no such judge is available, any other judge of the court (including the vacation judge).

NOMINATED JUDGE

As at July 1, 2014 the nominated judges are Lords Malcolm, Woolman and Doherty.

Procedure in causes under the 2010 Act

100.3. Subject to the provisions of the Scottish Arbitration Rules and this Chapter, the procedure in a cause under the Scottish Arbitration Rules shall be such as the judge dealing with the cause shall determine.

GENERAL NOTE

This rule applies to applications or appeals under the SAR and not under the main body of the 2010 Act. Therefore it does not apply to petitions to enforce awards or to other applications which are covered by the main body of the 2010 Act. It is unclear why the rule does not cover such applications.

Rule 100.3 gives the judge a discretion to decide on the procedure in the application or appeal consistent with the interests of justice. The intent is that the procedure is as flexible as possible (*Arbitration Application No. 3 of 2011*, 2012 S.L.T. 150 at [9]).

Rule 100.3 must be read with the subsequent rules 100.4 and 100.5. Rule 100.5 provides that an application or appeal under the Act (except for the enforcement of a Convention award) is to be made by petition unless a petition is already depending before the court in relation to the same arbitration process.

Rule 100.4 excludes the application of the default rules for petitions which require an automatic first order for intimation, service or advertisement of the petition to be made upon its presentation to the court, the lodging of answers by a respondent and, upon the lodging of answers, the making of a motion by the petitioner to move the court for further procedure. The petition procedure is inherently flexible and it is unclear why these default rules, which would have been quite appropriate for arbitration appeals and applications (subject to exclusion in particular cases), have been excluded in their entirety.

Disapplication of certain rules

100.4. The following rules shall not apply to a cause under this Part—
rule 6.2 (fixing and allocation of diets in Outer House);
rule 14.5 (first order in petitions);
rule 14.6 (period of notice for lodging answers);
rule 14.8 (procedure where answers lodged).

General Note

A2–21   This rule applies to all applications or appeals under the 2010 Act whether or not under the SAR; see also para.A2–18.

Application or appeal under the 2010 Act

100.5.—(1) Subject to paragraph (2), an application or appeal under the 2010 Act shall be made by petition.

(2) If proceedings are depending before the court under paragraph (1) in relation to the same arbitration process, an application under the 2010 Act shall be made by note in the process of the petition.

(3) Upon lodging a petition or note under paragraph (1) or (2), the petitioner or noter must enrol a motion for intimation and service of the petition or note and the court may make such order as is appropriate in the circumstances of the case.

(4) The court may make an order for intimation and service of the petition or note at the address of a party's agent or other person acting for that party in the arbitration process and the service will be effective if carried out in accordance with that order.

(5) Upon expiry of any period of notice following intimation and service of the petition or note, the petitioner or noter shall enrol a motion for further procedure and the court may make such order as is appropriate in the circumstances of the case, including, where appropriate, an order disposing of the petition or note.

General Note

A2–22   Rule 100.5 does not apply to applications for the enforcement of a Convention award. Instead, r.62.57 provides that such an application is to be made by petition or, in certain cases, by note and, in relation to such applications, the reader is referred to r.62.57.

The basic rule is that all applications or appeals under the 2010 Act are to be made by petition. This approach is flawed in so far as it fails to take account of the various applications under both the main body of the Act and the SAR that can be made which are incidental to ongoing court proceedings or an ongoing petition process. For example, an application for a sist under s.10, an application for anonymous reporting under s.15, an application for the provision of security for expenses under r.71(10) and an application for payment into court of sums awarded or provision of other security under r.71(12). It surely cannot have been intended that a fresh petition or even a note is required for every incidental application under the Act. It would seem very odd, for example, that a fresh petition is required to seek a sist of an ordinary litigation where, until the enactment of Ch.100, a mere motion was required. The solution is to identify the applications or appeals that are true fresh processes and to restrict RCS r.100.5 to them. Incidental applications can then continue to be dealt with by motion under RCS r.23.11.

Petition or Note

As noted the basic form of application or appeal is in the form of a petition. However, where there is a petition which is still "depending" before the court which relates to the same arbitration process, the application must be by note. A petition is depending before the court from the time that the court makes its first order in the petition process and it ceases to be depending when the final decree is made. The final decree is the interlocutor which, taken by itself or along with previous interlocutors, disposes of the whole subject matter of the cause including the liability for expenses (costs) but not the quantification of their amount.

A2–23

"Petition"

A petition is presented to the Outer House (RCS r.14.2(h)). The petition must be on Form 14.4 using the official printed form (RCS rr.4.1 and 14.4). The petition must be signed by counsel or other person having a right of audience (RCS r.4.2); and see RCS r.1.3(1) (definition of "counsel" and "other person having a right of audience"). Aside from compliance with RCS r.14.4, if the petition is a referral to the Outer House under rr.22 or 41 of the SAR, or an appeal under rr.67, 68 or 69 thereof, it must comply with r.100.8 of RCS 1994.

A2–24

The petitioner must lodge the petition with the required steps of process (RCS r.4.4). A fee is payable on lodging.

On petitions generally, see Ch.14 but it must be remembered that RCS rr.14.5, 14.6 and 14.8 do not apply to petitions under the 2010 Act.

"Note"

For procedure by note, see RCS r.15.2 but it must be remembered that RCS rr.14.5, 14.6 and 14.8 do not apply to notes under the 2010 Act.

A2–25

Motion for intimation and service

Given that a petitioner or noter must, at the outset, lodge a motion for intimation and service, it is unclear why the presumed automatic intimation and service provisions of RCS r.14.5 has been disapplied to petitions and notes under the 2010 Act. There may be situations where intimation and service may be inappropriate. In such a situation under RCS r.14.5 the petitioner or noter would have enrolled a motion with the court for dispensation with intimation and service. Under RCS r.100.5(3) the petitioner and noter is put to the needless trouble and expense of having to enrol a motion for intimation and service and, if necessary, seek dispensation with that very requirement.

A2–26

The usual order for service requires answers to be lodged within 21 days of intimation where it is in Europe. If, in relation to a particular application (e.g. an application for leave to make a legal error appeal) a shorter period is required, then this can be provided for in a special rule of the RCS.

Intimation and service to party's agent or representative

A2–27   Normally intimation and service must be made to a party unless the party's agent (solicitor) has authority to accept intimation and service. Where there is an ongoing arbitration, its conduct may be in the hands of a party's solicitor or an unqualified representative who will have the party's mandate to do so. Given that many applications under the 2010 Act will be in relation to ongoing arbitrations (before the final award), in order to expedite matters the court has a power to order intimation and service to the party's solicitor or other representative acting in the arbitration process.

The position may be different once a final award has been issued and there is no longer an ongoing arbitral process.

Motion for further procedure

A2–28   For motions, generally, see Ch.23 of the RCS. The purpose of intimation and service is to allow the intimation of opposition to the petition or note. In a standard process, the order for intimation and service requires intimation of opposition to be made through the lodging of answers and the petitioner or noter then seeks an order for further procedure (RCS rr.14.6 and 14.8). Even though RCS rr.14.6 and 14.8 are disapplied, this is what is contemplated in RCS r.100.5: *Arbitration Application No.3 of 2011*, 2012 S.L.T. 150 at [10]. The further procedure sought will depend on the nature of the application or appeal, whether answers have been lodged and, if so, the nature of the opposition expressed in the answers.

Thus where there are no disputed facts the further procedure may take the form of a hearing which is a debate. If there are disputed facts, then further adjustment of petition and answers may be required either generally or restricted to the specific factual issue which is in dispute, with the fixing of a hearing thereafter. The court can order witness statements or affidavits to be produced: *Arbitration Application No.3 of 2011*, 2012 S.L.T. 150 at [10]. Ultimately it can order a hearing to take place in the form of a proof (civil trial involving oral evidence).

Application for attendance of witnesses or disclosure of evidence

100.6. In relation to a petition or note lodged under rule 45 of the Scottish Arbitration Rules (court's power to order attendance of witnesses and disclosure of evidence), intimation and service of the petition or note is not required.

General Note

A2–29   The purpose of RCS r.100.6 is unclear and its effect is, with great respect, bizarre. Rule 45 of the SAR allows a party or an arbitrator to apply to the court for an order requiring any person (a) to attend a hearing for the purposes of giving evidence in the arbitration or (b) to disclose documents or other material evidence to the arbitrator or arbitrators. Rule 45 of the SAR also makes it clear that the court is not to order any person to give any evidence or to disclose anything which the person would be entitled to refuse to give or disclose in civil proceedings. This exception is presumably directed at issues of confidential privilege: see the various categories in *Greens Annotated Rules of the Court of Session* (Edinburgh: W. Green), para.35.2.7.

If a party seeks the attendance of a witness then r.45 of the SAR contemplates that objection may be taken to the witness being ordered to attend on the grounds that the evidence sought to be obtained from him is privileged and confidential. In addition, objection may be taken on the grounds of the irrelevance of the evidence. How is such an objection to be made by a witness or a haver over whom the arbitrator has no jurisdiction and to whom, by virtue of RCS r.100.6, the application has not been intimated?

The making of a binding court order to attend to give evidence or disclose evidence against a witness or haver who has had no notice of the order being made against him would appear to be contrary to natural justice under Scots common law and possibly incompatible with art.6 of the ECHR in so far as it determines the witness' or haver's civil rights and obligations. Such a court order differs from a common law citation in that it involves an order with the potential sanction of a contempt of court being made on the witness to attend rather than a warrant being given to a party to enable citation. Failure to comply with a citation may result in arrest but is not prima facie a contempt of court.

The position is even more unsatisfactory in relation to the recovery of documents. Clearly objection can be taken to the disclosure of documents on the grounds of privilege and confidentiality and immateriality (e.g. fishing for evidence). How, if intimation is not required, is a party or a haver to be given an opportunity to object to a proposed order?

Averments in petitions and notes under the 2010 Act

100.7.—(1) The petitioner or noter must set out in the petition or note the facts and circumstances on which the petition or note is founded and the relief claimed.

(2) In particular, any—

(a) application under rule 22 (referral of point of jurisdiction) or rule 41 (referral of point of law) of the Scottish Arbitration Rules, or
(b) appeal under rule 67(1) (jurisdictional appeal), rule 68(1) (serious irregularity appeal) or rule 69(1) (legal error appeal) of the Scottish Arbitration Rules,

should, so far as is necessary, identify the matters referred to in paragraph (3).

(3) The following matters should be identified—

(a) the parties to the cause and the arbitration from which the cause arises;
(b) the relevant rule of the Scottish Arbitration Rules or other

Arbitration (Scotland) Act 2010

provision of the 2010 Act under which the petition or note has been lodged;
(c) any special capacity in which the petitioner or noter is acting or any special capacity in which any other party to the proceedings is acting;
(d) a summary of the circumstances out of which the application or appeal arises;
(e) the grounds on which the application or appeal proceeds;
(f) in the case of an appeal under rule 67(1), whether the appellant seeks the variation or the setting aside of an award (or part of it);
(g) in the case of an appeal under rule 69(1), whether the appeal is made with the agreement of the parties to the arbitration;
(h) any relevant requirements of the Scottish Arbitration Rules which have been met.

GENERAL NOTE

A2–30   Rule 100.7 can be seen as applicable to referrals under rr.22 and 41 of the SAR and to appeals under rr.67, 68 and 69 thereof. For some reason it is not applied expressly to an appeal under r.21 but it is suggested that its additional requirements for petitions or notes should be followed for such an appeal also. Rule 100.7(1) merely re-states the generality of RCS rr.14.4(2)(a) and 15.2(2) which apply to all petitions and notes respectively and its purpose is unclear.

The provisions of RCS r.14.4 (for petitions) and r.15.2 (for notes) should be followed in addition to the provisions of RCS r.100.7. Subject to the terms of those rules, it should not be necessary to set everything out at length in the petition or note: *Arbitration Application No.3 of 2011*, 2012 S.L.T. 150 at [9]. As was observed in the last mentioned case, the basis of the challenge, placed (so far as relevant) in the context of the underlying dispute and what has happened in the arbitration, should be set out as simply as possible since, by the time that an appeal comes to be made, the underlying dispute will usually be very familiar to all of the parties. Cross reference to the award should be made: *Arbitration Application No.3 of 2011*, 2012 S.L.T. 150 at [11].

Appeals against arbitral award on ground of legal error

100.8.—(1) In addition to complying with rule 100.5(3) and (5), upon lodging a petition or note under rule 69 of the Scottish Arbitration Rules (legal error appeal), the petitioner or noter shall at the same time—
(a) except in a case where an appeal is made with the agreement of the parties, enrol a motion for leave to appeal; and
(b) lodge any documents that the petitioner or noter intends to rely on in the application for leave (if applicable) and in the appeal.
(2) A motion for leave to appeal under paragraph (1) shall—

(a) identify the point of law concerned; and
(b) set out the grounds that are relied on for the giving of leave.

(3) Within 14 days of service of the petition or note, or such other time as the court may allow, a respondent may lodge and intimate to all other parties grounds of opposition, including any evidence to be relied upon in opposition to the application for leave.

(4) The application for leave to appeal shall be dealt with without a hearing unless the court considers that a hearing is required.

(5) Where the court considers that a hearing is required, it may give such further directions as it considers necessary.

[1](6) Rule 41.2 (applications for leave to appeal), rule 41.3 (determination of applications for leave to appeal) and rule 41.5 (competency of appeals) do not apply to an application for leave to appeal under this rule.

NOTE

1. As amended by the Act of Sederunt (Rules of the Court of Session Amendment No. 6) (Miscellaneous) (SSI 2011/385) para.6 (effective November 28, 2011).

GENERAL NOTE

RCS r.100.8 is a rule that causes confusion. Just as RCS r.100.6 requires to be redrafted to align it with RCS rr.100.5 and 100.7, RCS r.100.8 seeks to regulate applications for leave to make legal error appeals. SAR r.70(2) provides that a legal error appeal may be made only with the agreement of the parties or with leave of the Outer House and SAR r.71(4) provides that an application for leave must be made to the Outer House within the 28 day time limit specified therein. RCS r.100.5 provides that an application must be made by petition (a note being unlikely in these circumstances). RCS r.100.7 provides that the circumstances on which the petition is founded must be set out and this will include the point of law founded upon and how the criteria for leave in SAR r.70 are satisfied. RCS r.100.5 also provides that, upon lodging a petition, a motion for intimation and service must be enrolled. In these circumstances, it is unclear why, with the requirements for leave already having been identified in the petition, there has to be another motion in terms of RCS r.100.8 re-indentifying the point of law and grounds of appeal.

A2–31

MOTION FOR LEAVE

Rule 70(4) of the SAR requires the motion to identify the point of law on which it is said that the tribunal has erred and to state why leave should be granted. The reasons for granting leave should be tied to the requirements of r.70(3) of the SAR. For further details of the requirements in r.70(3) of the SAR, see the commentary thereon at paras R70–10 to R70–25 above.

For motions under r.100.8, see Pts 3 and 4 of Ch.23. However, given that

A2–32

there is no provision for intimation of the motion to be made in accordance with Part 4 of Ch.23, the intimation provisions of that Part do not apply to a motion for leave. The motion for leave should therefore seek an order for intimation and service on the respondent with a standard time of 14 days to lodge grounds of opposition and evidence in support thereof: see r.100.8(3). If the time is to be less than 14 days, then the motion should give reasons. For further procedure see Part 4 of Ch.23.

The interlocutor for intimation and service of the motion should require the petitioner to lodge in process the certificate of service on the respondent within a specified period of time: *Arbitration Application No.3 of 2011*, 2012 S.L.T. 150 at [16].

GROUNDS OF OPPOSITION

A2-33 Following intimation and service in ordinary petition and note procedure the respondent is given an opportunity to lodge answers to the petition or note. It is not intended, however, that this be the case for legal error appeals: *Arbitration Application No. 3 of 2011*, 2012 S.L.T. 150 at [15]. Instead the respondent is given an opportunity to lodge and intimate "grounds of opposition" and "evidence to be relied upon" in opposition to the motion for leave. The grounds of opposition are to the motion rather than to the appeal itself: *Arbitration Application No. 3 of 2011*, 2012 S.L.T. 150 at [15] and [16].

DETERMINATION OF MOTION

A2-34 The general rule is that a motion is to be determined without a hearing unless the Lord Ordinary is satisfied that a hearing is required (SAR r.70(5) and r.100.8(4) of RCS 1994). It has been suggested that once the period for intimation of opposition has expired agents should intimate this to the court to allow the motion to be dealt with as expeditiously as possible. In *Arbitration Application No. 3 of 2011*, 2012 S.L.T. 150 at [16], per Lord Glennie, it was explained that:

> "[A] system has been initiated for ensuring that motions for leave are dealt with promptly after the expiry of the time for lodging grounds of opposition. The process will be marked in the petition department with a note to the effect that, upon the lodging of grounds of opposition, the process is to be passed to the commercial clerks to place before an arbitration judge at the earliest opportunity for a decision on the application for leave."

FURTHER PROCEDURE

A2-35 If the Lord Ordinary grants leave, it is for him to make the next order for procedure in relation to the appeal: r.100.3. This may entail the fixing of a By Order hearing at which parties can address the court on a timetable to be fixed for notes of argument or any further procedure necessary for the determination of the petition or note forming the legal error appeal itself.

Anonymity in legal proceedings
100.9.—(1) Where a petition or note is lodged under the 2010 Act, any application to the court under section 15 of the 2010 Act (anonymity in legal proceedings) shall be made not later than the hearing of a motion for further procedure under rule 100.5(5).

(2) Until an application under section 15 of the 2010 Act has been determined or, where no such application has been made, the time at which a motion for further procedure is made under rule 100.5(5) and, thereafter, if the court grants an order under section 15 of the 2010 Act—

(a) the petition or note shall not be available for inspection, except by court staff and the parties;
(b) the petition or note shall be referred to publicly, including in the rolls of court, as "Arbitration Application" or "Arbitration Appeal" (as the case may be) and by reference to a number and the year in which it was lodged;
(c) the court proceedings shall be heard in private.

(3) Unless the court grants an order under section 15 of the 2010 Act, all applications and appeals made under the 2010 Act shall be heard in public.

GENERAL NOTE
One of the innovative aspects of the 2010 Act was the introduction of a duty in the SAR (which the parties may agree to exclude) on the tribunal and the parties not to disclose any information relating to the dispute, the arbitral proceedings and any award which is not and has never been in the public domain (2010 Act Sch.1 r.26) and see the commentary thereon at paras R26–07 to R26–27 above.

A2–36

Information relating to the dispute includes the identity of the parties. This is seen as part of the keeping of the arbitration confidential which is one of the perceived benefits of arbitration. Whilst there are a number of exceptions to the duty of non-disclosure (including the necessity to comply with any rule of the RCS 1994 for petitions and notes), it was felt that an option for further protection to prevent information about the dispute and parties reaching the public domain was desirable.

That option was expressed in s.15 of the 2010 Act which allows any party to civil proceedings relating to an arbitration to apply to the court for an order prohibiting the disclosure of the identity of a party to the arbitration in any report of the proceedings. Civil proceedings are not restricted to applications or appeals under the Act and could potentially include an ordinary action which has been sisted for the dispute to be resolved by

Arbitration (Scotland) Act 2010

arbitration although such an application would not be made under RCS r.100.9. See, in general, paras S15–08 to S15–21.

FORM OF THE APPLICATION

A2–37 Neither the Act nor, surprisingly, RCS r.100.9 specifies the form that the application under s.15 of the 2010 Act should take. Given that the application is to be made by a party to civil proceedings to anonymise a party in a report of those proceedings, one would expect that the application would be by motion in those proceedings pursuant to RCS r.23.11. Unfortunately that is contrary to RCS r.100.5 which seems an unfortunate drafting error. Until that error is cured it would appear that most applications under s.15 require to be made by note in those civil proceedings.

TIMING OF THE APPLICATION

A2–38 The application must be made no later than the hearing of a motion for further procedure under r.100.5(5). There may, of course, not be a hearing on such a motion and, in legal error appeals where leave is refused, there may not even be such a motion. The court has, however, indicated that, regardless of the making of an application, it will not publish any decision on the grant or refusal of leave unless it raises issues of law or practice. Nevertheless, it is prudent for the application for anonymisation to be made no later than the motion for the first order in the petition or note. If no such application is made then, in the unusual case of a hearing on an application for leave, it will be heard in private: r.100.9(2)(c).

Rule 100.9(2) contains an attempt to provide provisional anonymisation pending the determination of an application or the expiry of the period for the making of the motion, whichever is the later. The effect of interim anonymisation is equated to permanent anonymisation for which see below.

EFFECT OF ORDER UNDER S.15

A2–39 An order under s.15 of the 2010 Act prohibits the disclosure of the identity of a party to the arbitration in any report of the proceedings. This is given practical effect by r.100.9(2). The cases of *Arbitration Application No. 3 of 2011*, 2012 S.L.T. 150 and *Arbitration Application No. 2 of 2011* [2011] CSOH 186; [2011] Hous. L.R. 72 are examples of the effect.

Applications for enforcement of a tribunal's award under the 2010 Act

100.10.—(1) A petition or note under section 12 of the 2010 Act for enforcement of a tribunal's award shall—

    (a) identify the parties to the cause and the arbitration process from which the cause arises;

    (b) specify that the award is not currently the subject of—

Rules of the Court of Session

      (i) an appeal under Part 8 of the Scottish Arbitration Rules (challenging awards);
      (ii) any arbitral process of appeal or review; or
      (iii) a process of correction under rule 58 of the Scottish Arbitration Rules; and
  (c) specify the basis on which the tribunal had jurisdiction to make the award.

(2) There shall be produced with such a petition or note—

  (a) the original tribunal's award or a certified copy of it; and
  (b) the documents founded upon or adopted as incorporated in the petition or note.

GENERAL NOTE

This rule deals with an application under s.12 of the 2010 Act seeking an order that an award may be enforced as if it were an extract registered decree bearing a warrant for execution granted by the court. It does not apply to Convention awards for which separate provision is made in s.19 of the Act and RCS rr.62.56 to 62.60. The enforcement procedure under s.12 of the 2010 Act and RCS r.100.10 is quicker than that for Convention awards in that, upon the granting of the s.12 application, there is no need for the deemed decree (judgment order) to be registered in the Books of Council and Session. **A2–40**

The provisions of RCS rr.14.4 (for petitions) and 15.2 (for notes) should be followed in addition to the provisions of RCS r.100.10.

INDEX

AAR
see **Arbitral appointments referee (AAR)**
Additional awards
  correction of awards, R58–08
Ad factum praestandum
see **Specific implement**
Administrative matters
see **Clerks**
Admissibility
  evidence
    tribunal to determine, R28, R28–15 to R28–16
Advertisements
  formal communications
    newspapers, R83–20
Advisers
see **Agents; Clerks; Employees; Experts**
Affirmations
  default rule, R36, R36–01 to R36–06
Agents
  administrative matters, R32–03 to R32–19
  appointment, R32, R32–01 to R32–20
  arbitral proceedings, R32, R32–01 to R32–20
  consent, R32
  default rule, R32, R32–01 to R32–20
  delegation, R32–06 to R32–08
  fees and expenses, R32–20
  immunity, R75, R75–01 to R75–05
Agreements
see **Arbitration agreements; Contracts**
Ambiguity
  challenging awards, R58–29
  clarification, R58, R58–18, R58–19
  discretion of tribunal, R58–29
  time limits, R58–25
Amiable compositeur
  decision according to justice, fairness, equity, R47–30
  legal error appeal, exclusion of, R69–15
Ancillary provisions
  Scottish Ministers
    powers, S32–01 to S32–04
Annulment
see **Reduction**
Anonymity
see also **Confidentiality**
  legal proceedings
    appeals, S15–22
    application to court for orders, S15, S15–04 to S15–07
    appointment of arbitrators, S15–09
    arbitration agreements, S15–11
    civil proceedings, S15–08 to S15–13
    conditions for disclosure, S15, S15–14 to S15–21
    criminal proceedings, S15–08

exceptions, S15–14
generally, S15–01 to S15–07
interests of justice, S15–21
lawful interests, disclosure to protect, S15–17
public functions exception, S15–15 to S15–16
public interest exception, S15–18 to S15–20
removal of arbitrators, S15–09
Appeals
  anonymity in legal proceedings, S15–22
  annulment appeals, S11–11
  arbitral appointments referee, R7–04
  arbitrators
    appointment, R7–04, R68
    resignation, R16–04
  awards S14–14, R51–50 to R51–56, R58–29
    legal error, R69, R69–01 to R69–30, R70, R70–01 to R70–51
    other challenges, R71, R71–01 to R71–59
    serious irregularity, R68, R68–01 to R68–97
    substantive jurisdiction, R67, R67–01 to R67–39
  clarification or removal of ambiguity in awards, R58–29
  enforcement of awards, S12, S12–23 to S12–28
  evidence, R28–12 to R28–17
  expenses, R62–06 to R62–09
  failure of appointment procedure, R7–04, R7–06, R7–11
  fees and expenses
    generally, S12–14, S12–25
    non-payment, R56, R56–23, R56–24
    recoverable arbitration expenses, R61, R61–01 to R61–22
  fraud, R68–54
  impartiality, R24–20
  judges, S25–15, S25–16
  jurisdictional appeals, R21, R21–01 to R21–16, R67, R67–01 to R67–39
  legal error, R69, R69–01 to R69–30, R70, R70–01 to R70–51
  Outer House, S12–22
  reconsideration by tribunal, R72, R72–02 to R72–06
  Scottish Arbitration Rules, S13, S13–04
  security for expenses of appeal, S12–27
  serious irregularity, R68, R68–01 to R68–97
  setting aside, partial, R67–33
  Sheriff Court, R45–36
  stated case procedure, S29–01

527

Index

time limits, R70–35, R71–09 to R71–22
umpires, S25
variation of awards, R67–32 to R67–39
Appointments
see also **Arbitral appointments referee (AAR)**
arbitrators
  anonymity in legal proceedings, S15–09
  appeals, R7–04, R68
  challenges to appointments, R10, R10–01 to R10–20, R24–14 to R24–22
  civil law, R3–10
  companies, R3–08
  conflict of interests, R8–01 to R8–20
  court intervention, S13–09
  death of arbitrator, R3–10
  default rules, S9–03, R2–01, R5–01, R6–01, R9–01, R10–01
  duty to disclose, R8–01 to R8–20
  eligibility for appointment, R4, R4–01 to R4–09, R16–03, R76, R76–08
  emergency arbitrators, R6–20, R35–07
  failure of appointment procedure, S29–01, R7, R7–01 to R7–11, R10, R10–20
  fairness, R10, R10–11
  guidelines on selection, R6–13 to R6–17
  impartiality, R7–11, R10–11
  interviews, R6–13 to R6–17
  judges, S25, S25–01 to S25–16
  limited liability partnerships, R3–08
  method of appointment, R6, R6–01 to R6–20
  multi–party arbitrations, R6–18 to R6–19
  notice, S20–42, R68–02
  number of arbitrators, S20–63, R5, R5–01 to R5–07, R6–19, R11–05, R30–07
  partnerships, R3–08
  party–appointed arbitrators, R6–09 to R6–12
  party autonomy, R6–16
  personal appointment, R3–12 to R3–14
  reasons for appointment, S25–03
  revocation of appointment, R9, R11–09, R16–03
  serious irregularity appeals, R68, R68–02
  sole arbitrators, R5, R6, R6–04
  striking out names, R10–05
  tenure, R9, R9–01 to R9–05
  time limits, S20–42, R6–06, R10–15 to R10–16, R10–20, R43–06
  umpires, S24, S24–01 to S24–08, S25, S25–01 to S25–16
challenges to appointment
  confirmation of appointment, R10–17 to R10–19

factual basis of objection, R10, R10–14
fairness, R10, R10–11
impartiality, R10, R10–10 to R10–11, R24–14 to R24–22
notice, R10, R10–16
party's right of challenge, R10–05 to R10–09
qualifications, R10, R10–12 to R10–13
revocation of appointment, R10–17 to R10–19
striking out names, R10–05
time limits, R10, R10–15 to R10–16, R10–20
tribunals
  default rule, R2, R2–01 to R2–04
  institutional rules, R2–03
Arbiter
see **Arbitrators**
Arbitrability
choice of law, S30–19 to S30–24
criminal law, S30–14
family law, S30–05, S30–13
contra bonos mores, S30–10
fraud, S30–11
governing law, S30–19 to S30–24
international approaches, S30–14 to S30–15
international arbitration, S30–16 to S30–18
jurisdiction, S30–19 to S30–24
non-arbitrability
  effect, S30–25 to S30–26
  employment disputes, S30–08 to S30–09
  family law matters, S30–05
  other jurisdictions, S30–14, S30–15
  social security claims, S30–07
  winding up, S30–06
New York Convention 1958, S20–104, S30–17
partnership law, S30–12
property rights, S30–12
Arbitral appointments referee (AAR)
appeals, R7, R7–04 to R7–11, R68, R68–45
arbitration agreements, R7–03
conflicts of interest, R8
disciplinary procedures, S24, S24–07
failure of appointment procedure, R7, R7–01 to R7–11
fees and expenses, R56–07 to R56–08, R59
immunity, R74, R74–01 to R74–10
ministerial authorisation of AARs, S24–03
notice of referral, R7
qualifying bodies, S24–04, R7–07
removal of arbitrators, R11–09
serious irregularity appeals, R68, R68–45
training, S24–05
Arbitral proceedings
admissibility of evidence, R28–15
affirmations, R36, R36–01 to R36–06

528

Index

amendment of claims or defences, R28
applicable rules, R28–18
arbitration agreements
    failure to comply, R39, R39–01 to R39–18
claims,
    delay, R37, R37–01 to R37–12
    exchange, R28–22
    time for submission, R28
clerks, agents or employees
    power to appoint, R32, R32–01 to R32–16
consolidated proceedings, R40, R40–01 to R40–12
decisions, R30, R30–01 to R30–08
defences,
    delay, R37, R37–01 to R37–12
    exchange, S28–22
    time for submission, R28
delay in submission of claim or defence, R37, R37–01 to R37–12
determination by tribunal, R28–07 to R28–11
directions, R31, R31–01 to R31–05, R39, R39–01 to R39–18
disclosure, R28, R28–25 to R28–34
documents
    recovery, R28–25 to R28–34
evidence, R28, R28–01 to R28–60, R45, R45–01 to R45–36
experts, R34, R34–01 to R34–12
failure to comply, R39, R39–01 to R39–18
foreign procedural law, invoking a, S9–10
hearings
    documents–only basis, R28–44 to R28–45
    oral hearings, R28–46
    failure to attend, R38, R38–01 to R38–10
improperly conducted arbitration, S20–67 to S20–70
jurisdiction, R23, R23–01 to R23–21
language, R28–06, R28–57
legal error appeals, R70, R70–01 to R70–51
location of arbitration, R28–19 to R28–20
oaths, R36, R36–01 to R36–06
parties
    questioning of, R28–35 to R28–39
party representatives, R33, R33–01 to R33–09
place of arbitration, R28, R29, R29–01 to R29–06
pleadings, R28–21 to R28–24
clerks, agents or employees
    power to appoint clerks, agents or employees, R32, R32–01 to R32–20
powers of tribunal, R28–40 to R28–43
property

powers relating to, R35, R35–01 to R35–08
submissions, R28–50 to R28–53, R37, R37–01 to R37–12
timing of arbitration, R28–19 to R28–20
Arbitration
see also **Arbitration awards; Fees**
definition, S2–01 to S2–20
mediation distinguished, S2–07
statutory arbitration
    consensual arbitrations, S16–11, S16–19
    consolidated proceedings, S16–19
    death of parties, S16
    definition, S16
    generally, S16–01 to S16–05
    power to adapt enactments providing for statutory arbitration, S17, S17–01 to S17–03
    scope, S16–06 to S16–19
    seat of arbitration, S16, S16–13 to S16–15
    special provisions, S16, S16–01 to S16–19
    time limits, extension of, S16–17
tribunals
    composition, S20–63 to S20–66, 106–107
    jurisdiction, R19, R19–01 to R19–20, R20, R20–01 to R20–29, R21, R21–01 to R21–16, R22, R22–01 to R22–06, R23, R23–01 to R23–21
Arbitration agreements
see also **Arbitral agreements; Consumer arbitration; Validity**
appeals, R68, R68–17, R68–28, R68–40, R68–51, R68–93 to R68–97, R69, R69–01 to R69–30
applicable law, R19–14 to R19–15
appointment of tribunal, R2, R2–01 to R2–04, R18
arbitration clauses
    categories, S4–11
    choice of law, S6–01 to S6–15
    commencement of arbitration, R1–05, R1–08 to R1–12
    consumer agreements, S4–22 to S4–27, A1–01 to A1–11
    coverage by 2010 Act, S36, S36–01 to S36–17
    definition, S4, S4–01 to S4–02
    executry clauses, S4–11
    failure to comply, R39, R39–01 to R39–18, R68, R68–24 to R68–30
    frustration, R47–10
    general clauses, S4–11
    generally, S4–03 to S4–06
    governing law, S6, S6–01 to S6–15, R19–14 to R19–15
    importation, S4–12 to S4–13
    illegality, S4–19, S6–09

incapable of being performed, agreements which are, S10–52 to S10–56
incorporation, S4–11 to S4–12
inoperative, where agreement is, S10–50 to S10–51
interpretation, S3–06 to S3–09
jurisdiction, S11–04, R19, R19–01 to R19–20
jus quaesitum tertio, S4–10, S10–42 to S10–43
New York Convention 1958, S18, S18–01 to S18–15
nominated arbitrators, R18, R18–01 to R18–03
oral agreements, S4–14 to S4–16
original agreements, S21, S21–13
public policy, S4–19
Scott v *Avery* clauses, S10–69 to S10–71, R46–01
seat of arbitration
  law governing agreements, S6–01 to S6–15
separability, S5, S5–01 to S5–12
time limits
  variation, R43, R43–01 to R43–09
translations, S21–14 to S21–16
uncertainty, S4–20, S10–48 to S10–49
universal clauses, S4–11
validity, S4–19 to S4–21, S12–21 to S12–34
void, voidable or otherwise unenforceable, not, S10–44
writing
  foreign enforcement, S4–17 to S4–18
Arbitration awards
see also **Appeals**
ambiguity, R58–18 to R58–19, R68–46 to R68–50
authentication of awards, S21, S21–01 to S21–16
binding nature
  generally, S11, S11–03
  right of appeal, S11–11
  third parties, S11–04
certificated awards
  refusal of recognition or enforcement, S21, S21–01 to S21–81
challenges
  appeals, S11–11, S12–21 to S12–30, R51–50 to R51–56, R58–29
  correction of awards, R58–11 to R58–17
  discretion, S12–16 to S12–19
  draft awards, R55, R55–01 to R55–16
  generally, S11–11, S12–21 to S12–30, R71, R71–01 to R71–06
  Inner House, R71–39 to R71–48
  no part in proceedings, S14, S14–01 to S14–14
  part awards, R54, R54–01 to R54–11
  provisional awards, R71–08
  reasons for awards, R51–33 to R51–56

  refusal of recognition or enforcement, S20–85 to S20–91
  serious irregularity appeals, R68, R68–01 to R68–97
  substantive jurisdiction, R67, R67–01 to R67–39
  time limits, R71–09 to R71–22
choice of law
  applicable law, R47–19
  application by tribunal, R47–22 to R47–28
  choice of tribunal, R47–22 to R47–34
  chosen by parties, R47–12 to R47–18
  generally, R47–08 to R47–11
  unlawful choice of law, R47–20 to R47–21
confidentiality, R26, R26–01 to R26–27
consumer agreements, S4–22 to S4–27, A1–01 to A1–11
contents of awards, R51, R51–01 to R51–63
contrast with ruling or direction, R20–24 to R20–29, R37–10
correction
  ambiguity, R58–18 to R58–19
  clarification, R58–18 to R58–19
  clerical errors, R58–11 to R58–17
  enforcement of awards, S12–21 to S12–28
  errors arising by accident or omission, R58–11 to R58–17
  generally, S12–21 to S12–28, R58–01 to R58–10, R58–21 to R58–38
  time limits, R58–31 to R58–35
court intervention, S13 to S13–06
coverage by 2010 Act, S36, S36–01 to S36–17
custom and usage, R47
damages, R48, R48–01 to R48–12
date of award, R51–24 to R51–32
declaratory awards, R49–07
default rule, R47–01
delivery to parties, R51–60 to R51–63
discretion, S12–16 to S12–19, R57–15 to R57–20
disputes
  applicable law, R47–19
  choice of law, R47–22 to R47–28, R47–20 to R47–21
dissenting opinion, R51–14 to R51–18
draft awards, R55, R55–01 to R55–16
enforcement
  application to enforce, S12–09 to S12–15
  court discretion, S12–16 to S12–19
  effect of appeal, review or correction, S12–21 to S12–28
  generally, S12–01 to S12–08
  non-Scottish awards, S12–34
fairness, R47, R47–29 to R47–34

Index

fees and expenses, R68–88 to R68–92
final award, R57, R57–01 to R57–28
foreign awards, S12–34
form requirements, R51, R51–01 to R51–63
fraud, R68–52 to R68–72
generally, R47–04 to R47–11
governing law, S6–01 to S6–15
institutional rules, R47–02
interdicts, R49–08 to R49–16
interest, R50, R50–01 to R50–25
jurisdictional appeals, R21, R21–01 to R21–06
last award, R57, R57–01 to R57–28
legal error appeals
  generally, R69, R69–01 to R69–30
  procedure, R70, R70–01 to R70–51
new awards, making, R72–07
New York Convention awards, R68–55 to R68–58
no part in proceedings, persons who take, S14–09
non-enforcement
  lack of jurisdiction, S12–29 to S12–30
  pending appeal, S12–21 to S12–22
  time limits, S12–23, S12–26
non-payment of fees or expenses
withholding awards, R56, R56–01 to R56–24
part awards, R54, R54–01 to R54–11
payment and damages
  payment into court, R71–49 to R71–59
  power to award, R48, R48–01 to R48–12
place of arbitration, R52, R52–01 to R52–08
previous awards, R51–57 to R51–59
provisional awards, S11–12, R53, R53–01 to R53–22
public policy, R68–52 to R68–72
reasons for awards
  form, quality and extent, R51–47 to R51–49
  generally, R51–33 to R51–46
  order for reasons, R71–24 to R71–37
  power to order reasons, R51–50 to R51–56
  request for reasons, R58–12, R58–19
reconsideration, R72, R72–01 to R72–07
rectification, S11–07 to S11–09, R49–17 to R49–22
reduction, S11–07, S11–08, S12–20, R49–17 to R49–22
registration, S12–31 to S12–33
remedies other than damages, R49, R49–01 to R49–22
Scotland
  award treated as made in, R52, R52–01 to R52–08

scrutiny of awards under institutional rules, S11–11
seat, R51–19 to R51–23
serious irregularity appeals, R68, R68–01 to R68–97
setting aside awards
see **Appeals**
settlements, R57, R57–01 to R57–28
signature of awards, R51–05 to R51–13
specific implement, R49–08 to R49–16
substance of dispute, R47, R47–01 to R47–44
substantive jurisdiction, R67, R67–01 to R67–39
termination of arbitration, R57, R57–01 to R57–28
translations, S21–14 to S21–16
withholding awards, R56, R56–01 to R56–24

Arbitrators
see also **Appointments; Impartiality; Removal; Resignation; Tenure**
age, R4, R4–03 to R4–04
capacity, R4, R4–03, R4–05 to R4–09
Code of Ethics, R6–09
conflict of interests, R8, R8–01 to R8–20
damages and payments
  power to award, R48, R48–01 to R48–12
death, R3–10
eligibility
  age, R4, R4–03 to R4–04
  capacity, R4, R4–03, R4–05 to R4–09
  mandatory rules, R4–01
  qualifications, R10, R10–12, R12, R68
emergency arbitrators, R6–20
fees and expenses
  arbitration expenses, R59, R59–01 to R59–13
  generally, R60, R60–01 to R60–15
  recoverable expenses, R61, R61–01 to R61–22, R62, R62–01 to R62–27
identity unknown, S20–44
immunity, R73, R73–01 to R73–15
individuals, R3, R3–01 to R3–14
institutional rules, R5–02, R6–03 to R6–04
interviews, R6–13 to R6–17
judges, as, S25, S25–01 to S25–16
liability
  at end of tenure, R16, R16–01 to R16–20
  immunity, R73, R73–01 to R73–15
  resignation, R73, R73–13 to R73–14
  vicarious liability, R74–08
number of arbitrators, S20–63, R5, R5–01 to R5–07
  appointment of arbitrators or tribunal, R6, R6–01 to R6–20
  default rules, R5–01
  institutional rules, R5–02

531

Index

international arbitration, R5–04, R5–05
multi-party arbitrations, R6–18 to R6–19
party autonomy, R5–05
removal of arbitrators, R11
party-appointed, R6–09 to R6–12
qualifications, R10, R10–12, R12, R68
removal by court, R12, R12–01 to R12–20, R14, R14, R14–04
removal by parties, R11, R11–01 to R11–10
remuneration, R60–07
resignation, R15, R15–01 to R15–23, R73–13, R73–14
signing awards, R51–05 to R51–13
sitting simultaneously as judge, S25–13
sole arbitrators, R5–04, R6, R6–06
tenure, R9, R9–01 to R9–05, R16, R16–01 to R16–20
termination of tenure, R16–01 to R16–20
umpires, S25, S25–01 to S25–16
Awards
see **Arbitration awards**
Bias
see **Impartiality; Independence**
Capacity
corporations, S20–16 to S20–18
curator ad litem, R46–18, R46–20
eligibility to act as arbitrators, R4, R4–03, R4–05 to R4–09
public authorities, S20–20
refusal of recognition or enforcement, S20–13 to S20–26
removal of arbitrators, R12–18
safeguarders
appointment, R46–18 to R46–21
Case management
delay, R24–48 to R24–49
directions, R31–03
Caution
see **Security**
Choice of law
arbitrability, S30–01 to S30–24
arbitration agreements, S6–01 to S6–15
awards
applicable law, R47–19
application by tribunal, R47–22 to R47–28
chosen by parties, R47–12 to R47–18
generally, R47–08 to R47–11
unlawful choice of law, R47–20 to R47–21
confidentiality, R26–18
conflict of laws, R47–12 to R47–18
default rules, S9–09
foreign procedural law, S9–09 to S9–10
forum
law of the, S6–14
governing law, S6, S6–01 to S6–15
habitual residence, R47–21

implied choice of law, S6–12 to S6–13, R47–14
inoperative agreements, S10–44
international arbitration agreements, S6–05
main agreements, S6–03, S6–05
non-specification of governing law, S6–03
renvoi, R47–15 to R47–16
Rome Convention 1980, S6–06, R47–16
Rome I Regulation, S6–06, R47–16
seat of arbitration, S20–28 to S20–31
unlawful choice of law, R47–21
Claims
counterclaims, S2–17, S31, R28–24, R54–08
failure to submit, R37, R37–01 to R37–12
submission of, R28–21 to R28–24
time for submission, R37, R37–01 to R37–12
Clerical errors
correction of awards, R58–11 to R58–17
Clerks
administrative matters, R32–03 to R32–19
appointment, R32, R32–01 to R32–20
arbitral proceedings, R32, R32–01 to R32–20
consent, R32
default rule, R32, R32–01 to R32–20
delegation, R32–06 to R32–08
fees and expenses, R32–20
immunity, R75, R75–01 to R75–05
Clerks, agents or employees
see **Agents; Clerks; Employees**
Commencement
Royal Assent, S35
transitional provisions, S36, S36–01 to S36–18
Commissioners
appointment, R45–05, R45–08 to R45–13
witnesses, R45–04 to R45–13, R46–36, R46–74
Communications
see also **Electronic communications**
default rule, R83, R83–01 to R83–23
email, fax or other electronic means, R83–09
fairness, R83–21
first class post, R83–16 to R83–17
formal communications
definition of, R83–06
hand delivery, R83–11 to R83–15
impartiality, R83–21
institutional rules, R83–02, R84–02
newspaper advertisements, R83–20
not reasonably practicable, R83–19 to R83–23
private postal services, R83–18
privileged confidentiality, R45–28 to R45–32
time limits, R84, R84–01 to R84–13

532

Index

writing, R83–08 to R83–09
Companies
 appointment of arbitrators or tribunal, R3–08
 capacity, S20–16 to S20–18
 expert determination, R3–08
Competition
 EU law
  breach, S20–128
Concurrent hearings
 see **Consolidated proceedings**
Confidentiality
 absolute privilege, R26
 actionability, R26–25 to R26–27
 anonymity in legal proceedings, S15–08 to S15–13
 arbitral proceedings, R26
 authorisation of disclosure, R26
 awards, R26
 banking confidentiality, R26–14, R26–16
 categories of confidential information, R45–28
 civil proceedings under section 15 of Act, R26
 common law, R26–20 to R26–24
 defamation, R26
 default rule, R26, R26–01 to R26–27
 definition, R26
 disclosure
  interdict, R26–27
 discretion, R26–14, R26–17
 disputes, information relating to, R26
 enactments or rules of law
  compliance with, R26
 implied obligation, R26–14
 informing parties of obligations, R26
 institutional rules, R26–02
 interests of justice, R26
 parties,
  disclosure by, R26
 privacy distinguished, R26–14
 privileged confidentiality, R45–27 to R45–32
 waiver, R45–29
 public interest, S15–18 to S15–20, R26, R26–14, R26–17, R26–21 to R26–23, R46–50
 third parties,
  disclosure, by, R26
 trade secrets, R26–14, R26–21
 tribunal, R26
Conflict of laws
 see **Choice of law**
Conflict of interest
 appointment of arbitrators or tribunal, R8, R8–01 to R8–20, R24–03
 arbitral appointments referee, R8
 arbitrators, R8, R8–01 to R8–20, R24–04 to R24–22

common basis of disclosure, R8–17 to R8–20
 duty to disclose R8, R8–01 to R8–20, R24–04 to R24–22
 European Convention on Human Rights, R8–04
 excessive disclosure, R8–13
 fair hearings, R8
 governing law, R47–22, R47–44
 guidelines, R8, R8–01 to R8–20
 impartiality, R8, R8–01 to R8–20, R24–04 to R24–22
 institutional rules, R8–03 to R8–08
 prospective arbitrators, R8
 relevance, R8, R8–01 to R8–20
 trivial associations, R8–19
Consolidated proceedings
 see also **Parallel proceedings**
 default rule, R40, R40–01 to R40–12
 statutory arbitrations, S16–19
Consumer arbitration
 fairness test, A1–05
 legal person, A1–07, A1–09
 natural person, A1–08, A1–09
 specified amount, A1–04
 SSFARs, A1–11
 Unfair Terms in Consumer Contracts Regulations, S4–22 to S4–27, A1–03
Contempt of court
 interdicts or interim interdicts, R46–48
 witnesses, R45–07
Contracts
 see also **Arbitration agreements**
 amiable compositeurs, R47–30
 awards, R47
 choice of law, R47–12 to R47–21
 fees and expenses, R60–11 to R60–12
 readjustment of contracts, R47–30
 rectification of, R49–17 to R49–20
 reduction (annulment) of, R49–17 to R49–20
 Rome Convention 1980, R47–16
 Rome I Regulation, S6–06, R47–16
 specific implement, R49–11, R49–13
 unfair contract terms, R47–21
Costs
 see **Expenses**
Counterclaims
 arbitral proceedings, R28–24,
 claims as including counterclaims, S31
 part awards, R54–08
Courts
 see also **Tribunals**
 anonymity in legal proceedings, S15–08 to S15–13
 appointment of tribunal, S13–09
 confidentiality, R26–02, R26–07 to R26–19
 disclosure of evidence, R45–01 to R45–13, R45–27 to R45–36

533

Index

dismissal of tribunal, R13, R13–01 to
   R13–06, R14, R14–01 to R14–13
fees and expenses, R56, R56–01 to R56–24
interim measures, R46, R46–01 to R46–75
payments into court, R71–49 to R71–58
points to law referral, R41, R41–01 to
   R41–17, R42, R42–01 to R42–20
removal of arbitrators, R12, R12–01 to
   R12–20, R14, R14–01 to R14–14
restricted intervention, S13–03 to S13–06
seat of arbitration, S3–15 to S3–25
time limits, R43, R43–01 to R43–09, R44,
   R44–01 to R44–16
witnesses, R45, R45–01 to R45–26

Crime
anonymity in legal proceedings, S15–08
fraud, S30–11, S30–14, R68, R68–52 to
   R68–72
perjury, S20–119, R68–70

Cross-examination
civil law, R28–37
common law, R28–46 to R28–47

Crown application
binding the Crown, Act as, S34
Her Majesty, representation of, S34
Prince and Steward of Scotland, S34

Crown proceedings
interdicts or interim interdicts, R49–09
specific implement, R49–12

Currency
awards, R48, R48–09 to R48–12

Custom and usage
awards, R47

Damages
see also **Awards**
mandatory rule, R48, R48–01 to R48–12
penal or exemplary damages, R48–06

Death
arbitrators, R3–07, R3–10, R79, R79–01
   to R79–06
executors, R79–01, R79–03, R80, R80–05
legal persons, R3–07
mandatory rule, R79, R79–01 to R79–06
parties, R80, R80–01 to R80–07

Decrees
see also **Awards**
decreets arbitral and, S36–13
Scottish court judgment, S12–09
use of term, S36–13

Decrees *ad factum praestandum*
see **Specific implement**

Default rules
agreement of parties, S9–08
appointment of tribunal, S9–03
arbitration rules, S9–04 to S9–07
choice of law, S9–09 to S9–10
disapplication, S9–01 to S9–03
foreign procedural law, S9–09 to S9–10
modification, S9–01 to S9–03
overriding rules, S13–08

party autonomy, S9–01
writing, S9–02

Defences
arbitral proceedings, R28, R28–22 to
   R28–24
delay, R37, R37–01 to R37–12
exchange of defences, R28–22 to R28–24
failure to lodge claims timeously, R37,
   R37–01 to R37–12
New York Convention 1958, S19–02
refusal of recognition or enforcement,
   S20–12 to S20–70
time for submission, R28, R37, R37–01 to
   R37–12

Delay
active case management, R24–48, R24–49
arbitral proceedings, R37, R37–01 to
   R37–12
avoidance of unnecessary delay, R24,
   R24–43 to R24–48, R25
claims
   submission, R37, R37–01 to R37–12
defences
   submission, R37, R37–01 to R37–12
fairness, R24–23 to R24–39
founding principle, S1, S1–06, S1–07,
   S3–11
general duties of tribunal, R24, R24–43 to
   R24–48
jurisdiction, R20, R20–25, R20–26, R23
liability of arbitrators, R16–05, R16–09,
   R16–10
mandatory rule, S8–03
objections, R76, R76–01 to R76–13
payments into court, R71–49 to R71–59
performable agreements, S10–52 to
   S10–56
points of law referral, R42, R42–01 to
   R42–20
sist, S10–07
time limits, R44–12 to R44–14, R44–16,
   R71–09 to R71–22

Delegation
clerks, agents or employees, R32–05 to
   R32–08

Depositions
interim measures, R46–55

Diligence on the dependence
court's powers, R46–22 to R46–32,
   R46–37 to R46–45

Directions
general, R31, R31–01 to R31–05
non-compliance with decisions
   adverse inferences, R39–15
   consequences, R39–18
   continuing with arbitration, R42,
      R42–19
   default rule, R39, R39–01 to R39–18
   defence submissions, service of, R39–17
   final awards, R39–16

534

Index

part awards, R39–16
party fails to comply, R39, R39–01 to R39–18
proportionality, R39–14
directions to parties, R31, R31–01 to R31–05, R39, R39–01 to R39–18

Disclosure
see also **Documents**
anonymity in legal proceedings, S15, S15–04 to S15–08
appointment of arbitrators or tribunal, R8–05, R8–08
confidentiality, S15, R26, R26–14, R26–17, R26–24
conflicts of interest, R8–01 to R8–20
evidence, R28, R28–25, R28–26, R28–34, R45, R45–01 to R45–36
lawful interests
protection of S15–17

Dispute
definition, S2–15 to S–2–17

Documents
civil proceedings, R46–33 to R46–36
commissioners, appointment of, R45–05 to R45–13
common law for recovery of, R28–28, R28–29
confidentiality, R45–27 to R45–32
court's powers, R45, R45–04 to R45–06
documents-only arbitration, R28–44, R28–45
E-disclosure protocol, R28–33
evidence, R28–31, R28–54, R46–33
failure to disclose documents, R39–14
fishing diligence, R28–29, R45–12
IBA Rules of Evidence, R28–31
inspection, R28–31, R28–54, R46–33
originals, R28–31
presentation, R28–31, R46–33
recovery of, R28–25 to R28–34, R45–18, R45–34, R45–35, R46–33
reduction or rectification, R49–17 to R49–22
specification of, R28–29, R45–11 to R45–13
calls, R45–21
Tribunal's powers, R28–25 to R28–34

Domestic arbitration agreements
definition, S2–14

Due process
failure, S20–32 to S20–36
public policy and, S20–37 to S20–38

Duress
sist, S10–27, S10–47

ECHR
see **European Convention on Human Rights**

Electronic communications
see also **Communications**
commencement of arbitration, notice of, R1–11

formal communications, R83–09

Employees
administrative matters, R32–03 to R32–19
appointment, R32, R32–01 to R32–20
arbitral proceedings, R32, R32–01 to R32–20
consent, R32
default rule, R32, R32–01 to R32–20
delegation, R32–06 to R32–08
fees and expenses, R32–20
immunity, R75, R75–01 to R75–05

Enforcement
see also **New York Convention on Recognition and Enforcement of Foreign Arbitral Awards 1958**
arbitral awards
adjournment, S20–145 to S20–149
anonymity in legal proceedings, S15–08 to S15–13
appeals, S12–21 to S12–28, R67–24, R68–49, R71–50, R71–51
applications, S12–09 to S12–15
common law, S12–02, S12–04, S12–20, S12–28
corrections, S12–21 to S12–28
Court of Session, S13, S13–08
discretion, S12–16 to S12–19
final and binding nature of awards, S11, S11–01 to S11–04
foreign awards, S18–01 to S19–11, S30–16 to S30–34, R67–24, R68–49
jurisdiction, S12–29 to S12–30, S12–34, R67–24
New York Convention awards, S19, S19–04 to S19–11
no part in proceedings, persons who take, S14–01 to S14–14
part awards, R54–10
prohibition on enforcement, S12–16 to S12–19
registration, S12–31 to S12–33
review, S12–21 to S12–28
setting aside by exception not contemplated, S12–42
transitional provisions, S36–09 to S36–12
due process
failure, S20–32 to S20–36
public policy and, S20–37 to S20–38
evidence for recognition and enforcement of awards
authenticated original awards, S21–07 to S21–12
generally, S21, S21–01 to S21–06
original arbitration agreements, S21–13
translated documents, S21–14 to S21–16
New York Convention awards, S12–03, S12–05
partial enforcement, S20–129 to S20–132
recognition or enforcement

535

Index

binding nature, S19
enforcement, S19–04 to S19–11
evidence for, S21, S21–01 to S21–16
recognition, S19–02 to S18–03
security, S20–144 to S20–149
sisting decisions, S20–134 to S20–143
refusal of recognition or enforcement
arbitration improperly conducted, S20–55 to S20–62
award not yet binding, S20–85 to S20–91
defences, S20–12
due process, S20–32 to S20–36, S20–37 to S20–38
excess of jurisdiction, S20–82 to S20–84
exclusive grounds for, S20–09 to S20–11
failure of due process, S20–32 to S20–36
form of tribunal, S20–63 to S20–66
generally, S20, S20–01 to S20–08
inability to present case, S20–32 to S20–36, S20–47 to S20–54
incapacity, S20–13 to S20–26
invalid agreements, S20–27 to S20–31
lack of jurisdiction, S20–72 to S20–81
lack of notice, S20–39 to S20–46
matters not attributable under Scots law, S20–104 to S20–105
notice, S20–39 to S20–46
partial enforcement, S20–129 to S20–132
procedural irregularity, S20–67 to S20–70
public policy, S20–106 to S20–128
public policy, S20–37 to S20–38
setting aside, S20–92 to S20–101
resisting enforcement
award not binding, S20–85 to S20–91
award set aside, S20–92 to S20–101
excess of jurisdiction, S20–82 to S20–84
failure, S20–32 to S20–36
lack of jurisdiction, S20–72 to S20–80
no part in proceedings, persons who take, S14–14
public policy and, S20–37 to S20–38
Equality
fairness, R24–24
full opportunity to present case, R24–24
general duties of tribunal, R24–02, R24–24
inequality of arms, R33–04
neutrality of arbitrator, R24–38
provisional awards, R53–12
Equity
awards, R47, R47–29
Estoppel
see **Personal bar**
Ethics
appointment of arbitrators or tribunal, R10–12
Code of Ethics,
disclosure, R8–07

impartiality, R6–09
public policy, S20–113 to S20–117
European Convention on Human Rights (ECHR)
appointment of arbitrators, R10–08
arbitration agreements
interpretation of, S4–10
validity, R19–17
conflicts of interest, R8–04
effect on the Act, S1–11 to S1–22
impartiality, R8–04, R24–04 to R24–12
interpretation of the Act, S1–14 to S1–17
leave to appeal, R70–30, R70–31, R70–46
reasons for award, R51–33
right to a fair trial, S16–03, R8–04, R24–25, R24–27, R24–30, R24–31, R67–38, R68–92, R68–96
statutory arbitration, S16–03, S17–02
EU law
breach
unfair competition, S20–128
Brussels Convention, R46–58, R64–09, R64–12
cautions, R46–60, R46–61
choice of law, R47–12 to R47–18
Civil Jurisdiction and Judgments Act, S3–21, S12–10, R43–09, R44–10, R45–19, R46–64
Lugano Convention, S3–22, R46–58, R64–09, R64–12
Rome Convention I Regulation, S6–06, R47–16
Evidence
see also **Documents, Experts**
Administration of Justice (Scotland) Act 1972 section 1, R46–33 to R46–36
admissibility, R28, R28–15 to R28–16
appeals, R28–14 to R28–16, R67–11, R70–17
arbitral proceedings, R28, R28–01 to R28–60
arbitration agreements
original, S21–13
awards
authentication or certification, S21, S21–01 to S21–16
improperly obtained awards, S20–119
common law, R28–58, R45–27
confidentiality, R45–27 to R45–32
cross–examination, R28–40 to R28–43
failure to provide evidence R38, R38–01 to R38–10
fairness, R24–27, R45–14, R45–33
finality of decisions, R45, R45–36
fishing diligence, R28–29, R45–12
impartiality, R12–14, R12–16, R45–14
inability to present case, S20–47, S20–49, S20–50, S20–53
inquisitorial system, R28–40 to R28–43

Index

inspection documents, R28, R28–54 to R28–56
inventories, production of, R42–15, R45–23
materiality, R28, R28–15 to R28–16
oral evidence, R28–36 to R28–39, R28–45 to R28–47, R32–04, R67–31
orders for disclosure, R45, R45–01 to R45–36
originals, S21–07, R28–31
presentation of evidence, R28, R28–54 to R28–56
procedure and, R28, R28–01 to R28–60
recovery of evidence, R28, R28–25 to R28–34, R45, R45–01 to R45–36, R46–33 to R46–36
recognition or enforcement, S21, S21–01 to S21–16
relevance, R28, R28–15 to R28–16
rules of evidence, R28, R28–58 to R28–60
sist
  objections to, S10–26, S10–32
submission of evidence, R28, R28–25 to R28–34,
translations, S21–14 to S21–16, R28
weight, R28, R28–12 to R28–14
witnesses
  attendance, R45, R45–01 to R45–36
  material evidence, S15–21
  questioning, R28–35 to R28–39
Executors
death, R79–01, R79–03, R80, R80–05
Expenses
allocation of liability, R62–10 to R62–16
appeals, S12–25, R56, R56–06, R56–24, R60–14, R62–06 to R62–09
  Auditor of Court of Session, R60, R60–11, R61, R61–08 to R61–09
arbitral appointments referee, R59, R59–04, R60, R60–06, R60–08, R61
arbitration expenses
  application expenses, R14–09
  awards on, R66, R66–01 to R66–05
  default rule, R59, R59–01 to R59–13
  definition, R59–02, R59–04
  guidance, R55–13
  legal and other costs distinguished, R59–05
  reasonableness, R59–12
  recoverable, R61, R61–01 to R61–22, R62, R62–01 to R62–27, R66, R66–01 to R66–05
Auditor of Court of Session, R60, R60–11, R61, R61–08 to R61–09
arbitrators' fees and expenses
  agreement, R60–11 to R60–12
  liability of parties, R60–06 to R60–10
  mandatory rule, R60, R60–01 to R60–15
  security, R60–04

withholding of award, R56, R56–01 to R56–24
awards
  binding nature, S11, S11–03, S11–04, S11–11
  recoverable arbitration expenses, R66, R66–01 to R66–05
common law, R61–08 to R61–22
death of arbitrator, R16–05 to R16–06
joint and several liability, R60–09, R62–26
judges arbitrators, S25–14
liability for arbitration expenses
  allocation of liability, R62–10 to R62–16
  default rule, R62, R62–01 to R62–27
  joint liability, R62–26
  pre-dispute agreements, R63, R63–01 to R63–05
  several liability, R62–26
  termination of arbitrators' tenure, R16, R16–04
  tests for awards of expenses, R62–17 to R62–25
limitation of recoverable arbitration expenses, R65, R65–01 to R65–17
mandatory rule, S8
non-payment
  power to withhold awards for, R56, R56–01 to R56–24
part awards, R65, R65–01 to R65–17
pre-dispute agreements on liability
  mandatory rule, R63, R63–01 to R63–05
provisional awards, R65, R65–01 to R65–17
power to withhold on non-payment
  mandatory rule, R56, R56–01 to R56–24
reasonableness, R59–12, R61–17 to R61–20
recoverable arbitration expenses
  default rule, R61, R61–01 to R61–22
  quantum of expenses, R61–04, R61–05
  quantifying expenses, R61–12 to R61–16
  reasonableness, R61–17 to R61–20
  awards on, R66, R66–01 to R66–05
  liability for, R62, R62–01 to R62–27
  limitation, R65, R65–01 to R65–17
removal of arbitrators, R11–04, R12–03, R13–03, R16–05, R16–06
resignation of arbitrators, R15–07, R15–09, R15–13, R16–08 to R16–13, R16–05, R16–06
security
  enforcement of awards, S12–27
  arbitrators' fees and expenses, R60–04
several liability, R60–09, R62–26
taxation of expenses, R61–06 to R61–11
tenure

Index

termination of, R4–09
Experts
arbitral proceedings, R34, R34–01 to R34–12
Civil Procedure Rules, R34–04
default rule, R34, R34–01 to R34–12
expert determination, S2–03 to S2–06
fees and expenses, R56–07, R60
hot-tubbing, R28–43
immunity, R75, R75–01 to R75–05
tribunal-appointed experts (TAE), R34–04 to R34–06, R34–11, R34–12
Fairness
see also **Equality**
arbitrators
challenges to appointment, R10, R10–11
impartiality, R8–03, R12–17, R15–15
removal, R12, R12–06, R12–08, R24–40, R24–41
awards, R47, R47–29 to R47–34
claims
failure to lodge, R37
confidentiality, R26–23
consumers, S4–22 to S4–27, R24–37 to R24–39, A1–04 to A1–07
default rule, R81, R81–01 to R81–03
defences
failure to lodge, R37
delay, R24–48 to R24–50
EU law, S20–128
European Convention of Human Rights, S1–14, S1–19, S1–21, R24–25, R24–27, R24–30 to R24–31
experts, R34–09
founding principle, S1
general duties of tribunal, R24, R24–05, R24–10, R24–13, R24–18, R24–23 to R24–33
mandatory rules, S8–03
natural justice, R62–08, R68–92
object
loss of right to, R76, R76–08
party autonomy, S1–08
procedure, R28–07, R28–31, R28–37, R28–42, R45–14
representatives, R33–04, R33–07
time limits, R44–12 to R44–14
unfair treatment, R81, R81–01 to R81–03
Fees
see **Expenses**
Foreign law
see also **International arbitration**
arbitrability of disputes, S30–16 to S30–24
misapplication of foreign law, R47–20, R51–41
part awards, R54–09
points of law referral and appeal, R41–10, R69–14 to R69–16
procedural law, R3–25

provisional awards, R53–14
reasons for awards, R51–41
seat of arbitration, R3–25
Formal communications
see **Communications**
Fraud
serious irregularity appeals, R68–52 to R68–72
Freezing orders
see also **Diligence on the dependence**
interim measures, R46–12
Frustration
see also **Impossibility**
arbitration agreements, R47–10
Functus officio
termination of arbitration, R57–04, R57–07 to R57–08
Governing law
see **Choice of law**
Guardian *ad litem*
appointment, R46–18 to R46–19
expenses of administration, R46–20
Hearings
see also **Oral hearings**
anonymity in legal proceedings, S15–03 to S15–05
attendance as witness
courts' power to order, R45, R45–01 to R45–46
civil proceedings, S15–12
concurrent hearings, S16, S16–19, R40
confidentiality, R26–02, R26–03, R26–12
consolidated hearings, S15, S16–09, R40, R40–01 to R40–12
cross-examination, R28, R28–36, R26–38, R26–42
de novo hearings, R67–12, R67–14
evidential hearings, R28–44 to R28–49
expenses
arbitration, R62–24, R65–11
hearing facilities, R60
immunity of tribunal, R73–08
experts, R34–03, R34–11
failure to attend, R37–06, R38, R38–01 to R38–10
fair hearings
procedural irregularity, S20–68, R68–24 to R68–28
improperly obtained awards, S20–119
interim interdict, R46–52
jurisdictional disputes, R20–11
legal error appeals, R70, R70–07, R70–30
oral hearings, S20–51, R28–21, R28–46 to R28–47, R67–31
party representatives, R33–04 to R33–06
points of law referral, R41–09, R42–11, R42–18
public hearings, S1–21, R26–05
Scottish Arbitration Centre, R28–20
submissions, R28–52

Index

Human rights
see **European Convention on Human Rights; Human Rights Act 1998**
Illegality
  arbitration agreement, S4–19
  contra bonos mores, S30–10, S30–14, S30–22
  effect on arbitrability, S20–114, S30–10, S30–22
  effect on enforcement of foreign award, S20–113 to S20–117
  presentation of evidence, R28, R28–54 to R28–56
  public policy, S20–113 to S20–117
  separability, S20–114
Immunity
  appointing arbitral institutions, R74, R74–01 to R74–10
  arbitral appointments referee, R75–05
  arbitrators, R14–10, R15–17, R16–08, R16–11 to R16–13
  bad faith, R73–10
  clerks, agents or employees, R73–15 to R74–10
  experts, witnesses and legal representatives, R75, R75–01 to R75–05
  institutional rules, R73–02
  judicial immunity, R74–10
  mandatory rules
    appointing arbitral institution immunity, R74, R74–01 to R74–10
    experts, R75, R75–01 to R75–05
    legal representatives, R75, R75–01 to R75–05
    tribunal immunity, R73, R73–01 to R73–15
    witnesses, R75, R75–01 to R75–05
  privilege
    public interest immunity, R45–28
  resignation of arbitrators, R73, R73–13 to R73–14
  state or sovereign immunity, S20–23 to S20–24
  third parties, R74–10
  tribunal, of, R73, R73–01 to R73–15
  vicarious liability, R74–08
Impartiality
  see also **Independence**
  arbitrator
    appointment, R7–11, R10–11
    challenges to appointment, R10, R10–10 to R10–11
    independence, R77, R77–01 to R77–05, R78, R78–01 to R78–07
  communications, R83–21
  conflict of interest, R8, R8–01 to R8–20, R24–04 to R24–22
  European Convention of Human Rights, R8–04, R24–04 to R24–12

examples, R12–14, R12–16, R24–14 to R24–22, R45–14
founding principle, as, S1
general duty of tribunal, as, R24, R24–04 to R24–22
hearings, R24–05, R24–24 to R24–30
institutional rules, R8–06, R69–09
justifiable doubts, R8–02
objection
  loss of right, R76, R76–08
umpires, R82–04
Impossibility
  incapable of being performed agreements, S10–52 to S10–56
  sist, S10
Incapacity
  see **Capacity**
Independence
  see also **Impartiality**
  appeals, R24–20
  arbitrator
    appointment, R7–11, R10–11
    challenges to appointment, R10, R10–10 to R10–11, R24–14 to R24–22
    independence, R77, R77–01 to R77–05, R78, R78–01 to R78–07
  code of ethics, R8–07
  communications, R83–21
  conflict of interest, R8, R8–01 to R8–20, R24–04 to R24–22
  European Convention of Human Rights, R8–04, R24–04 to R24–12
  examples, R12–14, R12–16, R45–14
  founding principle, as, S1
  general duty of tribunal, as, R24, R24–04 to R24–22
  hearings, R24–05, R24–24 to R24–30
  institutional rules, R8–06, R69–09
  justifiable doubts, R8–02
  objection
    loss of right, R76, R76–08
  umpires, R82–04
Injunctions
  see **Interdicts; Specific implement**
Inquisitorial proceedings
  evidence, S28, R28–40 to R28–43
Insolvency
  see also **Security**
  diligence on the dependence, R46–22 to R46–32
  lodging security in court, R46–23, R46–31 to R46–32
Inspection
  evidence, R28
Interdicts
  courts' powers, R46–46 to R46–54
  effectiveness abroad, R49–16
  interim measures, R46–46 to R46–54

539

Index

Interest
awards, R50–10 to R50–16
calculation, R50, R50–18
compound interest, R50–19 to R50–23
correction of awards, R58
discretion, R50–12
expenses, R50–16
mandatory rule, R50, R50–01 to R50–25
no effect on other power to award interest, R50–25
outstanding sums, R50–16
post-award interest, R50–16
rate of interest, R50–17

Interim measures
see also **Diligence on the dependence, Security, Freezing orders**
Administration of Justice (Scotland) Act, R46–33 to R46–36
arbitral proceedings, R46, R46–01 to R46–75
arrestment on the dependence, R46–37 to R46–45
consent of tribunal, R46–09 to R46–14
continuation of arbitration, R46–72
default rule, R46, R46–01 to R46–74
determinations pending, R46–72
diligence on the dependence, R46–23 to R46–27, R46–31, R46–27 to R46–38, R46–44 to R46–45, R46–65
freezing orders, R46–12
inhibition on the dependence, R46–37 to R46–45
interdicts or interim interdicts, R46–46 to R46–54
property, R46–21
safeguarders
appointment, R46–18 to R46–20
sale of property, R46–21
security, R46–03 to R46–04, R46–23, R46–26, R46–31 to R46–32, R46–44 to R46–45
sheriff court, R46–08, R46–18 to R46–53, R46–64, R46–70
specific implement, R46–16, R46–55
warrants to arrest, R46–37 to R46–45

International arbitration
see also **Independence**
juridical seat, S3–03

Interpretation
arbitration agreements, S4–07 to S4–10, S6–10
definitions in 2010 Act, S2, S31

Interviews
appointment of arbitrators or tribunal, R6–13 to R6–17

Interim interdicts
see **Interdicts**

Intimation
see **Communications**

Irregularity
see **Procedural irregularity; Serious irregularity**

Joinder
consolidated proceedings, R40–04

Joint liability
tribunal's fees and expenses, R62–26

Judges
arbitrators and umpires
appeals, S25–15
commercial disputes, S25, S25–09
expertise, S25–03
fees, S25–14
appointment, S25–01, S25–03, S25–10 to S25–11, S25–14
Inner House, S25, S25–15
national security, S25–03
power to act as arbitrator or umpire, S25, S25–01 to S25–16
reasons for appointment, S25–03
sitting simultaneously as arbitrator, S25–13
Technology and Construction Court, S25–03, S25–09

Judicial review
exclusion of, S13–03 to S13–06, R46–13
fees and expenses decision of Auditor of Court of Session, R60–14

Jurisdiction
jurisdictional appeals, R21–01 to R21–26, R67, R67–01 to R67–39
conditions for valid application, R23–05 to R23–12
Court of Session, S13–05, R22, R22–01 to R22–06
default rule, R22, R22–01 to R22–06
determination
Outer House determination, R22, R22–01 to R22–06
discretion to continue proceedings, R23–14 to R23–17
finality of Outer House decision, R23–18 to R23–21
jurisdiction referral
Outer House determination, R22, R22–01 to R22–06
procedure, R23, R23–01 to R23–21
limit of court's intervention, S13–07
mandatory rule, R23, R23–01 to R23–21
objections to tribunal's jurisdiction
appeals against tribunal rulings, R21, R21–01 to R21–26
effect of upholding objections, R20–21 to R20–23
mandatory rule, R20, R20–01 to R20–29
method of ruling on objections, R20–24 to R20–29
timing of objections, R20–04 to R20–20
Outer House

Index

final decision, R23–18 to R23–21
determining jurisdiction, R22, R22–01 to R22–06
power of tribunals to rule on
  constitution of tribunal, R19–18
  extent of matters submitted, R19–19 to R19–20
  mandatory rule, R19, R19–01 to R19–20
  validity of arbitration agreements, R19–10 to R19–17
procedure
  mandatory rule, R23, R23–01 to R23–21
tribunals
  kompetenz-kompetenz (competence-competence), R19–01 to R19–20
  lack of jurisdiction, S20–72 to S20–81
  power to rule on own jurisdiction, R19, R19–01 to R19–20
  tribunal jurisdiction, R22, R22–01 to R22–06

Language
arbitral proceedings, R28–06
awards, translation of, S21–14 to S21–16

Legislation
repeals, S29, S29–01, Sch.2

Liability
see also **Immunity**
at end of tenure, R16, R16–01 to R16–20
immunity, R73, R73–01 to R73–15
mandatory rule, R16, R16–01 to R16–20
resignation, R73, R73–13 to R73–14
vicarious liability, R74–08

Limitation
see **Time limits**

Limited liability partnerships (LLPs)
appointment of arbitrators or tribunal, R3–09

Litigation
see **Civil proceedings**

Location
contrast with seat, S3–03, R29–04
generally, R28–19

Mandatory rules
see also **Default rules**
agreement of parties, S9–08
arbitration rules, S9–04 to S9–07
default rules, S9, S9–01 to S9–10
foreign procedural law
  choice of law, S9–09 to S9–10
list of rules, S9
modification, S9–01 to S9–03

Mistake
clerical errors, R58, R58–04
correcting awards, R58–11 to R58–17, R58–21, R58–28, R58–36
draft awards, R55–04
reasons for awards, R51–35, R51–41, R51–52, R51–53, R51–56

seat of arbitration, R51–19 to R51–23

Moveable property
security, R46–21, R46–24 to R46–26

Multi–party disputes
appointment of arbitrators or tribunal, R6–18 to R6–19
interpretation, S31–02

National security
judges as arbitrators or umpires, S25–03

Nationality
appointment of arbitrators or tribunal, R3–05, R6–05

Natural justice
see **Fairness**

Neutrality
see **Impartiality**

New York Convention on Recognition and Enforcement of Foreign Arbitral Awards 1958
amendments, S26, S26–01 to S26–05
awards
  awards made at seat of arbitration, S18–12 to S18–15
  binding nature of awards, S19
  convention awards, S18–05 to S18–08
  generally, S18, S18–01 to S18–04
  pursuance of written agreements, S18–09 to S18–11
burden of proof, S20–03, S20–38, S20–41, S20–57, S20–73
due process
  failure, S20–32 to S20–36
  public policy and, S20–37 to S20–38
enforcement, S12–03, S12–05
evidence for recognition and enforcement of awards
  authenticated original awards, S21–07 to S21–12
  generally, S21, S21–01 to S21–06
  original arbitration agreements, S21–13
  translated documents, S21–14 to S21–16
jurisdiction
  excess of jurisdiction, S20–82 to S20–84
  lack of jurisdiction, S20–72 to S20–81
New York Convention awards, S12–03, S12–05
partial enforcement, S20–129 to S20–132
recognition or enforcement
  binding nature, S19
  enforcement, S19–04 to S19–11
  evidence for, S21, S21–01 to S21–16
  recognition, S19–02 to S19–03
  security, S20–144 to S20–149
  sisting decisions, S20–134 to S20–143
oral agreements and, S4–16, S6–14
recognition or enforcement
  binding nature, S19
  enforcement, S19–04 to S19–11
  evidence for, S21, S21–01 to S21–16
  recognition, S19–02 to S19–03

541

Index

security, S20–144 to S20–149
sisting, S20–134 to S20–143
procedure, S12–03, S12–05, S19–04 to S19–11, A2–01
public policy
  breach of EU law, S20–128
  generally, S20–106
  illegality, S20–113 to S20–117
  improperly obtained awards, S20–118 to S20–125
  international public policy, S20–108 to S20–111
  national public policy, S20–112
  procedural irregularity, S20–126
refusal of recognition or enforcement
  arbitration improperly conducted, S20–55 to S20–62
  award not set aside or suspended, S20–92 to S20–101
  award not yet binding, S20–85 to S20–91
  defences, S20–12
  due process, S20–32 to S20–36, S20–37 to S20–38
  excess of jurisdiction, S20–82 to S20–84
  exclusive grounds for, S20–09 to S20–11
  failure of due process, S20–32 to S20–36
  form of tribunal, S20–63 to S20–66
  generally, S20, S20–01 to S20–08
  inability to present case, S20–32 to S20–36, S20–47 to S20–54
  incapacity, S20–13 to S20–26
  invalid agreements, S20–27 to S20–31
  lack of jurisdiction, S20–72 to S20–81
  lack of notice, S20–39 to S20–46
  matters not attributable under Scots law, S20–104 to S20–105
  notice, S20–39 to S20–46
  partial enforcement, S20–129 to S20–132
  procedural irregularity, S20–67 to S20–70
  public policy, S20–106 to S20–128
  public policy, S20–37 to S20–38
  setting aside, S20–92 to S20–101
  tribunal improperly constituted, S20–63 to S20–66
  unknown members of the tribunal, S20–44
resisting enforcement
  award not binding, S20–85 to S20–91
  award set aside, S20–92 to S20–101
  excess of jurisdiction, S20–82 to S20–84
  failure, S20–32 to S20–36
  lack of jurisdiction, S20–72 to S20–80
  no part in proceedings, persons who take, S14–14
  public policy and, S20–37 to S20–38
seat of arbitration, S3–03
sist

effect of sist, S10–06
generally, S10–01, S10–03
lodging of defences, S10–61
necessity and form of application, S10–10
non-Scots arbitrations, S10–72
void, inoperative or incapable of being performed, S10–44
writing
  foreign enforcement, S4–17 to S4–18
Non-residents
security for expenses, R64–09
seat of arbitration, R52–04
sist, S10–72, R46–57
witnesses, R45–08
Notification
see **Communications**
Oaths
default rule, R36, R36–01 to R36–06
Objections
appointments, R10, R10–01 to R10–20
awards
  legal error, R69, R69–01 to R69–30
  serious irregularity, R68, R68–01 to R68–97
  substantive jurisdiction, R67, R67–01 to R67–39
default rules, R67, R67–01 to R67–39, R68, R68–01 to R68–97, R69, R69–01 to R69–30
factual basis, R10–14
grounds for, R10–12 to R10–13
loss of right to object
  justified by circumstances, R76–12 to R76–13
  mandatory rule, R76, R76–01 to R76–13
  reasonable practicability, R76–12
  timeous objections, R76–04 to R76–13
right to object, R10–05
time limits, R10–15 to R10–16
tribunal jurisdiction
  mandatory rule, R20, R20–01 to R20–29
Oral hearings
choice of written or oral submissions, R28–50 to R28–53
civil law countries, R28–52
credibility, assessment of, R17–08
evidential hearings, R28–44 to R28–49
expert evidence, R34
presentation of evidence, S28–54
Parallel proceedings
consolidation, S16, S16–19, R40
Parties
see also **Capacity, Consumer arbitration**
anonymity, S15–08 to S15–13
arbitral proceedings
  time limits set by parties, R43, R43–01 to R43–09

542

Index

autonomy, S1–08, S8–03, S9–01, R5–04, R6–16, R15–08, R19–05, R28–04, R48–07, R69–02
death, R80, R80–01 to R80–07
financially weak parties, R65–05
founding principles of Act, S1, S1–05
general duties, R25, R25–01 to R25–05
multi–party arbitrations, R6–18 to R6–19
no part in proceedings, S14, S14–01 to S14–14
questioning of parties, R28, R28–35 to R28–39
removal of arbitrators, R11
representation, R33, R33–01 to R33–09
unfair treatment by tribunal or arbitrator, R81, R81–01 to R81–03
Partnerships
appointment of arbitrators or tribunal, R3–09
dissolution, arbitrability of, S30–12
Payments
see also **Damages; Fees**
fees and expenses
power to withhold, R56, R56–01 to R56–24
payments into court, R46–22, R46–31, R64–12, R71–49 to R71–59
Perjury
improperly obtained awards, S20–119, R68–70
Personal bar
refusal of recognition or enforcement, S20–05 to S20–07
sist, S10–50, S10–62
Place of arbitration
see also **Seat of arbitration**
awards, R52, R52–01 to R52–08
default rules, R29, R29–01 to R29–06
Prescription
effect of Act on prescription and limitation, S23–13 to S23–15
interruption by arbitration, S23, S23–02 to S23–03, S23–05 to S23–08
negative prescription, S23, S23–09 to S23–12
positive prescription, S23, S23–04 to S23–08
Privacy
see also **Confidentiality**
common law, R26–20 to R26–24
confidentiality distinguished, R26–08, R26–14
consequences, R26–13, R26–20
context of decisions, R26–14
default rule, R26, R26–01 to R26–26
institutional rules, R26–02
Privilege
defamation, R26
evidence, R45–27 to R45–32, R46–33
legal privilege, R26–14

waiver, R45–29
Procedural irregularity
see also **Serious irregularity**
amiable compositeurs, S20–69
improperly conducted arbitration, S20–126 to S20–127
refusal of recognition or enforcement, S20–126 to S20–127
signature of awards, R51–11
witnesses, R28–42
Procedure
see **Arbitral proceedings; Fairness; Procedural irregularity**
Proof
see **Hearings**
Property
arrestment on the dependence, R46–37 to R46–46
default rule, R35, R35–01 to R35–08
emergency arbitrators, R35–07 to R35–08
evidence
preservation, R35–04
inhibition on the dependence, R46–37 to R46–46
inspection, R35
institutional rules, R35–02
preservation, R35
sale of property, R46–21
security, R46–22 to R46–36
tribunal powers relating to property, R35, R35–01 to R35–08
Public authorities
anonymity in legal proceedings, S15
capacity, S20–22
confidentiality, R26
proper performance of duties, R26
refusal of recognition or enforcement, S20–22
Public functions
confidentiality, R26
duty to disclose, S15–15 to S15–16
proper performance, R26
Public holidays
time periods, calculation of, R84, R84–08 to R84–13
Public interest
anonymity in legal proceedings, S15, S15–18 to S15–20
confidentiality, S15, R26, R26–14, R26–16, R26–21, R26–23
founding principles of Act, S1
interests of justice, S15–21 to S15–22
party autonomy and, S8–03, S10–28
Public policy
see also **Illegality**
contra bonos mores, S30–10, S30–22 to S30–23
due process, S20–37 to S20–38
EU law
breach, S20–128

543

Index

illegality, S20–113 to S20–117
improperly obtained awards, S20–118 to S20–125
international public policy, S20–108 to S20–111
natural justice, S20–37, S20–126
national public policy, S20–112
procedural irregularity, S20–126 to S20–127
refusal of recognition or enforcement, S20, S20–106 to S20–112
Qualifications
arbitrators, S3–18, R7, R10–12
Recognition of awards
see also **New York Convention on Recognition and Enforcement of Foreign Arbitral Awards 1958**
arbitral awards
adjournment, S20–145 to S20–149
anonymity in legal proceedings, S15–08 to S15–13
appeals, S12–21 to S12–28
applications, S12–09 to S12–15
common law, S12–02, S12–04, S12–20, S12–28
corrections, S12–21 to S12–28
Court of Session, S13, S13–08
discretion, S12–16 to S12–19
final and binding nature of awards, S11, S11–01 to S11–04
foreign awards, S18–01 to S19–11, S30–16 to S30–34
New York Convention awards, S19, S19–04 to S19–11
no part in proceedings, persons who take, S14–01 to S14–14
sisting decision, S20–134 to S20–143
transitional provisions, S36–09 to S36–12
due process
failure, S20–32 to S20–36
public policy and, S20–37 to S20–38
New York Convention awards, S19, S19–04 to S19–11
refusal to recognise
arbitration improperly conducted, S20–55 to S20–62
breach of EU law, S20–128
defences, S20–12
exclusive grounds, S20–09 to S20–11
failure of due process, S20–32 to S20–36
generally, S20, S20–01 to S20–08
illegality, S20–113 to S20–117
improperly obtained awards, S20–118 to S20–125
inability to present case, S20–47 to S20–54
incapacity, S20–13 to S20–26
invalid agreements, S20–27 to S20–31
lack of notice, S20–39 to S20–46

matter not arbitrable under Scots law, S20–102 to S20–105
procedural irregularity, S20–126 to S20–127
procedural irregularity, S20–67 to S20–70
public policy, S20–106 to S20–112
resisting enforcement, S20–72 to S20–101
tribunal not in agreed form, S20–63 to S20–66
resisting recognition
award not binding, S20–85 to S20–91
award set aside, S20–92 to S20–101
excess of jurisdiction, S20–82 to S20–84
lack of jurisdiction, S20–72 to S20–80
no part in proceedings, persons who take, S14–14
Rectification
awards, R49–17 to R49–22
decrees of court, R49–21
deeds or other documents, R49–18
effect on third parties, S11, S11–07
Reduction
awards, R49–17 to R49–22
deeds or other documents, R49–17
effect on third parties, S11, S11–07
Referral of points of law
arbitral proceedings, R41, R41–01 to R41–15, R42, R42–01 to R42–20
default rule, R41, R41–01 to R41–15
discretion to continue proceedings, R42–19
finality of decision, R42–20
mandatory rule, R42, R42–01 to R42–20
procedure, R42, R42–01 to R42–20
validity of application, R42–06 to R42–11
Referees
see **Arbitral appointments referee (AAR)**
Remedies
see **Appeals; Awards; Damages; Interdicts; Interest; Rectification; Reduction; Specific implement**
Removal
arbitrators
3 person tribunals, R11–05
arbitral appointment referees, R11–09
capacity, R12–18
conflicts of interest, R12–13 to R12–16
court removal of, R12, R12–01 to R12–20
default rules, R11, R11–01 to R11–10
impartiality, R12–13 to R12 to 16
institutional rules, R11–09
mandatory rule, R12, R12–01 to R12–20
natural justice, R11–04
notification, R11–10
parties removal of, R11, R11–01 to R11–10

544

Index

substantial injustice, R12–20
truncated tribunals, R11–06 to R11–07
unfair treatment by, R12–17
tribunals
  court removal of, R13, R13–01 to R13–06
  mandatory rule, R13, R13–01 to R13–06, R14, R14–01 to R14–13
  natural justice, R14–03
  third parties, R14–11
Remuneration
arbitrators, R60–07
fees and expenses, R60–07
guardian *ad litem*, R46–20
Renvoi
choice of law, R47–15, R47–16
Repeals
list, R29, Sch.2
Representatives
default rule, R33, R33–01 to R33–09
fairness, R33–04
immunity, R75
institutional rules, R33–02
notice, R33–04 to R33–06
objection to, R33–05
Res judicata
final and binding nature of awards, R69–10
jurisdictional appeals, R21–12, R23–19
New York Convention, S19–02
settlements, R57–12
Resignation
arbitrators
  appointment, challenges to, R15, R15–12 to R15–13
  authorisation by Outer House, R15, R15–03, R15–17 to R15–22, R16
  common law, R15–05
  consent of parties, R15, R15–08 to R15–09
  consequences, R15–07
  contractual right to resign, R15, R15–10 to R15–11
  fees and expenses, R15–07, R15–23, R60
  finality of Outer House decision, R15, R16, R16–20
  grounds, R15–06
  immunity of tribunal, R73, R73–13 to R73–14
  liability, R15–03, R16, R16–03 to R16–04, R16–08 to R16–13
  mandatory rule, R15, R15–01 to R15–23
  notice, R15
  reasons, R15–05
  refusal of resignation, R15–17
  tenure, R9, R9–05
Resources
differences, in, R24–37 to R24–39

financially weak parties, R65–05
agreements incapable of being performed, S10–52
Reviews
see also **Appeals; Judicial review**
challenging awards, R67–09, R67–16, R68–09, R68–11, R69–27, R70–17, R70–19, R71, R71–05
correction of awards, R51–51, R58–29 to R58–30
interim measures, R46–05
points of law referral, R42–20
withholding of award, R56, R56–23
Revocation
challenges to appointment, R9, R10, R10–18
tenure of arbitrators, R9
Royal Assent
date, S35, S35–01
Sampling
evidence, R35, R46–33
Savings provisions
ancillary provision, S32, S32–01 to S32–04
***Scott* v *Avery* clauses**
effect on interim measures, R46–01
sist, S10–69 to S10–71
Scottish Arbitration Rules
amendment, S26
approach of Act, S7–01
arbitral appointments referee, S24
default rules, S7, S9–01 to S9–10
foreign law, S9–09 to S9–10
founding principles of Act, S7
interpretation, S31
mandatory rules, S8–01 to S8–03
modification or disapplication, S9–01 to S9–03
other institutional rules distinguished, S9–04 to S9–07
party agreement, S9–08
procedural law, S9–09 to S9–10
seat of arbitration, S7, S7–01, S8, S9, S9–09 to S9–10
text, Sch.1
Seat of arbitration
arbitrability of disputes, S30–16 to S30–17, S30–23 to S30–24
arbitration agreements
  invalidity, S20–28 to S20–31
awards
  made at seat of arbitration, S18–12 to S18–13
  must state seat, R51, R51–19 to R51–23
contrast with location, R29–04
courts
  additional powers, R46–08
  death of arbitrator, R79–05
designation of seat
  court, by, S3–15 to S3–24
  parties, by, S3–07

545

Index

third parties, by S3–08
tribunal, by, S3–09, S3–11, S3–13
England, S3–10, S3–23, R61–07
foreign law, S3–10, S30–16 to S30–17
form of award, R51, R51–19 to R51–23
generally, S3–01 to S3–06
juridical seat
  purpose, S3–02
  determining applicability of national law, S3–03
legal error, R69–14
liability, R60–08
neutrality, S3–12
New York Convention 1958, S18, S18–03, S18–12 to S18–13, S19–02
place of arbitration, R29–04
refusal of recognition or enforcement, S20–28 to S20–31, S20–55 to S20–59, S20–92 to S20–100
Scotland, S3, S3–04 to S3–06, S23–15, R52–02 to R52–04, R52–07 to R52–08
serious irregularity, R68–56
sist, S10–25, S10–44, S10–72
statutory arbitrations, S3–06, S16, S16–13 to S16–15
substantive law, effect on, S3–25
time for designation, S3–14

Secretarial assistance
see **Clerks**

Security
see also **Diligence on the dependence**
adjournments, S20–144 to S20–149
appeals, S12–25 to S12–28, R71–42 to R71–48
arrestment on the dependence of moveable property, R46, R46–22 to R46–32
awards,
  enforcement, S12–25 to S12–28
  sums claimed in, R46–22
Brussels Convention, R64–12
caution
  court's power to order, R46–22, R46–46, R46–57 to R46–63, R71–42
consignation, R46–40
  diligence on the dependence, R46, R46–22 to R46–32
discretion, R46–22, R71–45
enforcement of awards, S12–25 to S12–28, S20–144 to S20–149
fees and expenses, R16–06 to R16–07, R46–46, R46–57 to R46–63, R64, R64–01 to R64–13, R71–39
  insolvency, R46, R46–22 to R46–32
interim measures, R46, R46–22 to R46–32
litigiosity, notice of, R46–26, R46–45
Lugano Convention, R64–12
mandatary, sist of, R46–58

moveable property, R46, R46–22 to R46–32
property
  recovery of, R46, R46–22 to R46–32
  refusal of recognition or enforcement, S20, S20–144 to S20–149
  tribunal's power to order, R64, R64–01 to R64–13
  warrants for arrestment or inhibition on the dependence, R46–22 to R46–32

Separability
arbitrable disputes, S5–12
arbitration agreements
  distinct agreements, S5, S5–07 to S5–10, R19–03, R19–04, R19–10
  generally, S5–03 to S5–06
  governing law, S5–01 to S5–02

Serious irregularity
admitted irregularity, R68–75
arbitral appointments referee, R68–45
arbitrators
  duty of fair treatment, R24–34 to R24–35
  removal, R12–05, R12–10, R12–16, R12–20, R24–20, R24–40
appeals, R68, R68–01 to R68–97
choice of law, R47–18
clarification or removal of ambiguity in awards, R58–36 to R58–37
clerks, agents or employees, R32–06
delay, R24–50
dissenting opinions, R51–16
draft awards, R55–12 to R55–13
evidence, R28–14, R28–47
fees and expenses, R61–12, R61–21, R62–07, R62–08, R62–15, R68–88 to R68–92
fraud, R68–52 to R68–72
mandatory rule, R68, R68–01 to R68–97
oral hearings, R28–47
part awards, R54–11
point of law referral, R42–20
provisional awards, R53–18
public policy, R68–52 to R68–74
qualifying irregularities, R68–15 to R68–22
remedies, R68–76 to R68–87
removal of arbitrators, R12–05, R12–10, R12–16, R12–20, R24–20
seat of arbitration, R51–20
substantial injustice, R68–15 to R68–23
third parties, R68–45
time limits, R44–14
tribunals
  acting outwith powers, R68–31 to R68–33
  dealing with all issues, R68–34 to R68–44
  failure to conduct as agreed, R68–24 to R68–30

546

Index

uncertainty or ambiguity of award, R68–46 to R68–51
Settlements
awards, R57–12 to R57–14
consent awards, R57–12 to R57–28
default rule, R57, R57–01 to R57–28
discretion to make an award, R57–15 to R57–20
early settlement, R57, R57–01 to R57–28
fees and expenses, R57–02, R57–28, R62–16
notification, R57–11
promotion by tribunal, R57–21 to R57–27
reasons for awards, R57–24
res judicata, R57–12
termination of arbitration, R57–04 to R57–10
Several liability
fees and expenses, R60–07, R60–09 to R60–10, R62–26
Sist
answers
lodging, S10–59 to S10–65
applications
form, S10–10 to S10–14
generally, S10–01, S14–10
notice of proceedings, S10–57 to S10–58
opposed applications, S10–19 to S10–34
timing, S10–59 to S10–68
arbitration agreements
litigated disputes, S10–36
not "void, inoperative or incapable of being performed", S10–44 to S10–45
parties, S10–37 to S10–43
arbitration seated outwith Scotland, S10–72
capacity, S10–52 to S10–56
common law, S10–02 to S10–03, S10–60
courts, S10–15 to S10–16
defences
lodging, S10–59 to S10–65
effect of sist, S10–06 to S10–09
form of application, S10–10 to S10–14
guardian *ad litem*, R46–20
generally, S10–02 to S10–04
incapable of being performed
arbitration agreement, S10–52 to S10–56
inoperative agreements, S10–50 to S10–51
interim orders, R46–57 to R46–60
jurisdiction, R19–05
legal proceedings, S10–17 to S10–18
lodging defences or answers, S10–59 to S10–65
mandatory sisting, R64–09 to R64–10
necessity, S10–10 to S10–14
non-arbitrability, S30–25 to S30–26
non-Scottish arbitrations, S10–72
notice of proceedings, S10–57 to S10–58

obligation to sist, S10–05, S10–35
point of law referral, R42–01
recognition or enforcement, S20, S20–134 to S20–143
Scott v *Avery* clauses, S10–69 to S10–71
seat of arbitration, S10–72
security, R64–09 to R64–10
tribunals, legal proceedings before, S10–16
void arbitration agreements, S10–47 to S10–49
Specific implement
effectiveness abroad, R49–16
remedies, R49, R49–08 to R49–16
Crown proceedings, R49–08 to R49–16
interim measures, R46–16, R46–55
land contracts, R49–13
permanent orders, R46–55
supervision, R49–16
State immunity
refusal of recognition or enforcement, S20–24
Stated case
draft awards, R55–06
fees and expenses, R59–06
points of law referral, R41–04, R42–03 to R43–04
procedure, S29–01
transitional provisions, S36–14
Statutory arbitration
consensual arbitrations, S16–11, S16–19
consolidated proceedings, S16–19
death of parties, S16
definition, S16
generally, S16–01 to S16–05
power to adapt enactments providing for statutory arbitration, S17, S17–01 to S17–03
scope, S16–06 to S16–19
seat of arbitration, S16, S16–13 to S16–15
special provisions, S16, S16–01 to S16–19
time limits, extension of, S16–17
Statutory instruments
negative procedure, S33–01
positive resolutions, S33–02
Stay of proceedings
see **Sist**
Striking out
want of prosecution, R37–10
Supreme Court
appeals, R21–14, R23–21
Suspension of legal proceedings
see **Sist**
Technology and Construction Court
judges as arbitrators or umpires, S25–03, S25–09
Tenure
arbitrators
default rule, R9, R9–01 to R9–05
termination, R16, R16–01 to R16–20
termination of

547

Index

appeals, R16–20
fees and expenses, R16–05, R16–06
liability, R16, R16–01 to R16–20
mandatory rule, R16, R16–01 to R16–20
procedure, R16–14 to R16–19
security, R16–07

Termination
arbitration
default rule, R57, R57–01 to R57–28
delay, R57–10
discretion, R57–15 to R57–20
functus officio, R57–04
jurisdiction, R57–08 to R57–11
last awards, on, R57, R57–01 to R57–28
objections to jurisdiction, R20, R20–21 to R20–23
partial termination, R20–21 to R20–23
settlement, R57, R57–01 to R57–28
time limits, R57–04 to R57–09

Third parties
confidentiality, R26, R26–14
consolidated proceedings, R40–04
disclosure, R6–14, R8, R8–08, R26, R26–14, R45–06
fees and expenses, R59, R59–04, R60, R60–06, R61, R61–17, R62
final and binding nature of awards, S11, S11–04
good faith, S11–07 to S11–10, S27–01
immunity, R74, R74–10
jus quaesitum tertio, S4–10, S10–42
payments into court, R71–55
removal of arbitrators, R9, R11, R14, R14–11, R16–03
seat of arbitration, S3, S3–07 to S3–14, S6–06
serious irregularity appeals, R68, R68–45
settlement, R57–25

Time limits
see also **Prescription**
appeals, R70–35, R71–09 to R71–22
appointment of arbitrators, S20–42, R6–06, R10–15 to R10–16, R10–20, R43–06
arbitral proceedings, R43, R43–01 to R43–09, R58–25
arbitration agreements, R43, R43–01 to R43–09
awards, R51–62, R71–09 to R71–22
calculation, R84–04, R84–07
challenges to arbitrators' appointments, R10, R10–15 to R10–16, R10–20
clarification or removal of ambiguity in awards, R58–25
communications, R84, R84–01 to R84–13
correction of awards, R58–31 to R58–35
courts, R43, R43–01 to R43–09, R44, R44–01 to R44–16
default rule, R43, R43–01 to R43–09

defences
failure to lodge, S10–65, R37–07
delay, R44–12 to R44–14, R44–16, R71–09 to R71–22
directions
failure to comply, R31–05
inclusion within, R39–08 to R39–09
evidence, S20–50
form of award, R51–25, R51–60
legal error appeals, R69–26, R70–04, R70–09, R70–35, R71–09 to R71–22
negative prescription, S23, S23–09 to S23–12
notice, S30–42, R1–14, R1–22
objections, R10–15 to R10–16
parties setting, R43
positive prescription, S23, S23–04 to S23–08
procedural irregularity, S20–67
procedure for variation
mandatory rule, R44, R44–01 to R44–16
reviews, R20–15, R44–16, R71–09 to R71–11, R71–15
serious irregularity, R44–14, R68–50, R71–09 to R71–22
setting limits, R84–04, R84–07
statutory arbitrations, S16, S16–17
termination of arbitration, R57–04 to R57–09
variation
procedure, R44
set by parties, R43, R43–01 to R43–09

Trade usages
see **Custom and usage**

Transitional provisions
arbiters
use of term, S36–13
arbitration agreements entered into prior to Act, S36–02
commencement of Act, S36–02 to S36–03, S36–07, S36–18
commencement of arbitration, S36, S36–06, S36–07
consultation by ministers, S36–11 to S36–12
decreets or decrees
use of term, S36–13
enforcement of foreign awards, S36–05
former regime, S36–10
stated case procedure
contracting out, S36–14 to S36–17

Tribunals
see also **Arbitrators; Directions; Impartiality; Jurisdiction; Seat of arbitration**
admissibility of evidence, R28, R28–15 to R28–16
consolidated proceedings, R40, R40–12
non-compliance with

548

Index

adverse inferences, R39–15
  consequences, R39–18
  continuing with arbitration, R42, R42–19
  default rule, R39, R39–01 to R39–18
  defence submissions, service of, R39–17
  final awards, R39–16
  part awards, R39–16
  party fails to comply, R39, R39–01 to R39–18
  proportionality, R39–14
confidentiality, R26, R26–02 to R26–27
correction of awards, R58–26 to R58–30
decision making
  default rule, R30, R30–01 to R30–08
delegation, R32, R32–01 to R32–20
deliberations, R27, R27–01 to R27–11
dismissal by court, R13, R13–01 to R13–06
evidence, R28, R28–01, R28–60
experts, R34, R34–01 to R34–12
general duties
  confidentiality, R26, R26–02 to R26–27
  cost control, R24–53 to R24–56
  delay, R24–43 to R24–52
  fairness, R24–23 to R24–39
  impartiality, R24–04 to R24–33
  mandatory rules, R24, R24–01 to R24–56
  removal of arbitrators, R24–40 to R24–42
immunity, R73, R73–01 to R73–15
inquisitorial power, R28–40 to R28–43
jurisdiction
  appeals against objections, R21, R21–01 to R21–16
  objections to jurisdiction, R20, R20–01 to R20–29
  ruling on own jurisdiction, R19, R19–01 to R10–20
objections to jurisdiction
  appeals, R21, R21–01 to R21–16
  rulings on, R20, R20–01 to R20–29
property
  powers relating to, R35, R35–01 to R35–08
reconsideration of awards, R72, R72–01 to R72–06
reconstitution, R17, R17–01 to R17–09
seat of arbitration
  designation by tribunal, S3–07 to S3–15
  generally, S3, S3–01, S3–04
serious irregularity appeals, R68, R68–24 to R68–33, R72
settlements
  discretion, R57–15 to R57–20
  promoted by tribunals, R57–21 to R57–27
truncated tribunals, R11–07

Umpires
  appointment, S29–01
  decisions of tribunal, R30–08
  fees and expenses, R56–09
  judge as umpire, S25, S25–01 to S25–06
  mandatory rule, R82, R82–01, R82–05
  number, R5–06, R30–08
  rules applicable to, S8, R82, R82–01, R82–05
UNCITRAL Model Law 1985
  see also **New York Convention on Recognition and Enforcement of Foreign Arbitral Awards 1958**
  amendments, S26, S26–01 to S26–04
  Model law jurisdiction, S1–09 to S1–10
Unfair contract terms
  unlawful choice of law, R47–21
Unfair treatment
  see **Fairness**
Unincorporated associations
  appointment as arbitrators or tribunal, R3–03 to R3–06
Validity
  agreements incapable of being performed, S10–52
  arbitrability, S4–19, S30–02 to S30–15, S30–25
  arbitration agreements, S4–08, S4–14, S6–05 to S6–10, S10–20, S10–29 to S10–30, S20–27 to S20–31
  capacity of parties, S6–07, R19–14, R71–22
  confidentiality, R45–32
  governing law, S6–05 to S6–10, S6–13 to S6–15
  inoperative, S10–50
  jurisdiction, R19–09 to R19–11
  oral agreements, S4–14
  points of law referral, R41–09, R41–15, R42–06,
  privilege, R45–32
  public policy, S4–19
  separability, S5, S5–02 to S5–06, S5–07, S5–11
  sist, S10–20, S10–29 to S10–30, S10–52, S10–70, S13–07
  void for uncertainty, S4–20, S10–48, S10–49, R19–13
Vicarious liability
  immunity, R74–08
Warrants
  arrestment on the dependence, R46, R46–37 to R46–45
  citation, for, R45–07 to R45–13
  diligence on the dependence, R46–27 to R46–32
  inhibition on the dependence, R46, R46–37 to R46–45
  interim attachment, R46–27 to R46–32
  security, R46, R46–37 to R46–45

Index

Weekends
  time periods, calculation of, R84
Witnesses
  affirmations, R36
  attendance
    court's power to order, R45, R45–01 to R45–36
    procedure, R45–19 to R45–26
  common law, R45–07, R45–27
  contempt of court, R45–07
  evidence, R8–22, R28, R28–01 to R28–60
  hearings, R28–44 to R28–49
  immunity, R75, R75–01 to R75–05
  mandatory rule, R45, R45–01 to R45–36, R75, R75–01 to R75–05
  oaths, R36, R36–03
  privilege, R45–27 to R45–32
  procedure, R28, R28–01 to R28–60, R45–19 to R45–26
  questioning, R28–35 to R28–39, R28–41 to R28–43
  reconstitution of tribunal, R17–07 to R17–08
  warrants for citation, R45, R45–08 to R45–11

Writing
  arbitration agreements, S4–01, S18–09 to S18–11
  foreign enforcement, S4–15 to S4–18
  New York Convention awards, S18–09 to S18–11
  formal communications, R57–11, R83, R83–03, R83–08 to R83–09
  signatures on awards, R51–05 to R51–13